THE ENCYCLOPEDIA OF
MIDDLE EAST WARS

THE ENCYCLOPEDIA OF
MIDDLE EAST WARS

The United States in the Persian Gulf, Afghanistan, and Iraq Conflicts

VOLUME II: E–L

Spencer C. Tucker
Editor

Priscilla Mary Roberts
Editor, Documents Volume

Dr. Paul G. Pierpaoli Jr.
Associate Editor

Colonel Jerry D. Morelock, USAR (retired)
Major General David Zabecki, USAR (retired)
Dr. Sherifa Zuhur
Assistant Editors

FOREWORD BY
General Anthony C. Zinni, USMC (retired)

A B C ⬥ C L I O

Santa Barbara, California Denver, Colorado Oxford, England

Library of Congress Cataloging-in-Publication Data

The encyclopedia of Middle East wars : the United States in the Persian Gulf, Afghanistan, and Iraq conflicts / Spencer C. Tucker, editor ; Priscilla Mary Roberts, editor, documents volume.
　　v.　cm.
　Includes bibliographical references and index.
　ISBN 978-1-85109-947-4 (hard copy : alk. paper) — ISBN 978-1-85109-948-1 (ebook)
　1. Middle East—History, Military—20th century—Encyclopedias.　2. Middle East—History, Military—21st century—Encyclopedias. 3. Middle East—Military relations—United States—Encyclopedias.　4. United States—Military relations—Middle East—Encyclopedias.　5. Persian Gulf War, 1991—Encyclopedias.　6. Afghan War, 2001—Encyclopedias.　7. Iraq War, 2003—Encyclopedias.　I. Tucker, Spencer, 1937–　II. Roberts, Priscilla Mary.
　DS63.1.E453 2010
　355.00956'03—dc22

2010033812

13 12 11 10 9　1 2 3 4 5

This book is also available on the World Wide Web as an ebook.
Visit abc-clio.com for details.

ABC-CLIO, LLC
130 Cremona Drive, P.O. Box 1911
Santa Barbara, California 93116–1911

This book is printed on acid-free paper ∞
Manufactured in the United States of America

About the Editors

Spencer C. Tucker, PhD, graduated from the Virginia Military Institute and was a Fulbright scholar in France. He was a U.S. Army captain and intelligence analyst in the Pentagon during the Vietnam War, then taught for 30 years at Texas Christian University before returning to his alma mater for 6 years as the holder of the John Biggs Chair of Military History. He retired from teaching in 2003. He is now Senior Fellow of Military History at ABC-CLIO. Dr. Tucker has written or edited 36 books, including ABC-CLIO's award-winning *The Encyclopedia of the Cold War* and *The Encyclopedia of the Arab-Israeli Conflict* as well as the comprehensive *A Global Chronology of Conflict*.

Priscilla Mary Roberts received her PhD from Cambridge University and is an associate professor of history and an honorary director of the Centre of American Studies at the University of Hong Kong. Dr. Roberts has received numerous research awards and was the documents editor of *The Encyclopedia of the Cold War* and *The Encyclopedia of the Arab-Israeli Conflict,* published by ABC-CLIO. She spent 2003 as a visiting Fulbright scholar at the Institute for European, Russian, and Eurasian Studies at the George Washington University in Washington, D.C.

ABC-CLIO Military History
Advisory Board Members

Contents

List of Entries

List of Maps

General Maps

MIDDLE EAST

TOPOGRAPHY OF THE MIDDLE EAST

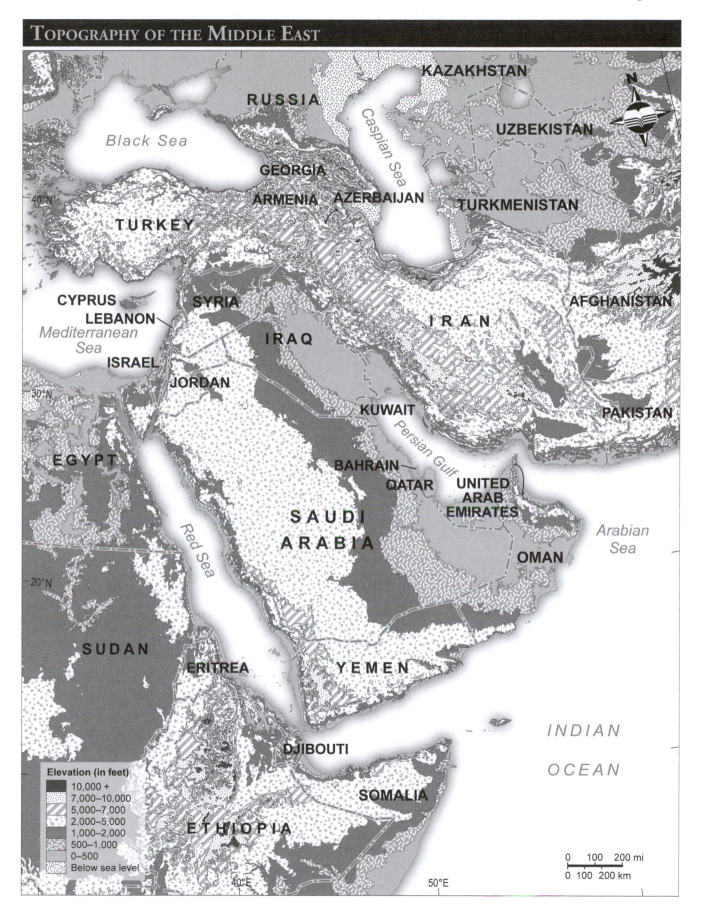

KAZAKHSTAN

RUSSIA

Black Sea

Caspian Sea

UZBEKISTAN

GEORGIA

40°N

ARMENIA   AZERBAIJAN

TURKMENISTAN

TURKEY

CYPRUS   SYRIA

AFGHANISTAN

LEBANON

*Mediterranean
Sea*

I R A N

IRAQ

ISRAEL

PAKISTAN

JORDAN

30°N

KUWAIT

EGYPT

Persian Gulf

BAHRAIN

*Arabian
Sea*

QATAR   UNITED
ARAB
EMIRATES

S A U D I
A R A B I A

Red Sea

OMAN

20°N

SUDAN

ERITREA   Y E M E N

INDIAN

DJIBOUTI

OCEAN

SOMALIA

Elevation (in feet)
10,000 +
7,000–10,000
5,000–7,000
2,000–5,000
1,000–2,000
500–1,000
0–500
Below sea level

E T H I O P I A

40°E   50°E

0   100   200 mi

0 100 200 km

COALITION AGAINST IRAQ, AUGUST 2, 1990–FEBRUARY 28, 1991

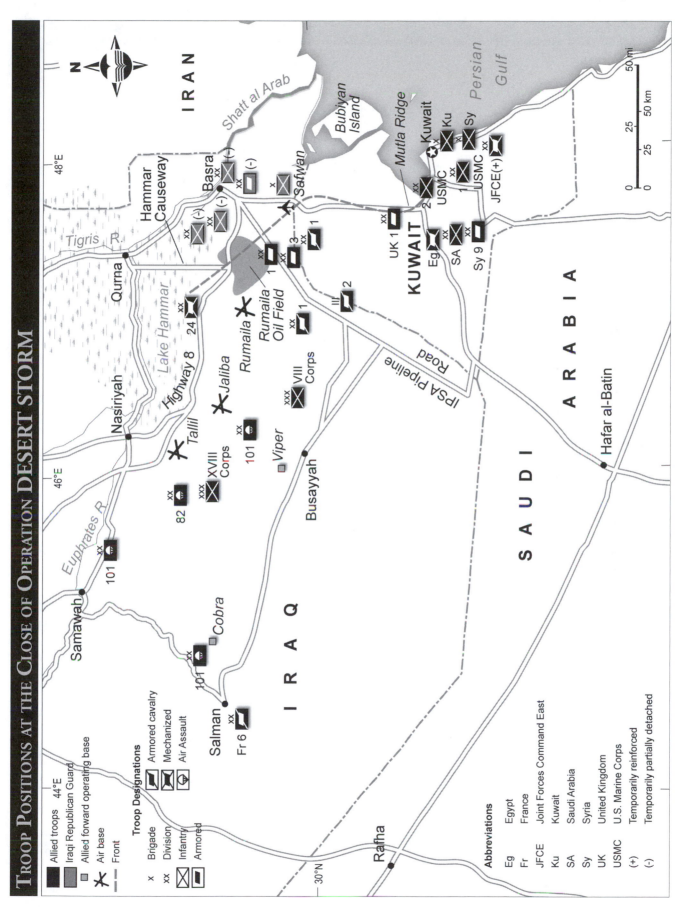

OPERATION ENDURING FREEDOM, 2001

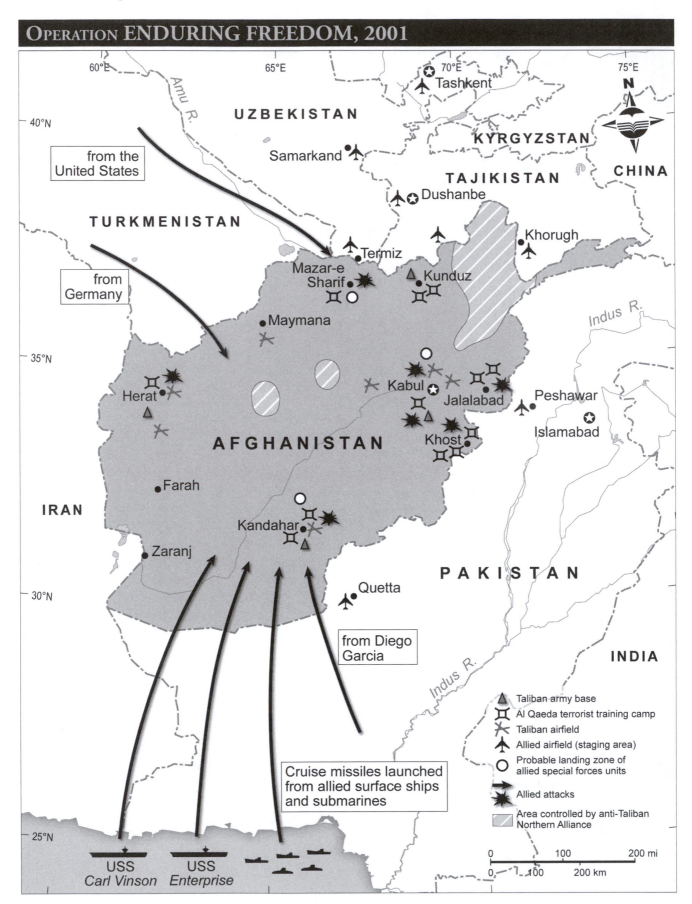

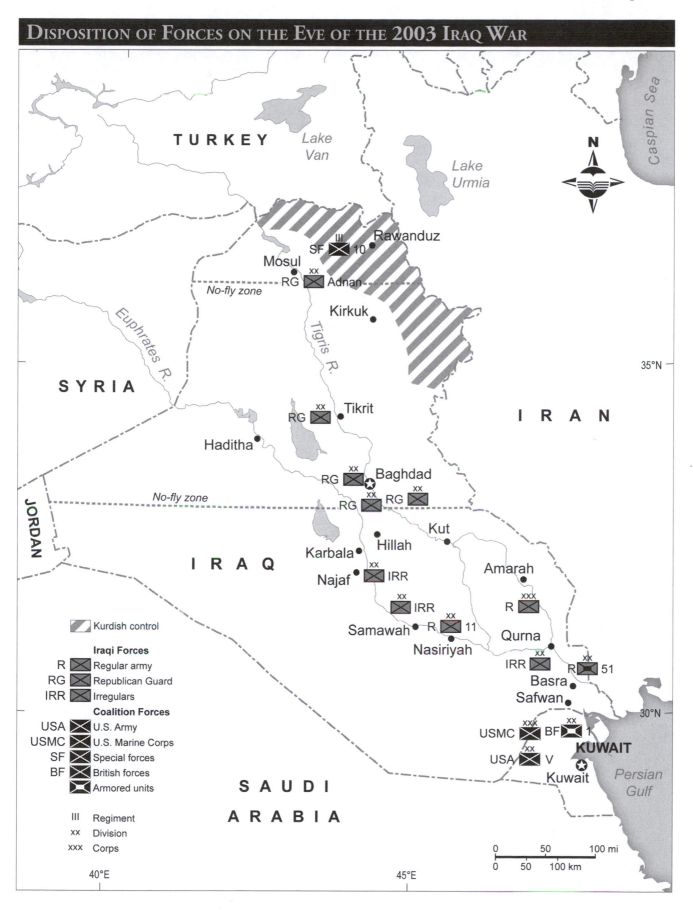

DISPOSITION OF FORCES ON THE EVE OF THE 2003 IRAQ WAR

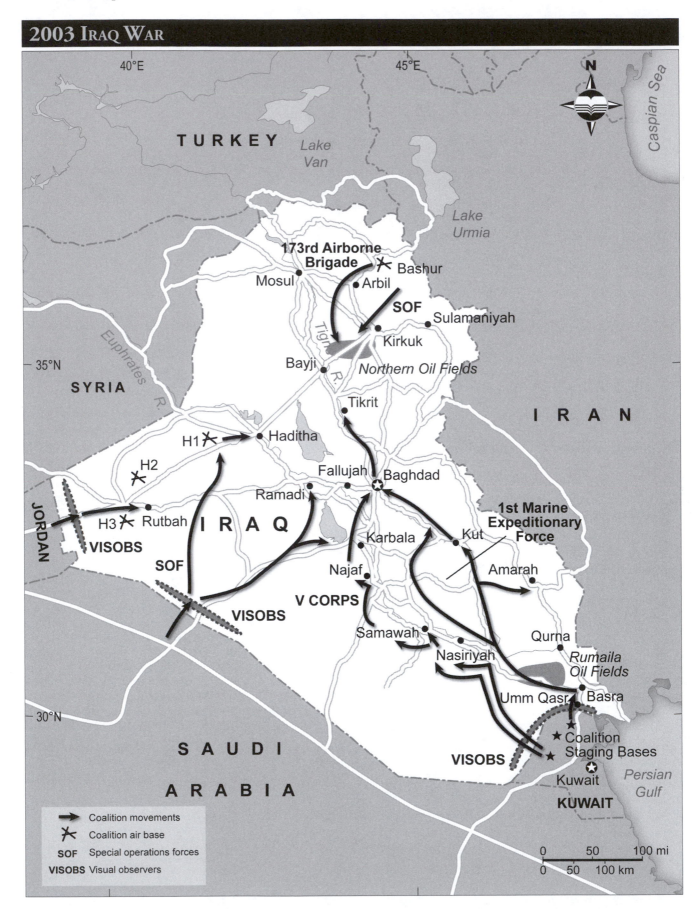

2003 IRAQ WAR

TURKEY

Lake Van

Caspian Sea

N

Lake Urmia

173rd Airborne Brigade

Mosul

Bashur

Arbil

SOF

Sulamaniyah

Kirkuk

Northern Oil Fields

Bayji

Tigris R.

— 35°N

Euphrates R.

SYRIA

Tikrit

I R A N

H1

Haditha

H2

Fallujah

Baghdad

Ramadi

1st Marine Expeditionary Force

Kut

JORDAN

H3   Rutbah

I R A Q

Karbala

Amarah

VISOBS

SOF

Najaf

V CORPS

VISOBS

Samawah

Qurna

Rumaila Oil Fields

Nasiriyah

— 30°N

Umm Qasr

Basra

S A U D I

★ Coalition Staging Bases

VISOBS

A R A B I A

Kuwait

Persian Gulf

KUWAIT

Coalition movements

Coalition air base

SOF   Special operations forces

VISOBS Visual observers

| 0 | 50 | 100 mi |

| 0 | 50 | 100 km |

E

Eagleburger, Lawrence Sidney
Birth Date: August 1, 1930

Diplomat, influential adviser to several U.S. presidents, and U.S. secretary of state (1992–1993). Lawrence Sidney Eagleburger was born in Milwaukee, Wisconsin, on August 1, 1930. He graduated from the University of Wisconsin–Madison with a BS in 1952 and immediately enlisted in the U.S. Army, serving during the Korean War (1950–1953) and attaining the rank of first lieutenant. Eagleburger returned to Madison to receive his MA in 1957. That same year he entered the U.S. Foreign Service, where we worked in Honduras and as a desk officer for Cuban affairs in the Department of State's Bureau of Intelligence and Research. Eagleburger served in Belgrade, Yugoslavia, from 1961 to 1965 and returned to Washington in 1965 to serve as the special assistant on North Atlantic Treaty Organization (NATO) affairs to presidential adviser Dean G. Acheson.

In 1969 President Richard M. Nixon's national security adviser Henry Kissinger appointed Eagleburger as his assistant. In September 1969 Eagleburger left the National Security Council to assume successive appointments in the Nixon administration to the U.S. mission to NATO, the Department of Defense, and the Department of State. Eagleburger served as the ambassador to Yugoslavia in the James (Jimmy) Carter administration from 1977 to 1980 before President Ronald Reagan appointed Eagleburger undersecretary of state for political affairs in 1982.

Retiring from the State Department, Eagleburger became the president of Kissinger Associates, Inc., a New York–based international consulting firm founded by Henry Kissinger, from 1984 to 1989. In 1989 President George H. W. Bush appointed Eagleburger deputy secretary of state, a position in which he served as Bush's chief adviser on Yugoslavia that, at the time, was descending into chaos as a result of the end of communist rule there. Controversy often marked Eagleburger's role as adviser on Yugoslavia. When he refuted reports that the Yugoslavian National Army and Serbian paramilitary forces had perpetrated war crimes, media outlets in both the United States and Europe labeled him a Serbian enthusiast.

In 1992 when Secretary of State James Baker resigned to manage Bush's unsuccessful reelection campaign, Eagleburger replaced him as acting secretary in August 1992. Eagleburger became secretary of state on December 8, 1992. When Bush left office in January 1993, Eagleburger joined the law firm of Baker, Donelson, Bearrnan and Caldwell as the senior foreign policy adviser. In 1998 he became the chairman of the International Commission on Holocaust-Era Insurance Claims, which offered $16 million to Holocaust victims and their heirs in 2005.

In 2002 Eagleburger publicly questioned the timing of a likely invasion of Iraq and stated that the evidence linking Saddam Hussein to weapons of mass destruction (WMDs) was not altogether conclusive. In 2003 after the Bush administration sharply reprimanded Syria and Iran, Eagleburger again openly warned that military action in either country could be disastrous. In 2006 he replaced Robert Gates in the Iraq Study Group, also known as the Baker-Hamilton Commission, charged by Congress with assessing the situation of the Iraq War. Eagleburger is currently the chairman of the board of trustees for the Forum for International Policy and serves on the Board of Advisors of the Washington Institute for Near East Policy.

CHRISTOPHER R. W. DIETRICH

393

See also

Baker, James Addison, III; Bush, George Herbert Walker; Bush, George Walker; Iraq Study Group; IRAQI FREEDOM, Operation; Kissinger, Henry Alfred; Weapons of Mass Destruction

References

Barilleaux, Ryan J., and Mark J. Rozell. *Power and Prudence: The Presidency of George H. W. Bush.* College Station: Texas A&M University Press, 2004.

Hess, Stephen, and Marvin Kalb, eds. *The Media and the War on Terrorism.* Washington, DC: Brookings Institution Press, 2003.

Langholtz, Harvey J. *The Psychology of Peacekeeping.* Westport, CT: Praeger, 1998.

EAGLE CLAW, Operation
Event Date: April 25, 1980

Failed U.S. mission to rescue American hostages being held in Iran on April 25, 1980, code-named Operation EAGLE CLAW. On November 4, 1979, during the Iranian Revolution, radical Iranian students seized the United States embassy in Tehran, taking 52 Americans captive. The ensuing hostage crisis created a division within the Jimmy Carter administration. National Security Advisor Zbigniew Brzezinski believed that the president had to take a hard stance and was an ardent proponent of a rescue operation. Secretary of State Cyrus Vance opposed military action and believed that persistent and carefully constructed negotiations could resolve the crisis. He maintained that a rescue attempt would in fact place the captives in greater danger. Vance considered the Iranian threats against their lives to be purely rhetorical, as dead hostages would be of no value to the Iranians. He argued that if the captives were rescued, the terrorists would simply take more hostages. The secretary of state also asserted that military action against Iran could turn the entire Muslim world against the United States.

President Carter resisted Brzezinski's initial pressure for a rescue mission. Carter, like Vance, feared that any military action would result in the execution of the hostages. The president did allow for tentative mission planning and preparation to begin, however.

On April 11, 1980, after the Iranian students publicly threatened the hostages, Carter gave his approval to a rescue attempt. Carter dismissed Vance's warnings about reprisals from other Middle Eastern countries, believing that Islamic fundamentalist Iran enjoyed little support from its Arab neighbors. The president determined that not taking action would be more costly than taking action. Indeed, he was especially concerned that the United States not appear soft on terrorism and weak in the eyes of leaders of the Soviet Union, with which relations had already rapidly deteriorated. Vance then resigned, having protested against the proposed rescue operation for nearly six months.

Carter and Brzezinski ordered the operation to proceed in accordance with four constraints: planning secrecy, protecting the lives of the hostages, keeping Iranian casualties to a minimum, and maintaining a small task force. The element of surprise was also encouraged. Carter met with the task force planners personally on April 16. The U.S. Army's Delta Force, commanded by Colonel Charles Beckwith, was charged with executing the raid, while Colonel James Kyle commanded the mission's air force elements. Meanwhile, White House Chief of Staff Hamilton Jordan met with representatives from Iran on April 18 in a final attempt to reach a diplomatic solution to the hostage crisis. He was informed that the Iranian government would not be able to address the issue until after parliamentary elections in mid-May. With his efforts to achieve an immediate diplomatic resolution frustrated, and under increasing pressure from the American public and media to take action, Carter authorized Operation EAGLE CLAW on April 23. He made a fateful pledge to the task force commanders that he would accept full responsibility for the mission.

The ill-fated rescue mission never reached Tehran. The plan failed because of weather conditions over the Iranian desert and an unfortunate set of circumstances that occurred at the mission's forward refueling point, code-named Desert One. On April 24, when the mission began, sandstorms caused the operation to fall an hour behind schedule. Mechanical failures reduced the eight navy RH-53D Sea Stallion helicopters in the mission to only five. Meanwhile, civilians in automobiles threatened operational secrecy by stumbling upon the forward refueling point. The decision to abort the mission because of the lack of serviceable helicopters had already been made when an accident occurred around 2:00 a.m. on April 25. A helicopter rotor struck an MC-130 transport aircraft on the ground, causing a massive explosion at Desert One. The task force, including five wounded, was evacuated immediately. Eight dead American servicemen and the four remaining Sea Stallions were abandoned in the desert.

The failed operation was a dark episode in Carter's presidency. In August 1980, an investigative body led by Admiral James L. Holloway analyzed Operation EAGLE CLAW. It concluded that the accident at the forward refueling point was the result of human error brought on by the dark, dusty, and cluttered conditions at Desert One. The government examined the state of U.S. special operations forces after the catastrophe at Desert One. The Senate Armed Services Committee consulted with Colonel Beckwith and drew several conclusions from the failed mission, including the importance of standardized training for all special operations forces and the need to create a permanent joint command. It also recommended the establishment of forward staging areas around the globe. These would allow special operations forces to be deployed faster and more efficiently. Based upon these findings, and those of the Holloway Committee, the Joint Special Operations Command (JSOC) was formed on December 15, 1980. In 1987, Congress created the position of Assistant Secretary of Defense

Six marine-piloted helicopters head from the U.S. aircraft carrier *Nimitz* to the rendezvous at Desert One in Iran in April 1980 as part of Operation EAGLE CLAW, the failed attempt to rescue U.S. hostages held by Iran. (U.S. Department of Defense)

for Special Operations and Low Intensity Conflict and The United States Special Operations Command (USSOCOM). Passage of this legislation guaranteed regular funding, standardized training, and specialized weapons and equipment for special operations forces in all branches of the U.S. military.

The American hostages were not released until January 20, 1981. The failure to secure their freedom earlier undoubtedly helped Republican Ronald Reagan win the presidency in the November 1980 elections.

JEFFREY LAMONICA

See also

Beckwith, Charles Alvin; Brzezinski, Zbigniew; Carter, James Earl, Jr.; Delta Force; Iranian Revolution; Reagan, Ronald Wilson

References

Beckwith, Charlie A., and Donald Knox. *Delta Force: The Army's Elite Counterterrorist Unit.* New York: Avon, 2000.

Carter, Jimmy. *Keeping Faith: Memoirs of a President.* Fayetteville: University of Arkansas Press, 1982.

Cogan, Charles. "Desert One and Its Disorders." *Journal of Military History* 67 (2003): 273–296.

Jordan, Hamilton. *Crisis: The Last Year of the Carter Presidency.* New York: Putnam, 1982.

Kyle, James, and John Eidson. *The Guts to Try: The Untold Story of the Iran Hostage Rescue Mission by the On-Scene Desert Commander.* New York: Orion Books, 1990.

Ryan, Paul. *The Iranian Rescue Mission.* Annapolis, MD: Naval Institute Press, 1985.

EARNEST WILL, **Operation**

Start Date: 1987
End Date: 1989

U.S. military operation designed to provide oil tanker escorts in the Persian Gulf from 1987 to 1989 during the last stages of the Iran-Iraq War (1980–1988). During the Iran-Iraq War, both the Iranians and Iraqis carried out attacks on tankers and other merchant shipping in the Persian Gulf. This became known informally as the Tanker War. The Tanker War was essentially designed to inflict economic damage on the enemy. Iraq, lacking a significant navy, used planes to attack Iranian tankers and ports. Iraq did not have a tanker fleet, so Iran targeted the shipping of countries that favored Iraq, such as Saudi Arabia and Kuwait. Iran used a variety of methods in its attacks, including small boats, mines, frigates, and aircraft. Kuwait was a nonbelligerent yet feared Iranian attacks on its tankers, which were critical to its status as a major oil and natural gas exporter.

In December 1986 and January 1987 Kuwait asked both the United States and the Soviet Union to protect 11 of its oil tankers from potential Iranian attacks. After much discussion, the United States agreed to place all 11 of the Kuwaiti-owned tankers under the U.S. flag and to escort them with warships through the Persian Gulf. The Ronald Reagan administration had three main motivations for agreeing to the escorts: to keep the Soviet Union out of

A line of reflagged Kuwaiti oil tankers transit the Persian Gulf under U.S. Navy escort in 1987 during Operation EARNEST WILL. (U.S. Department of Defense)

the oil-rich Persian Gulf, to improve diplomatic relations with Middle East allies, and to ensure the flow of oil to the West. Kuwait secretly agreed to provide free fuel for the escort operation.

Low-key planning for the operation, code-named EARNEST WILL, began in the spring of 1987. At the time, the United States had only a small naval contingent called the Middle East Force, consisting of seven ships, stationed in the Persian Gulf. Rear Admiral Harold Bernsen was the commanding officer of the Middle East Force. These ships were originally set to carry out the escorts with no augmentation. On May 17, 1987, during the EARNEST WILL planning stages, an Iraqi plane on a tanker attack mission mistakenly fired two missiles into the U.S. Navy Perry-class frigate *Stark,* one of the Middle East Force ships. This attack, held to be accidental, killed 37 U.S. sailors, drew increased public and congressional scrutiny to the upcoming escort operation, and led to increased coordination with Iraq in hopes of avoiding another such incident. The United States now sent more ships to the Persian Gulf and upgraded the capability of the Middle East Force in preparation for the late July start of EARNEST WILL.

The first official escort mission began on July 24, 1987, amid Iranian threats to disrupt the operation. The first Kuwaiti tankers to be reflagged and escorted were the *Bridgeton* and the *Gas Prince.* Three U.S. warships accompanied the two tankers from the Gulf of Oman to a position near Farsi Island in the northern

Persian Gulf. At that point, the *Bridgeton* struck a submerged sea mine on July 27, 1987. The explosion caused little damage to the massive tanker, which continued on to Kuwait after a short delay. The United States quickly determined that the Iranians had laid the mines in the path of the convoy. Iran denied any involvement but continued to make veiled threats. Despite criticism from Congress and even from segments of the U.S. military, the Reagan administration ordered EARNEST WILL to continue. The escorts were temporarily suspended while minesweeping operations began. The escorts resumed in early August, with improvised minesweepers leading the way.

The mine threat prompted the United States to bring in Special Forces units and to increase intelligence-gathering efforts to prevent further mining. On the night of September 21, 1987, U.S. helicopters spotted an Iranian ship *Iran Ajr* laying mines and took the ship under fire. Navy SEALs boarded the *Iran Ajr* the next morning and took the surviving crew members as prisoners. The Reagan administration presented the mines seized from *Iran Ajr* as proof of the Iranian mining campaign.

In early October 1987 U.S. Special Forces outfitted the first of two oil barges converted into heavily armed mobile sea bases in the northern Persian Gulf. Small boats and helicopters based on the barges patrolled the area, watching for Iranian minelayers and other activity that might threaten the convoys. These efforts virtually stopped the mining campaign in that area of the Persian Gulf. Iran periodically fired Silkworm missiles, and on October 16, 1987, one of the missiles struck a U.S.-flagged Kuwaiti tanker. The explosion blinded the captain, a U.S. citizen, and wounded several other members of the crew.

The United States retaliated with a naval bombardment of an offshore Iranian oil platform on October 19, 1987. According to intelligence reports, Iran used this platform along with others as command and control bases for tanker attacks. This bombardment was code-named Operation NIMBLE ARCHER and was commanded by Rear Admiral Dennis Brooks, who was stationed with a carrier task force in the Arabian Sea.

Following NIMBLE ARCHER, there were no confrontations between the United States and Iran for almost six months. The escorts continued with only minor problems throughout the winter of 1987–1988. In February 1988 the United States combined the forces in the Persian Gulf and the Arabian Sea into a joint command led by Vice Admiral Anthony Less.

On April 14, 1988, the U.S. Navy Oliver Hazard Perry–class guided missile frigate *Samuel B. Roberts* hit a mine while transiting through the central Persian Gulf alone. The mine severely damaged the ship and wounded 10 sailors. Only excellent damage control kept the ship afloat while it steered clear of the area. Further investigation found an extensive minefield with the same type of mines found on *Iran Ajr* and in other Iranian-laid minefields.

The United States planned a significant retaliatory measure, which took place on April 18, 1988. This day-long running battle was code-named Operation PRAYING MANTIS and involved nine American surface ships and a carrier air wing from the *Enterprise*. One of the mission goals was to sink an Iranian warship. The operation began with bombardments of two Iranian oil platforms. Iran sent various ships, boats, and planes to confront the U.S. ships throughout the day. Most of the Iranian force, including two frigates, were sunk or disabled by the Americans. The United States lost one helicopter with a two-man crew to an accident early in the evening. PRAYING MANTIS was the largest U.S. military combat operation to date in the Persian Gulf and the largest sea-air battle since World War II. Shortly after, the United States extended protection to all non-Iranian shipping in the Persian Gulf.

By the summer of 1988, Iraq clearly had the upper hand in the undeclared war with Iran. On July 3, 1988, the U.S. Navy Ticonderoga-class Aegis guided missile cruiser *Vincennes* accidentally shot down an Iranian passenger jetliner in the Strait of Hormuz. This incident was seen in Iran as further evidence that the United States was taking sides with Iraq, and it was one of the reasons the Iranian government decided to seek an end to the Tanker War and the Iran-Iraq War.

The Iran-Iraq War finally ended in August 1988, but the EARNEST WILL escorts continued until December 1989. Operation EARNEST WILL was mostly successful and laid the groundwork logistically and diplomatically for subsequent U.S. Persian Gulf operations.

HAROLD WISE

See also

Iran; Iran Air Flight 655; Iran-Iraq War; Iraq, History of, Pre-1990; Oil; Persian Gulf; PRAYING MANTIS, Operation; *Stark* Incident

References

Palmer, Michael A. *Guardians of the Gulf: A History of America's Expanding Role in the Persian Gulf, 1833–1992*. New York: Free Press, 1992.

Wise, Harold L. *Inside the Danger Zone: The U.S. Military in the Persian Gulf 1987–1988*. Annapolis, MD: Naval Institute Press, 2007.

EASTERN EXIT, **Operation**
Start Date: January 2, 1991
End Date: January 11, 1991

Military evacuation of U.S. embassy personnel and foreign nationals from Somalia in January 1991. By late 1990, the ongoing civil war in Somalia was threatening to undo all aspects of that nation's social and political infrastructure, especially as President Mohamed Siad Barre's forces were on the verge of collapse. As the situation in Mogadishu deteriorated, on January 1, 1991, the U.S. embassy in the besieged city requested that Washington provide an immediate evacuation mission to remove embassy workers and foreign nationals from Somalia. By then, chaos reigned in the capital city as competing groups vied for control of Mogadishu, and numerous Americans and other foreign nationals not working in the embassy had sought refuge there. In all, 281 individuals would have to be evacuated from the embassy compound.

The George H. W. Bush administration reacted quickly, and by January 2 Operation EASTERN EXIT was under way. The evacuation would involve USS *Guam* (LPH-9), an Iwo Jima–class amphibious ship, and USS *Trenton* (LPD-14), an Austin-class amphibious transport dock. Also involved in the operation were the 4th Marine Expeditionary Brigade, a nine-man Navy SEAL team, an air force Lockheed AC-130 gunship, and other support elements. Special operations helicopters in the region were placed on alert, as were other air force aircraft. Operation EASTERN EXIT was running concomitantly with Operation DESERT SHIELD, which in just a few weeks would morph into Operation DESERT STORM, the coalition invasion of Iraq.

Plans for the evacuation included an airlift of the Americans from the airport at Mogadishu; however, as the situation on the ground continued to worsen, it became clear that the Americans would probably not be able to make the trip from the embassy to the airport. Also, fighting in and around the airport would have imperiled any attempt at an airlift. A Marine Air-Ground Task Force (MAGTF) was hastily assembled from elements on the *Guam* and *Trenton*, which included a reinforced helicopter squadron comprised of two squadrons of Boeing CH-46 Sea Knight medium-lift transport helicopters and several Sikorsky CH53-E Super Stallion heavy transport helicopters. The only hope of evacuating the embassy was by flying directly to it via helicopter and extracting the Americans there.

In the early morning hours of January 5, several CH-53E helicopters lifted off from the *Guam,* bound for the Mogadishu embassy with a 60-person security force. The long flight required two midair refueling operations, as the *Guam* and *Trenton* were still some 400 miles distant from the Somali coast even though steaming there at full speed. Arriving at the embassy shortly after 7:00 a.m., the security force landed and began immediately to secure the embassy compound and its perimeter. The first CH53-E lifted off about an hour later with 61 evacuees on board, bound for the *Guam.*

On January 6 just after midnight, the *Guam* and *Trenton* had arrived off the coast of Somalia, making the remainder of the airlift far easier. CH-46 helicopters were launched, 20 in all, in four waves. The first three waves evacuated the remaining civilians, while the last evacuated the security force. Before 4:00 a.m. on January 6, the airlift had been completed. As the last helicopter left the scene, looters had already begun to penetrate the embassy compound.

On January 11 all the evacuees arrived at Muscat, Oman, and the operation was declared complete. Among the 281 rescued were individuals from some 30 nations. In the voyage from Somalia to Oman 1 evacuee gave birth, bringing the final count of persons evacuated to 282. The unqualified success of Operation EASTERN EXIT was all the more remarkable because it occurred in the looming shadow of the Persian Gulf War. At the time, however, it received scant attention because of the imminent war against Iraq.

PAUL G. PIERPAOLI JR.

See also

DESERT SHIELD, Operation; DESERT STORM, Operation; Somalia, International Intervention in

References

Allard, C. Kenneth. *Somalia Operation: Lessons Learned.* Washington, DC: National Defense University Press, 1995.

Simmons, Anna. *Networks of Dissolution: Somalia Undone.* Boulder, CO: Westview, 1995.

Stevenson, Jonathan. *Losing Mogadishu: Testing U.S. Policy in Somalia.* Annapolis, MD: Naval Institute Press, 1995.

Eberly, David William
Birth Date: May 26, 1947

U.S. Air Force officer and the senior-ranking allied prisoner of war during Operation DESERT STORM in 1991. William David Eberly was born on May 26, 1947. He earned a BS degree in business administration from Indiana University in 1969 and was commissioned a second lieutenant in the air force through the Reserve Officers' Training Corps (ROTC). After earning his pilot's wings at Columbus Air Force Base in Mississippi, he served in 18 locations around the world, including three assignments at the Pentagon, and logged more than 3,400 hours in fighter aircraft. He earned a master of arts degree from Central Michigan University in 1977.

Following flight school, Eberly was assigned as an instructor and staff officer in Air Training Command. He was then selected for a special one-year intern assignment in the Air Staff Training program (ASTRA) at the Pentagon. In 1977 he completed training in the McDonnell Douglas F-4 Phantom II at MacDill Air Force Base in Florida and was assigned to the 90th Tactical Fighter Squadron at Clark Air Base in the Philippines. In the spring of 1980 he graduated from the Armed Forces Staff College and then returned to fighter operations at Ramstein Air Base in West Germany, where he served as chief of standardization for the 86th Tactical Fighter Wing and as the operations officer of the 512th Tactical Fighter Squadron. In 1984 Eberly returned to the Pentagon, assigned to the Office of the Air Force Vice Chief of Staff.

After attending the Air War College in 1989, Eberly was selected to be deputy commander for operations of the 4th Tactical Fighter Wing at Seymour Johnson Air Force Base in Goldsboro, North Carolina. Within days of Iraq's invasion of Kuwait in August 1990, Colonel Eberly deployed to the Persian Gulf as the deputy commander of operations for the 4th Wing (Provisional) in Oman and Saudi Arabia.

On January 17, 1991, the air campaign of Operation DESERT STORM commenced, and Eberly took part in the initial night strikes into Iraq. On his second mission, January 19, his formation was targeted by seven Iraqi surface-to-air missiles, and his McDonnell Douglas F-15 Eagle was shot down over enemy territory. After ejecting, he and his weapons systems officer, Major Tom Griffin, evaded hostile forces for two days and three nights before being captured on the Syria-Iraq border. For the next 43 days, Eberly and 44 other allied prisoners were subjected to torture, starvation, and other forms of mistreatment in violation of the Geneva Conventions. After the cease-fire, Eberly and the final group of prisoners were released on March 5, 1991.

Eberly became the first commander of the newly activated 4th Operations Group at Seymour Johnson Air Force Base in April 1991 before returning to the Pentagon as a Joint National Security Council planner in 1992. Eberly's final assignment was as defense and air attaché at the U.S. embassy in Ottawa, Canada, from 1994 to 1997.

After retiring from the air force as a colonel in November 1997, Eberly wrote *Faith beyond Belief: A Journey to Freedom* (2002), detailing his experience as a downed airman and prisoner of war in Baghdad. He has appeared in a variety of Persian Gulf War specials on the History and Learning channels and has spoken to audiences across the country. Eberly also formed Main Street Vision, a company dedicated to continuing the fight against terrorism.

RANDY J. TAYLOR

See also

DESERT STORM, Operation, Coalition Air Campaign; Prisoners of War, Persian Gulf War

References

Atkinson, Rick. *Crusade: The Untold Story of the Persian Gulf War.* New York: Mariner Books, 1994.

Eberly, David. *Faith beyond Belief: A Journey to Freedom.* Richmond, VA: Brandylane Publishers, 2002.

Peters, John, John Nichol, and William Pearson. *Tornado Down.* London: Signet, 1993.

Simon, Bob. *Forty Days.* New York: Putnam, 1992.

Economic Effects of the Persian Gulf War on Iraq

For Iraq, the economic effects of the 1990–1991 Persian Gulf War were devastating. In 1988 Iraq emerged from an inconclusive eight-year war with its archenemy Iran deeply in debt, with much of its economy in ruins and having suffered hundreds of thousands of casualties. Iraq's invasion of Kuwait on August 2, 1990, had much to do with simple economics.

Iraqi president Saddam Hussein's subsequent refusal to withdraw unconditionally from its small wealthy neighbor led the United Nations (UN) four days later to impose broad economic sanctions on Iraq, which essentially amounted to an embargo on all Iraqi commercial and financial transactions. When economic sanctions failed to end Iraq's occupation of Kuwait, in January 1991 an international military coalition led by the United States attacked Iraq in a punishing one-month air campaign that destroyed much of Iraq's remaining infrastructure. That was followed by a 100-hour-long ground assault that evicted Iraqi military forces from Kuwait.

As a condition of ending the war and lifting the economic sanctions, Iraq agreed to account for and relinquish all of its stockpiles of weapons of mass destruction (WMDs) under the supervision of weapons inspectors operating under the UN. Because of repeated confrontations between Iraq and the United States along with Hussein's refusal to cooperate with UN weapons inspectors, economic sanctions remained in effect on Iraq for 13 years, until the overthrow of Hussein in April 2003.

On August 6, 1990, UN Security Council Resolution 661 prohibited both the importation and sale of any Iraqi products and goods "except payments exclusively for strictly medical or humanitarian

An Iraqi woman receives a ration of sugar. Food was in short supply after the United Nations (UN) imposed an embargo following the Iraqi invasion of Kuwait in August 1990. (AP/Wide World Photos)

purposes and, in humanitarian circumstances, foodstuffs." The sanctions were viewed as among the toughest ever imposed on a country and reflected the world's outrage over Iraq's unprovoked invasion and subsequent brutal occupation of Kuwait. The sanctions, however, failed to have any impact on Iraqi government policy and only further contributed to the misery and poverty of the Iraqi people. Iraq's economy was almost exclusively based on oil exports, and because the sanctions outlawed the international sale of Iraqi oil, this deprived Iraq of its principal source of hard currency.

In response to the sanctions the Iraqi government resorted to rationing food, but the rationing was insufficient to meet recommended daily nutritional and health needs. Along with dwindling food supplies, medical care and other social services began to collapse in Iraq, and malnutrition, disease, and death, particularly among infants and young children, rose to alarming levels. As a consequence, there was growing opposition in the world community to the sanctions.

Any hope that the sanctions would be lifted following the liberation of Kuwait and the defeat of Iraq in February 1991 were dashed by Hussein's defiance of the UN. This led to an extension of the sanctions imposed on August 6, 1990, and linkage to the dismantlement of Iraq's stockpiles of WMDs per Resolution 687.

With the massive destruction inflicted on Iraq by allied forces during the Persian Gulf War—including the destruction of much of the country's power-generating system and other types of infrastructure such as water treatment and sewage plants—the misery and suffering of the Iraqi people increased. It is estimated that Iraq suffered $230 billion in losses to its infrastructure alone during Operation DESERT STORM. Interestingly, between 1993 and 1995, owing to rising oil prices and the partial rejuvenation of the Iraqi petroleum industry, Iraq's gross domestic product (GDP) actually rose before falling again in the second half of the decade. This was also a result of Iraq's illegal and clandestine exports of oil. Because of rising international opposition to the seemingly endless confrontation and stalemate between Iraq and the United States and the UN along with international sympathy for the growing suffering of the Iraqi people, in 1997 Iraq was allowed to sell oil in exchange for food and medicine. This program was administered through the UN.

The effect of the Oil-for-Food Programme is difficult to gauge, but it did stabilize the rapidly deteriorating state of Iraqi living conditions. The program was criticized for its slow pace and the fact that so-called dual use technology—items that had both civilian and military uses, such as chemicals to treat sewage—was banned. In addition, although in theory Iraq could sell as much oil as it could produce, Iraq's oil infrastructure was in dire need of repair and modernization because of the war with Iran followed by the Persian Gulf War and then the sanctions. Thus, Iraq could refine and export only a fraction of its vast oil reserves. Moreover, it was later revealed that the Oil-for-Food Programme was rife with abuse, corruption, and fraud. It should be noted, however, that the Oil-for-Food Programme was never intended to be a cure for the ill

effects of the sanctions on Iraq but instead was intended to entice Hussein to finally cooperate fully with UN weapons inspectors.

Hussein, however, objected to the fact that sanctions were still in place years after the end of the Persian Gulf War and concluded—not without justification—that the United States and Great Britain would never lift the sanctions. Indeed, he professed to believe that the sanctions were designed to contribute to the overthrow of his regime. Besides that, the plight of the suffering Iraqis overshadowed external scrutiny of his repressive regime and review of his brutal human rights record, thereby providing him with a public relations weapon in his ongoing battle with the United States and Great Britain.

It is impossible to determine the overall effect of the sanctions on Iraq, but it is estimated that anywhere from tens of thousands to hundreds of thousands—perhaps even 1 million—Iraqis, disproportionately children, died under the sanctions regime during 1990–2003. Iraq was one of the few Arab states in the 1970s with an extensive middle class, a highly literate and college-educated population that included women, and a booming economy. Almost all of this was undone in the years leading up to 2003. It is important to note, however, that eight years of war with Iran, which preceded the Persian Gulf War, had already seriously damaged Iraq's economy. The sanctions most certainly made things even worse. By 2003, oil exports represented $7.4 billion of Iraq's total $7.6 billion in exports, meaning that Iraq was exporting virtually nothing beyond petroleum. These figures remained the same for much of the sanctions period, at least after the imposition of the Oil-for-Food Programme. This represented a loss of eight years of Iraq's total GDP simply from lost oil revenue. Some economists claim that Hussein's regime (1979–2003) effectively meant the loss of two decades' worth of GDP.

STEFAN M. BROOKS

See also

Iraq, History of, Pre-1990; Iraq, History of, 1990–Present; Iraq, Sanctions on

References

Alnasrawi, Abbas. *The Economic Consequences of the Gulf War.* Westport, CT: Greenwood, 1994.

Amstutz, Mark R. *International Ethics: Concepts, Theories, and Cases in Global Politics.* 2nd ed. Lanham, MD: Rowman and Littlefield Publishers, 2005.

Economic Impact of the September 11, 2001, Attacks

The financial impact of the September 11, 2001, terrorist attacks on the United States was particularly devastating to New York City and to the commercial airline industry. It was this economic damage as much as the physical damage that had appealed to Osama bin Laden when he helped plan the assaults. Indeed, he hoped to attack the United States at its source of strength and cause it considerable economic distress. Because New York City is the hub of the nation's financial industry, it was very high on Al Qaeda's list of targets.

Bin Laden was successful in achieving his goals. Property losses, particularly in New York City, were high. Southern Manhattan, where the World Trade Center was located, was the center of New York City's government and international finance, and both were paralyzed for weeks. Nearby office buildings remained empty, and the subways stopped running. Also, tens of thousands of New Yorkers who lived below Canal Street were prevented from going there. All of the city's schools and bridges were also closed.

The economic impact was greatest and most long lasting in the airline industry, because the attacks were carried out using commercial airliners. The airlines were hit by massive insurance and litigation claims from the thousands of families of those killed or wounded in the attacks, and greatly enhanced postattack airport security also cost the airlines millions of dollars to implement and administer.

It took the American airline industry nearly five years to recover completely from 9/11. Both American and United airlines lost two aircraft each to the hijackers, but insurance covered most of those losses. What hurt the airlines the most was the loss of customers, many of whom were afraid to fly. Airports had been shut down around the country for several days, meaning millions of dollars in lost revenue. Even 10 days after the September 11 attack, New York City's three main airports were only operating 80 percent of their flights but with only 35 percent of passenger seats filled. Lost revenue from the three New York airports alone was around $250 million a day.

Compounding the problem was the rocketing cost of oil and the higher aviation premiums from insurers. In the period from September 11, 2001, to September 2004, the airline industry lost $23 billion. In October 2001 airline passenger traffic had dropped 23.2 percent in comparison to October 2000. An infusion of $1.5 billion of federal aid helped the airline industry, but a series of bankruptcies and mergers occurred in the next few years. Only gradually were the airlines able to move back toward financial health.

New York City experienced massive job losses and saw many buildings damaged or destroyed. Job losses have been estimated at 143,000 a month, with lost wages of $2.8 billion. Nearly 70 percent of the jobs lost and 86 percent of the wages lost were to persons with well-paying positions in finance, insurance, and banking, the industries that were hit the hardest. Building and property-damage losses have been assessed at $34 billion, with only about half that insured at value. It has been estimated that the city lost $60 billion in revenue, with $82 million coming from lost parking ticket revenue alone.

Perhaps the least long-lasting economic impact was in the stock market. On September 11, 2001, the hijacked aircraft crashed into the World Trade Center complex before the opening of the stock market. Damage to communications, evacuation orders, and rescue efforts led to the closing of the market for the next four days. When the stock market reopened on Monday, September 17, there was an immediate sell-off. On September 10 the Standard & Poor's 500 Index had closed at 1,092.54; when trading closed on September 17, the index stood at 891.10. By September 24, however, the stock market was climbing again, and by October 11 the index closed at 1,097.43, having erased all of the earlier losses.

The American economy as a whole rebounded from the September 11 attacks within months. One reason that the attacks did not have a more lasting impact was that they had been concentrated by geography and industry. Whereas New York City, and to a much lesser extent Washington, D.C., suffered economic dislocation from unemployment and property damage, the rest of the country was left relatively untouched. The economy dipped into a mild recession; however, the situation significantly worsened by the end of 2008.

The most difficult area to assess is the economic cost of confronting Al Qaeda in military actions in Afghanistan and Iraq and in new procedures and agencies created worldwide to confront terrorism. Al Qaeda strategists have often pointed out the enormous sums of money now being expended by the United States and other Western countries on this effort as opposed to the relatively modest amounts for Al Qaeda in waging jihad.

Stephen A. Atkins

See also

September 11 Attacks

References

Griffiths, Katherine. "US Airline Industry in Tailspin to Disaster." *Independent* [London], September 10, 2004, 46.

Kawar, Mark. "9/11 Shock Didn't Bring Bears to Stock Market." *Omaha World Herald,* September 17, 2002, 1D.

Polgreen, Lydia. "Study Confirms 9/11 Impact on New York City Economy." *New York Times,* June 30, 2004, B6.

Zuckerman, Sam. "9/11 Before & After: It's the Rebound, Stupid." *San Francisco Chronicle,* December 30, 2001, D7.

Egypt

North African nation encompassing 386,660 square miles. Egypt has an estimated 2008 population of 81.713 million people. The country is bounded by the Mediterranean Sea to the north, Libya to the west, Sudan to the south, and the Red Sea, the Gulf of Aqaba, and Israel to the east and northeast.

Egypt boasts one of the world's oldest civilizations. In 1798 Napoleon Bonaparte invaded Egypt hoping to use it as a springboard to India. He defeated its Mamluk rulers but was then cut off there by British sea power. Upon the French departure, Ottoman military leader Muhammad Ali Pasha gained control over the country and secured the right to serve as its viceroy in return for suppressing rebellions in other Ottoman territories, the Arabian Peninsula, and Syria. Muhammad Ali's descendants ruled Egypt.

In 1869 a French company headed by Ferdinand de Lesseps, which had secured the concession from Egypt's ruler, opened the Suez Canal. It soon became of immense importance to Britain as

A view of the Cairo skyline, including Al-Azhar University and mosque. (iStockPhoto)

the imperial lifeline to India. In 1882 antiforeign riots gave the British government the excuse to send forces to the country and take control of Egypt. Although rising Egyptian nationalism led the British to cede nominal independence to Egypt in 1922, in effect the British government retained considerable control over the Egyptian government as well as maintained substantial military bases there. During World War II, Egypt remained an important Allied base. Its importance may be seen in that during the Battle of Britain, Prime Minister Winston Churchill diverted desperately needed military assets there. Axis and British forces clashed following an Italian invasion of Egypt in 1940, and the ensuing battles there were some of the most critical of the entire war. The expanded presence of Western troops in Egypt, however, fueled the fires of Egyptian nationalism and especially angered the Muslim Brotherhood, an antisecularist party that sought to dominate the country.

In 1952 a group of Egyptian Army officers overthrew King Farouk and seized power. Initially, the Free Officers chose as their leader Muhammad Najib, who was outmaneuvered by Gamal Abdel Nasser, who became president of Egypt. Nasser preached a populist and anti-imperialist philosophy that called for Arab unity and became known as Nasserism. Starting in 1961, he also promoted certain policies of Arab socialism.

Soon after becoming president, Nasser suppressed Egyptian Marxists, the labor movement, and the Muslim Brotherhood. In 1955 he signed an agreement with Czechoslovakia to purchase Soviet arms. This, his 1955 refusal to sign the pro-Western Baghdad Pact, and his association with the Non-Aligned Movement ran counter to British aims and also concerned policy makers, who did not differentiate local nationalisms from communism, which they hoped to contain in the region.

The United States rescinded its pledge to help fund Nasser's ambitious plan to build a high dam on the upper Nile at Aswan. Nasser then nationalized the Suez Canal to pay for construction of the canal. This step greatly angered British leaders. The French government was already upset over Nasser's perceived assistance to insurgent forces in Algeria who were fighting for independence there, and the Israelis were already angered over Nasser's decision to blockade the Gulf of Aqaba (Israel's access to the Indian Ocean) and Egyptian sponsorship of Palestinian fedayeen raids into the Jewish state. The British, French, and Israeli leaders then joined together to precipitate the 1956 Suez Crisis. Israeli forces then invaded the Sinai. When Egypt refused to allow the British to intervene to "protect" the Suez Canal, Britain and France attacked Egypt and landed troops.

The Soviet Union openly supported Egypt, and the administration of President Dwight D. Eisenhower also brought considerable pressure to bear, demanding that the British, French, and Israelis withdraw, which they did. Although Israel benefited from the crisis, Britain and France did not. And far from overthrowing

Nasser, the three nations had made him a hero in the Arab world. Nasser now expelled many foreigners and minorities and seized their property.

Nasser's government turned increasingly to the Soviet bloc, receiving both technical advisers and weaponry. Some 17,000 Soviet advisers eventually arrived in Egypt, and Egyptians were sent to the Soviet Union to receive advanced military training.

In 1958 Syrian officers and politicians prevailed on Nasser to join their country in the United Arab Republic, a three-year experiment in Arab unity. It was completely dominated by Egypt, and Syria withdrew from the union in 1961. That same year, the Egyptian government pursued more aggressive Arab socialist policies in the form of land reform, government seizure of private holdings, and further nationalizations. After 1962 the Arab Socialist Union, a single political party, dominated Egypt's bureaucratic and governmental structures. The party became even more important, for a time, after 1965.

The Egyptian military expanded throughout the Cold War and was equipped primarily by the Soviets. Egypt's chief military challenge was Israel's better funded and far better trained armed forces. During the Cold War a struggle developed between more progressive Arab states such as Egypt and Western-aligned monarchies such as Saudi Arabia; some scholars termed this the Arab Cold War. The Arab Cold War led Nasser to pursue secondary aims by supporting Yemeni republicans against the Saudi proxies of the royalists in Yemen in 1962. Egyptian forces were not highly successful in their intervention in Yemen, however, and were still bogged down there when the 1967 war with Israel began.

Convinced that Egypt was preparing to attack it because of second-country intelligence along with Egypt's closing of the Strait of Tiran, Israel mounted a preemptive strike that destroyed much of the Egyptian Air Force on the ground on June 5, 1967. Israel went on to defeat the Arab forces of Egypt, Syria, and Jordan and several Iraqi brigades in a six-day conflict. Egypt lost the Sinai, Jordan lost the entire West Bank of the Jordan River, and Syria lost the Golan Heights. The Israelis also secured Gaza from Egypt.

The debacle prompted Nasser to make the gesture of resigning, but wide-scale popular demonstrations by the Egyptian people blocked this. Recovering politically from the Six-Day War, Nasser then mounted a war of attrition against Israel that continued until 1970. Meanwhile, he continued to pursue his Arabist ideals and support the Palestinian cause. Palestinian and Syrian pressures in Jordan led to an inter-Arab crisis known as Black September (1970) in which militant Palestinians were expelled from that country. Nasser was personally involved in negotiating the aftermath of this crisis just prior to his death in 1970.

Nasser was succeeded by President Anwar Sadat, another member of the officer group that had come to power in 1952. Under Sadat, Egypt moved toward the West. Sadat expelled communist bloc advisers and purged Nasserists from the governmental elite. Egypt received more Arab aid and gradually opened its economy to foreign investment and joint partnerships.

Disillusioned with the lack of progress in the peace process, in 1973 Sadat joined forces with Syria to launch a surprise attack on Israel. The October 1973 Yom Kippur (Ramadan) War began successfully for the attackers. Egyptian troops crossed the Suez Canal, and Syrian forces moved into the Golan Heights. Israel eventually beat back both the Syrian and Egyptian attacks. The Israelis crossed the canal themselves and cut off Egyptian forces on the east bank. Heavy pressure from the United States, the Soviet Union, and the United Nations (UN) brought a cease-fire agreement.

Sadat had already effected economic and political changes and was modernizing the military. Egyptians regarded the 1973 war as an affirmation of the nation's strength, but Sadat knew that his nation country could not afford another costly war. He took the dramatic step of traveling to Jerusalem in 1977 to lay the groundwork for a peace agreement with Israel that was ultimately achieved in the 1979 Camp David Accords. This agreement returned the Sinai peninsula to Egyptian control. Egypt's participation in the bilateral agreement with Israel was very unpopular with other Arab nations, however, and they promptly cut off aid and tourism to the country for a time and expelled Egypt from the Arab League. Because of other political issues, including Sadat's failure to open the political system, the peace agreement soon became unpopular with many Egyptians.

New Islamic fundamentalist groups began to emerge in Egypt in the 1970s. Sadat had pardoned and released from jail members of the Muslim Brotherhood and allowed Islamist student groups to organize. One of these groups attempted to kill Sadat during a visit to the Military Technical Academy. The radical Islamic Jihad succeeded in assassinating Sadat in the course of a military review in October 1981.

Under Sadat's successor, Hosni Mubarak, the country continued its economic opening to the West via privatization and joint ventures, all the while maintaining a large military establishment. The most important challenge to the state internally in the decades of the 1980s and 1990s came from Islamist groups that mounted attacks against local officials and tourists. These groups as well as many professionals opposed normalized relations with Israel.

During the 1991 Persian Gulf War, Mubarak joined the international coalition to oppose Iraqi control of Kuwait, and Egyptian troops participated in the liberation of Kuwait in February 1991. As a result of its support, Egypt also received loan waivers from the United States, Western Europe, and several Persian Gulf states in excess of $20 billion. In the aftermath of the September 11, 2001, terror attacks, the Egyptian government voiced its support for the Global War on Terror but declined to deploy any troops to Operations ENDURING FREEDOM or IRAQI FREEDOM. Indeed, Egypt voiced its displeasure with the U.S.-led coalition invasion of Iraq; however, following the overthrow of Iraqi president Saddam Hussein, Egypt publicly supported the Iraqi Governing Council. Since 2003, U.S.-Egyptian relations have been periodically strained because of disagreements over the war in Iraq and the Israeli-Palestinian conflict, U.S. calls for increased democratization in Egypt, and suggestions that U.S. aid might be cut off. In December 2006 Egypt's foreign minister called for an end to what he termed "nuclear double standards," which saw economic sanctions imposed against Iran because of its alleged program to acquire nuclear weapons but allowed Israel to develop and deploy nuclear weapons with complete impunity.

Egypt, on U.S. insistence, helped to isolate the radical Palestinian organization Hamas in the Gaza Strip, which after 2007 was under an economic blockade mounted by Israel and Western nations. Egypt closed its borders with Gaza, yet widespread smuggling occurred into Gaza from Egypt through an extensive system of tunnels. Although Egypt took a tougher line with Hamas than that organization expected, Egypt also played a key role in negotiations with Hamas and has hosted various meetings aimed at securing a new truce between it and Israel and an end to the economic boycott.

Israeli's all-out attack on the Gaza Strip during December 2008–January 2009 imposed serious strains on Egyptian-Israeli relations. In the spring of 2008 a series of attacks and attempted attacks on tourists occurred, and there was mounting discontent in the Egyptian military, both of which were attributed to the Gaza debacle.

SHERIFA ZUHUR

See also

Arab-Israeli Conflict, Overview; Arab League; Arab Nationalism; Camp David Accords; Egypt, Armed Forces; Mubarak, Hosni; Muslim Brotherhood; Nasser, Gamal Abdel; Sadat, Muhammad Anwar; Suez Crisis

References

Aburish, Said. *Nasser: The Last Arab*. New York: St. Martin's and Thomas Dunne Books, 2004.

Al-Shumayry, Abd al-Wali. *Harb alf sa'at milhamah al-wihdah al-yamaniyah*. San'a: Maktabat al-Usr, 1995.

Beattie, Kirk J. *Egypt during the Sadat Years*. New York: Palgrave, 2000.

Gordon, Joel. *Nasser's Blessed Movement: Egypt's Free Officers and the July Revolution*. New York: Oxford University Press, 1992.

Rutherford, Bruce. *Liberalism, Islam, and Democracy in the Arab World*. Princeton, NJ: Princeton University Press, 2008.

Sullivan, Denis, and Kimberly Jones. *Global Security Watch Egypt: A Reference Handbook*. New York: Praeger, 2008.

Telhami, Ghada. *Palestine and the Egyptian National Identity*. Westport, CT: Praeger, 1992.

Waterbury, John. *The Egypt of Nasser and Sadat: Political Economy of Two Regimes*. Princeton, NJ: Princeton University Press, 1983.

Zuhur, Sherifa. *Egypt: Security, Political and Islamist Challenges*. Carlisle Barracks, PA: Strategic Studies Institute, 2007.

Egypt, Armed Forces

The Egyptian armed forces that emerged following World War II were organized and equipped largely on the British model. At the beginning of the Israeli War of Independence in May 1948, the Egyptian Army was the largest of the Arab invading armies. The Egyptians fielded 40,000 men supported by more than 50 combat aircraft. Initially the Egyptian expeditionary force included 10,000 troops in five infantry battalions and one armored battalion along with some field artillery. By the end of the war the expeditionary force had grown to 20,000 men, more than 100 armored vehicles, and 90 artillery pieces.

Despite the size of the Egyptian force, the heaviest fighting in the first months of the war occurred on Israel's northern and central fronts rather than in the south. The Egyptian military faced logistical difficulties in trying to move through the Sinai peninsula and the Negev desert. Although the Egyptians did capture several kibbutzim, they also sustained heavy losses in manpower and equipment and were eventually halted near Ashdod.

Following intervention by the United Nations (UN) on May 29, a truce went into effect on June 11, 1948. Folke Bernadotte, the UN mediator, proposed a partition of the region that would have placed the Negev desert under Arab control. Egypt and Israel promptly rejected the plan, and Egyptian units resumed their advance on July 8, ending the cease-fire. During the first truce Israel had obtained much-needed aircraft and weaponry, primarily from Czechoslovakia. The Israel Defense Forces (IDF) now concentrated most of its efforts in the Tel Aviv–Jerusalem corridor, but the Egyptian military failed to maintain the initiative in the south and only achieved a bloody stalemate by the time a second UN truce went into effect on July 18. After three months of negotiations the second cease-fire broke down, and the IDF initiated a series of operations to push the Arabs back.

On December 22, 1948, the IDF launched Operation HOREV, a massive push in the south to drive the Egyptian expeditionary force from Palestine. The operation succeeded in pushing the Egyptian Army out of the Negev and encircling it in the Gaza Strip. IDF troops also raided Egyptian territory in the Sinai, eventually obliging Egypt to accept a truce on January 7, 1949.

The two nations signed an armistice on February 24, 1949, the first between Israel and one of the Arab belligerents. According to the terms of the truce, the Gaza Strip remained under Egyptian occupation.

Conscription Policies of Selected Middle Eastern and North African Countries

Country	Military Obligation
Algeria	Males: 18 months
Bahrain	None
Egypt	Males: 18–30 months
Iran	Males: 18 months
Iraq	None
Israel	Males: 36 months
	Females: 24 months
Jordan	None
Lebanon	Males: 12 months
Morocco	Males: 18 months
Oman	None
Saudi Arabia	None
Syria	Males: 18–30 months
Tunisia	Males: 12 months
United Arab Emirates	None

During the early 1950s Egyptian and Israeli military units periodically raided and skirmished across the border, although no formal state of war existed. The Egyptian-Israeli armistice remained officially in place until 1956, when Egyptian president Gamal Abdel Nasser announced the nationalization of the Suez Canal. This action led to secret cooperation among Israeli, British, and French leaders in a plan to topple Nasser from power. Israel was to launch a drive into the Sinai, whereupon the British and French would intervene to save the canal. The plan called for British and French forces to assume control of a buffer zone extending 10 miles from the Suez Canal. The intended consequences also included the fall of Nasser's government.

On October 29, 1956, Israeli troops attacked the Gaza Strip and the Sinai peninsula, advancing quickly toward the Suez Canal. Britain and France offered to separate the warring armies, but Nasser refused. Two days later, British and French warplanes began bombing Egypt. Nasser thwarted the capture and reopening of the canal by ordering the sinking of 40 ships in the main channel. This forced the closure of the canal until 1957. The Soviet Union threatened to intervene on the side of Egypt, and the United States placed great diplomatic and economic pressure on Britain to withdraw its forces. The UN sent a peacekeeping force to the region, and by early 1957 all Israeli, British, and French forces had withdrawn from Egyptian soil. Nasser emerged from the Suez Crisis as a hero in the Arab world, which applauded him for having stood up to Israel and the Western powers.

The United Nations Emergency Force (UNEF) remained in the Sinai, separating Israel and Egypt, until 1967, although the force gradually shrank in size over time. In 1967 Nasser began remilitarizing the Sinai. He also demanded and secured the complete withdrawal of UNEF troops on May 18, 1967. He then announced that Egypt would close the Strait of Tiran to all Israeli shipping on May 23. On May 30 Egypt and Jordan signed a five-year mutual defense pact, joining an already-existing Egyptian-Syrian alliance. Jordan agreed to place its troops under Egyptian command, and the Jordanians were soon reinforced by Iraqi troops, also under temporary Egyptian control.

Once again, Egypt fielded the largest military force among the Arab belligerents arrayed against Israel. But almost half of Egypt's mobilized manpower of 200,000 was fighting in a civil war in Yemen and was thus unavailable for commitment against Israel. Egypt's air force consisted of more than 400 warplanes, most purchased from the Soviet Union. The force included a sizable number of medium-range bombers that could reach Israeli targets in a matter of minutes.

On June 5, 1967, in a masterful preemptive strike, the Israeli Air Force (IAF) attacked Egyptian airfields, committing virtually every Israeli warplane to the massive raid. More than 300 Egyptian aircraft were destroyed on the ground, almost completely wiping out the Egyptian Air Force. The Israelis lost only 19 aircraft. The air attack, followed by raids on Jordanian, Syrian, and Iraqi airfields, ensured Israeli air supremacy for the duration of the Six-Day War, which raged from June 5 to June 10, 1967.

The Egyptian army in the Sinai consisted of seven divisions, including four armored divisions, nearly 1,000 tanks, more than 1,000 armored personnel carriers, and 600 artillery pieces. They were opposed by three Israeli armored divisions with approximately 700 tanks. The Israelis, using combined-arms tactics and close air support, quickly moved to encircle Abu Aqila and bypass Egyptian positions. When Abu Aqila fell, Egyptian forces attempted to retreat from the Sinai but were cut off by Israeli armor units in the mountain passes of the western Sinai. IAF warplanes continually attacked Egyptian ground troops, and although some units escaped, the Egyptian army was routed in only four days at a cost of hundreds of Egyptian combat vehicles. Following the cease-fire, the Sinai remained under Israeli occupation.

From 1968 to 1970 Egypt and Israel fought a limited war. Known as the War of Attrition, it consisted of a series of raids across the Suez Canal, Egyptian bombardments of Israeli positions in the Sinai, and Israeli commando raids against Egyptian targets. Hostilities began with an Egyptian artillery barrage against the Israeli-held east bank of the Suez Canal in June 1968. During the period of protracted struggle Nasser sought assistance from the Soviet Union, which supplied surface-to-air missiles (SAMs), warplanes, and Soviet advisers and trainers. On August 7, 1970, a cease-fire went into effect that prohibited further military buildup in the Canal Zone. Egypt immediately violated the agreement by installing new SAM sites along the canal itself.

During a cease-fire between Israeli and Egyptian forces in September 1970, an Egyptian soldier stands guard along the banks of the Suez Canal. (AP/Wide World Photos)

In 1973 Egyptian leader Anwar Sadat's effort to secure the Sinai brought the Yom Kippur (Ramadan) War, fought during October 6–26, 1973. Egypt sought to regain control of the Sinai peninsula and end the Israeli threat to the Suez Canal. At the same time Syria hoped to regain the Golan Heights, seized by Israel in 1967. Egypt and Syria caught the Israelis by surprise, attacking without warning on October 6, 1973. The Egyptian assault force against the Bar-Lev Line, the Israeli system of fortifications along the east bank of the Suez Canal, included large numbers of infantry antitank guided missiles intended to neutralize Israel's armored vehicles.

The Egyptians had also established the most powerful air defenses in the region, which temporarily neutralized Israel's air superiority. Most of the air defense network consisted of fixed installations along the canal. The Egyptian Army initially did not intend to advance beyond its air defense umbrella. Instead, Egyptian forces breached the Israeli defenses along the Suez Canal and then dug in to repel the inevitable counterattack. When the attack came, Israeli commanders were stunned by the Egyptian antiair and antitank defenses. Egyptian SAMs exacted a heavy toll on Israeli aircraft.

On October 14 the Egyptians, in response to pleas from the Syrians, launched a massive offensive eastward into the Sinai. Although they advanced more than 10 miles, these forces suffered heavy losses when they moved beyond the range of their SAM batteries along the canal. They were soon battered by Israeli warplanes and antitank missiles. The next day an Israeli counterattack crossed the Suez Canal, destroying Egyptian air defense emplacements and opening the skies to Israeli warplanes. As Israeli armored units poured across the canal, they cut off Egyptian forces in the Sinai and inflicted yet another humiliating defeat upon the Egyptians. On October 22 a UN-mandated cease-fire went into effect, preventing further bloodshed but also trapping the Egyptian Third Army, now cut off without access to supplies. The Egyptians did not regard the Yom Kippur War as a defeat by any means but instead saw in it a psychological victory in that they had crossed the Suez. Indeed, as a direct result of the conflict, the Sinai was returned to Egypt.

The tremendous costs of war to Egypt, both in economic and human terms, convinced Sadat to do what no other Arab leader had done, both in traveling to Israel to meet with Israelis and in pursuing a peace agreement that culminated at Camp David in 1978. Ordinary Egyptians, while not favoring war and seeing it as a cynical outcome of debt and politics, had no political input into Sadat's decision. The Israel-Egypt Peace Treaty, signed in 1979, included provisions for an Israeli withdrawal from the Sinai and Egypt's recognition of Israel's right to exist. Egypt was subsequently expelled from the Arab League, and Sadat was assassinated in 1981 by army officers of the Islamic Jihad movement who opposed his policies, including his negotiations with Israel, and hoped to overthrow the government.

Assuming the Egyptian presidency upon Sadat's death, Hosni Mubarak, like all of Egypt's presidents a military officer, has sought to maintain a modern military force that is ready for combat. The Egyptian military is currently one of the largest forces in the Middle East and the world. All adult men are obliged to serve for three years in the military (although many serve a lesser period), with conscripts making up about half of the Egyptian active duty force at any given time. After the 1978 Camp David Accords, Egypt reduced its defense ties to the Soviet Union and rearmed with American, French, and British equipment. Some of this modern weaponry, including the American M-1 Abrams main battle tank, is assembled under license in Egyptian factories.

When Iraqi forces invaded and occupied Kuwait in August 1990, President Mubarak took his country into the international coalition that drove Iraq from Kuwait in 1991, ultimately providing about 35,000 troops to Operations DESERT SHIELD and DESERT STORM.

At present, the entire Egyptian military numbers some 450,000 active, 254,000 reserve, and 405,000 paramilitary personnel. Egypt's first-line armored and mechanized forces are equipped with almost 900 American M-1A1 and 1,700 M-60A3 main battle tanks and more than 2,600 M-113 armored personnel carriers. The Egyptians still operate a number of older Soviet armored vehicles, including 450 T-62 main battle tanks and more than 1,000 BTR-50 and BTR-60 armored personnel carriers. The Egyptian Army also maintains a substantial force of field artillery, including cannon, rockets, and missiles, as well as a continually upgraded arsenal of air defense systems. Egyptian field and air defense artillery remains a mixture of American and Soviet systems. Egyptian troops are armed with the M16, AKM, and Soviet AK-47 assault rifles as well as the Misr assault rifle.

As with all military forces built on the Soviet model, Egyptian decision making was rigid and highly centralized. The Egyptians, like their Soviet mentors, were capable of developing highly complicated and sophisticated plans, as they demonstrated so effectively when they crossed the Suez Canal in 1973. But once the initial phases of the plan unfolded, the Egyptians lacked the tactical flexibility and the lower-level command initiative to exploit any initial advantages. The Israelis took advantage of this weakness every time. Since moving away from the Soviet model, the Egyptians have made great strides in improving their command and operating systems. The United States and Egypt have also hosted biennial multinational military exercises in Egypt, known as BRIGHT STAR. The biggest Egyptian military handicap, however, remains the fact that a large number of the country's enlisted conscripts are illiterate and poorly equipped to learn how to operate modern high-tech weapons systems.

The Egyptian Air Force, with some 580 fixed-wing aircraft and 121 armed helicopters, primarily flies American and French aircraft, including the Dassault Mirage 2000 and some 220 American General Dynamics F-16 Fighting Falcon fighters. It also continues to operate older fighter aircraft, including the American McDonnell F-4 Phantom and the Soviet Mikoyan Gurevich MiG-21. The primary Egyptian cargo aircraft is the ubiquitous American Lockheed four-engine turboprop EC-130E Hercules. Egyptian attack

Egyptian rangers armed with AK-47 assault rifles in formation in the course of a demonstration for visiting dignitaries during Operation DESERT SHIELD. (U.S. Department of Defense)

helicopters include the American Hughes (McDonnell Douglas/Boeing) AH-64 Apache.

The Egyptian Navy is a relatively small coastal force with some 20,000 personnel. It operates destroyers, submarines, missile boats, and patrol boats. The navy relies on the air force for maritime aerial reconnaissance and all air support.

Egypt's various paramilitary groups include the Central Security Forces, which has about 350,000 troops, operates under the control of the Ministry of the Interior, and is used chiefly for law enforcement and intelligence; the National Guard, numbering some 60,000 personnel; the Border Guard Forces, with about 25,000 personnel; and the Coast Guard, with some 5,000 personnel.

In recent years Egypt has spent on average about $2.5 billion per year on defense, which translates roughly to 3.4 percent of the Egyptian gross domestic product (GDP). Egypt has remained at peace with Israel since 1973, which has reduced Egyptian standing in the Arab world. Nevertheless, Egypt has benefitted significantly by improved ties with the United States and most of the members of the European Union (EU).

PAUL JOSEPH SPRINGER

See also

Arab-Israeli Conflict, Overview; Arms Sales, International; Camp David Accords; DESERT SHIELD, Operation; DESERT STORM, Operation; Egypt; Mubarak, Hosni; Nasser, Gamal Abdel; Sadat, Muhammad Anwar; Suez Crisis

References

Abdel-Malek, Anouar. *Egypt: Military Society, the Army Regime, the Left, and Social Change under Nasser.* New York: Random House, 1968.

Bar-Siman-Tov, Yaacov. *The Israeli-Egyptian War of Attrition, 1969–1970: A Case-Study of Limited Local War.* New York: Columbia University Press, 1980.

Draper, Thomas. *Israel and the Middle East.* New York: H. W. Wilson, 1983.

El Shazly, Saad. *The Crossing of the Suez.* San Francisco: American Mideast Research, 1980.

Herzog, Chaim. *The Arab-Israeli Wars: War and Peace in the Middle East from the War of Independence to Lebanon.* Westminster, MD: Random House, 1984.

Vatikiotis, P. J. *The Egyptian Army in Politics: Pattern for New Nations?* Westport, CT: Greenwood, 1975.

Eikenberry, Karl W.
Birth Date: 1952

U.S. Army general who served during Operation ENDURING FREEDOM as commander, Combined Forces Command, Afghanistan, from

May 2005 to February 2006. Born in 1952 and raised in Indiana, Karl W. Eikenberry graduated from the U.S. Military Academy, West Point, in 1973 and was commissioned as a second lieutenant in the U.S. Army. His education includes master's degrees in East Asian studies from Harvard University and political science from Stanford University. He also studied at the British Ministry of Defence Chinese Language School in Hong Kong and at Nanjing University in China. Eikenberry was a national security fellow at the John F. Kennedy School of Government, Harvard University.

During his military career, Eikenberry has served as a commander and staff officer with mechanized, light, airborne, and ranger infantry units in both the continental United States and overseas in Hawaii, Korea, Italy, China, and Afghanistan. In 2001 he was promoted to major general and began direct support of Operation ENDURING FREEDOM. He served two tours of duty in Afghanistan. During his first Afghanistan assignment (2002–2003), he was instrumental in building up the Afghan Army following the displacement of the Taliban government.

During Operation IRAQI FREEDOM, under the direction of Secretary of Defense Donald Rumsfeld, Eikenberry led a survey team in Iraq during late 2003. The mission of the team was to determine the facts on the ground. Eikenberry reviewed the training of the Iraqi military and police and concluded that Iraqi security forces were not growing at a rate that could keep up with the burgeoning insurgency. At the time, Iraqi security training was controlled by the Coalition Provisional Authority. In the interest of centralized control over Iraqi security efforts, Eikenberry recommended that responsibility for the training and control of Iraqi security forces be given to the U.S. military instead. His recommendation was accepted by Rumsfeld and implemented by the U.S. commander in Iraq, Lieutenant General David Petraeus.

In 2005 Eikenberry was promoted to lieutenant general. During his second tour in Afghanistan (2005–2007), he served as commander of all North Atlantic Treaty Organization (NATO) troops in the nation (Combined Forces Command, Afghanistan). He has testified before Congress multiple times regarding the progress and challenges of coalition forces in that country.

Eikenberry is the former president of the Foreign Area Officers Association and is a member of the Council on Foreign Relations. He is widely published on national security subjects. His works include *Explaining and Influencing Chinese Arms Transfers* (1995) and *China's Challenge to Asia-Pacific Regional Stability* (2005). In January 2007 Eikenberry was assigned as deputy chairman of the NATO Military Committee in Brussels, Belgium.

BENJAMIN D. FOREST

See also

Combined Forces Command, Afghanistan; North Atlantic Treaty Organization in Afghanistan; Petraeus, David Howell; Rumsfeld, Donald Henry

References

Eikenberry, Karl W. *Explaining and Influencing Chinese Arms Transfers.* Washington, DC: National Defense University, 1995.

Ricks, Thomas E. *Fiasco: The American Military Adventure in Iraq.* New York: Penguin, 2006.

Woodward, Bob. *State of Denial: Bush at War, Part III.* New York: Simon and Schuster, 2006.

Eisenhower, Dwight David
Birth Date: October 14, 1890
Death Date: March 27, 1969

U.S. Army general and president of the United States (1953–1961). Born in Denison, Texas, on October 14, 1890, Dwight David Eisenhower grew up in Abilene, Kansas, and graduated from the U.S. Military Academy, West Point, in 1915. He did not serve in combat during World War I. Following the war, he remained in the army and served in a variety of assignments at home and overseas.

In 1939 Eisenhower became chief of staff of the newly established Third Army. Promoted to brigadier general in September 1941 and major general in April 1942, he transferred to London in June 1942 as commander of American and Allied forces in Britain and a month later was promoted to lieutenant general. In November 1942 he commanded the Allied invasion of North Africa. Promoted to full (four-star) general in February 1943, he then oversaw the invasions of Sicily and Italy. In December 1943 he was named to command the Allied forces that invaded France in June 1944 (D-Day invasion). In December 1944 he was promoted to the newly created rank of general of the army (five-star).

From 1945 to 1948 Eisenhower served as chief of staff of the U.S. Army. He was president of Columbia University from 1948 to 1952. During this time he was actively involved in foreign and military affairs and politics. He strongly endorsed President Harry S. Truman's developing Cold War policies, including intervention in Korea in 1950. In January 1951 Eisenhower took leave from Columbia to serve as the first supreme commander of the armed forces of the North Atlantic Treaty Organization (NATO).

In 1952 the Republican Party, desperate to choose a candidate who would be assured of victory, turned to Eisenhower. As a candidate, he promised to end the Korean War but otherwise continue Truman's Cold War policies. Eisenhower won the November 1952 elections.

Under Eisenhower, U.S. defense commitments around the world solidified into a network of bilateral and multilateral alliances. A fiscal conservative uncomfortable with high defense budgets, Eisenhower introduced the New Look strategy of relying heavily on nuclear weapons rather than conventional forces. Critics of the New Look complained that it left the United States unprepared to fight limited wars. As president, Eisenhower fulfilled his campaign pledge to end the Korean War, seemingly threatening to employ nuclear weapons unless an armistice agreement was concluded. The armistice was signed in July 1953.

After Soviet dictator Joseph Stalin's death in March 1953, Eisenhower tried, unsuccessfully, to reach arms control agreements with the Soviets. In February 1956 Soviet leader Nikita Khrushchev repudiated much of Stalin's legacy, a move suggesting that potential existed for a Soviet-American rapprochement. Soon afterward, Khrushchev expressed his faith that it might be possible for the East and West to attain a state of peaceful coexistence. Progress toward this end was patchy, however. From 1958 until 1961 he made repeated attempts to coerce and intimidate the Western powers into abandoning control of West Berlin. The May 1960 U-2 spy plane fiasco all but quashed peaceful coexistence and torpedoed any chances at arms control between the two superpowers.

Eisenhower consistently sought to entice nations in the developing world into the Western camp. Nowhere was this more apparent than in the Middle East. Of course, the Eisenhower administration had other motives in the region, not the least of which was the protection of vital oil supplies. If anticommunism and protection of oil were absolutes in America's Middle East policies, the suppression of Pan-Arabism (often linked to radicalism) was not far behind. Fond of using covert operations via the Central Intelligence Agency (CIA), Eisenhower and Secretary of State John Foster Dulles used the CIA to overthrow a reputedly leftist regime in Iran in August 1953. When Iranian prime minister Mohammad Mossadegh's policies began to go against the wishes of Mohammad Reza Shah Pahlavi—a staunch U.S. ally—Eisenhower came to suspect that Mossadegh had communist leanings at worst or Pan-Arab inclinations at best. Neither was acceptable to Washington. Operation AJAX, launched in August 1953, fomented violent street demonstrations in Iran and stirred up support for the shah, who had left the country only days earlier. Mossadegh was forced to give up power and was arrested and detained. The shah was back in power by month's end. Pro-American stability had returned to the country, and its vast oil resources had been secured.

Three years later another Middle East crisis embroiled the Eisenhower administration in the region's affairs. Egyptian president Gamal Abdel Nasser sought to purchase U.S. arms, and when the United States refused, Nasser brokered an arms barter deal with Czechoslovakia. This was followed by Egyptian recognition of the People's Republic of China (PRC) and fierce anti-U.S. rhetoric in the government-controlled Egyptian press. In response, in July 1956 the Eisenhower administration, followed by the British government, rescinded an earlier offer to grant Egypt a substantial loan for Nasser's project to build a dam on the Nile River south of Aswan.

Nasser then decided to nationalize the Suez Canal, a step that should not have surprised the Western powers. The British and French governments conspired with the Israeli government for the latter to launch an attack against Egypt that would threaten the canal. Britain and France then planned to intervene militarily themselves and overthrow Nasser.

The resulting Suez Crisis unfolded at the end of October and in early November. Enraged that France and Britain had not

General of the Armies Dwight D. Eisenhower was supreme commander of the Allied Expeditionary Forces, European Theater of Operations. He was subsequently the first commander of North Atlantic Treaty Organization (NATO) forces, then president of the United States (1953–1961). (Library of Congress)

consulted the United States and worried about a Soviet intervention, Eisenhower put heavy pressure on the three nations, especially Britain, to remove their forces, which they did in November.

Responding to Soviet threats of interference in future Middle East crises, in January 1957 Eisenhower put forth the Eisenhower Doctrine, pledging American military and economic assistance to any Middle Eastern country that sought to resist communism. Except for Lebanon and Iraq (prior to Iraq's 1958 revolution), few nations welcomed this doctrine, since most countries in the region believed that they had more to fear from Western imperialism than from Soviet expansionism. In April 1957 when Jordan's King Hussein came under intense pressure by Nasserists and other opponents, Eisenhower dispatched the Sixth Fleet to the eastern Mediterranean. His administration also provided the king with $10 million in economic aid.

The first significant test of the Eisenhower Doctrine came in 1958. In February of that year, Egypt and Syria whipped up Nasserist sentiments by their brief union in the United Arab Republic. This set the Eisenhower administration on edge, but it was events in Lebanon that activated the Eisenhower Doctrine. In May, Lebanon's Christian president, Camille Chamoun, who was opposed by a coalition of Muslim, Druze, and Christians in the Lebanese National Front, appealed to Washington for assistance.

Eisenhower's advisers decided to act in this instance, although too late to stave off revolution in Iraq or the Egyptian-Syrian political union. By July 15 the first contingent of some 15,000 U.S. marines landed on Beirut's beaches to restore order. U.S. forces departed Lebanon by the end of October.

Despite Republican claims during the 1952 presidential campaign that they would roll back communism, when workers rose against Soviet rule in East Berlin in June 1953 and again when Hungarians attempted to expel Soviet troops in October 1956, Eisenhower refused to intervene. Although he would not recognize the PRC, he reacted cautiously in the successive Taiwan Strait crises of 1954–1955 and 1958. His administration encouraged the government of South Vietnam in its refusal to hold the elections mandated for 1956 and provided military and economic assistance to bolster its independence. Eisenhower justified these actions by citing the domino theory, which holds that if one noncommunist area were to become communist, the infection would inevitably spread to its neighbors.

Besides the 1953 covert coup in Iran, the CIA supported a successful coup in Guatemala in 1954. Eisenhower and Dulles encouraged the CIA to undertake numerous other secret operations. These included plans for an ill-fated coup attempt against Cuba's communist leader, Fidel Castro.

After leaving office in 1961, Eisenhower backed American intervention in Southeast Asia, an area he specifically warned his successor John F. Kennedy not to abandon. Eisenhower died in Washington, D.C., on March 28, 1969.

PRISCILLA ROBERTS

See also

Dulles, John Foster; France, Middle East Policy; Hussein ibn Talal, King of Jordan; Lebanon, U.S. Intervention in (1958); Nasser, Gamal Abdel; Pan-Arabism and Pan-Arabist Thought; Russia, Middle East Policy, 1991–Present; Soviet Union, Middle East Policy; Suez Crisis; United Kingdom, Middle East Policy; United States, Middle East Policy, 1945–Present

References

Ambrose, Stephen E. *Eisenhower.* 2 vols. New York: Simon and Schuster, 1983–1984.

Chandler, Alfred D., Jr., and Louis Galambos, eds. *The Papers of Dwight D. Eisenhower.* 21 vols. to date. Baltimore: Johns Hopkins Press, 1970–.

Perret, Geoffrey. *Eisenhower.* New York: Random House, 1999.

Eisenhower Doctrine

Major Cold War foreign policy tenet regarding U.S. policy toward the Middle East enunciated by President Dwight D. Eisenhower on January 5, 1957, in the course of a special joint session of the U.S. Congress in which he addressed recent developments in the Middle East. Since the mid-1950s, both the United States and the Soviet Union had increasingly treated that area as a theater of Cold War competition. As the region decolonized, in 1950 Great Britain, the United States, and France had issued a statement expressing their hopes for continuing peace and stability in the Middle East and their desire to avoid an ever-escalating arms race there, especially between the Arab nations and the newly founded State of Israel. Such proclamations proved fruitless. When nationalist regimes resentful of their former colonial overlords won power in the region, most notably in Egypt, they increasingly looked to the Soviet bloc for economic and military aid, while Israel received substantial assistance from the United States. With American backing, in February 1955 Iraq, Turkey, Pakistan, Iran, and the United Kingdom signed the Baghdad Pact, a mutual security treaty widely perceived as a mechanism for preserving Western influence.

In the summer of 1956 American resentment of the fact that Egypt nationalist president and former army officer Gamal Abdel Nasser had accepted substantial amounts of Soviet bloc weaponry led the United States to cancel economic assistance previously promised for a showpiece Egyptian development project, the Aswan Dam. Nasser decided to meet the projected funding shortfall by nationalizing the Suez Canal, which was owned and managed by the British and French governments and thus was a constant source of irritation to Egyptian nationalist pride. This strategically and commercially valuable waterway linked the Mediterranean Sea with the Red Sea, enabling shipping to move between Europe and Asia without circumnavigating Africa. In November 1956 a brief war, usually called the Suez Crisis, erupted when Britain, France, and Israel invaded Egypt and tried to retake control of the canal, only to withdraw when Eisenhower and his secretary of state, John Foster Dulles, exerted heavy financial and diplomatic pressure to compel them to retreat.

During the Suez Crisis, the Soviet Union made what could be interpreted as threats of military action against Britain and France unless they removed their forces from Egypt. Soviet leader Nikita Khrushchev had also recently sent troops to the East European Soviet satellite Hungary to prevent its secession from the Warsaw Pact. Shortly afterward, Khrushchev also indulged in somewhat threatening proclamations that his country would win the Cold War and "bury the Western powers." The Middle East contained the world's most substantial oil reserves, resources that were increasingly essential to the heavily energy-dependent American domestic economy and also to U.S. military capabilities. Convinced that the Middle East, where rising anti-Western nationalism and Arab resentment of Israel compounded the tumultuous political situation, had become a Cold War battleground, Eisenhower advocated a high level of U.S. involvement in the region, and he demanded that Congress grant him military and financial resources to aid Middle Eastern powers attempting to fend off communism. Eisenhower also asserted that when required, the United States would deploy American military forces in the region to oppose "overt armed aggression from any nation controlled by International Communism." In March 1957 Congress passed a joint resolution endorsing Eisenhower's request, the beginning of extensive American involvement in the Middle East that would continue into the 21st century.

The Soviet Union was predictably hostile to the Eisenhower Doctrine, attacking it as a colonialist effort by the United States to replace British and French imperialism with its own hegemony, in defiance of the aspirations to national independence of the Arab peoples. Soviet officials were particularly incensed by the possibility of future American military interventions in the Middle East. The real objective of the United States, in Soviet eyes, was to impose a sort of military protectorate and protect its oil interests in the region. The Soviet Union reminded Arab countries of its own support for Egypt over Suez and urged them to look to themselves for protection against attempts at domination by outside powers. Clearly, the two Cold War superpowers now viewed the Middle East as a significant arena for strategic and economic competition, its various states constituting a potential sphere of influence from which each sought to exclude the other.

Many Arab states and radical nationalist elements were equally hostile to the Eisenhower Doctrine, condemning it immediately as a new form of Western colonialism. Proclamation of the Eisenhower Doctrine effectively dissipated any credibility that American actions during the Suez Crisis had won for the United States with Arab nationalist forces. The United States proved unable to prevent the Iraqi Revolution of July 1958, when radical army officers overthrew the Hashemite monarchy and killed the young king and several of his relatives. The Eisenhower administration did, however, intervene successfully in both Lebanon and Jordan in 1958 to shore up pro-Western governments that it feared might follow suit and succumb to radical leftist coups. These actions helped to reinforce the prevailing image of the United States in the Middle East as a conservative power wedded to the status quo and committed to supporting traditionalist and often illiberal regimes to resist more radical, progressive, and modernizing political forces.

PRISCILLA ROBERTS

See also

Arab Nationalism; Baghdad Pact; Dulles, John Foster; Eisenhower, Dwight David; Lebanon, U.S. Intervention in (1958); Nasser, Gamal Abdel; Soviet Union, Middle East Policy; Suez Crisis; United States, Middle East Policy, 1945–Present

References

Brands, H. W. *Into the Labyrinth: The United States and the Middle East, 1945–1993.* New York: McGraw-Hill, 1994.

Oikarinen, Jarmo. *The Middle East in the American Quest for World Order: Ideas of Power, Economics, and Social Development in United States Foreign Policy, 1953–1961.* Helsinki, Finland: Suomen Historiallinen Seura, 1999.

Salt, Jeremy. *The Unmaking of the Middle East: A History of Western Disorder in Arab Lands.* Berkeley: University of California Press, 2008.

Stivers, William. *America's Confrontation with Revolutionary Change in the Middle East, 1948–83.* London: Macmillan, 1986.

Yaqub, Salim. *Containing Arab Nationalism: The Eisenhower Doctrine and the Middle East.* Chapel Hill: University of North Carolina Press, 2004.

ElBaradei, Muhammad Mustafa
Birth Date: June 17, 1942

Egyptian diplomat, United Nations (UN) official, and director general of the International Atomic Energy Agency (IAEA) since 1997. Muhammad Mustafa ElBaradei (al-Baradei) was born in Cairo, Egypt, on June 17, 1942. His father was Mostafa ElBaradei, a lawyer and former president of the Egyptian Bar Association. The younger ElBaradei earned a bachelor's degree in law from the University of Cairo and a master's degree (1971) and doctorate (1974) in international law from the New York University School of Law.

ElBaradei joined the Egyptian Ministry of Foreign Affairs in 1964. He was twice in the Egyptian permanent missions to the UN in New York and Geneva with responsibilities for political, legal, and arms control issues. In between these postings, during 1974–1978 he was a special assistant to the Egypt foreign minister. ElBaradei became the senior fellow in charge of the International Law Program at the United Nations Institute for Training and Research in 1980, and in 1984 he became a senior

Muhammad ElBaradei, director general of the International Atomic Energy Agency (IAEA), shown here at a news conference in Vienna on February 12, 2003. (AP/Wide World Photos)

staff member of the IAEA Secretariat, where he served as its legal adviser (1984–1993).

During 1984–1987 ElBaradei was also the representative of the IAEA director general to the UN in New York. During 1981–1987 he also taught as an adjunct professor of international law at the New York University School of Law. ElBaradei served as the assistant director general for external relations for the UN during 1993–1997. In January 1997 he accepted the position of director general of the IAEA.

Prior to the beginning of the 2003 Iraq war, ElBaradei and Hans Blix, the Swedish diplomat who headed the United Nations Monitoring, Verification and Inspection Commission (UNMOVIC) from January 2000 to June 2003, led the UN inspection team in Iraq. ElBaradei and Blix asserted that Iraq had no weapons of mass destruction (WMDs).

ElBaradei has since publicly questioned the WMD rationale used by the George W. Bush administration to initiate the Iraq War (2003). ElBaradei has also served as the point man for the UN in the ongoing controversy over Iran's alleged drive to develop nuclear weapons. In September 2005, despite U.S. opposition, ElBaradei was appointed to his third term as director of the IAEA. The Bush administration contended that ElBaradei had been reluctant to confront Iran on its ability to turn nuclear material into weapons-grade fissionable material. Nevertheless, in October 2005 ElBaradei and the IAEA were jointly awarded the Nobel Peace Prize for efforts "to prevent nuclear energy from being used for military purposes and to ensure that nuclear energy for peaceful purposes is used in the safest possible way."

ElBaradei favored a diplomatic solution to Iran's developing nuclear weapons capability and worked diligently through European and Russian diplomats along with the UN Security Council to limit Iran's nuclear capability. ElBaradei favored the imposition of diplomatic and economic sanctions on Iran sufficient to bring it into compliance with the Nuclear Non-Proliferation Pact (NNPP) and the IAEA mission "Atoms for Peace." Despite criticism from Israel and the United States that his stance toward Iran was too lenient, in June 2008 Elbaradei issued a statement proclaiming that while the IAEA had been conducting exhaustive inspections there, it had not as yet been able to conclude with certainty that Iran had abandoned all plans for an atomic weapon. He urged Iran to be more forthcoming so that the verification process could be concluded. Not surprisingly, Elbaradei's comments were met with much derision in Washington and Tel Aviv. Elbaradei has also repeatedly dismissed any talk of the use of force against Iran, claiming that to do so would be counterproductive and invite a similar scenario that ensued after the 2003 invasion of Iraq.

RICHARD M. EDWARDS

See also

Blix, Hans; International Atomic Energy Agency; Iran; United Nations Monitoring, Verification and Inspection Commission; Weapons of Mass Destruction

References

Kile, Shannon N., ed. *Europe and Iran: Perspectives on Non-Proliferation.* SIPRI Research Reports. Oxford: Oxford University Press, 2006.

Timmerman, Kenneth R. *Countdown to Crisis: The Coming Nuclear Showdown with Iran.* New York: Three Rivers, 2006.

United Nations, ed. *Basic Facts about the United Nations.* New York: United Nations, 2003.

El Salvador, Role in Iraq War

Central American nation with a 2008 population of 7.066 million people. Covering an area of 8,124 square miles, El Salvador is bordered by Guatemala to the west, Honduras to the north and east, and the Pacific Ocean to the south. El Salvador is a representative democracy with a presidential-style government. The president serves as both head of government and head of state. The nation's politics in recent years have been dominated by the conservative National Republican Alliance Party (ARENA) and the opposition leftist Farabundo Martí National Liberation Front (FMLN). Since 2000, however, ARENA's power has been steadily eroded by that of the FMLN, particularly in the legislature.

During the Iraq War, El Salvador emerged as one of the staunchest supporters of the U.S.-led coalition and maintained troops in Iraq longer than any other Latin American nation. Relations between the United States and El Salvador have been very close since the Salvadoran Civil War (1980–1992). During that struggle, the United States deployed special operations forces and military advisers to the country and provided more than $6 billion in military and economic assistance to the conservative government. In addition, there is a substantial Salvadoran population in the United States whose remittances home totaled more than $2.5 billion in 2008, or approximately 17 percent of El Salvador's gross national product (GNP).

Following the September 11, 2001, terrorist strikes against the United States, El Salvador pledged intelligence and security cooperation to the George W. Bush administration's Global War on Terror. In August 2003 El Salvador dispatched elements of a battalion of troops to Iraq. Salvadoran troop strength peaked at 380 in 2004, and the government maintained that number until 2007, when forces were reduced to 280. Salvadoran personnel were subsequently reduced to 200 in August 2008. The soldiers served six-month rotations and were initially deployed in the southern area of Iraq near Najaf as part of a contingent of Latin American states that served under the command of the larger Spanish-speaking deployment. Later, Salvadoran units were stationed in the eastern cities of Najaf, Hillah, and Kut. Salvadoran staff officers were also assigned to the headquarters units of the Multi-National Force in Baghdad.

Salvadoran forces engaged in a variety of humanitarian and reconstruction operations in Iraq. The soldiers completed more than 430 projects, ranging from school and hospital construction to road building to the creation of potable water facilities. After

El Salvador minister of defense General Otto Romero speaks to his country's soldiers during a visit to Camp Charlie in Al Hillah, Iraq, on May 17, 2005. El Salvador was the only Latin American nation to furnish troops to the coalition forces in Iraq. (U.S. Department of Defense)

the Dominican Republic, Honduras, and Nicaragua all withdrew their forces in 2004, El Salvador became the only Latin American country with forces still stationed in Iraq.

Although the government of President Elias Antonio Saca of the ARENA party strongly supported the Iraq War, the conflict was unpopular among the domestic population. Opposition was led by the FMLN, the former insurgency group that had fought ARENA during the Salvadoran Civil War. The conflict in Iraq became an issue in the 2004 national elections, but ARENA won the balloting, led by Saca, a popular ex-sportscaster who received 58 percent of the vote. ARENA faced growing pressure to withdraw the country's forces ahead of the next national elections in 2009.

As other nations withdrew forces from Iraq in 2008 when the United Nations (UN) mandate ended, El Salvador announced that it would end its deployment, and the Salvadoran troops were withdrawn in December 2008. More than 3,000 Salvadoran soldiers served in Iraq in 11 contingents of troops. The United States provided funding to cover most of the costs of the Salvadoran deployments. During El Salvador's involvement in Iraq, 6 Salvadoran soldiers were killed and more than 50 were wounded.

TOM LANSFORD

See also

IRAQI FREEDOM, Operation, Coalition Ground Forces; Multi-National Force–Iraq

References

Allawi, Ali A. *The Occupation of Iraq: Winning the War, Losing the Peace.* New Haven, CT: Yale University Press, 2007.

Cockburn, Patrick. *The Occupation: War and Resistance in Iraq.* New York: Verso, 2007.

ENDURING FREEDOM, **Operation**

ENDURING FREEDOM was the code name given to the U.S.-led invasion of Afghanistan that began on October 7, 2001. The purpose of the invasion was to topple the Taliban government and kill or capture members of the Al Qaeda terrorist group, which had just carried out the terror attacks of September 11, 2001. The Taliban had sheltered Al Qaeda and its leader, Osama bin Laden, on Afghan territory and provided the terrorists with bases, training facilities, and quite possibly financial support.

The United States faced major problems in planning a war against the Taliban and Al Qaeda. Prime among these were

Soldiers from the 101st Airborne Division out of Fort Campbell, Kentucky, check local residents for possible weapons or contraband in the vicinity of Narizah, Afghanistan, on July 23, 2002. (U.S. Department of Defense)

logistical concerns, for Afghanistan is a landlocked country quite distant from U.S. basing facilities. American planners decided that an alliance would have to be forged with the Afghan United Front (also known as the Northern Alliance), an anti-Taliban opposition force within Afghanistan. The Northern Alliance would do the bulk of the fighting but would receive U.S. air support, along with assistance, advice, and cash from U.S. special operations forces.

The war began on October 7, 2001, with American air strikes from land-based B-52 and B-1 bombers, carrier-based F-14 Tomcat and F-18 Hornet aircraft, and Tomahawk cruise missiles. These attacks were intended to knock out the Taliban's antiaircraft defenses and communications infrastructure. However, desperately poor Afghanistan had a very limited infrastructure to bomb, and the initial air attacks had only minimal impact. Al Qaeda training camps were also targeted, although they were quickly abandoned once the bombing campaign began. U.S. special operations forces arrived in Afghanistan on October 15, at which time they made contact with the leaders of the Northern Alliance.

The first phase of the ground campaign was focused on the struggle for the northern city of Mazar-e Sharif, which fell to the Northern Alliance forces led by generals Abdul Dostum and Ustad Atta Mohammed on November 10, 2001. The fighting around Mazar-e Sharif was intense, but U.S. air strikes, directed by special operations forces on the ground, did much to break Taliban and Al Qaeda resistance.

As the fighting progressed, the Taliban and Al Qaeda improved both their tactics and combat effectiveness. Camouflage and concealment techniques were also enhanced, helping to counter American air power. However, the Taliban's limited appeal to the population meant that the regime could not withstand the impact of a sustained assault. The repressive rule of the Taliban ensured that the Taliban never widened its base of support beyond the Pashtun ethnic group from which they originated.

Northern Alliance forces captured the Afghan capital of Kabul without a fight on November 13. On November 26 a besieged garrison of 5,000 Taliban and Al Qaeda soldiers surrendered at Kunduz after heavy bombardment by American B-52s. Meanwhile, an uprising by captured Taliban fighters held in the Qala-e-Gangi fortress near Mazar-e Sharif prison was suppressed with great brutality in late November.

The scene of the fighting then shifted to the city of Kandahar in southern Afghanistan. Because the Taliban had originated in Kandahar in the early 1990s, they were expected to put up a stiff fight for the city. Kandahar was attacked by Northern Alliance forces led by generals Hamid Karzai and Guyl Agha Shirzai, with U.S. special operations forces coordinating the offensive. The Taliban deserted Kandahar on December 6, and Taliban leader Mohammed Omar and the surviving Taliban elements went into hiding in the remote mountain regions of Afghanistan and Pakistan. The fall of Kandahar marked the end of Taliban rule in Afghanistan, only nine weeks after the beginning of the bombing campaign. On December 22, 2001, an interim administration, chaired by Hamid Karzai, took office.

Despite the rapid and efficient progress of Operation ENDURING FREEDOM, Taliban and Al Qaeda elements remained at large in Afghanistan, and the operation failed to capture or kill either Osama bin Laden or Mohammed Omar. Bin Laden was believed to be hiding in mountain dugouts and bunkers located in the White Mountains near Tora Bora. A 16-day offensive in early December 2001 failed to find bin Laden. For this offensive, the United States once again relied on Northern Alliance ground troops supported by U.S. special operations forces and American air power. Later there would be charges that this offensive was mishandled, and an opportunity to take bin Laden was lost. Bin Laden escaped, probably into Pakistan through the foreboding but porous border that separates Afghanistan from Pakistan.

Despite the failure to capture or kill bin Laden, the United States could point to notable success in the so-called War on Terror by the end of 2001. The Taliban had been deposed and Al Qaeda was on the run, with many of its members and leaders having been killed or captured. This occurred despite the fact that the United States deployed only about 3,000 service personnel, most of them special operations forces, to Afghanistan by the end of the year. The U.S. death toll was remarkably light, with only 2 deaths attributed to enemy action. Estimates of Afghan fatalities are approximate, at best. As many as 4,000 Taliban soldiers may have been killed during the campaign. Afghan civilian deaths have been estimated at between 1,000 and 1,300, with several thousand refugees dying from disease and/or exposure. Another 500,000 Afghans were made refugees or displaced persons during the fighting.

The United States attempted a different approach in March 2002, when Al Qaeda positions were located in the Shahi-Kot Valley near Gardez. On this occasion, U.S. ground troops from the 10th Mountain Division and the 101st Airborne Division led the way, along with special operations forces from Australia, Canada, and Germany, and Afghan government troops, in an offensive code-named Operation ANACONDA. Taliban reinforcements rushed to join the Al Qaeda fighters, but both were routed from the valley with heavy losses.

Since 2002 the Taliban and Al Qaeda remnants have maintained a low-level insurgency in Afghanistan. Troops from the United States and allied countries, mainly from North Atlantic Treaty Organization (NATO) member states, remain in Afghanistan operating ostensibly under the banner of Operation ENDURING FREEDOM. An upsurge of Taliban insurgent activity beginning in 2006, however, has necessitated a series of coalition offensives.

PAUL W. DOERR

See also

Afghanistan; Al Qaeda; Bin Laden, Osama; ENDURING FREEDOM, Operation, Initial Ground Campaign; ENDURING FREEDOM, Operation, U.S. Air Campaign; Northern Alliance; Omar, Mohammed; Taliban

References

Biddle, Stephen. *Afghanistan and the Future of Warfare: Implications for Army and Defense Policy.* Carlisle, PA: Strategic Studies Institute, 2002.

Hanson, Victor Davis. *Between War and Peace: Lessons from Afghanistan to Iraq.* New York: Random House, 2004.

Kagan, Frederick. *Finding the Target: The Transformation of American Military Policy.* New York: Encounter, 2006.

Maley, William. *The Afghanistan Wars.* New York: Palgrave Macmillan, 2002.

ENDURING FREEDOM, Operation, Coalition Naval Forces

Following the September 11, 2001, terrorist attacks on targets in New York and Washington, the United States launched Operation ENDURING FREEDOM, which included six components: Operation ENDURING FREEDOM–Afghanistan (OEF-A), Operation ENDURING FREEDOM–Philippines (OEF-P), Operation ENDURING FREEDOM–Horn of Africa (OEF-HOA), Operation ENDURING FREEDOM–Trans Sahara (OEF-TS), Operation ENDURING FREEDOM–Kyrgrzstan (OEF-K), and Operation ENDURING FREEDOM–Pankisi Gorge (OEF-PK). OEF-K ended in 2004,

OEF-PK ended in 2007, and like OEF-TS, none involved more than very limited naval forces, all of which were from the U.S. Navy.

Prior to initiating action against the Taliban and Al Qaeda in Afghanistan on October 7, 2001, U.S. leaders assembled a coalition of forces from 50 nations, 12 of which contributed naval forces for varying lengths of time. The largest contributor to OEF has been the United States, which has deployed aircraft carrier battle groups in support of ENDURING FREEDOM operations in Afghanistan including, at varying times, the 9-ship *Enterprise* (CVN-65) battle group, the 10-ship *Carl Vinson* (CVN-70), and the 12-ship *Theodore Roosevelt* (CVN-71) battle group. France contributed a carrier battle group, consisting of the aircraft carrier *Charles de Gaulle;* the frigates *La Motte-Picquet, Jean Bart,* and *Jean de Viernne;* the attack submarine *Rubis;* the antisubmarine patrol ship *Commandant Ducuing;* and the tanker *Meuse* in 2002. The United Kingdom committed an aircraft carrier, 1 destroyer, 1 frigate, 1 amphibious ship, and 3 fleet submarines. Germany sent 3 frigates, a fast patrol boat group of 5 ships, and 4 supply ships. Canada dispatched 3 ships, while New Zealand and the Netherlands sent 2 frigates each. Other nations—including Australia, Bahrain, and Greece—provided a number of smaller warships. India dispatched a frigate to escort coalition shipping through the Strait of Melaka, and Japan provided naval support for noncombat reinforcement of OEF. Additional naval forces have come in the form of U.S. and French naval special forces and U.S. Seabee construction units at varying times.

On October 7, 2001, operations began with carrier-based Grumman F-14 Tomcats and McDonnell Douglas/Boeing/Northrop F/A-18 Hornets joining U.S. Air Force bombers and Tomahawk missiles being fired from American and British surface ships and submarines. Three months later (December 20, 2001), the United Nations (UN) Security Council formed the International Security Assistance Force–Afghanistan (ISAF) to direct operations inside Afghanistan, which would be administered through the North Atlantic Treaty Organization (NATO). The following May, the United States formed Combined Joint Task Force 180 (CJTF-180) to coordinate all coalition operations.

Warships coordinated their activities but did not combine to form a single operational unit, although in April 2002 ships from five nations sailed in formation for a photograph. They included the French aircraft carrier *Charles de Gaulle,* the U.S. carrier *John C. Stennis,* the Italian destroyer *Luigi Durand de la Penne,* the U.S. cruiser *Port Royal,* the French destroyer *De Grasse,* the Italian frigate *Maestrale,* the French frigate *Surcouf,* the Dutch frigate *Van Amstel,* and the British helicopter amphibious assault ship *Ocean.*

In January 2002, 1,200 U.S. Special Operations forces were dispatched to the southern Philippines in OEF-P with the aim of assisting Philippine forces in eradicating terrorist organizations operating in the area. U.S. Navy SEALs were included in the forces, which received logistical support from elements of the U.S. Seventh Fleet. In October 2002 Operation ENDURING FREEDOM was expanded to include Somalia and adjacent areas in the Horn of Africa with the formation of Combined Joint Task Force–Horn of Africa (CJTF-HOA).

Combined Task Force 150 (CTF-150) was formed in 2002 to support OEF-HOA and Operation IRAQI FREEDOM (OIF). The focus of CTF-150 was the monitoring of shipping and countering piracy in the northern Persian Gulf, but it also has trained units of the Iraqi Navy. Warships from Australia, Canada, Denmark, France, Germany, Italy, the Netherlands, New Zealand, Pakistan, Turkey, the United Kingdom, and the United States have participated in CTF-150, which usually numbers about 15 ships and the command of which rotates among the participating navies in four- to six-month intervals. Commanders have included Spanish rear admiral Juan Moreno, British commodore Tony Rix, French vice admiral Jacques Mazars, Dutch commodore Hank Ort, Pakistani rear admiral Shahid Iqbal, German rear admiral Heinrich Lange, British commodore Bruce Williams, British commodore Duncan Potts, and U.S. rear admiral Kendall Card.

Ships of CTF-150 patrol the north Persian Gulf boarding and inspecting suspicious merchant ships. From 2006 onward, antipiracy operations became a focus of operations, as attacks on merchant vessels in the area increased dramatically from Somali pirates. In January 2007 elements of the *Dwight D. Eisenhower* U.S. carrier battle group joined CTF-150 to stand offshore to prevent the escape by sea of Al Qaeda members as air strikes were launched against suspected Al Qaeda targets in Somalia.

JAMES C. BRADFORD

See also

ENDURING FREEDOM, Operation; United States Navy, Afghanistan War

References

Cooke, Leonard W. W. "A Deployment to Remember: The Navy's Seabees in Afghanistan." *Sea Power* 45 (October 2002): 55–57.
Peterson, Gordon I. "Bush: 'The Might of Our Navy Is Needed Again.'" *Sea Power* 45 (January 2002): 13–23.
Wisecup, Phil, and Tom Williams. "Enduring Freedom: Making Coalition Naval Warfare Work." *U.S. Naval Institute Proceedings* 128(9) (September 2002): 52–55.

ENDURING FREEDOM, Operation, Initial Ground Campaign

Start Date: October 7, 2001
End Date: December 17, 2001

Operation ENDURING FREEDOM opened on October 7, 2001, less than a month after the September 11, 2001, terror attacks perpetrated by Al Qaeda. The invasion of Afghanistan occurred when the Taliban government ruling the country refused to hand over Al Qaeda terrorist organization leader Osama bin Laden or cooperate with American efforts to bring those responsible for the attacks to justice. The stated goals of the operation were the capture of bin Laden and other Al Qaeda leaders, the destruction of terrorist training camps and infrastructure within Afghanistan, and an end to all terrorist activities there.

In the invasion the United States and its allies opted for an asymmetric strategy, which on the ground relied heavily on indigenous warlords who were opposed to the Taliban and Al Qaeda, especially the Northern Alliance, comprised mainly of Tajik, Uzbek, and Hazara forces.

Having first severely reduced the Taliban war machine in cruise missile attacks and air strikes, the U.S. Air Force then provided close ground support for the Northern Alliance. From the beginning of the war, the U.S. Air Force, supported by coalition tanker, cargo, and surveillance aircraft, enjoyed complete command of the air. With this and the fact that the fighting forces involved were relatively few in number, the country was vast, and the front lines were porous, the ground situation changed very quickly.

The general strategy was to cut off the Taliban lines of communications between the northern part of the country and their stronghold in the south, liberate those areas, and then eliminate the remnants of resistance in remote mountain areas. The ground fighting was left largely to the Northern Alliance, with U.S. and non-Afghan coalition military involvement during the initial phase of the ground war limited mainly to special operations and focusing on assisting the Northern Alliance's advance and coordinating it with the air strikes.

To oversee the allied land campaign, the U.S. Central Command (CENTCOM) established the Combined Forces Land Component Command (CFLCC), led by Lieutenant General Paul T. Mikolashek, that moved to Camp Doha (Kuwait) on November 20, 2001. In order to provide direct assistance to Northern Alliance forces and to conduct special operations, the Joint Special Operation Task Force Dagger, under Colonel John Mulholland, was deployed to Karshi Kandabad air base in Uzbekistan. It included the 5th Special Forces Group (Airborne); elements of the 160th Special Operations Aviation Regiment; Special Tactics personnel from Air Force Special Operations Command; the 1st Battalion, 87th Infantry; and the 10th Mountain Division (Light). The British furnished unspecified numbers of special forces, including units of the Special Air Service (SAS) and Special Boat Service (SBS).

U.S. Special Forces began their operations on October 19, 2001, when they joined the 6,000-strong Northern Alliance force under General Abd al-Rashid Dostum in its attack on the strategic city of Mazar-e Sharif along with some 10,000 troops under Fahim Khan and Bissmullah Khan advancing through Panjsher Valley to Kabul. The Special Forces teams called and coordinated close air support provided by Rockwell/Boeing B-1 Lancer and Boeing B-52 Stratofortress bombers, Grumman F-14 Tomcat, McDonnell Douglas/Boeing F-15 Eagle and McDonnell Douglas/Boeing/Northrop F-18 Hornet fighter-bombers, and Fairchild Republic A-10 Thunderbolt II combat support aircraft. These attacked key Taliban command posts, tanks and armored vehicles, artillery pieces, troop concentrations, bunkers, and ammunition storage areas. The heavy application of airpower had a huge and demoralizing psychological effect on the Taliban

Residents look for their belongings amid the rubble of their destroyed houses in Kabul, Afghanistan, on October 17, 2001. (AP/Wide World Photos)

fighters and allowed Northern Alliance forces to soon seize key strategic targets. On November 9, 2001, the anti-Taliban forces secured Mazar-e Sharif.

From the north coalition forces carried out a rapid advance, surprising and outflanking the Taliban defenders. Boosted by large-scale defections among the local Taliban commanders, Northern Alliance forces ware able to retake many towns and villages without firing a shot. On November 14, 2001, Northern Alliance troops took the capital city of Kabul.

After that in just a few days of quick and fierce fighting and negotiated surrenders, all central and western Afghan provinces including the key city of Herat were liberated from Taliban control. To assist command and control functions in providing assistance to the Afghan forces, supplies and humanitarian aid via Task Force Bagram was organized at Bagram air base under the command of Colonel Robert Kissel. At the same time, a number of U.S. Delta Force commandos, Central Intelligence Agency (CIA) agents, and British SAS and SBS and French intelligence agents were deployed in central Afghanistan to conduct strategic reconnaissance of targets linked to Al Qaeda.

On November 16, 2001, the siege of Kunduz, the remaining Taliban stronghold in the north, began with heavy air strikes over a nine-day period. During the siege the U.S. Green Berets along with British SAS and SBS forces assisted Northern Alliance troops under General Mullah Daud in the destruction of Taliban tanks, cargo trucks, bunker complexes, and personnel. On November 23, 2001, remaining Taliban forces in the Kunduz area surrendered. Some 3,500 prisoners of war (POWs) were transported to the fortress-prison in Mazar-e Sharif, where they subsequently rebelled and were only suppressed after several days of heavy fighting in which coalition airpower and U.S. and British Special Forces took part. This last battle of Mazar-e Sharif saw the first introduction of coalition conventional ground troops in Afghanistan: the 1st Battalion, 87th Infantry of the 10th Mountain Division (Light) from Uzbekistan, which helped to secure the perimeter around the fortress and secured the local airfield.

The next phase in the ground campaign was aimed at defeating the Taliban in its political and spiritual birthplace, the Pashtun heartland around the city of Kandahar. There, as early as October 19–20, 2001, a detachment of the U.S. Army Rangers who had flown in from bases in southern Pakistan and Oman conducted swift assaults in Kandahar and secured a deserted airstrip, known as Camp Rhino, as a future forward operational base for hit-and-run raids. Following the scheme already tested in the north, the U.S. Special Forces established contacts with and supplied ammunition, weapons, and close air support to some 3,000 anti-Taliban Pashtun forces under Hamid Karzai and Gul Afha Sherzai, effectively establishing a new front by November 19, 2001.

On November 25 nearly 1,000 U.S. marines of Task Force 58 were ferried in from a carrier group in the Arabian Sea. Establishing a forward operational base at Camp Rhino, they joined the fight by cutting off the Taliban supply lines. In early December U.S. Army special operations troops, U.S. Navy SEALs, Navy Seabee construction teams, and Australian Special Forces reinforced the marines at Camp Rhino. Taliban forces surrendered Kandahar on December 6, and the marines secured its airport by December 13.

By mid-December, the remnants of the Taliban and Al Qaeda forces (about 2,000 militants) were besieged in pockets of resistance in the mountainous area of Tora Bora, with its extensive fortifications and stockpiles of weapons and ammunition, in the eastern part of Afghanistan. The operation in the Tora Bora area involved U.S. and British Special Forces, CIA paramilitaries, and about 2,000 Afghan tribesmen under Hazrat Ali. The U.S.-led coalition also employed Lockheed/Boeing AC-130 Spectre gunships for close air support and intense bombing of the underground tunnels with bunker-busting bombs. By December 17, 2001, the last cave complex in Tora Bora was cleared of enemy fighters.

From the point of view of its immediate and purely military aims, the ground component of Operation ENDURING FREEDOM was a highly successful effort that toppled the Taliban and inflicted severe damage to Al Qaeda and its Afghan allies. The joint application of air and ground assaults as well as intelligence operations and psychological warfare, frequently called synergetic warfare, strengthened the coalition's abilities to challenge the Taliban forces asymmetrically. The combination of familiar strategic and tactical approaches, including the application of overwhelming airpower assets, stealthy commando raids, and active and multifaceted support of proxy ground forces, allowed the United States and its allies to avoid committing a large number of their own troops in combat and prevented significant American losses (12 U.S. servicemen were killed in action in 2001) while creating necessary conditions for the swift and decisive destruction of the Al Qaeda sanctuary in Afghanistan.

At the same time, as the continued and even spreading Taliban-led insurgency has demonstrated since 2002, the broader task of stabilizing the country, even militarily, would be much more difficult, complicated by the fact that key Al Qaeda leaders, including Osama bin Laden, were allowed to escape.

PETER J. RAINOW

See also

Al Qaeda; ANACONDA, Operation; Casualties, Operation ENDURING FREEDOM; Coalition Force Land Component Command–Afghanistan; Dostum, Abd al-Rashid; ENDURING FREEDOM, Operation, Planning for; ENDURING FREEDOM, Operation, U.S. Air Campaign; Hekmetyar, Gulbuddin al-Hurra; Karzai, Hamid; McKiernan, David Deglan; Taliban; Taliban Insurgency, Afghanistan

References

Biddle, Stephen. *Afghanistan and the Future of Warfare: Implications for Army and Defense Policy*. Carlisle, PA: Strategic Studies Institute, 2002.

Boaz, John, ed. *The U.S. Attack on Afghanistan*. Detroit: Thompson/Gale, 2005.

DeLong, Michael, with Noah Lukeman. *Inside CENTCOM: The Unvarnished Truth about the Wars in Afghanistan and Iraq*. Washington, DC: Regnery, 2004.

Franks, Tommy, with Malcolm McConnell. *American Soldier*. New York: Regan Books, 2004.

Stewart, Richard W. *Operation Enduring Freedom: The United States Army in Afghanistan, October 2001–March 2002*. Washington, DC: U.S. Army Center of Military History, 2003.

ENDURING FREEDOM, **Operation, Planning for**

Planning for Operation ENDURING FREEDOM, the U.S.-led invasion of Afghanistan, began immediately after the connection had been established between the terrorist network Al Qaeda, which struck the United States on September 11, 2001, and the Taliban regime that had harbored Al Qaeda in Afghanistan. The initial name of the operation—Operation INFINITE JUSTICE—was dropped in deference to Muslim belief that only Allah can provide people with infinitive justice.

There were several relatively low-risk retaliatory options discussed at the U.S. Central Command (CENTCOM), which has primary responsibility for the region militarily. These included cruise missile strikes from ships, submarines, and aircraft; attacking Taliban and Al Qaeda training camps, barracks, command and control facilities, communications centers, and support complexes; and a combination of cruise missile assaults and a bombing campaign of 3–10 days to take out specific targets. At the same time, the declared strategic goals of the operation—to topple the Taliban regime, disrupt Al Qaeda's base of operations, and bring Al Qaeda's leader Osama bin Laden and his associates to justice—unavoidably determined the planning for the operation as a combination of air war with some sort of ground invasion.

From the very beginning, the strategic conditions in the Afghan theater presented serious challenges to the planners at CENTCOM, which was led by U.S. Army general Tommy R. Franks. Indeed, there were a number of daunting peculiarities and complexities. Afghanistan was already in the midst of the civil war. This conflict pitted Taliban forces (25,000–45,000 troops, 650 tanks and armored vehicles, 15 combat planes, 40 cargo planes, 10 transport helicopters, and some 20 missiles, old Soviet SA-7 and American-made Stingers), supported by some 3,000 Al Qaeda militants, who controlled about 80 percent of the country's territory, against their opponents of the Northern Alliance, a loose confederation of warlords and factions (12,000–15,000 troops, 60–70 tanks and armored vehicles, 3 cargo planes, 8 transport helicopters, and some 25 surface-to-surface and short-range ballistic missiles), concentrated in the remote northern parts of Afghanistan.

The difficult mountainous terrain and harsh climate of Afghanistan and its archaic infrastructure shattered by more than 20 years of war enormously limited maneuverability and complicated the logistics of any modern military force. At the same time, these very conditions led light and mobile Taliban forces to believe that they could engage and exhaust any invader in sudden ambushes and attacks. Afghans had a history of successfully repelling invaders, particularly the British in the 19th century and, more recently, the Soviets in the 1980s.

Bearing in mind the harsh conditions of the theater and the fanatical character of the enemy, some military observers and analysts foresaw a long and bloody campaign in Afghanistan. According to some estimates, it would take as many as 100,000 U.S. troops to occupy and control the country. Such a large-scale operation would be put under additional risk by approaching winter, which limited the time available. The Taliban, for its part, expected that the United States would follow the Soviet example of a massive ground invasion. The Taliban therefore prepared to lure the Americans in and outmaneuver them, employing its key tactic of using highly mobile strike squads mounted on pickup trucks.

The general strategic scheme of the U.S. operation in Afghanistan was designed to avoid a Vietnam War–style gradual escalation and involvement in a long and bloody ground war. Thus, instead of committing a large number of U.S. ground troops, the Americans sought to execute the operation with a combination of air strikes and special operations, which would be closely coordinated with the U.S.-backed ground assault by the anti-Taliban Northern Alliance forces.

The American war plan for Afghanistan had important new elements, which reflected distinctive local realities and the intention of the U.S. command to engage the enemy asymmetrically, exploiting its vulnerabilities and outmaneuvering its strengths. The plan envisaged the use of the most advanced military and communications technology in the world on one of the world's most primitive battlefields. The dispersed nature of warfare in the Afghan deserts, high plateaus, and foreboding mountains as well as the decentralized structure of the Taliban and Al Qaeda forces demanded a major emphasis on special operations to take the fight to the enemy, keeping it off balance as well as seizing and maintaining the initiative on the battlefield. In coordination with an intense bombing campaign and military pressure from the Northern Alliance, this, it was hoped, would swiftly reshape the situation on the ground.

The political dimension of the war was of much importance also. The United States actively exploited the unpopularity and vulnerability of the Taliban regime inside and outside Afghanistan as a result of its violent character and extreme interpretation of Islamic law. To isolate the Taliban further, the United States publicly emphasized the just and defensive character of its war on terror and stressed the puppet role of the Taliban under Al Qaeda. U.S. representatives established contacts with the exiled Afghan king Zahir Shah, then living in Rome, who had some influence in the country, particularly among the Pashtuns, Afghanistan's largest ethnic group. Additionally, the military campaign would be paralleled by a large-scale humanitarian effort, with U.S. cargo planes conducting massive food drops for starving Afghans.

The United States would also work on managing the tremendous logistics problems of waging a war over such a long distance and in a landlocked country. The measures to undertake this would include access to bases and facilities in Bahrain, Oman, Pakistan, and Uzbekistan; flight rights over these and other countries; and efforts to achieve understanding with major regional players—India, China, and Russia—about American motives, aims, and actions. U.S. airlift capability using its midair refueling abilities (employing the McDonnell Douglas KC-10 Extender and Boeing KC-135 Stratotanker) was to play a critical role during the 2001 Afghan campaign. The logistical challenges of ENDURING FREEDOM also prompted the seizure of airfields inside Afghanistan at earlier stages of the campaign, and that was an important and integral part of the plan.

In planning and preparing for ENDURING FREEDOM and the Global War on Terror, the United States received active support from the North Atlantic Treaty Organization (NATO) and other allied countries, including intelligence cooperation and offers to put troops on the ground. The allied naval presence in the Arabian Sea was instrumental in creating additional pressure on Pakistan to join the coalition. Nevertheless, the Pentagon tried to avoid the multilateral bureaucratic wrangling it had experienced during the 1999 NATO bombing of Yugoslavia and carefully crafted the operation as a primarily American effort. The only exceptions were with the British and, to a lesser extent, the Australians. The British role in ENDURING FREEDOM (code-named Operation VERITAS by the British), while modest by comparison, had aims virtually identical with those of the Americans. The United States also placed much value on British contributions thanks to the professionalism and experience of the British military, particularly Special Operations forces.

The completed plan was to occur in four consecutive phases while simultaneously executing multiple lines of operation. In Phase One, the United States planned to set conditions for the operation, including interservice coordination; buildup of forces; coalition-building, basing, and staging arrangements; and providing support for the Northern Alliance. The coalition had assembled a formidable U.S. force (three aircraft carrier battle groups with cruisers, destroyers, attack submarines, frigates, and support ships; more than 400 aircraft; and some 50,000 sailors, airmen, marines, and soldiers including Special Forces, about 4,000 of them deployed inside Afghanistan by the beginning of 2002); a British force (3 Royal Navy attack submarines, 1 support aircraft carrier, a naval task group, and 4,200 military personnel, including

A U.S. Navy F-18 Hornet aircraft carries out air-to-air refueling with a U.S. Air Force KC-10 Extender aircraft during Operation ENDURING FREEDOM, 2001. (U.S. Department of Defense)

sailors, marines, and Special Forces), and a small detachment of the Australian Special Operations Forces.

The actual war (Phase Two) would begin with 3–5 days of a U.S.-British bombing campaign across Afghanistan using cruise missiles, jets from aircraft carriers, and strategic bombers (Northrop Grumman B-2 Spirit and Boeing B-52 Stratofortress aircraft) flying concurrently from the United States and Diego Garcia. Then the Northern Alliance forces would begin its attack on Taliban strongholds in the northern part of the country, securing the area for further movements. The Special Operations forces drawn from the Central Intelligence Agency (CIA) Special Activities Division, U.S. Army Green Berets, and U.S. Navy SEALs were to execute reconnaissance and direct-action line of operation, making contact with the Northern Alliance troops on the ground and providing training and tactical support for them. The U.S. Air Force combat air controllers would also infiltrate the area to pinpoint enemy targets for the coalition strike aircraft (operational fires line of operation).

During Phase Three a limited number of coalition conventional troops would move in to eliminate the remaining pockets of enemy resistance. Even the conventional forces were to be employed unconventionally, by flexible and rapid-reaction airborne and helicopter-borne night assaults. The concluding Phase Four would concentrate on stabilization and rebuilding efforts in Afghanistan.

While the planning of Operation ENDURING FREEDOM did demonstrate creative and innovative approaches in addressing numerous challenges in Afghanistan and succeeded in eliminating Al Qaeda sanctuaries in the country, the continuing guerrilla war there, which followed the fall of the Taliban, has stimulated critical evaluations of the plan and the operation. Critics maintain that by putting so much effort in the quick and impressive toppling of the Taliban regime, the United States underestimated the complexity and urgency of the stabilization efforts needed in Afghanistan to consolidate the coalition's initial victory and bring Al Qaeda and Taliban top commanders to justice. Some critical assessments also blame the initial American plan for its failure to capitalize on the interim disagreements between Al Qaeda and Taliban and within the Taliban structure itself. There have also been critical overviews of U.S. coalition-building efforts. Some have argued that the Pentagon's determination to carry out the operation largely alone set the stage for the rift between the United States and Europe on the critically important issue of burden sharing that was to deepen the longer the war progressed.

PETER J. RAINOW

See also

Afghanistan; Al Qaeda; Bin Laden, Osama; Central Intelligence Agency; ENDURING FREEDOM, Operation; Franks, Tommy Ray; Global War on Terror

References

DeLong, Michael, with Noah Lukeman. *Inside CENTCOM: The Unvarnished Truth about the Wars in Afghanistan and Iraq.* Washington, DC: Regnery, 2004.

Franks, Tommy, with Malcolm McConnell. *American Soldier.* New York: Regan Books, 2004.

Woodward, Bob. *Bush at War.* New York: Simon and Shuster, 2002.

ENDURING FREEDOM, Operation, U.S. Air Campaign
Event Date: October 2001

Following the September 11, 2001, attacks on the World Trade Center and the Pentagon, the United States requested that the Taliban-controlled government of Afghanistan hand over leaders of Al Qaeda, the terror organization responsible for the attacks. Among these was Al Qaeda leader Osama bin Laden. The administration of President George W. Bush considered the Taliban's failure to extradite bin Laden and his compatriots to the United States with no preconditions as sufficient justification for invading Afghanistan.

Prior to the ground assault led by the Northern Alliance, the U.S.-led alliance began an aerial bombing campaign of Afghanistan in October 2001. The targets selected during the first wave of bombings in the initial phase of Operation ENDURING FREEDOM provide insights into the political bargaining by the United States to enlist support from Afghanistan's neighbors, Uzbekistan and Pakistan, into the antiterror coalition. In order to gain access to Uzbekistan's military facilities, the United States agreed to destroy the bases of the Islamic Movement of Uzbekistan (IMU), located in Taliban-controlled Afghanistan. Several IMU bases in the Balkh and Kunduz provinces near the Uzbek border were among the first targets hit in Afghanistan. To secure the cooperation of Pakistan, the U.S.-led alliance agreed not to target key Taliban defensive positions in and around Kabul.

On October 7, 2001, American and British forces began the aerial bombing of Al Qaeda training camps as well as the Taliban air defenses. Initial strikes focused on the heavily populated cities of Kabul, Kandahar, and Herat. Within a few days most of the Al Qaeda training camps had been destroyed, and the Taliban air defenses had been neutralized. The bombing campaign then shifted toward communications and the command and control structure of the Taliban government. Two weeks into the bombing campaign, America's Afghan ally, the Northern Alliance, sought and received aerial support in its efforts to attack Taliban frontline positions. The bombing of population centers caused a refugee problem, however, as large numbers of Afghans fled to avoid the strikes.

In the next phase of the aerial campaign, Taliban frontline positions were bombed with 1,500-pound daisy cutter bombs and cluster bombs that caused extensive casualties. By early November, Taliban frontline positions had been wiped out. In the last remaining Taliban stronghold, Mazar-e Sharif, the United States carpet-bombed the Taliban defenders, enabling the Northern Alliance to take the city after several days of fierce fighting.

The early success of the bombing campaign in destroying Taliban positions was not without controversy. The relentless aerial bombing of Afghanistan led to a high number of civilian casualties, estimated at between 3,700 and 5,000. In fact, the civilian death toll surpassed those incurred during the 1999 North Atlantic Treaty Organization (NATO) bombing campaign of Kosovo and Serbia. When credible reports of bombing mishaps and accidental civilian casualties emerged, U.S. policy makers and military spokespersons consistently denied these claims. Nevertheless, the U.S. willingness to bomb heavily populated areas in Afghanistan using heavy ordnance bombs stoked fierce criticism of U.S. foreign policy. Allied and Muslim nations alike complained that the bombing victimized the innocent, exacerbated the humanitarian disaster in Afghanistan, and created widespread resentment across the Muslim world. Worse still, reports that U.S. troops participated in a massacre of Taliban prisoners of war in Mazar-e Sharif in late November 2001 further inflamed world opinion. In spite of the apparent success of the air campaign, however, Al Qaeda mastermind Osama bin Laden was not captured or killed and still remains at large.

KEITH A. LEITICH

See also

Afghanistan; Al Qaeda; Bin Laden, Osama; ENDURING FREEDOM, Operation; ENDURING FREEDOM, Operation, Initial Ground Campaign; Global War on Terror; September 11 Attacks; Taliban

References

Docherty, Bonnie L. *United States/Afghanistan: Fatally Flawed: Cluster Bombs and Their Use by the United States in Afghanistan.* New York: Human Rights Watch, 2002.

Fiscus, James W. *America's War in Afghanistan.* New York: Rosen, 2004.

Dudley, William, ed. *The Attack on America, September 11, 2001.* San Diego: Greenhaven, 2002.

Miller, Raymond H. *The War on Terrorism: The War in Afghanistan.* Chicago: Lucent Books, 2003.

Schroen, Gary. *First In: An Insider Account of How the CIA Spearheaded the War on Terror in Afghanistan.* Novato, CA: Presidio, 2005.

Environmental Effects of the Persian Gulf War

The Persian Gulf War of 1991 made history as the most environmentally damaging war of modern times. On August 2, 1990, Iraqi forces invaded Kuwait, a country of about 1.7 million people that controlled some 10 percent of the world's oil reserves. When the Iraqi government refused to withdraw from Kuwait, a coalition headed by the United States launched Operation DESERT STORM on January 17, 1991, to force Iraqi troops to quit Kuwait.

It was not long thereafter that environmental disasters began to occur. As early as January 19–23, 1991, Iraq was accused of releasing large amounts of crude oil into the Persian Gulf. Then, starting on January 22, 1991, a number of Kuwaiti oil wells were set ablaze, beginning with the Wafra field and moving northward. By February 1991 reports indicated that retreating Iraqi forces had ignited some 190 oil wells, and by the time coalition forces pushed out the last invaders from Kuwait in February 1991, Iraqi troops were alleged to have set alight 732 oil wells. It was estimated that 6 million barrels of oil per day were burning simultaneously. Although skeptics claimed that it could take years to extinguish all the fires, the last well fire was capped by coalition forces or contracted firefighters on November 8, 1991.

As a consequence of these Iraqi actions, oil droplets, soot, and smoke devastated large regions of the Persian Gulf. Moreover, other wells that retreating Iraqi troops had unsuccessfully tried to set afire spewed out oil that formed stagnant pools on the desert floor. Other environmental damage resulted from the effects of military and firefighting activity on the desert surface. For instance, Iraqi forces dug deep into the Kuwaiti land surface to build defensive fortifications, and roadbeds built to access blazing oil wells caused further wind- and water-erosion hazards.

The short- and long-term environmental impacts of the Persian Gulf War were immense, and its effects continue to this day. On land, these include groundwater contamination from sabotaged oil wells and seawater used to douse the fires. Desert vegetation was disrupted or killed. The release of approximately 11 million barrels of oil into the Persian Gulf from January 1991 to May 1991—an amount that doubled the previous world oil spill record—and the sinking of some 80 ships loaded with oil and munitions caused an unprecedented marine disaster that killed wildlife and washed up oil on more than 800 miles of Kuwaiti and Saudi Arabian beaches.

Scientific studies have indicated, however, that the effects on the global environment have been less damaging than initially feared. For example, German scientist Paul Crutzen had predicted that the fires would produce enough soot and smoke to cover half the Northern Hemisphere, while American researcher Carl Sagan had foreseen that the oil fires would alter monsoon patterns in Southern and Central Asia, leading to disastrous harvests and the equivalent of a nuclear winter. Nevertheless, these predictions largely ignored wind directions in the Persian Gulf region. Moreover, the weight of particulates from the burning wells prevented them from rising into the stratosphere. The climatic effects consequently were largely limited to the Persian Gulf region. Temperatures cooled in Kuwait, and physicians observed a rising incidence of asthma and other respiratory and eye ailments. The long-term effects of toxic exposure on area residents continue to be monitored.

The health effects of toxic exposure on U.S. Persian Gulf War veterans remain an area of medical controversy. Returning veterans reported symptoms such as fatigue, skin rashes, muscle and joint pain, headache, loss of memory, shortness of breath, and gastrointestinal problems, which collectively became known as the Gulf War Syndrome. It was conjectured that exposure to pesticides, debris from Scud missiles, chemical and biological warfare agents, and smoke or oil rain from fires may well lie at the root of this mysterious illness.

Another area of controversy involves the precise extent of Iraqi responsibility for the ecological disaster. For instance, former U.S. attorney general Ramsey Clark later argued that the United States, not Iraq, was primarily responsible. Even though as early as September 1990 Iraqi president Saddam Hussein had threatened to release large amounts of oil into the Persian Gulf, Clark contended that U.S. bombing targeted oil tankers and storage facilities. He also claimed that coalition military action, and not the Iraqis, started many of the oil well fires. Clark's conclusions, however, remained controversial and disputed. While it is a given that the coalition's Operation DESERT STORM unleashed certain environmental perils, the Iraqis themselves were responsible for the worst of them.

ANNA M. WITTMANN

See also

DESERT STORM, Operation; Gulf War Syndrome; Oil Well Fires, Persian Gulf War

References

Clark, Ramsey. *The Fire This Time: U.S. War Crimes in the Gulf.* New York: Thunder's Mouth, 1994.

El-Baz, Farouk, and R. M. Makharita, eds. *Gulf War and the Environment.* London: Taylor and Francis, 1994.

Lange, Jeffrey L., et al. "Exposures to the Kuwait Oil Fires and Their Association with Asthma and Bronchitis among Gulf War Veterans." *Environmental Health Perspectives* 110(11) (November 2002): 1141–1146.

Proctor, S. P., et al. "Health Status of Persian Gulf War Veterans: Self-Reported Symptoms, Environmental Exposures and the Effect of Stress." *International Journal of Epidemiology* 27(6) (December 1998): 1000–1010.

Sagan, Carl, and Richard P. Turco. "Nuclear Winter in the Post-Cold War Era." *Journal of Peace Research* 30(4) (November 1993): 369–373.

Estonia, Role in Afghanistan and Iraq Wars

Baltic nation that was part of the Soviet Union from 1940 until its independence in 1990. Covering 17,462 square miles, Estonia is bordered by Latvia to the south, Russia to the East, and the Baltic Sea and the Gulf of Finland to the west and north, respectively. The nation's population in 2008 was some 1.308 million people. A pro-Western nation since its independence, Estonia has a democratic representative government run in parliamentary fashion; the prime minister serves as head of government and is nominated by the president in consultation with parliament. The president, nominally the head of state, is strictly limited in his executive powers.

Coalitions have dominated the Estonian government since 1991. Almost all of these have been formed by centrist, center-left, or center-right parties. Estonia's transition to a free-market economy was sometimes difficult, but in recent years its economic institutions have been lauded for their openness, and government social and economic reforms have produced a modern nation that harnesses high technology and free-market mechanisms.

Along with its fellow Baltic nations of Latvia and Lithuania, Estonia was a strong supporter of the United States in both Operation ENDURING FREEDOM and Operation IRAQI FREEDOM. Thanks to the long-standing U.S. support of Baltic independence during the Cold War and subsequent efforts by the United States to integrate these nations into the institutional framework of the West, including membership in the North Atlantic Treaty Organization (NATO), Estonia enjoyed close relations with the United States.

When terrorists struck the United States on September 11, 2001, Estonia immediately pledged increased intelligence and logistics cooperation and the use of its airspace for any U.S.-led military operations. In July 2002 Estonia deployed a small force of 10 soldiers to support Operation ENDURING FREEDOM in Afghanistan. Estonia later expanded its presence in Afghanistan as part of the NATO-led International Security Assistance Force (ISAF). By December 2008, Estonia had 150 troops in Afghanistan.

Estonian forces were engaged mainly in humanitarian and reconstruction projects. Estonian ordnance-disposal units also undertook minesweeping operations in and around Kabul as part of the ISAF. The Estonian government also provided the Afghan government with material donations to aid refugees. Through December 2008, Estonia had suffered three soldiers killed during its operations in Afghanistan.

During the diplomatic wrangling by the United States to develop a multilateral coalition against Saddam Hussein's Iraqi regime in 2002 and 2003, Estonia endorsed military action in Iraq and signed the Vilnius Letter, a document by eight Central and Eastern European countries that backed the George W. Bush administration. The letter was published on February 6, 2003, and highlighted divisions between the aspirant nations of the European Union (EU) and NATO, which generally supported military intervention, and existing members of both organizations, such as France and Germany, that opposed the invasion.

In June 2003 Estonia deployed an infantry platoon and a cargo unit to Iraq. Since its initial mission, the country has maintained about 40 troops in Iraq. Although the deployment was relatively small, it was a significant contribution from a nation whose total active duty military force numbered just 3,800. Estonian troops served six-month rotations. The infantry contingent was regularly assigned to operate with U.S. troops in security missions, and the Estonians received high praise from their American counterparts for their professionalism and conduct in Iraq. Most of the Estonian operations were in the Baghdad area and around Abu Ghraib. Estonia also stationed a small number of troops as part of the NATO-led mission to train Iraqi security forces.

In 2004 Estonia and the other Baltic nations became members of NATO and the EU. Estonia was one of the last members of the "coalition of the willing" to maintain its troop deployment in Iraq; however, in 2008 the government announced that it would end its mission in Iraq during the summer of 2009. Two Estonian soldiers had been killed during the nation's involvement in Iraq through the end of 2008.

TOM LANSFORD

See also

Afghanistan, Coalition Combat Operations in, 2002–Present; IRAQI FREEDOM, Operation, Coalition Ground Forces; Multi-National Force–Iraq; North Atlantic Treaty Organization in Afghanistan

References

Cockburn, Patrick. *The Occupation: War and Resistance in Iraq.* New York: Verso, 2007.

Feickert, Andrew. *U.S. and Coalition Military Operations in Afghanistan: Issues for Congress.* Washington, DC: Congressional Research Service, 2006.

Keegan, John. *The Iraq War: The Military Offensive, from Victory in 21 Days to the Insurgent Aftermath.* New York: Vintage, 2005.

Euphrates Valley

See Tigris and Euphrates Valley

Europe and the Afghanistan and Iraq Wars

In the first decade of the 21st century, the United States, with significant assistance from Great Britain, launched wars in Afghanistan in October 2001 and then against Iraq in March 2003 to overthrow governments those powers considered intolerable threats to their own interests and replace them with more amenable regimes. In the first conflict, the administration of President George W. Bush initially received almost unanimous support from European governments as it sought to deprive the radical Islamist Al Qaeda forces of the safe haven they had found in Afghanistan under the sympathetic Taliban regime. Al Qaeda had been responsible for the September 11, 2001, terror attacks on the United States. The second war, designed to overthrow President Saddam Hussein of Iraq, proved more problematic, dividing European nations and provoking serious internal dissent and criticism in even those European countries whose governments supported American policies against Iraq.

By the time Bush had completed his second term in January 2009, even the British government, once Bush's strongest backer, had grown weary of involvement in what seemed to be one—if not two—almost interminable wars that produced a low level but constant toll of casualties among British troops.

The immediate reaction of Europeans to the terrorist attacks of September 1l, 2001, upon the United States was one of near-unalloyed sympathy for the American people and their government. For the first time in its more than 50-year history, the North Atlantic Treaty Organization (NATO) invoked the provision in its charter whereby an attack upon one member state constituted war against all. The source of the suicidal air raids upon the World Trade Center Towers in New York and the Pentagon building in Washington, D.C., was soon identified as Al Qaeda, headed by Osama bin Laden. The Taliban leaders refused to repudiate Al Qaeda and surrender bin Laden and his followers to the United States. With strong support from other NATO members, in October 2001 a coalition of American, British, Australian, and anti-Taliban Afghan Northern Alliance forces launched an invasion of Afghanistan. By the end of the year they had taken Kabul, the capital, and driven Taliban and Al Qaeda forces into the mountainous areas of Afghanistan bordering on Pakistan. In December 2001 the United Nations (UN) established the International Security Assistance Force (ISAF) to help restore order in Afghanistan, first in the area around Kabul and eventually throughout the country. In the following years, many other European nations outside the original coalition contributed troop contingents to the ISAF.

Much has been made of America's failure to enthusiastically embrace NATO's early offers of support. In largely going it alone at first, the United States lost a lot of goodwill. Undoubtedly, this was a major political error that only reinforced many of the world's deeply held prejudices about American arrogance and unilateralism. On the operational level, however, there were reasons for this approach. The command and control of NATO's war against Serbia over Kosovo was a nightmare of command decision by committee. After that experience, U.S. military and political leaders vowed not to repeat it. The second reason is that with the exceptions of Britain and France, the rest of NATO's armies, navies, and air forces have sharply declined since the end of the Cold War. Although still impressive on paper, those armies—especially the German Bundeswehr—have been starved of funds and resources for almost two decades since the end of the Cold War. Much of their equipment is obsolete; their soldiers are untrained, unskilled, and unmotivated; and their communications systems are completely incompatible with modern systems. They have almost no logistics capability and no strategic lift.

While the invasion of Afghanistan attracted massive international support and almost every European country subsequently participated in some manner in the ISAF, the invasion of Iraq slightly less than 18 months later failed to win comparable backing. Before September 11, 2001, the Bush administration had focused primarily on the possibility of overthrowing President Saddam Hussein of Iraq, whose regime still remained in power a decade after his country's defeat in the 1991 Persian Gulf War. Once apparent victory had been attained in Afghanistan, American officials quickly returned to their preoccupation with Iraq, erroneously arguing that close links existed between Hussein and Al Qaeda and that Iraq already possessed large quantities of weapons of mass destruction (WMDs) and was well on the way to

producing many more, which would enable Hussein to destabilize and dominate the Middle East.

Bush's national security team sought to persuade the UN to pass resolutions demanding that Iraq allow inspection teams full access to all its potential weapons facilities and surrender or destroy all WMDs and authorizing the use of military force should Iraq refuse to comply. Bush argued that even if Iraq did not at that time pose a real military threat to the United States and its allies, it might do so in future, and preemptive action to overthrow Hussein's rule was therefore justified.

The Bush administration's efforts were energetically seconded by Tony Blair, the Labour prime minister of Britain, who had established a very close relationship with Bush. The two men shared what appeared to be an almost visceral hatred of Hussein and a passionate desire to overthrow his regime. Blair faced strong opposition from within his own Labour Party, many of whom rejected his rationale for war, including former foreign secretary Robin Cook, who resigned in protest as leader of the House of Commons. In March 2003 Blair won a parliamentary majority in favor of war, including most of the opposition Conservative Party, while some 135 Labour members voted against him. Broader public support for the war in Britain was at best lukewarm, with massive public demonstrations against an invasion of Iraq organized shortly before Britain and the United States launched their invasion.

Similar demonstrations took place across most of Western Europe, as Bush and Blair signally failed to convince the people and often the leaders of many other European countries that war against Iraq was either desirable or justified. In early 2003 they were unable to win a resolution from the UN fully endorsing military action against Iraq to enforce the existing ban on its possession or development of WMDs. Germany, France, and Russia (the latter two countries holding permanent UN Security Council seats with veto power) all strongly opposed the passage of such a resolution and were entirely unwilling to contribute troops to any invasion force. This stance attracted fierce verbal criticism from U.S. secretary of defense Donald Rumsfeld, who derisively condemned the nations of "Old Europe"—meaning such long-established noncommunist West European nations as France and Germany—as being effete, spineless, and decadent, corrupted by too many years of comfortable prosperity, and contrasting them unfavorably with those of "New Europe"—such as postcommunist states including Albania, Azerbaijan, Bosnia, Bulgaria, the Czech Republic, Georgia, Hungary, Latvia, Lithuania, Macedonia, Poland, Romania, and Ukraine—that were prepared to join in the "Coalition of the Willing," led by the United States and Britain, that went to war against Iraq in late March 2003.

The invasion itself was undertaken by U.S., British, and Australian military forces, but numerous other countries subsequently dispatched modest contingents of troops to assist in postinvasion efforts to restore order. Since Denmark, Italy, the Netherlands, Norway, Portugal, and Spain had all done so by the end of 2003, the correlation between Old Europe and nonparticipation was by no means precise. Rumsfeld's words, and such American actions as informal suggestions that patriotic Americans should refuse to eat French wine or cheese and should speak of "freedom fries" rather than "French fries," generated great resentment as well as ridicule in France and much of Europe.

At this juncture Robert Kagan, a well-known American political commentator and former diplomat, stirred up further controversy with a provocative article, arguing that whereas Americans possessed, respected, and were willing to deploy muscular military power to maintain global order, Europeans had a totally different mind-set, being relatively weak in terms of defense and thus placing a higher value on diplomacy, conciliation, cooperation, and tolerance. Kagan feared that unless the United States abandoned its growing unilateralism and displayed greater regard for European sensitivities, the ranks of the world's liberal democratic powers would be divided and ineffective on the international stage.

The apparently rapid coalition victory in Iraq and the overthrow of Hussein's government initially seemed to vindicate the invasion, somewhat moderating European governmental and popular opposition to it. Widely publicized revelations of the deposed regime's use of terror and brutality to maintain itself in power and crush antagonists gave some credibility to American and British claims that the dictator's removal was a victory for human rights. The failure to locate any substantial stores of WMDs in Iraq did, however, prove to be a continuing basis for controversy over the purpose of the war. At best it cast doubt on the reliability of the intelligence data they had been cited to support their case for military intervention in Iraq, and at worst it cast doubt on the good faith of top American and British political leaders. Official discomfiture in both countries was compounded by public revelations in May 2003 that Blair and his advisers, like the Bush administration, had massaged intelligence data so as to greatly exaggerate the strategic threat from Iraq to its neighbors and others. The suicide in July 2003 of David Kelly, a scientist in the British Ministry of Defense suspected of leaking this information to the media, added further bitterness to this controversy, which the January 2004 report of a public inquiry headed by Lord Hutton failed to resolve.

These revelations were only one reason why popular disillusionment with the conflict in Iraq became steadily more pronounced throughout much of Europe. The tactics that the United States used to prosecute suspects in both Iraq and the Global War on Terror aroused widespread public revulsion and destroyed much of the credibility of American claims that the invading forces were defending liberal democracy and human rights. In 2004 photographs and videotapes of the abuse, torture, and humiliation of Iraqi political detainees by American troops at Abu Ghraib prison were widely circulated in the international media and proved particularly embarrassing to the United States. So too did the Bush administration's sanction of so-called enhanced interrogation techniques, considered torture and disreputable by many, in disregard of the Geneva Conventions; the detention without trial

or legal redress at the U.S. overseas military facility at Guantánamo, Cuba, of hundreds of alleged terrorists; and the rendition, or kidnapping, in foreign jurisdictions of individuals suspected for some reason of involvement in terrorist activities and their physical transfer to countries where harsh interrogation methods were employed. Most European governments, even those such as Germany that declined to sanction the invasion of Iraq, permitted American intelligence and security operatives to undertake such renditions within their countries. Anti-American sentiment mounted almost across the board in Europe, and condemnation of American disregard for liberal values and human rights and the insensitive unilateralism of the United States in international affairs was widespread.

Most European nations, including France and Germany, which had opposed the war in Iraq, nonetheless contributed funding and sometimes personnel to aid and training programs intended to assist both Iraq and Afghanistan. While refraining from any military involvement in Iraq, in October 2003 the German Bundestag did vote to send German forces to Afghanistan, and by February 2009 Germany had the third-largest national contingent of troops in the ISAF, although these were restricted to reconstruction rather than combat operations.

In most European nations, war weariness with what seemed unwinnable conflicts also steadily intensified. Although Bush

Demonstrators in Amsterdam march in protest of U.S. involvement in Iraq. One protester wears a George W. Bush mask. (Shutterstock)

declared an end to major combat operations in Iraq early in May 2003, for several years the situation in Iraq remained extremely unstable, with the country deeply divided among majority Shiite, Sunni, and Kurdish political groupings. The new coalition-backed Iraqi government initially failed to win military or political control of large swaths of territory. Violence and insurgency, sometimes involving Al Qaeda operatives from outside Iraq, had escalated by 2006 to a point where a state of virtual civil war existed in much of the country. Casualties among the foreign occupation forces as well as deaths among Iraqi government personnel and civilians mounted steadily, and significantly more coalition troops died in action after the supposed end of major hostilities than before. Foreigners of all nationalities, including journalists, civilian security personnel, businesspeople, and others, also became repeated targets of kidnappings and murder by a variety of Iraqi insurgent elements, as increasingly were Iraqis themselves, causing a huge number to flee the country. Anglo-American preoccupation with the war in Iraq meant that fewer resources of every kind, personnel, economic assistance, or attention, were devoted to Afghanistan. By 2005 Taliban and other insurgent forces in Afghanistan had regrouped, posing a major military threat to that country's stability and undermining the authority of the Afghan government in substantial areas of its own territory.

In many European nations, radical Islamic elements of the population deeply resented their governments' involvement in hostilities in Iraq and Afghanistan and, more broadly, what they perceived as disrespect for their own religious faith and values. The emergence of Muslim extremists ready to resort to violence aroused growing concern across Western Europe. One consequence was increased official security surveillance of the Muslim communities in each nation, generally undertaken in conjunction with government-sponsored efforts to reach out to and enter into dialogues with the less radicalized portions of their substantial Muslim populations. In March 2004 extremist Spanish Muslims exploded several bombs on commuter trains at the Madrid railway station, killing 191 people and injuring 1,800. In July 2005 British Muslims launched similar suicide bombing attacks on the London transport system, leaving 56 dead and around 700 injured. Further terrorist attempts took place in Britain in the summer of 2007 shortly after Gordon Brown replaced Blair as Labour prime minister. Violence against individuals who were seen as unfriendly to Islam also occurred. In May 2002 the independent Dutch politician Pim Fortuyn, who had condemned Islam as intolerant and called for an end to further Muslim immigration into the Netherlands, was assassinated. Two years later, in November 2004, the Dutch filmmaker Theo van Gogh, another well-known personality who had strongly criticized Islam, was likewise assassinated by a Muslim extremist. In 2005 a Danish newspaper published uncomplimentary cartoons of the Prophet Muhammad, provoking massive demonstrations from Muslims within Denmark and outside Danish embassies across the Middle East on the grounds that these were racist. Most European governments found the emergence of indigenous Muslim terrorism among their own populations an ominous development.

As the wars in Afghanistan and Iraq continued with little apparent prospect of any conclusive resolution, European governments bent to popular pressure and became less willing to contemplate indefinite military involvements in those countries. Three days after the Madrid bombings, a new government won power in Spanish elections and shortly afterwards withdrew the remaining Spanish troops from the occupation of Iraq. Hungary, the Netherlands, and Portugal likewise withdrew their forces from Iraq in 2005; Italy and Norway followed suit in 2006. Early in 2007 the United States adopted a new policy of a surge of temporary troop increases in Iraq combined with intensive efforts to strengthen the Iraqi government, eradicate hard-line opponents, win over potentially friendly elements, and train Iraqi security and other personnel in the hope of stabilizing the country. The withdrawals of European forces continued, with Lithuania and Slovakia removing their troop contingents in 2007. In 2008 the Iraqi government itself requested the gradual removal of coalition forces, and all remaining military personnel from Albania, Armenia, Azerbaijan, Bosnia, Bulgaria, the Czech Republic, Denmark, Estonia, Georgia, Latvia, Macedonia, Moldova, Poland, and Ukraine were gone by December of that year. By early 2009 only Romania and Britain still had troops in Iraq.

Brown, the new British premier, was widely believed to be a far less enthusiastic supporter than Blair of both wars. To the dismay of American officials, in late 2007 Brown withdrew British forces from Basra Province and the city of Basra in Iraq and restricted their mission to training the Iraqi military. Brown also reduced the number of British troops in Afghanistan.

In November 2008 the election as president of the United States of Barack Obama, a Democrat who had not voted for intervention in Iraq and planned a phased withdrawal of virtually all American forces in that country, brought at least temporarily a new warmth, even euphoria, to U.S. relations with Europe. European officials and the public generally welcomed Obama's decisions to end the use of so-called enhanced interrogation techniques against terrorist suspects and to close the detention center at Guantánamo Bay, Cuba. They also applauded his efforts to reach out to Islamic leaders and populations around the world and his emphasis on multilateral rather than unilateral solutions to international problems. Less popular with European governments and their people was Obama's belief that while the situation in Iraq was under control, mounting military and political problems in Afghanistan and across the border in neighboring Pakistan warranted a major boost in American and allied forces deployed in Afghanistan as a preliminary to stabilizing those countries. In the spring of 2009, Obama announced his intention of temporarily increasing American deployments in Afghanistan from 32,000 to between 50,000 and 60,000 personnel, and he called upon other countries that belonged to the NATO alliance to send additional troops to the ISAF.

In February 2009, 34 European countries still had more than 30,000 military personnel in Afghanistan, with the largest

London Muslims march to protest a Danish newspaper's publication of a cartoon portraying the Prophet Muhammad wearing a bomb-shaped turban, February 16, 2006. (iStockPhoto)

contingent, 8,300, coming from Britain. Their response to Obama's request for greater manpower was decidedly unenthusiastic. Belgium promised an additional 150 men and four jet fighters; France pledged to send a few hundred troops, with additional personnel for the European Gendarmerie Force, to help train the new Afghan police, plus some Eurocopter Tiger attack helicopters; Italy contributed an additional 800 support troops to assist with police training and economic development; Poland offered 320 additional combat troops to help with the security of forthcoming Afghan elections; Spain offered a further 450 for the same purpose; Slovakia promised up to 176 more troops; Georgia promised as many as 500 troops; and Sweden promised between 100 and 125 troops. In early 2009 British premier Brown increased British troops levels from 8,000 to 8,300, a number he pledged to increase temporarily to 9,000 until after the August 2009 elections in Afghanistan. Overall, these new forces amounted to perhaps 4,000 additional personnel altogether, well below the major boost for which Obama had hoped.

It was clear, moreover, that some European nations, including the Netherlands, intended to bring all their troops home within two years, and several, including Britain, Poland, and Spain, planned to reduce their Afghan commitments once the summer 2009 elections were over. Across Europe, governments and the public alike had been worn down by a steady trickle of casualties and believed that almost a decade of inconclusive war in Afghanistan was long

enough. As Taliban and Al Qaeda forces enjoyed a resurgence in Afghanistan and even more in neighboring Pakistan, it was clear that while most European governments wished the Obama administration well, the United States itself would have to find the great bulk of whatever resources were needed to bring the war in Afghanistan to a conclusion that American officials considered acceptable.

PRISCILLA ROBERTS

See also

ENDURING FREEDOM, Operation; Europe and the Persian Gulf War; France, Middle East Policy; Germany, Federal Republic of, Middle East Policy; International Security Assistance Force; IRAQI FREEDOM, Operation; Russia, Middle East Policy, 1991–Present; United Kingdom, Middle East Policy

References

Andrews, David M., ed. *The Atlantic Alliance under Stress: US-European Relations after Iraq.* Cambridge: Cambridge University Press, 2005.

Baylis, John, and Jon Roper, eds. *The United States and Europe: Beyond the Neo-Conservative Divide?* London: Routledge, 2006.

Campbell, Alastair, and Richard Stott, eds. *The Blair Years: Extracts from the Alastair Campbell Diaries.* London: Hutchinson, 2007.

Cook, Robin. *The Point of Departure.* New York: Simon and Schuster, 2003.

Joffe, Josef. *Uberpower: The Imperial Temptation of America.* New York: Norton, 2006.

Judt, Tony, and Denis Lacorne, eds. *With Us or against Us: Studies in Global Anti-Americanism.* New York: Palgrave Macmillan, 2005.

Lindberg, Tod, ed. *Beyond Paradise and Power: Europe, America and the Future of a Troubled Partnership.* New York: Routledge, 2005.

Merkl, Peter H. *The Rift between America and Old Europe: The Distracted Eagle.* London: Routledge, 2005.

Serfaty, Simon. *Architects of Delusion: Europe, America, and the Iraq War.* Philadelphia: University of Pennsylvania Press, 2008.

Europe and the Persian Gulf War

The invasion of Kuwait by Iraq on August 2, 1990, caught Europe in the midst of a major political transformation. Indeed, the sudden unraveling of the Cold War and the implosion of the Soviet bloc had created a political vacuum in a region whereby old habits and rivalries were giving way to a new European configuration.

By 1990 the sudden collapse of Soviet domination over Eastern Europe, the accepted unification of Germany (the Federal Republic of Germany and the German Democratic Republic would formally reunite on October 1, 1990), and the end of the Warsaw Pact all created a major political shift, leaving European countries uncertain about their future course of action. In such a context, French and Germans saw the period as an opportunity to reaffirm European influence. On the other hand, nations such as Great Britain expressed concern—shared by the United States—about a reinforced European community and feared the emergence of a rival force that would diminish both the North Atlantic Treaty Organization (NATO) and British influence within it.

The nature of West European collaboration before the collapse of the Soviet bloc made the undertaking of common European military operations outside Europe difficult. First and foremost, West European countries were from the outset prepared to act and intervene only within the context of the NATO partnership. Furthermore, France and Britain were the only two states that had military forces capable of mounting and sustaining relatively large-scale overseas operations. Italy and Spain had naval units operation in the Mediterranean but not the capability of sending large troop deployments abroad. Finally, except for Britain and France, no European nations had the resources to face a powerful and large Iraqi Army, and most European nations did not have an infrastructure capable of supporting a foreign intervention.

In addition, public opinion in most European countries was hostile to any form of military intervention outside Europe. Not only did France, Italy, and Spain wish to maintain an autonomous Middle Easy policy, but a foreign intervention posed the serious risk of dividing public opinion. The British stood alone and presented a different picture. The 1982 Falklands War had shown that a foreign intervention, supported by the United States, could indeed gain public support.

When Iraq invaded Kuwait, European reaction was initially limited and somewhat subdued. There was, of course, official condemnation of the invasion and support for United Nations (UN) Security Council Resolution 661. France, Great Britain, and the Federal Republic of Germany all froze Iraqi funds but did little else. It took a month for the West European nations to coordinate their policy. Although Britain, France, Greece, Italy, and the Netherlands decided to send naval forces to the Persian Gulf, it was only on September 9, more than five weeks after the invasion, that they were able to coordinate this step with U.S. forces already in the area. By the end of September, approximately 30 European warships were in place enforcing the UN embargo on Iraq. France and Great Britain joined Belgium, Germany, Italy, and the Netherlands in the air defense of Turkey, a fellow NATO member. France and Britain were, however, the only West European nations to dispatch ground forces to protect Saudi Arabia (Operation DESERT SHIELD) and also take part in the subsequent coalition invasion of Iraq (Operation DESERT STORM).

Difficulties in coordinating a common European policy and diplomacy demonstrated the limited diplomatic influence and capacity of the Europeans. In fact, the Persian Gulf War clearly demonstrated the limited nature of European integration in 1990; the shifting balance of power and reconfiguration of the political structure hindered a common and strong European response to the crisis, leaving leadership largely in the hands of the United States.

MARTIN LABERGE

See also

DESERT SHIELD, Operation; DESERT STORM, Operation; France, Role in Persian Gulf and Iraq Wars; Germany, Federal Republic of, Middle East Policy; Italy, Armed Forces in Iraq and Afghanistan; North Atlantic Treaty Organization; Spain, Role in Persian Gulf, Afghanistan, and Iraq Wars; Turkey, Role in Persian Gulf and Afghanistan Wars; United Kingdom; United Nations Security Council Resolution 661

References

Gordon, Philip H. *France, Germany, and the Western Alliance.* Boulder, CO: Westview, 1995.

De Nooy, Gert C., ed. *The Role of European Ground and Air Forces after the Cold War.* Leiden, Netherlands: Martinus Nijhoff, 1997.

Explosive Reactive Armor

Explosive reactive armor (ERA) is a common form of add-on armor employed in many armored fighting vehicles (AFVs), such as tanks. AFVs utilize an armor casing to protect the crew and the machinery against strikes from enemy antitank weapons. The antitank weapons, in turn, work by piercing the armor and killing the crew or damaging hardware and software. ERA is only effective against chemical energy antiarmor weapons, such as high-explosive antitank (HEAT) rounds. ERA is not effective against kinetic energy weapons, such as sabot rounds.

In the late 1970s the Israel Defense Forces (IDF) developed the new ERA technology to protect AFVs. The concept underlying ERA was accidently discovered in 1967–1968 by a German researcher, Manfred Held, who was then working in Israel. Held and his team conducted tests by firing shells at wrecked tanks left over from the 1967 Six-Day War. They noticed that tanks that still contained live ordnance exploded and that this explosion could disrupt the penetration of a shaped charge. This insight led to the manufacture of ERA.

ERA utilizes add-on protection modules, called tiles, made from thin metal plates layered around a sloped explosive sheath. The sheath explodes when it senses the impact of an explosive charge, such as a HEAT projectile. By creating its own explosion the HEAT warhead detonates prematurely, which prevents the plasma jet of molten metal from the shell penetrating into the crew compartment of the AFV. Explosive reactive armor is most effective against HEAT rounds. Once used, an ERA tile has to be replaced.

The early ERA models effectively defended tanks and other AFVs from single strikes. However, after they performed their task, the explosive sheath was spent, leaving the AFV vulnerable to another shell in the same location. More recent reactive armor uses a combination of energetic and passive materials to withstand multiple strikes. These modern designs employ smaller tiles and more complex shapes to offer optimal plate slopes to counter potential threats including missile warheads, exploding shells, and rocket-propelled grenades (RPGs).

In early 1991 technicians installed ERA on the nose and glacis plate of Challenger 1, the main battle tank of the British Army. Likewise, the U.S. Army Materiel Command applied reactive armor plates to the U.S. Marine Corps M60-series tanks. Since that time, modern AFVs such as the Abrams M-1A2, the British Challenger 1 and 2, and a variety of Russian tanks have all demonstrated excellent protection by using ERA.

New generations of antitank guided missiles continue to pose a threat. In addition, in urban combat such as that which occurred in the Iraq War after 2003, enemy infantry armed with RPGs fired from multiple directions at close range have the potential to overwhelm the target's ERA. One downside to the use of ERA is the potential to harm nearby friendly troops. In times past, infantry soldiers commonly used tanks as a means of transport. They would even ride on the tanks as they entered combat. ERA-equipped tanks made this practice too dangerous.

During the 1991 Persian Gulf War, the Iraqi military fielded almost 6,000 main battle tanks ranging from the obsolete T-55 to the modern T-72. Iraqi tanks lacked ERA. The main Iraqi battle tank, the T-72, had reactive armor but not ERA.

Development of ERA technology has continued. Advanced versions of ERA were based on better understanding of the science associated with ERA systems, and they utilized lower masses of explosives. These considerations have had significant implications on the logistics, storage, and handling of AFVs and protection systems without a reduction in the protection levels. Future ERA models are likely to employ so-called smart armor concepts that will integrate sensors and microprocessors embedded into the armor. These devices will sense the location, type, velocity, and diameter of the projectile or jet and trigger smaller explosive elements precisely tailored to defeat a specific penetrator.

JAMES ARNOLD

See also

Challenger Main Battle Tanks; M1A1 and M1A2 Abrams Main Battle Tanks; Medina Ridge, Battle of; T-54/55 Series Main Battle Tank; T-62 Main Battle Tank; T-72 Main Battle Tank

References

Dunnigan, James F., and Austin Bay. *From Shield to Storm: High-Tech Weapons, Military Strategy, and Coalition Warfare in the Persian Gulf.* New York: William Morrow, 1992.
Hutchison, Kevin Don. *Operation Desert Shield/Desert Storm: Chronology and Fact Book.* Westport, CT: Greenwood, 1995.
Jane's Armour and Artillery, 1990–1991. London: Jane's Information Group, 1990.
Jane's Armour and Artillery, 2001–2002. London: Jane's Information Group, 2001.

F

Fadhila Party

Shia Iraqi political party headed by Abd al-Rahim al-Husayni since May 2006 and part of the United Iraqi Alliance (UIA) until March 2007. Nadim al-Jabiri presided over Fahdhila (Islamic Virtue Party) prior to May 2006. Although the Fadhila Party is Islamist in focus, it does not follow Iraq's Grand Ayatollah Sayyid Ali Husayn al-Sistani but instead remains loyal to Ayatollah Muhammad al-Yaqubi, a follower of Grand Ayatollah Muhammad Sadiq al-Sadr (murdered on the orders of Saddam Hussein in 1999). Yaqubi's faction is technically a branch of the Sadrist Movement, but neither he nor Fadhila are adherents of Muqtada al-Sadr. In fact, they are seen as a rival faction to Sadr's followers.

The party's principal base of power is in southern Iraq, and it is most prevalent in the southern city of Basra. The majority of Fadhila's adherents are relatively poor Shiites, and its slogan is "made in Iraq," to differentiate it from the Shia parties linked to Iran. Prior to the January 2005 elections in Iraq, the first nationwide plebiscite since the Anglo-American–led invasion in March 2003, Fadhila joined the Shia-dominated UIA, a political coalition representing more than 20 groups and parties. The UIA won a majority of seats in the interim Iraqi National Assembly, and in the December 2005 elections, which chose a permanent parliament, Fadhila captured 15 seats. In the January–December 2005 interim government, a prominent member of Fadhila, Hashim al-Hashimi, was given the important Ministry of Oil in the new government. Charges of inefficiency and corruption, however, plagued that office. In Basra, where Fadhila was important in the provincial government, it joined with the Dawa movement (distinguished from the main Dawa Party) and the secular Wifaq movement in order to best the Supreme Council for the Islamic Revolution in Iraq (SCIRI) party.

When Husayni took control of the party in May 2006, he pulled Fadhila out the new Iraqi government, meaning that it had no clout in the governmental structure. Husayni alleged that there was "too much interference" in Iraqi internal affairs by U.S. occupation forces. The more likely reason for Fadhila's intransigence was the fact that the party did not secure control of the Ministry of Oil when the permanent government was seated after the December 2005 elections.

In May 2007 Fadhila withdrew from the UIA, claiming that the latter was too secular and was fanning the flames of sectarianism in Iraqi politics. The move angered the UIA and caused Prime Minister Nuri al-Maliki to worry that other parties might quit the UIA and weaken the government. The party disagrees with the Supreme Islamic Iraqi Council (SIIC, formerly SCIRI) idea of a "Shiite" region based on southern and central provinces. In March 2008 the Iraqi Army moved against the Mahdi Army in Basra, leaving Fadhila and the Badr Corps alone there.

PAUL G. PIERPAOLI JR.

See also

Allawi, Iyad; Maliki, Nuri Muhammed Kamil Hasan al-; Sadr, Muqtada al-; Sistani, Sayyid Ali Husayn al-; United Iraqi Alliance

References

Nasr, Vali. *The Shia Revival: How Conflicts within Islam Will Shape the Future.* New York: Norton, 2006.

Packer, George. *The Assassins' Gate: America in Iraq.* New York: Farrar, Straus and Giroux, 2005.

Stansfield, Gareth. *Iraq: People, History, Politics.* Cambridge, UK: Polity, 2007.

Visser, Reidar. "Basra, the Reluctant Seat of Shiastan." *Middle East Report* 242 (Spring 2007): 23–28.

Fahd, King of Saudi Arabia
Birth Date: ca. 1922
Death Date: August 1, 2005

King of Saudi Arabia (1982–2005) and 11th son of the founder of Saudi Arabia, Abd al-Aziz ibn Abd al-Rahman al-Saud (commonly known as Ibn Saud). Fahd ibn Abdel Aziz al-Saud was born in 1922 or 1923 in Riyadh, the current capital of Saudi Arabia. At the time of his birth his father was in the process of building modern Saudi Arabia, and during the 1920s Ibn Saud gained control over the Hejaz, the western region where the Holy Cities of Mecca and Medina are located.

Fahd was one of Ibn Saud's 37 officially recognized sons. According to the Kingdom of Saudi Arabia's 1992 Basic Law, only sons and grandsons of monarchs are eligible to be kings of Saudi Arabia. Fahd was the eldest of the so-called Sudayri Seven, the seven sons fathered by Ibn Saud with his favorite wife, Hussah bint Ahmad al-Sudayri. These seven brothers formed a close-knit group within the Saudi royal family. Fahd's full brothers include Sultan bin Abd al-Aziz, the minister of defense since 1963 and crown prince since August 1, 2005; Nayif bin Abd al-Aziz, the interior minister since 1975; and Salman bin Abd al-Aziz, the governor of Riyadh. All of his brothers are considered potential future kings of Saudi Arabia.

As the absolute monarch of Saudi Arabia, King Fahd ibn Abdel Aziz al-Saud (1982–2005) pursued close relations with the United States and oversaw Saudi Arabia's transformation from poverty to riches during the post–World War II oil boom. (AP/Wide World Photos)

Fahd was educated at the Princes' School, which was established by Ibn Saud to educate members of the royal family. In 1945 Fahd accompanied his half brother Faisal to New York City to attend the first session of the General Assembly of the United Nations (UN). At the time Faisal, who eventually became Saudi Arabia's third king, was the foreign minister.

From 1953 to 1960 Fahd served as the minister of education. In 1959 he led the Saudi delegation to the meeting of the League of Arab States. In 1964 he became interior minister. In this capacity, he ordered mass arrests after several terrorist attacks on oil facilities and government ministries. He also reportedly put down a coup attempt in 1968. Later he assumed the post of second deputy prime minister.

Following the assassination of King Faisal by his nephew on March 25, 1975, Fahd was named crown prince of Saudi Arabia. He assumed full control of daily management of the government in that year. It was assumed that King Khalid would abdicate in 1978 after hip and open heart surgery, but his health then improved. Nonetheless, by 1981, because of King Khalid's incapacitating illness, Fahd became the de facto ruler of Saudi Arabia. In August 1981 Crown Prince Fahd advanced an eight-point plan to solve the Israeli-Palestinian-Arab dispute consisting of Israeli withdrawal from 1967 to 1948 boundaries, dismantling of post-1967 Israeli settlements, guaranteed freedom of worship for all religious groups at the holy sites, affirmation of the right of return for Palestinians and compensation for those who did not wish to return, and a transitional UN authority over the West Bank and the Gaza Strip leading to an independent Palestinian state with Jerusalem as its capital, a guarantee of peace for all nations in the region, and a guarantee of the agreements by the UN or selected UN member states. Israel rejected the proposal.

Following the death of King Khalid on June 13, 1982, Fahd formally assumed the throne. During his reign, Fahd pursued a policy of open friendship with the United States while also attempting to take a leading role in Islamic and Arab issues in the Middle East. He encouraged fairly aggressive economic development policies in Saudi Arabia based on the nation's vast oil wealth and consistently sought to develop plans for economic diversification. Although Saudi Arabia remained one of the most traditional Islamic societies during Fahd's rule, advancements were nevertheless realized in technology, infrastructure, and education. Within Saudi Arabia, Islamic fundamentalists were the king's greatest critics.

On November 22, 1979, heavily armed ultra-Wahhabists, led by Juhayman Utaybi, seized the Haram, or Grand Mosque, at Mecca and held hostages there for two weeks until the Wahhabists were ousted. Utaybi and 62 others were subsequently beheaded. The rebels had accused the Saudi royal family of bowing to secularism and had proclaimed one of their leaders to be the Mahdi. Later, Iranian Islamic revolutionaries made similar claims in a propaganda war against the Saudis.

In August 1990 after Saddam Hussein's forces invaded and occupied Kuwait, Fahd agreed to allow U.S. and allied troops into

Saudi Arabia. He did this mainly out of concern that Hussein also had his eye on Saudi Arabia and its vast oil reserves. Fahd's decision earned him the condemnation of many Islamic conservatives in his own country as well as extremists such as the terrorist leader Osama bin Laden. Bin Laden himself was from a wealthy Saudi family.

After 1990 Fahd and Hussein became implacable enemies. Fahd was an avid supporter of the UN. Indeed, that organization's backing of the plan to expel Iraqi forces from Kuwait helped Fahd in his decision to allow U.S. troops access to his country. He also supported the Palestinian cause and repeatedly criticized the Israeli government's policies toward the Palestine Liberation Organization (PLO).

After Fahd suffered a debilitating stroke in 1995, many of his official duties as monarch were delegated to his brother, Crown Prince Abdullah. Although Fahd still attended government meetings, he spent increasing amounts of time on his 200-acre estate in Marbella, Spain. After the terrorist attacks of September 11, 2001, Fahd's government fully supported the Global War on Terror and mounted its own counterterrorism campaign against the Al Qaeda in the Arabian Peninsula movement within Saudi Arabia. Fahd died of pneumonia in Riyadh on August 1, 2005. At the time of his death, he was considered one of the richest men in the world, with a personal fortune worth more than $20 billion. He was succeeded by his brother Abdullah.

MICHAEL R. HALL

See also

Abdullah, King of Saudi Arabia; DESERT STORM, Operation; Faisal, King of Saudi Arabia; Hussein, Saddam; Iran-Iraq War; Saudi Arabia

References

Farsy, Fouad. *Custodian of the Two Holy Mosques: King Fahd bin Abdul Aziz.* New York: Knight Communications, 2001.

Henderson, Simon. *After King Fu'ad: Succession in Saudi Arabia.* Washington, DC: Washington Institute for Near East Policy, 1994.

Fahrenheit 9/11

Documentary film released on June 25, 2004, by Michael Moore that sharply criticized the George W. Bush administration's handling of the Global War on Terror and rationale for the March 2003 invasion of Iraq. *Fahrenheit 9/11* earned record box office receipts for a documentary but did not achieve the filmmaker's goal of preventing the reelection of Bush.

Moore is an iconoclastic author, filmmaker, and liberal activist whose controversial work enjoys considerable commercial success. His best-selling books—*Stupid White Men* (2002) and *Dude, Where's My Country* (2003)—both satirized and challenged the nation's political establishment. Moore's excellent documentary *Roger & Me* (1989) focused on the director's efforts to secure a meeting with General Motors chief executive officer Roger Smith. Moore had accused Smith of abandoning the filmmaker's hometown of Flint, Michigan. In *Bowling for Columbine* (2002), Moore addressed the subject of guns and violence in American society. At the 2003 Oscar Awards, Moore received an Academy Award for *Columbine* as best documentary feature. The filmmaker used the occasion to make a brief speech criticizing the U.S. invasion of Iraq.

Moore's controversial Oscar appearance was the beginning of a political firestorm that engulfed his next feature, *Fahrenheit 9/11*. On May 22, 2004, *Fahrenheit 9/11* was awarded the prestigious Palme d'Or at the 57th Cannes Film Festival. Moore's detractors sneered that the award was another example of French anti-Americanism; however, there was only one French citizen on the nine-person jury. Prerelease publicity for the film was also assured when executives of the Disney Corporation blocked their subsidiary Miramax from distributing the film. Lion's Gate, however, was willing to replace Disney. Moore asserted that Disney was bowing to political pressure from the Bush administration.

Fahrenheit 9/11 earned $23.9 million on its first weekend of release in Canada and the United States, making it the number one box office hit of the weekend. This was all the more remarkable because the film was in limited release. In fact, those weekend receipts alone exceeded the total amount earned by Moore's *Bowling for Columbine*, which was the largest-grossing documentary film before *Fahrenheit 9/11*. By the weekend of July 24, 2004, the film was in European release and had grossed more than $100 million.

In *Fahrenheit 9/11*, Moore indicts the Bush administration for manipulating the outcome of the 2000 presidential election as well as mishandling the Global War on Terror and the occupation of Iraq. Employing information from Craig Unger's *House of Bush, House of Saud* (2004), Moore critiques the close relationship between the Bush family and Saudi officials, observing that most of the 9/11 hijackers were Saudis rather than Iraqis. Moore also chastises the U.S. military for targeting the poor and minorities in recruitment campaigns for the Iraq War.

Moore focuses on the story of Lila Lipscomb from Flint, Michigan. Lipscomb was initially a strong supporter of the Iraq War, but she began questioning the war after her son was killed in the conflict. A grieving Lipscomb asks Moore why her son had to die in a needless conflict. Moore concludes the film by asserting that the nation must never again send its brave young men unnecessarily into harm's way. This theme was reiterated by Moore in his book *Will They Ever Trust Us Again?* (2004).

Critics on the political Right labeled the film as in-your-face propaganda, attacking Moore and the accuracy of his arguments. Moore responded that his critics failed to understand that documentaries were not objective and that *Fahrenheit 9/11* might be best described as an op-ed piece. Although acknowledging that his film was indeed opinionated, Moore defended the accuracy of his case. Perhaps Moore's condemnation of corporate media's support for the war accounted for the growing criticism of the film in the mainstream press and media. Historian Robert Brent Toplin asserts that Moore's detractors were successful in casting doubt upon the veracity of the film. Accordingly, many Americans who

A moviegoer looks at a poster of director Michael Moore peering over an envelope stamped "confidential" in an advertisement for the controversial documentary *Fahrenheit 9/11*. The film takes a critical look at the policies of the administration of U.S. president George W. Bush. (AP/Wide World Photos)

firmly supported the war effort refused to see the film. The negative political reaction to the film was also apparent in its failure to garner any Academy Award nominations. Moore did not submit his film for consideration as a documentary, hoping to attain a Best Picture nomination.

However, those who shared Moore's political perspective flocked to the film. By January 2005 it had grossed $220 million in world distribution. And more than 2 million DVD copies, record sales for a documentary, were purchased upon the DVD's release on October 5, 2004. Although a target of the political Right, Moore remains politically active and in 2007 released *Sicko,* a scathing documentary that indicts the state of the American health care industry. He was criticized by some when it became known that he had filmed part of the movie in Cuba, a potential violation of the long-standing U.S. embargo against that island nation.

RON BRILEY

See also

Bush, George Walker; IRAQI FREEDOM, Operation; Moore, Michael

References

Moore, Michael. *Will They Ever Trust Us Again?* New York: Simon and Schuster, 2004.

Toplin, Robert Brent. *Michael Moore's Fahrenheit 9/11: How One Film Divided a Nation.* Lawrence: University Press of Kansas, 2006.

Failed States and the Global War on Terror

A failed state is characterized as a nation whose governing institutions do not provide minimum services to its population, especially in terms of security. Although still not accepted by many political experts, the concept of failed states gained currency during the George W. Bush presidency as a way of rationalizing interventionism in the Global War on Terror or explaining how 9/11 could have arisen. The concept of failed states was discussed in a volume edited by Robert Rotberg and then became part of an index in the influential journal *Foreign Policy* to measure certain facts in a number of countries.

In the popularized concept of failed or collapsed states, they may be paralyzed by corruption, unable to initiate or maintain economic or development programs, and have ineffective judicial systems and little democracy. The novel factor now of interest as supposedly the true test of failure is the presence of large-scale endemic violence. The concept of failed states was specifically crafted to explain the rise of Osama bin Laden, so it was employed to identify ungoverned or poorly governed areas that harbor those who are violent.

A primary function of the state is to provide security for its citizens by means of what German sociologist Max Weber referred to as a monopoly on the legitimate use of violence. Failure to maintain this monopoly, by permitting or being unable to prevent nonstate groups to exercise violence on a large scale within the borders of the state, calls into question the existence of the state as a system of governance.

Those who employ the label "failed states" may point to Afghanistan, Lebanon, and perhaps Pakistan. Failed states became an issue in the years following World War II as new nation-states were established in the European powers' former colonial empires and as former colonies rebelled and abruptly gained their independence. Some of these new states lacked strong central-governing bureaucratic institutions or well-trained government officials and civil servants. They were unable to govern their territories and populations in an efficient manner, leaving many of their citizens to search for other sources of basic services and security.

Many of the new states' borders were not aligned with ethnic or tribal boundaries, which had been in place for decades and in some cases centuries, creating new territorial conflicts or making old ones worse. This resulted in groups within the states attempting to take on some of the powers normally held by the state, either as a means to provide security for themselves and their constituents or simply to attain autonomous power within the state's boundaries.

One supposed central characteristic of a failed state is the breakdown of law and order. This is often the result of the increased power of criminal organizations such as drug cartels, militias, insurgents, and terrorist organizations arrayed against the poor-quality military and security forces of the state.

With the weakening and failure of the state, areas of these nations may come under the control of these organizations, especially as they become more capable of imposing their will on the security forces and leadership of the state. The concept of failed states has been particularly important in the U.S. approach to the Global War on Terror because most terrorist organizations seek areas of weak governmental control, which they take advantage of for the purposes of training, organization, and staging attacks.

Terrorist organizations may take advantage of state weakness in a number of ways. Terrorists often seek to operate from regions that are difficult to reach due to geographical distances from the country's center or because of difficult, typically mountainous, terrain, or both. In some cases, such as in Afghanistan under the Taliban, the central government may welcome a terrorist organization such as Al Qaeda as an ideological ally. Sometimes the terrorists will come to an informal agreement of "live and let live" with the government, promising not to challenge government authority or get involved in domestic politics in return for

a free hand to operate in their sanctuaries. Attacks in Pakistan by a rebuilt Taliban in 2008 have led to attempts by the Pakistani government to arrange such an agreement with the terrorists. Because failed states are still considered sovereign by their citizens and governments, military action by other states against terrorist organizations in their territory involve issues of international law and politics that relate to interstate conflict and war.

While the American-led invasion of Afghanistan in 2001 was aimed at Al Qaeda, it was premised on the overthrow of the Taliban regime and reconstructing Afghanistan so that it would no longer serve as a haven for terrorist organizations. However, the Taliban remain active in Afghanistan, and the insurgency that followed the quick 2001 American victory over the Taliban and Al Qaeda illustrates how difficult it can be to establish a strong state until adequate leadership and institutions can be established, positioned, and strengthened.

ELLIOT P. CHODOFF

See also
Afghanistan; Al Qaeda; Democratization and the Global War on Terror; Global War on Terror; Hezbollah; Lebanon; Pakistan; Taliban; Terrorism

References
Fearon, James D., and David D. Laitin. "Ethnicity, Insurgency, and Civil War." *American Political Science Review* 97 (2003): 75–76.

Hironaka, Ann. *Neverending Wars: The International Community, Weak States, and the Perpetuation of Civil War.* Cambridge: Harvard University Press, 2005.

Jones, Seth G. "The Rise of Afghanistan's Insurgency: State Failure and Jihad." *International Security* 32 (2008): 7–40.

Rotberg, Robert I., ed. *When States Fail: Causes and Consequences.* Princeton, NJ: Princeton University Press, 2003.

Faisal, King of Saudi Arabia
Birth Date: ca. 1903
Death Date: June 1975

Third king of Saudi Arabia, reigning from 1964 to 1975. King Faisal ibn Abd al-Aziz al-Saud was born in Riyadh in 1903 (some sources claim 1906), the fourth son of King Abd al-Aziz ibn Saud, founder of the Saudi dynasty. In 1925 Faisal, in command of an army of Saudi loyalists, won a decisive victory over Hussein ibn Ali in the Hejaz region of western Arabia. In reward Faisal was made the governor of Hejaz the following year. After the new Kingdom of Saudi Arabia was formalized, he was named minister of foreign affairs in 1932, a post he would hold until 1964.

During the first oil boom of 1947–1952, Faisal played a key role in shaping Saudi policies. In 1953 when his elder half brother Saud became king, Faisal was declared crown prince and continued as foreign minister. In 1958 during an economic and internal political crisis, a council of princes within the Saud family sought to oust Saud and replace him with Faisal. Faisal was unwilling to endorse

During his reign as king of Saudi Arabia from 1964 to 1975, Faisal ibn Abd al-Aziz al-Saud raised his country from near-feudal status to a modern society that still strongly adhered to Islamic teachings. (Library of Congress)

this political change. Instead, Faisal received full executive powers as president of the reconstituted Council of Ministers. Saud and some supporters seized executive authority again in 1960 when Faisal was out of the country, and in response Faisal resigned.

Faisal returned to the government in 1962, when he assumed virtually full executive authority. When Saud's health began to fail, Faisal was appointed regent, assuming office on March 4, 1964. On November 2 of that year he became king after his brother Saud was finally officially forced to abdicate by the ruling family and left for Greece.

Although a traditionalist in many ways, King Faisal proved to be a farsighted innovator and administrator who modernized the ministries of government and established for the first time an efficient bureaucracy. In the course of his reign he also initiated a number of major economic and social development plans. Under Faisal, the industrial development of the Kingdom of Saudi Arabia began in earnest.

Using Saudi Arabia's vast oil revenues, which grew from $334 million in 1960 to $22.5 billion in 1974, Faisal established state benefits, including medical care and education to the postgraduate level. His government subsidized food, water, fuel, electricity, and rents. Faisal also introduced reforms such as girls' schools and television, which were hotly protested. Indeed, these reforms were

opposed by many Saudis, including members of the royal family, who saw them as counter to the tenets of Islam.

Saudi Arabia joined the Arab states in the Six-Day War of June 1967, but Faisal was devastated when Israel won the conflict. In 1973 he began a program intended to increase the military power of Saudi Arabia. On October 17 he withdrew Saudi oil from world markets, quadrupling the price of oil worldwide. Reacting to U.S. assistance to Israel during the 1973 Yom Kippur (Ramadan) War, Faisal's action was the primary force behind the 1973–1974 oil crisis, which limited American and European access to Saudi oil. It also empowered the Organization of Petroleum Exporting Countries (OPEC), which was further empowered to set the supply and price of oil supplies. In 1974 Faisal was named *Time* magazine's Man of the Year.

On March 25, 1975, Faisal was shot and killed by his nephew, Prince Faisal ibn Musad. It is generally believed that the prince wanted to avenge his elder brother, who was killed by security forces in a clash over the introduction of television into the kingdom in 1966. Ibn Musad's father had sought vengeance against his son's killer, but the ruler had deemed that the authorities were in the right. Some speculated that when the younger Faisal was in the United States, drug use might have further impaired his judgment. Musad was captured shortly after the attack. Declared sane, he was tried and found guilty of regicide and was beheaded in a public square in Riyadh in June 1975. King Faisal was succeeded by his half brother, Crown Prince Khalid ibn Sultan.

JAMES H. WILLBANKS

See also

Arab-Israeli Conflict, Overview; Oil; Organization of Petroleum Exporting Countries; Saud, Khalid ibn Sultan ibn Abd al-Aziz al-; Saudi Arabia

References

Beling, William A., ed. *King Faisal and the Modernization of Saudi Arabia.* Boulder, CO: Westview, 1980.

De Gaury, Gerald. *Faisal: Biography of a King.* New York: Praeger, 1967.

Holden, David, and Richard Johns. *The House of Saud.* New York: Holt, Rinehart and Winston, 1982.

Faisal II, King of Iraq
Birth Date: May 2, 1935
Death Date: July 14, 1958

King of Iraq from 1939 to 1958. Faisal was born in Baghdad on May 2, 1935, the only son of the second king of Iraq, Ghazi II, who died in an automobile accident in 1938. Until Faisal turned 18, his uncle, Abd al-Ilah, served as regent of Iraq and de facto head of state.

Faisal meanwhile studied at the Harrow School in Great Britain with his cousin, the future King Hussein of Jordan. The two men enjoyed a close relationship, and their two countries based on their Hashimite lineage retained important commercial and political ties. In 1952 Faisal graduated and returned to Iraq.

Current and Former Monarchs of Selected Middle Eastern and North African States

Current Monarchies

Country	Type of Monarchy	Current Ruler	Ruling Since
Bahrain	Constitutional	King Hamad bin Isa al-Khalifa	1999
Jordan	Constitutional	King Abdullah II	1999
Kuwait	Constitutional	Emir Sabah al-Ahmad al-Jabir al-Sabah	2006
Morocco	Constitutional	King Muhammad VI	1999
Oman	Absolute	Sultan Qabus ibn Said	1970
Qatar	Absolute	Emir Sheik Hamad ibn Khalifa al-Thani	1995
Saudi Arabia	Absolute	King Abdullah bin Abdulaziz al-Saud	2005
United Arab Emirates	Absolute	Sheik Khalifa bin Zayed Al Nahayan	2004

Former Monarchies

Country	Monarchy Until	Last Monarch
Egypt	1953	King Fuad II
Iran	1979	Mohammad Reza Shah Pahlavi
Iraq	1958	Faisal II
Libya	1969	Sayyid Hasan ar-Rida al-Mahdi as-Sanussi
Tunisia	1957	Muhammad VIII al-Amin
Yemen	1962	Muhammad al-Badr

Following World War I, the British received a League of Nations mandate over Iraq. The British were soon confronted with a fierce rebellion against their rule during 1920–1922, however. In restoring order and stability in Iraq, they installed on the Iraqi throne a member of the Hashimite family, Faisal I (the grandfather of Faisal II), to whom they had earlier promised the throne of Syria. Some Iraqis viewed the members of the Iraqi royal family as foreigners, as they hailed from the Hejaz, a western area of the Arabian Peninsula. Others supported Faisal I, who had symbolized the Arab cause for independence in the Arab Revolt. Many political followers of Faisal I accompanied him from Syria to Iraq, including Iraqi former Ottoman Army officers who provided a base of power for him. His son Ghazi was popular with Iraqis but was not an adept ruler. The royal family's pro-British policies and those of Nuri al-Said Pasha, who had held as many as 48 cabinet positions, including repeated stints as prime minister, caused Faisal II and the regent to be viewed by Iraqis as puppets of the British government.

By 1940 the most powerful group in Iraqi politics was the Golden Square of four army colonels, led by Colonel Salah al-Din al-Sabagh, an Arab nationalist who supported the Palestinian cause. The British regarded the Golden Square as a distinct threat and sympathetic to the Axis cause. In April 1941 Colonel Rashid Ali al-Gaylani, part of this group, engineered a military coup in Iraq, sent Abd al-Ilah into exile, and proclaimed himself regent. Gaylani sought to pursue a foreign policy independent of the United Kingdom. The young King Faisal went into seclusion outside of Baghdad. Within a month, however, a combined force of the Royal Iraqi Air Force, Jordan's Arab Legion, and a contingent of British troops defeated Gaylani's forces and restored Abd al-Ilah as regent. Faisal II then returned to Baghdad. In May 1953, upon his 18th birthday, he assumed full governing responsibility over Iraq.

In his policies, Faisal II was guided by his mentor and uncle, Abd al-Ilah, and pro-British prime minister Nuri al-Said. Many Iraqis became disillusioned with Faisal's foreign policy during the 1950s, however. Arab nationalists opposed the government's pro-Western stance on diplomatic issues. In 1955 Iraq joined the U.S.-inspired anti-Soviet Middle East Treaty Organization (also known as the Baghdad Pact). Its members included Iraq, the United States (as an associate member), the United Kingdom, Turkey, Pakistan, and Iran. The Arab nationalist president of Egypt, Gamal Abdel Nasser, strongly opposed the pact, arguing that threats to the Middle East originated in Israel rather than in the Soviet Union. During the 1956 Suez Crisis, Iraqis supported Egypt's resistance to the coordinated attack undertaken by Great Britain, France, and Israel. The Iraqi government's relationship with Great Britain, however, caused tensions concerning the rise of Nasserists and Pan-Arabists in Iraq after this crisis.

In response to Egypt's February 1, 1958, union with Syria known as the United Arab Republic (UAR), the Hashimite monarchs of Jordan and Iraq created the Arab Federation of Iraq and Jordan on February 14, 1958. Faisal II became head of state of the new federation.

In June 1958 King Hussein of Jordan requested military assistance from Iraq to quell disturbances fueled by Arab nationalists. Faisal ordered troops to Jordan, including a division of the Iraqi Army under the command of General Abd al-Karim Qasim, a staunch opponent of British ambitions in the Middle East. On July 14, 1958, using the troop movements as a cover, Qasim overthrew the monarchy and proclaimed a republic. Members of the royal family, including King Faisal II, were murdered and their bodies mutilated. Prince Zayid, the youngest brother of Faisal I, was in London at the time of the coup and became the heir-in-exile to the

Iraqi throne. When Zayid died in 1970, he was succeeded as heir-in-exile by his son, Raad, an adviser to Jordan's King Abdullah.

MICHAEL R. HALL AND SHERIFA ZUHUR

See also

Baghdad Pact; Hussein ibn Talal, King of Jordan; Iraq, History of, Pre-1990; Nasser, Gamal Abdel; Nuri al-Said; Pan-Arabism and Pan-Arabist Thought; Suez Crisis; United Arab Republic; United Kingdom, Middle East Policy

References

Eppel, Michael. *Iraq from Monarchy to Tyranny: From the Hashemites to the Rise of Saddam.* Gainesville: University Press of Florida, 2004.

Marr, Phebe. *The Modern History of Iraq.* 2nd ed. Boulder, CO: Westview, 2003.

Fallon, William Joseph
Birth Date: December 30, 1944

U.S. Navy officer and commander, U.S. Central Command (CENTCOM), during 2007–2008. William Joseph "Fox" Fallon was born in East Orange, New Jersey, on December 30, 1944, and grew up in Merchantville, New Jersey. He was commissioned in the U.S. Navy through the Navy ROTC program after graduating from Villanova University in 1967. That December he completed flight training and became a naval aviator. He later graduated from the Naval War College, Newport, Rhode Island, and the National War College, Washington, D.C. Fallon also earned an MA degree in international studies from Old Dominion University in 1982.

Fallon's career as a naval aviator spanned 24 years, with service in attack squadrons and carrier air wings. He logged more than 1,300 carrier-arrested landings and 4,800 flight hours. Fallon began his career in naval aviation flying an RA-5C Vigilante in Vietnam, later moving on to pilot the A-6 Intruder beginning in 1974. He served in the Mediterranean and the Atlantic, Pacific, and Indian oceans on the carriers *Saratoga, Ranger, Nimitz, Dwight D. Eisenhower,* and *Theodore Roosevelt.*

Fallon's commands included Attack Squadron 65, deployed aboard the *Dwight D. Eisenhower* (May 3, 1984–September 5, 1985); Medium Attack Wing One at Naval Air Station, Oceana, Virginia; Carrier Air Wing Eight, aboard the *Theodore Roosevelt* deployed in the Persian Gulf during Operations DESERT SHIELD and DESERT STORM (Fallon led 80 strike air missions into Iraq and Kuwait during August 1990–February 1991); Carrier Group Eight (1995); Battle Force Sixth Fleet as part of the *Theodore Roosevelt* Battle Group during the North Atlantic Treaty Organization (NATO) combat Operation DELIBERATE FORCE (August 29–September 14, 1995) in Bosnia; and Second Fleet and Striking Fleet Atlantic (November 1997–September 2000).

Fallon held numerous staff assignments. He also served as deputy director for operations, Joint Task Force, Southwest Asia in Riyadh, Saudi Arabia; deputy director, aviation plans and requirements on the staff of the chief of Naval Operations in Washington, D.C.; assistant chief of staff, plans and policy for Supreme Allied Commander, Atlantic (his first flag officer position); deputy and chief of staff, U.S. Atlantic Fleet; and deputy commander in chief and chief of staff, U.S. Atlantic Command.

Fallon was promoted to full (four-star) admiral and became the 31st vice chief of naval operations, a post he held from October 2000 to August 2003. While serving in that capacity, he publicly apologized to the president of Japan following a collision between the U.S. submarine *Greeneville* and the Japanese fishing training ship *Ehime Maru* off the coast of Hawaii in February 2001. In 2002 Fallon asserted before the U.S. Senate Committee on Environment and Public Works Committee that the ability to conduct military operations superseded obedience to environmental laws. He then took command of the U.S. Fleet Forces Command (October 2003–February 2005) and the U.S. Pacific Command (February 2005–March 2007), where his approach to the People's Republic of China (PRC) was less confrontational than previous commanders and was not well received by some American policy makers who favored a tougher stance toward the PRC.

In March 2007 Fallon replaced General John P. Abizaid of the U.S. Army to become the first naval officer to take command of CENTCOM. Fallon's tenure lasted only one year, from March 16, 2007, to March 28, 2008. Although the impetus for his abrupt retirement as CENTCOM commander is not disputed, its voluntariness is. Despite the fact that Fallon was publicly lauded by President George W. Bush and Secretary of Defense Robert Gates, Gates noted that Fallon's resignation was due in part to controversy surrounding an article by Thomas P. M. Barnett titled "The Man between War and Peace," published in *Esquire* magazine on March 11, 2008. In it, Fallon was quoted as having disagreements with the Bush administration on the prosecution of the war in Iraq and over a potential conflict with Iran regarding its nuclear weapons program. The article portrayed Fallon as resisting pressure from the Bush administration for war with Iran over the latter's pursuit of a nuclear weapons program. Besides Fallon's rather open opposition to Bush's war policies, the admiral purportedly disagreed with General David Petraeus over Iranian covert exportation of weapons to Iraqi insurgents and the pace of future American troop reductions in Iraq. Many believed that Fallon was forced out principally because his superiors blamed him for the failure to halt Iranian weapons from entering Iraq.

RICHARD M. EDWARDS

See also

Abizaid, John Philip; Bush, George Walker; Gates, Robert Michael; Petraeus, David Howell

References

Barnett, Thomas P. M. "The Man Between War and Peace." *Esquire,* March 11, 2008, 1–4.

Dorsey, Jack. "Navy Taps 2nd Fleet's Adm. William J. Fallon for 4-Star Pentagon Post." *Virginian Pilot,* September 7, 2000, 1.

Lambeth, Benjamin S. *American Carrier Air Power at the Dawn of a New Century.* Santa Monica, CA: RAND Corporation, 2005.

Fallujah

City located in central Iraq, within the so-called Sunni Triangle, and a center of insurgency activity after the March 2003 Anglo-American–led invasion of Iraq. On the eve of the Iraq War, Fallujah had a population of approximately 440,000 people, the great majority of whom were Sunni Muslims. The city is located along the Euphrates River about 42 miles to the west of the capital city of Baghdad. The city consisted of more than 2,000 city blocks laid out in regular grid fashion. A typical block grid featured tenements and two-story concrete houses surrounded by courtyard walls and divided by narrow alleyways. Highway 10, a two-lane road that runs through the city, becomes a four-lane throughway in the city's center.

The area encompassing Fallujah has been inhabited for many centuries, and its history can be traced back at least as far as the reign of the Babylonian king Hammurabai, during 1780–1750 BCE. After the Babylonian captivity of the Jews and beginning in circa 219 CE, the area now encompassed by Fallujah became a center of Jewish learning and scholarship that included many Jewish academies. This lasted until circa 1050. The city was a crossroads during the many centuries of Ottoman rule.

Following World War I the British established a mandate over the area of Iraq. With a rise of Iraqi nationalism, in April 1941, during World War II, there was a coup that brought Rashid Ali al-Gaylani to power. He formed a cabinet that contained a number of individuals with Axis connections. Encouraged by hints of Axis aid, Gaylani refused to honor a 1930 treaty that allowed the transportation of British troops from Basra across Iraq. The Iraqi government also positioned troops and artillery around British bases in Iraq. In the ensuing fighting, British troops defeated the Iraqi Army near Fallujah.

In 1947 the city had just 10,000 inhabitants, but it grew exponentially in the decades to follow because of Iraq's growing oil wealth, Fallujah's strategic position along the Euphrates, and Iraqi dictator Saddam Hussein's program designed to make it a centerpiece of his power base beyond Baghdad. Many Sunnis from the city held positions within the government, and the ruling Baath Party claimed many important ties to Fallujah. The city came to be highly industrialized under Hussein's rule, although westward-running Highway 1, a four-lane divided superhighway, bypassed the city and caused the city to decline in strategic importance by the early 2000s. Fallujah retained its political importance thanks to the many senior Baath Party members from the area.

During the 1991 Persian Gulf War, bridges spanning the Euphrates River in Fallujah were targeted by coalition aircraft. In

Members of the U.S. Navy assigned to a mobile construction battalion patrol a Fallujah street one day before the January 30, 2005, national elections in Iraq. (U.S. Navy)

the process several markets were hit, resulting in substantial civilian casualties. As many as 200 Iraqi civilians may have been killed in these bombing raids.

During the initial stages of Operation IRAQI FREEDOM Fallujah remained largely unaffected by the fighting because Iraqi troops who had garrisoned the city fled, leaving considerable military equipment behind. However, as the war progressed and Hussein's regime was toppled, Fallujah was struck by a spasm of violence and looting, with individuals sacking military storage areas, stores, hospitals, and restaurants. To make matters worse, Hussein had released all political prisoners held in the nearby Abu Ghraib Prison, which flooded the area with an assortment of bitter political exiles and criminals who delighted in the anarchy of Fallujah in the spring and summer of 2003. Inhabitants fled the city by the thousands, leaving behind the remnants of their lives and livelihoods. A large percentage of the male population of Fallujah was unemployed, and they proved to be a major source of recruits for the Iraqi insurgency movement. The Iraqis of Falluja perceived themselves as having lost the status they had enjoyed under Hussein and believed that they had little to gain in a new governmental system dominated by his former enemies.

In April 2003 U.S. occupation forces finally attempted to exert control over the city, but by then the major damage had already been done, and the city was increasingly anti-American. Sunni rebels had soon taken root in Fallujah, as had foreign insurgents allied with Al Qaeda. Operation VIGILANT RESOLVE (the First Battle of Fallujah), launched in April 2004 by U.S. forces, failed to wrest the city away from the insurgents. During November–December 2004 U.S. and Iraqi security forces launched Operation PHANTOM FURY (the Second Battle of Fallujah), a large and bloody affair that caused the insurgents to flee the city. However, the coalition and Iraqi forces had to conduct yet another operation in Fallujah in June 2007.

Since then Fallujah's population has trickled back into the city, but they have returned to a disaster zone. Half of the city's housing was destroyed, much of its infrastructure lay in ruins or disrepair, and city services were absent. Reconstruction has advanced slowly, and it is estimated that almost 150,000 refugees still reside in massive tent cities on the outskirts of Fallujah. In 2009 the Iraqi government estimated the population of the city at 350,000, but Fallujah struggles to return to normalcy.

PAUL G. PIERPAOLI JR.

See also

Al Qaeda in Iraq; Baath Party; Fallujah, First Battle of; Fallujah, Second Battle of; Hussein, Saddam; Iraqi Insurgency; Sunni Triangle

References

Buzzell, Colby. *My War: Killing Time in Iraq.* New York: Putnam, 2005.

Keegan, John. *The Iraq War: The Military Offensive, from Victory in 21 Days to the Insurgent Aftermath.* New York: Vintage, 2005.

Ricks, Thomas E. *Fiasco: The American Military Adventure in Iraq.* New York: Penguin, 2006.

Fallujah, First Battle of

Start Date: April 4, 2004
End Date: May 1, 2004

A U.S. offensive, the principal goal of which was to retake the Iraqi city of Fallujah after insurgents had seized control of it. Codenamed VIGILANT RESOLVE, it occurred during April 4–May 1, 2004. Sunni insurgents, including Al Qaeda fighters, had steadily destabilized Anbar Province in Iraq in the aftermath of the 2003 U.S.-led invasion. Fallujah, located some 42 miles west of Baghdad in the so-called Sunni Triangle, emerged as a focal point for anticoalition attacks. The town was dominated by salafist groups who were extremely suspicious of all outsiders, particularly foreigners; family and clan ties dominated personal relationships. The collapse of Iraqi president Saddam Hussein's regime had left some 70,000 male inhabitants in the city unemployed, providing a major source of recruits for the Iraqi insurgency movement.

Growing violence in Fallujah in March 2004 led the U.S. military to withdraw forces from the city and conduct only armed patrols. On March 31 insurgents ambushed four contractors working for Blackwater USA, a private contracting company that provided security personnel to the Coalition Provisional Authority (CPA). The insurgents dragged the bodies through the streets and then hanged them from a bridge. Television cameras transmitted the grisly images around the world, prompting a strong response to offset the perception that coalition forces had lost control of the area.

In an effort to regain control of the city and the surrounding province, the U.S. military launched a series of operations against suspected insurgent groups and their bases. The lead unit was the I Marine Expeditionary Force (I MEF), which had been deployed to Anbar in March. The ground forces were supported by coalition aircraft and helicopter units. U.S. lieutenant general James Conway had overall command of the operation. On April 4 some 2,200 marines surrounded Fallujah. They blockaded the main roads in and out of the city in an effort to allow only civilians to escape the fighting. The commanders on the ground believed that the marines should remain outside of the city because they lacked the troops to effectively control the area and the population; nevertheless, they were ordered to seize the city.

In the opening days of the operation, U.S. forces conducted air strikes on suspected targets and undertook limited incursions into Fallujah, including a strike to take control of its main radio station. At least one-quarter of the civilian population fled the city as insurgents used homes, schools, and mosques to attack the marines, who responded with devastating firepower that often produced high collateral damage and civilian casualties.

Within the city there were an estimated 15,000–20,000 insurgent fighters divided among more than a dozen insurgent groups of various origins. Some were former members of Hussein's security forces. They were armed with a variety of weapons, including light arms, rocket-propelled grenades (RPGs), mortars, and

U.S. Army armor withdraws from the U.S. military checkpoint at the entrance to Fallujah, Iraq, April 30, 2004. (AP/Wide World Photos)

improvised explosive devices (IEDs). The insurgents used guerrilla tactics against the marines, including ambushes, mortar attacks, and mines and IEDs. Sniper fire was common throughout the operation. U.S. forces responded with artillery and air strikes, including the use of heavily armed Lockheed AC-130 gunships. Support from Bell AH-1W Super Cobra attack helicopters, however, was limited because of significant ground fire. Meanwhile, the marines attempted to secure neighborhoods one or two blocks at a time using air support and tanks.

There were problems coordinating movements in the dense urban environment, especially because maps were not standardized between the various units. Meanwhile, many of the remaining Iraqi security forces within the city either joined the insurgents or simply fled their posts. After three days of intense fighting, the marines had secured only about one-quarter of Fallujah.

In response to the escalating violence, the failure of the marines to make significant progress in the city, growing pressure from Iraqi political leaders, and increasing domestic pressure on the George W. Bush administration that was largely the result of media coverage, the U.S.-led CPA ordered a unilateral cease-fire on April 9 and initiated negotiations with the insurgent groups. The marines allowed humanitarian aid into the city; however, in spite of the cease-fire, sporadic fighting continued. Throughout

the negotiations, it was decided that the United States would turn over security for the city to a newly formed ad hoc Iraqi militia force, the Fallujah Brigade. The United States agreed to provide arms and equipment for the brigade, which included former soldiers and police officers of the Hussein regime.

On May 1 U.S. forces completely withdrew from Fallujah, but they maintained a presence outside of the city at an observation base. More than 700 Iraqis had been killed in the fighting (the majority of these, perhaps as many as 600, were civilians), while 27 U.S. marines were killed and 90 were wounded.

The Fallujah Brigade failed to maintain security and began to disintegrate during the summer of 2004. Many of its members joined or rejoined the insurgency, and the military announced that Abu Musab al-Zarqawi, the leader of Al Qaeda in Iraq, was headquartered in Fallujah. The coalition undertook a second campaign in Fallujah in the autumn of 2004, code-named Operation PHANTOM FURY.

TOM LANSFORD

See also

Fallujah; Fallujah, Second Battle of; Iraqi Insurgency; United States Marine Corps, Iraq War

References

Afong, Milo. *Hogs in the Shadows: Combat Stories from Marine Snipers in Iraq.* New York: Berkley, 2007.

Cockburn, Patrick. *The Occupation: War and Resistance in Iraq.* New York: Verso, 2007.

O'Donnell, Patrick K. *We Were One: Shoulder to Shoulder with the Marines Who Took Fallujah.* New York: Da Capo, 2007.

West, Bing. *No True Glory: A Frontline Account of the Battle for Fallujah.* New York: Bantam, 2006.

Fallujah, Second Battle of
Start Date: November 7, 2004
End Date: December 23, 2004

Major battle fought in and around the city of Fallujah, some 42 miles west of Baghdad, between U.S., Iraqi, and British forces and Iraqi insurgents (chiefly Al Qaeda in Iraq but also other militias). Following the decision to halt the coalition assault on Fallujah in Operation VIGILANT RESOLVE (the First Battle of Fallujah) during April–May 2004, the U.S. marines had withdrawn from the city and turned over security to the so-called Fallujah Brigade, an ad hoc force of local men who had formerly served in the Iraqi Army. The Fallujah Brigade failed dismally in this task, giving the insurgents another chance to claim victory and attract additional recruits. During the summer and autumn months, the Fallujah police turned a blind eye as the insurgents fortified positions inside Fallujah and stockpiled supplies. The Iraqi interim government, formed on June 28, 2004, then requested new efforts to capture and secure Fallujah.

A U.S. marine at an observation post in Fallujah, Iraq, during Operation NEW DAWN on November 10, 2004. (U.S. Army)

In preparation for the ground assault, coalition artillery and aircraft began selective strikes on the city on October 30, 2004. Coalition ground forces (American, Iraqi, and British) cut off electric power to the city on November 5 and distributed leaflets warning people to stay in their homes and not use their cars. This was a response to insurgent suicide bombers who had been detonating cars packed with explosives. On November 7 the Iraqi government announced a 60-day state of emergency throughout most of Iraq. Because of all these warnings, between 75 and 90 percent of Fallujah's civilian population abandoned the city before the coalition ground offensive began. Many of these fled to Syria, where they remain as refugees.

The Americans initially labeled the assault Operation PHANTOM FURY. Iraqi prime minister Ayad Allawi, however, renamed it AL-FAJR (New Dawn). The operation's main objective was to demonstrate the ability of the Iraqi government to control its own territory, thereby bolstering its prestige. The American military focused on the important secondary objective of killing as many insurgents as possible while keeping coalition casualties low. About 10,000 American soldiers and marines and 2,000 Iraqi troops participated in Operation AL-FAJR. Some Royal Marines also took part. The American forces involved had considerable experience in urban combat.

The assault plan called for a concentration of forces north of Fallujah. Spearheaded by the army's heavy armor, army and marine units would attack due south along precisely defined sectors. The infantry would methodically clear buildings, leaving the trailing Iraqi forces to search for insurgents and assault the city's 200 mosques, which coalition tacticians suspected would be used as defensive insurgent strong points. Intelligence estimates suggested that some 3,000 insurgents defended the city, one-fifth of whom were foreign jihadists. Intelligence estimates also predicted fanatical resistance.

Ground operations associated with the Second Battle of Fallujah commenced on November 7, 2004, when an Iraqi commando unit and the Marine 3rd Light Armored Reconnaissance Battalion conducted a preliminary assault. The objective was to secure the Fallujah General Hospital to the west of the city and capture two bridges over the Euphrates River, thereby isolating the insurgent forces inside the city. This preliminary assault was successful, allowing the main assault to commence after dark the following evening. The American military chose this time because it knew that its various night-vision devices would provide it a tactical advantage over the insurgents. Four marine infantry and two army mechanized battalions attacked in the first wave. M-1A2 Abrams tanks and M-2A3 Bradley infantry fighting vehicles provided mobile firepower for which the insurgents had no answer. The M-1A2 Abrams tanks exhibited the ability to absorb enormous punishment and keep operating. The speed and shock of the massed armor overwhelmed the insurgents, enabling the American soldiers to drive deep into Fallujah. Iraqi forces also performed surprisingly well. After four days of operations, coalition forces had secured about half the city.

By November 11 the methodical American advance had driven most of the insurgents into the southern part of Fallujah. Three days of intense street fighting ensued, during which time the Americans reached the southern limits of the city. On November 15 the Americans reversed direction and attacked north to eliminate any insurgents who had been missed in the first pass and to search more thoroughly for insurgent weapons and supplies. For this part of the operation, the ground forces broke down into squad-sized elements to conduct their searches. By November 16 American commanders judged Fallujah secured, although the operation would not end officially until December 23, by which time many residents had been allowed to return to their homes.

U.S. casualties in the Second Battle of Fallujah were 95 killed and 560 wounded; Iraqi Army losses were 11 killed and 43 wounded. Insurgent losses were estimated at between 1,200 and 2,000 killed, with another 1,000 to 1,500 captured. The disparity in the casualties indicated the extent of the coalition's tactical advantage. Indeed, postbattle army and marine assessments lauded the tremendous tactical skill in urban warfare displayed by American forces. However, the intense house-to-house fighting had caused the destruction of an estimated 20 percent of the city's buildings, while another 60 percent of the city's structures were damaged. The tremendous damage, including that to 60 mosques, enraged Iraq's Sunni minority. Widespread civilian demonstrations and increased insurgent attacks followed the Second Battle of Fallujah. Although the 2005 Iraqi elections were held on schedule, Sunni participation was very low partially because of the Sunnis' sense of grievance over the destruction in Fallujah.

JAMES ARNOLD

See also

Al Qaeda in Iraq; Allawi, Iyad; Fallujah; Iraqi Insurgency; Sunni Islam; Sunni Triangle

References

Ballard, John R. *Fighting for Fallujah: A New Dawn for Iraq.* Westport, CT: Praeger Security International, 2006.

Bellavia, David. *House to House: An Epic Memoir of War.* New York: Free Press, 2007.

Gott, Kendall D., ed. *Eyewitness to War: The U.S. Army in Operation Al Fajr; An Oral History.* 2 vols. Fort Leavenworth, KS: Combat Studies Institute Press, 2006.

Falwell, Jerry
Birth Date: August 11, 1933
Death Date: May 15, 2007

Conservative and often controversial American fundamentalist Baptist pastor, educator, author, televangelist, and pro-Israel activist. Jerry Lamon Falwell was born in Lynchburg, Virginia, on August 11, 1933, and graduated with a degree in Bible studies from the Baptist Bible College in Springfield, Missouri, in 1956. That same year he returned to Lynchburg and founded the Thomas Road Baptist Church (TRBC). Church membership grew from the original 35 members in 1956 to more than 24,000 members by 2007. Falwell also founded Lynchburg Baptist College (now Liberty University) in 1971.

In 1979 Falwell and Ed McAteer founded the Moral Majority, a conservative Christian lobbying group that stood against abortion, pornography, feminism, and homosexuality and advocated for an increased role of religion in public schools and traditional family values. The Moral Majority was highly influential in the election of Republican Ronald Reagan to the presidency in 1980 and also championed continued American support of Israel. Meanwhile, Falwell had developed a national following through his television and radio programming. The *Old Time Gospel Hour,* still in production and aired nationally until 2004, broadcasts the TRBC's Sunday morning services. Since 2004, the television program has aired only locally in the Lynchburg market. *Listen America Radio* produces three-minute news and commentary segments featuring the opinions of various conservatives.

During the 1990s Falwell was a vehement opponent of President Bill Clinton and First Lady Hillary Clinton. Falwell actively promoted a video titled *The Clinton Chronicles* that accused the Clintons of complicity in the suicide death of White House counsel Vincent Foster.

Falwell's resolute support of Israel has been referred to as an example of the Christian Zionism common among fundamentalist Christians. He and other American Christian Zionists contend that conservative American Christians are the staunchest and most loyal supporters of Israel and that this bloc, 70 million strong, will closely monitor American policies toward Israel. In January 1998 Falwell stated that if need be he could contact 200,000 evangelical pastors on behalf of Israel. He proved this point when he responded to President George W. Bush's April 2002 prodding of Israel to remove its tanks from Palestinian towns on the West Bank with a personal letter of protest followed by more than 100,000 e-mails from Christian conservatives. The tanks remained, and Bush issued no follow-up call for their withdrawal.

Falwell believed that the return of the Jews to their homeland would initiate a prophetic cycle that began with the destruction of Jerusalem and the temple in 70 CE. The formation of the State of Israel in 1948 was the necessary component that restarted the prophetic cycle, which will end with the Second Coming of Jesus. Israel's retaking of the Western (Wailing) Wall, the only remaining wall of Solomon's original temple, and of the Temple Mount during the 1967 Six-Day War were seen as a further progression of the cycle that would ultimately lead to the end of the world. Falwell viewed the continued war and upheaval in the Middle East as drawing the world closer to Armageddon, the final battle played out as prophesied in the Revelation of John.

Reverend Jerry Lamon Falwell (1933–2007), American fundamentalist Baptist pastor, educator, author, televangelist, and pro-Israel activist. (AP/Wide World Photos)

Falwell viewed Israel as the catalyst necessary for the completion of this cycle. To this end, he agreed with former Israeli prime minister Menachem Begin that the boundaries of ancient Judea and Samaria must be maintained at all costs. Falwell therefore opposed all land concessions to the Palestinian National Authority (PNA), including the West Bank and the Gaza Strip. He thus saw Prime Minister Yitzhak Rabin's signing of the 1993 Oslo Accords and offer to trade land for peace as a terrible sin.

Falwell also asserted that Islam is not a religion of peace and that the Prophet Muhammad was a "terrorist." In an act that was perceived by Falwell's followers as proving his point, a fatwa encouraging the murder of Falwell was promptly issued by Iranian clerics on October 11, 2002, after Falwell's incendiary characterization was aired on CBS on national television in October 2002. Falwell continued to lobby for the interests of the Christian Right and remained an important emblem to advance its agenda up until his death in Lynchburg on May 15, 2007.

RICHARD M. EDWARDS

See also

Begin, Menachem; Rabin, Yitzhak

References

Falwell, Jerry. *Falwell: An Autobiography.* New York: Liberty House, 1996.

Harding, Susan Friend. *The Book of Jerry Falwell: Fundamentalist Language and Politics.* Princeton, NJ: Princeton University Press, 2001.

Simon, Merrill. *Jerry Falwell and the Jews.* New York: Jonathan David, 1999.

Fao Peninsula

See Faw Peninsula

Fast Combat Support Ships

Underway replenishment ships that combine the capabilities of fleet oilers, combat stores ships, and ammunition ships in servicing fast aircraft carrier battle groups. In 1953 the U.S. Navy converted the *Conecuh* (AO-110, the former German supply ship *Dithmarschen*) into the first replenishment oiler. Its characteristics influenced the design of the purpose-built U.S. fast combat support ships. Eight ships were built. The first four were the Sacramento-class (AOE-1 through AOE-4). These joined the fleet during 1964–1970. In addition to the *Sacramento* (AOE-1), these included the *Camden* (AOE-2), *Seattle* (AOE-3), and *Detroit* (AOE-4). Their dimensions were length, 794.75 feet; beam, 107 feet; and draft, 39.3 feet. They displaced 18,700 tons (light) and 53,600 tons (full load). They had a speed of 27.5 knots and a range of 10,000 nautical miles at 17 knots or 6,000 nautical miles at 26 knots. Complement was 601 (27 officers and 574 enlisted). Cargo capacities were 177,000 barrels of fuel, 2,150 tons of munitions, 500 tons of dry stores, and 250 tons refrigerated stores. They carried two UH-46 Sea Knight helicopters and were armed with a North Atlantic Treaty Organization (NATO) Sea Sparrow 8-cell surface-to-air missile (SAM) launcher, two Vulcan Phalanx close-in weapons systems (CIWs), and four 12.7-millimeter (mm) machine guns.

The four Supply-class ships (T-AOE-6, T-AOE-7, T-AOE-8, and T-AOE-10) were commissioned during the period 1994–1998. In addition to the *Supply* (T-AOE-6), they included the *Rainier* (T-AOE-7), *Arctic* (T-AOE-8), and *Bridge* (T-AOE-10). Dimensions for this class were length, 754.75 feet; beam, 107 feet; and draft, 39 feet. They displaced 19,700 tons (light) and 48,800 tons (full load). They were capable of 26 knots and had a range of 6,000 nautical miles at 22 knots. Complement was 188 (160 civilians and 28 naval personnel). Cargo capacities were 156,000 barrels of fuel, 1,800 tons of munitions, 400 tons of refrigerated stores, and 250 tons of dry stores. Each carried three UH-46 Sea Knight helicopters. Weapons were removed upon their transfer to the Military Sealift Command (MSC).

Originally based on a late 1950s' plan to convert battleships of the Iowa-class to fast underway replenishment ships that incorporated the capabilities of the *Conecuh*, the *Sacramento, Camden, Seattle,* and *Detroit* were finally developed from an alternate new-construction design after the prohibitive complications and costs of adapting the heavily armored and compartmented battleship hulls for service as auxiliaries became evident. Maintaining a link to the Iowa-class nonetheless, these ships' hull lines mirrored the sleek aspect of the fast battleships. Their graceful clipper-bowed hulls supported minimal superstructure, which was punctuated by the distinctive M-framed cargo and hose-handling posts, and was capped aft with a funnel that would be equally at home atop a cruise liner. A large helicopter pad covered each ship's stern. The *Sacramento* and *Camden* each were powered by half of the main machinery from the unfinished battleship *Kentucky,* which led to their engine rooms acting as seagoing classrooms in the 1980s for engineering crews assigned to the newly reactivated Iowa-class ships.

The Sacramento-class ships were the largest underway replenishment ships in naval service anywhere, and their hull designation

"AOE" combined the "AO" of a fleet oiler with the ammunition ship's "AE" in order to express their unique capabilities, which also included supplying stores along with fuel and munitions to aircraft carriers, battleships, cruisers, destroyers, and virtually any other ship type in the fleet. Not only did their improved fuel transfer systems and advanced cargo handling stations revolutionize and accelerate the connected underway replenishment via cables and support lines to ships maneuvering alongside, but their helicopters were also capable of the rapid ship-to-ship resupply to other vessels in the formation of ordnance and stores via vertical replenishment at rates up to three tons per minute. A single AOE of either the Sacramento or Supply class would be capable of sustaining a conventionally powered aircraft carrier, its air group, and three escort vessels cruising nearly halfway around the world. Their speed and enormous capacity quickly made the AOEs indispensable to the operations and flexibility of the modern carrier battle group.

For most of their operational years, the *Sacramento* and *Camden* were based on the U.S. west coast (Bremerton, Washington); the *Seattle* and *Detroit* were based on the east coast (at Norfolk, Virginia). All but the *Camden* took part in Operations DESERT SHIELD and DESERT STORM: the *Sacramento* was on station from January to March 1991 with the *Saratoga* (CV-60) battle group, the *Seattle* operated from September 1990 to March 1991 with the *John F. Kennedy* (CV-67) battle group, and the *Detroit* moved from its Mediterranean station into the Red Sea on August 24, 1990, and was on hand with the *Saratoga* battle group for DESERT STORM operations until early February 1991.

The four original AOEs also participated in the early stages of Operation ENDURING FREEDOM: the *Sacramento* served with the *Carl Vinson* (CVN-70) battle group (October–December 2001), the *Detroit* serviced the *Theodore Roosevelt* (CVN-71) battle group (October 2001–March 2002) and the *Enterprise* (CVN-65) battle group (October 2003–March 2004), the *Seattle* joined the *Kennedy* battle group (March 2002–July 2002 and again during June–December 2004), and the *Camden* operated with the *Abraham Lincoln* (CVN-72) battle group (July 2002–May 2003) and was on station at the outset of Operation IRAQI FREEDOM on March 20, 2003.

The *Camden* made a final deployment with the *Vinson* battle group from January through August 2005. The *Sacramento* was decommissioned in 2004, while the *Camden, Seattle,* and *Detroit* left service in 2005.

The characteristics of the U.S. Navy's next group of four fast combat support ships were based on the design and capabilities of the Sacramento class, but the Supply-class ships are powered by gas turbines, whose demands for internal engineering space are less than those posed by the Sacramento-class boilers and turbines and allow for a slightly smaller ship with nearly equal capacities (see specifications above). Only a pair of blunter, squarer funnels and a straighter bow distinguish this class visually from its forebears. Plans in 1992 called for an AOE-9 (the name *Conecuh*

The combat support ship USS *Camden* and the nuclear-powered aircraft carrier *Carl Vinson* flank the Military Sealift Command combat stores ship USNS *Mars* and oiler USS *Pecos* during a vertical replenishment operation off the coast of Sri Lanka, 1994. (U.S. Department of Defense)

was proposed) to follow the *Arctic,* but the funding was diverted to other uses, and the construction was cancelled. In 1993 AOE-10 was authorized and named the *Bridge.*

The Supply class, like the Sacramento class, employs connected underway replenishment and vertical replenishment, and each can replenish up to four ships simultaneously. The Fast Automated Shuttle Transfer (FAST) system for connected underway replenishment was first employed by the U.S. Navy in the Sacramento-class and was replaced by the more capable and automated Standard Tensioned Replenishment Alongside Method (STREAM) system, which has greatly increased the rate of fueling at sea. The Supply-class ships were delivered to the fleet with the STREAM system as standard equipment.

The *Supply* (AOE-6), *Rainier* (AOE-7), *Arctic* (AOE-8), and *Bridge* (AOE-10) were designed with many automated features that reduced the size of their crews relative to those of the Sacramento-class, and their phased transfer to the MSC involved transitional modifications that would lead to even smaller and more efficient blended naval and civilian crews managing the ships' systems at a reduced cost. USS *Supply* was decommissioned from the U.S. Navy in July 2001 for refit and direct transfer to the MSC's

Naval Fleet Auxiliary Force, emerging as USNS *Supply* (T-AOE-6), followed in June 2002 by USNS *Arctic* (T-AOE-8), USNS *Rainier* (T-AOE-7) in August 2003, and USNS *Bridge* (T-AOE-10) in June 2004. The prefix "USNS" stands for "United States Naval Ship," denoting an MSC vessel with a largely civilian crew. All weapons as well as some radar and communication systems were removed during the ships' preparations for transfer to the MSC, and improved accommodations characterized the renovations to all crew areas.

During the early stages of Operation ENDURING FREEDOM, the *Arctic* operated with the *Enterprise* carrier battle group from October to November 2001, the *Bridge* maintained station with the *John C. Stennis* (CVN-74) battle group (December 2001–May 28 2002), and the *Supply* deployed to the Persian Gulf and the Mediterranean with the *George Washington* (CVN-73) battle group from June through December 2002. The *Rainier* joined the *Constellation* (CV-64) battle group for that carrier's last deployment, in support of Operation ENDURING FREEDOM and Operation IRAQI FREEDOM (November 2002–June 2003), and *Arctic* accompanied the *Roosevelt* carrier battle group in theater from February through May 2003. All four Supply-class fast combat support ships continue their deployments in support of ongoing naval operations associated with Operations ENDURING FREEDOM and IRAQI FREEDOM. The *Supply* and *Arctic* are based on the east coast, with home ports at Earle, New Jersey, and Norfolk, Virginia, respectively. The *Rainier* and *Bridge* are both stationed at Bremerton, Washington.

During Operations DESERT SHIELD and DESERT STORM and Operation ENDURING FREEDOM, smaller but analogous combat support ships from other coalition navies also were on station, including the Royal Australian Navy's *Success* (OR-304); the Royal Canadian Navy's *Protecteur* (AOR-509); the French Navy's *Durance* (A-629), *Marne* (A-630), and *Var* (A-608); the Royal Netherlands Navy HNLMS *Zuiderkruis* (A-832); and the Portuguese Navy's *Sao Miguel* (A-5208).

GORDON E. HOGG

See also

Aircraft Carriers; Battleships, U.S.; DESERT STORM, Operation, Coalition Naval Forces; ENDURING FREEDOM, Operation, Coalition Naval Forces; IRAQI FREEDOM, Operation, Coalition Naval Forces; Military Sealift Command; Support and Supply Ships, Strategic; Underway Replenishment Ships

References

Marolda, Edward, and Robert Schneller. *Shield and Sword: The United States Navy and the Persian Gulf War.* Annapolis, MD: U.S. Naval Institute Press, 2001.

Polmar, Norman. *The Naval Institute Guide to the Ships and Aircraft of the U.S. Fleet.* 18th ed. Annapolis, MD: Naval Institute Press, 2005.

Saunders, Stephen, ed. *Jane's Fighting Ships, 2005–2006.* Coulsdon, Surrey, UK: Jane's Information Group, 2005.

Sharpe, Richard, ed. *Jane's Fighting Ships: 1991–1992.* London: Jane's Information Group, 1991.

Wildenberg, Thomas. *Gray Steel and Black Oil: Fast Tankers and Replenishment at Sea in the U.S. Navy, 1912–1995.* Annapolis, MD: Naval Institute Press, 1996.

Fatah

Highly influential political, military, and governing faction within the Palestine Liberation Organization (PLO). Fatah, meaning "victory" or "conquest," is a reverse acronym of Harakat al-Tahrir al-Watani al-Falastini (Palestinian National Liberation Movement) and was formally organized on December 31, 1964.

For much of its official history Yasser Arafat (also PLO chairman from 1969 until his death in 2004) served as the party's leader, although the beginnings of Fatah date to the late 1950s when Palestinian groups began fighting the Israelis during their occupation of the Gaza Strip. Fatah's founders include Arafat, Salah Khalaf (Abu Iyad), Khalil al-Wazir (Abu Jihad), and Khalid Hassan. Fatah was a combination of a political organization and paramilitary cells, the objective of which was the liberation of Palestine, armed resistance to Israel, and the creation of a Palestinian state. From the late 1960s, Fatah was larger than many of the other groups under the umbrella of the PLO because their Marxist-Leninist doctrines limited their recruiting. Consequently, Fatah

has experienced a larger Muslim-to-Christian ratio than the small progressive parties. Indeed, all of its founders with the exception of Arafat were members of the Muslim Brotherhood. And because Fatah controlled much of the monetary resources of the PLO, it wielded considerable influence.

Fatah has undergone many transformations over the years and until very recently hardly resembled a political party in the traditional sense. In its first years the group eschewed the establishment of a formal organizational structure and indirectly appealed to the Palestinian diaspora in Syria, Jordan, Egypt, Lebanon, Iraq, the Gulf States, and Western countries. Fatah had a following not only in the diaspora but also in the important structures such as the General Union of Palestinian Students, the General Union of Palestinian Workers, and the General Union of Palestinian Women. Fatah published an occasional periodical titled *Filasti-nuna* (Our Palestine).

Early on and from the 1967 defeat in the Six-Day War until about 1974, Fatah embraced the concept of armed confrontation as the primary means of achieving a unified independent Palestine. Fatah's pragmatism ensured it a large base of support and also created a de facto ideology that stressed Palestinian unity, with the idea that although Palestinians might have varied approaches to their problems, they could all be united in their three major goals: the destruction of Israel, political freedom from Arab nations, and the creation of a Palestinian state.

Although Fatah did not initially maintain an organizational hierarchy (it was more along the lines of an uncoordinated series of factions, each led by a different head), it did quickly establish a coherent military force capable of harassing the Israelis. Several militant groups based in Jordan were involved in attacks on Israel, among them the Asifah group, and their actions and the Israeli response caused a crackdown and their expulsion by King Hussein of Jordan. That expulsion in 1970, known as Black September, did, however, create fissures between the rightists and leftists within Fatah and with the broader Palestinian movement. When Fatah reconstituted itself in Lebanon beginning in 1970, it found that resisting involvement in the internal machinations of its host country was impossible. This made it more prone to pressure from other Arab states. Soon enough, conflict among Fatah members surfaced when some in the group began to espouse a two-state solution to the Palestinian-Israeli conflict.

Soon embroiled in the Lebanese Civil War that began in 1975, the Palestinian resistance groups continued to sponsor attacks against Israeli interests, including two massive assaults on Israeli territory in 1975 with the loss of many lives. In 1982 the PLO (and thus Fatah) was forced out of Lebanon by the Israeli invasion of that country. From 1982 to 1993 the Fatah leadership, along with the PLO, was located in Tunisia. In 1983 an anti-Arafatist revolt occurred that was led by Said Muragha (Abu Musa). He created a splinter group known as Fatah Uprising, which was backed by Syrian officials. Meanwhile, Fatah's Revolutionary Council and the Revolutionary Council Emergency Command both broke with

Fatah over policy issues. Despite these setbacks, Fatah remained the preeminent Palestinian faction, and Arafat maintained an iron grip over Fatah.

Many in Fatah's leading group had supported a two-state solution ever since the Rabat Conference of 1974 and realized that this meant tacit recognition of Israel. Fatah's leadership also concluded that armed conflict was not moving the organization any closer to its goal of a Palestinian state. By 1988 Arafat had recognized Israel's right to exist explicitly and proposed the pursuit of diplomacy and a land-for-peace arrangement.

Arafat supported Iraqi dictator Saddam Hussein in the 1991 Persian Gulf War because of Hussein's support of Fatah. This support, however, led to the mass forced exile of Palestinians from Kuwait after the war and difficult economic times for the Palestinians in general. Consequently, as the effort to reach a comprehensive accord in Madrid was occurring, Arafat had agreed to a secret Palestinian-Israeli track in Oslo, Norway.

The 1993 Oslo Accords and the 1994 creation of the Palestinian National Authority (PNA) witnessed the relocation of the PLO and Fatah to Gaza and the West Bank. This finally centered the Palestinian power base in Palestine after almost 50 years of transience. By this time, however, the Palestinians were no longer entirely represented by the Tunisian old guard of Fatah. Younger leaders were frustrated with the policies of the longtime exiles and with major financial difficulties and corruption. They acquired experience in the First Intifada and represented grassroots interests in the West Bank and Gaza. Also, Islamist organizations such as Islamic Jihad of Palestine and especially Hamas had begun to attract more support from the Palestinian population than Fatah was attracting. Arafat clung to power, still recognized for his many years of devotion to the Palestinian cause. In January 1996 he was elected as the PNA's first president. He now simultaneously held the positions of PLO chairman, PNA president, and leader of Fatah.

Fatah essentially controlled the PNA bureaucracy, although the fissures within the organization began to grow deeper. While Fatah attempted to push ahead with the Palestinian-Israeli peace process, certain members who were opposed to it began to sabotage Arafat. Now the group was divided by hard-liners versus peace proponents, old guard versus youths, and bureaucrats versus revolutionaries. The Second (al-Aqsa) Intifada, which broke out in September 2000, saw the embattled Fatah become even more divided against itself. Fatah member Marwan Barghuti was accused of organizing a militia called al-Tanzim, the goal of which was to attack Israeli forces. And in 2002 the al-Aqsa Martyrs Brigades, another faction consisting of local militias and theoretically aligned with Fatah, began launching major attacks against Israeli forces as well. To punish the PNA for a particularly heinous suicide bombing in the spring of 2002, the Israelis reoccupied much of the West Bank. Arafat was trapped in his own headquarters, and much of the rebuilding and the infrastructure in the West Bank was destroyed. Israeli officials had periodically launched campaigns against Arafat's leadership, and these were now revived.

Now under enormous pressure from Israel and the United States, Arafat reluctantly acquiesced to the creation of a new position within the PNA, that of prime minister. In April 2003 he named Mahmoud Abbas to the post. However, after months of infighting, Abbas resigned from office in September 2003. Then in February 2004, 300 Fatah members resigned in unison to show their contempt for their leadership. A hasty convening of Fatah's Revolutionary Council was called, but the meeting accomplished nothing and resulted in bitter recriminations from all sides.

Arafat died on November 11, 2004, and this threw Fatah and the PNA into more turmoil. Days after Arafat's death, Fatah's Central Committee named Farouk Qaddumi to replace him. This was in itself problematic because Qaddumi, unlike his predecessor, did not support the peace process. Meanwhile, Abbas was named to succeed Arafat as PLO chairman. For the first time, Fatah and the PLO were not controlled by the same person. After bitter political machinations, Fatah decided to put Abbas up as its presidential candidate in the January 2005 election. Abbas was strongly challenged in this by Barghuti, who vowed to run as an independent from a jail cell in Israel. Barghuti, who came under intense pressure to bow out, finally did so, opening the way for Abbas's victory in January 2005.

Abbas's victory, however, was not a harbinger of a resurgent and unified Fatah. In the December 2004 municipal elections for the PNA, Hamas had racked up impressive gains. Then, in December 2005 Barghuti formed a rival political alliance, al-Mustaqbal, vowing to run a new slate of candidates for the January 2006 PNA legislative elections. At the last moment the two factions decided to run a single slate, but this temporary rapprochement was not sufficient to prevent a stunning victory for Hamas. In fact, Hamas's strength did not rest simply on the divisions within Fatah. Indeed, Hamas won 74 seats to Fatah's 45, although Hamas had captured only 43 percent of the popular vote. The election allowed Hamas to form its own government and elect a prime minister, Ismail Haniyeh, who assumed the premiership in February 2006. As a result of the Hamas victory, the United States and some European nations cut off funding to the PNA in protest of the group's electoral success. This placed the PNA in a state of crisis, as no civil servants could be paid, and hospitals and clinics had no supplies. For more than a year, and despite an agreement between Hamas and Fatah, the U.S. government continued to state that only if Hamas renounced its violent intentions against Israel in a format satisfactory to Israel and the United States would any funds be allowed into the PNA.

On March 17, 2007, Abbas brokered a Palestinian unity government that included both Fatah and Hamas, with Hamas leader Haniyeh becoming prime minister. In May, however, violence between Hamas and Fatah escalated. Following the Hamas takeover of Gaza on June 14, Abbas dissolved the Hamas-led unity government and declared a state of emergency. On June 18, having been assured of European Union (EU) support, Abbas also dissolved the National Security Council and swore in an emergency Palestinian government. That same day, the United States

Palestinian Fatah supporters hold up flags with a picture of Marwan Barghuti, a popular Fatah leader jailed in Israel. They are attending a rally in the West Bank city of Ramallah in 2008, marking the movement's 43rd anniversary. (AP/Wide World Photos)

ended its 15-month embargo on the PNA and resumed aid in an effort to strengthen Abbas's government, which was now limited to the West Bank. On June 19 Abbas cut off all ties and dialogue with Hamas, pending the return of Gaza. In a further move to strengthen the perceived moderate Abbas, on July 1 Israel restored financial ties to the PNA.

Today Fatah is recognized by Palestinians as a full-fledged political party, with the attendant organizational structures that have in fact been in place for several decades. Competition between the PLO's four major parties caused problems in the past, but today it is Fatah's competition with Hamas that appears more pressing. Hamas does not belong to the PLO and refused to recognize its claim as the sole representative of the Palestinian people. The 2006 elections revealed greater support for Hamas than Fatah among Palestinians. The Israeli government refused to recognize the Hamas victory in the elections, however. Fatah and the U.S. government also refused to deal with Hamas. In June 2007 Hamas seized full control of Gaza, where its elected government had been ruling since January, and drove out Fatah. Gaza was now largely cut off economically from the rest of the world and more than ever was an economic basket case. Meanwhile a virtual civil war between Hamas and Fatah continued, and when Israel began

a major campaign against Hamas in December 2008, Fatah could do little but watch the killing of hundreds of Palestinians in Gaza.

The Fatah-Hamas split has impacted surrounding Arab states. Saudi Arabia initially pushed for a unity government, but U.S. secretary of state Condoleezza Rice opposed these efforts. In the wake of the Gaza War, Egypt and Saudi Arabia found themselves opposed by Qatar, Syria, and others but again tried to negotiate a unity government along terms that might satisfy the Israelis.

PAUL G. PIERPAOLI JR. AND SHERIFA ZUHUR

See also

Arafat, Yasser; Hamas; Intifada, Second; Islamic Jihad, Palestinian; Lebanon; Lebanon, Civil War in; Lebanon, Israeli Invasion of; Oslo Accords; Palestine Liberation Organization

References

Aburish, Said K. *Arafat: From Defender to Dictator.* New York: Bloomsbury, 1998.

Hart, Alan. *Arafat: A Political Biography.* Rev. ed. London: Sidgwick and Jackson, 1994.

Jamal, Amal. *The Palestinian National Movement: Politics of Contention, 1967–2005.* Bloomington: Indiana University Press, 2005.

Kurz, Anat N. *Fatah and the Politics of Violence: The Institutionalization of a Popular Struggle.* Eastbourne, East Sussex, UK: Sussex Academic, 2006.

Rubin, Barry. *The Transformation of Palestinian Politics: From Revolution to State-Building.* Cambridge: Harvard University Press, 2001.

Said, Edward W. *Peace and Its Discontents: Essays on Palestine in the Middle East Process.* New York: Vintage Books, 1995.

Zuhur, Sherifa. *Hamas and Israel: Strategic Interaction in Group Based Politics.* Carlisle, PA: Strategic Studies Institute, 2008.

Fatwa

The fatwa (singular, *responsa*) or fatawa (plural, *responsae*) is a question and answer process referred to in the Qur'an (4:127, 176) that began in early Islam as a means to impart knowledge about theology, philosophy, hadith, legal theory, religious duties, and, later and more specifically, Sharia (Islamic law). Fatawa may deal with a much broader series of subjects than did the Islamic courts, and a fatwa, unlike a court ruling, is not binding. The reason it is not binding is that in a court, a *qadi* (judge) is concerned with evidentiary matters and may actually investigate these and hear two sides to an argument, but a cleric or authority issuing a fatwa is responding instead to just one party, should the question involve a dispute, and as the question might be formulated in a particular way.

In modern times a fatwa is usually defined as a legal opinion given by someone with expertise in Islamic law. However, so long as a person mentions the sources he uses in a legal opinion, other Muslim authorities or figures may issue fatwa. A modern fatwa usually responds to a question about an action, form of behavior, or practice that classifies it as being obligatory, forbidden, permitted, recommended, or reprehensible. Traditionally, a fatwa could be issued by a Muslim scholar knowledgeable of both the subject and the theories of jurisprudence. These persons might be part of or independent from the court systems. However, other persons might issue fatawa as well. Muslim governments typically designated a chief mufti, who was in the role of the sheikh of Islam in the Ottoman Empire.

In the colonial period the Islamic madrasahs (madaris is the Arabic plural), which can mean either simply a school or a higher institute of Islamic education, began in some cases to include a fatwa-issuing office, a *dar al-ifta.* Muslim governments continued efforts to control and limit the issuing of fatawa, as in the Higher Council of Ulama or the Permanent Council for Scientific Research and Legal Opinions in Saudi Arabia or the Council of Islamic Ideology in Pakistan. However, many Muslim authorities—from lesser-trained sheikhs to political figures to legal specialists classified as *fuqaha* (specialists in jurisprudence), mujtahids, and muftis—issue fatawa. Some are no more than a short response to the inquiry, whereas others are recorded, published, or circulated along with explanations.

For many reasons, including the development of differing legal schools within Islam and the history of opinions concerning religious requirements as opposed to mere duties, fatawa may conflict with each other. For example, the legal opinions concerning women's inheritance under Jafari, or Twelver Shia law, and that given by a Hanafi Sunni jurist would differ. At times, even councils of jurists from a single sect may issue a complex opinion with, for instance, each indicating their agreement with or reservations about different implications or subquestions of a fatwa.

Muslim countries today may govern with civil laws that are partially dependent on principles of Islamic law or are derived in part from Ottoman law. When matters of civil legal reform are discussed, then the opinions of religious authorities might be consulted. A fatwa may also be issued by popular figures outside of the venue of civil authorities. Other countries, however, operate on the basis of uncodified Islamic law. At the supranational level, there is no single authoritative person or body that can settle conflicting issues or declare binding fatawa in Islamic law (as the pope and the Vatican issue religious decrees for Roman Catholicism).

In 1933 clerics in Iraq issued a fatwa that called for a boycott of all Zionist-made products. In 2004 the very popular Egyptian Sunni Muslim cleric and scholar Yusuf al-Qaradawi declared a fatwa similarly calling for a boycott of goods manufactured in Israel or the United States.

Other much-disputed questions have concerned the necessary resistance of Palestinians to Israeli rule or the actual status of Palestine and the status of Iraqi resistance to coalition forces. Many fatawa were issued earlier to confront foreign occupation in Muslim lands, in Morocco, Egypt, Syria, Iraq, Iran, and elsewhere. Modern responses that affect the right to wage jihad (holy war) concern the land's status (dar al-Islam) as an Islamic territory. That is the generally agreed status of Iraq and of Palestine because of the presence of the holy sites at the al-Aqsa Mosque complex, from which the Prophet Muhammad experienced the Miraj and the Isra (the Night Journey and the Ascent to Heaven, respectively), as well as other holy sites in Palestine. Because the country is an Islamic land and yet many Palestinian Muslims cannot visit their holy sites or practice their religion and have had their lands and properties seized, some fatawa assert that jihad is, in this context, an individual duty, incumbent on Muslims. Divergent fatawa identify the country, now Israel, as *dar al-kufr,* a land of unbelief (somewhat like India under British rule) from which Muslims should flee, as in a highly disputed fatwa by Sheikh Muhammad Nasir al-Din al-Albani. While Palestinian Islamic Jihad issued a lengthy fatwa in 1989 that legitimated suicide attacks by Palestinians in the context of jihad, no leading clerics actually signed this document. It could be countered by a statement by the grand mufti of Saudi Arabia, made on April 21, 2001, that Islam forbids suicide attacks and is referred to as if it were a formal fatwa. On the other hand, Sheikh Qaradawi issued a fatwa in 2002 that said women could engage in martyrdom operations in conditions when jihad is an individual duty.

PAUL G. PIERPAOLI JR. AND SHERIFA ZUHUR

See also
Jihad; Sharia

References
Coulson, Noel J. *A History of Islamic Law.* Edinburgh, UK: Edinburgh University Press, 1994.

Esposito, John L. *Islam: The Straight Path.* New York: Oxford University Press, 1991.

Messick, Brinkley. *The Calligraphic State: Textual Domination and History in a Muslim Society.* Berkeley: University of California Press, 1993.

Peters, Rudolph. *Islam and Colonialism: The Doctrine of Jihad in Modern History.* The Hague: Brill, 1979.

Faw Peninsula

Strategically important peninsula located in southeastern Iraq, adjacent to the Persian Gulf. The Faw (Fao) peninsula lies to the south and east of Basra, Iraq's principal port and second-largest metropolis, and west of the Iranian city of Abadan. The peninsula separates Iraq from Iran and lies to the immediate west of the critical Shatt al-Arab waterway, which is Iraq's only access to the sea and only seagoing route to the port at Basra. Control of the Faw peninsula has thus been strategically essential to Iraq, as loss of control there likely means being cut off from access to the Persian Gulf.

The Faw peninsula is also important because it has been home to some of Iraq's biggest oil installations, including refineries. The country's two principal terminals for oil tankers—Khor al-Amayya and Mina al-Bakr—are also located here. The only significant population center on the peninsula is Umm Qasr, the base of former Iraqi dictator Saddam Hussein's navy.

The Faw peninsula was a center of attention during the 1980–1988 Iran-Iraq War and was the site of several pitched battles, as both nations struggled to control the Shatt al-Arab waterway. In February 1986 Iranian forces were able to overwhelm the poorly trained Iraqi forces charged with guarding the peninsula. Despite desperate fighting the Iraqis were unable to dislodge the Iranians from the area, even in the face of numerous offensives. The Iranians were then able to threaten Basra and Umm Qasr and use the Faw peninsula as a base from which to launch missiles into Iraq, into naval and merchant assets in the Persian Gulf, and into Kuwait, which was backing Iraq in the war. In April 1988 the Iraqis launched a new and determined effort to dislodge the Iranians from the peninsula. With almost 100,000 troops, heavy artillery, and aerial bombing that included chemical weapons, the Iraqis finally drove the Iranians out after a 35-hour offensive.

In the lead-up to the 1991 Persian Gulf War, the Faw peninsula and Shatt al-Arab waterway became a bone of contention between Iraq and Kuwait, as both nations jockeyed to control access to Umm Qasr as well as two small adjacent islands. Hussein used the dispute as part of his justification for the August 1990 Iraqi invasion of Kuwait. When Operation DESERT STORM began in January 1991, coalition air forces heavily bombed the Faw peninsula, wiping out much of Iraq's naval assets and oil facilities. Although no significant ground actions occurred there, Iraqi shipping was closed down by the bombardment, meaning that Iraq was cut off from any seaborne trade or resupply efforts.

During Operation IRAQI FREEDOM, which began in March 2003, American and British plans called for the immediate seizure and occupation of the Faw peninsula to deny Iraq access to the Persian Gulf and to open Umm Qasr and Basra to humanitarian and military resupply missions. Military planners also hoped to secure the peninsula before Iraqi troops could damage or destroy its oil facilities.

The coalition attack on Umm Qasr, led by U.S. and British marines and Polish special land forces, began on March 21, 2003, but ran into unexpectedly heavy Iraqi resistance. After four days of sporadically heavy fighting, however, Umm Qasr and the Faw peninsula had been largely secured, and the adjacent waterway had been cleared of Iraqi mines. Pockets of Iraqi resistance endured in the "old city" of Umm Qasr until March 29, when the entire peninsula had essentially been occupied and secured. Almost immediately coalition forces opened the port at Umm Qasr, which then became the primary entrepôt for humanitarian and civilian aid to Iraq.

PAUL G. PIERPAOLI JR.

See also

Basra; DESERT STORM, Operation; Iran-Iraq War; Iraqi Claims on Kuwait; IRAQI FREEDOM, Operation; Kuwait; Kuwait-Iraq Diplomacy; Persian Gulf; Shatt al-Arab Waterway; Umm Qasr, Battle of

References

Keegan, John. *The Iraq War: The Military Offensive, from Victory in 21 Days to the Insurgent Aftermath.* New York: Vintage, 2005.

Tripp, Charles. *A History of Iraq.* Cambridge: Cambridge University Press, 2007.

Faylaka Island Raid
Event Date: February 1991

Aborted raid planned for February 22, 1991, to immediately precede the ground war component of Operation DESERT STORM. The raid was code-named DESERT DAGGER and later DESERT SLASH. Faylaka Island lies in the northern part of the Persian Gulf and is a key to control of the Kuwait Bay. More than 2,000 Faylakawis were expelled when the Iraqis invaded and established defenses on the island during 1990–1991.

The Faylaka Island Raid was intended as a diversionary attack to prevent the Iraqis from moving reinforcements to the west, against the main body of coalition forces. By mounting the raid the day before the ground attack was intended to begin, planners hoped to fix Iraqi coastal defenses in place. It was supposed to take place along with an amphibious assault of the Kuwaiti port of Shuaybah. In the end, the Faylaka Island raid was canceled over concerns about Iraqi minefields. The credible threat of an amphibious landing, however, was just as important to coalition commander General H. Norman Schwarzkopf's overall plan as an actual landing would have been.

By February 1991 the Iraqi forces on Faylaka Island consisted of the 440th Marine Infantry Brigade. Nominally the brigade included 2,500 troops along with supporting artillery, tanks, and air defense artillery. Unlike U.S. marines, however, the Iraqis were not considered elite troops. They were comparable to the American marine defense battalions of World War II, intended to build and man defenses but not to operate in offensive roles. The island was, however, strongly protected by minefields in the shallow waters offshore and minefields ashore on the most likely invasion beaches.

In the planning for DESERT STORM, American commanders expected to launch an amphibious assault at some point in time. This faced many problems, however. These included the shallow water along the Kuwaiti coast that would keep most American ships from approaching close enough to land to employ their main batteries against inland targets. They also feared the many sea mines known to have been laid by the Iraqis. Preliminary plans had suggested an amphibious assault at Shuaybah, a Kuwaiti industrial port, in order to establish a logistical supply center for forces driving up the coast. Improvements in the road network in northern Saudi Arabia, however, reduced the need for this. At a commanders' conference on February 2, 1991, Schwarzkopf agreed to hold off on the Shuaybah landing. Instead, he agreed with a proposal from Vice Admiral Stanley R. Arthur for a large-scale raid on Faylaka Island.

On February 6 Arthur issued orders to begin planning the raid. The core of the raid was to be a landing by two U.S. marine battalions by helicopter and surface craft. They would destroy as much Iraqi military equipment and defenses on the island as possible and then withdraw after about 12 hours. Another goal was to kill or capture as many Iraqi defenders as possible. To draw attention away from the forthcoming attack on the western flank, the raid was scheduled to occur one to two days before ground operations began.

The raiders were to be drawn from the 4th Marine Expeditionary Brigade (MEB), a regimental combat team that included artillery, armor, aircraft, and supporting units. One battalion would be landed by helicopter in a recreational area on the south side of Faylaka, supported by gunships. It would attack west and northwest toward Zawr. The other would come ashore in landing craft on the beach at the recreational area. These troops would secure the beach and assist in the destruction of nearby Iraqi forces and defenses. An armored force consisting of 35 lightly armored vehicles (LAV), 8 tanks, and 20 Humvee-mounted TOW antiarmor missiles would provide cover for the eastern flank and assist in the destruction of any armored targets. The landing was set for 2:30 a.m. because of the tides. After completing their mission, the marines would then withdraw after darkness that evening.

To provide additional support, tiny nearby Awhah Island would be captured by a special marine operations unit before the landing on Faylaka. Four 155-millimeter howitzers would then be landed on Awhah to provide direct fire support for the marines on Faylaka, to be withdrawn after the marines left that place.

Coalition aircraft had been granted permission to drop any unexpended ordnance on Faylaka Island during the air portion of DESERT STORM, so the defenses there had already been degraded.

The greatest threat to the amphibious raid was from Iraqi mines. To defeat them, a combined British and American minesweeping force would clear a lane 15 miles long. An area closer to Faylaka would then be cleared to provide maneuvering room for the gunfire support ships. Besides the amphibious assault ships and minesweeping craft, naval support for the raid included the Iowa-class battleships *Missouri* and *Wisconsin*. Each battleship had nine 16-inch guns that could lob 2,700-pound shells more than 17 miles.

Some confusion occurred on February 11 when Arthur issued an order for his ships to prepare to move. Schwarzkopf believed that it was an order to execute the raid, issued without his permission. After the misunderstanding was cleared up, planning went ahead. The raid was finally scheduled to take place on February 22. On February 18, however, the Iwo Jima–class amphibious assault ship *Tripoli* and the Ticonderoga-class guided missile cruiser *Princeton* both struck mines in an area believed to have been cleared of them. The minesweepers were brought back to clear this area, and the raid was postponed a day.

As the beginning of the ground war approached, the scale of the Faylaka Island Raid was revised downward. Each time, the landing force was made smaller until the commanders finally realized that the dangers of launching a diversionary raid against Faylaka were simply too great. The possible loss of life was also a real concern for military and political leaders. In the end, the *Missouri* simply shelled Faylaka Island on the night of February 23. The next day the ground war began. Many of the marines who had been assigned to the raid against Faylaka Island were used to form a reserve for marine units pushing up the coast of Kuwait.

TIM J. WATTS

See also

Arthur, Stanley; DESERT STORM, Operation; Schwarzkopf, H. Norman, Jr.; United States Marine Corps, Persian Gulf War; United States Navy, Persian Gulf War

References

Brown, Ronald J. *U.S. Marines in the Persian Gulf, 1990–1991: With Marine Forces Afloat in Desert Shield and Desert Storm.* Washington, DC: History and Museums Division, U.S. Marine Corps, 1998.

Marolda, Edward, and Robert Schneller. *Shield and Sword: The United States Navy and the Persian Gulf War.* Annapolis, MD: U.S. Naval Institute Press, 2001.

Pokrant, Marvin. *Desert Storm at Sea: What the Navy Really Did.* Westport, CT: Greenwood, 1999.

Fayyad, Muhammad Ishaq al-
Birth Date: 1930

One of the five grand ayatollahs who make up the *marjaiyya* (the highest level of Shiite clerics), the informal council of Iraq's senior resident Twelver Shia religious scholars, of Najaf. He has frequently served as the council's representative public voice in the post-2003 invasion of Iraq. Born in 1930 in a small village in the Afghan province of Ghazni to a family of farmers, Muhammad Ishaq al-Fayyad is an ethnic Hazara, a Dari-speaking people who reside in Afghanistan and parts of Iran and northwestern Pakistan. Despite this the grand ayatollah is fluent in Arabic, although Western reporters and scholars who have met him say that he speaks it with a distinct Dari Afghan accent. He is widely considered to be one of the most influential members of the *marjaiyya* (meaning those who can be emulated, or followed, as spiritual guides) and is also one of the most publicly engaged, arguably even more so than Grand Ayatollah Ali al-Husayni al-Sistani, Iraq's most senior Shia scholar.

Fayyad, like many young Muslims from religious families, began his informal religious studies early, at the age of 5, learning the Qur'an from the village mullah, the local religious scholar. According to some reports, Fayyad and his family moved to Najaf when he was 10 years old. As he grew older he began studying other subjects, including the Arabic language and grammar, rhetoric, logic, Islamic philosophy, *ahadith* (traditions of the Prophet Muhammad and the 12 Shiite Imams), and Islamic jurisprudence. He ultimately pursued his studies under the supervision of Grand Ayatollah Abu al-Qasim al-Khoi, one of Iraq's senior resident Shia scholars during the 1970s and the most senior during the 1980s until his death in 1992.

According to accounts from individuals close to both Fayyad and Khoi, the former excelled at his studies and is widely acknowledged to have been one of the latter's best students. Some reports hold that Fayyad was, in fact, Khoi's best student and now is the most senior member of the *marjaiyya*, but he did not seek to chair the council because scholars who are not Iraqi or Iranian have little chance of gaining followers among Arabs and Iranians, who make up the majority of the world's Shia. In 1992 when the *marjaiyya* was left without a chair after Khoi's death, Fayyad, along with the council's other members, supported Sistani for the position.

Following the March 2003 invasion and subsequent occupation of Iraq by the United States and Great Britain, aided by a relatively small coalition of other countries, Fayyad proved to be the most willing to engage with the Americans and British. Unlike Sistani, he has met occasionally with U.S. and British officials, both diplomatic and military, in order to relay the position of the *marjaiyya*. Fayyad has stated that Iraqi law must take into account Islamic religious law, particularly with regard to social and family issues. He has spoken out strongly against forced secularization of Iraqi society and has argued that there can be no absolute separation of the state from religion. However, like Sistani, Fayyad has also rejected the implementation of an Iranian-style governmental model for Iraq, one based on Grand Ayatollah Ruhollah Khomeini's concept of *wilayat al-faqih*, the governance of the supreme religious jurist in the absence of the twelfth Imam, Muhammad al-Mahdi, whom Twelver Shias believe went into a mystical "hiding" or occultation in the 10th century and who will return at a time appointed by God.

Thus, Fayyad has gone on record as being opposed to clerical rule in Iraq, although he does believe that the *ulama* (Muslim religious scholars) should exercise some influence over Iraqi society, specifically ensuring the protection of Muslim moral and social values. According to a December 2007 report from the Associated Press, Fayyad was supervising the seminary studies of Muqtada al-Sadr, the populist Iraqi Shia leader and head of the Sadr Movement, although Fayyad and the *marjaiyya* do not approve of Sadr's approach toward politics and have pressured him to clamp down on his more militant followers.

The *marjaiyya* backed the United Iraqi Alliance (UIA), a loose coalition of mainly Shiite Arab political parties that includes the Supreme Islamic Iraqi Council (SIIC) and the Party of Islamic Call (Hizb al-Da'wah al-Islamiyya), in the January 2005 interim elections and the December 2005 formal elections. Despite their early support, Fayyad and his council colleagues reportedly became increasingly critical of the UIA's performance, particularly the combative political sectarianism of the SIIC (then known as the Supreme Council for the Islamic Revolution in Iraq, or SCIRI) and the Islamic Dawa Party. The *marjaiyya*, through senior spokespeople for the various members, let it be known in the latter half of 2008 that it would not back any slate of candidates and would instead urge its followers to vote for the party or parties that had the best plan for improving the situation in Iraq.

CHRISTOPHER ANZALONE

See also

Iraq, History of, 1990–Present; Islamic Dawa Party; Khomeini, Ruhollah; Sadr, Muqtada al-; Shia Islam; Supreme Iraqi Islamic Council; United Iraqi Alliance

References

Cole, Juan R. I. *The Ayatollahs and Democracy in Iraq*. ISIM Paper 7. Leiden, Netherlands: Amsterdam University Press and the International Institute for the Study of Islam in the Modern World, 2006.

Hendawi, Hamza, and Qassim Abdul-Zahra. "Iraq's Maverick Cleric Hits the Books." *Associated Press*, December 13, 2007.

Khalaji, Mehdi. *Religious Authority in Iraq and the Election*. Policy Watch #1063. Washington, DC: Washington Institute for Near East Policy, 2005.

Nasr, Seyyed Vali Reza. "Iraq: The First Arab Shia State." *Missouri Review* 29(2) (2006): 132–153.

Visser, Reidar. *Shi'i Separatism in Iraq: Internet Reverie or Real Constitutional Challenge?* Oslo, Norway: Norwegian Institute of International Affairs, 2005.

Fedayeen

Term used to refer to various (usually Muslim) groups or civilians who have engaged in either armed struggle or guerrilla tactics against foreign armies. The term "fedayeen" is the English transliteration of the term *fida'iyuna*, which is the plural of the Arabic word meaning "one who is ready to sacrifice his life" (*fida'i*) and referred historically to different types of Muslim fighters, including Muslim forces waging war on the borders; freedom fighters; Egyptians who fought against the British in the Suez Canal Zone,

An overturned vegetable truck on the road to Beersheba, Israel. The driver was slightly wounded when the truck was fired upon by fedayeen on April 7, 1956. (Israeli Government Press Office)

culminating in a popular uprising in October 1951; Palestinians who waged attacks against Israelis from the 1950s until the present (including fighters of Christian background); Iranian guerrillas opposed to Mohammad Reza Shah Pahlavi's regime in the 1970s; Armenian fighters in Nagarno-Karabakh (also Christian); and a force loyal to Iraqi dictator Saddam Hussein (the Fedayeen Saddam) during the Iraq War that began in 2003.

Following the rejection by Jewish and Arab leaders of the 1947 United Nations (UN) partition plan that would have created a Palestinian state in the West Bank and the Gaza Strip and the resulting declaration of the State of Israel the following year, Palestinian refugees were driven from their homes and flooded into the areas surrounding the new Jewish state. Anti-Israel activity became prevalent, particularly in West Bank and Gaza Strip areas. Supported by money and arms from a number of Arab states, Palestinians carried out attacks against Israeli military forces and also Israeli settlers, and in 1951 the raids became more organized. These fighters were referred to as fedayeen since they were an irregular rather than a government force. The fighters created bases in Egypt, Jordan, and Lebanon, with Egyptian intelligence training and arming many of them. Between 1951 and 1956 the fedayeen orchestrated hundreds of raids along the Israeli border, killing an estimated 400 Israelis and injuring 900 others.

The fedayeen operated primarily out of Jordan and Lebanon, causing these countries to bear the brunt of the retaliation campaigns carried out by the Israel Defense Forces (IDF) and paramilitary groups. Fedayeen attacks and subsequent retaliations were significant factors in the outbreak of hostilities during the 1956 Suez Crisis. The fedayeen also launched attacks into Israel from the Jordanian-controlled territory of the West Bank. The fighters included those associated with the Palestine Liberation Organization (PLO), the Popular Front for the Liberation of Palestine (PFLP), and various other militant groups.

King Hussein of Jordan was initially supportive of the groups, but by 1970 he deemed their presence detrimental to Jordan and a threat to his own political power. Although based in refugee camps, the fedayeen were able to obtain arms and financial support from other Arab countries and therefore clashed with Jordanian government troops who attempted to disarm them beginning in 1968. The civil war that erupted in 1970 during what has been called Black September saw the eventual defeat and removal of the fedayeen from Jordanian soil.

The fedayeen were forced to recognize Jordanian sovereignty via an October 13, 1970, agreement between PLO leader Yasser Arafat and King Hussein. Although PLO members often participated in commando raids, the PLO denied playing a role in several terrorist attacks. After being ousted from Jordan, the PLO and the fedayeen relocated to Lebanon, where they continued to stage attacks on Israel. At present, the terms *fida'iyuna* and *fida'iyin* are still used by many Arabs for Palestinian militants, and the Arabs see the militants as freedom fighters who struggle for the return (*awda*) of their lands and property in Palestine.

Fidayan-e Islam (in Farsi there is an "e"; in Arabic there is none) was the name taken by a radical Islamist group opposed to the reign of Mohammad Reza Shah Pahlavi of Iran beginning in the 1940s. Between 1971 and 1983 these Iranian fedayeen carried out numerous attacks, including political assassinations, against people supportive of the Pahlavi regime. The same name was adopted by a radical group in Islamabad, Pakistan. The freedom fighter term was also given to a group created by ousted Iraqi leader Saddam Hussein. The Fedayeen Saddam was so-named to associate the force with patriotic self-sacrifice and anti-imperialism. Initially led by Hussein's son Uday in 1995, the group's leadership was handed over to his other son, Qusay, when it was discovered that Uday was diverting Iranian weaponry to the group. Many of them became part of the Iraqi resistance, or *muqawamah,* who following the March 2003 U.S.- and British-led invasion used rocket-propelled grenades, machine guns, and mortars to attack coalition forces, forces of the new Iraqi government, and Sadrists. In January 2007 the group recognized Izzat Ibrahim al-Duri as the rightful leader of Iraq and secretary-general of the Iraqi Baath Party following the execution of Saddam Hussein.

JESSICA BRITT AND SHERIFA ZUHUR

See also

Abu Daoud; Hussein, Qusay; Hussein, Saddam; Hussein, Uday; Hussein ibn Talal, King of Jordan; Iraq, History of, 1990–Present; Iraqi Insurgency; Jordan; Palestine Liberation Organization; Reza Pahlavi, Mohammad; Suez Crisis; Terrorism

References

Abdullah, Daud. *A History of Palestinian Resistance.* Leicester: Al-Aqsa Publishers, 2005.

Khoury, Elias. *Gate of the Sun.* Translated by Humphrey Davies from *Bab al-Shams.* New York: St. Martin's, 2006.

Laqueur, Walter, and Barry Rubin, eds. *The Israel-Arab Reader: A Documentary History of the Middle East Conflict.* London: Penguin, 2001.

Nafez, Nazzal, and Laila A. Nafez. *Historical Dictionary of Palestine.* Lanham, MD: Scarecrow, 1997.

O'Neill, Bard E. *Revolutionary Warfare in the Middle East: The Israelis vs. the Fedayeen.* Boulder, CO: Paladin, 1974.

Rubin, Barry. *Revolution until Victory? The Politics and History of the PLO.* Cambridge: Harvard University Press, 1996.

Feith, Douglas
Birth Date: July 16, 1953

Attorney, foreign and military policy expert, noted neoconservative, and undersecretary of defense for policy (2001–2005). Born on July 16, 1953, in Philadelphia, Douglas Feith attended Harvard University, earning a BA degree in 1975. In 1978 he earned a law degree from Georgetown University. While in law school, Feith interned at the Arms Control and Disarmament Agency, where he met Fred Iklé, John Lehman, and Paul Wolfowitz. After graduation Feith practiced law in Washington, D.C., and wrote articles on foreign policy. As Feith grew older, he developed positions on foreign policy that would eventually identify him as a neoconservative who believed in the use of force as a vital instrument of national policy.

Feith entered government service in 1981 during the Ronald Reagan administration, working on Middle East issues for the National Security Council. Feith then transferred to the Department of Defense as special counsel for Assistant Secretary of Defense Richard Perle and later served as deputy assistant secretary of defense for negotiations from March 1984 to September 1986. After that Feith left government to form a law firm, Feith & Zell, P.C., which he managed until 2001, although he continued to write and speak on international affairs.

In April 2001 President George W. Bush nominated Feith as undersecretary of defense for policy. Confirmed in July 2001, Feith held that position until August 2005. His tenure would prove to

Former U.S. undersecretary of defense Douglas Feith at a press conference at the U.S. Embassy in Kabul, Afghanistan, in September 2002. Feith and his staff were subsequently accused of developing dubious intelligence linking Iraqi leader Saddam Hussein and Al Qaeda as a justification for launching the Iraq War. (AP/World Wide Photos)

be highly controversial. At the Pentagon, Feith's position was advisory; he was not within the military chain of command, yet his office held approval authority over numerous procedures. He was the number three civilian in the Pentagon, next to Secretary of Defense Donald Rumsfeld and Deputy Secretary of Defense Paul Wolfowitz.

As undersecretary, Feith became associated with three projects that, although well known, did not bear fruit. First, he hoped to engage America's opponents in the Global War on Terror in a battle of ideas. In the late autumn of 2001 Feith supported the development of the Office of Strategic Influence (OSI), a division of the Department of Defense that would seek to counter propaganda sympathetic to terrorist groups such as Al Qaeda through psychological campaigns. The clandestine nature of the OSI and a lack of oversight forced Rumsfeld to close it down in February 2002.

Second, Feith advocated the arming of a force of Iraqi exiles to accompany the U.S. invasion of Iraq in 2003. According to Feith, the idea was not well received in the Pentagon, the State Department, or the Central Intelligence Agency (CIA). Third, before Operation IRAQI FREEDOM began, Feith and his staff developed a plan for the creation of an Iraqi Interim Authority (IIA), which would have allowed for joint American-Iraqi control of Iraq after the defeat of Saddam Hussein's regime, as a prelude to a new Iraqi government. This plan was nixed by U.S. administrator in Iraq L. Paul Bremer in the autumn of 2003.

During his time at the Pentagon, Feith became a lightning rod for criticism of the Bush administration's conduct of the Global War on Terror and the Iraq War. He has been blamed for a myriad of policy miscues in Afghanistan and Iraq, and some have accused him of pursuing policies that led to the highly damaging Abu Ghraib Prison scandal in 2004. Former vice president Al Gore called for Feith's resignation in a speech at New York University on May 26, 2004.

In various press accounts, Feith has been accused of setting up a secret intelligence cell designed to manipulate the prewar intelligence on Iraq to build a case for war. Feith's account of events in his memoirs differs considerably, however. He presented the Policy Counter Terrorism Evaluation Group, which evaluated prewar intelligence, as a small group of staffers tasked with summarizing the vast amounts of intelligence that had crossed his desk. Far from being a cadre of Republican political operatives, he argued, the small staff included Chris Carney, a naval officer and university professor who won a seat in Congress in 2006 as a Democrat.

In addition, Feith was accused of attempting to politicize intelligence and to find and publish evidence of links between Iraq and Al Qaeda that did not exist. In his memoirs, Feith states that he tasked career intelligence analyst Christina Shelton with reviewing intelligence on Iraqi–Al Qaeda connections and that she developed a view that was critical of the methods by which CIA analysts examined that intelligence. A subsequent Senate Intelligence Committee investigation concluded that staffers of the Office of the Undersecretary of Defense for Policy did not, in fact, pressure intelligence

analysts into changing their product. However, intelligence and military analysts as well as other policy experts and media were either concerned by the scrutiny of or influenced by Rumsfeld's and Feith's office, and this did in fact affect their products.

In August 2005, with both Rumsfeld and Wolfowitz gone and discredited and the Bush administration's war and national security policy under attack from both Democrats and Republicans, Feith tendered his resignation and left government service. In 2006 he took a position at Georgetown University as visiting professor and distinguished practitioner in national security policy. His contract at Georgetown was not renewed in 2008. Also in 2006, Feith published his memoirs, *War and Decision: Inside the Pentagon at the Dawn of the War on Terrorism*, which offered a sustained defense of his reputation and an explanation of the decisions that he made while serving in government. The book hardly appeased his legion of critics and detractors, however, and Feith now operates on the margins of policy, but his ideas still retain influence.

MITCHELL McNAYLOR

See also

Abu Ghraib; Bush, George Walker; Global War on Terror; Neoconservatism; Rumsfeld, Donald Henry; Wolfowitz, Paul Dundes

References

Feith, Douglas. *War and Decision: Inside the Pentagon at the Dawn of the War on Terrorism*. New York: Harper, 2008.

U.S. Senate. *Report of the Select Committee on Intelligence on the U.S. Intelligence Community's Prewar Assessments on Iraq*. Washington, DC: U.S. Government Printing Office, 2004.

Woodward, Bob. *State of Denial: Bush at War, Part III*. New York: Simon and Schuster, 2006.

Field Army Ballistic Missile Defense System

Prototype antiballistic missile defense system of the late 1950s and early 1960s built for the U.S. Army to provide battlefield defense against enemy tactical ballistic missiles. Although the army did not field the Field Army Ballistic Missile Defense System (FABMDS), the work on this system assisted in the development and fielding of the army's Patriot missile system.

After the end of World War II, the U.S. Army recognized the threat posed to its ground forces by enemy short- and medium-range ballistic missiles. In 1951 the army developed the criteria for a future mobile surface-to-air missile (SAM) system, which it designated the SAM-A-19 antimissile missile (AMM). The modern term for this AMM would be Theater Ballistic Missile Defense (TBMD).

In 1952 the army formally began the SAM-A-19 program as Project Plato. From 1953 to 1956 Sylvania Electric and Cornell Aeronautical Lab conducted the formal design studies, and in September 1956 the army selected Sylvania's XSAM-A-19 design as the basis for further development. Because the Plato missile would be designed for speeds of Mach 6 to 8, the main focus of the initial studies included the aerodynamic and thermodynamic problems of hypersonic flight.

The contractors continued the development of components for the Plato system until February 1959, when the army cancelled the program before building any further prototypes. As an interim measure, the army decided to upgrade the SAM-A-25/MIM-14 Nike Hercules with a very limited antimissile capability. Because the need for a defense system against ballistic missile attacks had not gone away, in September 1959 the army began the FABMDS program as a long-term replacement for the cancelled Plato system.

From September 1959 through May 1960 the army conducted an in-house study to properly define the future FABMDS. The resulting requirements included a fully mobile antiaircraft/anti-missile system that could engage at least four targets at the same time with a kill probability of over 95 percent against a ballistic missile. The army then asked for proposals from the defense industry and by July 1960 received seven proposals. Later, in September 1960, the army awarded contracts for a feasibility study to Convair, General Electric, Martin, Hughes, Sylvania Electric, and Raytheon. The following summer, the army reviewed the results of the studies and selected General Electric to develop its FABMDS.

The General Electric FABMDS was a relatively large and heavy system that reduced its mobility. However, it would have provided defense against the widest possible range of threats, including ballistic missiles with a range of 55–930 miles. Its guidance and control system was most probably some combination of semiactive radar and/or radio-command guidance. Because the FABMDS missile would have been armed with a nuclear warhead, it had obvious restrictions on minimum altitude and range.

The Department of Defense eventually concluded that the limited defense promised by the proposed FABMDS, using then state-of-the-art technology, did not warrant the high development time and cost. As a result, it did not issue a development contract to General Electric and formally cancelled the program in October 1962. However, the army immediately replaced the cancelled FABMDS program with a new program, the Army Air-Defense System-1970 (AADS-70). In actuality, the AADS-70 was essentially a continuation of the FABMDS under a different name. In 1964 the army renamed the AADS-70 the Surface-to-Air Missile-Development (SAM-D). This program eventually led in the development of the MIM-104 Patriot.

Robert B. Kane

See also

Patriot Missile System

References

Bullard, John W. *History of the Field Army Ballistic Missile Defense System Project, 1959–1962*. U.S. Army Redstone Arsenal, Huntsville, AL: Historical Branch, 1963.

Cullen, Tony, and Christopher F. Foss, eds. *Jane's Battlefield Air Defense, 1988–89*. Sussex, UK: Jane's Information Group, 1988.

Lennox, Duncan, ed. *Jane's Strategic Weapon Systems*. Sussex, UK: Jane's Information Group, 2001.

Film and the Middle East Wars

While the 1991 Persian Gulf War superseded the Vietnam War as America's great televised war, the Global War on Terror launched against perceived radical Islamist threats in the wake of the September 11, 2001, attacks against the United States and subsequent military campaigns in Afghanistan and Iraq may well become known as the first of the multimedia wars. With a plethora of online data available, the public has available to it a wide range of sources for images and analyses of the conflicts. Consequently, movies based on contemporary conflicts face a difficult task, that of competing with a flood of documentaries and Internet-based information. The documentary film has risen to unprecedented prominence, while many fictional movies have met with either failure or little more than modest success. Whether this failure is due to the success of documentaries, mounting criticism of ongoing conflicts in Afghanistan and Iraq, public rejection of the theatrical films' general antimilitary themes, or other factors is a difficult question to answer.

Certainly, earlier filmmakers faced problems in trying to sell the Korean War (1950–1953) to an indifferent public, and the one Korean blockbuster, *M*A*S*H* (1970), did not emerge until well after the armistice, when America was engaged in the even more controversial war in Vietnam. In fact, the film's director, Robert Altman, admitted later that *M*A*S*H* is actually a film about the Vietnam War but that he had to disguise it by setting it ostensibly during the less controversial Korean War or he would not have been allowed to make the film at all. Also, apart from John Wayne's prowar *Green Berets* (1968), the major Vietnam movie successes—such as *Coming Home* (1978), *The Deerhunter* (1978), *Apocalypse Now* (1979), *Platoon* (1986), and *Full Metal Jacket* (1987)—also emerged well after the conflict. Current filmmakers dealing with continuing wars in the Middle East lack the benefits of hindsight and are, in essence, forced to write a script of ongoing conflicts with unknown outcomes. Other limitations may well also influence the success of movies focusing on modern Middle Eastern wars: bleak desert and urban settings limit visual appeal, the heavily armored gear-laden soldiers of today are hard to distinguish as individual characters, and Middle Eastern combatants and civilians often function as little more than type characters. Moreover, it may well be that movies about ongoing conflicts have yet to find their voice.

1991 Persian Gulf War

The Persian Gulf War unleashed a great media spectacle whereby war itself gained the status of a blockbuster movie, directed by a governmental media giant with leading generals in a starring role and a dénouement celebrated by parades of triumphant returning forces. Unlike any other war in U.S. history, the Persian Gulf War unfolded in real time on American televisions screens in highly dramatic fashion. Before, during, and after the brief conflict, the documentary gained a new prominence in the genre of the war film. Propaganda preceded the war, as with *Saddam Hussein—Defying the World* (1990; updated 1992), and major television networks supplemented their 24-hour coverage with a spate of documentaries, all released in 1991, such as CNN's *Operation Desert Storm: The War Begins;* CBS's three-part *Desert Triumph;* and CNN's six-part *War in the Gulf: The Complete Story.* Other documentaries of the same year highlighted the star "actors" of the conflict, as in ITN's *General H. Norman Schwarzkopf: Command Performance;* ABC's *Schwarzkopf: How the War Was Won; Operation Welcome Home: Victory in the Gulf,* featuring General Colin Powell and the New York victory homecoming; and PBS's update of its 1983 *Frontline* program *Vietnam Memorial 1991,* which contrasted the homecoming of Vietnam veterans with those of the Persian Gulf War.

A similar patriotic fervor characterizes the IMAX documentary *Fires of Kuwait* (1992), which celebrates firefighters from 10 countries battling the oil field infernos that resulted from conflict. More critically, prominent German filmmaker Werner Herzog documented postwar devastation inside Kuwait in *Lessons of Darkness* (*Lektionen in Finsternis,* 1992). With little actual war footage apart from a series of images of bombs falling on cities, filmed through the surrealistic filter of night-vision cameras, the sparsely narrated episodes present an inferno of lakes and deltas of black oil and burning towers of flame. Furthermore, as a counterbalance to CNN renditions of Operation DESERT STORM, *Lines in the Sand* attacks government media control, seeing the war as a "national therapy session" to drive out memories of Vietnam, a critical stance also reflected in two other 1991 documentaries, *The Gulf Crisis Tapes* and *The Desert Bush.*

Media control is also the target of *Counterfeit Coverage* (1992), unveiling the collaboration between Kuwaiti citizens and the Hill and Knowlton public relations firm to promote U.S. intervention. The satirical *Gulf Bowl Cabaret: For All You Do, This Scud's for You* (1992) further reflects mounting criticism of the Persian Gulf War, a movement perpetuated some 10 years later on the eve of a new military campaign against Iraq by documentaries such as *The Hidden Wars of Desert Storm* (2001), which attacks the media war and questions the reasons for U.S. involvement. Ongoing controversy about Gulf War Syndrome among veterans and allegations of a significant rise in the rates of postwar Iraqi cancer and birth defects as a result of alleged chemical and germ warfare, alongside the effects of radioactive depleted uranium, continue to spur documentaries, such as the recent *Gulf War Syndrome: Killing Our Own* (2007).

Apart from documentaries, the Persian Gulf War inspired a handful of movies a few years after the end of the brief war. *Courage under Fire* (1996) centers upon an investigation to determine whether Captain Karen Walden deserves a Medal of Honor after she dies fighting Iraqis following the crash of her rescue helicopter. Amid conflicting evidence, Lieutenant Colonel Serling, in charge of the investigation, is forced to confront his own insecurities about his own Gulf deployment. The bizarre *Uncle Sam: I Want you . . . Dead* (1996) features the corpse of an American soldier killed in Kuwait that crawls out of his casket to torment his enemies, including crooked politicians and draft dodgers.

Three Kings (1999), another irreverent look at the Persian Gulf War, follows three U.S. soldiers who, led by a major from the U.S. Army Special Forces, set off into Iraqi territory in an attempt to steal Kuwaiti gold seized by the Iraqi Army. During their journey, however, they encounter and rescue civilians who have risen up against Saddam Hussein's regime and are now abandoned by the coalition. *Tactical Assault* (1999) is a revenge thriller about a deranged U.S. Air Force pilot who, after being shot down to stop him from shooting an unarmed passenger jet, tries to get even with his former commander. *Mad Songs of Fernanda Hussein* (2001) transposes the Persian Gulf War to the New Mexico desert by tracing the stories of three characters: a Latina previously married to Saddam Hussein's namesake, a teenage antiwar protestor, and a traumatized Persian Gulf War veteran.

Two British television movies, *The One That Got Away* (1995) and *Bravo Two-Zero* (1999), both based on Chris Ryan's book *The One That Got Away,* combine fact and fiction in the story of an eight-man Special Air Service (SAS) team delegated to take out Saddam Hussein's Scud missiles and sever Iraqi communication lines. In an arduous journey marked by technological breakdowns and bad weather, only one survivor manages to reach safety in allied Syria. Also based on fact, *Live from Baghdad* (2003) deals with two CNN journalists who remained in Baghdad once others had pulled out.

The Manchurian Candidate (2004) is a recycled version of the Korean War–based novel by Richard Condon (1959) and the subsequent film (1962). Here, however, international weapons manufacturers replace communist agents as the insidious forces who brainwash a Persian Gulf War platoon and plan to take over the White House. The similarly bizarre *Jacket* (2005) tells the story of a veteran who, falsely accused of murder, travels in time in an effort to escape impending death under the care of a sadistic doctor.

On a more realistic level, *Jarhead* (2005) deals with a war that never really happens for a group of marine recruits. This movie, perhaps the best to emerge about the Persian Gulf War to date, traces the shenanigans of a group of marines from boot camp to 175 days of waiting for action in Saudi Arabia before Operation DESERT STORM begins. After their deployment in Kuwait the war ends within five days but not without their exposure to harrowing images of charred enemy bodies and blazing oil derricks. Itching for real military action, two snipers are delegated to wipe out the sorry remnants of Iraqi Republican Guards, only to have the action countermanded by other forces determined to gain glory with an air strike.

From the Arab perspective, few significant films have emerged. *The Gulf War: What Next?* (1991), a collection of five brief films with Arab directors commissioned by British television, attempts to demonstrate the repercussions of Persian Gulf War developments throughout the Arab world. The response is overwhelmingly personal, as with Nejia Ben Mabrouk's *Research of Shaima,* which follows the filmmaker in an attempt to trace a Baghdad girl whose face she has seen on television. Shortly after the end of the

In a scene from the Sam Mendes film *Jarhead,* marines play football in the desert heat wearing full combat gear. (Francois Duhamel/Universal Studios/ Bureau L.A. Collection/Corbis)

Persian Gulf War, Saddam Hussein commissioned *Hafer al-Batin* to detail an alleged war crime, the burial by U.S. bulldozers of live Iraqi soldiers dug in along the Saudi border. Released some years later, *The Storm* (2000) deals with Egyptians' equivocal reactions to the Persian Gulf War, while *Dawn of the World* (2008) tells the story of an Iraqi Marsh Arab who, killed in battle, sends his cousin to care for his wife.

Afghanistan War

Cinematically, the conflict in Afghanistan, launched 10 years after the Persian Gulf War, could, like the Korean War, be termed the "forgotten war," for it has inspired relatively few movies to date. As with the Persian Gulf War, documentaries predominate. Released soon after September 11, 2001, the National Geographic documentary *Afghanistan Revealed* (2001) includes interviews with Afghan resistance leader Ahmad Shah Massoud, killed two days before the 9/11 attacks; Taliban prisoners with the Northern Alliance; and refugees from the Taliban. In support of the U.S. counterattack against Al Qaeda leader Osama bin Laden, Mullah Mohammed Omar, and the Al Qaeda network held responsible for 9/11, *Operation Enduring Freedom: America Fights Back* was released in 2002, supported by the U.S. Department of Defense and introduced by Secretary of Defense Donald Rumsfeld.

Soon, however, dissident voices sounded, as with Irish filmmaker Jamie Doran's *Massacre in Afghanistan—Did the Americans Look On?* (2002), amid protests and denials from the U.S. State Department. The documentary focuses on the alleged torture and slaughter of some 3,000 prisoners of war who had surrendered to U.S. and allied Afghan forces after the fall of Konduz. Some years later, the PBS *Frontline* documentary *Return of the Taliban* (2006) reported the resurgence of the Taliban on the Afghanistan-Pakistan border.

Focusing on international journalists covering the conflict, *Dateline Afghanistan: Reporting the Forgotten War* (2007) highlights the dangers and frustrations of war reporting. More controversially, Alex Gibney's *Taxi to the Dark Side* (2007) deals with a young Afghan taxi driver allegedly beaten to death at Bagram Air Base. In an attempt to counter mounting criticism of the U.S.-led engagement in Afghanistan, the 2008 episode of *War Stories,* a series narrated by Oliver North, focuses on "The Battle for Afghanistan." This episode follows a U.S. Marine Corps battalion deployed in Helmand Province. Concurrently, other documentaries from allied forces in the International Security Assistance Force–Afghanistan (ISAF) reflect growing disquiet about mounting casualties, as in *Waging Peace: Canada in Afghanistan* (2009).

One of the earliest movies dealing with Afghanistan is perhaps the most powerful, Michael Winterbottom's *In This World* (2002) that begins in the Shamshatoo refugee camp in Peshawar on Pakistan's North-West Frontier Province, where some 50,000 Afghan refugees, displaced either by the Soviet invasion of 1979 or the post-9/11 U.S. bombing, lead a miserable existence. Two teenagers set out on the ancient Silk Road in an attempt to reach London. The film was first shown at the Berlinale Film Fest, and the premiere of the film preceded a massive antiwar demonstration at the Brandenburg Gate.

September Tapes (2004) follows a filmmaker and his team in an attempt to find Osama bin Laden. Using a combination of real and spurious documentary footage to chronicle their way, the group eventually disappears as it approaches Taliban fighters. While the Danish movie *Brothers* (*Brødre,* 2004) powerfully probes sibling rivalry and post-traumatic stress disorder (PTSD) psychoses, little of this film actually deals with the Afghanistan War. Captured by Afghani rebel fighters after surviving a helicopter crash, the central character is manipulated into killing his feckless fellow prisoner to save his own life. Upon his return to Denmark after rescue, he is severely traumatized.

On a different tack, the American movie *Lions for Lambs* (2007) suggests dissent about the war by tracing three stories involving a warmongering Republican senator, a skeptical journalist, and a California university professor, two of whose students have been trapped behind enemy lies in Afghanistan and a third student who needs convincing to do something with his life. In a bizarre twist, the hero of *Ironman* (2008), a successful arms trader captured by Afghan insurgents, escapes only to return to America as a pacifist. He no longer wants weapons that he has designed to be deployed against American forces. *Lone Survivor* (2009) is based on the memoir of U.S. Navy Seal Marcus Luttrell, the lone survivor from his unit during Operation REDWING on the Afghanistan-Pakistan border. Yet another little-known movie release, *The Objective* (2008), is concerned with Special Operations reservists who go missing on a mission in Afghanistan. Although dealing with covert arms supplies to the mujaheedin after the Soviet invasion of Afghanistan in 1979, *Charlie Wilson's War* (2007) is still relevant in the current context, as its recent date of release suggests: by arming its anti-Soviet allies of the past, many of whom later joined the Taliban, the United States had been in essence aiding its present foes.

A number of Middle Eastern movies have also addressed the conflict. Set shortly before 9/11, Iranian producer Mohsen Makhmalbaf's *Kandahar* (originally titled *Safar-e Ghandehar,* 2001) follows an Afghan Canadian woman who sets forth on a disturbing journey to find her sister and displays the Taliban's savagery. Afghans also produced their own movie, *The White Rock* (2009), about a massacre of refugees by the Iranians in 1998. In a dark comedy, Afghani writer-director Siddiq Barmaq's *Opium War* (2008) is about two American airmen who crash into a remote poppy field and attack an old Soviet tank, which they assume shelters Taliban or Al Qaeda fighters. It turns out that this is the home of a family forced to grow opium poppies to survive.

Iraq War

The ongoing conflict in Iraq has inspired the bulk of documentaries and movies to date. Accompanying the intense debate about the presence of weapons of mass destruction (WMDs) in Iraq, United Nations (UN) weapons inspector Scott Ritter released a documentary, *In Shifting Sands: The Truth about UNSCOM and the Disarming of Iraq* (2001), for distribution in 2003. *Uncovered: The Whole Truth about the Iraq War* (2003) deals with media treatment of the developing push to invade Iraq; an expanded version appeared in 2004. One of the most controversial documentaries came from Al Jazeera, the Arab news network. *Control Room* (2004) follows the Iraqi war from the American military information station in Qatar to the streets of Baghdad during Operation IRAQI FREEDOM, showing Iraqi civilian casualties, dead American soldiers, and U.S. assaults that kill a number of journalists, including an Al Jazeera cameraman when the network's Baghdad office is attacked. Other documentaries, such as *Alpha Company: Iraq Diary* (2005), shot by Gordon Forbes as a journalist embedded with a reconnaissance battalion, and *The War Tapes* (2006), shot by soldiers themselves, deal with the everyday lives of U.S. forces in Iraq. An Emmy Award–winning documentary, *Baghdad ER* (2006), moves the perspective to a military hospital, while *Gunner Palace* (2005) consists of firsthand accounts of servicemen faced with a dangerous and chaotic military situation. A Veterans' Day special, *Last Letters Home: Voices of American Troops from the Battlefields of Iraq* (2005), features the families of eight men and two women killed in Iraq. Also with a personal focus, *The Ground Truth: After the Killing Ends* (2006) addresses the effects of the war, including PTSD, on veterans, family members, and friends.

As the conflict lengthened, criticism of the war's handling became more intense. In *Iraq for Sale: The War Profiteers* (2006), four major U.S. government contractors came under attack for profiteering and doing shoddy work. In a series of 35 interviews with former government officials alongside journalists and former servicemen, *No End in Sight* (2007) focuses on the major mistakes of the Iraqi occupation, which include disbanding the Iraqi Army and dismissing experienced bureaucrats. With *Ghosts of Abu Ghraib* (2007) yet another Iraq War scandal reached the screen, this time examining the events of the 2004 Abu Ghraib torture and prisoner abuse scandal, a theme also taken up in Errol Morris's *Standard Operating Procedure* (2008). In a further condemnation of the foreign policies of the George W. Bush administration, *Finding Our Voices* (2008) weaves together the voices of 8 people, including former government officials and soldiers who refused to return to Iraq.

Other documentaries focus on the effects of the conflicts on the people of Iraq. In *About Baghdad* (2004), exiled Iraqi writer Sinan Antoon returns to his city to probe recent developments in a collage of walking tours through war-ravaged streets, interviews with political prisoners tortured under the Hussein regime, conversations with intellectuals, and commentaries by the outspoken Antoon. Similarly, *In the Shadow of the Palms* (2005), shot by Australian filmmaker Wayne Coles-Janess, offers footage of the lives of Iraqis before Hussein's deposition, during the fall of the government, and throughout the U.S. occupation. An Iraqi-made documentary, *Dreams of Sparrows* (2005), follows director Haydar Daffar's team in encounters with Iraqi citizens, a project that results in a crew member's death. Two documentaries from 2006, *My Country, My Country* and *The Blood of My Brother,* focus on individual Iraqis caught up in the bloodshed of the growing Shia insurgency.

Predictably, studies of Saddam Hussein have accompanied the Iraqi conflict. Among these, *Our Friend Saddam* (2003) examines the dictator's earlier relationship with Western countries who supplied him with weapons, a theme also taken up in a 2004 French television documentary, *Saddam Hussein: Le procès que vous ne verrez pas* (Saddan Hussein: The Trial You Will Not See). *Saddam Hussein: Weapon of Mass Destruction* (2005) chronicles the rise and fall of the dictator, while *America at a Crossroads: The Trial of Saddam Hussein* (2008) raises questions on procedural aspects of the trial and the ethnoreligious differences within Iraq that it mirrors.

One of the earliest Iraqi War–based movies, *Saving Jessica Lynch* (2003), evoked accusations of media manipulation when it was revealed that the "rescue" of Private Lynch, supposedly captured in an ambush, did not take place; rather, the Iraqi hospital in which she was under treatment willingly handed her over to military forces. *Over There* (2005), a television series about a U.S. Army unit on its first tour of duty, met with little success in spite of explosions, amputations, and grisly footage. An Italian movie, *La tigre e la neve* (*The Tiger and the Snow*, 2005), is a love story about a man who attempts to court a woman writing the biography of an Iraqi poet in Baghdad. Unsuccessful in his attempt, he is finally mistaken as an Iraqi insurgent and arrested. *American Soldiers* (2005) deals with an American patrol's struggle against fedayeen fighters; eventually they release mistreated prisoners, running afoul of the Central Intelligence Agency (CIA).

Also a combat movie, *A Line in the Sand* (2006) deals with two soldiers with different views of the war who survive an ambush and struggle to reach safety. Based on an incident of November 19, 2005, *The Battle for Haditha* (2007) investigates the alleged murder of 24 Iraqi civilians by marine forces in retaliation for a roadside bombing. Using creative nonfictional filming techniques that combine a soldier's home movies, documentaries, newscasts, and Internet postings, *Redacted* (2007) is based on a real event wherein a squad persecutes an innocent Iraqi family and rapes a young girl.

Other recent movie releases focus on a chaotic battlefront, as in the seven-part television series *Generation Kill* (2008), where members of the U.S. Marine Corps 1st Reconnaissance Battalion face unclear conditions and military ineptitude. *The Hurt Locker* (2008) deals with the sergeant of a bomb disposal team who recklessly exposes his subordinates to urban combat, while *Green Zone* (2009) is a fictional treatment of a U.S. Army inspection squad hunting for WMDs, misled by covert and faulty intelligence. *No*

True Glory: Battle for Fallujah (2009) takes up the familiar theme of the confusion and frustration of the Iraqi insurgency in its account of the fighting in Fallujah in 2004 between insurgents and U.S. forces.

Increasingly, however, Iraq War movies have turned to the home front. After harrowing experiences in Iraq, for instance, four soldiers in *Home of the Brave* (2006) must deal with their physical and psychological trauma upon their return home. Similarly, *Four Horsemen* (2007) focuses on four high school friends: one is killed in action, another is permanently maimed, and the remaining two return to Iraq after leave. The main character in *Stop Loss* (2008), however, refuses to return when, as a decorated hero, he experiences PTSD following his first tour of duty. With a different twist, *In the Valley of Elah* (2007) is about a father's search to discover what has happened to his soldier son Mike, who has gone absent without leave (AWOL) after his return from Iraq. A complex investigation leads to shocking discoveries: first that Mike had been guilty of prisoner abuse in Iraq and second that his fellow soldiers have stabbed him and dismembered his body. Similarly, the British television movie *The Mark of Cain* (2007) follows three young men who suffer the effects of what they have seen and done after their tour of duty. Dealing with family bereavement, *Grace Is Gone* (2007) concerns a father's difficulty in breaking the news of his wife's death in Iraq to his two daughters.

Among Iraqi-made movies, *Ahlaam* (2005), directed by Mohamed Al-Daradji, an exile during Hussein's reign, was inspired by the sight of psychiatric patients let loose in the streets of Baghdad in the wake of Operation IRAQI FREEDOM. The movie focuses on a mental institution and interweaves the narratives of three characters. Filming in 2004 proved dangerous, for Al-Daradji and three crew members were once kidnapped twice in the same day. *Valley of the Wolves* (2006), based on a popular Turkish television series, is set in northern Iraq and begins with U.S. forces capturing 11 Turkish special forces soldiers.

An Egyptian black comedy, *The Night Baghdad Fell* (2006), was extremely popular. It lampooned American officials, and the story line dealt with preparations to prevent the United States from continuing its invasion into Egypt. Condoleezza Rice and U.S. marines figure in the repressed fantasies of the film characters. An earlier comedy, *No Problem, We're Getting Messed Over,* featured an Egyptian who sends his son to Iraq to deliver mangoes and then must rescue him from a U.S. prison. He falls into Hussein's hiding place and is fired on by insurgents, arrested by Americans, and taken to President Bush, who forces him to wear a beard and confess to bombing the U.S. embassy.

Global War on Terror

While films dealing with the ongoing conflicts in Afghanistan and Iraq are virtually inseparable from the Global War on Terror, other documentaries and movies address the conflict in a more general Middle Eastern context. Arabic films have portrayed this topic for several decades. A classic piece portraying a conventional view of

Matt Damon and Alexander Siddig, who starred in Stephen Gaghan's political thriller film *Syriana*. (Sygma/Corbis)

Islamist terrorists was *Irhabi* (The Terrorist) of 1993, starring Adel Imam. John Pilger's documentary *Breaking the Silence: Truth and Lies in the War on Terror* (2003) criticizes American and British involvement in the Middle East since 9/11, questioning the real motives for the Global War on Terror, as does Noam Chomsky's *Distorted Morality* (2003), which claims that America is the world's biggest endorser of state-sponsored terrorism. Most notably, Michael Moore's *Fahrenheit 9/11* (2004), which holds the current box office record for a political documentary, attacks the Global War on Terror agenda of the Bush government, alleging connections with Saudi royalty and the bin Laden family. The film provoked rebuttals, such as *Fahrenhype 11* (2004). Produced by the BBC in 2004, the documentary series *The Power of Nightmares: The Rise of the Politics of Fear* parallels the American Neo-Conservative movement with radical Islamism, arguing as well that the threat of Islamism is a myth perpetuated to unite the public through fear. Subsequent documentaries include *The Oil Factor: Behind the War on Terror* (2005), which examines the link between U.S. oil interests and current conflicts, and *The Road to Guantánamo* (2006), a docudrama on four Pakistani brothers who, in Pakistan for a wedding, venture into Afghanistan. Captured, they spend three years at Guantánamo Bay.

American movies have addressed the theme of rampant Muslim terrorism for decades, and recent films carry on the tradition. The global oil industry is the focus of *Syriana* (2005), a political thriller in which a CIA operative is caught up in a plot involving a Persian Gulf prince. Inspired by terrorist bombings in Saudi Arabia in 1996 and 2003, *The Kingdom* (2007) follows a Federal Bureau of Investigation (FBI) inquiry into the bombing of a foreign-worker complex. In *Rendition* (2007), a terrorist bomb kills an American envoy, and the investigation leads to an Egyptian American who, after arrest, is sent overseas for torture and interrogation. Touching upon all recent Middle Eastern conflicts, Oliver Stone's recent *W.* (2008) is not only a mildly entertaining biopic of President George W. Bush but also a withering representation of the decision making that preceded the declaration of a Global War on Terror and military deployments in Afghanistan and Iraq. Other of the film's episodes includes a flashback to President George H. W. Bush's decision to stop the Persian Gulf War early and pull out U.S. troops at the end of the conflict.

ANNA M. WITTMANN

See also

Abu Ghraib; Al Jazeera; Antiwar Movements, Persian Gulf and Iraq Wars; Bin Laden, Osama; DESERT STORM, Operation; ENDURING FREEDOM, Operation; *Fahrenheit 9/11;* Global War on Terror; Gulf War Syndrome; Hussein, Saddam; IRAQI FREEDOM, Operation; Iraqi Insurgency; Moore, Michael; Music, Middle East; Omar, Mohammed; Post-Traumatic Stress Disorder; Taliban Insurgency, Afghanistan; Vietnam Syndrome

References

Rollins, Peter C., and John E. O'Connor, eds. *Why We Fought: America's Wars in Film and History*. Lexington: University of Kentucky Press, 2008.

Slocum, J. David, ed. *Hollywood and War: The Film Reader*. New York: Routledge, 2006.

Westwell, Guy. *War Cinema: Hollywood on the Front Line*. London: Wallflower, 2006.

Firdaws Bunker Bombing

See Amariyah Bunker or Shelter Bombing

Fox M93 NBC Vehicle

See Fuchs M93 NBC Vehicle

France, Middle East Policy

France, whose interests in the Middle East date back many centuries, acquired extensive imperial interests in the region during the 19th century, gradually annexing or acquiring protectorates or special rights in Lebanon, Egypt, Algeria, Tunisia, and Morocco. During the 1854–1856 Crimean War, France protected Ottoman Turkey against Russian incursions, while French engineers and capital were later behind construction of the Suez Canal. France played a prominent role in Egyptian affairs until 1882, when the French government rejected a cooperative military effort against Egypt and when Britain occupied the country. France's stake in the former Ottoman Empire expanded under the World War I Sykes-Picot Agreement (1916), whereby France eventually gained mandates over the Levant (present-day Syria and Lebanon). It effectively administered the regions as colonial territories until World War II began in 1939.

After World War II France maintained substantial cultural influence in its former territories, but the French Middle Eastern empire rapidly shrank as its former colonies demanded and—sometimes humiliatingly for France, as in Algeria—gained independence. This process was also occurring in Africa, and active resistance to French rule occurred in Asia with the Indochina War (1946–1954). Meanwhile, France's 1956 effort with Britain and Israel against Egypt over the nationalization of the Suez Canal ended in fiasco. Over time, traditional ties to former colonies and economic self-interest made France broadly pro-Arab in the protracted Arab-Israeli conflict.

French interest in the Middle East dates back to the Crusades of 1096–1291, which received major backing and participation from the French monarchy. By the 16th century, French leaders considered the Ottomans a valuable counterbalance to rival Hapsburg power in Europe. In 1535 François I of France and Ottoman sultan Suleiman I signed a treaty of accord and friendship, whereby the latter effectively recognized France as the protector of Latin Christians in the Ottoman Empire. Suleiman granted France economic and legal privileges known as the capitulatory treaties, or capitulations, whereby France exercised legal jurisdiction over French merchants and received other most-favored nation commercial rights in Ottoman territories. One of these treaties had been forged with the rulers of Egypt centuries earlier in the aftermath of a crusade. Others were extended to King Louis XV in 1740 and Napoleon I in 1802. French commerce dominated the Mediterranean well into the mid-18th century.

By the late 18th century French leaders also viewed the eastern Mediterranean as an arena for imperial competition with Great Britain and other powers, usually at the expense of the increasingly crumbling Ottoman Empire. As a possible prelude to a drive on Britain's Indian territories, in 1798 General Napoleon Bonaparte invaded and conquered Mamluk-administered Egypt, which was then under Ottoman sovereignty. Napoleon's subsequent advances into Palestine and Syria halted when, thanks in large part to British sea power, he failed to take the city of Acre. Napoleon returned to France in 1799, and the remaining French troops in Egypt surrendered to the British in 1801, thereby ending the unpopular French occupation.

Throughout the 19th century Ottoman weakness provided opportunities for France and other European powers to acquire colonial possessions and quasi-imperial rights and privileges in the Middle East. Early 19th-century British ties with the Ottoman government were a major reason that, during the 1820s and 1830s, France backed the efforts of independent-minded Muhammad Ali Pasha of Egypt to gain greater autonomy from his Ottoman overlord. In 1840, however, the French declined to assist him when British and other European powers curbed his authority.

The Anglo-French entente that characterized Napoleon III's reign during the 1850s and 1860s led France and Britain to cooperate extensively in the Middle East. Seeking to restrain Russian ambitions against Ottoman territory, the two joined forces against Russia in the 1854–1856 Crimean War. In Lebanon, France claimed special rights as protector of the substantial Maronite Christian community and intervened to assist its clients during 1842–1845 and again in 1860, when it collaborated with Britain to end major civil strife. France's commercial interests in Lebanon, then part of Syria, were centered in the silk industry.

The Anglo-French entente was not permanent, as France's weakness after its 1870 defeat by Germany encouraged other powers to encroach upon its sphere of influence. In 1854 and 1856 French engineer Ferdinand de Lesseps obtained concessions from the Egyptian government to build a canal across the Isthmus of Suez, a waterway that would considerably shorten transit time between Asia and Europe by enabling ships to avoid circumnavigation of the African continent. The French and Egyptian governments provided the capital for the Suez Canal Company, which would own and operate the canal for 99 years and which, built with French expertise, opened with great fanfare in 1869.

At this time, French and British nationals jointly administered Egypt's debts. In 1875, however, the continuing financial

The decisive British victory at the Battle of the Nile on August 1, 1799, stranded Napoleon Bonaparte's army in Egypt and re-established Royal Navy dominance in the Mediterranean. (Clarke, James Stanier and John McArthur. *The Life and Services of Horatio, Viscount Nelson—from his Lordship's Manuscripts*, 1840)

difficulties of Viceroy (Khedive) Ismail Pasha of Egypt forced him to sell the Egyptian stake in the Suez Canal to the British government. Seven years later, to bitter French resentment, Britain occupied Egypt and took over its administration. This occupation had been planned as a joint British-French venture, but the fall of the French cabinet led the French to renege, and the British then went in alone. In the latter 19th and early 20th centuries, however, French bankers lent money to the Ottoman government. Under the terms of these loans, French nationals and other Westerners supervised and administered some Ottoman revenues.

During the 19th century France also acquired a North African empire at Ottoman expense. In 1830 France conquered Algeria, which was incorporated outright into France, to become three French departments. Four decades of sporadic military operations against the Muslim Arab and Berber populations ensued before French control was assured, and numerous French colonists settled in Algeria. During 1881–1883 France made neighboring Tunisia a protectorate. In 1912 Morocco also became a French protectorate. In East Africa, the French acquired Djibouti during the 1880s and sought to expand their African possessions into the southern Sudan, provoking the 1898 Fashoda Crisis with Great Britain, which considered the Sudan to be part of Egypt. In the aftermath of the crisis, France finally renounced all designs on the

Sudan. The net effect of this was to concentrate French imperial efforts in Africa and make possible an entente with Britain.

World War I intensified French appetites for colonial concessions in Ottoman-administered territory. In early 1915 Britain agreed to allow Russia to acquire Constantinople, the Ottoman capital that commanded the strategic Dardanelles Straits connecting the Black Sea to the Mediterranean. France responded by claiming much of the Levant and in 1916 concluded the Sykes-Picot Agreement with Britain. This allocated French rule over coastal Syria and Lebanon and much of the Anatolian province of Cilicia, a sphere of influence that would include the remainder of Syria and the Mesopotamian province of Mosul. The agreement also guaranteed French participation in an international administration of Palestine.

The 1919 Paris Peace Conference modified these provisions, and France abandoned Mosul and Palestine to be ruled as British mandates. In return, the French received a mandate that gave it full control over all the Levant, essentially comprising present-day Syria and Lebanon. Growing Turkish nationalism meant that although the 1920 Treaty of Sèvres recognized French control of Cilicia, France could not enforce its rule and abandoned this claim under the subsequent 1923 Treaty of Lausanne.

French rule over Syria and Lebanon proved contentious. During 1925–1926 French forces suppressed an armed rebellion in Syria. In

1936 France signed treaties granting both Syria and Lebanon independence within three years, although France retained military base rights in both states. But the treaties were never ratified or implemented, and instead in 1939 France restored colonial rule. After France's defeat by Germany in June 1940, French administrators in Syria and Lebanon supported the Vichy government, which negotiated an armistice with Germany. In June 1941, however, British and Free French forces took over the areas, and Free French representative General Georges Catroux promised independence to both. After a number of military and political clashes between French officials and the Lebanese and Syrians, France withdrew all its forces from the two states, which became fully independent in 1946.

The French position in North Africa was almost equally precarious. During the 1920s, capable French general Louis-Hubert Lyautey suppressed insurgencies in Morocco, but nationalist forces nonetheless burgeoned. Serious nationalist unrest occurred in Tunisia in 1938, and despite having been banned in the late 1930s, nationalist parties existed in Algeria. In June 1940 administrators in France's North African colonies backed the Vichy regime, but in November 1942 Allied forces launched a successful invasion there. Despite strong French opposition in all three states, Allied and Axis wartime propaganda alike encouraged independence movements.

Morocco's sultan adeptly headed his nationalist forces, eventually winning independence in 1956. A guerrilla war led by activist Habib Bourguiba began in Tunisia in 1952, bringing autonomy in 1955 and full independence in 1956. In Algeria, politically influential French settlers, known as *colons,* adamantly opposed independence, and a brutal eight-year conflict, led by the *Front de Libération Nationale* (FLN, National Liberation Front), began in 1954, killing between 300,000 and 1 million Algerians, and toppling the French Fourth Republic. Finally in 1962 French President Charles de Gaulle granted the country independence.

Most *colons* thereupon hastily returned to France, whose population split bitterly over the war. Under agreements reached in 1965, French companies retained control of Algerian oil and gas resources, but following repeated disputes, the Algerian government nationalized majority holdings in these companies in 1971.

Despite a vaunted close identification with Arab interests, in 1947 France voted to partition Palestine and in 1949 recognized the new State of Israel. In 1950 France joined Britain and the United States in the Tripartite Declaration, imposing an arms embargo on all parties in the Middle East conflict. This effectively preserved the existing status quo, and by 1955 France had become a major arms supplier to the Israeli military. Anger over perceived Egyptian support for the Algerian FLN was one reason that France, alarmed by Egyptian president Gamal Abdel Nasser's nationalization of the Suez Canal in July 1956, joined Britain and Israel in October 1956 in an abortive military expedition to Egypt intended to retake control of the canal. Within 10 days American economic pressure forced Britain and then France and Israel into a humiliating and much resented withdrawal.

In the late 1950s France helped Israel develop a nuclear capability, but once Algeria won independence, Franco-Arab tensions relaxed, and French strategic and economic interests brought a tilt away from Israel. Before the 1967 Six-Day War, de Gaulle sought to restrain Israel from launching a preemptive strike and in June imposed a complete arms embargo on all parties to the conflict, a measure that primarily affected Israel. An angry de Gaulle subsequently urged unconditional Israeli withdrawal from all occupied Arab territories, and from late 1969 onward France became a major arms supplier to several Arab states. During and after the 1973 Yom Kippur (Ramadan) War, France heeded Arab demands, reinforced by an oil embargo on offending nations, to cease supplying arms to Israel. French officials promoted a pro-Arab stance in the European Economic Community (EEC), urged admission of the Palestine Liberation Organization (PLO) to international bodies, and in October 1981 endorsed the Palestinian call for a national homeland.

During the 1980s French policies toward the Middle East conflict became more evenhanded as France became a target for assorted Lebanese, Iraqi, Iranian, Palestinian, and other terrorists. Although France had sheltered the exiled Iranian ayatollah Ruhollah Khomeini, who became head of the revolutionary Iranian government in 1979, France supplied significant quantities of arms to Iraq during the subsequent Iran-Iraq War (1980–1988), and the asylum France afforded various post-1979 Iranian political exiles strained relations with the new regime.

France still felt special responsibility for Lebanon and in July 1982 contributed troops to a multinational United Nations (UN) task force to oversee the evacuation of Syrian and PLO fighters, first from Beirut and later, in December 1983, from Tripoli. In 1984

French troops in Port Said on December 27, 1956, prior to their departure from the Suez Canal Zone after French and British forces had invaded Egypt during the Suez Crisis of that year. (AFP/Getty Images)

France also sent observers to monitor the Lebanese cease-fire, but heavy casualties brought their withdrawal two years later. From 1980 until 1987, when Libyan forces withdrew, France sought with only moderate success to exert political and military pressure on Libya to cease its incursions against neighboring Chad.

France acquiesced and participated in the 1991 Persian Gulf War when a U.S.-led international coalition drove Iraq out of oil-rich Kuwait, which Saddam Hussein had forcefully annexed. In 1993 France, along with Britain and the United States, also launched air strikes against Iraq to protest Hussein's infractions of UN sanctions; such operations recurred frequently throughout the 1990s. During the 1990s and early 2000s, French sales of arms and other goods to Iraq, Iran, and other regimes that the United States found unpalatable nonetheless provoked considerable U.S. rhetorical condemnation.

In the late 1990s the presence of several million North African immigrants and migrant workers in France contributed to the growing strength of extremist right-wing political groups who resented and campaigned against the immigrants' arrival. After the extremist Al Qaeda organization launched the September 11, 2001, terrorist attacks against the United States, the French government expressed full support for the United States in moves to track down terrorists and to invade Afghanistan, Al Qaeda's territorial base. Indeed, France feared that fundamentalist Muslims might launch similar attacks on French soil. In 2001 and again since 2003, French soldiers have taken part in various operations against Taliban fighters and other insurgents in Afghanistan. More than 4,000 French troops have served in Afghanistan. In 2004, with anti-Semitism burgeoning dramatically in France, the French government banned Muslim girls in state-run schools from wearing the hijab (or headscarf) in class, a measure that provoked spirited national and international debate.

French leaders nonetheless deplored and refused to endorse the spring 2003 U.S.-led invasion of Iraq, and for at least a year French and American officials engaged in bitter and highly undiplomatic attacks on each other's countries. Dominque de Villpin, French foreign minister from 2002 to 2004, was especially critical of the invasion of Iraq. The July 2005 Muslim terrorist attacks on London's transportation systems raised new fears that France would soon become a terrorist target and that French Muslims might become objects of popular suspicion and harassment. French Muslims for their part were thoroughly angered by official neglect, discrimination, and rising racist sentiment encouraged by leaders such as Étienne Le Pen. By summer 2007 Franco-American relations were on the rebound, largely as a result of Nicolas Sarkozy's election to the French presidency earlier in that year. Sarkozy promised to mend relations with Washington, and thus far he has made numerous substantive steps toward that end.

PRISCILLA ROBERTS

See also

Algerian War; Arab-Israeli Conflict, Overview; Egypt; ENDURING FREEDOM, Operation; Iran-Iraq War; IRAQI FREEDOM, Operation; Khomeini, Ruhollah; Kuwait; Lebanon; Libya; Morocco; Nasser, Gamal Abdel; September 11 Attacks; September 11 Attacks, International Reactions to; Suez Crisis; Syria; Terrorism; Tunisia; Turkey, Role in Persian Gulf and Afghanistan Wars; United Kingdom, Middle East Policy; United States, Middle East Policy, 1917–1945; United States, Middle East Policy, 1945–Present

References

Brown, L. Carl, and Matthew S. Gordon, eds. *Franco-Arab Encounters: Studies in Memory of David C. Gordon.* Beirut, Lebanon: American University of Beirut, 1996.

Gaunson, A. B. *The Anglo-French Clash in Lebanon and Syria, 1940–1945.* New York: St. Martin's, 1987.

Marlowe, John. *Perfidious Albion: The Origins of Anglo-French Rivalry in the Levant.* London: Elek, 1971.

Tal, David, ed. *The 1956 War: Collusion and Rivalry in the Middle East.* Portland, OR: Frank Cass, 2001.

Thomas, Martin. *The French North African Crisis: Colonial Breakdown and Anglo-French Relations, 1945–62.* Basingstoke, UK: Macmillan, 2000.

Wall, Irwin M. *France, the United States, and the Algerian War.* Berkeley: University of California Press, 2001.

Watson, William E. *Tricolor and Crescent: France and the Islamic World.* Westport, CT: Praeger, 2003.

Williams, Ann. *Britain and France in the Middle East and North Africa, 1914–1967.* London: Macmillan, 1968.

France, Role in Persian Gulf and Iraq Wars

West European nation covering 211,208 square miles, with a 2008 population of approximately 64.058 million. France is bordered to the west and northwest by the Atlantic Ocean and the English Channel; to the northeast by Belgium, Luxembourg, and Germany; to the east by Switzerland and Italy; and to the south by the Mediterranean Sea and Spain. A prosperous and highly industrialized nation whose economy is ranked eighth in the world, France is a democratic, semipresidential republic. Since the inauguration of the Fifth Republic in 1958, the French government has had a bicameral parliamentary system in which much executive power is vested in a popularly elected president, who is head of state. The prime minister, who is elected by parliament, serves as head of government. The French president wields considerable clout, especially in foreign and military affairs and national security. Since 1990 France has had three presidents: François Mitterand (1990–1995), Jacques Chirac (1995–2007), and Nicolas Sarkozy (2007–).

Following Iraq's invasion of Kuwait on August 2, 1990, France participated in Operation DESERT SHIELD and Operation DESERT STORM, which led to the liberation of Kuwait in February 1991. The French mission, code-named Operation DAGUET (French for a species of deer), involved army, air force, and navy personnel; however, the bulk of the forces came from the army. General Michel Roquejoffre commanded the French forces. France was, after Great Britain, the second-largest non-U.S. contributor of troops to the war. France contributed 18,000 troops (of whom 14,500 were army ground troops). France also supplied 2,100 vehicles of all types, including

In October 1990, following the Iraqi occupation of Kuwait, France sent aircraft to Qatar. Here, a Mirage F-1 of the Qatari Air Force is protected by U.S. troops with a grenade launcher. (U.S. Department of Defense)

45 tanks, 60 combat aircraft, 120 helicopters, and an aircraft carrier and other smaller naval ships. The bulk of the French troops were in the 6th Light Armored Division, but a cavalry unit and an engineering regiment from the French Foreign Legion were also attached to the division. French troops remained under French command, but in January 1991 they were placed under tactical control of and fought alongside the U.S. XVIII Airborne Corps during DESERT STORM.

After Iraq invaded Kuwait on August 2, 1990, French president François Mitterand dispatched to the Persian Gulf a French naval task force that included the aircraft carrier *Clemenceau*. Seven days later, the United Arab Emirates requested military aid from France, and later that same month France increased its naval strength in the Persian Gulf. As a military buildup of U.S.-led forces in Saudi Arabia continued, and Iraqi president Saddam Hussein seized French residents in Iraq and Kuwait as hostages and announced his intention to use them as human shields, the first French force contingent—about 100 troops and 10 helicopters—arrived in Saudi Arabia on September 10, 1991. Four days later Iraqi forces invaded the French ambassador's residence in

Kuwait, prompting Mitterand to deploy 4,000 French troops to Saudi Arabia and approximately 30 fighter aircraft (Sepecat Jaguars). By the end of October, French forces in Saudi Arabia numbered almost 6,500 men.

As Saddam showed no willingness to withdraw unconditionally from Kuwait, France increased its military presence in Saudi Arabia with an additional 5,000 troops and two dozen fighter aircraft in early December. By early January 1991 an additional 4,000 French troops arrived in Saudi Arabia. French forces now numbered more than 10,000 troops and 1,450 vehicles, including 45 AMX-30B2 tanks. Six weeks later, on the eve of Operation DESERT STORM, French forces numbered some 18,000 men.

The French army contingent of the 6th Light Armored Division was deployed with the U.S. XVIII Airborne Corps along the far western part of the Saudi-Iraqi border. Its objective was to invade and secure western Iraq and thereby protect the flank or rear of the bulk of the coalition ground forces deployed to the east along the Saudi-Kuwait and Saudi-Iraqi borders, where most of Iraq's army was entrenched. Most of the coalition ground forces were positioned to invade Kuwait or southern Iraq, but allied commanders feared that Iraqi forces, particularly the Republican Guard with a large contingent of tanks and armored vehicles, might try to outflank these forces and encircle coalition forces to the north and south. Accordingly, the 6th Light Armored Division was tasked with invading and securing western Iraq to prevent this from occurring.

After more than a month of a devastating air campaign against Iraqi forces and targets in Kuwait and Iraq, the ground campaign began on February 24, 1991. The initial objective of the French forces was the seizure of an Iraqi airfield at Salman. Although French forces crossed the border unopposed, they later encountered elements of the 45th Iraqi Mechanized Infantry Division. Supported by French helicopters, the French ground forces defeated the Iraqi forces, captured 2,500 prisoners, and secured the airfield at Salman. After achieving their initial objective on the first day, French forces, along with those of the United States, pushed deeper, occupying the central part of southern Iraq, including major highways connecting Baghdad to southern Iraq. Four days later, after a 100-hour ground offensive that completely overwhelmed Iraq's beleaguered forces, Kuwait was liberated, and the Persian Gulf War came to an end.

Nine French soldiers died during the Persian Gulf War, including during the ground campaign. Two soldiers were killed while clearing explosives near Salman on February 26, 1991, and about 50 French soldiers were injured during the four-day ground offensive.

Since early 2002 France has also contributed troops to Afghanistan as part of the some 50,000-strong North Atlantic Treaty Organization's (NATO) International Security Assistance Force–Afghanistan (ISAF). NATO's ISAF mission was to bring security and prosperity to Afghanistan by fighting terrorism and denying the Taliban and its Al Qaeda allies the use of that country as a sanctuary; promoting democracy by supporting the democratic government of Afghanistan, currently under President Hamid Karzai; and rebuilding the country's ruined economy after two decades of war. By early 2009 some 2,500 French troops were deployed in the country, mostly in the capital of Kabul but also in the southern city of Kandahar, where French fighter aircraft are based and provide air support for NATO ally troops. France has also trained more than 3,800 Afghan military officers and Afghan Special Forces units. In seven years, 25 French soldiers have died in Afghanistan, and more than 100 have been injured.

With mounting violence in Afghanistan and a rise in attacks by the Taliban, on March 26, 2008, French president Nicolas Sarkozy announced the deployment of an additional battalion of troops to eastern Afghanistan close to the Pakistan border, raising the number of French troops to about 3,300. Despite the death of 10 French troops and wounding of 21 in a Taliban ambush 30 miles east of Kabul on August 18, 2008, and polls showing strong public opinion against the French mission in Afghanistan, Sarkozy announced that his "determination remained intact" to continue France's mission in that country. A month later, the French parliament voted to continue that mission over the objections of the opposition Socialist Party. Foreign Minister François Fillon informed the National Assembly that withdrawing French troops from Afghanistan would mean that Paris is indifferent to Afghanistan's fate, no longer assumes its responsibilities, and abandons its allies.

In the wake of the August 18, 2008, attack on French forces, France sent transport and attack helicopters, drones, surveillance equipment, mortars, and 100 additional troops. By year's end it had drawn down some of its troops, which then numbered about 2,700 men.

The French government under Jacques Chirac refused to sanction the Anglo-American–led invasion of Iraq in 2003. As a result, France did not participate in that endeavor, and it has steadfastly refused to send troops, even for postwar reconstruction and humanitarian efforts. France's unwillingness to support the United States and Great Britain in the Iraq War severely strained relations with the United States for several years. Making matters even worse was persistent public criticism of the war effort emanating from Paris. Since President Sarkozy assumed office in 2007, there have been efforts by both sides to heal the rift, and Franco-American relations have steadily improved.

STEFAN M. BROOKS

See also

Chirac, Jacques René; DESERT STORM, Operation; ENDURING FREEDOM, Operation; France, Middle East Policy; International Security Assistance Force; North Atlantic Treaty Organization in Afghanistan

References

Atkinson, Rick. *Crusade: The Untold Story of the Persian Gulf War.* New York: Mariner Books, 1994.

Crocker, H. W., III. *Don't Tread on Me.* New York: Crown Forum, 2006.

Rottman, Gordan. *Armies of the Gulf War.* London: Osprey, 1993.

Ryan, Mike. *Battlefield Afghanistan.* London: Spellmount, 2007.

Franks, Frederick Melvin, Jr.
Birth Date: November 1, 1936

U.S. Army officer and commander of VII Corps during the 1991 Persian Gulf War (Operation DESERT STORM). Born in West Lawn, Pennsylvania, on November 1, 1936, Frederick Melvin Franks Jr. graduated from the United States Military Academy, West Point, and was commissioned as an armor officer in June 1959. Following an initial assignment in Germany with the 11th Armored Cavalry Regiment, he attended the Armor Officer Advanced Course at Fort Knox, Kentucky, and then entered Columbia University, earning master's degrees in both English and philosophy before returning to West Point as an English instructor in 1966.

In 1969 he rejoined the 11th Armored Cavalry Regiment, then stationed in Vietnam, and served as an operations officer. Seriously wounded during the Cambodian incursion in 1970, he fought to remain on active duty and as an armor officer, in spite of the amputation of his left leg. Following tours at the Armed Forces Staff College and the Department of the Army Staff, he took command of the 1st Squadron, 3rd Armored Cavalry Regiment, at Fort Bliss, Texas, in 1975. In 1982, after an assignment with the U.S. Army Training and Doctrine Command, he returned to the 11th Cavalry, stationed in Germany, as its commander. Promoted to brigadier general in July 1984, Franks commanded the Seventh Army Training Command and in 1985 returned to the United States as the deputy commandant of the Army's Command and General Staff College at Fort Leavenworth, Kansas. There he was instrumental in implementing small-group instructional techniques in the Regular Course and inaugurating a staff procedures course for senior captains (Combined Arms and Services Staff School, CAS3). In addition, he oversaw the expansion and refinement of the School of Advanced Military Studies into one of the U.S. Army's most important educational institutions.

Franks returned to the Pentagon and in August 1987 became the first J-7 (Plans) on the newly reorganized Joint Staff as a major general. Returning to Europe in 1988, he assumed command of the 1st Armored Division and, a year later, following his advancement to lieutenant general in August 1989, VII Corps. During the next year he transformed the corps staff from essentially a garrison organization to a more agile, mobile command headquarters, just in time for its deployment to the Middle East in November 1990 during Operation DESERT SHIELD. While in Saudi Arabia, VII Corps grew into the largest and most powerful tactical command ever fielded by the U.S. Army, with more than 3,000 tanks, 700 artillery pieces, and 142,000 soldiers organized into five heavy divisions, an armored cavalry regiment, an aviation brigade, and the supporting organizations needed to execute the army's AirLand Battle Doctrine.

After breaking through the Iraqi defenses at the beginning of Operation DESERT STORM, Franks maneuvered the VII Corps to confront and destroy two of the Iraqi Republican Guard Force's best units, the Tawakalna Mechanized and Medina Armored Divisions. Overall coalition commander General H. Norman Schwarzkopf

U.S. Army lieutenant general Frederick M. Franks commanded VII Corps, the powerful formation that included several armor divisions, during Operation DESERT STORM in 1991. (U.S. Army)

publicly criticized Franks for moving too slowly and allowing elements of the Republican Guard to escape destruction by withdrawing toward Basra. In his later memoirs, written with Tom Clancy, Franks rebuts Schwarzkopf's criticisms and gives his own version of events.

Advanced to four-star rank in August 1991, Franks headed the Training and Doctrine Command (TRADOC) and directed the army's educational and doctrinal programs, adjusting them to meet the needs of the post–Cold War era. He retired from the service in November 1994.

Since his retirement from active duty, Franks has continued to serve as an army consultant, particularly for the Battle Command Training Program. He has served as chairman of the VII Corps Desert Storm Veteran's Association and has traveled extensively to speak and lecture. Franks has also served on a number of boards, including the board of trustees for West Point. Since January 2005 he has been chairman of the American Battle Monuments Commission, the organization responsible for managing and maintaining America's overseas military cemeteries from World Wars I and II.

STEPHEN A. BOURQUE

See also
AirLand Battle Doctrine; DESERT STORM, Operation; Republican Guard; Schwarzkopf, H. Norman, Jr.

References
Atkinson, Rick. *Crusade: The Untold Story of the Persian Gulf War.* New York: Mariner Books, 1994.
Bourque, Stephen A. *Jayhawk! The VII Corps in the Persian Gulf War.* Washington, DC: Department of the Army, 2002.
Clancy, Tom, with General Fred Franks Jr. *Into the Storm: A Study in Command.* New York: Putnam, 1997.
Gordon, Michael R., and General Bernard E. Trainor. *The Generals' War: The Inside Story of the Conflict in the Gulf.* New York: Little, Brown, 1995.

Franks, Tommy Ray
Birth Date: June 17, 1945

U.S. Army general. Tommy Ray Franks was born in Wynnewood, Oklahoma, on June 17, 1945. After studying briefly at the University of Texas, Franks joined the U.S. Army in 1965 and went into the artillery. He served in Vietnam, where he was wounded three times. He again attended the University of Texas but dropped out and rejoined the army after being placed on academic probation. Franks later earned a master's degree in public administration at Shippensburg University (1985). He also graduated from the Armed Forces Staff College in 1967, and in 1972 he attended the Field Artillery Center at Fort Sill, Oklahoma.

From 1976 to 1977 Franks attended the Armed Forces Staff College in Norfolk, Virginia, and in 1984–1985 he attended the U.S. Army War College at Carlisle Barracks, Pennsylvania. He advanced through the ranks, and by the time of Operation DESERT STORM in 1991 he was serving as an assistant division commander of the 1st Calvary Division. Franks was appointed brigadier general in July 1991 and major general in April 1994. From 1994 to 1995 he was assistant chief of staff for combined forces in Korea. Franks was advanced to lieutenant general in May 1997 and to general in July 2006.

After the September 11, 2001, terrorist attacks on the United States, Franks was named U.S. commander of the successful Operation ENDURING FREEDOM to topple the Taliban in Afghanistan. In early 2003 he took command of Central Command (CENTCOM) for Operation IRAQI FREEDOM, the invasion of Iraq that began in March 2003.

Franks was a principal author of the war plans for the ground element of the invasion of Iraq and was an advocate of the lighter, more rapid mechanized forces that performed so well during the ground campaign. Franks designed a plan for the 125,000 U.S., 45,000 British, 2,000 Australian, 400 Czech and Slovak, and 200 Polish troops under his command. His plan involved five ground thrusts into Iraq, with two main thrusts—one by the I Marine Expeditionary Force up the Tigris River and one through the western desert and up the Euphrates by the army's 3rd Armored Division.

The plan allowed for great flexibility, and even though CENTCOM advertised a shock-and-awe bombing campaign, in fact there

As commander of the U.S. Central Command, Army general Tommy Franks led the successful military efforts that toppled the Taliban in Afghanistan in 2001 and overthrew Saddam Hussein in Iraq in 2003. (U.S. Department of Defense)

all simultaneously employed by commanders in the field to defeat the enemy.

Although sources suggest that Secretary of Defense Donald Rumsfeld offered Franks the post of army chief of staff when the ground war ended in late April 2003, Franks wanted to leave the army to pursue other interests. He retired in late May 2003 and subsequently wrote his memoir, *American Soldier* (2004). Franks's departure was fortuitous for him, as he left Iraq prior to the start of the Iraqi insurgency and thus avoided most of the criticism that it engendered. In retirement, Franks started his own consulting firm that deals in disaster recovery operations. He also sits on the boards of several large corporations.

LARRY SCHWEIKART

See also

Bush, George Herbert Walker; ENDURING FREEDOM, Operation; Hussein, Saddam; Iraq, History of, 1990–Present; IRAQI FREEDOM, Operation; Iraqi Insurgency; Rumsfeld, Donald Henry; September 11 Attacks; United States Central Command

References

Cordesman, Anthony H. *The Iraq War: Strategy, Tactics, and Military Lessons.* Westport, CT: Praeger, 2003.
Fontenot, Gregory, et al. *On Point: The United States Army in Iraqi Freedom.* Annapolis, MD: Naval Institute Press, 2005.
Franks, Tommy, with Malcolm McConnell. *American Soldier.* New York: Regan Books, 2004.
Murray, Williamson, and Robert H. Scales Jr. *The Iraq War: A Military History.* Cambridge, MA: Belknap, 2005.
Woodward, Bob. *Plan of Attack.* New York: Simon and Schuster, 2004.

was never any such intention. Franks's plans called for a near-simultaneous ground and air assault. When missiles struck Iraqi president Saddam Hussein's compound on March 19, 2003, ground forces moved into Iraq. Franks emphasized speed, bypassing cities and Iraqi strong points. Contrary to media reports that coalition forces were "bogged down" and had not occupied many cities, Franks maintained that this was by design: CENTCOM did not want the Iraqis to see the method and tactics by which coalition forces planned to take Baghdad demonstrated in advance in Basra or Najaf.

Franks's campaign was an unqualified success, going farther, faster, and with fewer casualties than any other comparable military campaign in history. This reflects what Franks calls "full-spectrum" war, in which troops not only engage the enemy's military forces, but also perform simultaneous attacks on computer/information facilities, the banking/monetary structure, and public morale.

During the campaign, American forces operated in true "joint" operations, wherein different service branches spoke directly to units in other service branches. The plans also featured true "combined arms" operations in which air, sea, and land assets were

Friendly Fire

Friendly fire, fratricide, or blue-on-blue are attacks involving troops firing on their own units, usually unknowingly, in which they wound or kill members of their own force. Although military establishments work hard to prevent such incidents, they are inevitable in the fog of war. Of the 613 American casualties in the 1990–1991 Persian Gulf War (including Operations DESERT SHIELD and DESERT STORM), 146 were killed in action, and 35 died in so-called friendly fire incidents. Of 467 wounded, 78 were as a result of friendly fire. Nine British soldiers were killed in such incidents, and 11 others were wounded during DESERT SHIELD/DESERT STORM. Remarkably, with thousands of coalition aircraft flying missions in the Kuwaiti theater of operations, no coalition aircraft were lost in the conflict to friendly fire.

A total of 28 separate incidents of friendly fire were recorded during the war. Sixteen of these occurred in ground-to-ground engagements in which coalition ground forces mistakenly fired on other coalition ground forces. In these incidents, 24 coalition troops were killed and 27 were wounded. Nine died in friendly fire incidents involving aircraft striking ground targets. In all, 11 servicemen were killed and 27 were wounded by air-to-ground friendly fire incidents.

Nonhostile Deaths in the U.S. Military during Operations DESERT SHIELD **and** DESERT STORM

	U.S. Air Force	U.S. Army	U.S. Marine Corps	U.S. Navy	Total
Operation DESERT SHIELD	9	21	18	36	84
Operation DESERT STORM	6	105	26	14	151
Total	15	126	44	50	235

In the air-to-ground incidents, the majority of the incidents involved fixed-wing aircraft; two involved attack helicopters. Four attacks involved U.S. Air Force planes. One U.S. Marine Corps aircraft was also involved, while two U.S. Army attack helicopters were involved in friendly fire attacks. Three incidents involved air-to-ground attacks from undetermined sources. Coalition naval forces also experienced three friendly fire attacks, although no personnel were injured or killed in these cases.

The majority of the friendly fire incidents during the war involved armored units and personnel; the majority of these were U.S. Army armored units and crew members. One tank crew of 4 men, 15 men in an armored fighting vehicle, 1 armored personnel carrier crewman, and 4 infantrymen were killed by friendly fire. The majority of these casualties involved armor-piercing tank rounds designed to destroy targets using kinetic energy. Of the 65 soldiers wounded in friendly fire incidents, only 9 were not in armored vehicles at the time of the incident.

Two incidents involving friendly fire were particularly deadly. The first serious friendly fire incident resulting in deaths during the Persian Gulf War involved U.S. Marine LAV-25 units fighting near the city of Kafji. Anti-tank missiles fired by other vehicles in the unit struck two Marine LAV-25 vehicles, destroying both. Twelve marines were killed in the attack. The second incident involved British Army armored units of the C Company, 3rd Royal Regiment of Fusiliers, that were mistakenly attacked by a U.S. Air Force Republic-Fairchild A-10 Thunderbolt II (Warthog) aircraft. In that case, the aircraft fired anti-armor missiles at vehicles thought to be Iraqi. The aircraft were flying at 8,000 feet to avoid Iraqi antiaircraft fire and were not able to visually identify the vehicles as British. Two British vehicles were hit, resulting in 9 soldiers killed and 11 wounded. The number killed equaled those killed by enemy fire in the entirety of the war.

Friendly fire incidents have also occurred in the Afghanistan War (Operating ENDURING FREEDOM) and the Iraq War (Operation IRAQI FREEDOM). In the Afghanistan War four Canadian soldiers were killed and eight others wounded on the night of April 18, 2002, when a U.S. Air Force Lockheed Martin F-16 Fighting Falcon dropped a bomb on their unit during a night-firing exercise near Kandahar. Subsequently court-martialed, Air National Guard pilot Major Harry Schmidt blamed the accident on drugs ("go pills," which he said the pilots were encouraged to take during missions) and the fog of war. Found guilty of dereliction of duty, he was fined and reprimanded.

The best-known friendly fire incident in Afghanistan was the killing of Pat Tillman, who left a promising and lucrative National Football League (NFL) career to serve in the army following the September 11, 2001, terrorist attacks on the United States. Tillman was serving as a corporal with the 2nd Ranger Battalion when he was shot and killed at close range by three shots to the forehead on April 22, 2004, in what was initially reported as an ambush on a road outside the village of Sperah, about 25 miles southwest of Khost near the Pakistan border. An Afghan militiaman was also killed, and two other rangers were wounded. The subsequent cover-up regarding the circumstances of his death ultimately caused great outrage in the United States. The first investigation held that the deaths were the result of friendly fire brought on by the intensity of the firefight, but a second, and more thorough, investigation held that no hostile forces were involved in the firefight and that two allied groups had fired on each other in confusion following the detonation of an explosive device. The incident continues to be the subject of considerable speculation.

Among numerous other friendly fire incidents in Afghanistan, a U.S. Air Force F-15 called in to support British ground forces dropped a bomb into the same British unit, killing two British soldiers and wounding two others. Two Dutch soldiers were also shot and killed by men from their same unit, and British Javelin anti-tank missiles killed two Danish soldiers during an operation in Helmand Province. On July 9, 2008, nine British soldiers were wounded during patrol when a British helicopter fired upon them.

The so-called Black Hawk Incident was the most costly single incident of friendly fire during U.S. and coalition operations in Iraq. It occurred during Operation PROVIDE COMFORT—the effort to protect the Kurds of northern Iraq from Iraqi military attack. On April 14, 1994, two U.S. Air Force F-15s mistakenly identified two U.S. Army UH-60 Black Hawk helicopters flying over the northern part of the country as Iraqi Mil Mi-24 Hind helicopters and shot them down. The attack killed all 26 U.S., United Kingdom, French, Turkish, and Kurdish military personnel and civilians aboard.

During the Iraq War (Operation IRAQI FREEDOM), U.S. aircraft attacked Kurdish and U.S. special forces, killing 15 people, including a British Broadcasting Corporation (BBC) reporter. As the result of a design flaw, which rendered missile operators unable to identify friendly aircraft, a Patriot missile downed a Lockheed F-18 Hornet aircraft near Karbala, killing the pilot. Another Patriot shot down a British Panavia Tornado, killing its 2-man crew.

In fighting at Nasiriyah on March 23, 2003, an A-10 Warthog supporting the ground effort there attacked marines on the north side of a bridge after mistaking them for Iraqis, killing six. Among other incidents, an American air strike killed eight Kurdish soldiers, and a British Challenger II tank came under fire from another British tank during a nighttime battle; the Challenger's turret was blown off, and two crew members were killed.

The incidents related above demonstrate only friendly forces firing against their own side and do not include the numerous casualties inflicted by mistake on noncombatants.

STEVEN F. MARIN AND SPENCER C. TUCKER

See also

Casualties, Operation DESERT STORM; Casualties, Operation ENDURING FREEDOM; Casualties, Operation IRAQI FREEDOM; PROVIDE COMFORT, Operation; Tillman, Patrick Daniel

References

Coonjohn, Jeffery J. *Operation Desert Storm: Stories from the Front.* Fresno, CA: Military Press, 1991.

Friedman, Norman. *Desert Victory: The War for Kuwait.* Annapolis, MD: Naval Institute Press, 1991.

Summers, Harry. *Persian Gulf War Almanac.* New York: Facts on File, 1995.

Front de Libération Nationale

See National Liberation Front in Algeria

Fuchs M93 NBC Vehicle

Military reconnaissance, armored personnel vehicle designed to detect and protect its crew against nuclear, biological, or chemical (NBC) materials on a battlefield and other areas of military activity. Until 1989 or so, the U.S. military focused on countering the Soviet threat, especially in Central and Western Europe. Soviet use of chemical and biological weapons was never discounted, but following the 1973 Yom Kippur (Ramadan) War, that threat was reassessed. During the Yom Kippur War Israel captured many Soviet armored vehicles that had the capacity of operating in a chemical environment without the crew being encumbered by unwieldy protection suits and filtering masks. Because these same weapons were designed for use in a war in Europe, the conclusion was that Soviet military doctrine included use of offensive chemical agents, requiring protection for Soviet forces passing through already contaminated areas.

The result of these findings was a program begun in the 1980s to develop a reconnaissance vehicle that would detect, identify, and provide warning to friendly forces of chemical contamination, as well as the hazards of biological agents and radiological contamination. The U.S. Chemical Corps had responsibility for this program.

In 1979 the Federal Republic of Germany (FRG, West Germany) fielded a new armored personnel carrier (APC), the Tpzl (Transportpanzer1) Fuchs. This vehicle was a successor to the 1960s-era American M-113 tracked APC. The Fuchs, known in the United States as the Fox, was a wheeled vehicle manufactured by Thyssen-Henschel. The original Fox had a crew of 2 and could carry 10 soldiers, the same capacity of the tracked M-113. Like the M-113, the Fox could serve as a platform for a wide range of military needs. West Germany had already configured the Fox as an NBC reconnaissance vehicle.

The U.S. Army, as the lead agency for NBC defense, decided to explore the use of the M-113 or the Fox as a platform upon which to build an NBC reconnaissance vehicle to identify and mark hazards from weapons of mass destruction (WMDs). In September 1986 the Army began a program to lease 48 German Fox vehicles and in October cancelled the M-113 program. Negotiations with the Germans led to an agreement in March 1990 for General Dynamics to manufacture the Fox in the United States. Until it could be type classified, the Fox was identified as the XM-93 Fox NBC Reconnaissance Vehicle.

The XM-93 required a four-man crew. It was a 6-by-6 wheeled vehicle with sloped armor and featured six-wheel drive, with the forward four wheels providing steering. It weighed 37,400 pounds and measured 22.2 feet long, 9.74 feet wide, and 8 feet high. It had an overpressure system that allowed the crew to operate in a contaminated area without being encumbered by bulky NBC protective suits and masks. The Mercedes-Benz-built eight-cylinder diesel engine provided 320 horsepower to propel the vehicle at speeds of up to 65.2 miles per hour (mph) and up a 60 percent slope. It had armor to protect against small-arms fire of up to 14.5 millimeters, as well as mine protection. It was amphibious at a speed of 6.2 mph and had a maximum range of 497 miles.

The Fox featured a chemical mass spectrometer programmed to identify a wide range of chemical hazards and a remote marking device that could mark the hazards. Radiological detection equipment allowed the crew to identify and mark radiological hazards. There was no capability to identify biological hazards, but the overpressure system provided crew protection.

After August 1990, when Iraq invaded Kuwait, the XM-93 moved from the regular pace of research, development, testing, and fielding to a high-priority item for immediate use. It became evident that the United States would deploy forces to the Persian Gulf to contain the Iraqis and potentially expel them from Kuwait. Iraq had used chemical weapons in its war with Iran from 1980 to 1988 and had also employed them against its own Kurdish population.

On August 7, 1990, Brigadier General Robert D. Orton, chief of the chemical corps and commandant of the Chemical School, directed the establishment of a command center in the school to coordinate NBC defense support for deploying forces. The 24th Infantry Division had already been alerted for movement to the Persian Gulf, and on August 8 it requested use of the XM-93s at Fort McClellan for testing. Two experts from Germany flew to Fort McClellan to assist in "Americanizing" the vehicles by equipping them with U.S. machine guns, radios, and smoke grenade launchers. The vehicles, painted in desert camouflage, left to join the 24th on August 12 and were loaded onto ships for deployment. Eight soldiers from the school also left to man the vehicles and train the 24th

The Fuchs (Fox) M93 NBC Vehicle. Built in Germany, both the United States and Great Britain purchased the Fuchs, which is used to test for nuclear, biological, and chemical contamination on the battlefield. (U.S. Department of Defense)

in their use. All this was possible because of the close coordination of the NBC defense organizations in Germany and the United States. There were liaison officers at both NBC schools, and on August 4 General Orton advised the liaison officer at Sondhofen that requests for assistance with the XM-93 were likely to come soon.

Eventually the Germans provided 60 of these vehicles. These were "Americanized" and also equipped with air conditioning for operation in the heat of the Persian Gulf. The German NBC School at Sondhofen also translated operating manuals and trained eight U.S. Army and Marine platoons. By the start of Operation DESERT STORM in January 1991, there were about 40 Fox vehicles in the theater, a number that increased to 61 by the end of hostilities in February. Crews trained specially for their operation manned the vehicles.

The XM-93 performed reasonably well, but the rapid deployment did lead to problems. Among these were a lack of a doctrine regarding its use; overestimation of its capabilities to detect chemical vapors while the vehicle moved faster than 5 mph; a lack of time to train operators fully and to test their performance before deployment; a Vehicle Orientation System that was not useful in off-road operations over long distances; problems with the sampling wheel in off-road conditions; and false alarms caused by diesel fuel, smoke from burning oil fields, and vehicle exhaust. A normal development and fielding program would have probably precluded these problems, and all were noted for further

development of the NBC Reconnaissance Vehicle, which in 1998 entered into service as the M-93A1 Fox.

The M-93A1, of which there are currently more than 120 in the U.S. military, corrected the deficiencies of the XM-93 that were identified in 1990 and 1991. It features updated, more automated chemical and radiological equipment that reduces the crew requirement to three. The M-21 remote sensing chemical alarm allows 180-degree rotation, and there is a monitor for the vehicle commander that provides either the screen from the MM-1 mass spectrometer or the M-21's aiming camera. A separate screen is provided to the crew member operating the MM-1 in the rear of the vehicle. There is a Global Positioning System (GPS) that more accurately locates the vehicle and allows precise marking of hazards. This, along with the communications system in the new vehicle, provides automatic production and broadcast of NBC warning reports. The M-93A1 is manufactured in both the United States, by General Dynamics, and Germany, by Thyssen Henschel. Other North Atlantic Treaty Organization (NATO) countries, as well as several nations in the Middle East, have acquired the M-93A1. Research is ongoing to add a credible biological weapons detection capability.

DANIEL E. SPECTOR

See also
Biological Weapons and Warfare; Chemical Weapons and Warfare; Weapons of Mass Destruction

References

Cordesman, Anthony H., and Abraham R. Wagner. *The Lessons of Modern War*, Vol. 4, *The Gulf War*. Boulder, CO: Westview, 1996.

Hogg, Ian V. *The Greenhill Armoured Fighting Vehicles Data Book.* London: Greenhill Books, 2002.

Spector, Daniel E. *U.S. Army Chemical School Annual Historical Review: 1 January through 31 December 1990*. Fort McClellan, AL: U.S. Army Chemical School, 1991.

———. *U.S. Army Chemical School Annual Historical Review: 1 January through 31 December 1991*. Fort McClellan, AL: U.S. Army Chemical School, 1992.

———. *U.S. Army Chemical School Annual Historical Review: 1 January through 31 December 1992*. Fort McClellan, AL: U.S. Army Chemical School, 1993.

Funk, Paul Edward
Birth Date: March 10, 1940

U.S. Army officer. Paul Edward Funk was born in Roundup, Montana, on March 10, 1940, and graduated from Roundup High School in 1957. Interested in ranching, he entered Montana State University, where he joined the Reserve Officers' Training Corps (ROTC). In 1961 he earned a bachelor's degree in animal husbandry with ambitions of becoming a veterinarian but was also commissioned a second lieutenant in the U.S. Army. After completing Army Officers' Basic Training, the Armor Advanced Training School, and Helicopter Flight School, Funk saw combat during the Vietnam War. He then returned to Montana State University, where he earned a master's degree in psychological counseling in 1972 and a doctorate in education in 1973.

As a commander, Funk always looked for ways to improve his troops' performance. Convinced that rigorous training was the key to battlefield success, he designed a training program that ensured his troops were among the army's most prepared. Funk held a variety of posts both in the United States and abroad. He was promoted to brigadier general in 1987 and to major general in 1990.

In 1990–1991, when President George H. W. Bush decided to drive Iraqi occupation forces from Kuwait, Major General Funk was ordered to Saudi Arabia to prepare for a likely invasion of Iraq and Kuwait. His 3rd Armored Division of 22,553 men was then the most powerful armored division in U.S. history. As commanding officer of the division, Funk immediately began training his troops when they arrived in Saudi Arabia. Funk's division was assigned to VII Corps, commanded by Lieutenant General Frederick Franks. VII Corps' mission was to destroy the Iraqi Republican Guard's mechanized forces.

On February 24, 1991, the first day of the ground war of Operation DESERT STORM, the 3rd Armored Division encountered only light resistance. Late in the afternoon of the second day, however, Funk's troops engaged the Tawakalna Division of the Republican Guard. During the next 48 hours the fighting was fierce, with weather deteriorating and sand storms packing 60-mile-per-hour winds. As such, ground forces had to accomplish the mission without air support. After two nights of intense mounted combat, the Iraqi commanders surrendered. The 100-hour-war ended on February 28, 1991. Funk's "Spearhead Division," as it was known, inflicted massive equipment and personnel losses on three Iraqi divisions, while sustaining only minimal equipment losses and personnel losses itself. The 3rd Division had only seven men killed in the fighting.

After the war, Funk was reassigned to Washington, D.C., where he worked with the Joint Chiefs of Staff (JCS). He was promoted to lieutenant general in 1993 and retired from military service at that rank on January 1, 1996.

Funk now breeds Herford cattle at his Spearhead Ranch near Fort Hood, Texas, and works at the Institute for Advanced Technology of the University of Texas at Austin. He has been active as a television consultant and military affairs analyst and a speaker at veterans' events.

RANDY TAYLOR

See also

DESERT STORM, Operation; DESERT STORM, Operation, Ground Operations; Franks, Frederick Melvin, Jr.; Republican Guard

References

Bourque, Stephen A. *Jayhawk! The VII Corps in the Persian Gulf War.* Washington, DC: Department of the Army, 2002.

Hallion, Richard P. *Storm over Iraq: Air Power and the Gulf War.* Washington, DC: Smithsonian Institution Press, 1997.

Hiro, Dilip. *Iraq: in the Eye of the Storm.* New York: Thunder's Mouth Press/Nation Books, 2002.

Huchthausen, Peter A. *America's Splendid Little Wars: A Short History of U.S. Military Engagements, 1975–2000.* New York: Viking, 2003.

Yetiv, Steven A. *The Persian Gulf Crisis.* Westport, CT: Greenwood, 1997.

G

Gadahn, Adam Yahya
Birth Date: September 1, 1978

American indicted in October 2006 by a U.S. federal court for treason, providing material support to the Al Qaeda terrorist organization, and aiding and abetting terrorists because of his ties to Al Qaeda. It is alleged that Gadahn worked as a translator and a media adviser for Al Qaeda, possibly attended an Al Qaeda training camp, and acted as a spokesman for the organization.

Adam Yahya Gadahn (also known as or referred to as Abu Suhayb al-Amriki, Abu Suhayl al-Amriki, Abu Suhayb, and Azzam al-Amriki [meaning Azzam the American]) was born Adam Pearlman in Oregon on September 1, 1978. His father, born Jewish, had become a Christian before his son's birth and changed his last name to Gadahn. Adam spent his early life on a goat farm in rural Winchester, California. Home-schooled by his parents, he moved in with his grandparents as an adolescent in Santa Ana, California, and became a Muslim during a period of involvement with the Islamic Society of Orange County. In the late 1990s he left the United States for Pakistan, maintaining intermittent contact with his family until 2001.

By early 2004 Gadahn was wanted by the Federal Bureau of Investigation (FBI) for questioning. He appeared in his first Al Qaeda video that October. He is believed to have remained in Pakistan until at least 2008.

The 2006 indictment in *U.S. v. Gadahn* cites excerpts from Gadahn's videos as evidence of his crimes, including his declaration of membership in Al Qaeda, which he describes as "a movement waging war on America and killing large numbers of Americans," on October 27, 2004; his warning of attacks on Los Angeles and Melbourne, on September 11, 2005; his admonition

to Muslims on July 7, 2006, that they should not "shed" any "tears" over attacks on Western targets; his lament on September 2, 2006, about the state of America's "war machine"; and his reflection on September 11, 2006, about the September 11, 2001, terror attacks, in which he refers to the U.S. as "enemy soil." After the indictment, Gadahn continued to appear in more videos. On May 29, 2007, he referenced the shooting massacre at Virginia Tech, which occurred on April 16, 2007, and intimated that Al Qaeda had even grislier plans. On January 7, 2008, he urged attacks on President George W. Bush during the president's visit to the Middle East.

In early 2008 Internet rumors began to circulate that Gadahn had died in the Central Intelligence Agency (CIA) Predator strike that killed Abu Laith al-Libi. The FBI was unable to confirm or deny these reports, and intensified its efforts to gather intelligence on Gadahn's whereabouts. Suspicions of Gadahn's death were reinvigorated in September 2008, when he failed to release a video marking the anniversary of 9/11; however, in early October Gadahn appeared in a message focusing on the U.S. relationship with Pakistan and the American economic crisis.

Gadahn's primary service to Al Qaeda has been as a propagandist, whether by conveying Al Qaeda's official messages in English; providing Arabic-to-English translations for others' messages, including perhaps those of Al Qaeda leader Osama bin Laden; or by capitalizing on his status as an American convert to their cause. He remains high on the FBI's list of Most Wanted Terrorists. Gadahn is the first American to be charged with treason since World War II, and he remains the only person currently charged with this capital crime. Even John Walker Lindh, an American captured in Afghanistan during the 2001 invasion of that nation, was charged with less serious crimes.

Despite the gravity of the charges against Gadahn, most observers contend that they are largely symbolic, citing significant obstacles to capturing and prosecuting him. Although Gadahn has not been implicated in any violence against Americans, his actions underscore the importance of media in the Global War on Terror, and the difficulty in controlling it.

REBECCA A. ADELMAN

See also

Al Qaeda; Bin Laden, Osama; Global War on Terror; Terrorism

References

Greenberg, Karen J., ed. *Al Qaeda Now: Understanding Today's Terrorists.* Cambridge: Cambridge University Press, 2005.

Stern, Jessica. "Al Qaeda, American Style." *New York Times,* July 15, 2006, A:15.

Galloway, Joseph Lee
Birth Date: November 13, 1941

Newspaper correspondent and writer. Joseph Lee Galloway was born on November 13, 1941, in Refugio, Texas. He became a newspaper reporter at age 17 and within two years was a bureau chief for United Press International (UPI), in the Kansas City office. In early 1965, as U.S. involvement in Vietnam intensified, Galloway undertook the first of his three tours as a war correspondent for UPI in Vietnam.

In September 1965 the 1st Cavalry Division departed Fort Benning, Georgia, for its base camp at An Khe in the Central Highlands of the Republic of Vietnam (RVN, South Vietnam). In late October, a large People's Army of Vietnam (PAVN, North Vietnamese Army) force attacked the Plei Me Special Forces Camp, and U.S. forces then began an effort to locate and destroy the PAVN forces. On November 14 Lieutenant Colonel Harold G. Moore and the lead elements of the 1st Battalion, 7th Cavalry Regiment (Airmobile), were airlifted by helicopters into the Ia Drang Valley, initiating the first major battle of the Vietnam War between the U.S. Army and PAVN forces. Soon after Moore's troopers arrived at Landing Zone (LZ) X-Ray, they were surrounded by 2,000 PAVN regulars. Another 2,000 awaited other U.S. troops as they arrived later.

From November 14 to 18, U.S. forces at LZ X-Ray and later LZ Alpha, supported by air strikes, managed to hold their positions. On the evening of November 14, Galloway joined the engagement, intending to gather information for a newspaper article. He soon found himself aiding wounded American soldiers while under heavy fire and, with a borrowed M-16, returning fire at PAVN troops attempting to overrun the position. After suffering heavy casualties, the PAVN eventually broke off the attack. In the aftermath of the battle, the surviving Americans withdrew from the area. While Moore considered the battle a draw, since the enemy ultimately reoccupied the Valley, General William Westmoreland, commander of Military Assistance Command, Vietnam (MACV),

hailed it as a victory. Many believe that this battle set the pattern for U.S. ground operations during most of the war.

Galloway spent more than 40 years as a foreign correspondent and bureau chief for UPI, and as senior editor and writer for *U.S. News & World Report.* His reports from Vietnam were invariably accurate, highly informed, and unbiased. Besides his tours in Vietnam, Galloway spent time overseas in Japan, Indonesia, India, Singapore, and the Soviet Union.

In 1990–1991 Galloway covered the Persian Gulf War, accompanying the 24th Infantry Division during its famous end-run around Iraqi defenses. Allied commander General H. Norman Schwarzkopf called Galloway "the finest combat correspondent of our generation—a soldier's reporter and a soldier's friend." *Vietnam* magazine once called Galloway "the Ernie Pyle of the Vietnam War," a reference to the legendary World War II war reporter and relentless champion of the American G.I.

In 1992 Galloway and Lieutenant General Harold G. Moore coauthored the best-selling book *We Were Soldiers Once . . . And Young* about their experiences in the Ia Drang Valley in 1965. In 2002 the book was made into a popular film with Barry Pepper playing Galloway and Mel Gibson portraying Moore. Both the book and film received critical acclaim. The coauthors recently collaborated again on the 2008 sequel, *We Are Soldiers Still: A Journey Back to the Battlefields of Vietnam.*

On May 1, 1998, Galloway received the Bronze Star Medal with the Valor Device for his actions at Ia Drang. He is the only civilian to receive such a medal for the Vietnam War. Shortly thereafter, Vietnam Veterans Memorial Fund (VVMF) members created the Joseph L. Galloway Award, which is presented to war correspondents serving with U.S. troops overseas. In the autumn of 2002 Galloway joined Knight Ridder as its senior military correspondent, working in the organization's Washington bureau. During this time he also served as a special consultant to Secretary of State Colin L. Powell. More recently, Galloway was an outspoken critic of President George W. Bush and his Iraq War policies, including a caustic commentary titled "When Will It End?" published on March 13, 2008. Perhaps more significantly, Galloway was an unrelenting critic of Secretary of Defense Donald Rumsfeld and his management of the wars in Iraq and Afghanistan. He was especially critical of what he regarded as Rumsfeld's general lack of concern for the needs and welfare of the troops sent to fight those wars; Rumsfeld's theories of war fighting that initially condemned U.S. forces to fight without adequate equipment; and the shoddy and disgraceful health care provided to wounded veterans. As one of the very few American journalists with a widely respected command of the details of military matters, as well as the tremendous respect of the U.S. military itself, Galloway is far more difficult to dismiss than most other critics of the Bush administration.

WILLIAM P. HEAD

See also

Bush, George Walker; Media and Operation DESERT STORM; Schwarzkopf, H. Norman, Jr.; War Correspondents

References

Galloway, Joe. "A Reporter's Journal From Hell." In *The Greatest U.S. Army Stories Ever Told: Unforgettable Tales of Courage, Honor and Sacrifice,* edited by Ian C. Martin, 215–222. Guilford, CT: Lyons, 2006.

Moore, Harold G., and Joseph L. Galloway. *We Were Soldiers Once . . . and Young: Ia Drang, the Battle That Changed the War in Vietnam.* New York: Random House, 1992.

Garner, Jay Montgomery
Birth Date: April 15, 1938

U.S. Army general who, after retirement from active duty, in 2003 served as the first civilian director of the Office for Reconstruction and Humanitarian Assistance (ORHA) for Iraq. Jay Montgomery Garner was born on April 15, 1938, in Arcadia, Florida. After service in the U.S. Marine Corps, he earned a degree in history from Florida State University and secured a commission in the army. He later earned a master's degree from Shippensburg University in Pennsylvania.

Garner rose steadily through the ranks, holding a series of commands in the United States and in Germany and rising to major general by the time of the Persian Gulf War (Operation DESERT STORM) in 1991. Garner helped develop the Patriot antimissile system and oversaw the deployment of Patriot batteries in Saudi Arabia and Israel during the Persian Gulf War. Garner subsequently managed efforts to improve the Patriot systems and to finalize and deploy the joint U.S.-Israeli Arrow theater antiballistic missile systems. He also worked with Israel, Kuwait, and Saudi Arabia on the sale of the Patriot system. Garner next commanded Operation PROVIDE COMFORT, the coalition effort to provide humanitarian assistance to Kurds in northern Iraq. He directed international forces that included U.S., British, French, and Italian troops in the delivery of food, medicine, and other supplies, and in efforts to prevent reprisals by Iraqi government forces. Garner was subsequently named to command the U.S. Space and Strategic Defense Command.

Garner retired in 1997 as a lieutenant general and assistant vice chief of staff of the army. In September 1997 he was named president of SY Technology, a defense contractor, and he served on a variety of advisory boards on security issues, including the Commission to Assess United States National Security Space Management and Organization.

In March 2003 Garner was named head of ORHA for the Coalition Provisional Authority of Iraq, to coincide with Operation IRAQI FREEDOM and the allied postwar occupation. In this post, Garner was the senior civilian official during the initial period after the overthrow of Saddam Hussein in April 2003. He reported directly to the U.S. military commander in Iraq, General Tommy Franks. Garner's previous service in the region and work during Operation PROVIDE COMFORT made him an attractive candidate for the position,

Former U.S. Army general Jay Garner, who was named by U.S. president George W. Bush director of the Office of Reconstruction and Humanitarian Assistance in Iraq following the overthrow of Saddam Hussein. (U.S. Department of Defense)

and the George W. Bush administration hoped that he would be able to integrate civilian and military occupation efforts in Iraq.

Garner's occupation strategy emphasized a quick turnover of appropriate authority to the Iraqis and a withdrawal of U.S. and coalition forces to protected bases outside of major urban areas. He also advocated early elections to create an interim Iraqi government with widespread popular legitimacy. Senior defense officials opposed his plans, however, and argued that too rapid a withdrawal of coalition forces would create a power vacuum and might lead to increased sectarian strife. U.S. officials also sought to ensure that former political and military officials linked to Saddam's Baath Party would be purged from their positions (a policy known as de-Baathification). Meanwhile, Garner's status as a former general and his close ties to Secretary of Defense Donald Rumsfeld undermined his ability to work with nongovernmental organizations and non-U.S. officials. Both groups saw him as an indication that the United States was not committed to democratic reform in Iraq.

Garner was confronted with a range of challenges. There was a growing insurgency being waged by Saddam loyalists and foreign fighters, and the country's infrastructure was in worse condition than anticipated as a result of the international sanctions of the 1990s, coalition military action, and a scorched-earth policy carried out by the former regime to deny assets to the invading forces. As a result, Garner was unable to restore basic services in a timely manner.

After initially dismissing the nation's security forces, Garner recalled policemen and initiated a new recruitment and screening process to expedite both the return of former police officers without close ties to the regime and the hiring of new officers. This was part of a broader effort to counter growing lawlessness in major cities, such as Baghdad. Garner also made the initial Iraqi appointments to various ministries as part of the foundation of a transitional government.

Garner was critical of the failure of the United Nations (UN) to immediately end sanctions on Iraq, and he called for the world body to act quickly to facilitate economic redevelopment and the rebuilding of the country's oil-producing infrastructure. Nevertheless, the blunt and plainspoken Garner faced increasing criticism for the deteriorating conditions in Iraq. He was replaced on May 11, 2003, by career diplomat L. Paul Bremer, who reported directly to Rumsfeld instead of to the coalition's military commander. Most members of Garner's senior staff were also replaced. Garner returned to the United States to work in the defense industry. He has remained largely silent on his short and tumultuous tenure in Iraq.

TOM LANSFORD

See also

Bremer, Jerry; Iraq, History of, 1990–Present; IRAQI FREEDOM, Operation; Patriot Missile System; PROVIDE COMFORT, Operation; Rumsfeld, Donald Henry

References

Allawi, Ali A. *The Occupation of Iraq: Winning the War, Losing the Peace.* New Haven, CT: Yale University Press, 2007.

Bremer, L. Paul, with Malcolm McConnell. *My Year in Iraq: The Struggle to Build a Future of Hope.* New York: Simon and Schuster, 2006.

Garrison, William F.
Birth Date: June 27, 1944

U.S. army general and major figure in special operations who commanded Operation GOTHIC SERPENT in 1993, the failed effort to capture Somali warlord Mohammed Farrah Aidid (Aideed). William F. Garrison was born on June 27, 1944, in Palo Pinto County, Texas, and joined the U.S. Army as a private in 1966. He was selected for officer candidate school and received his commission the next year. His education includes a bachelor's degree from Pan-American University and an MBA from Sam Houston University. During two tours of duty in Vietnam, Garrison was wounded and decorated for valor.

The Vietnam War led Garrison to believe that the U.S. Army needed to develop its special operations capabilities more fully. He spent the majority of his career in special operations forces and was regarded as an innovative tactician and strong advocate for unconventional forces. Garrison rose steadily through the ranks, and upon promotion he became one of the youngest army officers to be promoted to colonel, brigadier general, and major general. He held posts in army intelligence and in the 1st Special Forces Operational Detachment–Delta (Delta Force).

Garrison had correctly foreseen that the army needed to transition from its reliance on heavy, conventional forces and weapons systems to a leaner, more mobile fighting force that could adapt to different missions around the globe. Garrison sought to better integrate the rapid advancements in communications and technology into unconventional tactics. He also urged greater integration and collaboration between the special operations forces of the different services.

In 1992 U.S. forces led an international peacekeeping mission in Somalia dubbed RESTORE HOPE, which had as its goals the ending of a bitter civil war and amelioration of the attendant humanitarian crisis. Fighting between warlords in the capital of Mogadishu had prevented repeated efforts to end the conflict. In June 1993 an ambush killed 24 Pakistani peacekeepers; in response the United Nations (UN) Security Council passed Resolution 837, which called for the capture of Somali warlord Mohammed Farrah Aidid (Aideed) and others held responsible for the brutal attack.

International efforts were now directed at apprehending warlord Aidid and his senior aides. In August 1993 Garrison was placed in command of a task force, code-named Operation GOTHIC SERPENT, that included army rangers, members of Delta Force, and other special operations forces. The general's main mission was to conduct operations to suppress the warlords and capture Aidid. When intelligence indicated that a major meeting of senior Aidid supporters was about to take place in Mogadishu, Garrison ordered a task force into the city on October 3.

The strike was a coordinated attack that included the insertion of a Delta Force unit to capture the warlords, supported by helicopters and rangers who were to create a perimeter around the target site. Meanwhile, a motorized ranger column was to travel through Mogadishu and extract the prisoners being held by Aidid's men and the U.S. forces. The American forces included 160 men, 16 helicopters, 3 aircraft, and 12 mechanized vehicles. Garrison wanted to ensure the element of surprise and believed that a small, mobile force would be able to move quickly through the streets and achieve its objectives. Consequently, he did not seek to involve the slower, heavily armored units of other UN forces in the area. Meanwhile, officials in President Bill Clinton's administration, who sought to avoid the perception of escalating the conflict, denied Garrison's requests for infantry fighting vehicles and aerial gunships.

The operation initially went off as planned, including the capture of several senior aides to Aidid; however, Somali clan fighters quickly surrounded American forces and engaged them. The Somalis shot down first one, and then another, U.S. helicopter with shoulder-launched rocket-propelled grenades. The task force became bogged down by efforts to reach and rescue the crews of the downed helicopters, and several pockets of U.S. forces were cut off from each other. Eventually, a relief column that included UN troops and the U.S. 10th Mountain Division was assembled to extract the remnants of Task Force Ranger.

Garrison oversaw the conduct of the engagement from his base on the outskirts of the city. The so-called Battle of Mogadishu resulted in 19 U.S. dead, 73 wounded, and 1 captured. Televised footage of U.S. dead being dragged through the streets of Mogadishu created substantial domestic pressure in the United States for an end to the U.S. presence in Somalia. All U.S. forces were withdrawn by 1995.

After Operation GOTHIC SERPENT, Garrison was appointed commander of the John F. Kennedy Special Warfare Center at Fort Bragg, North Carolina. On August 3, 1996, the day after Aidid was killed in Somalia, Garrison retired from the army as a major general. He has since been involved in private business ventures and lecturing.

TOM LANSFORD

See also

Aidid, Mohammed Farrah; Delta Force; Somalia, International Intervention in; United States; United States Special Operations Command

References

Bowden, Mark. *Black Hawk Down: A Story of Modern War.* 1st ed. New York: Atlantic Monthly Press, 1999.

Stewart, Richard W. *The United States Army in Somalia, 1992–1994.* Fort Lesley J. McNair: U.S. Army Center for Military History, 2003.

Gates, Robert Michael
Birth Date: September 25, 1943

U.S. Air Force officer, president of Texas A&M University, director of the Central Intelligence Agency (CIA), and secretary of defense from 2006. Robert Michael Gates was born in Wichita, Kansas, on September 25, 1943. He graduated in 1965 from the College of William and Mary with a bachelor's degree in history, then earned a master's degree in history from Indiana University in 1966, and a PhD in Russian and Soviet history from Georgetown University in 1974.

Gates served as an officer in the U.S. Air Force's Strategic Air Command (1967–1969) before joining the CIA in 1969 as an intelligence analyst, a post he held until 1974. He was on the staff of the National Security Council (NSC) from 1974 to 1979, before returning to the CIA as director of the Strategic Evaluation Center in 1979. Gates rose through the ranks to become the director of central intelligence (DCI)/deputy director of central intelligence (DDCI) Executive Staff (1981), deputy director for intelligence (DDI) (1982), and deputy director of Central Intelligence (1986–1989).

Nominated to become director of the CIA in 1987, he withdrew his nomination when it appeared that his connection with the Iran Contra Affair might hamper his Senate confirmation. He then served as deputy assistant to the president for National Security Affairs (March–August 1989) and as assistant to the president and deputy national security adviser from August 1989 to November 1991.

The Iran Contra Affair erupted in 1987 when it was revealed that members of President Ronald Reagan's administration had sold weapons to Iran and illegally diverted the funds to the Nicaraguan Contras, the rightist anti-Sandinista rebels. Gates's political enemies assumed that he was guilty because of his senior status at the CIA, but an exhaustive investigation by an independent counsel determined that Gates had done nothing illegal, and on September 3, 1991, the investigating committee stated that Gates's involvement in the scandal did not warrant prosecution. The independent counsel's final 1993 report came to the same conclusion. In May 1991 President George H. W. Bush renominated Gates to head the CIA, and the Senate confirmed Gates on November 5, 1991.

Gates retired from the CIA in 1993 and entered academia. He also served as a member of the Board of Visitors of the University of Oklahoma International Programs Center, and as an endowment fund trustee for William and Mary. In 1999 he became the interim dean of the George Bush School of Government and Public Service at Texas A&M University, and in 2002 he became president of Texas A&M University, a post he held until 2006.

Former Central Intelligence Agency (CIA) director Robert Gates replaced the controversial Donald Rumsfeld as U.S. secretary of defense in 2006. New president Barack Obama continued Gates in the post. (U.S. Department of Defense)

U.S. Secretaries of Defense, 1989–Present

Name	Dates of Service
Dick Cheney	March 21, 1989–January 20, 1993
Les Aspin	January 21, 1993–February 3, 1994
William Perry	February 3, 1994–January 24, 1997
William Cohen	January 24, 1997–January 20, 2001
Donald Rumsfeld	January 20, 2001–December 18, 2006
Robert Gates	December 18, 2006–present

Gates remained active in public service during his presidency, cochairing in January 2004 a Council on Foreign Relations task force on U.S.-Iran relations, which suggested that the United States engage Iran diplomatically concerning that nation's pursuit of nuclear weapons. Gates was a member of the Iraq Study Group (also known as the Baker-Hamilton Commission; March 15, 2006–December 6, 2006), a bipartisan commission charged with studying the Iraq War, when he was nominated to succeed the controversial and discredited Donald Rumsfeld as defense secretary. Gates assumed the post on December 18, 2006.

In addition to the challenges of the Iraq War, Gates was faced in February 2007 with a scandal concerning inadequate and neglectful care of returning veterans by Walter Reed Army Medical Center. In response, he removed both Secretary of the Army Francis J. Harvey and Army Surgeon General Kevin C. Kiley from their posts. Gates further tightened his control of the Pentagon when he did not recommend the renomination of U.S. Marine Corps general Peter Pace as chairman of the Joint Chiefs of Staff (JCS) that June. Pace would have certainly faced tough questioning by Congress. It was also Gates's job to implement the so-called troop surge initiated by Bush in January 2007.

In March 2008 Gates accepted the resignation of Admiral William Joseph "Fox" Fallon, commander of the U.S. Central Command (CENTCOM), a departure that was due in part to the controversy surrounding an article by Thomas P. M. Barnett titled "The Man between War and Peace," published in *Esquire* magazine on March 11, 2008. The article asserted policy disagreements between Fallon and the Bush administration on the prosecution of the war in Iraq and potential conflict with Iran over that nation's nuclear arms program. Gates rejected any suggestion that Fallon's resignation indicated a U.S. willingness to attack Iran in order to stop its nuclear weapons development.

Unlike his abrasive predecessor, Gates has brought an era of calm and focus to the Pentagon and has appeared far more willing to engage in discussion and compromise over matters of defense and military policy. In April 2009 Gates proposed a major reorientation in the U.S. defense budget, which would entail deep cuts in more traditional programs that provide for conventional warfare with such major military powers as Russia and China, and shift assets to those programs that would aid in fighting the insurgencies in both Iraq and Afghanistan. Among his proposed cuts were missile defense, the army's Future Combat Systems, navy shipbuilding, new presidential helicopters, and a new communications satellite system. Gates would delay development of a new air force bomber and order only 4 additional F-22 fighters for a total of 197, while purchasing as many as 513 of the less expensive F-35 strike fighters over the next five years. Purchases of large navy ships would be delayed. At the same time, the new budget would provide for a sharp increase in funding for surveillance and intelligence-gathering equipment, to include the Predator-class unmanned aerial vehicles, and increase manpower in the army to include special forces and the Marine Corps. These decisions triggered major debate in Congress over defense spending and priorities. In December 2009 Gates was the first senior U.S. official to visit Afghanistan after President Barack Obama announced his intention to deploy 30,000 additional military personnel to that country.

RICHARD M. EDWARDS

See also

Bush, George Herbert Walker; Bush, George Walker; Central Intelligence Agency; Fallon, William Joseph; Iran-Contra Affair; Iraq Study Group; IRAQI FREEDOM, Operation; Iraqi Insurgency; National Security Council; Pace, Peter; Reagan, Ronald Wilson; Rumsfeld, Donald Henry

References

Barnett, Thomas P. M. "The Man between War and Peace." *Esquire,* March 11, 2008, 1–4.

Gates, Robert M. *From the Shadows: The Ultimate Insider's Story of Five Presidents and How They Won the Cold War.* New York: Simon and Schuster, 1996.

Gates, Robert M. *Understanding the New U.S. Defense Policy through the Speeches of Robert M. Gates, Secretary of Defense.* Rockville, MD: Arc Manor, 2008.

Oliphant, Thomas. *Utter Incompetents: Ego and Ideology in the Age of Bush.* New York: Thomas Dunne Books, 2007.

Georgia, Role in Iraq War

Nation located in Transcaucasia and a Soviet republic until 1991. Encompassing 26,911 square miles, Georgia borders Russia to the north; Azerbaijan to the east; Armenia and Turkey to the south; and the Black Sea to the west. Its 2008 population was estimated at 4.631 million people. Georgia's transition to independence and freedom was fraught with violence, beginning with a Soviet crackdown against independence protestors in April 1989 that resulted in 20 deaths and hundreds of injured. Tensions between Georgians and Abkhazians and South Ossetians, two autonomous non-Georgian ethnic groups within greater Georgia, resulted in a brief but violent civil war from December 1991 to July 1992 in which hundreds died.

Georgia is a representative democracy with a unitary, semi-presidential government. The president is head of state, and the prime minister is head of government. The president holds the preponderance of executive power. In recent years, Georgia's political landscape has been dominated by the United National

Movement, a center-right party that is pro-Western and nationalist in outlook. The Rightist Opposition coalition is the other major political force. It strongly supports pro-business elements in Georgia, and favors low taxes and reduced regulation of industry, as well as increased defense spending.

Georgia provided one of the largest military contributions to the U.S.-led Operation IRAQI FREEDOM. Georgia's military deployment was undertaken as part of a broader effort to improve relations with the United States to offset Russian influence in the Caucasus region. The Georgian government also hoped that involvement in Iraq would bolster its chances for membership in the North Atlantic Treaty Organization (NATO).

Beginning in 2002 Georgia engaged in a broad, multiyear effort to reform and modernize its military. The United States provided $64 million in military aid and dispatched approximately 200 advisers to assist the Georgians through the Georgia Train and Equip Program (GTEP). The U.S. assistance was part of the broader Global War on Terror and was initially designed to enhance the counterterrorism capabilities of the Georgian military through training and advanced equipment for four battalions. GTEP ended in 2004, but a follow-up initiative, the Georgia Sustainment and Stability Operations Program, continued until 2007 and provided U.S. training and assistance for units preparing to deploy to Iraq.

Georgia strongly supported the U.S.-led invasion of Iraq and deployed troops to the country in August 2003. Georgia's initial deployment grew to about 800 troops and then peaked at 2,300 soldiers in mid-2008. In addition to participation in Operation IRAQI FREEDOM, from 2005 to 2008 Georgia also contributed a battalion of approximately 550 troops to the United Nations Assistance Mission in Iraq (UNAMI). At first, the Georgians deployed for Operation IRAQI FREEDOM were stationed in Baghdad and undertook general security missions; however, beginning in 2007, Georgian forces were deployed along the border with Iran and tasked to interdict smuggled weapons, goods, and narcotics. The battalion assigned to UNAMI remained stationed in Baghdad within the "Green Zone." Georgian units worked primarily within the U.S. area of operations.

Georgian troops served six-month deployments; service in Iraq was voluntary. More than 6,000 Georgian troops served in Iraq. Unlike the domestic constraints faced by other members of the coalition, the Georgian government's decisions to participate in IRAQI FREEDOM generally enjoyed public support. Georgia had long sought NATO membership, and in a 2008 referendum, 77 percent of Georgians voted in favor of NATO accession. Although the United States endorsed Georgia's NATO bid, other members of the alliance blocked the effort at the April 2008 Bucharest Summit. Instead, NATO issued a pledge that Georgia would eventually be able to join the alliance.

In August 2008, when fighting between Georgian troops and separatists in South Ossetia escalated, Georgia announced that it would redeploy 1,000 of its troops back to Georgia. When Russia then intervened in the fighting and invaded Georgia, the remaining forces were recalled, and Georgia ended its mission in Iraq.

The United States provided logistical support for the withdrawal, drawing a sharp protest from Russia. However, the United States did not take stronger action against the Russian move, to the disappointment of the Georgian government. Five Georgian soldiers were killed during the nation's involvement in Iraq.

TOM LANSFORD

See also
IRAQI FREEDOM, Operation, Coalition Ground Forces; Multi-National Force–Iraq

References
Cockburn, Patrick. *The Occupation: War and Resistance in Iraq.* New York: Verso, 2007.

Keegan, John. *The Iraq War: The Military Offensive, from Victory in 21 Days to the Insurgent Aftermath.* New York: Vintage, 2005.

Germany, Federal Republic of, Middle East Policy

Three major factors determined the Middle East policies of the Federal Republic of Germany (FRG, West Germany) from its foundation in 1949 until German reunification in 1990. The first factor, one that led to what has often been called West Germany's special relationship with the State of Israel, was *Schuldgefühl*, or the sense of culpability for the destruction of Jewish life and property before and during World War II. During 1949–1950, the newly established West German government, under pressure from Israel and Western allies, held itself morally responsible for the crimes of the Third Reich and therefore obligated to provide financial and material restitution to Israel.

The second factor lay in West Germany's solid placement in the Western sphere of influence during the Cold War, an alliance reinforced when the West German government received full sovereignty in 1955 and joined the North Atlantic Treaty Organization (NATO). In seeking to maintain amicable relations with the Arab states, thereby blocking the growth of Soviet influence in the area, West Germany's Middle East policy by and large reflected that of the Western allies and, from the 1970s onward, that of the European Economic Community (EEC), or the European Union (EU), as it was renamed in 1993. Since the end of the Cold War, however, the focus has shifted to preventing the spread of regional conflict, international terrorism, and an exacerbation of refugee crises.

The third factor lay in West Germany's rapid development as a major industrial nation, which made it increasingly dependent on Middle Eastern oil resources and eager to maintain bilateral trade. West German policy thus had to tread a fine line to fulfill its moral obligations to Israel without compromising relations with Arab oil producers.

Although a controversial move in Israel, in September 1951, with the new state in economic crisis, Israeli officials approached the West German government for reparations payments. Eager to mark a decisive break with the Nazi past, West German chancellor

West German chancellor Konrad Adenauer and Israeli prime minister Moshe Sharett sign the Luxembourg Reparations Agreement of 1952. The Bonn government agreed to provide Israel 3 billion German marks in commodities and services over a 12-year period. (AP/Wide World Photos)

Konrad Adenauer saw in such reparations a chance to rehabilitate the international image of the new Germany. Negotiations led to the signing of the Luxembourg Reparations Agreement in September 1952 and its ratification in March 1953. West Germany thereby promised to pay the State of Israel 3 billion German marks (DM) in commodities and services over the next 12 years. Israel agreed to place orders with West German firms, which in turn would receive direct payment from the West German government. A provision allowed for about one-third of the payments to be made to British oil companies for shipments to Israel. Israel also promised to distribute about 450 million DM to the Conference on Jewish Material Claims against Germany, a body that represented almost two dozen Jewish organizations with headquarters outside Israel.

German technological assistance also strengthened the faltering Israeli economy. Five power plants quadrupled Israel's generating capacity from 1953 to 1956. Other assistance included oil supplements, installations of industrial plants, railroad tracks and cars, improved telegraph and telephone communications, irrigation pipelines for the Negev desert project, and more than 60 ships.

The subsequent decade proved, however, the difficulty of maintaining good relations with both Israel and the Arab states. In 1955 moves to establish diplomatic relations between West Germany and Israel prompted Egyptian president Gamal Abdel

Nasser to threaten to recognize East Germany. According to the West German Hallstein Doctrine, which was in effect from 1955 to 1969, West Germany claimed the exclusive right to represent the German nation. The West German government was also obligated to break off diplomatic relations with any state that recognized East Germany. Fear of antagonizing the Arab world and spurring the growth of Soviet influence in the Middle East forced West Germany to back down and delay recognition of Israel.

Other problems ensued when the United Nations (UN), the United States, and several Arab countries asked West Germany to withhold payments under the Luxembourg Agreement during Israel's advance on the Suez Canal in the Sinai Campaign of 1956. This time West Germany refused, holding fast to the initial treaty. Nevertheless, tension with Israel erupted with the disclosure that a number of scientists at a Stuttgart institute were involved in developing missiles for Egypt. Although the West German cabinet dismissed the scientists, it was unwilling to intercede when a number of the researchers relocated to Cairo. The conflict ended only when most of the scientists, fearful for their safety or lured by more profitable contracts, returned to West Germany.

A crisis with Egypt came to a head when it was revealed in 1964 that West Germany had secretly been training Israeli troops and supplying weapons to Israel. Although the Bonn government, under public pressure, soon stopped the shipments, it now made good its delayed decision to recognize Israel. No sooner had West Germany and Israel exchanged ambassadors in 1965 than Algeria, Lebanon, Jordan, Syria, Saudi Arabia, Yemen, Iraq, Kuwait, Sudan, and Egypt severed diplomatic relations with Bonn.

In an attempt to mollify the Arab states at the end of 1965, Chancellor Ludwig Erhard promised neutrality in future Arab-Israeli disputes, a move reinforced by Chancellor Kurt Kiesinger's emphasis on the need for good relations with Arab countries during his inaugural address of 1966. Nevertheless, diplomatic ties with the Arab world were restored only after the new government of Chancellor Willy Brandt abandoned the Hallstein Doctrine after 1970 and adopted new foreign policies.

With West Germany's awareness of the Arab world's growing political and economic power in the 1970s, the Ostpolitik (Eastern Policy) launched by the government of Brandt sought to improve relations with the Arab nations and West European states. Thus, it announced that West German foreign policy would reflect that of the EEC. While stressing that West Germany would not forget its responsibilities to Israel in light of the Nazi past, Brandt emphasized that West Germany's Middle East policy would address the legitimate rights of all states, Arab and Israeli alike.

Consequently, West Germany supported the EEC's call for Israel to withdraw from areas it had occupied during the June 1967 Six-Day War. Declaring itself neutral during the October 1973 Yom Kippur (Ramadan) War, West Germany protested against the U.S. use of port facilities at Bremen to resupply Israel. These moves led to improved German-Arab relations, and by 1974 all the Arab states that had broken off diplomatic ties with West Germany in 1965 resumed relations with Bonn. Consequently, when the Organization of Petroleum Exporting Countries (OPEC) announced its oil embargo on October 17, 1973, West Germany faced only relatively light cutbacks of 5 percent per month.

Within five years, West Germany more than doubled its exports to Arab states, and an increasing flow of economic delegations and diplomatic visits ensued. Other indications of a shift in West Germany's Middle East policy occurred when Chancellor Helmut Schmidt publicly voiced criticism of Israel's settlement policy to Israeli premier Menachem Begin in June 1979. The following month, former chancellor Brandt and Austrian chancellor Bruno Kreisky met with Palestine Liberation Organization (PLO) leader Yasser Arafat. In June 1981 West German spokespersons expressed dismay at the Israeli bombing of Iraq's nuclear installations at Osiraq and a year later, upon Israel's invasion of Lebanon, joined other EEC members in short-term economic sanctions against Israel. Nevertheless, pressure from his cabinet and Israel forced Schmidt to abandon a tentative arms deal with Saudi Arabia in 1981.

Under Chancellor Helmut Kohl, who voiced a determination to improve German-Israeli relations, West German Middle East policy adopted a more subdued tone, even though unfortunate wording marred the chancellor's first visit to Israel in January 1984. He stated that as the first chancellor of the postwar generation, he enjoyed "the grace of late birth" and thus had not been involved in the crimes committed under the Third Reich. This faux pas laid him open to accusations that he was trying to escape responsibility for German actions between 1933 and 1945. Tensions rose again in 1987 when Israeli president Chaim Herzog expressed concern about West German weapons sales to Saudi Arabia. By and large, however, Middle Eastern policy during the mid- to late 1980s played a relatively minor role in West Germany's Foreign Office, overshadowed by relations with the crumbling Soviet bloc in Central and Eastern Europe.

Years earlier, in 1967, Iran had acquired a 5MWe nuclear reactor, intended for research, from the United States and established its Atomic Energy Foundation in 1975. In a pattern somewhat similar to German involvement in Egypt, a West German company, a subsidiary of Siemens, helped the Iranians in their endeavor to build a nuclear power plant at Bushehr. This plant was crippled and bombed in the Iran-Iraq war. Given the change in the Iranian regime, the United States pressured the Germans and others to cease involvement in reconstruction at Bushehr in 1991.

Reunified Germany had also faced a major international crisis with Iraq's August 1990 invasion of Kuwait and the subsequent wider Persian Gulf War early in 1991. Following the Iraqi seizure of several hundred hostages, many of whom were German, Chancellor Kohl's government came under intense public pressure to negotiate with Iraqi dictator Saddam Hussein, in spite of EEC resolutions to hold firm. Kohl therefore hesitantly backed Brandt's mission to Baghdad, which led to the release of 175 hostages from 11 countries on November 9, 1990, but Kohl also faced criticism for Germany's unilateral action.

The German government found itself in a further difficult position in the face of a U.S. request to contribute troops to a UN-backed effort to drive Iraq from Kuwait. The German *Grundgesetz* (Basic Law) precluded German military involvement, as it limited the Bundeswehr (German armed forces) to defensive actions within the traditional area covered by NATO. Furthermore, massive public antiwar demonstrations and parliamentary opposition impeded Kohl's efforts to amend the constitution.

Nevertheless, the German government voiced full support for alliance efforts and, in place of military participation, resorted to checkbook diplomacy, contributing the equivalent of about $7 billion to the American-led intervention. In addition, Germany extended to the United States full use of its territory for transport and resupply, contributed substantial amounts of military equipment, and deployed a minesweeping unit in the eastern Mediterranean. Also, Germany not only sent jet fighters and antiaircraft missile units to Turkey but also stationed more than 1,000 troops there to protect Turkish airfields.

In the wake of Hussein's threats of chemical warfare against Israel and the launching of Scud missile attacks on January 18, 1991, Germany reacted promptly, sending to Israel 250 million DM in humanitarian aid, Fox armored reconnaissance vehicles for antichemical warfare, and air defense missiles. This reaction was prompted, at least in part, by public exposure that German companies had earlier contributed to Iraq's store of missiles and chemical agents. After the end of the war, German minesweepers operated in the Persian Gulf from April through July 1991, and following the March 1991 Kurdish uprising, Bundeswehr personnel assisted in founding refugee camps in Iran and Iraq.

Germany's Middle East policy remained relatively passive for the remainder of Kohl's chancellorship, even though Germany was the first country to establish a diplomatic mission, temporarily in Jericho and later in Ramallah, in 1994 with the founding of the Palestinian National Authority (PNA), in the wake of the Madrid Peace Process (1991) and the Oslo Accords (1993). Germany soon became the most important European economic supporter of the PNA, contributing about 23 percent of EU total funding.

Another significant development during the Kohl administration paved the way for a stronger German military role in the Middle East and other parts of the world. On July 12, 1994, Germany's Federal Constitutional Court declared that German troops could participate in UN peacekeeping missions and out-of-area NATO or Western European Union (WEU) undertakings backed by the UN, provided that a majority vote in the Bundestag approved such actions.

Even though Kohl's successor, Chancellor Gerhard Schröder, stated in his inaugural address of 1998 that Germany's historical responsibilities to Israel and peace in the Middle East would best be furthered by economic aid, bilateral trade, and infrastructure measures, Germany now began to assume a more active diplomatic role. This was largely prompted by the escalation of Palestinian-Israeli conflict after the failure of the U.S.-led negotiations at the 2000 Camp David Summit. After a suicide attack on March 27, 2002, killed 29 people in Netanya, Israel, and Israel responded with a massive campaign against cities in the West Bank, German foreign minister Joschka Fischer presented a proposal titled "Ideas for Peace in the Middle East." In it he called for a roadmap laying out a timetable for Israelis and Palestinians to arrive at a two-state solution, overseen by a quartet consisting of the United States, the EU, the UN, and Russia. Fischer's proposal evolved into the Road Map to Peace presented on April 30, 2003, to Israeli prime minister Ariel Sharon and newly elected Palestinian prime minister Mahmoud Abbas.

Further signs of a more involved German role included Arafat's visit to Berlin in the spring of 2000 and Schröder's return visit in the fall of that year. Several months later, following a suicide bombing outside a Tel Aviv discotheque in June 2001, Fischer began a course of shuttle diplomacy, appealing to Arafat for a swift condemnation of the violence and urging Sharon against retaliation. The Second (al-Aqsa) Intifada of 2002, however, led to a significant cooling of relations with Israel when on April 9 Chancellor Schröder announced the suspension of arms sales, called for the early creation of a Palestinian state, and asked that Israel immediately withdraw from recently seized territory. Outspoken criticisms of Israel's role among German political figures, most notably from Jürgen Möllemann, deputy chairman of the Federal

German chancellor Gerhard Schröder, right, and Palestinian leader Yasser Arafat, left, on their way to a press conference after discussions regarding the Middle East peace process and bilateral relations in the Chancellery in Berlin, March 27, 2000. (AP/Wide World Photos)

Democratic Party, further exacerbated tensions with Israel and were only defused by Möllemann's forced resignation.

After the September 11, 2001, terrorist attacks on the United States, Germany's Middle East policy focused on international terrorism. Pledging unconditional political and military support for President George W. Bush's War on Terror, Schröder made an initial commitment of 3,900 German troops to Afghanistan. Less than a year later, however, the German government refused to commit troops to the U.S.-led coalition invasion of Iraq on the grounds that with 10,500 soldiers already serving in foreign countries (out of a total active force of 284,500), the Bundeswehr was spread thin. In addition, the Schröder government objected to the absence of a UN mandate, inconclusive evidence of weapons of mass destruction in Iraq, and the lack of a clear post-victory plan. Schröder was joined in his criticism of Operation IRAQI FREEDOM by France, perhaps Germany's closest ally. Schröder's refusal to join IRAQI FREEDOM cooled relations with Washington but aided his bid for reelection in the autumn of 2002. Nevertheless, since the coalition takeover of Iraq, Germany has conducted training programs for Iraqi military, police, security, technical, and medical personnel. In addition, Germany's financial contributions have included $652,000 for program funding and airlift of Iraqi personnel, $155 million to the coalition and UN/World Bank Trust Fund, and $8 million toward Iraqi elections.

With Chancellor Angela Merkel's grand coalition government taking office on November 22, 2005, German foreign policy has undergone a pronounced shift, particularly by way of strengthened ties with Washington and Israel. Soon after her inauguration and shortly after the Islamic militant party Hamas won the Palestinian parliamentary elections on January 26, 2006, Merkel paid a state visit to Israel and met with acting prime minister Ehud Olmert and with Abbas, now the Palestinian president. At the time Merkel took a tough stand, emphasizing that no negotiation with Hamas should occur unless the organization recognized Israel and renounced terrorism. She also stated that Iran had "crossed a red line" in its nuclear policy and constituted a threat to Israel and all democratic countries. Subsequently, Germany supported the EU decision to suspend direct aid to the PNA on April 10, 2006.

The 2006 Lebanese War prompted yet another major change in Germany's Middle East policy. On September 13 Merkel announced her cabinet's "historic decision" to send troops to the Middle East to enforce a truce between Lebanon and Israel. Continuing sensitivity about Germany's role in the Holocaust, however, limited the rules of engagement, which stipulated that German forces would not be placed in combat that could involve Israeli forces. Consequently, German naval forces were delegated to patrol the Lebanese coastline. As of November 18, 2006, Germany had deployed 1,021 troops in Lebanon.

Meanwhile, German public opinion has favored a pullout of German forces from Afghanistan, and by late 2007 polls indicated widespread support—both from the left and right—for a German withdrawal. Merkel, however, has made no promises or moves that would indicate a German withdrawal from Afghanistan, and at least 2,000 German troops continue to serve with the International Security Assistance Force (ISAF), the military arm of the North Atlantic Treaty Organization (NATO) that has been operating in Afghanistan for several years. However, the so-called national caveat applied to the deployment of Bundeswehr troops means in effect that they can only be committed in the northern part of Afghanistan and not in the south, where the main security threat is located. German efforts to build an effective Afghan police force have largely been a failure so far.

ANNA M. WITTMANN

See also

Abbas, Mahmoud; Arafat, Yasser; DESERT STORM, Operation; ENDURING FREEDOM, Operation; France, Middle East Policy; Hamas; Intifada, Second; Lebanon; Oil; Organization of Petroleum Exporting Countries; September 11 Attacks, International Reactions to; Sharon, Ariel; Suez Crisis; United States, Middle East Policy, 1945–Present

References

Erlanger, Steven, et al. *German and American Perspectives on Israel, Palestine, and the Middle East Conflict.* AICGS German-American Issues 06. Washington, DC: American Institute for Contemporary German Studies, 2006.

Feldman, Lily Gardner. *The Special Relationship between West Germany and Israel.* Boston: Allen and Unwin, 1984.

Gray, William Glenn. *Germany's Cold War: The Global Campaign to Isolate East Germany, 1949–1969.* Chapel Hill: University of North Carolina Press, 2003.

Hacke, Christian. "The Foreign Policy of the Schröder/Fischer Administration in Historical Perspective." *American Foreign Policy Interests* 27(4) (August 2005): 289–294.

Lewan, Kenneth M. "How West Germany Helped to Build Israel." *Journal of Palestine Studies* 4(4) (Summer 1975): 41–64.

Müller, Harald. "German Foreign Policy after Unification." In *The New Germany and the New Europe,* edited by Paul B. Stares, 126–173. Washington, DC: Brookings Institution, 1992.

Overhaus, Marco, Hanns W. Maull, and Sebastian Harnisch, eds. "German Foreign Policy and the Middle East Conflict." Special issue of *German Foreign Policy in Dialogue: A Quarterly Newsletter on German Foreign Policy* 3(7) (2002).

Ghilzai Tribe

The largest and best-known Afghan tribe, a subset of the predominant Pashtun tribe. Also known as Khilji or Ghalji, the Ghilzai peoples are located mainly in the southeastern portion of Afghanistan, roughly between Ghazni and Kandahar. There are also large numbers to be found in western Pakistan and the Suleiman Mountains. In the last several decades, they have staunchly opposed Durrani-led Afghan governments and supported the Taliban regime, before it was toppled by U.S.-led forces in late 2001.

Although the Ghilzai's precise origins are uncertain, some ethnologists believe that they are descended from Turkish bloodlines and can trace that relationship to at least the 10th century CE. Most Ghilzai speak Pashto and/or Dari, a form of Persian. By the early 18th century, the group had become ascendant in what is now Afghanistan, and Mirways Khan Hotak, a Ghilzai, ruled the region from 1709 to 1738. By the late 1800s, however, many Ghilzai had been driven into northern and eastern Afghanistan by the Durrani, which explains their continuing antipathy toward that group. In 1978 the Ghilzai were the major instigators of the revolt against Mohammad Daoud Khan's government, which triggered the Soviet intervention and occupation of Afghanistan that began the following year. Although the succeeding three rulers of Afghanistan, all backed by the Kremlin, were Ghilzai, a large number of the mujahideen fighting the Soviet occupation were themselves Ghilzai. Historically, the group has been nomadic, in opposition to its chief rival tribe, the Durrani, which tends to be sedentary.

During the 1990s, while Afghanistan was convulsed by civil war after the Soviet withdrawal in 1989, the Ghilzai dominated the rising Taliban movement, which sought to institute an Islamic theocracy over Afghanistan. Indeed, Taliban leader and head of state, Mullah Mohammed Omar, was a member of the Ghilzai tribe. Today, the Ghilzai's population in Afghanistan is thought to number about 9 million, with an additional 1 million located in western Pakistan. They thus make up as much as one quarter of the total Afghan population. Almost all Ghilzai adhere to Sunni Islam (of the Hanafi School), and most are devoutly religious. In present-day Afghanistan, the Ghilzai oppose the government of President Hamid Karzai, who is Durrani, and many are part of the resurgent insurgency movement that is attempting to topple the government, rid the nation of Western (chiefly U.S.) influences, and reinstall a Taliban regime.

PAUL G. PIERPAOLI JR.

See also

Afghanistan; Karzai, Hamid; Mujahideen, Soviet-Afghanistan War; Omar, Mohammed; Soviet-Afghanistan War; Taliban

References

Ewans, Martin. *Afghanistan: A Short History of Its History and Politics.* New York: Harper Perennial, 2002.

Tanner, Stephen. *Afghanistan: A Military History from Alexander the Great to the Fall of the Taliban.* New York: Da Capo, 2003.

Glaspie, April
Birth Date: April 26, 1942

U.S. diplomat. April Glaspie was born on April 26, 1942, in Vancouver, Canada. She graduated from Mills College in 1963 with a bachelor's degree and from the John Hopkins University Paul H. Nitze School of Advanced International Relations in 1965 with a master's degree. She entered the U.S. diplomatic corps in 1966 and held a variety of posts, mainly in the Middle East. From 1989 to 1990 Glaspie served as ambassador to Iraq, appointed to that post by President George H. W. Bush. She was the first woman appointed as a U.S. ambassador to an Arab state.

Fluent in Arabic, Glaspie is best remembered for a meeting with then-Iraqi president Saddam Hussein on July 25, 1990, eight days before the Iraqi invasion of Kuwait. Two transcripts exist of this meeting: excerpts provided by the government of Iraq to the *New York Times* and published on September 23, 1990, and an American version from a cable, sent by the U.S. embassy in Baghdad, summarizing the meeting.

Some have alleged, based on both transcripts but particularly the Iraqi version, that Glaspie's statements to Saddam Hussein encouraged him to invade Kuwait by giving him the impression that the United States was disinterested in Iraq's feud with Kuwait, including its military buildup along the Kuwaiti border. According to the Iraqi transcript, Glaspie allegedly gave Hussein a "green light" to invade Kuwait by telling him that "we have no opinion on the Arab-Arab conflicts, like your border disagreement with Kuwait . . . and [Secretary of State] James Baker has directed our official spokesmen to emphasize this instruction." The American transcript, however, has Glaspie first asking Hussein about his intentions, given his declaration that recent Kuwaiti actions were the equivalent of military aggression and his deployment of troops along Kuwait's border. Only then did she say, "We take no position on these Arab affairs," without specifically mentioning the border dispute between Iraq

and Kuwait. According to the U.S. cable, however, the ambassador made clear that the United States could "never excuse settlements of dispute by other than peaceful means."

Because Iraq's invasion of Kuwait was unexpected in Washington, Glaspie's words were seen by some as encouraging Hussein to invade Kuwait. Although she clearly did not take a position regarding Iraq's border dispute with Kuwait, this neutrality is not equivalent to an endorsement of an Iraqi invasion. Also, it should be remembered that no one other than the Iraqi leadership expected an invasion—not the United States, Kuwait, the rest of the Arab world, nor Egyptian president Hosni Mubarak, who was mediating the dispute and had brokered a series of upcoming meetings between Iraq and Kuwait. Instead, most believed that Hussein was merely bluffing to intimidate Kuwait into forgiving Iraq's large debts, amassed during its eight-year war with Iran (1980–1988), and into lowering its oil production to raise the price of oil and thus enhance Iraqi revenues.

Even if Hussein had indeed asked to meet with Glaspie to gauge her response regarding America's position on Iraq's dispute with Kuwait and she had communicated U.S. opposition, it is highly unlikely that Hussein would have been deterred from invading Kuwait by mere words alone, particularly given the fact that the United States had scant military resources to back up any such warnings. On the other hand, the meeting between Hussein and Glaspie raises a cautionary note from which all diplomats can learn: that is, what one does not say can be just as telling as what one actually utters.

After leaving Iraq following the Iraqi invasion of Kuwait, Glaspie was posted to the U.S. Diplomatic Mission to the United Nations (UN). She concluded her diplomatic career as consul general in Cape Town, South Africa, retiring in 2002.

STEFAN BROOKS

See also

Baker, James Addison, III; Bush, George Herbert Walker; DESERT SHIELD, Operation; DESERT STORM, Operation; Hussein, Saddam; Iran-Iraq War; Iraq, History of, 1990–Present; Kuwait; Kuwait, Iraqi Invasion of; Kuwait-Iraq Diplomacy

References

Bush, George, and Brent Scowcroft. *A World Transformed.* New York: Knopf, 1998.

Freedman, Lawrence, and Efraim Karsh. *The Gulf Conflict, 1990–1991: Diplomacy and War in the New World Order.* Princeton, NJ: Princeton University Press, 1993.

Sifry, Michah, and Christopher Cerf, eds. *The Gulf Reader: History, Documents, Opinions.* New York: Random House, 1991.

Global War on Terror

Term used to describe the military, political, diplomatic, and economic measures employed by the United States and other allied governments against organizations, countries, or individuals that are committing terrorist acts, that might be inclined to engage in terrorism, or that support those who do commit such acts. The Global War on Terror is an amorphous concept and a somewhat indistinct term, yet its use emphasizes the difficulty in classifying the type of nontraditional warfare being waged against U.S. and Western interests by various terrorist groups that do not represent any nation. The term was coined by President George W. Bush in a September 20, 2001, televised address to a joint session of the U.S. Congress, and has been presented in official White House pronouncements, fact sheets, State of the Union messages, and such National Security Council (NSC) position papers as the National Security Strategy (March 2006) and the National Strategy for Combating Terrorism (February 2003 and September 2006 editions). Since 2001, the Global War on Terror has been directed primarily at Islamic terrorist groups but has also been expanded to include actions against all types of terrorism. During the Bush administration, Secretary of Defense Robert Gates also called it the "Long War."

As with the Cold War, the Global War on Terror is being waged on numerous fronts, against many individuals and nations, and involves both military and nonmilitary tactics. President George W. Bush's September 20, 2001, announcement of the Global War on Terror was in response to the September 11, 2001, terror attacks against the United States, which led to the deaths of some 3,000 civilians, mostly Americans but representing civilians of 90 different countries.

Although the war constitutes a global effort, stretching into Asia, Africa, Europe, and the Americas, the Middle East remains a focal point of the effort. The ongoing conflict and the manner in which it has been waged has been the source of much debate. There is no widely agreed-upon estimate regarding the number of casualties during the Global War on Terror because it includes the invasion of Afghanistan in 2001 and the war in Iraq, as well as many acts of terrorism around the world. Some estimates, which include the U.S.-led coalition invasion of Afghanistan in 2001 and the invasion of Iraq in March 2003, claim that well over 2 million people have died in the struggle.

Following the September 11, 2001, terror attacks, the United States responded quickly and with overwhelming force against the organizations and governments that supported the terrorists. Evidence gathered by the U.S. government pointed to the Al Qaeda terrorist organization. Al Qaeda at the time was being given aid and shelter by the Taliban regime in Afghanistan. On September 20, 2001, President George W. Bush announced to a joint session of Congress that the Global War on Terror would not end simply with the defeat of Al Qaeda or the overthrow of the Taliban but only when every terrorist group and terrorist-affiliated government with a global reach had been defeated. These broad aims implied attacks on countries known to support terrorism, such as Iran and Syria. Bush further assured the American people that every means of intelligence, tool of diplomacy, financial pressure, and weapon of war would be used to defeat terrorism. He told the American people to expect a lengthy campaign. Bush also put down an ultimatum to every other nation, stating that each had to choose whether they were with the United States or against it. There would be no middle ground. Clearly Bush's pronouncements were far-reaching, yet the enemies were difficult to identify and find.

Less than 24 hours after the September 11 attacks, the North American Treaty Organization (NATO), declared the terrorist attacks of 9/11 to be against all member nations, the first time the organization had made such a pronouncement since its inception in 1949.

On October 7, 2001, U.S. and coalition forces (chiefly British) invaded Afghanistan to capture Osama bin Laden, the head of Al Qaeda, to destroy his organization, and to overthrow the Taliban government that supported him. Eventually Canada, Australia, France, and Germany, among other nations, joined that effort. However, when a U.S.-led coalition invaded Iraq in March 2003, there was considerable international opposition to this campaign being included under the rubric of the Global War on Terror. One problem for national leaders who supported President Bush's policies was that many of their citizens did not believe that the overthrow of Iraqi dictator Saddam Hussein was really part of the Global War on Terror and questioned other reasons stated by the Bush administration to justify the U.S.-led invasion. International opinion polls have shown that support for the War on Terror has consistently declined since 2003, likely the result of opposition to the Bush administration's preemptive invasion of Iraq in 2003 and later revelations that Iraq possessed neither ties to Al Qaeda nor weapons of mass destruction.

The Global War on Terror has also been a sporadic and clandestine war since its inception in September 2001. U.S. forces were sent to Yemen and the Horn of Africa in order to disrupt terrorist activities, while Operation ACTIVE ENDEAVOR is a naval operation intended to prevent terror attacks and limit the movement of terrorists in the Mediterranean. Terrorist attacks in Pakistan, Indonesia, and the Philippines led to the insertion of coalition forces into these countries as well and concerns about the situation in other Southeast Asian countries. In the United States, Congress has also passed legislation intended to help increase the effectiveness of law enforcement agencies in their search for terrorist activities. In the process, however, critics claim that Americans' civil liberties have been steadily eroded, and government admissions that the Federal Bureau of Investigation (FBI) and other agencies have engaged in wiretapping of international phone calls without requisite court orders and probable cause have caused a storm of controversy, as have the methods used to question foreign nationals.

The Bush administration has also greatly increased the role of the federal government in the attempt to fight terrorism at home and abroad. Among the many new government bureaucracies formed is the Department of Homeland Security, a cabinet-level agency that counts at least 210,000 employees. The increase in the size of the government, combined with huge military expenditures—most of which are going to the Iraq War—has added to the massive U.S. budget deficits.

Attorney General John Ashcroft, center, is seen on video screens discussing the secret Foreign Intelligence Surveillance Court's wiretap ruling on November 18, 2002, in Washington, D.C. (AP/Wide World Photos)

Proponents of the Global War on Terror believe that proactive measures must be taken against terrorist organizations to effectively defeat global terrorism. They believe that in order to meet the diverse security challenges of the 21st century, a larger, global military presence is needed. Without such a force, they argue, terrorist organizations will continue to launch strikes against innocent civilians. Many of the people argue that the United States, Great Britain, Spain, and other countries, which have been the victims of large-scale attacks, must go on the offensive against such rogue groups and that not doing so will only embolden the attackers and invite more attacks. Allowing such organizations to gain more strength may allow them to achieve their goal of imposing militant Islamist rule.

Critics of the Global War on Terror claim that there is no tangible enemy to defeat, as there is no single group whose defeat will bring about an end to the conflict. Thus, it is virtually impossible to know if progress is being made. They also argue that "terrorism," a tactic whose goal is to instill fear into people through violent actions, can never be truly defeated. There are also those who argue against the justification for preemptive strikes, because such action invites counterresponses and brings about the deaths of many innocent people. Many believe that the Iraqi military posed

no imminent threat to the United States when coalition forces entered Iraq in 2003, but the resultant war has been disastrous for both the Iraqi and American people. Civil right activists contend that measures meant to crack down on terrorist activities have infringed on the rights of American citizens as well as the rights of foreign detainees. Furthermore, critics argue that the war and the amount of spending apportioned to military endeavors negatively affects the national and world economies. Others argue that the United States should be spending time and resources on resolving the Arab-Israeli problem and trying to eradicate the desperate conditions that feed terrorism.

As support for the Global War on Terror effort has diminished, the debate over its effectiveness has grown. From late 2007 to the beginning of 2009, terrorist attacks have continued, and the deliberation over the best way to ensure the safety of civilian populations around the world continues.

As of March 2009, the new Barack Obama administration is not using the terms "Global War on Terror" or "Long War" in defense fact sheets. It has instructed U.S. government agencies to use the term "Overseas Contingency Operations." White House press secretary, Robert Gibbs, has explained that Obama is "using different words and phrases in order to denote a reaching out to many moderate parts of the world that we believe can be important in a battle against extremists." However, the term "Global War on Terror" is still deeply embedded.

GREGORY W. MORGAN

See also

Counterterrorism Strategy; ENDURING FREEDOM, Operation; IRAQI FREEDOM, Operation; September 11 Attacks; Terrorism

References

Bacevich, Andrew J. *The New American Militarism: How Americans Are Seduced by War.* New York: Oxford University Press, 2005.
Mahajan, Rahul. *The New Crusade: America's War on Terrorism.* New York: Monthly Review, 2002.
Woodward, Bob. *Bush at War.* New York: Simon and Schuster, 2002.

Glosson, Buster C.
Birth Date: March 14, 1942

U.S. Air Force officer and director of campaign plans for U.S. Central Command Air Forces (CENTAF) in Riyadh, Saudi Arabia, and commander of the 14th Air Division (Provisional), U.S. Central Command (CENTCOM), during the 1991 Persian Gulf War. Buster C. Glosson was born on March 14, 1942, in Greensboro, North Carolina. He graduated from North Carolina State University in 1965 and entered the U.S. Air Force through the Reserve Officers' Training Corps (ROTC).

Glosson received his pilot's wings in 1966. By the end of his career he had accumulated more than 3,600 flying hours in the Cessna T-37 Tweet, Northrop T-38 Talon, Northrop F-5 Freedom

Fighter, and the McDonnell Douglas F-15C/E Eagle. Glosson flew numerous combat missions during the Vietnam War, commanded the Air Force Fighter Weapons Squadron and two tactical fighter wings, and held a variety of major command and Air Staff assignments. He was promoted to brigadier general on July 1, 1988.

When the Iraqi army invaded Kuwait in August 1990, Glosson had just completed a one-year assignment as deputy commander, Joint Task Force Middle East, CENTCOM. On August 20, 1990, Colonel John A. Warden briefed Lieutenant General Charles A. Horner, the Joint Air Forces Component commander (JFACC), in Riyadh on the INSTANT THUNDER air campaign plan. Not enamored with the plan, Horner asked Warden to return to Washington. Within two days, however, Horner appointed Glosson as the director of CENTAF Campaign Plans and assigned to him the three lieutenant colonels that Colonel Warden had brought with him.

Glosson, together with Colonel David A. Deptula, guided the air-campaign planning, blending Warden's ideas with the existing operational situation. Within two weeks, Glosson's planning group, soon known as the "Black Hole," had completed an executable plan, using INSTANT THUNDER as the foundation. In early September, Glosson briefed General H. Norman Schwarzkopf, commander of CENTCOM, on the plan, the central concept of which was to allocate CENTCOM's limited air assets to neutralize specific target groups, but not necessarily to destroy them. On October 10 Glosson presented an updated and more detailed plan to President George H. W. Bush, Secretary of Defense Dick Cheney, and Chairman of the Joint Chiefs of Staff (JCS) General Colin Powell.

In late December 1990 General Horner created the Directorate of Campaign Plans, with Glosson as its chief, to transition the plans into a higher state of readiness in preparation for possible combat. The new organization combined the former Black Hole with portions of the CENTAF Combat Operations Planning Staff, which performed D-Day defensive planning in case of an Iraqi attack; the Air Tasking Order (ATO) staff, which prepared the daily training ATO; and the Airborne Combat Element (ACE) staff, which manned the Airborne Warning and Control System (AWACS) aircraft. The new organization had three elements: the Guidance, Apportionment, and Tasking (GAT) Division; the ATO Division; and the ACE Division.

Within the GAT Division, Colonel Deptula reviewed, selected, and assembled the completed targeting recommendations into a final Master Attack Plan (MAP). He then reviewed the MAP with Glosson and gave the approved MAP to the GAT Division night shift, which transcribed the MAP onto target-planning worksheets, which, in turn, the ATO Division used to create the daily ATO. When the air campaign began in January 1991, the GAT Division oversaw last-minute updates to the MAP and ATO to ensure minimal impact of these changes to the approved ATO. To take care of last-minute high priority changes, Glosson created an alert force of eight General Dynamics F-111F Aardvarks on the ground.

On December 5, 1990, the air force activated the 14th Air Division (Provisional) (AD[P]), consisting of the deployed air force fighter wings. Horner selected Glosson, who retained his position as director of campaign plans, as its commander. As a result, Glosson directly commanded the fighter squadrons while he simultaneously planned their commitment in the upcoming air campaign.

The strategic air campaign began on January 17, 1991, and lasted 10 days. As early as January 24, Glosson began planning the shift of sorties to Phase III, the attrition of Iraqi ground forces in Kuwait. On January 27, 1991, CENTAF declared air supremacy and shifted to Phase III, but both Glosson and Deptula thought that the phase had begun too early. From January 27 on, the broad systematic attack concept of INSTANT THUNDER transitioned to a more traditional battle of attrition in which aircraft concentrated on bombing well-defined target sets. Glosson received major credit for the efficacy of the air campaign, which ensured a quick allied victory over Iraqi forces. On June 1, 1991, he was promoted to major general.

In 1992 Glosson became air force deputy chief of staff for plans and operations, responsible for the development of the requirements and force structure to support U.S. forces with air and space power. He was promoted to lieutenant general on June 1, 1992.

In December 1993 Secretary of the Air Force Sheila Widnall admonished General Glosson for improper intervention with a promotion board, and he retired six months later at the rank of lieutenant general. In 2003 Glosson wrote a book titled *War with Iraq: Critical Lessons.*

ROBERT B. KANE

See also

Deptula, David A.; DESERT STORM, Operation, Coalition Air Campaign; DESERT STORM, Operation, Coalition Air Forces; DESERT STORM, Operation, Planning for; Horner, Charles; INSTANT THUNDER, Plan; Warden, John Ashley, III

References

Davis, Richard G. *On Target: Organizing and Executing the Strategic Air Campaign against Iraq.* Washington, DC: U.S. Air Force History and Museums Program, 2002.

Glosson, Buster C. *War with Iraq: Critical Lessons.* Greensboro, NC: Carolina Gardener, 2003.

Jamieson, Perry D. *Lucrative Targets: The U.S. Air Force in the Kuwaiti Theater of Operations.* Washington, DC: U.S. Air Force History and Museums Program, 2001.

Keaney, Thomas A., and Eliot A. Cohen. *Gulf Air Power Survey Summary Report.* Washington, DC: Department of the Air Force, 1993.

Mann, Edward C., III. *Thunder and Lightning: Desert Storm and the Airpower Debates.* Maxwell Air Force Base, AL: Air University Press, 1995.

Gog and Magog

Apocalyptic term appearing in both the Hebrew Bible and the Christian New Testament, as well as in the Qur'an. Gog and Magog also appear in folklore. They are variously identified as supernatural beings, national groups, or even lands.

The first reference to Magog appears in the "Table of Nations" in Genesis 10:2, with Magog given as one of the sons of Japheth. The first reference to Gog and Magog together is in Ezekiel 38:2–3, where Yahweh (God) warns the prophet, "Son of man, set thy face against Gog the land of Magog, the chief prince of Meshech and Tubal, and prophesy against him. . . . Behold, I come against thee, O Gog, the chief prince of Meshech and Tubal." The same command is repeated at the beginning of Chapter 39, but there is no clear identification of either the ruler or his country. In Chapter 39:5–6, Gog is identified as being accompanied in his invasion of Israel by the nations of Persia, Ethiopia, Libya, and Gomer, as well as the house of Thogorma.

Because of the sheer number of peoples identified by Ezekiel as taking part in the invasion of Israel, some have asserted that Gog is simply a generic figure for all the enemies of Israel and that reference to it in the Apocalypse denotes the enemies of the Church. The book of Revelation 20:7–8 reads: "And when the thousand years are expired, Satan shall be loosed out of his prison, and shall go out to deceive the nations what are in the four quarters of the earth, Gog and Magog, to gather them to battle: the number of whom is as the sand of the sea." The Qur'an refers in 18:94 to Yajuj and Majuj (Gog and Magog) and claims in 21:96–97 that they will be "let loose" when "the True Promise," meaning the Day of Resurrection, "shall draw near."

Scholars have endeavored to identify Gog historically. One possible source is the Lydian king known to the Greeks as Gyges, or in Assyrian inscriptions as Gu-gu. Others say that Gog and Magog are two tribes and refer to either the Khazar kingdom in the northern Caucasus or the Mongols. Apparently, Gog may also have been used in ancient Israel to identify any northern population. Throughout history there have been repeated claims that Gog and Magog represent particular peoples, including the Goths.

Some extremists in the Arab-Israeli conflict have used the phrase "Gog and Magog" to justify the unjustifiable. Some have claimed that Ezekiel's prophesy of the invasion of Israel by a vast number of enemies refers to the present conflict in the Middle East, in which the Islamic nations will all invade Israel, and that this great conflict will see the rise of the Antichrist and end with the destruction of Israel's enemies by God Himself. At the outbreak of World War II, Avraham Stern, founder of the terrorist group Lehi, declared that the war was a struggle between Gog and Magog and that this justified increased violent action against the British Mandate for Palestine.

SPENCER C. TUCKER

See also
Bible; Qur'an

References
Berner, Douglas. *The Silence Is Broken: God Hooks Ezekiel's Gog and Magog.* London: Lulu, 2006.
The Catholic Encyclopedia, Vol. 6. New York: Robert Appleton, 1909.

Goldwater-Nichols Defense Reorganization Act

Congressional act, formally known as the Department of Defense Reform Act of 1986, designed to enhance the ability of the U.S. Armed Services to operate more effectively in joint operations. This act, named for its lead sponsors Senator Barry M. Goldwater (R-Ariz.) and Congressman William "Bill" Nichols (D-Ala.), was designed to address lingering problems associated with the compromises made in the crafting of the National Security Act of 1947, which established the Department of Defense structure. Congressional sponsors and defense reform advocates had pushed for the changes to address problem areas generated by bureaucratic inefficiencies and interservice competition, as well as issues that had been identified in prior combat operations, ranging from the Korean War to Operation URGENT FURY (the U.S. invasion of Grenada in 1983).

The primary objectives of the Goldwater-Nichols Act were to strengthen civilian authority, improve the military advice provided to senior civilian leaders, reduce the effects of service parochialism and interservice rivalry, enhance the role of the chairman of the Joint Chiefs of Staff (JCS) and the Joint Staff, and improve the operational authority of the commanders in chief (CINCs) of the unified combatant commands.

The Goldwater-Nichols Act strengthened the authority of the Secretary of Defense and made the chairman of the JCS the "principal military adviser" to the president, secretary of defense, and the National Security Council (NSC). Previously, under a system requiring unanimity, the JCS had provided collective recommendations, which were often watered-down compromises made among the service chiefs. Prior to the passage of Goldwater-Nichols, any service chief, to protect the parochial interests of his own service, could block a Joint Staff action. The new act established the chairman as the final approval authority for all Joint Staff actions, allowing the chairman to override any service objections. Although the chairman and the individual service chiefs remained outside the formal operational chain of command (which flows from the president, through the secretary of defense, directly to the combatant commanders in the field), the reforms allowed the president and the defense secretary to pass operational orders to the combatant commanders, including both the geographic theater joint commanders and the functional joint command commanders through the JCS chairman.

The act also established a vice chairman position for the JCS and revised the Joint Staff responsibilities to clarify and enhance the staff's role in the planning and decision-making process. Goldwater-Nichols also adjusted the defense personnel system to encourage service in joint organizations and to require that senior officers have career experiences and professional education that provide a joint perspective in their leadership roles. Additionally, the act clarified and enhanced the roles of the CINCs. At the time the act was passed, the JCS chairman was Admiral William J. Crowe Jr., although the first chairman to be appointed under the new structure was General Colin L. Powell.

The effects of Goldwater-Nichols were clearly evident in the conduct of Operation DESERT SHIELD and Operation DESERT STORM, in 1990 and 1991 respectively, in response to the Iraqi invasion of Kuwait. During the conflict, General Powell played a key role in the national leadership as the principal military adviser. Additionally, President George H. W. Bush and Secretary of Defense Dick Cheney used Powell as the primary conduit for orders flowing to the theater CINC, General H. Norman Schwarzkopf. Schwarzkopf also found it useful to pass information back through the JCS chairman, as well as to report directly to the defense secretary and the president.

Within the theater itself, Schwarzkopf fully exploited the Goldwater-Nichols authority and the emphasis on joint efforts to create a highly effective joint and coalition force structure and to conduct a well-coordinated joint campaign for the liberation of Kuwait. Operation DESERT STORM was viewed by many analysts as a validation of the wisdom of the reforms implemented by the Goldwater-Nichols Act. In October 2002 Secretary of Defense Donald Rumsfeld directed that the functional and regional CINCs be referred to as "combat commanders" or "commanders," arguing that there can be but one commander in chief—namely the president of the United States. During U.S. military operations in Afghanistan (Operation ENDURING FREEDOM) in 2001 and Iraq (Operation IRAQI FREEDOM) in 2003, the wisdom of Goldwater-Nichols was once again clearly evident, as both operations were conducted with a great deal of efficiency and joint effort.

JEROME V. MARTIN

See also

Bush, George Herbert Walker; Cheney, Richard Bruce; DESERT SHIELD, Operation; DESERT STORM, Operation; ENDURING FREEDOM, Operation; IRAQI FREEDOM, Operation; Powell, Colin Luther; Schwarzkopf, H. Norman, Jr.

References

Lederman, Gordon Nathaniel. *Reorganizing the Joint Chiefs of Staff: The Goldwater-Nichols Act of 1986.* College Station: Texas A&M University Press, 2002.

Locher, James R. *Victory on the Potomac: The Goldwater-Nichols Act Unifies the Pentagon.* College Station: Texas A&M University Press, 2002.

Gorbachev, Mikhail
Birth Date: March 2, 1931

Last president of the Soviet Union (1988–1991) and general secretary of the Communist Party of the Soviet Union (CPSU) during 1985–1991. Born on March 2, 1931, in Privolnoye, Stavropol Province, Russia, to a peasant family, Mikhail Sergeyevich Gorbachev joined the Komsomol (Communist Union of the Young) in 1946. That same year he began driving a harvester for an agricultural cooperative. In 1951 he entered the Law Faculty of Moscow State University, where he earned a law degree in 1955.

Returning to Stavropol following his studies in Moscow, Gorbachev enjoyed a remarkably rapid rise within the ranks of the CPSU, first through various posts in the Komsomol and then in the party apparatus in Stavropol during the second half of the 1950s and the first half of the 1960s. Gorbachev became a member of the CPSU Central Committee in 1971, a candidate member of the Politburo in 1979, a full member in 1980, and general secretary of the CPSU Central Committee in March 1985. A keen politician, Gorbachev's political ascendancy was further promoted by Mikhail Suslov and particularly by Yuri Andropov, one-time head of the Committee for State Security (KGB) and general secretary of the CPSU from 1982 to 1984.

Once in power, Gorbachev consolidated his position within the party and proceeded to move forward with internal reforms. He termed his reform agenda perestroika (restructuring) and glasnost (openness). What soon became called the "politics of perestroika" was a process of cumulative reforms, ultimately leading to results that were neither intended nor necessarily desired.

Perestroika had three distinctive phases. The first phase was aimed mainly at the acceleration of economic development and the revitalization of socialism. The second phase was marked by the notion of glasnost. During this period, Gorbachev emphasized the need for political and social restructuring as well as the

Former president of the Soviet Union Mikhail Gorbachev, who is widely credited with playing a key role in ending the Cold War. (Library of Congress)

necessity of dealing openly with the past. Media freedoms were enhanced considerably as part of this process. In the economic arena, limited market-oriented elements were introduced, and greater latitude was given to state-owned enterprises. The third and final phase of perestroika was aimed at democratizing the Soviet political process. Reformers created a new bicameral parliament, and new procedures allowed for the direct election of two-thirds of the members of the Congress of People's Deputies. In March 1990 the Congress abolished the CPSU's political monopoly, paving the way for the legalization of other political parties.

Perestroika's third phase was also marked by some incongruous paradoxes. While the power of the CPSU was waning, Gorbachev's power was on the increase. In October 1988 he replaced Andrei Gromyko as head of the Presidium of the Supreme Soviet. Seven months later, Gorbachev became chairman of the new Supreme Soviet. Finally, in March 1990 the Congress elected him president of the Soviet Union, a newly established post with potent executive powers. At the same time, Gorbachev's economic reforms were yielding little fruit. Civil unrest, interethnic strife, and national and regional independence movements, particularly in the Baltic and Caucasus regions, were already overshadowing perestroika.

Although his domestic reforms had been disappointing in their results, Gorbachev enjoyed remarkable successes in foreign policy. He quickly eased tensions with the West. Two summits with U.S. president Ronald Reagan (Geneva in 1985 and Reykjavik in 1986) paved the way for historic breakthroughs in Soviet-U.S. relations and nuclear arms reductions. On December 8, 1987, the Intermediate-Range Nuclear Forces (INF) Treaty, the first agreement in history that eliminated an entire class of nuclear weapons, was signed by both nations.

In succeeding years, Gorbachev's international stature continued to grow, although his popularity at home plummeted. In 1988 he ordered the withdrawal of Soviet troops from Afghanistan, ending his nation's disastrous decade-long struggle there. He also promised publicly to refrain from military intervention in Eastern Europe. In fact, Gorbachev embraced the new democratically elected leadership in the region. Especially significant was his agreement to the reunification of Germany and the inclusion of the new united Federal Republic of Germany (FRG, West Germany) in the North Atlantic Treaty Organization (NATO). Awarded the Nobel Peace Prize in 1990, Gorbachev is generally considered by some in the West to be the driving force behind the end of the Cold War. While others do not go that far, attributing the Soviet Union's collapse to the inherent weaknesses in the Soviet system, Gorbachev is praised for managing the collapse without undue bloodshed.

The Iraqi invasion of Kuwait in August 1990 triggered Operation DESERT SHIELD, a huge multinational military buildup led by the United States. Gorbachev was generally sympathetic to the coalition's mission of expelling Iraqi forces from Kuwait. In the lead-up to the war, however, Gorbachev urged caution in the use of military force and asked that the coalition powers allow adequate time for sanctions to work. In the weeks immediately preceding the war, he attempted but was unsuccessful in efforts to mediate a peaceful end to the conflict. When the conflict began in January 1991, Gorbachev did not attempt to block the military intervention. Such a development would have seemed unthinkable during the Cold War.

While Gorbachev's foreign policy was being hailed abroad, problems within the Soviet Union continued unabated. Old-line communists considered Gorbachev's policies as heresy, while economic dislocations multiplied. In 1990 several Soviet-controlled republics, including that of Russia, declared their independence. Gorbachev tried to stem this tide but was unsuccessful. Talks between Soviet authorities and the breakaway republics resulted in the creation of a new Russian federation (or confederation), slated to become law in August 1991.

Many of Gorbachev's reforms were tainted by an attempted coup of reactionary opponents to perestroika in August 1991. Led by high-ranking officials, among them the chief of the KGB, the defense minister, the prime minister, and the vice president, Gorbachev was placed under house arrest in his home in Foros after rejecting any negotiations with the putsch leaders. With the courageous intervention of Russian Republic leader Boris Yeltsin, the coup collapsed after two days. Gorbachev returned to Moscow but was now dependent on Yeltsin, who banned the CPSU from the Russian Republic. On August 24, 1991, Gorbachev resigned as CPSU general secretary. On December 7, 1991, the presidents of Russia, Ukraine, and Belarus created a loose confederation called the Community of Independent States (CIS). Soon thereafter, eight other republics joined, and the CIS treaty was concluded on December 21. Gorbachev resigned as Soviet president on December 25, and the Soviet Union became extinct on December 31, 1991.

Since leaving office, Gorbachev has tried to stay active in Russian politics, but his efforts have produced only very modest results. He lost a bid for the presidency in 1996. He is a much sought-after speaker in the West and remains engaged in numerous endeavors related to foreign policy and international security. He formed the Gorbachev Center, a think tank for studies in socioeconomic issues, in San Francisco, California, in 1992. The next year he founded Green Cross International, an environmental organization that played a key role in drafting the Earth Charter.

MAGARDITSCH HATSCHIKJAN

See also

Bush, George Herbert Walker; DESERT STORM, Operation; Reagan, Ronald Wilson; Soviet-Afghanistan War; Soviet Union, Middle East Policy; Yeltsin, Boris Nikolayevich

References

Brown, Archibald Haworth. *The Gorbachev Factor*. Oxford: Oxford University Press, 1996.

D'Agostino, Anthony. *Gorbachev's Revolution*. New York: New York University Press, 1998.

Gorbachev, Mikhail. *Memoirs*. Translated by Georges Peronansky and Tatjana Varsavsky. New York: Doubleday, 1996.

Matlock, Jack F., Jr. *Reagan and Gorbachev: How the Cold War Ended*. New York: Random House, 2004.

Gordon, Gary

Birth Date: August 30, 1960
Death Date: October 3, 1993

U.S. Army master sergeant posthumously awarded the Medal of Honor; as a member of the 1st Special Forces Operational Detachment–Delta (Delta Force), he fought and died in the Battle of Mogadishu on October 3–4, 1993. Gary Gordon was born in Lincoln, Maine, on August 30, 1960. Known as "Bugsy" to his friends while growing up, he demonstrated an early interest in the military. After graduating from high school in February 1978, Gordon enlisted in the U.S. Army. After completing basic training, he was assigned to the combat engineers and selected for U.S. Army Special Forces two years later. He was eventually assigned to the 2nd Battalion, 10th Special Forces Group, garrisoned at Fort Carson, Colorado. Master Sergeant Gordon's military career reached its zenith with his selection to Delta Force.

In December 1992 U.S. forces deployed to Somalia to aid United Nation (UN) forces in Operation RESTORE HOPE, a mission to restore order in Somalia and feed victims of a multiyear famine. The operation took a more violent turn on June 5, 1993, when rebel forces loyal to Mohammed Farrah Aidid (Aideed) killed 24 Pakistani troops in an ambush in Mogadishu. The next day the UN Security Council issued Resolution 837, calling for the arrest of Aidid and anyone else responsible for the ambush. Toward that end, the United States deployed Task Force Ranger, commanded by Major General William F. Garrison in Operation GOTHIC SERPENT. Task Force Ranger included Delta Force as well as other army, navy, and air force elements. The task force conducted several successful nighttime raids. The next raid, however, occurred during daylight hours, and with disastrous results.

On October 3, 1993, Task Force Ranger received intelligence that several members of Aidid's clan were meeting at a location in Mogadishu. The task force immediately launched a daylight raid, against established practices. The initial capture was successful; however, during the extraction that followed, two Lockheed UH-60 Black Hawk helicopters were shot down. Army Rangers secured the first crash site, but the second crash site was farther away, and no combat and rescue units were available to secure it. In an MH-6 Little Bird helicopter orbiting the area, Delta operators Sergeant First Class Randy Shugart and Master Sergeant Gordon asked twice for permission to land and secure the crash site. The pair finally received permission after a third request. Shugart and Gordon removed the crew, including Chief Warrant Officer Mike Durant, to relative safety. The pair then set up a perimeter and engaged Somali clansmen. The firefight lasted until the Delta men ran out of ammunition and were killed. Their bodies and those of the dead Blackhawk crew were later desecrated and dragged through the streets of Mogadishu. Durant was taken captive and later released.

For heroic action in the defense of a fellow serviceman, Gordon and Shugart were both awarded the Medal of Honor. President Bill Clinton presented the posthumous award to Gordon's family on May 23, 1994. Two further honors were bestowed upon Gordon: the naming of U.S. Navy transport USNS *Gordon* (T-AKR 296) and the naming of the Shugart Gordon Military Operations Urbanized Terrain Complex (MOUT) training center at Fort Polk, Louisiana.

SHAWN LIVINGSTON

See also

Aidid, Mohammed Farrah; Somalia, International Intervention in

References

Anderson, Cindy. "Leaving Lincoln," *Yankee* 59(11) (1995): 56–68.
Bowden, Mark. *Black Hawk Down: A Story of Modern War.* 1st ed. New York: Atlantic Monthly Press, 1999.
Eversmann, Matt Schilling. *The Battle of Mogadishu: Firsthand Accounts from the Men of Task Force Ranger.* Novato, CA: Presidio, 2004.

Gore, Albert Arnold, Jr.

Birth Date: March 31, 1948

U.S. representative, senator, vice president (1993–2001), unsuccessful presidential candidate (2000), and noted environmentalist. Albert (Al) Arnold Gore Jr. was born on March 31, 1948, in Washington, D.C. His father, Albert Gore Sr., had a long and distinguished career as both a U.S. representative and senator from his native Tennessee. Gore spent much of his youth in Washington, D.C., but often returned to his family's extensive farm near Carthage, Tennessee, where he worked during the summer. In 1969 he received an undergraduate degree from Harvard University.

Although he did not support the Vietnam War, Gore nevertheless enlisted with the U.S. Army in August 1969; he chose not to use his significant family connections to avoid military service. Gore was soon made a reporter for *The Army Flier* at Fort Rucker (Alabama). In January 1971, with just seven months left in his enlistment period, he shipped off to Vietnam, where he served in the 20th Engineer Brigade headquartered at Bien Hoa.

When his enlistment was up, Gore returned to the United States, began study at Vanderbilt University's divinity school, and worked the night shift as a reporter/writer for the *Tennessean*, one of Nashville's main newspapers. He distinguished himself as a young journalist, and in 1972 he left the divinity school, after holding a Rockefeller Foundation Scholarship for a year, to devote his full energies to newspaper reporting. For two years, from 1974 to 1976, he attended Vanderbilt Law School but did not complete his studies. Instead, he decided to run for the U.S. House of Representatives. Gore won the 1976 election and served in the House until 1985. Considered a southern centrist, Gore's tenure in the House was competent but not spectacular. He was on record as being opposed to the Ronald Reagan administration's support of Iraq during the Iran-Iraq War (1980–1988), citing Iraqi president Saddam Hussein's quest to secure weapons of mass destruction (WMDs), his sponsorship of terrorism, and the use of poison gas during the conflict.

Former vice president Al Gore during a speech on November 9, 2003, in Washington, D.C. Gore charged that the George W. Bush administration had failed to make the country safer after the September 11 World Trade Center and Pentagon attacks and was using the antiterrorism fight as a pretext to consolidate political power. (AP/Wide World Photos)

In 1984 Gore ran successfully for the U.S. Senate, taking office in January 1985. He quickly learned the ins and outs of the Senate and became a highly effective legislator. In 1988 he cosponsored the Prevention of Genocide Act, which would have effectively cut off all U.S. aid to the Hussein regime. The bill was largely a reaction to Hussein's genocidal al-Anfal Campaign, which employed chemical weapons against Iraqi Kurds. The legislation was vigorously resisted by the Reagan White House, which launched a successful campaign to defeat the bill. In 1988 Gore, just 40 years old, ran for the Democratic presidential nomination, winning early primaries in several southern and western states before dropping out to allow the presumptive nominee, Governor Michael Dukakis, to square off against Vice President George H. W. Bush in the November elections.

Gore continued in the Senate, and in 1992 he became the Democratic nominee for vice president, alongside Arkansas governor Bill Clinton, who was the presidential nominee. The Democratic ticket, aided by third party candidate Ross Perot, went on to win the November 1992 elections with a plurality but not a majority of the popular vote, and Gore took office as vice president in January 1993.

Gore had unparalleled access to the Oval Office and was an actively engaged vice president, probably the most engaged in American history. Only Vice President Dick Cheney, who took office in 2001, was more central to administration policies than Gore. Gore worked hard to reduce and then eliminate the federal budget deficit, and he was a key player in the passage of the North Atlantic Free Trade Agreement (NAFTA) in the autumn of 1993. Despite allegations that he had engaged in questionable money-raising endeavors, for which he was never indicted, Gore maintained a rather unblemished public image, especially when compared to Clinton. During the late 1990s, Clinton embroiled himself in a tawdry sex scandal involving White House intern Monica Lewinsky, for which he was impeached but acquitted on February 12, 1999.

Gore was the presumptive Democratic presidential nominee in 2000, and indeed he received his party's nomination in July. Choosing Connecticut senator Joseph Lieberman as his running mate, Gore ran on his eight years' experience as vice president, but at the same time he tried to distance himself from Clinton, whom he believed to be a political liability because of the Lewinsky affair. This tactic may have been a mistake, however, as Gore struggled to gain the upper hand against Texas governor George W. Bush, the Republican nominee. To many voters, Gore appeared wooden and ill at ease, despite his considerable experience. In the end, the 2000 election became one of the most bitter and disputed in U.S. history, and after more than a month of ballot recounts and court decisions, the U.S. Supreme Court suspended the recounts, essentially giving the election to Bush. Gore's supporters were outraged, citing the fact that their candidate had won some 500,000 votes more than Bush. Nevertheless, Gore, who voiced his dismay with the court's decision, accepted Bush's electoral college victory, to the disgruntlement of many in his own party, for what he thought to be the good of the country.

Gore was very active in his postgovernment years, becoming a crusader for environmental issues, especially global warming. He was also sharply critical of the Bush administration, criticizing both its justification of the war against Iraq and its flawed execution of it, and supporting allegations that increased security measures taken in the wake of the September 11, 2001, terror attacks threatened individual constitutional liberties.

In 2006 Gore released his documentary film about global warming, *An Inconvenient Truth*, which won the praise of environmentalists and movie critics. In 2007 Gore won an Academy Award for the film. An even greater honor came in the form of the 2007 Nobel Peace Prize for his environmental activism.

Gore continued to pursue his environmental causes and to excoriate the Bush administration for its policies in Iraq, as well as its authorization of wiretaps without the requisite court orders. Several Democratic groups tried to draft Gore into running for the White House in 2008, but he demurred. He did not, however, close the door to future political endeavors.

PAUL G. PIERPAOLI JR.

See also

Bush, George Herbert Walker; Bush, George Walker; Clinton, William Jefferson; Hussein, Saddam; Iran-Iraq War; Iraq, History of, Pre-1990; Iraq, History of, 1990–Present; Kurds; Kurds, Massacres of

References

Berman, William C. *From the Center to the Edge: The Politics and Policies of the Clinton Administration.* Lanham, MD: Rowman and Littlefield, 2000.

Marannis, David, and Ellen Nakashima. *The Prince of Tennessee: The Rise of Al Gore.* New York: Simon and Schuster, 2000.

Goss, Porter Johnston
Birth Date: November 26, 1938

Politician, intelligence operative, Republican congressman (1989–2004), and director of the Central Intelligence Agency (CIA) from

2004 to 2006. Porter Johnston Goss was born on November 26, 1938, in Waterbury, Connecticut, to a well-to-do family. His early education was at the exclusive Fessenden School in West Newton, Massachusetts, and the equally elite Hotchkiss High School in Lakeville, Connecticut. He attended Yale University, graduating in 1960.

Most of Goss's early career was with the CIA, specifically with the Directorate of Operations (DO), which carries out the clandestine operations of the agency. Goss worked as a CIA agent in the DO from 1960 to 1971. Most of his activities in the CIA are still classified, but it is known that his area of operations included Latin America, the Caribbean, and Europe. In 1970, while he was stationed in London, health problems led him to resign his post.

Goss began his political career in 1975, serving as mayor of Sanibel City, Florida, from 1975 to 1977 and again during 1981–1982. In 1988 he ran for the U.S. House seat in Florida's 13th congressional district and retained it until 1993. In 1993 he became the congressional representative from Florida's 14th congressional district, and he held this seat until September 23, 2004, when he resigned it to head the CIA. During his 16 years in Congress, Goss served on specialized committees that had oversight on intelligence. Although Goss had always been supportive of the CIA, he

Porter Goss is the director of the Central Intelligence Agency (CIA). He was a CIA operative for most of the 1960s and served as a member of the House of Representatives from 1989 to 2004. (U.S. House of Representatives)

endorsed legislation in 1995 that would have cut intelligence personnel by 20 percent over a five-year period as a budget-cutting measure. Goss served as chair of the House Permanent Committee on Intelligence from 1997 to 2005, and he helped to establish and then served on the Homeland Security Committee. Throughout his political career, Goss defended the CIA and generally supported budget increases for it. He also was a strong supporter of CIA director George Tenet.

The September 11, 2001, attacks brought Goss to the political forefront. He, along with his colleague and friend U.S. Senator Bob Graham (D-Fla.), began to call for a bipartisan investigation into the events surrounding September 11. Both in the Senate and in the House of Representatives there was reluctance to proceed, however. Opposition was even stronger in the George W. Bush administration against such an investigation. Most feared that an investigation would invite finger pointing and be tainted by politics. This fear on both the Republican and the Democratic sides slowed down the creation of a Senate-House Joint Inquiry on Intelligence, and the length of time provided to produce a report was unrealistically short. Despite the short time span—and reluctance or refusal to cooperate on the parts of the CIA, the FBI, and the White House—a valuable report was finally issued, with sections of it censored.

Goss ultimately opposed the creation of the September 11 Commission and many of its recommendations. Like many of his fellow Republicans, he was fearful that the commission would become a witch hunt against the Bush administration. Even after it was apparent that the commission was bipartisan, Goss opposed its recommendations on intelligence matters. His biggest concern was the report's recommendation to create the position of national intelligence director, whose job would be to oversee all intelligence agencies. As a conservative Republican, Goss defended the Bush administration in its War on Terror and was a severe critic of what he called the failures of the Bill Clinton administration.

The Bush administration noted Goss's loyalty. When George Tenet resigned as director of the CIA on June 3, 2004, Goss was nominated to become director of the CIA. Despite opposition from some Democratic senators, Goss won confirmation on September 22, 2004. During his confirmation hearings, Goss promised that he would bring change and reform to the CIA.

Goss's tenure as head of the CIA provided a mixed record. He began on September 24, 2004, with a mandate for change, but the top leadership of the CIA showed reluctance to accept him. These leaders were already distressed by how the CIA had been made a scapegoat for past mistakes by both the Clinton and Bush administrations. Several of Goss's top subordinates, particularly his chief adviser Patrick Murray, clashed with senior CIA management, leading three of the CIA's top officials to resign. An attempt by Goss to make the CIA more loyal to the Bush administration also brought criticism. His memo to CIA staff that it was their job "to support the administration and its policies" became a cause of resentment. Finally, Goss's promotion of his friend Kyle Dustin

"Dusty" Foggo from the ranks to a high CIA position and his links to former congressman Randy "Duke" Cunningham, who was convicted of accepting bribes, lowered morale in the CIA.

Eventually, Goss lost out in a power struggle with his nominal boss, John Negroponte. One of the reforms called for in the final report of the September 11 Commission was coordination of intelligence efforts. This recommendation led to the creation of the position of director of national intelligence (DNI) and the appointment of Negroponte, a career diplomat, to that post. Goss and Negroponte had disagreements about how to reform intelligence gathering. Goss was reluctant to transfer personnel and resources from the CIA to the National Counterterrorism Center (NCTC) and the National Counter Proliferation Center (NCPC). These disagreements led to Goss's surprising resignation on May 5, 2006, after only a 19-month tenure. His replacement was Negroponte's principal deputy director for national intelligence, Air Force general Michael Hayden.

STEPHEN A. ATKINS

See also

Bush, George Walker; Central Intelligence Agency; Clinton, William Jefferson; Counterterrorism Center; Negroponte, John Dimitri; September 11 Commission and Report; Tenet, George John

References

Graham, Bob. *Intelligence Matters: The CIA, the FBI, Saudi Arabia, and the Failure of America's War on Terror.* New York: Random House, 2004.

Risen, James. "Rifts Plentiful as 9/11 Inquiry Begins Today." *New York Times,* June 4, 2002, A1.

GRANBY, **Operation**
Event Date: 1991

Name given by the British to their military operations during the 1991 Persian Gulf War. Operation GRANBY covers both the British deployments to defend Saudi Arabia and the subsequent liberation of Kuwait, known to Americans as the separate Operations DESERT SHIELD and DESERT STORM.

The British contribution to Operation DESERT STORM, code-named Operation GRANBY, involved the British Army, Royal Navy, Royal Marines, and Royal Air Force (RAF), which deployed some 43,000 troops in total to the war zone. Operation GRANBY took its name from John Manners, Marques of Granby, a British commander in the Seven Years' War (1756–1763). The overall commander of British forces in the Middle East, based in Riyadh, Saudi Arabia, was initially Air Vice-Marshal Andrew Wilson. Wilson was replaced by army Lieutenant-General Sir Peter de la Billiére. British air forces were initially under the command of Air Vice-Marshal R. A. F. Wilson, then under Air Vice-Marshal William Wratten. British naval forces in the theater were under the command of Captain Anthony McEwen, then Commodore Paul Haddocks, and finally Commodore Christopher Craig.

The Royal Navy contingent initially included the destroyers *York*, *Battleaxe*, and *Jupiter*; three mine countermeasures ships; and the tanker *Orangeleaf*. As the deployment grew, three more mine countermeasure ships were added. The frigates *London* and *Brazen* were added as well as the training ship *Argus*, which was converted to a hospital ship. Two submarines, the *Opossum* and *Otus*, were also deployed to provide assistance for special operations troops. Also, the Royal Navy had various helicopters with support and attack capabilities. A total of 12,500 Royal Navy personnel served during Operation GRANBY, including a contingent of Royal Marines. In the course of the conflict, the Royal Navy suffered no losses in ships or submarines.

The Royal Air Force deployed six squadrons of aircraft to the Persian Gulf. The squadrons were based all around the Kuwaiti theater of operations in Saudi Arabia. Ground attack variants of the Panavia Tornado (GR.1), as well as the air defense variant (F.3) and Jaguar ground attack aircraft, were all deployed. After the initial air campaign, which began on January 16, 1991, the RAF also deployed 12 *Buccaneer* attack aircraft to assist the GR.1 Tornados in locating and striking ground targets with laser designators. Overall, the RAF deployed 158 aircraft and helicopters and 5,500 personnel to the Gulf. Six RAF aircraft were lost in combat, and 1 was lost in a noncombat accident.

The British Army initially deployed the 7th Armoured Brigade, the successor to the famous Desert Rats of the North African campaign during World War II, to the Persian Gulf. The 7th was initially attached to the U.S. 1st Marine Division and was eventually attached to the British 1st Armoured Division. The British Army's contribution to the ground component included 25,000 troops. The 1st Armoured division was charged with protecting the flank of the U.S. VII Corps that moved into Iraq through the breach in the Iraqi lines made by the U.S. 1st Infantry Division. With more than 43,000 men under arms deployed to the Gulf during Operation GRANBY, 25 British military personnel were killed in action, and an additional 45 were wounded in action.

STEVEN F. MARIN

See also

Billiére, Sir Peter Edgar de la; DESERT STORM, Operation; DESERT STORM, Operation, Coalition Nations' Contributions to; United Kingdom, Air Force, Persian Gulf War; United Kingdom, Army, Persian Gulf War; United Kingdom, Marines, Persian Gulf War; United Kingdom, Navy, Persian Gulf War

References

Black, Jeremy. *A Military History of Britain: From 1775 to the Present.* Westport CT: Greenwood, 2006.

Bratman, Fred. *War in the Persian Gulf.* Riverside, NJ: Millbrook, 1992.

De la Billière, General Sir Peter. *Storm Command: A Personal Account of the Gulf War.* London: HarperCollins, 1992.

Grand Council, Afghanistan

See Loya Jirga, Afghanistan

Gray, Alfred M., Jr.
Birth Date: June 22, 1928

U.S. Marine Corps officer and the 29th commandant of the corps (1987–1991). Gray is credited with changing the culture and attitudes of the Marine Corps during his tenure from one that emphasized careerism and bureaucracy to one that tried to instill the warrior spirit. Alfred M. Gray Jr. was born on June 22, 1928, at Rahway, New Jersey. He was raised in Point Pleasant Beach, New Jersey, and attended Lafayette College. Gray dropped out of college and enlisted in the Marine Corps in 1950. He saw action in the Korean War and soon attained the rank of sergeant. His superiors recognized his intelligence and leadership qualities, along with his aggressive combat skills, and he was commissioned a second lieutenant in April 1952. After completing officer training at Quantico, Virginia, Gray was sent to the Army Field Artillery School. He returned to Korea as an artillery officer with the 1st Marine Division before the 1953 armistice was signed.

During the 1950s Gray was trained as a communications officer and rotated through a number of postings. With the commitment of marine units to the defense of the Republic of Vietnam (RVN, South Vietnam), beginning in October 1965, Major Gray saw service with the 3rd Marine Division. He served in a number of different communications, artillery, and infantry posts before returning to Quantico to help develop advanced sensor technology for the battlefield. Gray returned to Vietnam in June 1969 and was assigned to reconnaissance duties. Staff and field commands followed. In April 1975 Gray commanded the 33rd Amphibious Brigade and Regimental Landing Team 4. His unit assisted in the final evacuation of U.S. personnel from Saigon (now Ho Chi Minh City).

Gray was promoted to brigadier general in March 1976 and to major general in February 1980, when he took command of the 2nd Marine Division at Camp Lejeune, North Carolina. Following promotion to lieutenant general in August 1984, Gray commanded the Fleet Marine Force, Atlantic, and the II Marine Expeditionary Force. He was promoted to full (four-star) general and became commandant of the Marine Corps on July 1, 1987.

Gray's experience in rising through the ranks from noncommissioned officer to commandant of the Marine Corps was unusual, but it gave him a background that was unique. Although he had earned a bachelor of science degree from the State University of New York, Gray did not have the reputation of being an intellectual. Nonetheless, he proved to be one of the most thoughtful commandants in Marine Corps history. His appointment was enthusiastically sponsored by James Webb, secretary of the navy under President Ronald Reagan.

After the Vietnam War, the Marine Corps suffered from declining morale and a loss of vision concerning what its mission should be. The process had already begun of clearing the deadwood and improving personnel in the corps. Although many improvements had been made, the corps had been badly shaken by the terrorist bombing of the marine barracks at Beirut, Lebanon, on October 23, 1983, which killed 241 marines and other Americans.

Gray believed that officers who had spent most of their careers in staff positions were too influential, and he immediately took a number of steps to reintroduce the "warrior spirit" into the corps. He ordered that boot camp for all marines include combat training. Previously, only those troops who were assigned to the infantry received combat training, and that was after boot camp. Gray believed that every marine, whatever his or her duty, should be a rifleman first. Aggressiveness and hard training were actively encouraged.

Gray worked to improve the quality and attitudes of the officers as well, and a number of generals were encouraged to retire. He introduced formal reading lists for all officers, to encourage them to think outside their usual patterns.

Noncommissioned officers received special attention from Gray. As a former sergeant, he recognized them as the heart of the corps. Gray spent much of his time traveling and meeting with enlisted men and listening to their suggestions and comments. He possessed a good memory for faces and names, and used it to cultivate a devoted following.

Finally, Gray emphasized that the marines should fight smart and use maneuver and mobility tactics to defeat their opponents whenever possible. He favored the fielding of light armored vehicles because of their utility in the limited conflicts traditionally fought by marines. Gray also supported enhanced amphibious capabilities.

During the Persian Gulf War, Gray as a service chief had no direct role in the planning and conduct of the war. He did, however, campaign for a greater role for the marines. Gray hoped to see an amphibious landing that would outflank the Iraqi defenses in southern Kuwait. When that option was rejected, he continued to push for a series of raids from the sea by marine units to tie down Iraqi troops. In the end, the amphibious operation was largely limited to a deception, although the 1st and 2nd Marine Divisions distinguished themselves in the land campaign.

The success of marine units in the war was seen by many as vindication of Gray's efforts to reorganize and reinvigorate the Marine Corps, and his successors have continued many of his reforms. Gray retired in 1991 and has since served on a number of corporate boards.

TIM J. WATTS

See also

DESERT STORM, Operation; United States Marine Corps, Persian Gulf War

References

Brown, Ronald J. *U.S. Marines in the Persian Gulf, 1990–1991: With Marine Forces Afloat in Desert Shield and Desert Storm.* Washington, DC: History and Museums Division, U.S. Marine Corps, 1998.

Ricks, Thomas E. *Making the Corps.* New York: Touchstone, 1997.

Greece, Role in Persian Gulf and Afghanistan Wars

Southeast European nation encompassing 50,942 square miles. Greece had a 2008 population of 10.723 million people. The country lies between the Ionian Sea and the Aegean Sea and is bordered by Albania, Macedonia, and Bulgaria to the north and Turkey to the east. Greece is a parliamentary democracy with a pro-Western orientation. The prime minister is the head of government, while the president, elected by parliament, is the head of state. The presidency in modern times has been largely ceremonial, however. Greece has multiple political parties. The largest and most influential ones include the New Democracy Party, the Panhellenic Socialist Movement, the Communist Party, the Coalition of the Radical Left, and the Popular Orthodox Rally.

Greece supported the U.S.-led coalitions during the 1991 Persian Gulf War and Operation ENDURING FREEDOM (2001–); however, it strongly opposed the 2003 Iraq War. Following the August 1990 Iraqi invasion of Kuwait, Greece deployed naval vessels as part of the multilateral squadron that enforced the United Nations (UN) economic sanctions against the regime of Saddam Hussein. Greece provided further support to the U.S. coalition by allowing the multilateral forces to use its air and naval facilities at Souda Bay in Crete. Greece also allowed a large number of its merchant ships to be chartered for use by the allied forces and sent approximately 200 troops to Saudi Arabia. Within the country, the government's cooperation with the United States met protests and civil disobedience. The domestic terrorist group November 17 carried out a series of bombings and other attacks against government facilities and Western targets. Greece deployed military forces to bolster its domestic police units and provide increased security against terrorism.

As with other West European states, Greece condemned the September 11, 2001, terrorist attacks against the United States. In the aftermath of the attacks, Greece increased intelligence cooperation with the United States and initiated reforms to the nation's intelligence agencies to better address the threat of Islamic terrorism. Greece also agreed to contribute troops to the International Security Assistance Force (ISAF) in Afghanistan. In January 2003 Greece deployed 124 troops, engineers, and security forces, along with 63 vehicles, as part of the ISAF. As of the end of 2009, there were 175 Greek troops in Afghanistan. The Greek force was stationed in Kabul along with a small staff contingent that operated as part of the ISAF headquarters. Greece also dispatched two Lockheed C-130 Hercules aircraft to Karachi, Pakistan, to provide logistical support to the coalition and stationed two frigates and a minesweeper in the Mediterranean.

Greece opposed military intervention in Iraq without UN authorization. There were also large public demonstrations against the war and two general strikes. In January 2003 Greece took over the rotating presidency of the European Union (EU) and endeavored unsuccessfully to develop a joint approach among the member states of the EU. Once the conflict in Iraq began in March 2003, domestic opposition to the conflict constrained the ability of the government to provide any support to the U.S.-led coalition. Greece declined to deploy troops as part of the invasion or subsequent occupation. However, Greece did not oppose the North Atlantic Treaty Organization (NATO) mission to train Iraqi security forces.

Meanwhile, Athens had been selected as the host of the 2004 Summer Olympic Games, and the government launched new security measures to protect the events from terrorist attacks. In March 2004 the Greek government formally requested security assistance from NATO to help safeguard the Olympics. NATO agreed to help monitor the no-fly zone that was established over Olympic events, provide intelligence cooperation, and assist with both maritime and ground security. NATO naval units involved in supporting Operation ENDURING FREEDOM were redeployed to patrol the Greek coast. The alliance further pledged support in the event of a catastrophic nuclear, biological, or chemical attack. The United States provided approximately $25 million in support for security for the Olympic Games, including training and enhanced intelligence cooperation.

TOM LANSFORD

See also

Afghanistan, Coalition Combat Operations in, 2002–Present; International Security Assistance Force; IRAQI FREEDOM, Operation, Coalition Ground Forces; North Atlantic Treaty Organization in Afghanistan

References

Cockburn, Patrick. *The Occupation: War and Resistance in Iraq.* New York: Verso, 2007.

Feickert, Andrew. *U.S. and Coalition Military Operations in Afghanistan: Issues for Congress.* Washington, DC: Congressional Research Service, 2006.

Keegan, John. *The Iraq War: The Military Offensive, from Victory in 21 Days to the Insurgent Aftermath.* New York: Vintage, 2005.

Green Zone in Iraq

Highly fortified walled-off section of central Baghdad (Iraq), also know as the International Zone, that is the location of many of Iraq's government buildings. The Green Zone was established soon after the March 2003 invasion of Iraq by U.S. and coalition forces and became the area in which most U.S. and coalition occupation authorities worked and lived. The Green Zone is approximately four square miles in land area.

The Green Zone is entirely surrounded by reinforced concrete walls capable of absorbing explosions from car and truck bombs, improvised explosive devices (IEDs), and suicide bombers. The walls are topped by barbed and concertina wire to foil anyone attempting to scale them. In areas where the likelihood of insurgent infiltration is high, the blast walls are supplemented by thick earthen berms. There are fewer than a half dozen entry and exit points into and out of the zone, all of which are manned around the clock by well-trained and well-armed civilian guards and military police.

Since 2006, Iraqi forces have begun to bear the largest burden of protecting the Green Zone. They are aided in their mission by

M1-Abrams tanks, Humvees, and armored personnel carriers equipped with .50-caliber machine guns.

The Green Zone is home to many of Iraq's most important government buildings and ministries, including the Military Industry Ministry. The Green Zone encompasses several presidential palaces and villas used by former president Saddam Hussein, his sons Uday and Qusay, and other Baath Party loyalists. The Republican Palace, the largest of Hussein's residences, is located there. Considered Hussein's principal base of power, it was akin to the White House for the U.S. president. For that reason, it was a key target for coalition forces as they moved into Iraq in 2003.

The zone includes several large markets, stores, shops, restaurants, and large hotels and a convention center. Also found in the Green Zone are the former Baath Party headquarters, a military museum, and the Tomb of the Unknown Soldier. There is also an elaborate underground bunker constructed to shield key government officials during time of war.

Since the coalition invasion, the Green Zone has housed all the occupation officials' offices and residences. It is also currently home to the Iraqi government. The vast majority of civilian contractors and independent security firm personnel are also located there. The American, British, Australian, and other international embassies and legations as well as most media reporters are located within the Green Zone.

Despite the elaborate security measures within the Green Zone, the area has been targeted on numerous occasions for attacks by truck bombs, suicide bombers with explosives-laden backpacks, and rockets and mortars. After measures were taken to further limit egress into the Green Zone such incidents declined, although they were not entirely eliminated. Nevertheless, rebels and insurgents continue to attack the Green Zone, employing rocket-propelled grenades (RPGs), IEDs, and even Katuysha rockets.

Some Iraqis and those in the international community have criticized the existence of the Green Zone because it entirely isolates occupation officials and Iraqi government officials from the grim and perilous realities of life in Iraq. Outside the Green Zone lies what has come to be called the Red Zone, an area into which occupation authorities rarely venture and lawlessness and chaos abound. Although occupation forces have been criticized for having established an artificial oasis in a worn-torn nation, the Green Zone will likely remain for some time, walled off from the remainder of Iraq unless or until violence perpetrated by insurgents and terrorists comes to an end.

PAUL G. PIERPAOLI JR.

See also

Baghdad; Improvised Explosive Devices; Iraqi Insurgency; Rocket-Propelled Grenade

References

Chandrasekaran, Rajiv. *Imperial Life in the Emerald City: Inside Iraq's Green Zone.* New York: Viking Books, 2007.

Mowle, Thomas S., ed. *Hope Is Not a Plan: The War in Iraq from Inside the Green Zone.* Westport, CT: Praeger, 2007.

Griffith, Ronald Houston
Birth Date: March 16, 1936

U.S. Army general and commander of the 1st Armored Division during Operations DESERT SHIELD and DESERT STORM. Ronald Houston Griffith was born in Lafayette, Georgia, on March 16, 1936. While studying at the University of Georgia, he joined the U.S. Army's Reserve Officers' Training Corps (ROTC). Graduating with a BS degree in 1960, he was commissioned a second lieutenant.

Griffith's introduction to combat began early in his military career. From 1964 to 1965, as a first lieutenant, he served as an infantry unit adviser with the Army of the Republic of Vietnam (ARVN, South Vietnamese Army). Later he spent a second tour in Vietnam (1969–1970) as executive officer of the 2nd Battalion, 8th Infantry Regiment, 4th Infantry Division.

Griffith rose steadily through the ranks while serving in both command and staff positions. Known for his administrative and strong leadership skills, he led platoons at Fort Hood, Texas, and in South Korea; was a company commander in the 2nd Armored Division at Fort Hood; and commanded the 1st Battalion, 32nd Armored Regiment in West Germany and the 1st Brigade, 2nd Infantry Division, in South Korea. He also received an MA degree in public administration from Shippensburg University in Pennsylvania and attended both the Command and General Staff College and the Army War College.

In the mid-1980s Griffith served in the Pentagon in the Operations Division of the Department of the Army. On December 1, 1987, he was promoted to brigadier general and was subsequently appointed assistant division commander of the 1st Armored Division in West Germany. The following year he became its commander. Griffith received his second star on October 1, 1990, just prior to the Persian Gulf War.

During Operations DESERT SHIELD and DESERT STORM, Griffith's division played a prominent role in land operations. In 1990–1991 the United States had deployed to the Persian Gulf a total of 527,000 personnel and 2,000 tanks, many of them the M-1A1 Abrams tanks. After a withering aerial assault against Iraqi government buildings and fixed military entrenchments, U.S. Central Command commander General H. Norman Schwarzkopf ordered the land offensive to begin driving Iraqi troops from Kuwait.

The action commenced on February 24, 1991. Griffith's 1st Armored Division was directly involved in the massive highly mobile left-hook maneuver around and through Iraqi positions to the west of Kuwait in an effort to envelop and destroy the elite Republic Guard forces of Iraqi president Saddam Hussein. The maneuver was carried out by combined U.S., British, and French armored and airborne forces. VII Corps deployed four armored divisions including Griffith's, which occupied the northernmost position. Quickly and decisively, U.S. armored and mechanized units and attack helicopters advanced practically unscathed toward the city of Basra on the leading edge of the left hook. Griffith was known for his aggressiveness in combat, and his 1st Armored Division soon defeated the Medina Armored Division and the Iraqi 26th Infantry Division.

On February 23 three of Griffith's maneuver brigades destroyed 300 Iraqi armored vehicles and only lost one soldier. The 2nd Brigade alone destroyed 60 Iraqi T-72s and dozens of personnel carriers. Although some Republican Guard units fought well, they were no match for the lethal U.S. tanks and mechanized vehicles. Kuwait City was liberated, and U.S. forces had advanced into Iraq.

On August 1, 1991, Griffith was promoted to lieutenant general and reassigned to the Pentagon. In 1995 while serving as the inspector general of the U.S. Army, he became the first person in that position to be promoted to four-star rank (June 6, 1995). From 1995 to 1997 Griffith served as vice chief of staff of the U.S. Army.

Griffith retired from the U.S. Army on November 1, 1997. He has since served as executive vice president of Military Professional Resources, Inc. (MPRI). He also serves on the board of directors of the Allied Defense Group, and in 2008 he was reelected to the Board of Visitors of the Virginia Military Institute. Griffith and his wife reside in Alexandria, Virginia.

CHARLES F. HOWLETT

See also

Armored Warfare, Persian Gulf and Iraq Wars; Basra; Busayyah, Battle of; DESERT STORM, Operation; DESERT STORM, Operation, Ground Operations; M1A1 and M1A2 Abrams Main Battle Tanks; T-72 Main Battle Tank

References

Atkinson, Rick. *Crusade: The Untold Story of the Persian Gulf War.* New York: Mariner Books, 1994.

Bourque, Stephen A. *Jayhawk! The VII Corps in the Persian Gulf War.* Washington, DC: Department of the Army, 2002.

Cordesman, Anthony H. "The Persian Gulf War." In *The Oxford Companion to American Military History,* edited by John W. Chambers II, 544–546. New York: Oxford University Press, 1999.

Scales, Robert H. *Certain Victory: The U.S. Army in the Gulf War.* Washington, DC: Brassey's, 1994.

Swain, Richard. *Lucky War: The Third Army in Desert Storm.* Fort Leavenworth, KS: U.S. Army Command and General Staff College Press, 1999.

Woodward, Bob. *The Commanders.* New York: Simon and Schuster, 1991.

Guantánamo Bay Detainment Camp

Detainment camp operated by the U.S. government to hold enemy combatants taken prisoner during the Global War on Terror, which began in late 2001 after the September 11, 2001, terror attacks against the United States. The Guantánamo Bay Detainment Camp is situated on the Guantánamo Bay Naval Base, operated by the United States in southeastern Cuba. The base is an area of 45 square miles that has been formally occupied by the United States since 1903, a result of the 1898 Spanish-American War. The original intent of the base was to serve as a coaling station for the

U.S. military police escort a detainee to his cell at the naval base at Guantánamo Bay, Cuba, on January 11, 2002. (U.S. Department of Defense)

U.S. Navy. A subsequent lease was signed on July 2, 1906, on the same terms. A new lease was negotiated between the Cuban and U.S. governments in 1934.

Shortly after the 1959 Cuban Revolution, the Castro government demanded that the Guantánamo Bay area be returned to Cuban sovereignty, but the U.S. government refused, citing that the lease required the agreement of both parties to the modification or abrogation of the agreement. Since then, the United States has continued to send a check to the Cuban government for the lease amount every year, but the Cuban government has steadfastly refused to cash them.

During its invasion of Afghanistan that began in October 2001, the U.S. military captured a large number of Al Qaeda fighters and other insurgents. The George W. Bush administration determined that those captured were enemy combatants, not prisoners of war.

This decision came after lawyers from the White House, the Pentagon, and the Justice Department issued a series of secret memorandums that maintained that the prisoners had no rights under federal law or the Geneva Conventions. In this ruling, enemy combatants could be held indefinitely without charges. A number of conservative lawyers in the Justice Department's Office of Legal Counsel (OLC) provided the legal opinions for this decision. The Bush administration issued this decision on January 22, 2002.

Finally, after considering several sites to hold these prisoners, the U.S. military decided to build a prison at Guantánamo Bay, Cuba, the Guantánamo Bay Detention Camp. Camp X-Ray was the first facility, and the first 110 prisoners arrived there on January 11, 2002. They were held in wire cages. Later Camp Delta was constructed, but neither camp was up to standards for prison inmates in the United States. At their peak, the camps held 680 prisoners.

The Bush administration selected Guantánamo Bay for a specific reason. If the prisoners were held on U.S. soil, then the prisoners might claim access to legal representation and American courts. Guantánamo Bay fell under a unique legal situation because the land is leased from Cuba and thus is not technically American soil. Furthermore, because the United States has no diplomatic relationship with Cuba, the prisoners had no access to the Cuban legal system. There the prisoners reside in legal limbo with few if any legal rights.

The detainment camp is run by the U.S. military. At the beginning, command responsibility for the base was divided between Major General Michael Dunlavey, an army reservist, and Brigadier General Rick Baccus, of the Rhode Island National Guard. Dunlavey maintained a hard-line attitude toward the detainees, but Baccus was more concerned about their possible mistreatment. They often quarreled over interrogation techniques and other issues. This situation changed when U.S. Army major general

Geoffrey Miller replaced them and established a unitary command at Guantánamo in November 2003.

Miller had no experience running a prison camp, and he was soon criticized for allowing harsh interrogation techniques including the controversial waterboarding technique, which the Bush administration insisted was not torture. Later Miller was transferred to Iraq, where he took over responsibility for military prisons there.

After Camp Delta was built, the detainees lived in better but still restrictive conditions. At Camp X-Ray, the original camp, the detainees lived behind razor wire in cells open to the elements and with buckets in place of toilets. At Camp Delta the detainees were held in trailerlike structures made from old shipping containers that had been cut in half lengthwise, with the two pieces stuck together end to end. Cells were small, six feet eight inches by eight feet, with metal beds fixed to the steel mesh walls. Toilets were squatting-style flush on the floor, and sinks were low to the ground so that detainees could wash their feet before Muslim prayer. There was no air conditioning for the detainees, only a ventilation system that was supposed to be turned on at 85 degrees but rarely was. Later a medium-security facility opened up, and it gave much greater freedom and better living conditions to the detainees.

The Bush administration gave the Central Intelligence Agency (CIA) responsibility for interrogations. Because these enemy combatants had no legal standing in American courts, they were treated as merely sources of intelligence. President Bush had determined this stance after deciding that Al Qaeda was a national security issue, not a law enforcement issue. Consequently, the Federal Bureau of Investigation (FBI) was completely left out of the loop. But this did not mean that the FBI gave up on questioning prisoners. For various reasons, FBI personnel did interrogate the detainees on occasion.

To encourage cooperation, levels of treatment for detainees are determined by the degree of a detainee's cooperation. Level one was for cooperating prisoners, and they received special privileges. Level two included more moderately cooperative detainees, and they received a few privileges, such as a drinking cup and access to the library. Level three was for the detainees who absolutely refused to cooperate. They were given only the basics: a blanket, a prayer mat and cap, a Qur'an, and a toothbrush.

The CIA ultimately determined that the most important Al Qaeda prisoners should not be held at the Guantánamo Bay Detention Camp. There were simply too many American officials from too many agencies trying to interrogate the prisoners. Moreover, it was too public. CIA leaders wanted a secret location where there would be no interference in the interrogations. Several secret interrogation sites were then set up in friendly countries where the CIA could do what they wanted without interference.

Soon after the prisoners had been transferred to the Guantánamo Bay Detention Camp, reports began to surface about mistreatment of the detainees, which caused considerable consternation abroad. In the late spring of 2002, a CIA analyst visited the camp and was aghast at the treatment of the prisoners. Because he spoke Arabic, he was able to talk to the detainees. In his report the analyst claimed that half of the detainees did not belong there. This report traveled throughout the Bush administration, but no action was taken regarding it. The American public was still upset over the September 11 attacks, and public reports about mistreatment of those held at Guantánamo Bay garnered little sympathy.

The Bush administration decided in the summer of 2006 to transfer the top captured Al Qaeda leaders to the Guantánamo Bay Detention Camp. In September 2006 the transfer of these 14 detainees was complete. Then, beginning in March 2007, court proceedings were begun to determine their status. In the most important case, that of Khalid Sheikh Muhammed, the accused made a total confession of all his activities both in and outside Al Qaeda. However, his confessions were elicited through torture and physical abuse. Among these were the planning for the September 11 attacks and the execution of U.S. journalist Daniel Pearl. Muhammed's justification was that he was at war against the United States. Proceedings against the other detainees continued in the spring of 2007.

Meanwhile, growing public criticism in the United States and elsewhere about the status of the detainees led to a series of court cases in the United States in 2007 and 2008 that tried to establish a legal basis for them. Finally, in June 2008 the U.S. Supreme Court ruled that Guantánamo detainees were indeed subject to protection under the U.S. Constitution. By that time the situation in Cuba had become a public relations fiasco for the Bush administration. In October 2008 a federal court judge ordered the release of five Algerians being held at Guantánamo because the government had shown insufficient evidence for their continued incarceration. More detainees were likely to be reevaluated, which would result in their potential release or a trial. Experts have recommended exactly such a process, which they termed R2T2: (1) review, (2) release or transfer, and (3) try. In January 2009 President Barack Obama firmly declared that his administration would close the prison at Guantánamo but conceded that doing so presented unique challenges and would take some time. Since 2008, discussions have taken place with other countries that have agreed to take prisoners. Some have already been released to other countries, where they are incarcerated.

STEPHEN A. ATKINS

See also

Bush, George Walker; Coercive Interrogation; Global War on Terror; Mohammed, Khalid Sheikh; Torture of Prisoners

References

Epstein, Edward. "Guantanamo Is a Miniature America." *San Francisco Chronicle,* January 20, 2002, A6.

Hansen, Jonathan M. "Making the Law in Cuba." *New York Times,* April 20, 2004, A19.

Hersh, Seymour. *Chain of Command: The Road from 9/11 to Abu Ghraib.* New York: HarperCollins, 2004.

Saar, Erik, and Viveca Novak. *Inside the Wire: A Military Intelligence Soldier's Eyewitness Account of Life at Guantanamo.* New York: Penguin, 2005.

Mendelsohn, Sarah E. *Closing Guantanamo: From Bumper Sticker to Blueprint.* Washington, DC: Center for Security and International Studies, 2008.

Yee, John. *War by Other Means: An Insider's Account of the War on Terror.* New York: Atlantic Monthly, 2006.

Gulf Act

See Persian Gulf Conflict Supplemental Authorization and Personnel Benefits Act of 1991

Gulf Cooperation Council

Middle Eastern mutual security and economic cooperation organization. The Gulf Cooperation Council (GCC) was formed by Arab states on May 25, 1981, mainly as a counter to the threat posed from the Islamic Republic of Iran. At the time, Iran was in the early stages of its fundamentalist Islamic revolution and was involved in fighting Iraq in the Iran-Iraq War of 1980–1988. In general, the region's Arab nations eyed Iran with great suspicion and hoped to contain Islamic fundamentalism to that state.

The GCC is made up of six member states: Bahrain, Kuwait, Oman, Qatar, Saudi Arabia, and the United Arab Emirates (UAE). Among these countries, the political systems, socioeconomic forces, and overall culture are quite similar, making cooperation among them relatively easy to achieve. Led by Saudi Arabia, together these states possess roughly half of the world's known oil reserves.

The GCC's power is therefore principally economic, and its main goal is to boost the economic might of its members. On the military side, the GCC established a collective defense force in 1984 (effective since 1986), sometimes called the Peninsula Shield, based in Saudi Arabia near King Khalid Military City at Hafar al-Batin and commanded by a Saudi military officer. Even before the mutual security pact was established, joint military maneuvers had been carried out since 1983.

The Peninsula Shield comprises one infantry brigade and is currently maintained at an estimated 7,000 troops. Oman's proposal to extend the force to 100,000 troops in 1991 was turned down. The force did not participate in the 1991 Persian Gulf War as a distinct unit. Through the GCC, military assistance has been extended to Bahrain and to Oman, funded mostly by Kuwait and Saudi Arabia. Plans to integrate naval and ground radar systems and to create a combined air control and warning system based on Saudi Airborne Warning and Control System (AWACS) aircraft have been repeatedly delayed until just recently.

While all GCC members agree in their desire to become more independent from U.S. security arrangements, they have yet to find consensus as to how this could best be achieved. This became a contentious issue during the conflict with Iraq in 1991, with some states, foremost Kuwait and Saudi Arabia, forming parts of the international coalition against Iraq, while others remained opposed to the action. Notably, in March 1991 just weeks after the Persian Gulf War ended, the GCC agreed—together with Egypt and Syria—to form a security alliance to protect Kuwait against renewed aggression.

Deep divisions also exist as to whether or how Iran, Iraq, and Yemen could be brought into the GCC. The same is true on the issue of political reforms. Militant Islam is seen as a significant threat by Saudi Arabia, while some other members would like to speed up liberalization of the political process, including the admittance of Islamic parties. Since 2004 the GCC countries also share intelligence in the fight against terror but to a limited extent. In November 2006 Saudi Arabia proposed expanding the GCC's military force to 22,000 troops, so far to no effect.

The GCC's structure includes the Supreme Council, the highest decision-making body, composed of the heads of the six member states. Meetings are held annually; the presidency of the council rotates in alphabetical order. Decisions by the Supreme Council on substantive issues require unanimous approval. The council also appoints a secretary-general for a three-year term, renewable once. The secretary-general supervises the day-to-day affairs of the GCC. Currently, Abd-al-Rahman al-Attiya from Qatar is the secretary-general. The Ministerial Council convenes every three months, proposes policies, and manages the implementation of GCC decisions. The Ministerial Council is usually made up of the member states' foreign ministers. Should problems among member states arise, the Commission for the Settlement of Disputes meets on an ad hoc basis to seek a peaceful solution to disagreements. The Defense Planning Council also advises the GCC on military matters relating to its joint armed forces.

THOMAS J. WEILER

See also

Bahrain; DESERT STORM, Operation; Iran-Iraq War; Iranian Revolution; Iraq, History of, Pre-1990; Iraq, History of, 1990–Present; Kuwait; Middle East, History of, 1945–Present; Middle East Regional Defense Organizations; Oman, Role in Persian Gulf and Iraq Wars; Qatar; Saudi Arabia; Saudi Arabia, Armed Forces; United Arab Emirates

References

Dietl, Gulshan. *Through Two Wars and Beyond: A Study of the Gulf Cooperation Council.* New Delhi: Lancer Books, 1991.

Ramazani, Rouhollah K. *The Gulf Cooperation Council: Record and Analysis.* Charlottesville: University Press of Virginia, 1988.

Gulf War Syndrome

Name given to a host of physical symptoms and maladies among U.S. and British veterans who fought in the 1991 Persian Gulf War. The exact origins of these is unknown. Gulf War Syndrome (GWS) is a progressive neuron-degenerative and immunological multisymptom condition that apparently is not explainable by posttraumatic stress disorder (PTSD) or other variables. GWS may afflict as many as tens of thousands of people, and some estimates run as high as 150,000. The cause of GWS is unclear; indeed, its very existence is still questioned in some governmental and scientific circles. As the research and the debate continue, the continuing decline of those who suffer from GWS could push the total number of American fatalities from the Persian Gulf War past the total number of those lost in the Vietnam War.

Operation DESERT STORM was seen as a dazzling tactical success for U.S.-led coalition forces. The Iraqis were routed in four days of ground combat, and Kuwait was liberated at the cost of just a few coalition causalities. The troops returned home, at least to the United States, to waves of hyperpatriotism. However, within months some veterans began reporting unusual physical symptoms. Those few became, over time, thousands and then tens of thousands. Persian Gulf War veterans reported symptoms such as chronic fatigue, loss of muscle control, persistent headaches, sleep disorders, memory loss, chronic pain, and other chronic and disabling conditions.

Later, medical research began to show that Persian Gulf War veterans were developing amyotrophic lateral sclerosis (ALS, or Lou Gehrig's disease) at two times the rate of soldiers who had not deployed to the Gulf. Studies have also shown greater than normal risks for multiple sclerosis, fibromyalgia, brain cancer, and, perhaps most frightening, birth defects in children born to parents who were Persian Gulf War vets.

Despite years of official denial of the existence of GWS by the U.S. Department of Defense and the British Ministry of Defense, the two organizations have now funded an enormous number of medical, military, and scientific investigations into the causes of GWS. In a comprehensive 452-page report of November 2008, the Research Advisory Committee on Gulf War Veterans' Illnesses, conducted by the U.S. Department of Veterans Affairs, declared the syndrome real. Causative agents included exposure to the drug pyridostigmine bromide, meant to protect against nerve gas and pesticides. In addition, exposure to nerve agents, smoke, and other agents may have contributed to the victims' conditions.

Some other theories have blamed vaccines. Before heading off to service in the Gulf, troops received multiple vaccinations to provide protection against a number of communicable diseases. The vaccines that may have been most problematic were those for anthrax. Concerns have been voiced about the combination and number of vaccines as well as the chemical used in the immunizations. After the war, troops who had never been to the Gulf but had been given the anthrax vaccine began to develop GWS-like symptoms. In 2004 a federal judge ruled that the Pentagon must stop administering the anthrax vaccine because there was good reason to believe that it was harmful. It should be noted that French troops, who were not vaccinated, have not reported GWS. However, the November 2008 report issued by the U.S. Department of Veterans Affairs holds that there is little reason to believe that the anthrax vaccine, or depleted uranium, played a role in the syndrome.

Some troops in the field may have been exposed to repeated low-level doses of chemical weaponry such as sarin or other nerve

An ammunition specialist examines a 105-mm armor-piercing sabot round to be used in an M-1 Abrams main battle tank during Operation DESERT STORM. Many antitank projectiles contain depleted uranium, but the U.S. Department of Veterans Affairs holds that there is little reason to believe that depleted uranium played a role in causing Gulf War Syndrome. (U.S. Department of Defense)

agents or mustard gases. Low-level exposures were common, and Iraqi troops did, ineffectively, attempt to use chemical weapons on coalition troops. But the exposure may also have been the result of coalition bombing of Iraqi chemical weapon depots, which would have resulted in a wide dispersal of a thin cloud of dust and a low dose of sarin, soman, or one of the mustard gasses. One report claims that the British NIAD (Nerve-Agent Immobilised Enzyme Alarm and Detector) chemical and biological weapons detection systems went off 18,000 times during the war. Such repeated low-dose exposures could be a causative factor, yet it seems unlikely that such widespread exposures would have been overlooked by the military.

Pesticides, both government issued and locally purchased, were used widely by American and British troops. They sprayed them on their bodies, tents, and buildings and on prisoners of war. As a result, Persian Gulf War vets received varying degrees of long-term exposure to organophosphate and carbamate pesticides. Studies reviewed by the RAND Corporation for the Research

Advisory Committee on Gulf War Veterans' Illnesses suggest that the pesticides could be a potentially contributing factor in GWS.

A few studies have suggested parasites such as leishmaniasis as a possible culprit in GWS. Many researchers are now pursuing the difficult-to-detect mycoplasma bacteria, while others theorized that GWS may be the result of some as yet unknown virus or bacterial agent. This theory has been given some support by gastrointestinal diseases caused during the war. Many reports of troops drinking from local water supplies or eating local vegetables that were watered or cleaned with contaminated local water have surfaced. Because this theory deals with intangibles, it is difficult to rule in or out.

Battlefield stress and PTSD have certainly always been a part of warfare. The stress that a soldier faces in battle most certainly has a negative effect on his or her health. To assert that GWS was the modern equivalent of shell-shock or battle fatigue, however, would simply be wrong, and research indicates that stress alone does not cause GWS. Be that as it may, stress may play a role in intensifying the symptoms of GWS.

Pyridostigmine bromide (PB) was administered to coalition troops as a pretreatment against exposure to the nerve agent soman. PB was only the first part of the treatment; if a soldier was exposed to militarily effective doses of soman, then a second treatment would be administered that was designed to combine with the PB already in the body. Because of the lack of knowledge of pyridostigmine bromide's short- or long-term effects on the nervous system, it cannot be ruled out as a possible factor.

Depleted uranium (DU) is a by-product of the enrichment of natural uranium to produce reactor fuel and weapons-grade isotopes. It is used as a projectile because it can tear through nearly any armor thanks to its density and self-sharpening nature. It also is a perfect metal to enhance one's one armor. DU shells were routinely employed in the Persian Gulf War, and many vehicles also used it to augment their armor. Some researchers claim that between its natural low-level radioactivity and the dust and uranyl oxide gas it creates on impact, DU is a health hazard and could be a cause of GWS. However, medical and scientific research seems to show that DU is safe and causes no negative long-term health effects. All the while, other studies claim that DU is a neurotoxin.

As Iraqi forces retreated from Kuwait, they set the oil fields, containing hundreds of wells, ablaze. The fires burned for nine months. Many theorists point to those sky-darkening infernos as a possible cause for GWS. While many short-term respiratory problems were reported at the time, studies since have shown that even though there was a great deal of airborne particulate matter,

U.S. Marine Corps major Randy Hebert testifies on Capitol Hill on December 10, 1996, before a subcommittee hearing on Persian Gulf veterans' illnesses. Hebert, who was diagnosed with Lou Gehrig's disease, believes his exposure to low levels of a chemical weapons agent in February 1991 caused his medical problems. Gulf War Syndrome is a term used to describe a number of different and mysterious ailments suffered by veterans of that conflict. (AP/Wide World Photos)

the amount of pollutants in the air, according to RAND, was lower than U.S. recommended occupational standards.

There exist dozens of other theories concerning the cause of GWS ranging from the plausible (inhibited red fuming nitric acid from Iraqi Scud missiles) to the hardly plausible (illicit experimentation by the U.S. military). The interesting fact to note about GWS is that it has been clustered among American and British troops. Why is that so? Some researchers point to the simple facts that American and British troops used more pesticides, were involved in more combat, used the anthrax vaccine, and reported by far the most chemical attack warnings. They were also arrayed on the battlefield in such a way that the prevailing winds pushed the airborne clouds of dust and debris from allied bombings, much of which was dispersed as high as the upper atmosphere, right overtop of them. From there it fell like a slow dusty rain from the front lines all the way to Saudi Arabia and Kuwait.

Both the U.S. and British governments met the initial GWS claims from ill veterans with skepticism. Both governments initially also refused to pay veterans' disability claims for GWS. Veterans knew that they were facing a battle against time, because seven years after a U.S. soldier leaves the service he or she can no longer report combat-related illnesses and get government assistance.

American veterans, however, finally met with modest success in their battle to be heard. In 1998 Congress established the Research Advisory Committee on Gulf War Veterans' Illnesses. In 2002 the Department of Defense ad'mitted that Persian Gulf War vets were showing signs of neural damage. By 2004 the U.S. government, through the Research Advisory Committee on Gulf War Veterans' Illnesses, seemed to make the recognition of GWS official policy. The committee's 2004 report admitted that between 26 and 32 percent of all Persian Gulf War veterans do manifest a multisymptom progressive neurodegenerative condition that is neither psychiatric nor stress related. The report also supports the idea that soldiers' exposure to chemical agents and pesticides seem to be the most plausible causative factors.

The report seemed to create a new openness between government and veterans. In 2005 the Department of Defense sent letters to 100,000 veterans informing them that they had been exposed to low levels of a chemical agent when a munitions dump at Khamisiyah, Iraq, was destroyed. By 2006 the U.S. federal budget included $15 million per year over a five-year period dedicated to research into Persian Gulf War illnesses. Legislation is even being considered that would eliminate the seven-year cutoff rule for U.S. Persian Gulf War vets.

British GWS veterans, on the other hand, have received little sympathy from their government. Soon after the war, the official line was that GWS was a PTSD. Then, after seeing military specialists, soldiers were told that their problems had nothing to do with the war. In 2003 the Media Research Council concluded that GWS was no single syndrome but rather merely each ill veteran's individual perception of his or her own health. As of 2004, the British Ministry of Defense still insisted that there was no link between GWS and service in the Gulf. Nevertheless, in 2005 the British Pension Appeals Tribunal ordered the Ministry of Defense to acknowledge the existence of GWS as a disability and to pay the veterans afflicted with GWS their appropriate pension. As of 2006 the Ministry of Defense had simply ignored the decision. This means that the government will save millions of pounds now and, if it survives legal challenges, could push retired servicemen past the length of time they are allowed to claim compensation for service-induced disability.

B. Keith Murphy

See also
Biological Weapons and Warfare; Chemical Weapons and Warfare; desert storm, Operation; Post-Traumatic Stress Disorder; Scud Missiles, U.S. Search for during the Persian Gulf War

References
Harley, Naomi H., Ernest C. Foulkes, Lee H. Hilborne, Arlene Hudson, and C. Ross Anthony. *Depleted Uranium: Gulf War Illnesses Series,* Vol. 7, *A Review of the Scientific Literature as It Pertains to Gulf War Illnesses.* Santa Monica, CA: National Defense Research Institute/ RAND Corporation, 1999.

Johnson, Alison. *Gulf War Syndrome: Legacy of a Perfect War.* Brunswick, ME: MCS Information Exchange, 2001.

Research Advisory Committee on Gulf War Veteran's Illnesses, U.S. Department of Veteran's Affairs. *Gulf War Illness and the Health of Gulf War Veterans: Scientific Findings and Recommendations.* Washington, DC: U.S. Department of Veteran's Affairs, November, 2008.

Wheelwright, Jeff. *The Irritable Heart: The Medical Mystery of the Gulf War.* New York: Norton, 2001.

H

Haass, Richard Nathan
Birth Date: July 28, 1951

Foreign policy expert, prolific author, and national security/foreign policy official in the George H. W. Bush and George W. Bush administrations. Richard Nathan Haass was born in Brooklyn, New York, on July 28, 1951. He received his BA degree from Oberlin College (Ohio) in 1973. Selected as a Rhodes Scholar, he continued his education at Oxford University, from which he ultimately earned both a master's and a doctoral degree. Haass subsequently held a series of academic posts at Hamilton College and the John F. Kennedy School of Government at Harvard University. He also served as vice president and director of foreign policy studies at the Brookings Institute and held posts with the prestigious Carnegie Endowment for International Peace and the International Institute for Strategic Studies. Although Haass's interests and research are wide reaching, most of it deals with foreign policy and national security issues. By the end of the 1980s, he had become especially interested in the Middle East.

Haass began his government service in 1979 as an analyst for the Department of Defense, a post he held until 1980. Concomitantly, he was a legislative aide for the U.S. Senate. In 1981 he began serving in the U.S. State Department, where he remained until 1985. By 1989 Haass had earned a reputation as a thoughtful yet cautious foreign policy adviser. That year he began serving as a special assistant to President George H. W. Bush as senior director for Near East and East Asian Affairs on the National Security Council (NSC). As such, Haass was deeply involved in the policy decisions surrounding Operations DESERT SHIELD and DESERT STORM. Indeed, he helped facilitate the Bush administration's success in cobbling together an impressive international coalition that ultimately defeated Iraq in 1991 and reversed that nation's occupation of Kuwait. In 1991 Haass was given the Presidential Citizens Medal for his work before and during the Persian Gulf War. Haass resigned his post in 1993 at the end of Bush's term in office.

When President George W. Bush took office in January 2001, Haass was appointed the State Department's director of policy planning, arguably the most influential foreign policy post next to that of secretary of state. Haass's main role during this time was to act as Secretary of State Colin L. Powell's chief adviser. Remaining in this post until June 2003, Haass had a significant role in the U.S. reaction to the September 11 terror attacks, the subsequent war in Afghanistan (Operation ENDURING FREEDOM), and the lead-up to war with Iraq in March 2003. Perhaps reflecting Powell's caution and skepticism toward the implementation of a second war with Iraq, Haass was not seen as a war hawk, at least not in the same league as neoconservatives such as Deputy Secretary of Defense Paul Wolfowitz, Secretary of Defense Donald Rumsfeld, or Vice President Richard (Dick) Cheney. While Powell's more cautious stance was cast aside in the months leading up to the war, Haass nevertheless remained publicly loyal to Bush's foreign policy.

For a brief time Haass served as policy coordinator for U.S. policy in Afghanistan after the fall of the Taliban regime there. He also served as special U.S. envoy to the Northern Ireland peace process, succeeding Senator George Mitchell. In late 2003 Haass chose to step down from government service and was awarded the Distinguished Honor Award from the U.S. Department of State. In July 2003 he accepted the post of president of the Council on Foreign Relations (CFR), and upon his departure from government he dedicated all of his efforts to the CFR. The CFR is a nonpartisan independent think tank and publisher dedicated to studying and articulating the foreign policies of the United States and other nations of the world. The author of 12 books by 2008, Haass lives in New York City.

PAUL G. PIERPAOLI JR.

See also

Bush, George Herbert Walker; Bush, George Walker; Cheney, Richard Bruce; DESERT SHIELD, Operation; DESERT STORM, Operation; ENDURING FREEDOM, Operation; IRAQI FREEDOM, Operation; Neoconservatism; Powell, Colin Luther; Rumsfeld, Donald Henry; Wolfowitz, Paul Dundes

References

DeYoung, Karen. *Soldier: The Life of Colin Powell*. New York: Knopf, 2006.

Haass, Richard. *The Opportunity: America's Moment to Alter History's Course*. PublicAffairs, 2006.

———. *War of Necessity, War of Choice: A Memoir of Two Iraq Wars*. New York: Simon and Schuster, 2009.

Habib, Philip
Birth Date: February 25, 1920
Death Date: May 25, 1992

Noted U.S. diplomat, perhaps best known for his work in brokering a tenuous—and short-lived—peace in Lebanon in the early 1980s. Born in Brooklyn, New York, on February 25, 1920, to a Lebanese Maronite Christian family, Philip Habib grew up in a Jewish neighborhood. In his formative years he straddled cultural barriers. For a short while he worked as a shipping clerk in New York before enrolling in a forestry program at the University of Idaho. He earned his degree in 1942 and immediately joined the U.S. Army, where he served until his discharge as a captain in 1946.

Upon his return to civilian life Habib enrolled at the University of California at Berkeley, where he studied agricultural economics. He earned his PhD there in 1952. In the meantime, in 1949 he joined the U.S. Foreign Service. He began a long and highly distinguished career with the U.S. State Department that included service in Canada, New Zealand, South Korea, Saigon, South Vietnam, and various other State Department posts. In 1968 he began serving on the U.S. delegation to the Vietnam Peace Talks.

Habib became the U.S. ambassador to South Korea in 1971, a post he held until 1974. During 1974–1976 he was assistant secretary of state for East Asian and Pacific affairs, and during 1976–1978 he served as undersecretary of state for political affairs. Following a heart attack, he retired from public service in 1978.

Just a year later, in 1979, Habib came out of retirement to serve as a special adviser to President Jimmy Carter on Middle East affairs. In the spring of 1981 newly elected president Ronald Reagan tapped Habib to serve as U.S. special envoy to the Middle East. Widely known for his tough but scrupulously fair negotiating prowess, Habib received the assignment of brokering a peace arrangement in the ongoing civil war in Lebanon.

During a series of tortuous negotiations and endless bouts of shuttle diplomacy, Habib managed to broker a cease-fire in Lebanon and resolved the mounting crisis over control of West Beirut. His efforts not only brought some semblance of order to Lebanon, albeit temporarily, but also served as a building block for the ongoing Arab-Israeli peace process. In September 1982 the Reagan administration awarded Habib with the Presidential Medal of Freedom for his diplomatic service. In 1986 Habib once again became a special envoy, this time to Central America. His task was to resolve the continuing conflict in Nicaragua. Realizing perhaps that U.S. policies in the region were a significant impediment to lasting peace there, he resigned his post after just five months on the job. Habib died suddenly on May 25, 1992, while on vacation in Puligny-Montrachet, France.

PAUL G. PIERPAOLI JR.

See also

Lebanon; Lebanon, U.S. Intervention in (1982–1984); Reagan, Ronald Wilson; Reagan Administration, Middle East Policy

References

Boykin, John. *Cursed Is the Peacemaker: The American Diplomat versus the Israeli General, Beirut 1982*. Belmont, CA: Applegate, 2002.

Laffin, John. *The War of Desperation: Lebanon, 1982–1985*. London: Osprey, 1985.

Haditha, Battle of
Start Date: August 1, 2005
End Date: August 4, 2005

Military engagement during August 1–4, 2005, between U.S. marines and Iraqi insurgents belonging to Ansar al-Sunnah, a militant Salafi group operating in and around Haditha, Iraq. Haditha is a city of some 100,000 people located in Anbar Province in western Iraq about 150 miles to the northwest of Baghdad. The city's population is mainly Sunni Muslim.

The battle was precipitated when a large force of insurgents ambushed a six-man marine sniper unit on August 1; all six marines died in the ensuing fight. The rebels videotaped part of the attack, which included footage allegedly showing one badly injured marine being killed. On August 3 the marines, along with a small contingent of Iraqi security forces, decided to launch a retaliatory strike against Ansar al-Sunnah, dubbed Operation QUICK STRIKE. Those involved included about 1,000 personnel from Regimental Combat Team 2.

The operation commenced with a ground assault against insurgent positions southwest of Haditha; this was augmented by four Bell AH-1 Super Cobra attack helicopters. U.S. officials reported at least 40 insurgents killed during this engagement. The next day, August 4, insurgents destroyed a marine amphibious vehicle using a large roadside bomb; 15 of the 16 marines inside it were killed, along with a civilian interpreter. Meanwhile, the marines had conducted a raid on a house suspected of harboring insurgents outside Haditha. In so doing, they discovered a large weapons cache containing small arms and improvised explosive devices (IEDs) and detained seven insurgents for questioning. Later, six of the men admitted to having ambushed and killed the six marines on August 1.

After the roadside bombing, coalition forces decided to regroup for a more concerted attack on Haditha itself, which would come in early September. In total, the marines suffered 21 killed; insurgent losses were estimated at 400.

On September 5, 2005, the 3rd Battalion, 1st Marines, launched a full-scale assault against Haditha, expecting heavy resistance. The resistance did not materialize, however, and the marines took the entire city in four days with very minimal insurgent activity. The operation uncovered more than 1,000 weapons caches and resulted in the detention of an additional 400 militants. Four marines were casualties. In early 2006 eight Iraqis suspected of involvement in the initial attack on the marine snipers were tried by an Iraqi court, found guilty, and executed.

PAUL G. PIERPAOLI JR.

See also

Iraqi Insurgency; United States Marine Corps, Iraq War

References

Hashim, Ammed S. *Insurgency and Counter-insurgency in Iraq.* Ithaca, NY: Cornell University Press, 2006.

Tracy, Patrick. *Street Fight in Iraq: What It's Really Like Over There.* Tucson: University of Arizona Press, 2006.

Haditha Incident
Event Date: November 19, 2005

The alleged murder of 24 Iraqi civilians in Haditha, in Anbar Province, on November 19, 2005, by U.S. marines of the 1st Squad, 3rd Platoon, K Company, 3rd Battalion, 1st Marine Regiment, 1st Marine Division. The incident gained international notoriety when it eventually became public knowledge, fueling critics' attacks on the conduct of the U.S.-led coalition's counterinsurgency operations in Iraq and raising charges that the U.S. Marine Corps had initially attempted to cover up the killings before reporters broke the story. Domestic and international pressure to investigate the incident fully and to prosecute those involved gained increasing momentum, as public knowledge of the Haditha Incident in early 2006 coincided with other allegations of unnecessary violence against Iraqi civilians by U.S. military personnel during military operations elsewhere in the country. Strong criticism of the incident and the U.S. Marine Corps' handling of its aftermath by congressional opponents of the George W. Bush administration was led by U.S. congressman John Murtha (D-Pa.). Murtha's status as a former marine combat veteran of the Vietnam War has frequently made him the Democrats' point man in attacks on the Bush administration's handling of the Global War on Terror. Murtha was subsequently sued by one of the alleged marine

participants in the Haditha Incident. Although several marine participants were eventually brought up on criminal charges for their roles in the incident, as of 2009 only one of them still faced prosecution and court-martial for the killings.

In November 2005 Anbar Province was one of the most dangerous places in Iraq, the heart of the Iraqi insurgency. The murders are alleged to have been in retaliation for the death of U.S. Marine Corps lance corporal Miguel Terrazas and the wounding of two other marines on November 19 after a four-vehicle U.S. convoy triggered the detonation of an improvised explosive device (IED) and came under attack by small-arms fire.

The U.S. Marine Corps initially reported that 15 civilians had been killed by the bomb's blast and that 8 or 9 insurgents had also been killed in the ensuing firefight. However, reports by Iraqi eyewitnesses to the incident, statements by local Iraqi officials, and video shots of the dead civilians in the city morgue and at the houses where the killings occurred contradicted the initial U.S. military version of events. Some of the Iraqi eyewitness reports were particularly compelling, such as testimony by a young girl who said she saw marines shoot her father while he was praying. The vividness and detail of Iraqi eyewitness reports gave substantial credibility to their claims, making it virtually impossible for U.S. military authorities to ignore them. The Iraqi claims contradicting the official military report prompted *Time* magazine to publish a story alleging that the marines deliberately killed 24 Iraqi civilians, including women and 6 children.

Although *Newsmax* questioned *Time*'s sources for the story, claiming that the dead were known insurgent propagandists and insurgent-friendly Haditha residents, based on the *Time* report and the international outcry it generated, on February 24, 2006, the U.S. military initiated an investigation. Led by U.S. Army major general Eldon Bargewell, the investigation was charged with determining how the incident was reported through the chain of command. On March 9 a criminal investigation was also launched, led by the Naval Criminal Investigative Services (NCIS) to determine if the marines deliberately targeted and killed Iraqi civilians. As *Newsweek* stated in a report on the Haditha Incident dated October 9, 2007, "the sinister reality of insurgents' hiding among civilians in Iraq has complicated the case" and was one of the main obstacles military investigators have faced in trying to determine if any Iraqi civilians were deliberately killed.

Marines on patrol in Haditha initially reported that 1 marine and 15 Iraqi civilians had been killed from an IED, whereupon insurgents opened fire on the marines, who proceeded to kill the 8 or 9 alleged insurgents. The U.S. Marine Corps then subsequently reported that the 15 Iraqi civilians had instead been accidentally killed as marines cleared four nearby houses in front of the road where the IED had exploded and in which they believed the insurgents were firing from and/or hiding in. According to Iraqi accounts, however, after the IED explosion, the incensed marines went on a rampage, set up a roadblock, and first killed 4 Iraqi students and a taxi driver who were all unarmed and surrendering to

Two Iraqis examine the charred side of a home a day or two after the Haditha Incident of November 19, 2005. (AP/Wide World Photos)

the marines at the time. The marines then stormed the four nearby houses and killed numerous people (accounts vary as to the exact number), including perhaps as many as 5 women and 6 children. Details beyond that remain sketchy and changeable.

On April 9, 2007, one marine, Sergeant Sanick De La Cruz, was granted immunity from prosecution for unpremeditated murder in exchange for his testimony. He testified on May 9, 2007, that he and others, including his squad leader, Staff Sergeant Frank Wuterich, killed the four Iraqi students and the driver of a white taxi who were attempting to surrender. De La Cruz further testified that Wuterich then told the men under his command, including De La Cruz, to lie about the killings. According to De La Cruz, the five Iraqis, including the driver, had been ordered out of a taxi by Wuterich and himself after the marines had put up a roadblock following the ambush of the convoy.

Other marines, however, reported that shortly after the explosion of the IED they noticed a white unmarked car full of "military-aged men" arrive and then stop near the bombing site. Suspecting the men of being insurgents or having remotely detonated the IED, Wutterich and De La Cruz ordered the five men to stop and surrender, but instead they ran; they were all shot and killed. As

reinforcements arrived, the marines began taking small-arms fire from several locations on either side of their convoy, and while taking cover they identified at least one shooter in the vicinity of a nearby house. Lieutenant William Kallop ordered Wuterich and an ad hoc team to treat the buildings as hostile and to "clear" them. They forced entry and shot a man on a flight of stairs and then shot another when he made a movement toward a closet. The marines say that they heard the sound of an AK-47 bolt slamming, so they threw grenades into a nearby room and fired; they killed five occupants, with two others wounded by grenade fragments and bullets. Wuterich and his men pursued what they suspected were insurgents running into an adjacent house. They led the assault with grenades and gunfire, in the process killing another man. Unknown to the marines, two women and six children were in a back room. Seven were killed. It was a chaotic and fast-moving action conducted in the dark in close-range quarters, causing accounts to diverge on the precise chronology and exact sequence of events.

After the firefight ended around 9:30 p.m., the marines noted men suspected of scouting for another attack peering behind the wall of a third house. A marine team, including Wuterich and Lance Corporal Justin Sharratt, stormed the house to find women and children inside (who were not harmed). They moved to a fourth house off a courtyard and killed two men inside wielding AK-47s, along with two others.

Thirty minutes after the house clearing, an intelligence unit arrived to question the marines involved in the operation. Shortly after the IED explosion, an unmanned aerial vehicle (UAV) flew over the blast area and for the rest of the day transmitted views of the scene to the company command headquarters and also the to battalion, regimental, and divisional headquarters. *Newsmax* reported that the UAV recorded marines sweeping the four houses for suspected insurgents and also showed four insurgents fleeing the neighborhood in a car and joining up with other insurgents. Based on Staff Sergeant Wuterich's account that in the first house he cleared he observed a back door ajar and believed that the insurgents had fled to another nearby house, it is possible that the four fleeing insurgents seen by the UAV were probably the same ones who left through the back door of the first house that Wuterich and other marines were clearing. The UAV followed both groups of insurgents as they returned to their safe house, which was bombed around 6:00 p.m. and then stormed by a squad from K Company.

On December 21, 2006, in accordance with U.S. Marine Corps legal procedures, criminal charges were brought against eight marines for war crimes in the Haditha killings. Four enlisted marines (including Wuterich) were accused of 13 counts of unpremeditated murder, and four officers were charged with covering up their subordinates' alleged misdeeds by failing to report and investigate properly the deaths of the Iraqis. In 2007 the charges against three of the four enlisted marines were dismissed, and by the summer of 2008 the charges against three of the officers were dismissed; the other was found not guilty by court-martial. Kallop was never charged with a crime.

On June 17, 2008, military judge Colonel Steve Folsom dismissed all charges against Lieutenant Colonel Jeffrey R. Chessani, the most senior officer to face charges, because the officer overseeing the Haditha investigation, Lieutenant General James Mattis, had been improperly influenced by legal investigator Colonel John Ewers, who was a witness to the case and later became a legal adviser to Mattis. The judge ruled that Ewers should not have been allowed to attend meetings and discussions with Mattis because Ewers's participation prejudiced and tainted the decision to charge and prosecute Chessani, who was accused of failing to report the incident and investigate the alleged killing of civilians by marines under his command. The U.S. Marine Corps has appealed the ruling to the Navy and Marine Court of Criminal Appeals, postponing indefinitely Chessani's case.

Of the eight marines originally charged on December 21, 2006, Staff Sergeant Frank D. Wuterich, the platoon sergeant implicated in the Haditha killings, remains the lone defendant facing prosecution and court-martial; he was initially charged with multiple counts of murder, but after a hearing the charges were reduced to nine counts of voluntary manslaughter. His court-martial, however, has been indefinitely postponed to allow prosecutors time to appeal a judge's decision to throw out a subpoena for unaired footage from a CBS *60 Minutes* program interview with Wuterich. Military prosecutors argued that the additional footage shows that Wuterich may have admitted to his role in the killings. In addition, the dismissal of all charges against Chessani has implications for Wuterich's case because Colonel Ewers also investigated Wuterich's case before becoming a legal adviser to Mattis, who recommended prosecuting Wuterich.

Wuterich insists his unit followed the rules of engagement and did not purposefully attack civilians and that his squad entered the houses to suppress insurgent fire and pursue gunmen who had opened fire on them. He further asserts that the civilian deaths occurred during the sweep of nearby homes in which fragmentation grenades and clearing fire were used before entering the houses. Wuterich also said that his unit never attempted to cover up the incident and immediately reported that civilians had been killed in Haditha.

The Department of Defense has said that the rules of engagement in effect at Haditha prohibited unprovoked attacks on civilians, but this of course assumes that the marines knew that the homes were populated by civilians. In addition, marines are trained as a matter of combat survival to suppress enemy fire with overwhelming force, including the tossing of grenades into a room before entering. The lead investigator of the Haditha incident has confirmed that some training the marines received conflicted with their rules of engagement and led them to believe that if fired upon from a house, they could clear it with grenades and gunfire without determining whether civilians were inside.

The Haditha Incident stands as a classic example of the profound difficulties and the immense potential for human tragedy encountered by conventional military forces engaged in combating an insurgency in which the insurgents' very survival depends upon blending in with—and often becoming indistinguishable from—the local civilian population. Indeed, even when conventional forces win a tactical battle against insurgents, they risk incurring a more important strategic loss when they kill civilians (intentionally or accidentally) in the process. Inevitably, conventional forces conducting counterinsurgency operations are confronted by an unavoidable double standard: while being held strictly accountable to observing all of the internationally accepted laws of war, they must fight an enemy whose tactics principally rely on terror and indiscriminate killing of civilians and combatants alike. The very thought that Al Qaeda or other terrorist group leadership would conduct war crimes investigations for atrocities committed by its members as the U.S. Marine Corps has done in the wake of the Haditha Incident seems absurd; atrocities are the insurgents' main tactic, not aberrations occurring during the heat of battle. The Haditha Incident also emphasizes that a conventional counterinsurgency force's major actions and policies must be in place in order to prevent or at least limit civilian deaths: effective training, strict discipline and individual accountability, rigidly enforced rules of engagement, and competent leaders at every level of command who remain totally involved in the conduct of all combat operations. Not even one of these critical elements can be lacking or ignored, as that raises the risk of a repeat of such incidents as that which occurred at Haditha. When an atrocity occurs or is even suspected to have taken place, it must be rigorously investigated and, whenever warranted, vigorously prosecuted. A cover-up (or even the appearance of one) not only denies justice to the victims but, in a practical military sense, is also ultimately counterproductive.

STEFAN M. BROOKS

See also

Improvised Explosive Devices; Iraqi Insurgency; United States Marine Corps, Iraq War

References

Brennan, Phil. "New Evidence Emerges in Haditha Case." *Newsmax,* June 26, 2006.

Ephron Dan. "Haditha Unraveled." *Newsweek,* October 29, 2007.

McGirk, Tim. "Collateral Damage or Civilian Massacre at Haditha." *Time,* March 19, 2006.

"What Happened at Haditha." Editorial. *Wall Street Journal,* October 19, 2007.

White, Josh. "Marine Says Rules Were Followed." *Washington Post,* June 11, 2006.

Hadley, Stephen John
Birth Date: February 13, 1947

Attorney, national security and defense expert, and national security adviser to President George W. Bush (2005–2009). Stephen John Hadley was born in Toledo, Ohio, on February 13, 1947. He earned a BA degree from Cornell University in 1969 and a law degree from Yale University in 1972. From 1972 to 1975 he served in the U.S. Navy. Hadley ultimately became a senior partner in the law firm of Shea & Gardner in Washington, D.C., but also became involved in defense and national security work for Republican administrations, including those of Richard Nixon, Gerald Ford, Ronald Reagan, and George H. W. Bush. Between 1995 and 2001 Hadley was also a principal in the Scowcroft Group, an international advisory company specializing in international business development and consultation. Brent Scowcroft, founder of the concern, had been national security adviser to presidents Ford and George H. W. Bush and was a mentor to Hadley.

From 1989 to 1993 Hadley worked under Paul Wolfowitz as assistant secretary of defense for international security policy. In this post Hadley was involved with numerous arms-control agreements, including START I and START II, and he worked closely with Secretary of Defense Richard Cheney and Secretary of State James Baker. From 1986 to 1987 Hadley served as counsel to the Special Review Board created by President Reagan to investigate the Iran-Contra Affair (popularly known as the Tower Commission).

In 2000 Hadley served as a foreign policy and national security adviser to George W. Bush's presidential campaign. When Bush won, Hadley also served on the president-elect's transition team. In 2001 Bush named Hadley deputy national security adviser, meaning that he reported to National Security Advisor Condoleezza Rice. Just prior to his taking office, Hadley had served on a prominent conservative think tank panel that had urged the United States to make small tactical nuclear weapons a centerpiece of its nuclear arsenal. The group advocated the use of such weapons against nations that harbored illicit weapons of mass destruction (WMDs). Having worked for Cheney, Wolfowitz, and other neoconservatives, Hadley generally shared their get-tough approach to U.S. defense and national security policy, although he tended to be somewhat less rigid and dogmatic than they, probably the result of his relationship with Scowcroft, who believed in a more measured approach to defense policy.

Hadley reportedly was a member of the White House Iraq Group in 2002; the group's primary aim was to shape public opinion for a possible war with Iraq. In July 2003, some four months after the invasion of Iraq, Hadley offered his resignation to President Bush, claiming that he had allowed Bush to use in his January 2003 State of the Union address the now-discounted document showing that Iraq had tried to buy yellow-cake uranium from Niger. The document had been used as proof of Iraq's alleged nuclear weapons program. The president refused to accept the resignation. Later on Hadley was mentioned as the possible source of the leak that precipitated the Valerie Plame Wilson controversy, but he was cleared of any wrongdoing in that scandal. Nevertheless, Hadley has been blamed for a number of botched intelligence reports that were used to justify the Iraq War.

In 2005 Hadley became national security adviser when Rice was tapped to become secretary of state. Hadley kept a relatively low profile during Bush's second term, especially given the departure of two hard-core neoconservatives: Secretary of Defense Donald Rumsfeld and Deputy Secretary of Defense Paul Wolfowitz. Hadley is believed to have supported a change in strategy in the Iraq War that resulted in the 2007 troop surge, and he worked quietly behind the scenes to mend political fences with some of the disgruntled U.S. allies.

PAUL G. PIERPAOLI JR.

See also

Bush, George Herbert Walker; Bush, George Walker; Cheney, Richard Bruce; Iran-Contra Affair; IRAQI FREEDOM, Operation; Neoconservatism; Niger, Role in Origins of the Iraq War; Reagan, Ronald Wilson; Rice, Condoleezza; Rumsfeld, Donald Henry; Surge, U.S. Troop Deployment, Iraq War; Wilson, Valerie Plame

References

Mann, James. *Rise of the Vulcans: The History of Bush's War Cabinet.* New York: Viking, 2004.

Woodward, Bob. *State of Denial: Bush at War, Part III.* New York: Simon and Schuster, 2006.

———. *The War Within: A Secret White House History, 2006–2008.* New York Simon and Schuster, 2008.

Hagenbeck, Franklin L.
Birth Date: November 25, 1949

U.S. Army general and commander of coalition Joint Task Force Mountain during Operation ENDURING FREEDOM in Afghanistan. Born in Morocco on November 25, 1949, the son of a U.S. Navy officer, Franklin L. Hagenbeck attended high school in Jacksonville, Florida, and went on to graduate from the United States Military Academy, West Point, in 1971, when he was commissioned a second lieutenant. His subsequent military education included courses at the U.S. Army Command and General Staff College and the Army War College. Hagenbeck also earned a master's degree in exercise physiology from Florida State University and a master's degree in business administration from Long Island University.

Among Hagenbeck's earlier staff assignments were tours as director of the Officer Personnel Management Directorate and assistant division commander of the 101st Airborne Division. He also served abroad as an instructor in tactics at the Royal Australian Infantry Center. Having previously commanded at company, battalion, and brigade levels, Hagenbeck assumed command as a major general of the 10th Mountain Division at Fort Drum in New York in the autumn of 2001. He entered the public spotlight in the aftermath of the September 11, 2001, terror attacks on the United States. With the commencement of Operation ENDURING FREEDOM in Afghanistan in October 2001, the 10th Mountain Division received a warning that it would provide the first conventional forces to support ongoing special operations against the Taliban regime. After initially sending a small security element, the 10th Mountain contributed a portion of the 1,200 infantrymen who took part in Operation ANACONDA in March 2002 under Hagenbeck's immediate command.

Although a tactical success, ANACONDA was not without its problems in intelligence and fire-support coordination. Thus, a debate over the operation and the responsibility for its shortcomings occurred in which Hagenbeck would play a prominent role. In particular, in an interview published in *Field Artillery* magazine in 2002 he called into question the effectiveness of fire support provided solely by the U.S. Air Force, the problem being that the 10th Mountain Division was not allowed to deploy to Afghanistan with its organic artillery, and thus tactical air support was the division's sole source of fire support. His analysis drew a sharp rejoinder from U.S. Air Force spokespersons. Whatever the problems, they almost certainly stemmed in part from a hasty planning process as well a long-standing history of imperfect interservice coordination.

Hagenbeck next assumed the post of U.S. Army deputy chief of staff, personnel (G-1). In this position he testified several times before Congress on the challenges facing the army in recruitment and retention resulting from waging concurrent wars in Iraq and Afghanistan. In 2006 Lieutenant General Hagenbeck became the superintendent of the United States Military Academy, West Point.

ROBERT F. BAUMANN

See also

ANACONDA, Operation; ENDURING FREEDOM, Operation

References

"Afghanistan: Fire Support for Operation Anaconda, an Interview with MG Franklin L. Hagenbeck." *Field Artillery* (September–October 2002): 5–9.

Andres, Richard, and Jeffrey Hukill. "Anaconda: A Flawed Joint Planning Process." *Joint Forces Quarterly* 47 (4th Quarter 2007): 135–140.

Lambeth, Benjamin S. *Air Power against Terror: America's Conduct of Operation Enduring Freedom.* Santa Monica, CA: RAND Corporation, 2005.

Naylor, Sean. *Not a Good Day to Die: The Untold Story of Operation Anaconda.* New York: Berkley Trade, 2006.

Haifa Street, Battle of
Start Date: January 6, 2007
End Date: January 9, 2007

A two-staged combined-arms action by American and Iraqi troops against Sunni insurgents in central Baghdad during January 6–9, 2007. In the Battle of Haifa Street, U.S. Army infantry and cavalry units fought alongside Iraqi soldiers to successfully dislodge enemy insurgents from key urban areas. The engagement pitted about 1,000 U.S. and Iraqi troops against an undetermined number of insurgent fighters.

Haifa Street, a broad boulevard located in central Baghdad, runs northwest from the Green Zone, the home of the Coalition Provisional Authority (CPA), for two miles along the west bank of the Tigris River. Many of the buildings along the street, including the former residences of wealthy Sunni government officials, are 20-story high-rise apartments. Amid increasing sectarian violence in 2006, Sunni and Al Qaeda in Iraq insurgents had taken control of the street and its surrounding neighborhood. They also made use of the high-rise apartment buildings from which they were able to fire down into the streets, posing a serious hazard to civilians and coalition troops. Throughout 2006 insurgents sporadically engaged American and Iraqi forces by sniper fire and grenades lobbed from the residential and office buildings.

The catalyst for the Battle of Haifa Street occurred on January 6, 2007, when Iraqi troops killed 30 Sunni insurgents after discovering a fake checkpoint manned by insurgents. In retaliation, the insurgents executed 27 Shia and distributed leaflets threatening to kill anyone who entered the area. Following an unsuccessful attempt by Iraqi soldiers to clear the neighborhood on January 8, American troops prepared a full-scale offensive to assist the Iraqis.

The first stage of the battle involved approximately 1,000 American and Iraqi troops. On January 9 a reinforced U.S. Army battalion from the 2nd Infantry Division joined the Iraqi 6th Infantry Division to engage in pitched street-by-street combat to clear buildings from north to south along Haifa Street. During the intense one-day operation, the Americans employed snipers and

Stryker combat vehicles to methodically clear insurgent strongholds. Ground troops were supported by Boeing/McDonnell
Douglas AH-64 Apache attack helicopters and precision-guided
munitions. The U.S. and Iraqi forces mounted a successful retaliation effort against the strong insurgent resistance that included
machine-gun fire, rocket-propelled grenades, and coordinated
mortar fire. In the course of the battle approximately 70 insurgents
were killed or captured, including several foreign fighters. Some
25 others were captured.

U.S. troops subsequently withdrew, leaving Iraqi forces to
patrol the area. However, insurgents reinfiltrated the area over
the next two weeks. Before dawn on January 24, 2007, Iraqi troops
joined a larger American force comprised of two reinforced battalions from the 2nd Infantry and 1st Cavalry divisions to clear
the street again. This second stage of the battle, named Operation
TOMAHAWK STRIKE 11, lasted less than one day. U.S. army units used
both Bradley and Stryker combat vehicles to control the street,
supported by Iraqi and American troops who cleared apartments
while taking sniper and mortar fire. By evening the street and surrounding buildings had been cleared, and a large weapons cache
had been seized. Approximately 65 insurgents, including numerous foreign fighters, were killed or captured on January 24. Iraqi
forces suffered 20 killed during both engagements. Although a
substantial American presence remained for several days following the second battle, control and responsibility for the sector had
been relinquished to the Iraqi Army by February 1, 2007.

WILLIAM E. FORK

See also

Al Qaeda in Iraq; Baghdad; Green Zone in Iraq; Iraqi Insurgency

References

Cave, Damien, and James Glanz. "In a New Joint U.S.-Iraqi Patrol, the
   Americans Go First." *New York Times,* January 25, 2007.
Kagan, Kimberly. "The Iraq Report; From 'New Way Forward' to New
   Commander." *Weekly Standard,* January 10, 2007–February 10,
   2007, 7–10.
Zavis, Alexandra. "The Conflict in Iraq: Military Offensive in Baghdad;
   U.S.-Iraqi Forces Strike 'Sniper Alley.'" *Los Angeles Times,* January
   25, 2007.

Hakim, Abd al-Aziz al-
Birth Date: 1950

Mid-level Iraqi Arab Shia cleric, leader of the Supreme Islamic Iraqi
Council, and sayyid (descendant of the Prophet Muhammad). Abd
al-Aziz al-Hakim was born sometime in 1950 in the southern Iraqi
city of Najaf, a descendant of the Prophet Muhammad and the
fourth caliph, Ali ibn Abi Talib. Hakim is a hujjat al-Islam (literally
"proof of Islam") and the lower-level ranking of cleric, not a *mujtahid.* More importantly, he is the current leader of the Supreme
Islamic Iraqi Council (SIIC), one of the two largest Iraqi Shia political parties, a position he inherited upon the assassination of his

brother, Ayatollah Muhammad Baqir al-Hakim, who was killed by
a massive car bomb in Najaf in August 2003.

Abd al-Aziz's father was Grand Ayatollah Sayyid Muhsin al-
Hakim (1889–1970), the preeminent Shia religious scholar and
authority in Iraq from 1955 until his death in 1970. The family has
deep roots in Iraq as one of the premier Arab Shia scholarly families based in Najaf, where Imam Ali's shrine is located, although the
family originally came from the Jabal Amil in southern Lebanon.
Abd al-Aziz's brother, Sayyid Muhammad Mahdi (1940?–1988),
another activist, was also assassinated in Khartoum, Sudan, most
likely on the orders of Iraqi president Saddam Hussein. All three
of the Hakim brothers studied religious subjects under both their
father and then Ayatollah Sayyid Muhammad Baqir al-Sadr (1935–
1980), one of their father's leading students and an activist scholar
who was one of the intellectual founders of the Islamic Dawa Party
(Hizb al-Da'wah al-Islamiyya), Iraq's other large Shia political party.

Abd al-Aziz's earliest social and political activism occurred
in tandem with his father and older brothers, all of whom were
actively opposed to the growing influence of the Iraqi Communist
Party (ICP) among segments of Shia youth during the 1950s and
1960s. Grand Ayatollah Hakim was an outspoken critic of communism, and he passed a juridical opinion (fatwa) against membership in the ICP in February 1960. He was also instrumental in
the formation and support of the Jamaat al-Ulama (Society of Religious Scholars), a coalition of religious scholars (*ulama*) opposed
to the growing influence of the ICP and other Iraqi secular political
parties. Due to his age, Abd al-Aziz was not actively involved in the
Jamaat al-Ulama and the earlier stages of the Islamic Dawa Party,
although his brothers were.

Following the Iraqi invasion of Iran in September 1980 and the
outbreak of the Iran-Iraq War (1980–1988), when Hussein issued
orders calling for the execution of members of the Dawa Party, Abd
al-Aziz and his brother Muhammad Baqir left Iraq for Iran along
with thousands of other Iraqi Shias, many of them political activists. The Iraqi government claimed that it might face traitorous
actions by Iraq's long-disenfranchised Shia Arab majority. Ayatollah Baqir al-Sadr had been executed along with his sister, Amina
bint Haydar al-Sadr (also known as Bint al-Huda), in April 1980.

In November 1982 Baqir al-Hakim announced the formation of the Supreme Council for the Islamic Revolution in Iraq
(SCIRI), which initially was an umbrella organization that brought
together officials from the various Iraqi exiled opposition movements, although it eventually became its own political party as
other groups broke away over policy and ideological disputes.
SCIRI's leadership were based in Tehran, and it was more heavily
influenced by Iranian individuals and political competition than
the Dawa Party. In 1982–1983 SCIRI's paramilitary wing, the Badr
Organization, was founded under Abd al-Aziz's leadership. Badr
was made up of recruits from among the Iraqi exile community
living in Iran as well as Iraqi Shia prisoners of war, who received
training and equipment from the Iranian Revolutionary Guard
Corps on the instructions of Grand Ayatollah Ruhollah Khomeini,

Abd al-Aziz al-Hakim, leader of the Supreme Islamic Iraqi Council, casts his vote in Baghdad on January 30, 2005. (U.S. Department of Defense)

Iran's revolutionary leader. On the eve of the U.S.- and British-led invasion of Iraq of March 2003, Badr reportedly fielded 10,000–15,000 fighters, with a core elite group of several thousand fighters.

Abd al-Aziz and Muhammad Baqir returned to Iraq on May 12, 2003, making their way to the southern Iraqi port city of Basra, where the ayatollah gave a rousing speech in front of an estimated 100,000 Iraqi supporters in the main soccer stadium, rejecting U.S. postwar domination of the country. The Hakims were soon joined by thousands of SCIRI members and Badr fighters who flooded into southern Iraq. Following his brother's assassination on August 29, 2003, Abd al-Aziz assumed control of the SCIRI, which several years later was renamed the Supreme Iraqi Islamic Council (SIIC). He has maintained a close relationship with the U.S. government. In fact, he was the favorite of various American figures to succeed Ibrahim al-Jafari, perhaps due to his English skills and demeanor, but was not as popular with Iraqis, as was demonstrated at the polls. During Abd al-Aziz's tenure as party chief, then-SCIRI achieved a key electoral victory in December 2005 as part of the United Iraqi Alliance, a loose coalition of primarily Shia political parties that, together with the Kurdish political list, dominates Iraqi politics today. In the past, he has supported attempts to create a decentralized federal system. He has vocally supported the creation of an autonomous Shia region in southern and central Iraq, a move

that has been repeatedly opposed by other Shiite parties such as Fadhila and by Sunni Arab politicians and Tayyar al-Sadr (Sadr Movement), the sociopolitical faction led by Muqtada al-Sadr.

Badr officials and fighters are heavily represented in the Iraqi state security forces and important ministries, including the Ministry of the Interior. They were blamed for summarily arresting, kidnapping, torturing, and murdering Sunni Arabs, often political rivals and random civilians off of the streets particularly in mixed Sunni-Shia neighborhoods, which they sought to cleanse of Sunni Arabs. The SIIC leadership denies involvement in such attacks despite strong evidence to the contrary.

Beginning in 2004 and reaching its apogee in the spring of 2008, Badr fighters, many of them while in their capacity as Iraqi state security, engaged in running street battles with the Sadrists over political power, reportedly seeking to weaken them before the 2009 municipal elections. Heavy fighting under the direction of the official Iraqi state, backed by Prime Minister Nuri al-Maliki and the U.S. military, took place between SIIC-dominated Iraqi security forces and Sadrist fighters in Baghdad in 2007 and in Basra during the spring and early summer of 2008.

Abd al-Aziz is aided by his two sons, Muhsin (1974–) and Ammar (1972–), who both head various offices and departments within the SIIC. Ammar is the secretary-general of the al-Mihrab

Martyr Foundation, an SIIC affiliate organization that has built mosques, Islamic centers, and schools throughout southern Iraq and Shia areas of Baghdad, the Iraqi capital; he is also the second-in-command of the SIIC.

The SIIC publicly recognizes Grand Ayatollah Sayyid Ali al-Sistani, Iraq's senior resident Shia religious authority, as its official religious guide and scholar, although the degree to which it actually follows his religious edicts is unclear because SIIC and Sistani have their own networks of mosques, which reinstituted Friday sermons after the fall of Hussein. SIIC and Badr fighters have notably ignored Sistani's calls for intercommunal harmony and a cessation of sectarian/intercommunal killings by both Sunnis and Shias. Hakim and other SIIC leaders have also publicly denied that they seek to establish a religious state in Iraq, as this was the original goal of the SIIC. The party has insisted on a prominent role for Islamic morals, Sharia, and institutions, particularly Shia ones, in the present and future Iraqi state.

CHRISTOPHER ANZALONE

See also

Baath Party; Badr Organization; Hakim, Muhammad Baqir al-; Hussein, Saddam; Islamic Dawa Party; Maliki, Nuri Muhammed Kamil Hasan al-; Shia Islam; Sistani, Sayyid Ali Husayn al-; Sunni Islam; Supreme Iraqi Islamic Council; United Iraqi Alliance

References

Dagher, Sam. "Rising Player with a Vision for Shiite Iraq." *Christian Science Monitor,* November 20, 2007.

Jabar, Faleh A. *The Shi'ite Movement in Iraq.* London: Saqi Books, 2003.

Samii, A. William. "Shia Political Alternatives in Postwar Iraq." *Middle East Policy* 10 (May 2003): 93–101.

Visser, Reidar. *Shi'a Separatism in Iraq: Internet Reverie or Real Constitutional Challenge?* Oslo: Norwegian Institute of International Affairs, 2005.

Hakim, Muhammad Baqir al-
Birth Date: ca. 1939
Death Date: August 29, 2003

Iraqi ayatollah and founding leader of the Supreme Council for Islamic Revolution in Iraq (SCIRI), since renamed the Supreme Islamic Iraqi Council (SIIC), one of the two largest Iraqi Shia political parties. Muhammad al-Hakim Baqir was born in Najaf, Iraq, either in 1939 or 1944. His father was Grand Ayatollah Sayyid Muhsin al-Hakim (1889–1970), the preeminent Shia religious scholar and authority in Iraq from 1955 until his death in 1970. The Hakim family is one of Iraq's preeminent Shia scholarly families, with deep roots in the southern Iraqi shrine city of Najaf, where the first Shia imam and fourth Muslim caliph, Ali ibn Abi Talib, is buried. The family originally came from the Jabal Amil region of historical Syria in present-day southern Lebanon.

Muhammad Baqir was one of three sons, the others being his younger brother Abd al-Aziz (1950–), the current SIIC leader, and Muhammad Mahdi (1940?–1988), commonly known simply as "Mahdi," who was assassinated in Khartoum, Sudan, probably at the behest of the ruling Iraqi Baath Party under President Saddam Hussein. All three of the Hakim brothers were born in Najaf and studied under both their father and Ayatollah Sayyid Muhammad Baqir al-Sadr (1935–1980), one of their father's premier students and an activist scholar who was one of the intellectual founders of the Islamic Dawa Party (Hizb al-Da'wah al-Islamiyyah), Iraq's other large Shia political party. Both Muhammad Baqir and his brother Mahdi were involved in the formation of the Dawa Party, and the latter was also active in the Jamaat al-Ulama, a clerical association formed in Najaf during the 1950s to combat the rising popularity of communism among Iraqi Shiite youth.

Muhammad Baqir was a well-known Shiite activist throughout the 1960s and 1970s. He was arrested, tortured, and imprisoned in 1972 and again from February 1977 to July 1979. He left Iraq for Iran with his brother Abd al-Aziz and thousands of other Iraqi Shia, mainly political activists, in the autumn of 1980 following the execution of Ayatollah Muhammad Baqir al-Sadr and his sister, Amina bint Haydar al-Sadr (also known as Bint al-Huda), in April and the outbreak of the Iran-Iraq War that September. In November 1982 Muhammad Baqir al-Hakim announced the formation of the SCIRI, which initially was envisioned as an umbrella organization that would bring together the various exiled Iraqi opposition movements, topple Hussein, and bring about an Islamic state.

The SCIRI eventually was transformed into its own political party as other parties broke away over policy and ideological disputes. Grand Ayatollah Ruhollah Khomeini, Iran's revolutionary leader, was actively supportive of the new group, seeing it as a tool to harass the Saddam Hussein regime. In 1982–1983 the Badr Organization was founded under the leadership of Abd al-Aziz al-Hakim, forming the paramilitary wing of the SIIC. Officers from the Iranian Revolutionary Guard Corps provided military training and equipment for the several thousand Iraqi Arab exiles and prisoners of war who filled Badr's ranks.

During his 23 years in exile, Muhammad Baqir built up the SCIRI networks among the tens of thousands of Iraqi exiles living in Iran. On the eve of the U.S.- and British-led invasion of Iraq in March 2003, SCIRI officials claimed to have 10,000 armed fighters in the Badr Corps. The organization's networks inside Iraq were not as developed as SCIRI propaganda claimed, however, because Baath Party security forces had been largely successful in limiting their growth inside the country. Prior to 2003, Badr agents carried out attacks on Iraqi government targets both inside and outside of Iraq, and Badr fighters were active participants in northern Iraq (Iraqi Kurdistan) during the Iran-Iraq War. Muhammad Baqir and the SCIRI were criticized by segments of the Iraqi Shia community for siding with Iran against Iraq during the war; unlike Dawa Party members, some in SCIRI fought Iraq, and many Iraqi Sunnis have therefore alleged that the organization is controlled by the Iranians.

Muhammad Baqir and Abd al-Aziz al-Hakim, together with other SCIRI leaders and members, returned to southern Iraq on May 12, 2003. Muhammad Baqir delivered a rousing speech in front of an estimated 100,000 Iraqis in the main soccer stadium in the southern Iraqi port city of Basra, publicly thanking Iran for its longtime support in resisting Saddam Hussein and rejecting U.S. postwar domination of the country. The Hakims were soon joined by thousands of SCIRI members and Badr fighters who flooded into southern and central Iraq's cities, towns, and villages.

In his public pronouncements and interviews, Muhammad Baqir was supportive of the role of the *marjaiyya,* the informal council of Iraq's five senior grand ayatollahs based in Najaf. He also did not call for his followers to fight the U.S. and British forces in the country, although he remained opposed to their long-term presence in the country. He called for the establishment of an Islamic state in Iraq but did not call for any immediate implementation of such a state. He acknowledged that the *marjaiyya* (whose religious leadership is senior to any other in Iraq) should occupy a major advisory role for the government.

On August 29, 2003, Muhammad Baqir was assassinated by a massive car comb following Friday prayers, before which he delivered the requisite sermon, at the Imam Ali Shrine in Najaf. Between 84 and 125 other people were also killed, and scores more were wounded in the bombing. This attack is believed to have been carried out by the Tawhid wa al-Jihad organization, later renamed Al Qaeda in the Land of the Two Rivers (al-Qa'ida fi Bilad al-Rafhidayn), led by the Jordanian Abu Musab al-Zarqawi (1966–2006). Muhammad Baqir's brother Abd al-Aziz al-Hakim then took up the leadership of the SCIRI.

CHRISTOPHER ANZALONE

See also

Baath Party; Hakim, Abd al-Aziz al-; Islamic Dawa Party; Khomeini, Ruhollah; Supreme Iraqi Islamic Council

References

Jabar, Faleh A. *The Shi'ite Movement in Iraq.* London: Saqi Books, 2003.

Hijazi, Ihsan A. "Iraqi's Death in Sudan Linked to Iran Faction." *New York Times,* January 24, 1988.

Joffe, Lawrence. "Ayatollah Mohammad Baqir al-Hakim." *Guardian,* August 30, 2003.

Samii, A. William. "Shia Political Alternatives in Postwar Iraq." *Middle East Policy* 10 (May 2003): 93–101.

Halliburton

A multinational corporation based in Houston, Texas, that provides specialty products and services to the oil and gas industries and also constructs oil fields, refineries, pipelines, and chemical plants through its main subsidiary KBR (Kellogg, Brown, and Root). Although Halliburton conducts operations in more than 120 countries, controversy regarding Halliburton Energy Services has focused on U.S. government contracts awarded to the company following the 2003 Iraq War and allegations of conflict of interest involving Vice President Richard (Dick) Cheney, who was a former Halliburton chief executive officer (CEO).

In 1919 during the midst of the oil boom in Texas and Oklahoma, Mr. and Mrs. Erle P. Halliburton began cementing oil wells in Burkburnett, Texas. That same year the Halliburtons established their business in Dallas, Texas. They then moved the business to Ardmore, Oklahoma. In 1924 the Halliburton Oil Well Cementing Company was incorporated. A significant expansion of the company occurred in 1962 with the acquisition of Brown & Root, a construction and engineering firm that became a wholly owned subsidiary of Halliburton. Brown & Root had been established in 1919 by brothers George and Herman Brown along with their brother-in-law Dan Root. Employing political patronage with influential figures such as Lyndon B. Johnson, Brown & Root grew from fulfilling small road-paving projects to garnering military contracts constructing military bases and naval warships. Brown & Root was part of a consortium responsible for providing approximately 85 percent of the infrastructure required by the U.S. military during the Vietnam War.

Halliburton headquarters, Houston, Texas. (AP/Wide World Photos)

Price of a Share of Halliburton Stock, 2000–2010

Date	Price of a Share of Stock
March 1, 2000	$20.47
September 1, 2000	$26.81
March 1, 2001	$20.11
August 31, 2001	$13.93
March 1, 2002	$8.45
August 30, 2002	$7.60
February 28, 2003	$10.13
August 29, 2003	$12.09
March 1, 2004	$16.26
September 1, 2004	$14.94
March 1, 2005	$21.43
September 1, 2005	$31.58
March 1, 2006	$34.69
September 1, 2006	$32.93
March 1, 2007	$31.34
August 31, 2007	$34.59
February 29, 2008	$38.30
August 29, 2008	$43.94
February 27, 2009	$16.31
August 31, 2009	$23.71
February 28, 2010	$30.15

The relationship between Halliburton and the U.S. military establishment was enhanced in 1992 when the Pentagon, under the direction of Secretary of Defense Dick Cheney, offered the company a contract for the bulk of support services for U.S. military operations abroad. Three years later Cheney was elected chairman and CEO of Halliburton. One of his first initiatives at Halliburton was the acquisition of rival Dresser Industries for $7.7 billion. Halliburton, however, also inherited the legal liabilities of Dresser for asbestos poisoning claims. The asbestos settlement caused Halliburton's stock price to plummet 80 percent in 1999. Nevertheless, during Cheney's five-year tenure at Halliburton (1995–2000), government contracts awarded to the company rose to $1.5 billion. This contrasts with just $100 million in government contracts from 1990 to 1995.

Upon assuming the vice presidency in the George W. Bush administration in 2001, Cheney declared that he would be severing all ties with the company. He continued, however, to earn deferred compensation worth approximately $150,000 annually along with stock options worth more than $18 million. Cheney assured critics that he would donate proceeds from the stock options to charity.

Even if Cheney did not personally profit, Halliburton secured several lucrative government contracts to rebuild Iraq and support the U.S. military presence in that nation following the U.S.-led invasion of Iraq in March 2003. It is estimated that Halliburton's Iraq contracts are worth as much as $18 billion. The company had also received contracts worth several hundred million dollars for support work in Afghanistan after the beginning of Operation ENDURING FREEDOM in late 2001. Although the company enjoys relatively low profit margins from its military contracts, Halliburton stock hit a record high in January 2006.

These profits have been subject to charges of corruption. For example, in 2003 a division of Halliburton overcharged the government by some $61 million for buying and transporting fuel from Kuwait into Iraq. Halliburton insisted that the high costs were the fault of a Kuwaiti subcontractor. Halliburton also received criticism for a $7 billion no-bid contract to rebuild Iraqi oil fields. This endeavor was largely a failure, as Iraq's oil production grew only slowly, and international access to Iraqi oil supplies has been limited. An effort to construct a pipeline under the Tigris River at Fatah was a dismal failure and was undertaken against the advice of experts who cautioned that the area was geologically unstable and could not support such a project. Halliburton spent $75.7 million dollars on the failed project, including approximately $100,000 per day as its crews were idle because of broken drill bits and other damaged equipment. Nevertheless, the U.S. government issued Halliburton another contract, for $66 million, to complete the pipeline. Once completed, the project will have cost 110 percent more than the original estimate.

Defenders of Halliburton insist that few companies have the resources and capital necessary to carry out the large-scale assignments given to Halliburton. Company executives also point out that if Halliburton were not providing support operations, far more troops would be needed in Iraq. The controversies surrounding Halliburton's role in the Iraq War continue to raise questions as to the rationale for the initial March 2003 invasion of Iraq, the mismanagement of the postwar stability and reconstruction efforts there, and the company's close relationship to the George W. Bush administration, whose wars in Afghanistan and Iraq have allowed the company to garner handsome profits.

RON BRILEY

See also

Bush, George Walker; Cheney, Richard Bruce; ENDURING FREEDOM, Operation; Iraq, History of, 1990–Present; IRAQI FREEDOM, Operation

References

Briody, Dan. The *Halliburton Agenda: The Politics of Oil and Money.* Hoboken, NJ: Wiley, 2004.

Purdum, Todd S., and the Staff of *The New York Times. A Time of Our Choosing: America's War in Iraq.* New York: Times Books/Henry Holt, 2003.

Hamas

Islamist Palestinian organization formally founded in 1987. The stated basis for Hamas (Harakat al-Muqawama al-Islamiyya, or Movement of Islamic Resistance) is currently to end the Israeli occupation of Palestinian territories and to institute a more truly Islamic way of life. Essentially, Hamas combines moderate Islamism based with Palestinian nationalism. Hamas secured an estimated 30–40 percent support in the Palestinian population within five years because of its mobilization successes and the general popular desperation experienced by the Palestinian population during the First Intifada. Hamas rejected the Oslo Accords because it did not believe that the Palestine Liberation Organization (PLO) should serve as the sole representative of the Palestinian people or that the PLO had the right to conclude peace without popular input. While Hamas refrained from participation in the first set of Palestinian elections, its leaders realized that this decision marginalized the group.

Hamas became increasingly popular among students and professionals, in part because of its opposition to the corrupt practices of many within Fatah but also because of its concern for the welfare of poor Palestinians and its demonstrated more efficient behavior toward constituents. In January 2006 Hamas won a majority in the Palestinian National Authority (PNA) general legislative elections, which brought condemnation from Israel and a protracted power struggle with PNA president Mahmoud Abbas and his Fatah Party.

The name "Hamas" is an acronym for Harakat al-Muqawamah al-Islamiyya, and the ordinary Arabic word *hamas* means "zeal." Hamas grew directly out of the Muslim Brotherhood, an Islamist organization that for historical and doctrinal reasons had given up militant resistance against the state (Egypt or Israel) after its suppression under Gamal Abdel Nasser. The growth of Islamist movements was delayed among Palestinians because of their status as a people without a state and the tight security controls imposed by Israel, which had strengthened the more secular nationalist expression of the PLO.

The Muslim Brotherhood, established in Egypt in 1928, had set up branches in Syria, Sudan, Libya, the Gulf states, Amman in Jordan (which influenced the West Bank), and Gaza. However, for two decades the Muslim Brotherhood focused on its religious, educational, and social missions and was quiescent politically. The Muslim Brotherhood advocated *dawa,* what may be called a re-Islamization of society and thought; *adala* (social justice); and an emphasis on *hakmiyya* (the sovereignty of God, as opposed to temporal rule). With Muslim Brotherhood supporters who became part of Hamas, this *dawa*-first agenda shifted to activism against Israel after Islamic Jihad had accelerated its operations during 1986 and 1987. Eventually Islamic Jihad split into three rival organizations. The new movement of Hamas, which emerged from the Jordanian and Egyptian Muslim Brotherhood groups, was able to draw strength from the social work of Sheikh Ahmed Yassin, a physically disabled cleric who had established the Mujamma al-Islami, a multifunctional organization that provided social, educational, and medical services. The Hamas founders were also active in establishing the al-Azhar University in Gaza.

Hamas supporters in the West Bank city of Ramallah celebrate the group's victory in Palestinian legislative elections on January 25, 2006. Hamas triggered a political earthquake with its sweeping election victory over the ruling Fatah party. (Pedro Ugarte/AFP/Getty Images)

In December 1987 Abd al-Aziz Rantisi, who was a physician and an educator at the Islamic University, and former student leaders Salah Shihada and Yahya al-Sinuwwar, who had been in charge of security for the Muslim Brotherhood, formed the first unit of Hamas. While Yassin gave his approval, as a cleric he was not directly connected to the new organization. In February 1988 as a result of a key meeting in Amman involving Sheikh Abd al-Rahman al-Khalifa (the spiritual guide of the Jordanian Muslim Brotherhood), Ibrahiam Ghawsha (the Hamas spokesperson and Jordanian representative), Mahmud Zahar (a surgeon), Rantisi (acting as a West Bank representative), Jordanian parliament members, and the hospital director, the Muslim Brotherhood granted formal recognition to Hamas.

In 1988 a Gazan member of Hamas wrote its charter. The charter condemns world Zionism and the efforts to isolate Palestine, defines the mission of the organization, and locates that mission within Palestinian, Arab, and Islamic elements. It does not condemn the West or non-Muslims but does condemn aggression against the Palestinian people, arguing for a defensive jihad. The charter also calls for fraternal relations with the other Palestinian nationalist groups. The Hamas leadership rarely refers to the charter, and many members no longer consider it valid because it has been replaced by key position papers.

Hamas is headed by the Political Bureau with representatives for military affairs, foreign affairs, finance, propaganda, and internal security. The Advisory Council, or Majlis al-Shura, is linked to the Political Bureau, which is also connected with all Palestinian communities; Hamas's social and charitable groups, elected members, and district committees; and the leadership in Israeli prisons.

Major attacks against Israel were carried out by the Izz al-Din al-Qassam Brigades of Hamas. Militants from Hamas, Islamic Jihad, and other smaller groups also employed Qassam rockets against Israeli civilian settlements in the Negev desert. However, much of Hamas's activity during the First Intifada consisted of participating within more broadly based popular demonstrations and locally coordinated efforts at resistance, countering Israeli raids, enforcing opening of businesses, and the like.

Hamas decried the autonomy agreement between the Israelis and the PLO in Jericho and the Gaza Strip as too limited a gain. By the time of the first elections for the PNA's Council in 1996, Hamas was caught in a dilemma. It had gained popularity as a resistance organization, but Oslo 1 and Oslo 2 (the Taba Accord of September 28, 1995) were meant to end the intifada. The elections would further strengthen the PLO, but if Hamas boycotted the elections and most people voted, then it would be even more isolated. Finally, Hamas's leadership rejected participation but without ruling it out in the future, and this gave the organization the ability to continue protesting Oslo. When suicide attacks were launched to protest Israeli violence against Palestinians, Hamas was blamed for inspiring or organizing the suicide bombers whether or not its operatives or those of the more radical Islamic Jihad were involved.

Hamas funded an extensive array of social services aimed at ameliorating the plight of the Palestinians. It provides funding for hospitals, schools, mosques, orphanages, food distribution, and aid to the families of Palestinian political prisoners who, numbering more than 10,000 people, constituted an important political force. When women of prisoner families who came to pick up their stipends were harassed by the authorities, Hamas took over these payments. Charitable and educational services constituted about 90 percent of the Hamas budget. Israel and Fatah deliberately targeted these services, closing, destroying, or taking them over beginning in 2007–2008 in order to destroy Hamas's popularity. The tactic largely failed, as the Fatah-based PNA in the West Bank did not properly staff the services or ran them in a partisan fashion.

Until its electoral triumph in January 2006, Hamas received funding from a number of sources. Palestinians living abroad provided money, as did a number of private donors in the Arab world and beyond. The U.S. government claims that Iran has been a significant donor to Hamas, but others assert that the relationship has been largely limited to political support. Much aid was directed to renovation of the Palestinian territories and was badly needed, and a great deal of that rebuilding was destroyed in the Israeli campaign in the West Bank in 2002, which in turn was intended to combat the suicide bombings.

Over the years, the Israel Defense Forces (IDF) has carried out targeted eliminations of a number of Hamas leaders. These include Shihada (July 23, 2002), Dr. Ibrahim Al-Makadma (August 3, 2003), Ismail Abu Shanab (August 21, 2003), Yassin (March 22, 2004), and Rantisi (April 17, 2004).

Hamas has had two sets of leaders, those inside the West Bank and the Gaza Strip and those outside. The West Bank leadership is divided along the general structure into political, charitable, student, and military activities. The political leadership is usually targeted for arrests because its members can be located, unlike the secret military units. That leadership has organized very effectively before and since PLO leader Yasser Arafat's 2004 death and has become more popular than the PLO in the West Bank, an unexpected development. A current Hamas leader, Khalid Mishal, is in Syria. Other senior Hamas leaders are there as well, and there is also some Hamas activity in refugee camps in Lebanon. Although Arafat was quickly succeeded by Abbas as the PLO leader, a sizable number of Palestinians had already begun to identify with Hamas, mainly because it was able to accomplish what the PNA could not, namely to provide for the everyday needs of the people.

Hamas won the legislative elections in January 2006. Locals had expected a victory in Gaza but not in the West Bank. Nonetheless, both Israel and the United States (which had supported the holding of an election) steadfastly refused to recognize the Palestinian government under the control of Hamas. The United States cut off $420 million and the European Union (EU) cut off $600 million in aid to the PNA's Hamas-led government, which created difficulties for ordinary Palestinians. The loss of this aid halted the delivery of supplies to hospitals and ended other services in addition to stopping the payment of salaries. To prevent total collapse, the United States and the EU promised relief funds, but these were not allowed to go through the PNA. The cutoff in funds was designed to discourage Palestinian support for Hamas.

On March 17, 2007, Abbas agreed to a Palestinian unity government that included members of both Hamas and Fatah in which Hamas leader Ismail Haniyeh became prime minister. Yet in May armed clashes between Hamas and Fatah escalated, as the United States supported an intended Fatah takeover of Gaza. To preempt that, on June 14 Hamas seized control of Gaza. Although lacking the authority under the PNA's constitution, Abbas dissolved the Hamas-led unity government. On June 18, having been assured of U.S. and EU support, Abbas also dissolved the National Security Council and swore in an emergency Palestinian government. That same day the United States ended its 15-month embargo on the PNA and resumed aid solely to Abbas in an effort to strengthen the Fatah wing of the PNA. Other governments followed suit. On June 19, 2007, Abbas cut off all ties and dialogue with Hamas, pending the return of Gaza.

Throughout 2007 Israeli and Western media reported that Hamas had imposed a more religiously conservative regime on Gaza, although these reports were without substance. Gaza, however, was now largely cut off economically from its donors and more than ever was an economic basket case. In the meantime, Israel had imposed a blockade against Hamas.

In June 2008 Hamas concluded a *tahdiya* (truce) with Israel that was supposed to end the boycott. It did not last. Hamas and other militant groups not party to the truce launched rockets into Israeli territory, while the IDF assassinated a number of Hamas leaders in November 2008. The Israelis retaliated against the growing number of rockets into its southern territory with a devastating series of air strikes late in the month that continued for several weeks. On January 3, 2009, Israel sent troops into Gaza.

The resulting two-week-long incursion, known as the Gaza War, killed an estimated 1,300 Palestinians (more than one-third of them children) and wounded another 5,400. Reportedly, 22,000 buildings were destroyed or damaged, including the American school, the Islamic University, and the United Nations (UN) school where Gazans had taken temporary shelter. The physical damage was estimated at more than $2 billion. On January 17, 2009, a shaky cease-fire again took hold, only to be broken by some rockets and additional Israeli air strikes concentrated on the tunnels that connect Gaza with Egypt.

Israel came under intense criticism from some quarters because of the high civilian casualties during its incursion, while in contrast only 3 Israeli civilians and 10 Israeli military had been killed. Rather than weakening Hamas as the Israeli government claimed, the scale of the human cost and physical damage in Gaza seemed, if anything, to have strengthened the prestige of Hamas among West Bank Palestinians at the expense of the more moderate Fatah.

HARRY RAYMOND HUESTON II, PAUL G. PIERPAOLI JR., AND SHERIFA ZUHUR

See also

Abbas, Mahmoud; Arafat, Yasser; Intifada, First; Intifada, Second; Islamic Jihad, Palestinian; Israel; Israel, Armed Forces; Jihad; Muslim Brotherhood; Palestine Liberation Organization; Terrorism

References

Gunning, Jeroen. *Hamas in Politics: Democracy, Religion, and Violence.* New York: Columbia University Press, 2008.

Hroub, Khaled. *Hamas: A Beginner's Guide.* London: Pluto, 2006.

International Crisis Group. "After Mecca: Engaging Hamas." Middle East Report No. 62. Amman, Jerusalem, and Brussels: ICG, February 28, 2007.

McGeough, Paul. *Kill Khalid: The Failed Mossad Assassination of Khalid Mishal and the Rise of Hamas.* New York: New Press, 2009.

Zuhur, Sherifa. "Gaza, Israel, Hamas and the Lost Calm of Operation Cast Lead." *Middle East Policy* 16(1) (Spring 2009): 40–52.

———. *Hamas and Israel: Strategic Interaction in Group Based Politics.* Carlisle, PA: Strategic Studies Institute, 2008.

Hamburg Cell

A terrorist cell formed by a group of radical Islamists affiliated with Al Qaeda in Hamburg, Germany. The Hamburg Cell, which played an important role in the September 11, 2001, terror attacks on the United States, began when Mohamed Atta, Ramzi bin al-Shibh, and Marwan al-Shehhi took up lodgings together on November 1, 1998, in an apartment on 54 Marienstrasse in Hamburg. They were members of a study group at the al-Quds Mosque run by Mohammad Belfas, a middle-aged postal employee in Hamburg who was originally from Indonesia. Both in the study group and at the apartment, the men began talking about ways to advance the Islamist cause. Soon the original three attracted others of a like mind. The nine members of this group were Mohamed Atta, Said Bahaji, Mohammad Belfas, Ramzi bin al-Shibh, Zakariya Essabor, Marwan al-Shehhi, Ziad Jarrah, Mounir al-Motassadez, and Abd al-Ghani Mzoudi.

At first Belfas was the leader of the group, but he was soon replaced by Atta and left the cell. Although Atta became the formal leader, Shibh was its most influential member because he was more popular within the Muslim community than Atta.

Initially the members of the Hamburg group wanted to join the Chechen rebels in Chechnya in their fight against the Russians. Before this move could take place, the leaders of the cell met with Mohamedou Ould Slahi, an Al Qaeda operative in Duisburg, Germany, who advised that they first undertake military and terrorist training in Afghanistan. Atta, Shibh, Jarrah, and Shehhi traveled to Kandahar, Afghanistan, where they underwent extensive training in terrorist techniques. They also met with Al Qaeda leader Osama bin Laden, at which time Atta, Jarrah, and Shehhi were recruited for a special martyrdom mission in the United States. Shibh was to have been a part of this mission, but he was never able to obtain a visa to travel to the United States. Instead, Shibh stayed in Hamburg, serving as the contact person between the Hamburg Cell and Al Qaeda. He also served as the banker for the hijackers in the September 11 plot.

What made those in the Hamburg Cell so important was that the individuals in it were fluent in English, well educated, and apparently accustomed to a Western lifestyle, so they were more likely to be able to live in a Western country without raising any suspicions. They also had the capability to learn with some training how to pilot a large aircraft.

Shibh ended communication with the Hamburg Cell as soon as he learned the date of the attacks. He made certain that all those connected with it were forewarned so that they could protect themselves. Shibh destroyed as much material as possible before leaving for Pakistan. Only later did German and American authorities learn of the full extent of the operations of the Hamburg Cell.

German authorities had been aware of the existence of the Hamburg Cell, but German law prevented action against its members unless a German law was violated. This restriction did not prevent Thomas Volz, a veteran U.S. Central Intelligence Agency (CIA) officer attached to the American consulate in Hamburg, from attempting to persuade German authorities to take action against the Islamist extremists who were allegedly part of the cell and known to be at the Hamburg mosque. Volz had become suspicious of several members of the group and their connections with other Muslim terrorists. He hounded the German authorities to do something until his actions alienated them to the point that they almost had him deported from Germany.

After the September 11 attacks German authorities began a serious investigation of the Hamburg Cell and its surviving members. By that time there was little to examine or do except to arrest whoever had been affiliated with it. German authorities finally learned the extent to which Al Qaeda had been able to establish contacts in Germany and elsewhere in Europe.

STEPHEN A. ATKINS

See also

Al Qaeda; Atta, Muhammad; Bin Laden, Osama; September 11 Attacks; Shibh, Ramzi Muhammad Abdallah ibn al-

References

Bernstein, Richard. *Out of the Blue: The Story of September 11, 2001, from Jihad to Ground Zero*. New York: Times Books, 2002.
McDermott, Terry. *Perfect Soldiers: The 9/11 Hijackers: Who They Were, Why They Did It*. New York: HarperCollins, 2005.
Posner, Gerald. *Why America Slept: The Failure to Prevent 9/11*. New York: Ballantine Books, 2003.
Sageman, Marc. *Understanding Terror Networks*. Philadelphia: University of Pennsylvania Press, 2004.

Hanjour, Hani

Birth Date: August 30, 1972
Death Date: September 11, 2001

The leader and probable pilot of the terrorist group that seized American Airlines Flight 77 and crashed it into the Pentagon on September 11, 2001; he was a last-minute recruit because the September 11 conspirators needed one additional pilot. Hani Saleh Husan Hanjour was born on August 30, 1972, in Taif, Saudi Arabia. His father was a successful food-supply businessman. Hanjour was a devout Muslim, and this colored virtually all of his conduct.

Because he was an indifferent student, Hanjour was only persuaded to stay in school by his older brother. This older brother, who was living in Tucson, Arizona, encouraged him to go to the United States. Hanjour arrived in the United States on October 3, 1991, and stayed in Tucson, where he studied English at the University of Arizona.

After completing the English program in three months, Hanjour returned to Taif. He spent the next five years working at his family's food-supply business. In 1996 he briefly visited Afghanistan. Following this visit, he decided to move back to the United States. He stayed for a time with an Arab American family in Hollywood, Florida. Then, in April 1996, Hanjour moved in with a family in Oakland, California. This time he attended Holy Names College and took an intensive course in English. He then decided to become a pilot and fly for Saudi Airlines. Hanjour also enrolled in a class at Sierra Academy of Aeronautics, but he withdrew because of the cost.

Leaving Oakland in April 1996, Hanjour moved to Phoenix, Arizona. This time he paid for flight lessons at CRM Flight Cockpit Resource Management in Scottsdale, Arizona, but his academic performance there was disappointing. His instructors found him to be a terrible pilot, and it took him a long time to master the essentials of flying.

While in Phoenix, Hanjour roomed with Bandar al-Hazmi. In January 1998 Hanjour took flying lessons at Arizona Aviation, and after a three-year struggle he finally earned his commercial pilot rating in April 1999 but was unable to find a job as a pilot. His Federal Aviation Administration (FAA) license expired in 1999 when he failed to take a mandatory medical test.

Frustrated in his job hunting, Hanjour traveled to Afghanistan. He arrived there just as Khalid Sheikh Mohammed's men were looking for another pilot for the September 11, 2001, terror plot. Hanjour seemed made to order. After his recruitment by Al Qaeda, he returned to the United States. In September 2000 when he moved to San Diego, California, Hanjour met up with Nawaf al-Hazmi. Hanjour returned to Phoenix to continue his pilot training at the Jet Tech Flight School. He was so inept as a flyer and his English was so poor that the instructors contacted the FAA to check on whether his commercial license was valid. The FAA confirmed this. Hanjour spent most of his time at Jet Tech on the Boeing 737 simulator. In the early spring of 2001 Hanjour moved to Paterson, New Jersey. There he met several times with other members of the September 11 conspiracy.

On September 11, 2001, Hanjour is believed to have served as the hijackers' pilot of American Airlines Flight 77. Despite his lack of flying ability, after the crew had been subdued he managed to fly that aircraft into the Pentagon. Hanjour put the Boeing 757 into a steep nose dive and slammed the jet into the building at 9:37 a.m. All 58 passengers aboard the plane perished, as did Hanjour and 4 other hijackers. An additional 125 people died on the ground upon and after impact.

STEPHEN A. ATKINS

See also

Mohammed, Khalid Sheikh; September 11 Attacks

References

Graham, Bob. *Intelligence Matters: The CIA, the FBI, Saudi Arabia, and the Failure of America's War on Terror.* New York: Random House, 2004.

McDermott, Terry. *Perfect Soldiers: The 9/11 Hijackers: Who They Were, Why They Did It.* New York: HarperCollins, 2005.

HARD SURFACE, **Operation**
Start Date: June 12, 1963
End Date: January 1964

U.S. military support to Saudi Arabia and the only John F. Kennedy administration projection of military power in the region. On June 12, 1963, President John F. Kennedy authorized Operation HARD SURFACE as part of his effort to deter Egyptian leader Gamal Abdel Nasser from expanding his nation's military participation in the North Yemen Civil War (1962–1970) to Saudi Arabia. Kennedy sought to protect long-standing U.S. strategic interests in the oil-rich kingdom, although the United States had formally recognized the newly declared Yemen Arab Republic on December 19, 1962.

The North Yemen Civil War broke out after republican Yemeni forces overthrew the newly crowned Mutawakkilite king of Yemen, Sayf al-Islam Mohammed al-Badr, actually the heir of the Zaydi imam. They then established the Yemen Arab Republic under Abdullah al-Sallal. The Mutawakkilite regime in northern Yemen had been created after the collapse of the Ottoman Empire at the end of World War I. Egypt provided troops and substantial military support to the Yemen Arab Republic, while Saudi Arabia financed the imam's royalist side with guerrilla forces trained by the British.

President Kennedy sought to press Crown Prince Faisal of Saudi Arabia, King Hussein of Jordan, President Sallal, and Nasser to bring about the removal of Egyptian troops through a pledge from Saudi Arabia and Jordan to halt their aid to Imam al-Badr. Nasser, however, responded that he would remove his forces only after Jordan and Saudi Arabia halted all military operations, while Faisal and Hussein rejected the U.S. president's plan outright because they claimed that it would mean U.S. recognition of the rebels who had ousted the imam and established the Yemen Arab Republic. Faisal also claimed that Nasser wanted to secure Saudi Arabia's oil and to use Yemen as a staging area for revolt in the rest of the

Arabian Peninsula. The situation was even more complicated, as Great Britain, a staunch ally of the Saudis, had its own designs in southern Saudi Arabia, which conflicted with various nationalist groups there. At the same time, United Nations (UN) diplomat Ralph Bunche was actively seeking to bring an end to the civil war.

Faisal was determined to secure U.S. military support, and Kennedy responded by assuring him in writing on October 25, 1962, of "full U.S. support for the maintenance of Saudi Arabian integrity." Twice U.S. aircraft staged brief shows of force over Saudi Arabia. In the first instance in November, six North American F-100 Super Sabre interceptors flew over the cities of Riyadh and Jeddah. On the second occasion two bombers and a transport flew over Riyadh on a return flight to Paris from Karachi.

Following an Egyptian Air Force strike against the Saudi city of Najran close to the Yemeni border in early January 1963 where Yemeni royalist base camps were located, Faisal again expressed his concerns to Washington, whereupon the United States again sent aircraft over Jeddah in a show of force on January 15. Washington also discussed the possibility of sending antiaircraft batteries to Najran.

Robert Komer, a senior staffer on the National Security Council (NSC), informed Kennedy that Faisal very much wanted the dispatch of U.S. aircraft to the desert kingdom. Officials at the Pentagon were unconvinced and noted that while the U.S. squadron might deter any Egyptian attack, it clearly lacked the military capability to defend Saudi Arabia. U.S. Air Force chief of staff General Curtis LeMay is said to have been especially opposed, claiming that the fighters would be sitting ducks and that in any case they were needed elsewhere.

Regardless, Komer and Secretary of State Dean Rusk urged that the squadron be sent, and on June 12 Kennedy signed off on Operation HARD SURFACE. Although it involved only a single squadron of eight North American F-100 Super Sabres, it also included 560 support personnel and 861.3 tons of equipment.

The Pentagon claimed that Kennedy's only military commitment to the Middle East was simply a token force. The rules of engagement called for the fighters to intercept any Egyptian aircraft violating Saudi airspace and try to escort them out of Saudi airspace or to a convenient runway. If the intruding aircraft were to bomb Saudi targets or attempt to engage the American aircraft, then the F-100 pilots were to shoot them down. The Pentagon insisted that the F-100s be fully prepared for combat and armed with Sidewinder missiles.

Plans hit a snag with the Saudi insistence that the U.S. personnel have passports and visas. This ran afoul of the long-running Saudi ban on Jews entering the Saudis' kingdom. Word of this soon got out and caused a minor flap in Congress and in the press. The Egyptian press picked it up, noting that the willingness of the Saudis to let Jews into Islam's holiest places was a sure sign of the weakness of the desert kingdom and its reliance on foreign support. On June 27 this impasse was broken by the adoption of a "don't ask, don't tell" policy. The Saudis would not ask if the American airmen were Jews; the Americans would not tell.

On July 2 the NSC asked for permission to send the F-100s to Saudi Arabia, and Kennedy approved. The eight F-100s did not entirely halt Egyptian attacks, leaving LeMay to grouse about the ineffectiveness of the operation, but Kennedy and the State Department downplayed these raids and styled the operation an effective deterrent at slight cost.

The U.S. aircraft never did engage Egyptian forces, and President Lyndon B. Johnson allowed the operation to end in January 1964. Nasser indeed increased Egyptian troop strength in Yemen, and the civil war there continued until 1970.

SPENCER C. TUCKER

See also

Kennedy, John Fitzgerald; Nasser, Gamal Abdel; Yemen, Civil War in

References

Bass, Warren. *Support Any Friend: Kennedy's Middle East and the Making of the U.S.-Israeli Alliance.* New York: Oxford University Press, 2003.

Patterson, Thomas G. *Kennedy's Quest for Victory: American Foreign Policy, 1961–1963.* New York: Oxford University Press, 1989.

United States Department of State. *Foreign Relations, 1961–1963,* Vol. 17, *Near East, 1961–1962.* Washington, DC: United States Department of State, 1991.

Harrell, Gary L.
Birth Date: ca. 1951

U.S. Army general who served for three decades in various special operations forces, including as Delta Force commander during operations in Somalia. Gary L. Harrell is a Tennessee native who enrolled in the Reserve Officers' Training Corps (ROTC) at East Tennessee State University as a means to pay for college. He did not plan on a military career but found the duty enjoyable and challenging. Commissioned after graduation with a BS degree in December 1973, Harrell was assigned to the 82nd Airborne Division at Fort Bragg, North Carolina. He participated in the U.S. invasion of Grenada in 1983 as a member of the 82nd Airborne Division. He later completed Ranger training and became a member of Delta Force. In 1989 he was a part of a team that rescued American Kurt Muse from a Panamanian prison during the U.S. invasion of Panama. Harrell also helped capture Pablo Escobar, an infamous drug lord in Colombia.

During Operation DESERT STORM in 1991, Harrell served with the Joint Special Operations Command and participated in the effort by special operations forces in western Iraq to locate and destroy Scud missiles used to attack Israel and Saudi Arabia. The effort was largely unsuccessful. Two years later Harrell was special assistant to the commander of the 1st Special Forces Operational Detachment–Delta (Airborne) in Somalia. During an attempt to capture warlords who were opposed to U.S. interests, two helicopters carrying U.S. Army Rangers were shot down. While a rapid reaction force battled toward one crash site, the other crash site was threatened by Somali militiamen. A Delta Force team providing oversight to the second downed helicopter requested permission to land and protect the survivors. Harrell twice refused permission but reluctantly gave in on the third request. The two Delta Force members, knowing their possible fate, were eventually killed by the Somalis, but they saved the pilot of the downed helicopter. The incident and Harrell's participation in it are portrayed in the book and movie *Black Hawk Down.*

During the 2001 invasion of Afghanistan to overthrow the Taliban, Harrell—promoted to brigadier general on November 1, 2001—commanded the U.S. Army Special Forces. In June 2002 he became the commander of Special Operations Command Central, a position with responsibility for the Middle East and Iraq. As war with Iraq approached, Harrell was charged with planning and overseeing special operations forces in Iraq.

Unlike the 1991 Persian Gulf War, special operations forces were expected to play a major role. Harrell devised the plans that employed more than 20,000 special operations troops. General Tommy Franks, in charge of Operation IRAQI FREEDOM, was open to Harrell's proposals, as was Secretary of Defense Donald Rumsfeld.

Harrell's plan built on his experiences in the Persian Gulf War. The 5th Special Forces Group was charged with securing the largely uninhabited western desert of Iraq and protecting the left flank of the main invasion force as it approached Baghdad. Most Scuds had been launched from this area in 1991, and Harrell hoped that more troops on the ground might control the area. The Special Forces employed specially modified vehicles that allowed them to move rapidly across the desert. The operation was a success, and no missiles were launched during the war.

The second part of Harrell's plan included using the 10th Special Forces Group to work with Kurdish forces to provide a credible threat in northern Iraq. Turkey's refusal to allow American forces passage into Iraq forced U.S. planners to rely on Special Forces teams working with the Kurds to tie down Iraqi forces and capture Mosul and the vital oil fields. Special Forces commanded by Colonel Charles Cleveland were completely successful in this. Using advanced weapons such as the Javelin fire-and-forget anti-armor missile, small teams were able to defeat much larger Iraqi regular forces.

Harrell was promoted to major general on November 1, 2004, and served as commander of the U.S. Army Special Operations Command at Fort Bragg. From April 2005 to March 2008 he was deputy chief of staff operations, Joint Force Command Headquarters, the Netherlands. He retired from the army on March 6, 2008. Harrell then took a position as vice president of business development for Pacer Health Corporation, a Miami-based owner-operator of acute-care hospitals.

TIM J. WATTS

See also

Cleveland, Charles T.; Delta Force; DESERT STORM, Operation; ENDURING FREEDOM, Operation; IRAQI FREEDOM, Operation; Scud Missiles, U.S. Search for during the Persian Gulf War; Somalia, International Intervention in; United States Special Operations Command

References

Murray, Williamson, and Robert H. Scales Jr. *The Iraq War: A Military History.* Cambridge, MA: Belknap, 2005.

Robinson, Linda. *Masters of Chaos: The Secret History of the Special Forces.* New York: PublicAffairs, 2004.

Hazmi, Nawaf al-

Birth Date: August 9, 1976
Death Date: September 11, 2001

One of the hijackers of American Airlines Flight 77, which crashed into the Pentagon on September 11, 2001. Nawaf bin Muhammad Salim al-Hazmi was born on August 9, 1976, in Mecca, Saudi Arabia. His father was a grocer, and his older brother was a police chief in Jizan. Hazmi became an Islamist militant at an early age, and as a teenager he traveled to Afghanistan. There he met Khalid al-Mihdhar. They subsequently joined Muslims in Bosnia fighting against the Serbs there in 1995. Then, with his brother Salem al-Hazmi, Hazmi and Mihdhar returned to Afghanistan to fight with the Taliban against the Afghan Northern Alliance. In 1998 Hazmi traveled to Chechnya, where he took part in fighting with the Chechen rebels against the Russian Army. Returning to Saudi Arabia in early 1999, Hazmi decided to go to the United States with Mihdhar and his brother Salem al-Hazmi, where they easily obtained visas.

By 1999 Hazmi had been recruited by the Al Qaeda terrorist organization for a special mission. Original plans had called for him to become a pilot, but he lacked the necessary competency in English and the ability to pass pilot's training. He thus teamed with Mihdhar to provide logistical support for the September 11 plot. On September 11, 2001, Hazmi was one of five hijackers on board American Airlines Flight 77. He helped subdue the crew and provided security while the airliner was crashed into the Pentagon. All 5 hijackers, in addition to 64 passengers and crew, died that day when the aircraft crashed into the Pentagon; another 125 people died on the ground.

STEPHEN A. ATKINS

See also

Al Qaeda; Mihdhar, Khalid al-

References

Graham, Bob. *Intelligence Matters: The CIA, the FBI, Saudi Arabia, and the Failure of America's War on Terror.* New York: Random House, 2004.

McDermott, Terry. *Perfect Soldiers: The 9/11 Hijackers: Who They Were, Why They Did It.* New York: HarperCollins, 2005.

Heavy Expanded Mobility Tactical Truck

Large heavy-duty, all-terrain, single-unit vehicle employed by the U.S. armed forces, first put into service in 1982. The Oshkosh Truck Corporation manufactures the Heavy Expanded Mobility Tactical Trucks (HEMTTs). These 10-ton trucks are produced in a half dozen different models: a general-purpose cargo truck, some of which feature a small crane mounted in the rear; a tanker, used to refuel tactical fighting vehicles and helicopters; a tractor tow, which pulls the M1M-104 Patriot missile battery; a generator truck capable of producing 30 kilowatts of power with a crane capable of towing the MGM-31 Pershing missile erector launcher; and a heavy-duty recovery vehicle with a built-in lift-and-tow system, a winch, and a small crane. All HEMTTs are 8×8 vehicles, meaning that power is distributed to all eight wheels, giving them the ability to operate in extremely rugged terrain as well as in deep mud, sand, and snow. Their huge wheels carry low-pressure puncture-resistant tires. HEMTTs have a crew of two men. Currently there are some 13,000 HEMTTs in use, and they have become the tactical workhorses of the U.S. Army.

Depending on their model and design, HEMTTs are anywhere from 29.25 feet long to 33.4 feet long. All are 96 inches wide and have a 2-foot ground clearance; maximum fording depth is 4 feet. Vehicle curb weights (without cargo) range from 32,200 pounds to 50,900 pounds. The trucks are powered by a V-8 diesel engine manufactured by Detroit Diesel Alison. The HEMTT produces 450 horsepower at 2,100 revolutions per minute. Top speed is 57 miles per hour, predetermined by a governor; range on one tank of fuel is approximately 300 miles. The transmission is an Alison-made 4-speed automatic with a single reverse gear. Brakes are air-activated internal expansion at all eight wheels. Mounted winches are capable of pulling 20,000–60,000 pounds. The most heavy-duty mounted crane is capable of lifting 14,620 pounds. Several models also include a self-recovery winch.

Affectionately known as the "Dragon Wagon," the HEMTT has repeatedly proven its mettle under combat situations, including those in Operation DESERT STORM and Operation IRAQI FREEDOM. The HEMTT frequently accompanies fast-moving units, typically led by the M1 Abrams tank, and also fulfills countless roles in logistical support, refueling, and cargo hauling. Several key weapons systems, including the Patriot missile, are often towed by HEMTTs. The M978 model serves as a highly mobile 2,500-gallon fuel tanker. A low-end general-purpose HEMTT (M977 or M985) costs approximately $140,000.

PAUL G. PIERPAOLI JR.

See also

M1A1 and M1A2 Abrams Main Battle Tanks; Patriot Missile System; Vehicles, Unarmored

References

Braulick, Carrie A. *U.S. Army Tanks.* Cottage Grove, MN: Blazers, 2006.

Kaelberer, Angie P. *U.S. Army Humvees.* Cottage Grove, MN: Blazers, 2006.

Hekmetyar, Gulbuddin al-Hurra
Birth Date: 1948

Former leader of the Islamic Party of Afghanistan (Hezb-e-Islami Afghanistan), prime minister of Afghanistan (1993–1994 and 1996–1997), and key figure in the Afghan jihad against the Soviet occupation (1979–1989). Born sometime in 1948 to a Kharuti Pashtun family in the Imam Saheb district of Kunduz Province in northern Afghanistan, Gulbuddin al-Hurra Hekmetyar attended the Mahtab Military School in Kabul. Fluent in Dari (Farsi), Urdu, Arabic, English, and Pashto, he was expelled within two years because of his political activities.

From 1970 to 1972 Hekmetyar attended the engineering school at Kabul University, although he was once more prevented from completing his studies because of his involvement in illicit political activity. Implicated in the murder of Saydal Sukhandan, a member of the pro-China Shola-e-Jawedan Movement, Hekmetyar was sentenced to two years in jail by the government of King Zahir Shah. Hekmetyar was freed from prison following a 1974 coup executed by the king's cousin, Mohammad Daud Khan.

Hekmetyar's interest in religious-political ideologies emerged early. As a high school student he had been a member of the communist People's Democratic Party of Afghanistan (PDPA), and later, as a student at Kabul University, his communist ideology was influenced by an extremist version of Islam nurtured through his membership in the Muslim Youths Movement (Nahzat-e-Jawanane Musalman). Although initially a leftist, Hekmetyar later became a disciple of the Egyptian author, socialist, and intellectual Sayyid Qutb and the Muslim Brotherhood movement.

Following his release from jail in 1974, Hekmetyar sought refuge in the Pakistan border city of Peshawar, accompanied by Burhanuddin Rabbani, Qazi Muhammad Amin Waqad, and a number of other jihadi leaders. Although members of the Muslim Youths Movement, the radical leaders nevertheless broke into competing factions and parties, and with the support of the Pakistani prime minister Zulfiqar Ali Bhutto, Hekmetyar established Hezb-e-Islami Afghanistan in 1976.

Also known as Hezb-e-Islami Gulbuddin (HIG), the movement was led by Hekmetyar and fellow jihadi leader Mawlawi M. Younus Khalis until 1979, when the two leaders parted ways and the new Hezb-e-Islami Khalis faction constituted a counter group to HIG. A significant ideological dichotomy inherent in the split resided in Khalis's conservative and traditional clerical approach, in contrast to Hekmetyar's more youthful and ideological activist stance. While Khalis walked away with the preponderance of the movement's most skilled commanders, HIG continued to dominate the Afghan resistance against the Soviets, with support from Pakistan. Drawing the majority of its membership from ethnic Pashtuns, the movement's ideology was influenced by the Muslim Brotherhood and the Sunni Pakistani theologian and political philosopher Abul Ala Mawdudi.

Advocating the notion that sustainable development and stability in Afghanistan could be achieved only through Sharia (Islamic law), throughout the 1980s and early 1990s the movement garnered substantial financial and arms support from Arab and Western countries, including Saudi Arabia, Pakistan, and the United States. Most notably, Hekmetyar received anti-aircraft Stinger missiles from the U.S. government through Pakistan's Inter-Services Intelligence (ISI), with which he facilitated the Afghan jihad against Soviet forces. Currently, the nonviolent faction of the Hezb-e-Islami is a registered political party in Afghanistan, led by Abd al-Hadi Arghandiwal, and is thought to be in decline.

During the Soviet occupation, Hekmetyar ascended to new heights of power. This posed a substantial threat to Dr. Mohammad Najibullah, the former chief of the Afghan government's security service, Khedamat-e Etelea'at-e Dawlati (KHAD), and the last president of the communist Democratic Republic of Afghanistan (1987–1992). Despite Najibullah's attempt to neutralize the threat posed by Hekmetyar by offering him 95 percent control of the regime, Hekmetyar refused, and in 1992 Najibullah's government was overturned by the leader of the Afghan National Liberation Front, Sebghantullah Mujadeddi, who then transferred power within two months to the leader of Jameet-e-Islami.

While Hekmetyar anticipated an easy transition to power, the Jabalurseraj Agreement, signed on May 25, 1992, enabled the strategic garrisons in Kabul to be seized by Tajik leader Ahmad Shah Masoud, Abdul Ali Mazari of the Hazaras, and Uzbek leader Abul Rashid Dostum. Left out of the city, Hekmetyar's forces shelled Kabul mercilessly in February 1993 before Hekmetyar joined a coordination council (Shora-e-Hamahangi) with Dostum and Mazari against President Burhaniddin Rabbani. Hekmetyar served as prime minister during 1993–1994 and 1996–1997. With the Hezb-e-Islami group weakened, Hekmetyar nevertheless kept up his rabid anti-American rhetoric while capitalizing on the weaknesses of his enemies, most notably through the exhortation of militants in Pakistan to attack American interests there rather than fighting across the border.

Hekmetyar was not always anti-American. During the 1980s the U.S. Central Intelligence Agency (CIA) had provided him and his allies with hundreds of millions of dollars in weapons and ammunition to help them battle the Soviet Army during its occupation of Afghanistan. In 1985 the CIA even flew Hekmetyar to the United States, and the agency considered him to be a reliable anti-Soviet rebel. Contrastingly, at the time of this writing, Hekmetyar has coordinated numerous attacks against United States and North Atlantic Treaty Organization (NATO) troops in Afghanistan while calling on Pakistani militants to attack U.S. targets from across the border. More recently, Hamid Karzai's government has extended a peaceful—if not controversially tentative—hand toward Hekmatyar in hopes of coaxing him to join its side. However, assertions by the former governor of Nooristan province, Tamim Nooristani, that Hekmetyar recently took part in a series of deadly attacks against U.S. soldiers, alongside Pakistani and Afghan Taliban fighters, may prove Hekmetyar's undoing.

K. LUISA GANDOLFO

See also

Afghanistan; Dostum, Abd al-Rashid; Kakar, Mullah; Muslim Brotherhood; Soviet-Afghanistan War; Taliban Insurgency, Afghanistan; Warlords, Afghanistan

References

Giraldo, Jeanne K., and Harold A. Trinkunas. *Terrorism Financing and State Responses: A Comparative Perspective.* Stanford, CA: Stanford University Press, 2007.

Appleby, Scott. *Fundamentalism and the State: Remaking Polities, Economies, and Militance.* Chicago: University of Chicago Press, 1996.

Emadi, Hafizullah. *Politics of the Dispossessed: Superpowers and Developments in the Middle East.* Westport, CT: Greenwood, 2001.

Friedman, Norman. *Terrorism, Afghanistan, and America's New Way of War.* Annapolis, MD: Naval Institute Press, 2003.

Helicopters

See Aircraft, Helicopters; Aircraft, Helicopters, Operations DESERT SHIELD and DESERT STORM; Aircraft, Helicopters, Soviet-Afghanistan War

Hersh, Seymour Myron
Birth Date: April 8, 1937

Controversial, Pulitzer Prize–winning journalist and author who in 2004 was among the various sources who publicized the mistreatment of Iraqi prisoners at Abu Ghraib and who has been a vocal critic of the Iraq War. Seymour Myron Hersh was born in Chicago on April 8, 1937. His parents were Jewish immigrants from Eastern Europe, and he grew up in a working-class, inner-city neighborhood.

Hersh graduated from the University of Chicago in 1959 and began his long journalism career as a police reporter in Chicago, working for the City News Bureau. Not long after, he joined United Press International (UPI) and by 1963 had become a UPI correspondent covering both Washington, D.C., and Chicago. Hersh soon earned the reputation as a hard-driving investigative reporter. In 1968, he served as Senator Eugene McCarthy's press secretary during his unsuccessful bid for the 1968 Democratic presidential nomination. After that, he became a reporter based in Washington, D.C., for the *New York Times.* It was here that he became internationally renowned for his investigative reporting.

In November 1969, it was Hersh who first revealed the story of the March 1968 My Lai Massacre in Vietnam, perpetrated by

Pulitzer Prize–winning journalist Seymour Hersh. (AP/Wide World Photos)

U.S. soldiers against South Vietnamese civilians. His scoop also included the bombshell that the Pentagon had engaged in a purposeful campaign to cover up evidence of the massacre to ensure that it did not become public knowledge. For his reporting of the incident and its aftermath, Hersh received the Pulitzer Prize in International Reporting for 1970. That same year, he published a well-read book on the subject, the first of many books he would author.

Hersh made it his business to seek out stories that he knew would be hard to break and that would generate a maximum amount of attention. In 1986, three years after a Korean Air Lines Boeing 747 jetliner was blasted out of the sky by Soviet jet fighters, Hersh published a book in which he alleged that the incident—coming as it did at the height of the renewed Cold War—was caused by Soviet stupidity and provocative U.S. intelligence operations that had been sanctioned by the Reagan administration. Later, Hersh's conclusions were somewhat vindicated by the subsequent release of classified government documents. Hersh's critics on the right, however, were outraged by his allegation that the tragedy had been brought about by U.S. policy.

Hersh continued his investigative reporting, often working independently of any publication or news agency so that he could be free to pursue those stories that most interested him. He did, however, develop a long-standing relationship with the *New Yorker* magazine, for which he has frequently provided articles and opinion pieces. In August 1998, Hersh once more drew the ire of the political establishment by blasting the Clinton administration for authorizing bombing a suspected chemical-weapons factory in Sudan, which Hersh concluded was in fact an important pharmaceutical-manufacturing facility. The bombing was in retaliation for the bombings of U.S. embassies by Al Qaeda terrorists, who were believed to be operating in Sudan.

The Iraq War, which began in March 2003, drew Hersh's attention and scrutiny. Since that time, he has launched numerous in-depth investigations into various events and developments in Iraq and into the Bush administration's interest in pursuing regime change against Syria and Iran. In the spring of 2004, Hersh published a series of articles illuminating the extent of the prisoner-abuse scandal in Iraq's Abu Ghraib prison. This unleashed a torrent of media attention, the release of photos showing prisoner abuse, and a major congressional investigation. Hersh also alleged that prisoners had been tortured in other holding facilities, including those in Afghanistan and at Guantánamo Bay, Cuba. That same year he also wrote that the invasion of Iraq in 2003 had been based on faulty intelligence about Iraq and that Vice President Dick Cheney and Secretary of Defense Donald Rumsfeld had purposely misused prewar intelligence to manufacture a justification of war. Hersh was intensely disliked by the George W. Bush administration, and some military analysts were not permitted to cite him. Richard Perle, a leading neoconservative and frequent adviser to the Bush White House, termed Hersh a journalistic "terrorist." In March 2007, Hersh excoriated the

Bush administration's surge strategy, alleging that it would only embolden Sunni extremists in Iraq.

Beginning in January 2005, Hersh began publishing a series of articles in which he alleged that the U.S. government was clandestinely preparing to launch preemptive air strikes against suspected nuclear weapons facilities in Iran. The Bush administration denied that such operations were being contemplated but did not deny that contingency plans existed. In 2006, Hersh wrote that the United States was preparing to use a nuclear bunker–busting bomb against Iranian nuclear facilities. This provoked a vehement denial from the White House and Pentagon. President Bush termed Hersh's allegations "wild speculation." In late 2007, Hersh drew the ire of many Democrats when he asserted that Senator Hillary Clinton's hawkish views on Iran were related to the large number of donations her presidential campaign had received from American Jews.

Hersh has sharply criticized both Democratic and Republican administrations. In 1997, Hersh was criticized in some circles for a book he published on President John F. Kennedy, both for its evidentiary value and its dubious allegations that Kennedy had been married before he wed Jacqueline Bouvier and that the president had had a long-standing relationship with Chicago mob boss Sam Giancana.

PAUL G. PIERPAOLI JR.

See also

Abu Ghraib; Bush, George Walker; Cheney, Richard Bruce; Clinton, William Jefferson; Perle, Richard; Rumsfeld, Donald Henry; Torture of Prisoners

References

Hersh, Seymour. *Chain of Command: The Road from 9/11 to Abu Ghraib.* New York: HarperCollins, 2004.

Lewis, Justin. *Shoot First and Ask Questions Later: Media Coverage of the 2003 Iraq War.* New York: Peter Lang, 2005.

Hester, Leigh Ann
Birth Date: 1982

Army National Guardsman and the first woman to earn the Silver Star for valor in combat in 60 years, since World War II. Born in Bowling Green, Kentucky, in 1982, Leigh Ann Hester later moved to Nashville. A varsity basketball and softball player in high school, she joined the Kentucky National Guard in April 2001 and was assigned to the 617th Military Police Company in Richmond, Kentucky, which was later deployed to Iraq.

Midday on March 20, 2005, Hester was patrolling with her unit in Humvees, providing security for a supply convoy of about 30 trucks near the town of Salman Pak south of Baghdad, when the convoy came under attack by about 50 insurgents. The insurgents attacked the convoy with assault-rifle and machine-gun fire and rocket-propelled grenades. In the ensuing 90-minute firefight, Hester participated in a dismounted flanking counterattack against the insurgents, helping with hand grenades and rifle grenade rounds to clear two trenches with insurgents. Hester personally shot and killed three insurgents with her M-4 carbine.

At the same time that Hester was awarded the Silver Star, her squad leader, Staff Sergeant Timothy F. Nein, was also awarded the Silver Star for his role in the same engagement. Another woman, Specialist Ashley J. Pullen, a driver, received the Bronze Star Medal. The battle reportedly resulted in the deaths of 27 insurgents and the capture of 7 others.

SPENCER C. TUCKER

See also

Vehicles, Unarmored; Women, Role of in Afghanistan and Iraq Wars

References

Shane, Leo, III. "Female Soldier Awarded Silver Star." *Stars and Stripes,* June 18, 2005.

Tyson, Ann Scott. "Soldier Earns Silver Star for Her Role in Defeating Ambush." *Washington Post,* June 17, 2005.

Hezbollah

Lebanese Shia Islamist organization. Founded in Lebanon in 1985, Hezbollah is a major political force in that country and, along with the Amal movement, a principal political movement representing the Shia community in Lebanon. There have been other smaller parties by the name of Hezbollah (Hizbullah) in eastern Saudi Arabia and Iraq, and their activities have been mistakenly or deliberately associated with the Lebanese party. Hezbollah in Lebanon also operates a number of social service programs, schools, hospitals, clinics, and housing assistance programs to Lebanese Shia. (Christians also have attended Hezbollah's schools and have run on their electoral lists.)

Some of those destined to be leaders and members of Hezbollah, meaning the "Party of God," were students of Islamic scholarship who fled from Iraq between 1979 and 1980 when Saddam Hussein cracked down on the Shia Islamist movements in the shrine cities. Lebanese as well as Iranians and Iraqis studied in Najaf and Karbala, and some 100 of these students returned to Beirut and became disciples of Sayyid Muhammad Husayn Fadlallah, a Lebanese cleric who also was educated in Najaf.

Meanwhile, in the midst of the ongoing civil war in Lebanon, a Shiite resistance movement developed in response to Israel's invasion in 1982. Israel's first invasion of southern Lebanon had occurred in 1978, but the invasion of 1982 was more devastating to the region, with huge numbers of casualties and prisoners taken and peasants displaced.

The earliest political movement of Lebanese Shia, known as the Movement of the Dispossessed, was established under the cleric Musa al-Sadr. The Shia were the largest but poorest sect in Lebanon and suffered from discrimination, underrepresentation, and a dearth of government programs or services that, despite some efforts by the Lebanese government, persist to this day.

After Sadr's disappearance on a trip to Libya, his nonmilitaristic movement was subsumed by the Amal Party, which had a military wing and fought in the civil war. However, a wing of Amal, Islamic Amal led by Husayn al-Musawi, split off after it accused Amal of not resisting the Israeli invasion.

On the grounds of resistance to Israel (and its Lebanese proxies), Islamic Amal made contact with Iran's ambassador to Damascus, Akbar Muhtashimi, who had once found refuge as an Iranian dissident in the Palestinian camps in Lebanon. A militant group began to organize in the Bekáa Valley. Somewhat later, Iran sent between 1,000 and 1,200 Revolutionary Guards to the Bekáa Valley to aid an Islamic resistance to Israel. At a Lebanese Army barracks near Baalbek, the Revolutionary Guards began training Shia fighters identifying with the resistance, or Islamic Amal.

Fadlallah's followers in Beirut now included displaced Beiruti Shia and displaced southerners, and some coordination between his group and the others in the South and in the Bekáa began to emerge in 1984. The Islamic Resistance in south Lebanon was led by Sheikh Raghib Harb, imam of the village of Jibshit who was killed by the Israelis in 1984. In February 1985, Harb's supporters met and announced the formation of Hezbollah, led by Sheikh Subhi Tufayli.

Prior to Hezbollah's emergence, a militant Shia group known as the Organization of the Islamic Jihad was led by Imad Mughniya. It was responsible for the 1983 bombings of the U.S. and French peacekeeping forces' barracks and the U.S. embassy and its annex in Beirut. This group received some support from the elements in Baalbek. Hezbollah, however, is to this day accused of bombings committed by Mughniya's group. Although Hezbollah had not yet officially formed, the degree of coordination or sympathy between the various militant groups in 1982 can be ascertained only on the level of individuals. Hezbollah stated officially that it did not commit the bombing of U.S. and French forces, but it also did not condemn those who did. Regardless, Hezbollah's continuing resistance in the south earned it great popularity with the Lebanese, whose army had split and had failed to defend the country against the Israelis.

With the Taif Accords, the Lebanese Civil War should have ended, but in 1990 fighting broke out, and the next year Syria mounted a major campaign in Lebanon. The Taif Accords did not end sectarianism or completely solve the problem of Muslim underrepresentation in government, but it represented regional and Lebanese efforts to negotiate an end to the war. Militias other than Hezbollah disbanded, but because the Lebanese government did not assent to the Israeli occupation of and use of proxy forces in southern Lebanon, Hezbollah's militia remained active.

The leadership of Hezbollah changed over time and adapted to Lebanon's realities. The multiplicity of sects in Lebanon meant that an Islamic republic there was impractical, and as a result elements in Hezbollah ceased public discussion of this goal. Also, the group stopped trying to impose the strictest Islamic rules and focused more on gaining the trust of the Lebanese community. The

Shiite Muslim members of Hezbollah beat their chests during a procession organized by the movement in the southern Lebanese town of Nabatiyeh on May 7, 1998. (AP/Wide World Photos)

party's Shura (Consultative) Council was made up of seven clerics until 1989; from 1989 to 1991 it included three laypersons and four clerics; and since 2001 it has been composed entirely of clerics. An advisory politburo has from 11 to 14 members. Secretary-General Abbas Musawi took over from Tufayli in 1991. Soon after the Israelis assassinated Musawi, Hassan Nasrallah, who had studied in Najaf and briefly in Qum, took over as secretary-general.

In 1985, as a consequence of armed resistance in southern Lebanon, Israel withdrew into the security zone. Just as resistance from Hezbollah provided Israel with the ready excuse to attack Lebanon, Israel's continued presence in the south built Lebanese resentment of Israel and support for Hezbollah's armed actions. In 1996 the Israelis mounted Operation GRAPES OF WRATH against Hezbollah in south Lebanon, pounding the entire region from the air for a two-week period.

Subhi Tufayli, the former Hezbollah secretary-general, opposed the movement's decision to participate in the elections of 1992 and 1996. He felt that transformation into a political party would compromise the movement's core principles, and in 1997 he launched the Revolt of the Hungry, demanding food and jobs

for the impoverished people of the upper Bekáa, and was expelled from Hezbollah. He and his fighters then began armed resistance, and the Lebanese Army was called in to defeat his faction.

In May 2000 after suffering repeated attacks and numerous casualties, Israel withdrew its forces from southern Lebanon, a move that was widely interpreted as a victory for Hezbollah and boosted its popularity hugely in Lebanon and throughout the Arab world. Hezbollah disarmed in some areas of the country but refused to do so in the border area because it contests Israel's control over villages in the Shaba Farms region.

Sheikh Fadlallah survived an assassination attempt in 1985 allegedly arranged by the United States. He illustrates the Lebanonization of the Shia Islamist movement. He had moved away from Ayatollah Ruhollah Khomeini's doctrine of government by cleric (*wilaya al-faqih*), believing that it is not suitable in the Lebanese context, and called for dialogue with Christians. Fadlallah's stance is similar to that of Ayatollah Sayyid Ali Husayn al-Sistani in Iraq. He, like some of the Iraqi clerics, called for the restoration of Friday communal prayer for the Shia. He has also issued numerous reform measures, such as issuing a fatwa against the abuse of women by men. Fadlallah is not, however, closely associated with Hezbollah's day-to-day policies.

Some Israeli and American sources charge that Iran directly conducts the affairs of Hezbollah and provides it with essential funding. While at one time Iranian support was crucial to Hezbollah, the Revolutionary Guards were subsequently withdrawn from Lebanon. The party's social and charitable services claimed independence in the late 1990s. They are supported by a volunteer service, provided by medical personnel and other professionals, and by local and external donations. Iran has, however, certainly provided weapons to Hezbollah. Some, apparently through the Iran-Contra deal, found their way to Lebanon, while Syria has also provided freedom of movement across its common border with Lebanon as well as supply routes for weapons.

Since 2000 Hezbollah has disputed Israeli control over the Shaba Farms area, which Israel claims belongs to Syria but Syria says belongs to Lebanon. Meanwhile, pressure began to build against Syrian influence in Lebanon with the constitutional amendment to allow Emile Lahoud (a Christian and pro-Syrian) an additional term. Assassinations of anti-Syrian, mainly Christian, figures had also periodically occurred. The turning point was the assassination of Prime Minister Rafic al-Hariri in February 2005. This led to significant international pressure on Syria to withdraw from Lebanon, although pro-Syrian elements remained throughout the country. Syria was allegedly linked to the murder.

Hezbollah became part of a coalition with Christian supporters of General Michel Aoun, an anti-Syrian Lebanese leader. But the party faced a new coalition of different Christians who were allied with Hariri along with Sunnis who sought to deny Hezbollah's aim of greater power for the opposition (in this case, Shia and Aounists) in the Lebanese government. The two sides in this struggle were known as the March 14th Alliance, for the date of a large anti-Syrian rally, and the March 8th Alliance, for a prior and even larger rally consisting of Hezbollah and Aoun supporters. These factions sparred since 2005, but the March 8th faction soon mounted street protests. Most were nonviolent, but one of these involved an attack on the media outlet of the Future Party.

Demanding a response to the Israeli campaign against Gaza in the early summer of 2006, Hezbollah forces killed three Israeli soldiers and kidnapped two others in a disputed border village, apparently planning to hold them for a prisoner exchange as had occurred in the past. The Israeli Defense Forces (IDF) responded with a massive campaign of air strikes throughout Lebanon, not just on Hezbollah positions. Hezbollah retaliated by launching rockets into Israel, forcing much of that country's northern population into shelters. In this open warfare, the United States backed Israel. At the conflict's end, Sheikh Nasrallah's popularity surged in Lebanon and in the Arab world. Even members of the March 14th Alliance were furious over the destruction of the fragile peace in post–civil war Lebanon and the terrible damage to infrastructure all over the country. Hezbollah offered cash assistance to those whose homes were destroyed, including Lebanese displaced from the south, and those in the districts of Beirut who were not eligible for reconstruction aid from the Lebanese government (which steered aid away from the Shia community). Hezbollah also disbursed this aid immediately. The government also extended assistance to other Lebanese, but it was delayed.

In September 2006, Hezbollah and its ally Aoun began calling for a new national unity government. The existing government, dominated by the March 14th Alliance forces, refused to budge, however. Five Shia members and one Christian member of the Lebanese cabinet also resigned in response to disagreements over the proposed tribunal to investigate Syrian culpability in the Hariri assassination. At the same time, Hezbollah and Aoun argued for the ability of a sizable opposition group in the cabinet to veto government decisions. Hezbollah and Aoun called for public protests, which began as gigantic sit-ins and demonstrations in the downtown district of Beirut in December 2006. There was one violent clash in December and another in January 2007 between the supporters of the two March alliances. In May 2008, the Lebanese political crisis finally ended, with Hezbollah gaining political capital. A new unity government was inaugurated in July 2008 in which Hezbollah controlled 1 ministry and 11 of 30 cabinet positions. Meanwhile, the United Nations Interim Force in Lebanon (UNIFIL) took up position in southern Lebanon. Its mission, however, is not to disarm Hezbollah but only to prevent armed clashes between it and Israel.

In August 2008, the new Lebanese government, led by Prime Minister Fouad Siniora, approved a draft policy statement that would guarantee Hezbollah's existence as an organization and ensure its right to "liberate or recover" occupied lands. This was a clear reference to Lebanese territory occupied by Israel. Meanwhile, U.S. officials continued to insist that Hezbollah has provided weapons to the Iraqi resistance fighting coalition forces in Iraq. In the summer of 2008, Iran denied that it had anything to do with operations in Iraq. When Lahoud's presidential term ended in November 2008, another political crisis began. The March 14th coalition wanted to elect one of their own. The strongest candidate for president was probably Michel Aoun, but that was unacceptable to the March 14th coalition and the United States. The compromise candidate, army chief of staff Michel Suleiman, eventually became president as part of a power-sharing deal between the two factions. The United States was extremely concerned that the March 8th coalition might win a majority in the 2009 Lebanese elections. This did not occur, but the March 8th coalition, made up of Hezbollah and the Aounists, did win 57 seats. This ensures its position as an important voice within the governmental opposition. In December 2009 a resolution toward a national unity government was taken, which implies that Hezbollah will continue on as an armed entity.

Harry Raymond Hueston II and Sherifa Zuhur

See also

Iran; Jihad; Lebanon; Lebanon, Armed Forces; Lebanon, Civil War in; Lebanon, Israeli Invasion of; Shia Islam; Suicide Bombings; Terrorism

References
Hajjar, Sami G. *Hezbollah: Terrorism, National Liberation, or Menace?*
    Carlise Barracks, PA: Strategic Studies Institute, U.S. Army War
    College, 2002.
Harik, Judith Palmer. *Hezbollah: The Changing Face of Terrorism.*
    London: I. B. Tauris, 2005.
Jaber, Hala. *Hezbollah: Born with a Vengeance.* New York: Columbia
    University Press, 1997.
Qassem, Naim. *Hizbullah: The Story from Within.* London: Saqi Books,
    2010.
Zuhur, Sherifa. "Hasan Nasrallah and the Strategy of Steadfastness."
    Terrorism Monitor 4(19) (October 5, 2006).

High Mobility Multipurpose Wheeled Vehicle

Multipurpose wheeled vehicle used by the U.S. armed forces. The High Mobility Multipurpose Wheeled Vehicle (HMMWV, popularly called the Humvee) has been in service since 1983. A commercial, civilian version was successfully marketed as the Hummer. The Humvee first saw service in Operation JUST CAUSE in Panama in December 1989. It has seen extensive service in Iraq and Afghanistan since the 1991 Persian Gulf War.

Since the invention of the internal combustion engine, the world's militaries have developed and used a wide variety of wheeled and tracked vehicles to transport personnel and cargo and to serve as platforms for weapons and other uses. During World War II the most common wheeled utility vehicle was the Jeep. Developed for the U.S. Army, the Jeep had various official designations and was a small, one-quarter-ton truck with four-wheel drive for off-road capability. It served through the 1970s with many changes over time. The Jeep's limited capacity and high center of gravity, which resulted in numerous rollovers, led the Army to develop other wheeled vehicles, such as the 6-wheel drive one-and-a-half-ton M-561 Gamma Goat and the M-715, a one-and-one-quarter-ton truck. The Army also procured commercial trucks like the three-quarter-ton Dodge, designated the M-880. In 1975 and 1976 the Army tested the commercial CJ-5 Jeep, the Dodge Ram Charger, Chevrolet Blazer, and Ford Bronco. Funding cuts in the post–Vietnam War era and the need for a platform for the TOW (tube-launched, optically tracked, wire-guided) missile led the Army to consider other options, such as the Cadillac Gage Scout, various dune buggies, and the Combat Support Vehicle (CSV) dedicated to the TOW mission. The plan was to produce 3,800 CSVs, but Congress scrapped that program in 1977, deeming that vehicle too limited.

Members of the U.S. Air Force 170th Security Police Squadron patrol an air base flight line in an M998 High Mobility Multipurpose Wheeled Vehicle (Humvee) mounting an M-60 machine gun during Operation DESERT STORM. (U.S. Department of Defense)

In 1980, Congress approved the development of the Humvee with the objective of producing 50,000 one-and-one-quarter-ton four-wheel drive vehicles to replace the multiplicity of vehicles, many worn out by years of use, in the Army inventory. This was a breakthrough, as up to this time the Army had opted for vehicles of varying sizes and carrying capacities. In 1981, three contractors were asked to bid on the Humvee: Chrysler Defense, Teledyne Continental, and AM General, whose parent company, American Motors, had purchased Kaiser-Jeep in 1969. All three produced prototypes for testing, which was done at Aberdeen Proving Ground, Maryland, and Yuma, Arizona, in 1982. The AM General model, nicknamed the "Hummer" as a play on the military designation and thought to be catchier than "Humvee," won.

The first production contract in 1983 was for 55,000 vehicles to be produced over 5 years, a number later raised to 70,000 vehicles. The Army received 39,000, the Marines 11,000, while the remainder went to the Air Force and Navy. By 1995 over 100,000 Humvees had been produced. Production would double by 2005 for both U.S. and foreign sales. American Motors began marketing the Hummer commercially in 1983, and the brand is still marketed by General Motors.

Designated the M-998, the Humvee four-wheel-drive vehicle weighs 5,200 pounds; measures 15 feet long, 7.08 feet wide, and 6 feet high (reducible to under 5 feet); and is powered by a 150-horsepower, 378-cubic-inch, V-8 diesel engine. Its ground clearance of more than 16 inches and four-wheel drive make the Humvee an effective off-road carrier. Its 25-gallon fuel tank allows for a range of 350 miles at speeds up to 65 miles per hour. It can ford water up to 2.5 feet deep and double that with a deep-water-fording kit. It can climb a 60 percent incline and traverse a 40 percent incline fully loaded. Its very wide stance and low center of gravity make it difficult to turn over.

The Humvee replaced several military vehicles and became a platform for many tasks. In addition to the Humvee's basic configuration as a truck with more than a ton of carrying capacity, there are variants, which function as an ambulance, a TOW-missile platform, a machine-gun or grenade-launcher platform, a prime mover for towing a 105-millimeter howitzer, and a shelter carrier. Some variants are equipped with a winch on the front, which provides additional capabilities, especially self-recovery. The Humvee can be delivered to the battlefield by helicopter. The weight of the vehicle can be reduced by using versions without roofs or with canvas roofs and sides. As the Humvee has matured over time, it has been reconfigured and manufactured in what the military calls M-A1 and M-A2 versions.

Not designed to be an armored combat vehicle, the Humvee in its original configuration posed serious problems in the conflicts in Iraq and Afghanistan. The military had already been exploring how to armor Humvees in light of experience in the peace-keeping mission in the Balkans in the 1990s. The canvas roofs and sides of some models offered no protection from small-arms fire, and the metal versions were little help against roadside mines. The solutions were not simple, but there have been several programs to alleviate this serious hazard in the M-1114 and M-1151 up-armored variants.

The up-armored vehicle is now in service in combat areas, and armor kits were made available for installation in the theater of operations. The basic upgrade in armament is a 2,000-pound kit that added steel plating and ballistic-resistant windows. The steel plating under the vehicle was designed to absorb an 8-pound explosive. The kit for in-theater installation weighs about 750 pounds. As the Humvee mission expanded, changes have been made in engine power, transmission, suspension, and engine cooling. Some changes can be made in theater, but many have to be done at depot level in the United States, as Humvees are modified for deployment or repaired after combat damage. The operational tempo in combat also produces vehicle wear seven times that in peacetime. This fact, the loss of 250 Humvees in combat, and the aging of the inventory stresses the ability of the military to maintain readiness and prepare for future challenges. The cost of updating the inventory as it rotates through the depot system is $52,000 per vehicle.

DANIEL E. SPECTOR

See also
Vehicles, Unarmored

References
Cordesman, Anthony H., and Abraham R. Wagner. *The Lessons of Modern War*, Vol. 4, *The Gulf War*. Boulder, CO: Westview, 1996.
Green, Michael, and Greg Stewart. *HUMVEE at War*. St. Paul, MN: Zenith, 2005.
Scales, Robert H. *Certain Victory: The U.S. Army in the Gulf War.* Washington, DC: Brassey's, 1994.
Thompson, Loren B., Lawrence J. Korb, and Caroline P. Wadhams. *Army Equipment after Iraq*. Arlington, VA: Lexington Institute, Center for American Progress, 2006.
Zaloga, Steven J. *HMMWV, Humvee, 1980–2005: U.S. Army Tactical Vehicle*. Oxford, UK: Osprey, 2006.

Holbrooke, Richard Charles Albert
Birth Date: April 24, 1941

U.S. diplomat, assistant secretary of state (1977–1981 and 1994–1996), ambassador to the United Nations (UN) (1999–2001), and diplomatic trouble shooter. Richard Charles Albert Holbrooke was born in New York City on April 24, 1941, and graduated from Brown University in 1962. Inspired by President John F. Kennedy's call for public service, Holbrooke entered the U.S. Foreign Service. Holbrooke served in the Republic of Vietnam, first in the Agency for International Development there and then as a staff assistant to U.S. ambassadors Maxwell Taylor and Henry Cabot Lodge. He returned to Washington in 1965 to be a member of a Vietnam study group in the National Security Council.

Holbrooke was next a special assistant to under secretaries of state Nicholas Katzenbach and Elliot Richardson before joining the U.S. delegation to the Paris Peace Talks in 1968. Holbrooke also drafted a volume of what became known as the Pentagon Papers, which traced the escalating U.S. involvement in Vietnam. During 1969–1970 he was a visiting fellow at the Woodrow Wilson School at Princeton University.

At his own request, in 1970 Holbrooke became the director of the Peace Corps in Morocco. He left government service two years later to become the managing editor of *Foreign Policy* magazine. Holbrooke was also a contributing editor to *Newsweek* magazine.

In 1976, Holbrooke left his publishing positions to become a foreign policy adviser to Democratic Party presidential candidate Jimmy Carter. Following Carter's victory, Holbrooke became assistant secretary of state for East Asian and Pacific Affairs, a post that he held from 1977 to 1981. During his tenure, in 1978 the United States established full diplomatic relations with the People's Republic of China. Holbrooke was also very much involved in the resettlement of hundreds of thousands of Southeast Asian refugees in the United States.

In 1981 Holbrooke became vice president of Public Strategies, a consulting firm in Washington, D.C. He also became a consultant to the investment firm Lehman Brothers, which led to him becoming managing director at Lehman Brothers. At the same time, he was a principal author of the bipartisan Commission on Government and Renewal, sponsored by the Carnegie Foundation.

In 1992, under the presidency of Bill Clinton, Holbrooke was a candidate to be ambassador to Japan. When that post went to former vice president Walter Mondale, Holbrooke was a surprise pick to be ambassador to the Federal Republic of Germany. He held that post until 1994, when he returned to the United States to become assistant secretary of state for European and Canadian Affairs. He held that position until 1996, the first individual in U.S. history to be an assistant secretary of state for two different areas of the world. While assistant secretary, Holbrooke led the effort to enlarge the North Atlantic Treaty Organization (NATO).

In 1995 Holbrooke was the principal figure in putting together the Dayton Peace Accords that ended the wars in Bosnia and Croatia. Upon leaving the State Department in 1996, Holbrooke joined Credit Suisse First Boston, becoming its vice chairman. President Clinton asked him to be a special envoy to the Balkans as a private citizen, and Holbrooke worked on a pro bono basis to try to resolve crises over Cyprus and Kosovo.

During 1999–2001 Holbrooke served as U.S. ambassador to the UN. During his tenure he brokered a deal with that body whereby the United States agreed to pay back dues in return for a reduction in future annual dues. He also secured a UN resolution that recognized HIV/AIDS as a threat to global security, the first time that body had so designated a public health issue. Upon leaving the UN, Holbrooke became the key figure in what is now the Global Business Coalition on HIV/AIDS, Tuberculosis, and Malaria, which seeks to mobilize the world business community to deal with pressing health issues. At the same time he continued his involvement with a wide variety of organizations and found time to speak on foreign affairs issues. Holbrooke is also the author of numerous articles and several books, including the acclaimed *To End a War* (1998), which details the efforts to end the fighting in Bosnia. He has been nominated for the Nobel Peace Prize on seven occasions.

During the 2004 presidential campaign, Holbrooke served as a foreign policy adviser to Democratic Party candidate John Kerry. He filled the same position for Senator Hillary Rodham Clinton when she ran for the Democratic presidential nomination in 2008. When she lost the nomination, he served in the same position for Barack Obama. In an article in the September–October 2008 issue of *Foreign Affairs*, Holbrooke said that the new U.S. government would need to reestablish the reputation of the United States in the world and he called U.S. policy in Afghanistan a failure. He listed four main problem areas: the tribal areas of northwestern Pakistan; the drug lords who dominate Afghanistan; the national police; and an incompetent and corrupt Afghan government. Shortly after becoming president, on January 22, 2009, Obama appointed Holbrooke to be Special Representative for Afghanistan and Pakistan.

SPENCER C. TUCKER

See also

Afghanistan; Obama, Barack Hussein, II; Pakistan

References

Clifford, Clark, and Richard Holbrooke. *Counsel to the President: A Memoir.* New York: Random House, 1991.

Holbrooke, Richard. "The Next President: Mastering a Daunting Agenda." *Foreign Affairs* 87(5) (September/October, 2008): 2–24.

———. *To End a War.* New York: Random House, 1998.

Holland, Charles R.
Birth Date: 1946

U.S. Air Force officer. Charles R. Holland was born in 1946 and graduated from the U.S. Air Force Academy in 1968. He went on to earn an MS degree in business management from Troy State University in 1976 and an MS degree in astronautical engineering from the Air Force Institute of Technology at Wright-Patterson Air Force Base, Ohio, in 1978. He also attended the Industrial College of the Armed Forces in 1986.

Holland held a series of flight-oriented positions and also increasingly responsible command posts. As a command pilot, he accumulated more than 5,000 flying hours in more than 100 combat missions, 79 of which were in Lockheed AC-130 Specter gunships during the Vietnam War. During the 1991 Persian Gulf War, Holland commanded the 1550th Combat Crew Training Wing, headquartered at Kirtland Air Force Base, New Mexico. On May 20, 1993, he was promoted to brigadier general and became deputy commanding general of the Joint Special Operations Command (Fort Bragg, North Carolina). In June 1995, Holland began serving as commander, Special Operations Command–Pacific, a post he held until 1997. Promoted to major general in 1997, he headed the Air Force Special Operation Command (Hurlburt Field, Florida) until August 1999. Until October 2000, Holland was vice commander, U.S. Air Forces in Europe; he was promoted to lieutenant general in November 1999.

In October 2000 Holland assumed the post of commander, headquarters, U.S. Special Operations Command (USSOCOM, MacDill Air Force Base, Florida), a position he held until his retirement in October 2003. Holland was promoted to four-star rank in December 2000. As commander of USSOCOM, Holland was a forceful spokesperson for the need to augment and improve U.S. special operations forces in order to allow the United States to be able to respond quickly to any military contingency. His advocacy proved prescient after the September 11, 2001, terrorist attacks against the United States, and his efforts to bolster USSOCOM aided rapid victories in Afghanistan in 2001 and the overthrow of the Saddam Hussein regime in Iraq in 2003.

Holland was an especially ardent proponent of the Bell/Boeing CV-22 Osprey, the controversial tilt-rotor, multimission, vertical take-off and landing aircraft. Since May 2004, Holland has been on the board of directors of a number of corporate and nonprofit organizations.

PAUL G. PIERPAOLI JR.

See also

United States Air Force, Afghanistan War; United States Air Force, Iraq War

References

Boyne, Walter J. *Beyond the Wild Blue: A History of the U.S. Air Force, 1947–2007.* 2nd ed. New York: Thomas Dunne Books, 2007.

Pushies, Fred J. *U.S. Air Force Special OPS.* Osceola, WI: Zenith, 2007.

Honduras

A Spanish-speaking country located in Central America, bounded by the Caribbean Sea to the north, Guatemala to the north and west, El Salvador to the west, the Pacific Ocean via the Gulf of Fonseca to the west, and Nicaragua to the west, south, and east. Honduran territory encompasses 43,227 square miles and can be roughly divided into five separate regions. The 2008 population of Honduras was estimated to be 7.639 million people.

Honduras is a democratic republic with a president, a unicameral legislative branch, and an independent judiciary. Although multiple political parties exist, the two most powerful and successful are the Partido Nacional de Honduras (PNH) and Partido Liberal de Honduras (PLH). Since 1982, the Honduran president has been a member of either the PNH or the PLH. Honduran military components include the army, navy, and air force. Historically, the military has been extremely active in national politics, actually seizing power and running the country over a number of years. The U.S. government has often worked closely with Honduras's military forces, and both nations have held a number of joint exercises since the 1960s. Honduras has also been willing to allow itself to be used as a staging point for military actions against other Central American countries. Not only has the United States trained foreign military personnel in Honduran territory but also Honduras has also allowed these forces the use of its bases to attack both Guatemala and Nicaragua.

Honduras's participation during the 1991 Persian Gulf War was limited to the deployment of 150 troops, which did not participate in combat operations. Although Honduras did not participate in the 2003 invasion of Iraq (Operation IRAQI FREEDOM), it did agree to send military forces, known as the Fuerza de Tarea Xatruch, to assist in peacekeeping and reconstruction missions in Iraq beginning in mid-2003. The 373 Honduran military personnel in Iraq became part of the Multinational Brigade Plus Ultra, which also included troops from El Salvador, Nicaragua, the Dominican Republic, and Spain. Specific duties for the Honduran contingent focused on peacekeeping, providing medical care, and minesweeping.

On April 20, 2004, Honduran President Ricardo Maduro announced the return of his country's forces, noting that all Honduran troops would return home prior to July 1, 2004. Honduras has played no direct role in Operation ENDURING FREEDOM in Afghanistan. Although Honduras continues to enjoy good relations with the United States, Honduran officials have become increasingly concerned over the lack of U.S. interest in providing nonmilitary foreign aid to their country.

WYNDHAM WHYNOT

See also

DESERT STORM, Operation; IRAQI FREEDOM, Operation

References

Anderson, Thomas P. *Politics in Central America: Guatemala, El Salvador, Honduras, and Nicaragua.* Rev. ed. New York: Praeger Paperback, 1988.

Booth, John A., Christine J. Wade, and Thomas Walker. *Understanding Central America: Global Forces, Rebellion, and Change.* 4th ed. Boulder, CO: Westview, 2006.

Hormuz, Strait of

Narrow body of water that connects the Persian Gulf to the Gulf of Oman and the Indian Ocean. The Strait of Hormuz is bounded in the north by Iran and on its south by the United Arab Emirates (UAE) and the Sultanate of Oman. The waters of the Strait of Hormuz are predominantly within the claimed territorial waters of these three nations because the United Nations Convention on the Law of the Sea (UNCLOS) defines territorial waters as 12 nautical miles from shore. At its narrowest point, the strait is 21 nautical miles wide, but there are islands throughout its length, most of which belong to Iran. The strait is designated as an international shipping lane. As such, ships are allowed to transit it under the rules of "innocent" or "transit" passage, which permit maritime traffic in key straits that separate international bodies of water.

Because of its location, the Strait of Hormuz is considered a strategic choke point. About 20 percent of world oil shipments transit the strait on any given day aboard commercial tankers. The key nation in this regard is Iran, whose largest port and naval base, Bandar Abbas, is located at the northernmost tip of the strait.

Iran has fortified several islands—the Tunb Islands and Abu Musa—that dominate the strait. Abu Musa, in particular, has long been a source of conflict between Iran and the UAE, especially since Iran's occupation of it in the early 1970s.

The Strait of Hormuz has always been a significant factor in modern wars. During World War II, it was the key conduit for American Lend-Lease aid through Iraq and Iran to the Soviet Union. Since then, the strait has been the chief avenue for U.S. seaborne trade into the Gulf region and oil out of it. The strait became even more an issue after the 1979 Islamic Revolution in Iran, which deposed pro-U.S. Mohammad Reza Shah Pahlavi. After that, the United States began to station a number of warships in the Persian Gulf to protect U.S. interests in the region.

Near the end of the Iran-Iraq War (1980–1988), Iran attempted to close the strait by mining it to deprive Iraq and other Gulf states of their oil revenues. The United States responded by reflagging oil tankers and forcibly reopening the strait in Operation ERNEST WILL. Not long after, the United States used the strait as the main conduit for sea-supplied military matériel in support of Operations DESERT SHIELD (1990) and DESERT STORM (the Persian Gulf War, 1991). Thereafter, the United States maintained a strong naval presence in the region, to include at least one, and often several, aircraft carrier battle groups.

Most recently, the strait was critical to the maritime power projection of Operation IRAQI FREEDOM, the 2003 Anglo-American-led invasion of Iraq. Without access to the Strait of Hormuz, the United States and other Western powers would be severely limited in influencing events in the Middle East. U.S. policymakers in particular continue to keep a wary eye on the Strait of Hormuz, especially given Iran's nuclear ambitions and the often harsh rhetoric coming from its rightist leaders.

JOHN T. KUEHN

See also

DESERT SHIELD, Operation; DESERT STORM, Operation; Iran-Iraq War; Iranian Revolution; IRAQI FREEDOM, Operation; Oil; Oman, Role in Persian Gulf and Iraq Wars; United Arab Emirates

References

Bowden, Mark. *Guests of the Ayatollah: The First Battle in America's War with Militant Islam.* New York: Atlantic Monthly, 2007.

Marolda, Edward, and Robert Schneller. *Shield and Sword: The United States Navy and the Persian Gulf War.* Annapolis, MD: U.S. Naval Institute Press, 2001.

Horner, Charles
Birth Date: October 19, 1936

U.S. Air Force officer responsible for U.S. and coalition air operations in the 1991 Persian Gulf War. Charles Horner was born in

Davenport, Iowa, on October 19, 1936, and earned a BA from the University of Iowa on an ROTC scholarship in 1958. In November 1959 he completed pilot training and was awarded his wings. His subsequent education included the College of William and Mary, where he earned an MBA (1972), and the Armed Forces Staff College (1972), the Industrial College of the Armed Forces (1974), and the National War College (1976).

Horner's primary distinction came as a tactical command pilot. He logged thousands of hours in a variety of fighter aircraft. He served two combat tours in Vietnam and participated in the bombing campaign against North Vietnam, Operation ROLLING THUNDER. During his second tour (May–September 1967) he flew the particularly dangerous "Wild Weasel" missions aimed at identifying and destroying North Vietnamese air defenses. Like many Vietnam veterans, Horner was embittered by the many restrictions placed on the air campaign by civilian officials. His Vietnam experience made him an outspoken critic of "absentee management" and a staunch advocate of the quick, overwhelming application of air power.

Following the Vietnam War, Horner served in various command and staff functions, where he gained attention as a leader

Lieutenant General Charles A. Horner, commander of U.S. Central Command Air Forces during Operation DESERT STORM. (U.S. Department of Defense)

of the movement to reform the Air Force's combat doctrine and overhaul civil-military relations. Horner was promoted to brigadier general on August 1, 1982, and to major general on July 1, 1985. He established professional and personal relationships with officers in other branches of the armed forces, including Army general H. Norman Schwarzkopf, who was to become his superior as commander of United States Central Command (CENTCOM) with responsibility for operations in the Middle East. On May 1, 1987, Horner was promoted to lieutenant general and given command of the Ninth Air Force and simultaneously appointed commander, Central Command Air Forces.

In the late 1980s, CENTCOM's mission underwent numerous changes. With the winding down of the Cold War and the end of the Iran-Iraq War in 1988, senior officers in CENTCOM began examining potential threats within the Middle East region, particularly Iraq, with its large and experienced army and President Saddam Hussein's ambition to dominate the Persian Gulf. At Schwarzkopf's urging, Horner developed plans for war with Iraq before Hussein's forces invaded Kuwait on August 1, 1990. Consequently, when that crisis broke, rudimentary plans for an American response were already in place.

Within a week of the Iraqi invasion, Horner and his planners had outlined a concept for an intensive air campaign code-named INSTANT THUNDER, a concept Schwarzkopf endorsed. It fell to Horner to oversee the translation of this concept into reality, including target selection, size of forces, types of ordnance to be used, and the integration of these packages into the complete air offensive. Horner selected Brigadier General Buster C. Glosson to direct the planning.

Many observers have pointed to the effectiveness of the air campaign as the most decisive factor in the quick victory by the United States and its allies in the Persian Gulf War and as a model for future conventional wars. After Schwarzkopf, Horner was perhaps the most important military leader on the coalition side in the war. Throughout both Operation DESERT SHIELD and Operation DESERT STORM, Horner had the complete support of Schwarzkopf, who gave him a virtual free hand in the direction of the air war. Horner later observed that the close working relationships he enjoyed with Schwarzkopf and other military branch commanders were the key to victory in the 1991 Persian Gulf War.

Horner has been increasingly critical of American military policy and diplomacy in the Middle East. He gained considerable attention when, on relinquishing his command in 1992 at the rank of general, he declared that war is folly. Following his retirement in 1994, Horner criticized American intelligence gathering in the Middle East, particularly as it related to weapons of mass destruction (WMDs). Even before the United States invaded Iraq in March 2003, Horner took issue with the George W. Bush and Bill Clinton administrations for maintaining a military presence in the Gulf after the 1991 war. He argued that by villainizing Saddam Hussein, American policymakers were, in fact, playing into his hands. Horner also criticized the focus on WMDs in Iraq, arguing that the

United States should be more concerned about nuclear proliferation in the former Soviet Union, Libya, Israel, and Iran. Horner remains active in retirement, writing and speaking extensively.

WALTER F. BELL

See also

DESERT SHIELD, Operation; DESERT STORM, Operation, Coalition Air Campaign; DESERT STORM, Operation, Planning for; Schwarzkopf, H. Norman, Jr.; United States Central Command; Weapons of Mass Destruction

References

Boomer, Walter E. "Ten Years After." *U.S. Naval Institute Proceedings* 127(1) (January 2001): 61–65.

Hallion, Richard P. *Storm over Iraq: Air Power and the Gulf War.* Washington, DC: Smithsonian Institution Press, 1997.

Hospital Ships

Unarmed and clearly marked ships with comprehensive medical facilities that operate near combat zones and have the capacity to take aboard and treat large numbers of casualties brought in by medical evacuation (MEDEVAC) helicopters. The only dedicated hospital ships currently in operation with the U.S. Navy are the two large vessels of the Mercy class. USNS *Mercy* (T-AH-19) entered naval service in 1986; its sister ship, the *Comfort* (T-AH-20), was commissioned the next year. Dimensions are length, 894 feet; beam, 105.75 feet; and draft, 33 feet. Speed is 17.5 knots with a range of 13,400 nautical miles at 17.5 knots. Crew complement (Reduced Operating Status in home port) is 16 civilian and 58 U.S. Navy support/communications (6 officers and 52 enlisted); active, deployed: 61 civilian, 58 Navy, and 1,100 medical/dental personnel.

Originally built at San Diego as the civilian tankers SS *Worth* and SS *Rose City,* these two ships were converted during 1984–1986 and 1985–1987, respectively. They entered service with the Military Sealift Command (MSC) as the largest hospital ships in the world, *Mercy* and *Comfort,* and the first dedicated hospital ships in U.S. service since USS *Sanctuary* (AH-17) was decommissioned in 1975. *Mercy* is based on the U.S. west coast at San Diego, and *Comfort* at the east coast port of Baltimore, placing their potential for combat or humanitarian medical support within range of critical need areas, whether nearby or overseas. Both ships are maintained in a state of readiness known as reduced operating status (ROS) within the MSC by caretaker crews when not deployed but can be fully staffed, outfitted, and supplied within five days when called on to proceed to a battle zone or the site of a disaster.

Each ship has 1,000 hospital beds, 80 of which are designated for intensive care, and the level of on-board care matches or outdoes that of a respectable land-based hospital with an extensive surgical center, albeit one with an exceedingly large trauma component. There are 12 operating theaters, a 50-bed triage area, 4 radiological units and a CT installation, a burn unit, a full medical laboratory, a blood bank, a pharmacy, as well as the on-board

U.S. Coast Guard boats pass in front of the hospital ship USNS *Mercy* during Operation DESERT SHIELD. (U.S. Department of Defense)

capacity to generate oxygen and distill 75,000 gallons of fresh water each day. When the ships are activated, medical personnel aboard *Mercy* generally are drawn from the naval medical center at Oakland, California, while Bethesda Naval Hospital in Maryland furnishes medical crews to *Comfort* in nearby Baltimore as predeployment work-up progresses. The majority of patients and casualties are typically airlifted by helicopter to each ship's large helipad, but there is also a limited ability to accept casualties from boats alongside when weather and sea-state allow. Maximum ingest is staked at 300 patients per day if half or more of that number require surgery, and the turnaround rate averages five days aboard the facility prior to discharge and return to action or MEDEVAC to the United States for further treatment.

Despite their great size, both *Mercy* and *Comfort* experience some limitations stemming from their original design as tankers, most notably in the internal transfer of patients. The impenetrable transverse bulkheads that once kept the oil cargo's wave action deep in the ship to a minimum now require the use of an awkward up-and-over technique when patients on lower-level wards need to be shifted forward or aft.

After Iraq's August 2, 1990, invasion of Kuwait, the *Mercy* and *Comfort* were activated. They arrived in the Persian Gulf by mid-September, remaining on station during Operations DESERT SHIELD

and DESERT STORM and returning to the United States in late March 1991. In June and July 1994, the *Comfort* was called to Jamaica and Guantánamo Bay to support and treat Haitian and Cuban refugees. The *Comfort* also joined the July 1998 NATO Partnership for Peace exercise Baltic Challenge 1998 and arrived in New York within six days of the terrorist attacks in New York on September 11, 2001, to augment regional hospitals' trauma capacities. From January to June 2003, the *Comfort* deployed in support of Operation IRAQI FREEDOM, during which the medical staff treated a great number of Iraqi civilians and prisoners of war as well as troops from the U.S. and coalition forces. In response to the destruction and health crisis resulting from the south Asian earthquake and tsunami on December 26, 2004, the *Mercy* was supplied and staffed for a humanitarian relief mission and departed San Diego on January 5, 2005, eventually assisting and treating over 200,000 victims. In 2006 the *Mercy* undertook a five-month humanitarian deployment to the Philippines and the South Pacific, while the *Comfort* spent four months of 2007 in the Caribbean and Latin America, treating nearly 100,000 patients in need of basic vaccinations, eye care, and dental work.

Hospital ships' medical capabilities have been regularly augmented by the facilities aboard U.S. amphibious assault ships of the *Tarawa* (LHA-1) class, which include medical facilities and a 300-bed capacity, and the newer Wasp (LHD-1) class, each with

600 beds. During Operations DESERT SHIELD and DESERT STORM, the Royal Navy's Royal Fleet Auxiliary (RFA) *Argus* (A-132), nominally an aircraft-training and -support vessel but reconfigured as a Primary Casualty Reception Ship with 100 hospital beds, served as part of the medical support network afloat.

As the *Mercy* and *Comfort* maintain their ROS readiness aspect and edge closer to retirement, the thought of building or converting similar replacement vessels has in recent year been overtaken by the U.S. Navy's preference for streamlining its auxiliary and support forces. The Maritime Prepositioning Force (MPF) has moved from concept to partial reality, including MSC cargo vessels that are kept in forward deployment and stocked with equipment, provisions, fuels, and matériel with which to supply all U.S. armed forces moving into an area. A current plan calls for the construction of MPF ships that would incorporate features of flagships, landing ships, supply ships, and fully equipped hospital ships, thus obviating the need for the *Mercy* or *Comfort* in the near future.

GORDON E. HOGG

See also

Amphibious Assault Ships; Amphibious Command Ships; DESERT STORM, Operation, Coalition Naval Forces; IRAQI FREEDOM, Operation, Coalition Naval Forces; Military Sealift Command; Support and Supply Ships, Strategic; United Kingdom, Navy, Persian Gulf War; United States Navy, Iraq War; United States Navy, Persian Gulf War

References

Baker, A. D. *The Naval Institute Guide to Combat Fleets of the World: Their Ships, Aircraft, and Armament.* Annapolis, MD: Naval Institute Press, 1995.

Marolda, Edward, and Robert Schneller. *Shield and Sword: The United States Navy and the Persian Gulf War.* Annapolis, MD: U.S. Naval Institute Press, 2001.

Polmar, Norman. *The Naval Institute Guide to the Ships and Aircraft of the U.S. Fleet.* 18th ed. Annapolis, MD: Naval Institute Press, 2005.

Saunders, Stephen, ed. *Jane's Fighting Ships 2002–2003.* Coulsdon, Surrey, UK, and Alexandria, VA: Jane's Information Group, 2002.

Houthi, Hussein Badr al-Din al-
Birth Date: Unknown
Death Date: September 10, 2004

Yemeni political and religious leader. Shaykh Hussein Badr al-Din al-Houthi was the charismatic leader of a Yemeni political movement that has opposed the national government. The members of Houthi's movement are drawn from the Zaydi Shia sect, which constitutes some 45–50 percent of Yemen's population. Followers of the Houthi movement, as it came to be called, are estimated at 30 percent of the population.

Between 1993 and 1999, Houthi was a member of parliament representing the Al-Haqq Party. In 1992, a movement known as the Shabab Mu'minin (Believing Youth) developed, apparently to counter growing salafist influence and to assert a new Zaydi identity. Houthi led this movement until 1997, when it split.

Following the U.S. invasion of Iraq in 2003, some members of the Zaydi community protested strongly against the U.S. occupation of Iraq and the Yemeni government's close ties with the United States. Houthi was identified as a leader of these protests. Since the attack on the U.S. Navy destroyer *Cole* in Aden in October 2000, the United States had become concerned about the growth of Al Qaeda in Yemen, and the Yemeni government took great strides to combat the Houthi movement, characterizing it as a deviant and terrorist group like Al Qaeda and claiming that it had links to Iran and Libya, which were never firmly established.

Houthi portrayed his movement as primarily one that sought social justice and basic human, political, and religious rights. His movement did not call for an end to the Saleh government, but it did oppose the Saleh government's alliances with the United States and the manipulation of salafi or Wahhabist elements in Yemen by that government. Houthi held that the government encouraged those groups but oppressed the Zaydis. Houthi's movement represented a challenge from within the Shia elite, for Houthi was a *sayyid,* a descendent of the Prophet Muhammad with roots in the Zaydi imamate that had dominated northern Yemen until the establishment of a Yemeni republic in 1962.

The Houthi rebellion was also known as the al-Sadah conflict. It took place in northern Yemen about 150 miles from Sanaa. In 2004, armed fighting among Houthi's followers broke out against the Yemeni government there. The Yemeni government employed force to crush the movement, which continued after Houthi's death in September 2004. After Houthi died, the movement came under the leadership of Abd al-Malik al-Houthi, his brother; Yusuf Madani, his son-in-law; and Abdullah Ayedh al-Razami; and it came under the spiritual leadership of Badr al-Din al-Houthi, his father.

Following 82 days of fighting in 2004, and after some 1,500 troops and civilians were killed and thousands had fled their villages, Yemeni government forces killed Houthi in Jarf Salman, a village in the Marraan mountains in Sadah on September 10, 2004. Fighting broke out again in March 2005. Some 400 persons were killed within two weeks, hundreds of locals were detained, hundreds of religious schools and religious summer camps were closed, and the government ordered that 1,400 charities be closed. Intermittent fighting has continued thereafter.

SHERIFA ZUHUR

See also

Al Qaeda in the Arabian Peninsula; *Cole,* USS, Attack on; Global War on Terror; Salafism; Yemen

References

Carapico, Sheila. *Civil Society in Yemen: The Political Economy of Activism in Modern Arabia.* Cambridge: Cambridge University Press, 2007.

Dresch, Paul. *A History of Modern Yemen.* Cambridge: Cambridge University Press, 2008.

Hill, Ginny. "Yemen: Fear of Failure." Chatham House Briefing Paper. London: Royal Institute of International Affairs, 2008.

Knickmeyer, Ellen. "In Yemen, A Mostly Concealed Sectarian Fight Endures." *Washington Post,* Foreign Service, Saturday June 7, 2008, A09.

Howe, Jonathan Trumble
Birth Date: August 24, 1935

U.S. Navy officer who served as the special representative for Somalia for United Nations (UN) general secretary Boutros Boutros-Ghali during 1993–1994. Jonathan Trumble Howe was born on August 24, 1935, in San Diego, California, the son of a rear admiral. Howe graduated from the U.S. Naval Academy at Annapolis in 1957. His early years in the Navy were spent in submarines. Howe earned an MS from Tufts University (1967) and both an MA (law and diplomacy) and a PhD from Tufts.

Howe commanded the guided missile destroyer *Berkeley* during 1974–1975, Destroyer Squadron 31 during 1977–1978, and Cruiser-Destroyer Group 3 Battle Group Foxtrot during 1984–1986. Howe also served as chief of staff, 7th Fleet, from 1978 to 1980. He was promoted to rear admiral on March 1, 1981, and served as director of the navy's Politico-Military and Planning Division from 1982 to 1984. Howe was promoted to vice admiral on June 18, 1986. He then served as deputy chairman of the Military Committee of the North Atlantic Treaty Organization (NATO) and later as assistant to the chairman of the Joint Chiefs of Staff. On June 1, 1989, he was promoted to admiral (four-star) and went on to serve as commander in chief, Allied Forces Southern Europe, and commander, U.S. Naval Forces Europe from 1989 to 1991. Howe retired from active service in 1992. From 1991 to 1993, Howe was the deputy assistant for National Security Affairs for President George H. W. Bush.

Howe took his foreign policy experience to the international arena when he became the special representative for Somalia for the UN secretary general on March 9, 1993, replacing Ismat Kittani from Iraq. Somalia was a failed state, wracked by famine and civil war. In an effort to stabilize the country, the UN undertook a humanitarian mission there to feed the populace and mediate peace between its warring factions. With the situation increasingly dire, in 1993 the UN took more direct action. The Security Council passed Resolution 814, calling for the extension of humanitarian aid by "all necessary means."

Howe's assignment was to oversee the transition from a United Task Force to a full, UN-sanctioned operation. This meant that Howe took over command of a multinational force mission for which there had been little preparation. The organization was called United Nations Operation in Somalia II (UNSOM II).

Howe's first task was to oversee an increase in the number of troops and support staff to carry out the expanded mission. Eventually, 68 nations agreed to participate. Howe then addressed enforcement of the 1993 Addis Ababa Accords. These had been signed by all 15 factions of the Somali clans operating in and about Mogadishu. For the first few weeks, humanitarian aid was delivered and Somalia moved toward a semblance of normalcy.

A few months into President Bill Clinton's administration, the mission of the UN forces shifted. In June 1993, Howe authorized the inspection of a radio station under the control of warlord Mohammed Farrah Aidid (Aideed), initiated to locate hidden weapons. Informed of the operation in advance, Aidid's followers ambushed and killed several Pakistani inspectors. Howe was now forced to go back to the UN Security Council on June 17, 1993, seeking an expansion of the UN mission to include bringing Aidid to justice. The mission expansion was granted and included a $25,000 reward for the capture of Aidid, issued by Howe. This action turned out to be the most controversial of Howe's Somali tenure, and he received criticism for this move because it compromised his impartiality.

UNOSOM II also received aid from U.S. armed forces to further the pacification mission. These forces performed their mission admirably and without major incident until October 3, 1993. On that day, U.S. forces pursued several Aidid aides. The raid turned out badly when American helicopters were shot down, resulting in several deaths and the capture of a U.S. pilot. Following this failure, the UN mission was reexamined and all UN troops were withdrawn from Somalia during the following year. Howe resigned his UN post in February 1994 and moved to Jacksonville, Florida, where he became the executive director of the Arthur Vining Davis Foundation; he still serves in this position.

SHAWN LIVINGSTON

See also
Aidid, Mohammed Farrah; Boutros-Ghali, Boutros; Somalia, International Intervention in

References
Casper, Lawrence E. *Falcon Brigade: Combat and Command in Somalia and Haiti.* Boulder, Co: Lynne Rienner, 2001.

Clarke, Walter S., and Herbst Jeffrey Ira. *Learning from Somalia: The Lessons of Armed Humanitarian Intervention.* Boulder, CO: Westview, 1997.

The United Nations and Somalia, 1992–1996. The United Nations Blue Books Series. New York: Department of Public Information, United Nations, 1996.

Howell, Wilson Nathaniel
Birth Date: September 14, 1939

Career U.S. diplomat and Foreign Service officer who was serving as ambassador to Kuwait when Iraqi forces invaded the small nation on August 2, 1990. Wilson Nathaniel Howell was born in Portsmouth, Virginia, on September 14, 1939. He earned an undergraduate degree from the University of Virginia in 1961 and a doctorate in government and foreign affairs from the same school in 1965. He then entered the U.S. Foreign Service, where he became an expert in Middle Eastern affairs and learned Arabic in Beirut, Lebanon, during 1970–1972.

Howell served in a variety of diplomatic posts and nations, including Egypt, the United Arab Emirates, Algiers, and Lebanon.

He also held high-ranking positions with the U.S. State Department in Washington, D.C., and served as political adviser to the commander in chief of the U.S. Central Command (CENT-COM) in 1986–1987. He also attended the National War College in Washington, D.C. Howell was well known for his extensive knowledge of the Middle East and his ability to link national security and regional security issues with broader foreign policy goals.

In May 1987, President Ronald Reagan named Howell U.S. ambassador to Kuwait, a position he assumed just a few weeks later. Kuwait was considered a highly desirable diplomatic posting at the time, as the United States enjoyed cordial relations with the Kuwaiti government. By 1990, Howell was painfully aware of the deteriorating relations between Iraq and Kuwait. Iraqi president Saddam Hussein had accused the Kuwaitis of "slant-drilling" into Iraqi oil fields and of manipulating the price of oil by overproducing and thereby worsening Iraq's tenuous financial situation. Be that as it may, the United States—and Howell—were surprised by Iraq's invasion of Kuwait on August 2, 1990.

Over the next several weeks, numerous Americans and foreign nationals sought refuge at the U.S. embassy in Kuwait City. Howell was able to accommodate them all but was concerned about their safety. He had good reason to be concerned. In late August, Saddam Hussein declared all foreign embassies in Kuwait closed and announced that foreign diplomats were free to leave the country. However, he refused to allow nondiplomats to leave, hoping to use these people as hostages to forestall air strikes by the United States or its allies. With the Bush administration's assent, Howell decided to keep the American embassy open and refused to leave the country. Howell's stand was nothing short of heroic given the fact that Iraqi troops were engaged in an orgy of rape and pillage in Kuwait.

In December 1990, Hussein reversed his earlier decision and stated that he would permit all of the people in the U.S. embassy to leave—both diplomatic personnel and civilians. Howell emptied the embassy and embarked for Baghdad by car, where he and the others who had been holed up in the embassy would leave for the United States. Howell retired from the foreign service in 1992. For his extraordinary service in Kuwait, that nation's government awarded him the Kuwait Decoration with Sash of the First Class. After leaving government service, Howell joined the faculty of the University of Virginia.

PAUL G. PIERPAOLI JR.

See also

Human Shields; Kuwait; Kuwait, Iraqi Invasion of; Kuwait, Occupation of by Iraq

References

Atkinson, Rick. *Crusade: The Untold Story of the Persian Gulf War.* New York: Mariner Books, 1994.

Time Magazine. *Desert Storm: The War in the Persian Gulf.* Boston, MA: Little, Brown, 1991.

Human Shields

The term "human shield" can refer to civilians who are forced by military or paramilitary forces to precede them in an attack. More recently, the media and others began using the term to refer to a person or group of people who are voluntarily or involuntary positioned at or near a potential military target as a means to deter enemy fire or attack. States and military establishments have often claimed that their opponents have employed civilians as human shields in order to explain civilian casualties resulting from military action.

A potential enemy may choose not to use force against the employers of the shield for fear of harming the person or persons who form the shield. A potential attacker's inhibition regarding the use of force depends on various considerations, such as fear for his or her own security, societal norms, the inclination to abide by international law forbidding attacks on civilians during an armed conflict, fear of negative international or national public opinion, or a close affiliation with the person or group of people forming the shield.

Human shields are similar to hostages, but there are important differences. In contrast to hostages, who are invariably taken involuntarily, human shields might be civilian volunteers utilized by a government at a particular site to deter an enemy from attacking it. The term also refers, however, to the involuntary use of civilians to shield combatants during attacks. In such incidents, the civilians are forced to move in front of the soldiers in the hope that the enemy force will be reluctant to attack, or if it does so and the civilians are killed, this might have propaganda value.

When there is a case of deliberate seizure of civilians to act as human shields, in most cases once the threat is over the seized are released. Usually, no ransom is involved. Historical records indicate that human shields have been used by state authorities, nongovernmental organizations, and terrorists alike.

The use of human shields is expressly prohibited by the Geneva Convention of 1949 and the Additional Protocols of 1977. Article 28 of the Fourth Geneva Convention states that: "The presence of a protected person may not be used to render certain points or areas immune from military operations." Article 3 of the Geneva Convention also forbids the taking of hostages. Furthermore, the Additional Protocols expanded the prohibitions. Protocol II, Part IV, Article 13 states: "The civilian population and individual civilians shall enjoy general protection against the dangers arising from military operations. . . . [They] shall not be the object of attack . . . unless and for such times as they take a direct part in hostilities."

Despite attempts to prevent the use of human shields through the development of international law during the second half of the 20th century, the use of human shields was recorded and discussed in the context of several conflicts, mainly in the 1991 Persian Gulf War, the Bosnian conflict of 1992–1995, the Kosovo War (1999), the Iraq War of 2003, as well as the ongoing Israeli-Palestinian conflict.

Both in Bosnia in 1995 and in Kosovo in 1999, human shields were used extensively by the Serbs. In the war in Bosnia, Bosnian-Serb armed units chained captured United Nations (UN) soldiers to potential North Atlantic Treaty Organization (NATO) air-strike targets. This strategy was effective in paralyzing the UN military forces' operations in Bosnia in May 1995. The nations participating in the UN operation refused to support the use of force against Serbian military targets, as their soldiers' lives were in jeopardy. In 1999, Serbian forces compelled civilian Kosovars to remain near Serb military bases to deter NATO from bombing the bases.

Iraqi dictator Saddam Hussein's regime used human shields of both Westerners and Iraqi civilians on several occasions during the 1990s and right up to the Anglo-American–led invasion of Iraq in March 2003 to safeguard potential military targets. After Iraq's armed forces occupied Kuwait on August 2, 1990, the Iraqi government held dozens of foreign nationals as human shields in strategic locations. To emphasize that human shields were in place, the Hussein regime released videos showing the human shields, some of them interacting with Hussein himself. Only after coming under intense international pressure did the Iraqi government allow these individuals to leave the country. The last human shields left Iraq by December 1991, several weeks before the beginning of Operation DESERT STORM.

In November 1997, a crisis developed between Iraq and the UN concerning weapons inspection in the country. There have been charges that the Iraqi government then encouraged hundreds of civilians to move into palaces and other strategic locations in order to deter attacks there.

Human shields were used again in Iraq in early 2003, but this time by antiwar protesters. The human shield operation was termed the Human Shield Action to Iraq, and it deployed several hundred Western volunteers to potential civilian strategic targets like water and power plants and a communications center.

When Operation IRAQI FREEDOM began on March 20, 2003, many of the volunteers left the country, but approximately 100 remained. The Human Shield Action to Iraq claimed that none of the strategic facilities to which it deployed volunteers were bombed while human shields were present.

In contrast to the examples given above, which emphasize the use of human shields by only one side in a conflict, during

Ken O'Keefe, an ex-U.S. marine who fought in the Persian Gulf War, speaks to the media in downtown Milan, Italy, on January 31, 2003, before preparing to travel to Iraq, where he and members of his group were determined to act as human shields. (AP/Wide World Photos)

the Israeli-Palestinian conflict both sides have employed human shields. There are records of Palestinians wanted by the Israeli government using civilians as a shield to prevent the Israeli Defense Forces (IDF) from firing at them. This tactic was repeated when leaders of Hamas—an Islamic Palestinian political faction that has controlled the Gaza Strip since June 2007—encouraged the Palestinian civilian population to gather near potential Israeli Air Force targets. Hamas also launched rockets on Israeli towns from civilian centers in Gaza. This practice was also reportedly employed by Hezbollah fighters during their war with Israel in July and August 2006, when they fired Katyusha rockets at Israel from civilian centers and fortified their positions inside villages.

Beginning in 2002, records kept by the Israeli human rights group B'Tselem indicate that some IDF units used Palestinian civilians as human shields during their operations in order to prevent Palestinian terrorists from firing at them. In these instances, the IDF forced persons held as hostages to precede them into buildings and certain areas. This practice was outlawed by the Israeli Supreme Court in October 2005. Nevertheless, since then, and on several occasions, human rights groups have recorded the use of Palestinian civilians as human shields by IDF units. In some cases, the IDF took disciplinary measures against its officers who employed this practice.

CHEN KERTCHER

See also

DESERT STORM, Operation; Global War on Terror; Hamas; Hezbollah; Hussein, Saddam; IRAQI FREEDOM, Operation; Israel

References

Ezzo, Matthew V., and Amos N. Guiora. "A Critical Decision Point on the Battlefield—Friend, Foe, or Innocent Bystander." *U of Utah Legal Studies Paper* 8(3) (2008).

Gross, Emmanuel. "Use of Civilians as Human Shields: What Legal and Moral Restrictions Pertain to a War Waged by a Democratic State Against Terrorism?" *Emory International Law Review* 16 (2002): 445–524.

Skerker, Michael. "Just War Criteria and the New Face of War: Human Shields, Manufactured Martyrs, and Little Boys with Stones." *Journal of Military Ethics* 3(1) (2004): 27–39.

Hungary, Role in Persian Gulf, Afghanistan, and Iraq Wars

Central European state with a 2008 population of approximately 9.9 million people. A democratic, parliamentary republic, Hungary covers 35,919 square miles and is bordered by Slovakia to the north, Croatia and Serbia to the south, Austria to the west, and Romania and Ukraine to the east. The prime minister is elected by a multiparty unicameral legislature. Currently, the two most powerful parties are the Hungarian Socialist Party and the Hungarian Civil Union (FIDESZ), a conservative Christian Democratic organization.

A former Soviet satellite state, Hungary emerged from the Cold War in 1989 as a staunch ally of the United States that supported U.S.-led efforts during the 1991 Persian Gulf War and the invasions of Afghanistan (2001) and Iraq (2003). During the Cold War, Hungary had little direct involvement in the conflicts of the Middle East, although it did produce weapons for export. In 1988, at the height of its output, the country's defense industry produced $370 million in arms and weapons. The majority of this production was sold or transferred to the Soviet Union and other Warsaw Pact nations; however, the country did sell small arms and light weapons to countries such as Egypt and Iraq. With the end of the Cold War, Hungary adopted a series of strict control mechanisms to prevent its stocks of Soviet-era weapons from being sold to regions in conflict. In 1988, Hungarian troops joined other United Nations (UN) peacekeepers as part of a force that monitored the cease-fire between Iran and Iraq, and a Hungarian officer commanded one of the three headquarters for the mission.

In 1989, Hungary transitioned from a pro-Soviet, communist regime to a pro-Western democracy. The government and military worked hard to develop closer ties to the West, in particular the United States, and to demonstrate its diplomatic autonomy. As part of this effort, Hungary supported the U.S.-led military coalition during the 1991 Persian Gulf War. It deployed a small force of 50 soldiers, who were part of a hospital unit. This was the first significant exposure of Hungarian personnel to Western medical technology and techniques. In addition, the superiority of U.S. military communications and weaponry reaffirmed the deficiencies in Warsaw Pact weapons and tactics and the necessity of closer cooperation with the West.

After the war, security ties between Hungary and the United States expanded significantly. During the Balkan conflicts of the 1990s, the United States used the former Soviet air base at Taszar, Hungary, to conduct NATO operations, and the facility would later be utilized for missions in Iraq and Afghanistan. At the peak of the Balkan operations, there were approximately 7,000 U.S. personnel stationed at the facility. Meanwhile, the United States supported Hungary's bid for membership in the North Atlantic Treaty Organization (NATO). Hungary, along with the Czech Republic and Poland (the so-called first tier of former Soviet satellites to be deemed eligible for NATO membership), joined the transatlantic alliance in 1999. The United States and other NATO partners supported efforts by successive Hungarian governments to modernize their military forces and ensure interoperability with NATO forces.

The Hungarian government strongly condemned the September 11, 2001, terrorist attacks on the United States, and it supported NATO's invocation of its collective defense clause, Article V, of the 1949 Washington Treaty. Although no Hungarian troops were involved in the initial invasion of Afghanistan during Operation ENDURING FREEDOM, Budapest granted the United States overflight rights for aerial missions and provided intelligence and logistical support. Beginning in 2003, Hungary maintained a small contingent (200–300 troops) in Afghanistan as part of the NATO-led International Security Assistance Force–Afghanistan (ISAF). Hungary also deployed a small police force to assist in the recruitment and training of Afghanistan's national police under the auspices of the European Union. In 2006, Hungary hosted an international conference of 35 nations in an effort to increase the global community's reconstruction aid and assistance to Afghanistan. Hungary then took command of the Provincial Reconstruction Team in Baghlan, in northern Afghanistan. The operation marked the first time in contemporary history that Hungarian forces operated outside of their home country in command of a major multilateral mission.

Budapest has allocated about $80 million per year for reconstruction and humanitarian missions in Baghlan Province since 2006. The majority of the population in the province is ethnic Tajiks, Uzbeks, and Hazaras. These groups were opposed to the Taliban and have been generally supportive of the Afghan national government. Consequently, Hungarian forces have not faced the same level of Taliban attacks as other NATO forces in the east and south of the country.

As part of the ISAF mission, Hungary assumed responsibility for security for Kabul airport in 2008 for a six-month period. It deployed an additional 60 troops for the mission. In 2008, Hungary suffered its first military fatality as part of ISAF, when a soldier was killed by a roadside bomb. Throughout Operation ENDURING FREEDOM and ISAF, Hungary has been a staunch proponent of increasing NATO's troop strength in Afghanistan. However, the government opposed U.S. plans for coalition forces to undertake a more active counternarcotics role in Afghanistan. In addition, in 2004, Hungary ended conscription as part of a broader military downsizing. One result was that the number of forces available for deployment in multilateral missions was reduced to about 2,000 total troops.

Hungary also supported the diplomatic efforts of the George W. Bush administration to organize a coalition to overthrow Iraqi dictator Saddam Hussein. In January 2003, Hungary joined with the Czech Republic in addition to five members of the European Union in a letter that accused Hussein's government of harboring weapons of mass destruction. The open document also pledged support for the U.S. policy of regime change in Iraq. Hungarian officials likened the removal of Hussein to the overthrow of the communists in the late 1980s. In addition, Budapest's support for the Bush administration was widely seen as a gesture of appreciation for the role the United States played during the end of the Cold War and the efforts by successive U.S. presidents to foster

The six-man advance team of some 300 Hungarians who joined international coalition forces in Iraq. The men are at Szolnok Air Base, east of Budapest, preparing to board a Soviet-built An-26 for Iraq on July 10, 2003. (AP/Wide World Photos)

Hungary's reintegration into Western Europe, including membership in NATO and the EU.

Hungary's stance put it at odds with EU partners such as France and Germany, however, and the government's position was not widely endorsed among the populace. Polls taken prior to the start of the war in March 2003 revealed that a consistent majority of about 70 percent opposed military action against Iraq without the explicit authorization of the UN. Nonetheless, the government undertook a number of concrete steps to affirm its support. In January 2003, some 3,000 Iraqi exiles underwent training at Taszar air force base prior to the invasion of Iraq. The majority of those trained were interpreters and noncombat personnel. U.S. forces were also authorized to use bases and facilities in Hungary from which to conduct the invasion.

Hungary did not contribute troops to the initial invasion of Iraq, but it deployed a battalion of 300 soldiers in August 2003. There were initial plans to dispatch a larger force, but Hungary was in the midst of a military reorganization program that resulted in constraints on the nation's deployable forces. The unit sent to Iraq was a logistics and transport battalion that specialized in humanitarian operations and had considerable experience in the peacekeeping missions in the Balkans. It served as part of the Multi-National Force in southern Iraq, under the command of Poland. Hungarian forces conducted general security and interdiction missions. In 2004, Hungary's center-right coalition government was replaced with one dominated by the left-of-center Social Democrats, but the new government continued to support the U.S.-led occupation of Iraq. But Hungary's military mission remained unpopular among the public and the government withdrew the troops at the end of December 2004 after it failed to gain the necessary two-thirds majority vote needed to extend the deployment. In addition, U.S. and NATO forces withdrew from Taszar air force base at the end of 2004.

In 2005, Hungary worked with its allies to gain approval for a NATO mission to train security forces in Iraq. The government then agreed to participate in NATO's security training mission in Iraq and deployed 150 military and police trainers, and a Hungarian general commanded NATO's training mission. The government also donated a significant amount of Soviet-era military equipment to Iraq's new security forces, including 77 T-72 main battle tanks and 36 BMPs (*boyevaya mashina pekhoty,* or infantry combat vehicles), as well as more than 1 million rounds of ammunition for the weapons systems. The donations were part of a NATO program to provide military equipment to the Iraqi government. Iraq paid Hungarian firms to refurbish and upgrade the equipment. In November 2008, Hungary announced that it would withdraw the remainder of its personnel from Iraq by the end of the year.

TOM LANSFORD

See also

Afghanistan, Coalition Combat Operations in, 2002–Present; International Security Assistance Force; IRAQI FREEDOM, Operation, Coalition Ground Forces; Multi-National Force–Iraq; North Atlantic Treaty Organization in Afghanistan; Provincial Reconstruction Teams, Afghanistan

References

Keegan, John. *The Iraq War: The Military Offensive, from Victory in 21 Days to the Insurgent Aftermath.* New York: Vintage, 2005.

Lansford, Tom. *All for One: NATO, Terrorism and the United States.* Aldershot, UK: Ashgate, 2002.

Michta, Andrew, ed. *America's New Allies: Poland, Hungary, and the Czech Republic.* Seattle: University of Washington Press, 1999.

Murray, Williamson, and Robert H. Scales Jr. *The Iraq War: A Military History.* Cambridge, MA: Belknap, 2005.

Husaybah, Battle of
Event Date: April 17, 2004

Battle near the Iraqi town of Husaybah, close to the Syrian border, on April 17, 2004, which involved U.S. Marines from the I Marine Expeditionary Force. The 14-hour battle occurred concurrently with the First Battle of Fallujah (April 4–May 1, 2004), an operation by the United States to capture the city of Fallujah, also known as Operation VIGILANT RESOLVE. From Husaybah, the insurgents had been attempting to launch an offensive against U.S. forces to divert resources from the attack against Fallujah. The insurgent force numbered about 300 and was operating from positions in the vicinity of the former Baath Party headquarters in Husaybah. U.S. forces numbered 150.

On April 17, the insurgents drew the Americans from their base on the outskirts of Husaybah with a roadside bombing and then with a mortar assault. When the marines retaliated, they encountered an ambush during which they were hit with small-arms and machine-gun fire. The marines then called in reinforcements. The resulting street fighting lasted the entire day and late into the night, with the marines having to advance block by block to clear buildings of insurgents. During the night, Bell AH-1 Cobra helicopter gunships also attacked insurgent positions in the city. The American forces defeated the insurgents after fierce fighting. Five marines were killed and nine wounded in the fight. The insurgents suffered an estimated 150 killed in action, an unknown number of wounded, and 20 captured. The insurgent losses represented more than 50 percent of their original strength.

RICHARD B. VERRONE

See also

Fallujah, First Battle of; Iraqi Insurgency

References

Murray, Williamson, and Robert H. Scales Jr. *The Iraq War: A Military History.* Cambridge, MA: Belknap, 2005.

Ricks, Thomas E. *Fiasco: The American Military Adventure in Iraq.* New York: Penguin, 2006.

West, Bing. *No True Glory: A Frontline Account of the Battle for Fallujah.* New York: Bantam, 2006.

Husayn, Zayn al-Abidin Mohamed

See Zubaydah, Abu

Hussein, Qusay

Birth Date: May 17, 1966
Death Date: July 22, 2003

Iraqi government and military official and son of Iraqi dictator Saddam Hussein. At the time of the U.S.-led invasion of Iraq in March 2003, Qusay Hussein was considered the second most powerful man in Iraq and the likely successor to his father. Qusay Hussein was born in Tikrit, Iraq, on May 17, 1966, the second son of Saddam Hussein and Sajida Talfah. As Arab custom dictates, Saddam Hussein's elder son, Uday, was the most prominent and was raised as his father's successor. Although out of the limelight, Qusay Hussein remained loyal to his father to the point of even imitating his dress and trademark mustache.

While Uday Hussein proved to be mentally unstable and a flamboyant sexual sadist whose antics embarrassed the ruling family, Qusay was much more reserved. Complying with his father's wishes, in 1987 he married the daughter of Mahir Abd al-Rashid, an influential military commander. The marriage produced four children. Although possessing numerous mistresses, Qusay Hussein portrayed himself as a devoted family man.

Qusay's loyalty and patience eventually bore dividends. When Uday's behavior became more erratic in the late 1980s, Saddam Hussein began to turn more to his second son. For example, Qusay was granted broad authority in crushing the Shiite Muslim and Marsh Arabs' uprisings following Iraq's defeat in the 1991 Persian Gulf War. He responded ruthlessly, using torture and executing entire families believed to be disloyal to the regime.

As Uday's position declined, Qusay began to emerge as the likely successor to Saddam Hussein. For his role in crushing the 1991 rebellions, Saddam entrusted Qusay with command of the Special Security Organization (SSO), including Internal Security and the Presidential Guard. In his role as security head, Qusay Hussein oversaw Iraqi's chemical, biological, and nuclear programs. He was also responsible for the repression of opponents of his father's regime. It is believed that Qusay, with his father's approval, had a hand in the attempted assassination of Uday on December 12, 1996.

Clearly Saddam Hussein's favorite, Qusay was named "caretaker" in the event of Saddam's illness or death and given command of the elite Republican Guard. Possessing no formal military training, Qusay Hussein refused to accept advice from more experienced commanders. None dared to question his orders for fear of the consequences, however. The dismal performance of the Republican Guard in failing to slow the American-led invasion in 1991 is often blamed on the lack of military experience of Qusay and his advisers.

Following the terror attacks of September 11, 2001, foreign pressure on Iraq began to increase, and the United States began preparing for a second invasion of Iraq, this time to topple the Hussein regime. Saddam Hussein and his sons temporarily rallied in the face of the overwhelming military force gathering to confront them. On March 18, 2003, U.S. president George W. Bush called on Saddam Hussein and his sons to leave the country, a demand that was rebuffed.

Following the invasion on March 20, 2003, Qusay Hussein went into hiding. On July 22, 2003, Qusay; his 14-year-old son, Mustapha; Uday; and their bodyguard were cornered in Mosul. During the course of a four-hour firefight, all were killed. Following identification, the bodies were buried in Awja.

ROBERT W. MALICK

See also

DESERT STORM, Operation; Hussein, Saddam; Hussein, Uday; Iraq, History of, 1990–Present; IRAQI FREEDOM, Operation; Marsh Arabs; Republican Guard; Shia Islam

References

Balaghi, Shiva. *Saddam Hussein: A Biography.* Westport, CT: Greenwood, 2006.

Bengio, Ofra. "How Does Saddam Hold On?" *Foreign Affairs* (July/August 2000): 90–103.

Bennett, Brian, and Michael Weisskopf. "The Sum of Two Evils." *Time,* June 2, 2003, 34.

Thomas, Evan, and Christopher Dickey. "Saddam's Sons." *Newsweek,* October 21, 2002, 34.

Woods, Kevin, James Lacy, and Williamson Murray. "Saddam's Delusions." *Foreign Affairs* (May/June 2006): 2–16.

Hussein, Saddam

Birth Date: April 28, 1937
Death Date: December 30, 2006

Iraqi politician, leading figure in the Baath Party, and president of Iraq (1979–2003). Born on April 28, 1937, in the village of Awja, near Tikrit, to a family of sheep herders, Saddam Hussein attended a secular school in Baghdad and in 1957 joined the Baath Party, a socialist and Arab nationalist party. Iraqi Baathists supported General Abd al-Karim Qasim's ouster of the Iraqi monarchy in 1958 but were not favored by President Qasim.

Wounded in an unsuccessful attempt to assassinate Qasim in 1959, Hussein subsequently fled the country but returned after the 1963 Baathist coup and began his rise in the party, although he was again imprisoned in 1964. Escaping in 1966, Hussein continued to ascend through the party's ranks, becoming second in authority when the party took full and uncontested control of Iraq in 1968 under the leadership of General Ahmad Hassan al-Bakr, a relative of Hussein's. The elderly Bakr gradually relinquished power to him so that Hussein eventually controlled most of the government.

Saddam Hussein, who ruled Iraq as national president and Revolutionary Command Council chairperson from July 1979 until he was driven from power by a U.S.-led coalition during the Iraq War, shown here in April 2003. (Reuters/Ina/Hulton Archive/Getty Images)

Hussein became president when Bakr resigned, allegedly because of illness, in July 1979. A week after taking power, Saddam led a meeting of Baath leaders during which the names of his potential challengers were read aloud. They were then escorted from the room and shot. Because Iraq was rent by ethnic and religious divisions, Hussein ruled through a tight web of relatives and associates from Tikrit, backed by the Sunni Muslim minority. He promoted economic development through Iraqi oil production, which accounted for 10 percent of known world reserves. Hussein's modernization was along Western lines, with expanded roles for women and a secular legal system based in part on Sharia and Ottoman law. He also promoted the idea of Iraqi nationalism and emphasized Iraq's ancient past, glorifying such figures as kings Hammurabi and Nebuchadnezzar.

Before assuming the presidency, Hussein had courted both the West and the Soviet Union, resulting in arms deals with the Soviets and close relations with the Soviet Union and France. He was also instrumental in convincing the Mohammad Reza Shah Pahlavi of Iran to curb his support of Iraqi Kurds. Hussein's efforts to take advantage of the superpowers' Cold War rivalry, including rapprochement with Iran, fell apart with the overthrow of the shah in the 1979 Iranian Revolution. The shah's successor, Ayatollah Khomeini, a radical, fundamentalist Muslim, bitterly opposed Hussein because of his Sunni background and secularism.

After a period of repeated border skirmishes, Iraq declared war on Iran in September 1980. Hussein's ostensible dispute concerned a contested border, but he also feared Iran's fundamentalism and its support for the Iraqi Shia Muslim majority. Initial success gave way to Iraqi defeats in the face of human-wave attacks and, ultimately, a stalemate. By 1982 Hussein was ready to end the war, but Iranian leaders desired that the fighting continue. In 1988 the United Nations (UN) finally brokered a cease-fire, but not before the war had devastated both nations. The war left Iraq heavily in debt, and Hussein requested relief from his major creditors, including the United States, Kuwait, and Saudi Arabia. He also sought to maintain high oil prices. His efforts were in vain; creditors refused to write off their debts, and Kuwait maintained a high oil output, forcing other oil-producing nations to follow suit.

Hussein responded by declaring Kuwait a "rogue province" of Iraq. He was also enraged by Kuwaiti slant drilling into Iraqi oil fields. Hussein's demands became more strident, and after securing what he believed to be U.S. acquiescence, he ordered Iraqi forces to attack and occupy Kuwait on August 2, 1990. Hussein miscalculated the U.S. reaction. President George H. W. Bush assembled an international military coalition, built up forces in Saudi Arabia (Operation DESERT SHIELD), and then commenced a relentless bombing campaign against Iraq in January 1991. The ground war of February 24–28, 1991, resulted in a crushing defeat of Iraqi forces. Although Hussein withdrew from Kuwait, coalition forces did not seek his overthrow and he remained in power, ruling a nation devastated by two recent wars.

Hussein retained control of Iraq for another decade, during which he brutally suppressed Kurdish and Shia revolts, relinquished limited autonomy to the Kurds, acquiesced to the destruction of stockpiles of chemical weapons, and pursued a dilatory response to UN efforts to monitor his weapons programs. Convinced—wrongly as it turned out—that Hussein had been building and stockpiling weapons of mass destruction, President George W. Bush asked for and received authorization from Congress to wage war against Iraq. U.S. and coalition forces invaded Iraq in March 2003. Coalition forces took Baghdad on April 10, 2003, and captured Hussein on December 14, 2003, to be brought to trial on charges of war crimes and crimes against humanity.

On November 5, 2006, the Iraqi Special Tribunal found Hussein guilty in the deaths of 148 Shiite Muslims in 1982, whose murders he had ordered. That same day, he was sentenced to hang. Earlier, on August 21, 2006, a second trial had begun on charges that Hussein had committed genocide and other atrocities by ordering the systematic extermination of northern Iraqi Kurds during 1987–1988, resulting in as many as 180,000 deaths. Before the second trial moved into high gear, however, Hussein filed an appeal, which was rejected by the Iraqi Court on December 26, 2006. Four days later, on December 30, 2006, the Muslim holiday of 'Id al-Adha, Hussein was executed by hanging in Baghdad. Before his death, Hussein told U.S. Federal Bureau of Investigation interrogators that he had misled the world to give the impression that Iraq had weapons of mass destruction in order to make Iraq appear stronger in the face of its enemy Iran.

DANIEL E. SPECTOR

See also

DESERT STORM, Operation; Iran-Iraq War; Iranian Revolution; Iraq, History of, Pre-1990; Iraq, History of, 1990–Present; IRAQI FREEDOM, Operation; Khomeini, Ruhollah; Kurds; Kuwait; Reza Pahlavi, Mohammad

References

Bengio, Ofra. *Saddam's Word: Political Discourse in Iraq.* New York: Oxford University Press USA, 1998.

Karsh, Efraim. *Saddam Hussein: A Political Biography.* New York: Grove/Atlantic, 2002.

Miller, Judith, and Laurie Mylroie. *Saddam Hussein and the Crisis in the Gulf.* New York: Times Books, 1990.

Wingate, Brian. *Saddam Hussein: The Rise and Fall of a Dictator.* New York: Rosen, 2004.

Hussein, Uday
Birth Date: June 18, 1964
Death Date: July 22, 2003

Iraqi government official, commander of the Fedayeen Saddam, and eldest son of Iraqi president and dictator Saddam Hussein. Uday Hussein was born in Baghdad on June 18, 1964, and was initially groomed to succeed his father as dictator of Iraq. Uday's mental instability, cruelty, and alcoholism, however, resulted in his being passed over for his younger brother, Qusay Hussein. Uday's fall from favor began in 1988. During a dinner party that year, he murdered his father's favorite bodyguard and food taster, Kamil Hanna Jajjo. Jajjo had supposedly introduced Saddam to his most recent mistress, which Uday viewed as insulting to his own mother. Originally sentenced to death, Uday was instead imprisoned and tortured. Upon his release, he was exiled to Switzerland as an assistant to the Iraqi ambassador. After six months, however, Swiss authorities quietly expelled Hussein after he threatened to kill a Swiss citizen in a restaurant.

Upon his return to Iraq, Uday attempted to rebuild his power base but was unable to control his sadistic and volatile nature. As head of the Iraqi Olympic Committee, he ordered the torture of athletes whom he believed were not performing to the best of their ability. In one instance, a missed soccer goal resulted in the offending athlete being dragged though gravel and then submerged in raw sewage. Uday also began to dominate the state-owned media, controlling state radio and the youth magazine *Babel*. As minister of youth affairs, Uday headed the paramilitary organization Fedayeen Saddam.

In 1994, Saddam granted Uday control of Iraq's oil-smuggling operations, which were in violation of sanctions by the United Nations (UN) that had been imposed following the 1991 Persian Gulf War. Supervising up to 150,000 barrels of smuggled oil a day provided a vast income. With this revenue, Uday lived a life of ostentatious luxury. He purchased hundreds of foreign sports cars, storing them in underground garages throughout Baghdad. At his numerous palaces, staffs were maintained around the clock, including a personal shopper and two trainers for his pet lions. At the palaces, Uday set up torture chambers, and he reportedly ordered the kidnapping, rape, and torture of scores of Iraqi women, including married women, even brides. Brides were sometimes taken from their wedding celebrations if Uday favored them sexually.

On December 12, 1996, a botched assassination attempt riddled Uday's sports car and two escort vehicles with bullets as they sped through the upper-class Baghdad neighborhood of Mansur.

Although hit eight times in the arm, leg, and stomach, Uday survived the attack. Official blame for the attack centered on Iran, although some sources claim Saddam or his other son, Qusay, were involved.

Following the terror attacks on the United States of September 11, 2001, foreign pressure on Iraq began to mount. President Hussein and his sons rallied in the face of the overwhelming military force gathering to confront them, however. On March 18, 2003, on the eve of the Iraq War, U.S. president George W. Bush demanded that Saddam Hussein and his sons leave the country immediately or face an invasion. After they refused this ultimatum, coalition forces invaded Iraq on March 20. Uday went into hiding following the invasion, but on July 22, 2003, he and his brother, Qusay, were cornered by Special Operations Task Force 20 and elements of the U.S. Army's 101st Airborne Division in Mosul, Iraq. After a four-hour firefight, Uday, Qusay, Qusay's 14-year-old son, and a bodyguard were shot dead. Saddam Hussein, meanwhile, was apprehended by American forces on December 13, 2003, and was executed for war crimes on December 30, 2006.

ROBERT W. MALICK

See also

Hussein, Qusay; Hussein, Saddam; Iraq, History of, Pre-1990; Iraq, History of, 1990–Present

References

Cockburn, Andrew, and Patrick Cockburn. *Out of the Ashes: The Resurrection of Saddam Hussein.* New York: HarperCollins, 2000.

Marr, Phebe. *The Modern History of Iraq.* 2nd ed. Boulder, CO: Westview, 2003.

Hussein ibn Talal, King of Jordan
Birth Date: November 14, 1935
Death Date: February 7, 1999

King of Jordan (1953–1999). Born in Amman on November 14, 1935, into the Hashimite family who had governed the holy cities in the Hijaz prior to the Saudi invasion, Hussein was the son of Prince Talal ibn Abdullah. Hussein ibn Talal was educated in Jordan and then at Victoria College in Alexandria, Egypt, before transferring to the prestigious Harrow School in Britain. He was with his grandfather King Abdullah when the king was assassinated in 1951.

Hussein's father was crowned king but was forced to abdicate the throne on August 11, 1952, because of mental illness. Hussein was proclaimed king as Hussein I and returned from Britain to take up his the throne at age 17. He formally ascended the throne on May 2, 1953.

Hussein's policies tended to be realistic and pragmatic. The nation's stability was threatened by the need to integrate the Palestinians who resettled in the East Bank and by the militancy of Palestinian refugees on the West Bank, which had been annexed by Jordan in a move that was not popular with the Israelis, the Palestinians, or other Arab states. In addition, Jordan still enjoyed considerable financial and military support from Britain, which also displeased Arab leaders who had fought British control over their countries and economies. Hussein continued the close ties with Britain until 1956. At that time, because of widespread resentment against the British over the Suez intervention in 1956, he was pressured to dismiss General John Bagot Glubb, the British head of the Arab Legion that had been formed in 1939 to fight in World War II.

The dismissal of Glubb was popular with Jordanians, but Hussein delayed another year before terminating the Anglo-Jordanian Treaty and signing the Arab Solidarity Agreement that pledged Egypt, Syria, and Saudi Arabia to provide Jordan with an annual subsidy of $36 million. When Hussein accepted U.S. aid in 1958, however, Egyptian and Syrian leaders began to campaign against him.

By the mid-1960s, Hussein was making attempts to alleviate the increasing isolation that separated Jordan from neighboring Arab states. After some hesitation, he linked his country with Egypt in war against Israel, permitting Jordanian long-range artillery fire against Jewish areas of Jerusalem and the suburbs of Tel Aviv in the 1967 Six-Day War. The Israelis had hoped that Jordan would remain neutral, but Hussein's steps brought retaliatory Israeli air strikes. Hussein later said that he made the decision because he feared that Israel was about to invade. The war was a disaster for Jordan, which lost the entire West Bank and its air force and suffered some 15,000 casualties. After the war, Hussein helped draft United Nations (UN) Resolution 242, which urged Israel to give up its occupied territories in exchange for peace.

In the early 1970s, Hussein was forced to challenge the presence of Palestinian commandoes in Jordan, because their raids into Israel were inciting retaliatory Israeli attacks on Jordan and because they challenged Hussein's authority over his own territory. After an assassination attempt on Hussein and the hijacking of four British airliners by the Popular Front for the Liberation of Palestine and the destruction of these aircraft in Jordan, the king decided that Palestinian militants were threatening the very survival of Jordan and that he must take action. In 1970, in what became known as Black September, Hussein began a controversial military campaign against the Palestinian militants, forcing them from Jordanian territory. Although he achieved his goal and the Palestinian resistance moved its headquarters to Lebanon, the unrest lasted until July 1971, and his action undermined his position as the principal spokesperson for the Palestinian people.

Hussein regained favor in the Arab world when he rejected the 1979 Israel-Egypt Peace Treaty. He received considerable international criticism for his neutrality regarding Iraqi leader Saddam Hussein's invasion of Kuwait and for not joining the coalition against Iraq in the 1991 Persian Gulf War. Jordan had to remain faithful to its own policy toward Iraq, which had resulted from their initial emergence as Hashimite kingdoms and was reflected in their close economic ties. King Hussein nonetheless continued to play a significant role in the ongoing Middle East peace talks. In July 1994 he signed a peace agreement with Israeli prime minister Yitzhak Rabin.

On the domestic front, Hussein was a popular but autocratic leader who guided his nation to relative prosperity. He saw to it that more Jordanians had access to running water, proper sanitation, and electricity. He also actively promoted education and dramatically increased the literacy rate. In the late 1960s he oversaw construction of a modern highway system in the kingdom.

In 1992 Hussein began to take some steps toward the liberalization of the political system and the development of a multiparty system. That same year he was diagnosed with pancreatic cancer. He underwent treatment several times in the United States, each time designating his brother Hasan as regent during his absence. Less than two weeks before his death in 1999, Hussein surprised the world by naming his eldest son, Abdullah, as crown prince and designated heir, publicly denouncing Hasan's performance as regent and ensuring his own immediate family's control of the throne.

Abdullah became King Abdullah II upon Hussein's death in Amman on February 7, 1999. Beloved by Jordanians for his attention to their welfare, Hussein had strengthened Jordan's position in the Arab world and contributed to the foundations of peace in the region.

JESSICA BRITT

See also

Camp David Accords; Jordan; Palestine Liberation Organization; Rabin, Yitzhak

References

Dallas, Roland. *King Hussein: A Life on the Edge.* New York: Fromm International, 1999.

Dann, Uriel. *King Hussein and the Challenge of Arab Radicalism: Jordan, 1955–1967.* Oxford: Oxford University Press, 1997.

Hussein, King of Jordan. *Uneasy Lies the Head: The Autobiography of His Majesty King Hussein I of the Hashemite Kingdom of Jordan.* New York: B. Geis, 1962.

Matusky, Gregory, and John P. Hayes. *King Hussein.* New York: Chelsea House, 1987.

Satloff, Robert B. *From Abdullah to Hussein: Jordan in Transition.* New York: Oxford University Press, 1993.

I

IMMINENT THUNDER, Operation

Start Date: November 15, 1990
End Date: November 21, 1990

Joint exercise conducted during November 15–21, 1990, by U.S. amphibious units and the Saudi military on the eve of the 1991 Persian Gulf War. Operation IMMINENT THUNDER was undertaken as part of a broader deception campaign against the Iraqi military.

On August 2, 1990, Iraq invaded Kuwait. Iraqi forces quickly overran that small country. In response to concerns that Iraq would also invade oil-rich Saudi Arabia, President George H. W. Bush ordered U.S. military forces to the region to protect the county's key Persian Gulf ally in what became known as Operation DESERT SHIELD. Two naval battle groups and elements of two marine amphibious units were among the forces sent to Saudi Arabia. Meanwhile, the Bush administration began to develop a diplomatic and military coalition to dislodge Iraqi forces. By October 1990, coalition military planners were convinced that Iraq would not invade Saudi Arabia. Consequently, U.S. and allied military leaders began to prepare for an offensive operation to drive the Iraqis from Kuwait.

The emerging plans for the liberation of Kuwait were centered on a massive air campaign to destroy Iraq's air defenses and weaken its ground defenses. The aerial campaign would be followed by a ground invasion. U.S. general H. Norman Schwarzkopf, overall coalition commander, was concerned about the number of casualties his forces might suffer at the hands of the Iraqis, who were in strong defensive lines along the Kuwaiti-Iraq border. Consequently, he ordered the several deceptive measures to mislead and divert Iraqi forces. For instance, the coalition created a mock base with elaborate decoys for the U.S. VII Corps, whose 1,200 tanks and armored personnel carriers were 200 miles away. In addition, in an effort to disperse Iraqi units in Kuwait, coalition military planners endeavored to deceive the Iraqis into believing that part of their plans called for a large amphibious assault. Central to this effort was Operation IMMINENT THUNDER.

If successful, the coalition's leaders hoped the deception would cause the Iraqis to maintain their coastal defense troops and also deploy additional forces to the coastal areas of Kuwait to defend against the assault, thereby weakening their lines along the Saudi border. In order to make the diversion convincing, U.S. Marines and naval units carried out a series of exercises, ostensibly in preparation for an assault on Kuwait.

Prior to IMMINENT THUNDER, coalition forces conducted two small amphibious training missions on the Omani Coast, in addition to carrying out shipboard training and other exercises. Intelligence reports affirmed that the Iraqi high command was paying close attention to the exercises and enhancing their coastal defenses. The culmination of the amphibious deception plan was to be Operation IMMINENT THUNDER, which would be the largest landing exercises conducted during the Persian Gulf crisis. A U.S. naval amphibious task force of 20 ships assembled in the Gulf of Oman under the command of U.S. Rear Admiral Daniel P. March, who was also the operational commander for coalition naval forces. At the core of the naval force was the aircraft carrier *Midway*. The task force included 10,000 sailors as well as some 8,000 marines from the 4th Marine Expeditionary Brigade and the 13th Marine Expeditionary Unit. The marines were supported by air units, including helicopter strike groups. The force was ordered to conduct a week-long series of practice landings and other maneuvers. The coalition publicly announced that the exercise was to be the final preparation before it launched the operation to liberate Kuwait.

IMMINENT THUNDER began on November 15, 1990, and continued through November 21. The operation was divided into five components. The first tested the ability of coalition air forces to operate in a coordinated manner to support the landings. The second involved a series of exercises to check the task force's logistics and support capabilities and to ensure service interoperability. The third component included practice landings, as well as training missions, to simulate the link-up with main ground forces. There were also casualty evacuation simulations and rescue exercises. The fourth part was centered on training to facilitate familiarity between the U.S. and Arab forces and to make sure that non-U.S. personnel were trained on U.S. weapons and communications systems. Finally, the fifth component was an extensive after-action effort to highlight those areas that needed further training or additional exercises.

IMMINENT THUNDER involved 16 ships, 1,100 aircraft and approximately 1,000 marines. A small number of Saudi and other Arab air and ground forces also participated. U.S. Navy, Marine, and Air Force personnel and assets were all part of the operation. The task force conducted landings and other exercises along the northeast coast of Saudi Arabia, along an area about 80 miles south of Kuwait. The exercise had originally been planned for Ras Al Mishab, only 20 miles from the Kuwaiti border and within Iraqi missile range, which prompted the transfer of IMMINENT THUNDER further south. Air units from the United States and Saudi Arabia conducted practice missions, while Saudi and other Arab amphibious forces participated in landings with the U.S. Marines. On the first day, coalition aircraft flew 115 sorties under the direction of air controllers on the battleship *Missouri,* who simulated coordination of air and naval strikes on land targets.

While the maneuvers were mainly to deceive the Iraqis, coalition planners did gain valuable information and experience from IMMINENT THUNDER. The exercise allowed the planners to test systems that had been developed to coordinate air, land, and sea elements. Especially important to U.S. planners was the opportunity to practice an operation that would allow amphibious forces to link with conventional ground forces. The inclusion of Saudi forces permitted the coalition to test its joint warfare capabilities and its interoperability in communications, logistics, and transport. Also, the operation provided a means for U.S. personnel to become acclimated to the region and to examine equipment for potential performance problems in the desert environment. The U.S. Navy was able to test successfully its Aegis Combat System, which allowed air controllers to coordinate multiple aircraft during the practice landings and reinforced the utility of the system for amphibious assaults. In addition, tests of communications equipment and procedures were successful, as were helicopter refueling exercises.

IMMINENT THUNDER also included tests of remote-controlled surveillance aircraft. Meanwhile, problems were discovered in the coalition's weather satellite and forecasting systems. Steps were taken to refine the weather system prior to the invasion. The navy had planned to use hovercraft during the exercises to highlight U.S. technological advantages; however, high seas and rough weather forced the abandonment of the effort after two attempts. This failure forced the navy to reconsider the conditions under which the vehicles could be utilized.

To maximize the deception, U.S. military planners launched a broad media campaign to highlight the exercises. Reporters and journalists from around the world were invited to observe the maneuvers, and the U.S. military provided transport for television crews to fly to the region and broadcast images of the practice landings. At the conclusion of IMMINENT THUNDER, President Bush traveled to Saudi Arabia and had a Thanksgiving service with the marines on November 23. Meanwhile, the stories and images were dutifully noted by Iraqi intelligence. The coalition's deception worked extraordinarily well. The Iraqi military positioned six divisions, some 80,000 troops, along the Kuwaiti coast prior to the invasion.

After IMMINENT THUNDER was concluded, coalition military planners finalized both their defensive plans—in the unlikely event that Iraq launched a preemptive strike against Saudi Arabia—and the plans for the liberation of Kuwait. While the initial planning had been for the task force to serve in a diversionary capacity, plans were developed for an amphibious assault near Ash Shuaybah in Kuwait, depending on the rate of the ground advance. If coalition forces met heavy resistance, the landings would serve as a second front. Meanwhile, and concurrent with Operation IMMINENT THUNDER, the U.S. naval amphibious task force participated in the continuing economic and weapons blockade against Iraq in the Arabian Sea and the Persian Gulf. After IMMINENT THUNDER, the task force conducted a smaller training mission, Operation SEA SOLDIER III, in Oman to further refine combined and joint communications and coordination capabilities. The follow-on exercise was also designed to continue the deception that the coalition still planned an amphibious assault and to provide coalition forces the opportunity to correct problems that emerged during IMMINENT THUNDER. It included more than 3,500 marines and 1,000 vehicles.

The international coalition commenced air strikes on January 17, 1991. The ground invasion followed on February 24. The speed of the coalition's advance eliminated the need for an amphibious second front, and the war was over by February 28.

TOM LANSFORD

See also

Amphibious Assault Ships; Amphibious Command Ships; Logistics, Persian Gulf War; DESERT SHIELD, Operation; DESERT STORM, Operation; DESERT STORM, Operation, Planning for; Fast Combat Support Ships; Support and Supply Ships, Strategic; Tank Landing Ships, U.S.; United States Marine Corps, Persian Gulf War

References

Bacevich, Andrew J., and Efraim Inbar, eds. *The Gulf War of 1991 Reconsidered.* Portland, OR: Frank Cass, 2003.

Brown, Ronald J. *U.S. Marines in the Persian Gulf, 1990–1991: With Marine Forces Afloat in Desert Shield and Desert Storm.* Washington, DC: History and Museums Division, U.S. Marine Corps, 1998.

Hoskins, Andrew. *Televising War: From Vietnam to Iraq.* London: Continuum, 2004.

MacArthur, John R. *Second Front: Censorship and Propaganda in the 1991 Gulf War.* Berkeley: University of California, 2004.

Marolda, Edward, and Robert Schneller. *Shield and Sword: The United States Navy and the Persian Gulf War.* Annapolis, MD: U.S. Naval Institute Press, 2001.

Pokrant, Marvin. *Desert Shield at Sea: What the Navy Really Did.* Westport, CT: Greenwood, 1999.

Improvised Explosive Devices

Improvised explosive devices (IEDs) have been employed in warfare almost since the introduction of gunpowder. They remain the weapon of choice for insurgent and resistance groups that lack the numerical strength and firepower to conduct conventional operations against an opponent. IEDs are the contemporary form of booby traps employed in World War II and the Vietnam War. Traditionally they are used primarily against enemy armor and thin-skinned vehicles.

A water cart filled with explosives was employed in a futile effort to assassinate Napoleon Bonaparte in Paris as he traveled to the opera on Christmas Eve 1800. The emperor escaped injury, but the blast killed the little girl the conspirators paid to hold the horse's bridle and killed or maimed a dozen other people. In more recent times, IEDs have been employed against civilian targets by Basque separatists and the Irish Republican Army. Molotov cocktails, or gasoline bombs, are one form of IED. The largest, most deadly IEDs in history were the U.S. jetliners hijacked by members of the terrorist organization Al Qaeda on September 11, 2001, and used to attack the World Trade Center in New York City and the Pentagon in Washington, D.C.

IEDs became one of the chief weapons employed by insurgents during the Iraq War (2003) and its aftermath to attack U.S. forces and Iraqi police to carry out sectarian violence. The simplest type of IED was a hand grenade, rigged artillery shell, or bomb triggered by a trip-wire or simple movement. It might be as simple as a grenade with its pin pulled and handle held down by the weight of a corpse; once the corpse is raised, the grenade explodes. Bombs and artillery shells are also used as IEDs. Such weapons may be exploded remotely by wireless detonators in the form of garage door openers and two-way radios or infrared motion sensors. More powerful explosives and even shaped charges can be used to attack armored vehicles. Casualty totals are one way to judge the effectiveness of a military operation, and growing casualties from IEDs in the 1980s and 1990s induced the Israeli Army to withdraw from southern Lebanon.

SPENCER C. TUCKER

Iraqi civilians and police officers examine the destruction wrought by a car bomb detonated in Baghdad on April 14, 2005. The attack was aimed at the Iraqi police force, but only 2 of 18 casualties were police officers. (U.S. Department of Defense)

See also
Antitank Weapons; Iraqi Insurgency

References
Crippen, James B. *Improvised Explosive Devices (IED)*. New York: CRC Press, 2007.
DeForest, M. J. *Principles of Improvised Explosive Devices*. Boulder, CO: Paladin, 1984.
Tucker, Stephen. *Terrorist Explosive Sourcebook: Countering Terrorist Use of Improvised Explosive Devices*. Boulder, CO: Paladin, 2005.

Infantry Fighting Vehicles, Iraqi

Iraq utilized mainly Soviet- and Warsaw Pact–manufactured infantry fighting vehicles from the 1980s through the early 2000s. Infantry fighting vehicles (IFVs) are used chiefly to transport soldiers, but IFVs differ from armored personnel carriers (APCs) because they have heavy armaments ranging from cannon to mortars to missiles. IFVs are usually assigned to armored or mechanized divisions.

In the Iraqi Army under the regime of Saddam Hussein, each armored division typically had one mechanized brigade that included IFVs and APCs. In addition, each mechanized division had one to two mechanized brigades. In 1980, at the beginning of the Iran-Iraq War, Iraq had six armored divisions and two mechanized divisions, as well as a number of independent armored and mechanized brigades. By the time of the 1991 Persian Gulf War, Iraq had more than 2,000 IFVs in addition to some 2,000 armored scout and reconnaissance vehicles in six armored and three mechanized regular divisions and three armored and six mechanized Republican Guard divisions. During the 2003 Iraq War, the country had approximately 1,000 IFVs, divided among six armored and four mechanized divisions, with a number of mechanized brigades assigned to Republican Guard divisions.

The main IFVs used by the Iraqi Army in its succession of conflicts were the BMP (*boyevaya mashina pekhoty*, Russian for "fighting vehicle for infantry") series BMP-1 and BMP-2, produced by the Soviet Union. The BMP-1 was in many ways the first true IFV, and it quickly gained in popularity after it was introduced in the 1960s. While many variations were produced, the basic BMP-1 had a crew of three and could carry eight soldiers. It was armed with a 73-millimeter (mm) recoilless cannon, an antitank guided missile system, and a 7.62-mm machine gun. The vehicle's armor was designed to withstand the heavy .50-caliber machine guns of the United States, as well as 20-mm cannon. It had an operational range of 300–375 miles and a top speed of 40 miles per hour (mph). It was also amphibious, with a speed through water of 4.3 to 5 miles per hour. During the 1973 Yom Kippur (Ramadan) War between Israel and an alliance of Arab states backing Egypt and Syria, the BMP-1 proved tough and reliable, and it was able to traverse areas where APCs and other armored vehicles became bogged down.

The rear of the BMP-1 was more vulnerable than the front because the armor was lighter there. The IFV was also prone to heavy damage from land mines on its left side, a flaw that was discovered during the Soviet occupation of Afghanistan (1979–1988), as well as the Iran-Iraq War. The BMP-1 was also difficult to operate in hot desert climates because it did not have an air conditioning system. This compelled crew members to leave the IFV's hatches open, increasing its vulnerability to small-arms fire.

To address these problems and update the design of the vehicle, the Soviets introduced the BMP-2. Production began in 1980. The new version of the popular IFV had a smaller main weapon, a 30-mm automatic cannon, but it also had its predecessor's antitank missile and machine gun. The new weaponry provided the IFV with an effective defense against helicopters. The BMP-2's speed and range were very similar to the older model's, but it had an improved engine and better armor. The BMP-2 also had a crew of three, but only carried seven troops because of a reconfiguration of the crew seating (the result of an effort to make the crew less vulnerable to injury from land mines).

Iraq began purchasing the BMPs in the early 1980s and had approximately 1,800 by the time of the Persian Gulf War. Iraq designed two upgrades for its BMPs. The first, dubbed the Saddam I, added additional armor. Before it entered production, the Saddam II was introduced. It had additional armor and was used mainly by Republican Guard units. Iraq also modified several dozen BMP-1s to serve as battlefield ambulances.

Iraq also acquired a large number of Soviet- and Warsaw Pact–produced BRDMs (*boyevaya razvedyvatelnaya dozornaya mashina*, Russian for "combat patrol and reconnaissance vehicle"). The amphibious BRDMs were primarily reconnaissance vehicles but were capable of carrying up to four passengers. There were several models, but most were armed with a heavy 14.5-mm machine gun and a lighter 7.62-mm machine gun. Some models had antitank missiles or surface-to-air missile systems. Iraq used a model that had a 23-mm cannon. Most of the vehicles had a crew of four, but Iraq purchased a Czech variation of the BRDM, known as the OT-65, that had a smaller crew of either two or three, depending on the model, and could carry a four-man deployable reconnaissance team. The vehicles had a range of 470 miles and a top speed of 55 mph (road); water range was 75 miles at a top speed of 5.5 mph. At the start of the Persian Gulf War, Iraq had approximately 1,200–1,300 BRDMs.

Iraq's IFVs performed well against its adversaries during the 1980–1988 Iran-Iraq War. However, in Iraq's two conflicts against U.S.-led coalitions, the Western IFVs proved vastly superior. U.S. forces used the M-2 and M-3 Bradley fighting vehicles, while the British used the Warrior IFV, and the French used the AMX-10. These IFVs generally had better communications capabilities, speed, and armaments. Iraqi IFV antitank guided missiles proved largely ineffective against coalition armor because of a combination of poor tactics and inferior weaponry. The average date at which coalition armored units, including both tanks and IFVs, were introduced was 1974, while among the Iraqi systems, the

Kuwaiti soldiers sit beside an Iraqi BMP-2 infantry fighting vehicle captured during Operation DESERT STORM in 1991. (U.S. Department of Defense)

average introduction date was 1964, giving the coalition forces a clear technological edge.

Among U.S. mechanized forces, the Bradleys actually destroyed more enemy armor, IFVs, and APCs than did the main battle tanks of the United States. Iraqi tactics also put their IFVs at considerable risk. Iraqi IFVs and other armored units lacked the autonomy of command and freedom of action that were common among their coalition opponents. This constrained offensive action. In addition, when coalition forces placed tanks or IFVs in defensive positions, they dug pits and placed the bodies of vehicles below the surface, creating a very low silhouette. In contrast, Iraqi practice was simply to place sand or earth around the armored units without affecting their silhouette. Iraqi minefields and antitank obstacles were also poorly deployed and did little to deter offensive action by coalition armor.

The coalition IFVs also had better air support, and significant numbers of Iraqi IFVs were destroyed in air strikes. For instance, on March 2, 1991, U.S. attack helicopters were able to destroy 49 IFVs in strikes on a Republican Guard division (the attacks also destroyed 32 main battle tanks). Large numbers of Iraqi IFVs were also destroyed in engagements with coalition main battle tanks, supported by IFVs. For example, on February 26, 1991, 9 M-1 tanks and 11 Bradleys destroyed 37 Iraqi tanks and 32 IFVs and APCs in one engagement. By the next day, the U.S. VII Corps had destroyed 1,350 Iraqi tanks and more than 1,200 IFVs and APCs, with the loss of only 36 of its armored vehicles. Approximately half of Iraq's IFVs were destroyed in the Persian Gulf War, by either combat or self-destruction by retreating Iraqi forces.

In the immediate aftermath of the 1991 conflict, Iraqi armor and IFV units played important roles in suppressing the Shiite uprising in the southern areas of the country. They were also used effectively against Kurdish forces in the north. However, United Nations (UN) sanctions precluded the purchase of new IFVs as well as spare parts or upgrades for the existing fleets of vehicles. Consequently, Iraq's IFV capabilities were seriously degraded, as were its other military resources.

During the 2003 Iraq War, Iraqi IFVs were not used extensively in offensive action. Instead, the vehicles were mainly utilized in static defensive positions and to move troops to new positions. Meanwhile, coalition IFVs were frequently used to make raids into urban areas and to secure positions. During the campaign, coalition armored units made some of the quickest advances in modern warfare, while Iraqi armor continued to be used in a defensive fashion. As was the case in the Persian Gulf War, Iraqi IFVs were highly vulnerable to coalition airpower and proved inferior against coalition armored units. By the time U.S. forces reached Baghdad in April 2003, Iraqi resistance had begun to transition to guerrilla-style insurgency tactics.

While the majority of Iraqi IFVs were destroyed during the 2003 invasion, the new Iraqi government has begun to acquire an updated version of the BMP-1 as its main IFV. Iraqi security forces have about 450 of the BMPs (including about 300 older models). Iraq has also acquired new versions of the BRDM-2. The new BRDMs, produced by Bulgaria, have twin 14.5-mm machine guns and updated armor protection. The IFVs and armored scout vehicles have enhanced the operational capabilities of the Iraqi Army, but remain vulnerable to roadside bombs and mines.

TOM LANSFORD

See also

Armored Warfare, Persian Gulf and Iraq Wars; BMP-1 Series Infantry Fighting Vehicles; DESERT STORM, Operation, Coalition Ground Forces; IRAQI FREEDOM, Operation, Coalition Ground Forces

References

Bacevich, Andrew J., and Efraim Inbar, eds. *The Gulf War of 1991 Reconsidered*. Portland, OR: Frank Cass, 2003.

Biddle, Stephen. *Military Power: Explaining Victory and Defeat in Modern Battle*. Princeton, NJ: Princeton University Press, 2004.

Cordesman, Anthony H. *The Iraq War: Strategy, Tactics, and Military Lessons*. Westport, CT: Praeger, 2003.

McNab, Chris, and Hunter Keeter. *Tools of Violence: Guns, Tanks and Dirty Bombs*. Oxford, UK: Osprey, 2008.

Zucchino, David. *Thunder Run: The Armored Strike to Capture Baghdad*. New York: Grove, 2004.

INFINITE REACH, **Operation**
Event Date: August 20, 1998

Retaliatory U.S. bombing raid on targets in Afghanistan and Sudan on August 20, 1998. The raids, which took place virtually simultaneously, were carried out by sea-based Tomahawk cruise missiles launched from 10 American warships and 5 submarines operating in the Red and Arabian seas. President Bill Clinton ordered the missile attacks (code-named Operation INFINITE REACH) in retaliation for the nearly simultaneous car bombings of the U.S. embassies in Nairobi, Kenya, and Dar es Salaam, Tanzania, on August 7, 1998. The two blasts all but destroyed both embassy compounds and killed a total of 257 people, including 12 Americans. An additional 5,000 were wounded.

Within just a few days of the embassy bombings, the Clinton administration concluded, with the help of foreign intelligence sources, that the terrorist attacks had been perpetrated by Al Qaeda, then headquartered in Afghanistan near the Pakistani border. National security officials also believed that Al Qaeda leader Osama bin Laden was the likely mastermind of the deadly explosions. To send a strong and unambiguous statement that the United States would not shrink in the wake of terrorism, Clinton ordered attacks against targets in Afghanistan—likely to be housing Al Qaeda terrorists and bin Laden himself—and against a suspected chemical weapons factory in Sudan that allegedly had links to bin Laden's network.

U.S. naval assets fired 70–75 Tomahawk cruise missiles into six terrorist training facilities located in and around Jalalabad and Khost, Afghanistan. The attacks were designed to coincide with a meeting that bin Laden had allegedly convened for August 20. Bin Laden, who was presumed to have been in one of the facilities, escaped unharmed.

Estimates of the number of deaths in the Afghanistan attacks vary widely. While the U.S. government claimed that 20 people died, Pakistani and Afghan journalists asserted at least 34 were killed in the raid. After the attack, the Central Intelligence Agency (CIA) learned that bin Laden had left the area only a few hours before the missiles fell. Afghanistan's Taliban government, which had given refuge to bin Laden and his followers, bitterly denounced the attacks, which also caused an anti-American stir in other Muslim nations.

Far more controversial was the cruise missile attack against the suspected chemical weapons plant in Khartoum, Sudan. The plant (known as El Shifa Pharmaceutical Industries), which the Sudanese government insisted was a pharmaceutical manufacturing center, was suspected of having links to Al Qaeda and the National Islamic Front, which was then operational in Sudan. U.S. intelligence sources alleged that the pharmaceutical factory was a cover for far more sinister purposes, namely the production of a potent nerve gas that could be easily weaponized or employed in terror attacks against civilians.

Approximately 13 Tomahawk cruise missiles hit the El Shifa factory, causing heavy damage. The Sudanese government reported one person dead and seven people injured in the attack, which it roundly condemned. The Sudanese insisted that the bombed plant had no chemicals capable of being used as weapons. Further, it claimed that the El Shifa facility was the nation's principal drug-manufacturing factory, and that its loss would cause a serious crisis in Sudan's health care system. Since the attack, many sources have suggested that the United States erred in linking the plant to chemical weapons and utilized weak intelligence. There was no clear link between bin Laden and anyone associated with El Shifa.

Sudan demanded an immediate apology from Washington, which was not forthcoming. The United States claimed that it did not know that the bombed plant was manufacturing drugs, a claim that was later called into question. Several days after the attack, thousands of Sudanese gathered in Khartoum to protest the U.S. bombing; Sudan's president, Omar Hassan Ahmad al-Bashir, personally led the anti-American demonstration. Since then, some in the United States continued to insist that the El Shifa plant was being used for nefarious purposes, despite evidence that the plant may not have been involved in the making of chemical weapons and was not linked to Al Qaeda or other terrorist groups.

For detractors of the United States—and of President Bill Clinton—the timing of the cruise missile attacks was more than curious, coming just three days after Clinton had been forced to admit that he had indeed had a sexual relationship with former White House intern Monica Lewinsky. The Lewinsky affair had endured since January 1998 and, until August, Clinton had maintained his innocence. He was later impeached but acquitted. Some argue that Clinton used the high-profile cruise missile attacks to deflect attention away from the scandal. The allegations that the administration tried to distract the public were also fueled by a 1997 movie titled *Wag the Dog,* in which an American president embroiled in a sex scandal employs a Hollywood producer to fabricate a war with Albania to take attention off his own personal problems.

PAUL G. PIERPAOLI JR.

See also

Afghanistan; Al Qaeda; Bin Laden, Osama; Chemical Weapons and Warfare; Clinton, William Jefferson; Dar es Salaam, Bombing of U.S. Embassy; Missiles, Cruise; Nairobi, Kenya, Bombing of U.S. Embassy; Sudan; Terrorism

References

Friedman, Thomas L. *Longitudes and Attitudes: The World in the Age of Terrorism.* New York: Anchor Books, 2003.

Halberstam, David. *War in a Time of Peace: Bush, Clinton, and the Generals.* New York: Scribner, 2001.

Hyland, William. *Clinton's World: Remaking American Foreign Policy.* Westport, CT: Praeger, 1999.

Rubin, Barry, and Judith Colp Rubin, eds. *Anti-American Terrorism and the Middle East.* New York: Oxford University Press, 2002.

Wright, Lawrence. *The Looming Tower: Al-Qaeda and the Road to 9/11.* New York: Vintage Books, 2007.

INSTANT THUNDER, Plan
Event Date: 1990

Initial air campaign plan developed in response to the Iraqi invasion of Kuwait on August 2, 1990, providing an initial offensive option for the theater commander, General H. Norman Schwarzkopf, if Iraqi forces continued on into Saudi Arabia. INSTANT THUNDER served as the conceptual foundation for the air offensive during Operation DESERT STORM. The plan was developed by United States Air Force (USAF) staff planners in Washington, D.C., in an organization generally referred to as CHECKMATE.

Formal planning began on August 8, 1990, and evolved over the course of the month. This was a controversial move as many in the U.S. military were determined to avoid a situation similar to the Vietnam War in which, they perceived, too many planning and operational decisions were made in Washington rather that by the theater commander and his staff.

However, in this case, theater commander General Schwarzkopf specifically requested this support. He believed that his component air staff under Lieutenant General Charles A. Horner would initially be swamped with the details of rapidly deploying and preparing the large Central Command Air Force (CENTAF) for combat operations. This situation was compounded by the fact that Schwarzkopf had designated Horner as the commander of the U.S. Central Command (CENTCOM) forward element, meaning that Horner would be the senior American in the theater and would be responsible for the disposition and logistical support for all of the U.S. forces arriving in the region. Schwarzkopf and the national leadership desired a strategic air campaign plan that could be implemented rapidly if needed, and that could become the core of a full CENTCOM campaign plan when time and circumstances allowed.

The USAF leadership assigned the task of developing the campaign plan to Air Force colonel Mike Warden, deputy director for war-fighting concepts on the Air Staff. Warden had actually directed his staff to begin a study of the Iraqi situation before being given the assignment, and he based the planning effort on a strategic concept for the use of air power that he had been developing. Warden's concept viewed a potential enemy as a system of centers of gravity that he described as a series of concentric rings, with the most important centers of gravity in the innermost ring. In this analytical construct, the inner ring of a country was its leadership, which could be directly attacked or specifically influenced by the targets that were attacked. Warden identified the second ring as essential industries, the third as transportation or infrastructure systems, the fourth as the population center and food sources, and the fifth, outermost ring as the fielded military forces.

Warden argued that traditional military plans and operations focused on the enemy military system, but the real key to victory was the mind of the enemy commander. Although the ring model was not formally used to explain the plan, Warden's planners used it to develop lists of target sets that were based on the concept, and the plan was presented to the national leadership and to Schwarzkopf as an offensively oriented approach to defeating the Iraqi state and forcing a withdrawal from Kuwait. The name INSTANT THUNDER was selected to differentiate the approach from the gradual escalatory effort of the Vietnam War, called Operation ROLLING THUNDER. The plan was accepted as an initial approach, although it was criticized for not including enough attacks on Iraqi ground forces in Kuwait.

INSTANT THUNDER was passed on to CENTAF planners, and it ultimately became the core of the air component within the DESERT STORM campaign plan. Changes and additions to the plan included the substantial expansion of missions against Iraqi ground forces and support for coalition forces during the ground offensive, which began in February 1991.

JEROME V. MARTIN

See also

DESERT SHIELD, Operation; DESERT STORM, Operation; DESERT STORM, Operation, Coalition Air Campaign; Horner, Charles; Schwarzkopf, H. Norman, Jr.; United States Air Force, Persian Gulf War; United States Central Command

References

Cohen, Eliot A., and Thomas A. Keaney. *Gulf War Air Power Survey: Summary Report.* Washington, DC: United States Department of the Air Force, 1993.

Hallion, Richard P. *Storm over Iraq: Air Power and the Gulf War.* Washington, DC: Smithsonian Institution Press, 1997.

Mann, Edward C., III. *Thunder and Lightning: Desert Storm and the Airpower Debates.* Maxwell Air Force Base, AL: Air University Press, 1995.

Murray, Williamson. *Air War in the Persian Gulf.* Baltimore: Nautical and Aviation Publishing Company of America, 1995.

Putney, Diane T. *Airpower Advantage: Planning the Gulf War Air Campaign, 1989–1991.* Washington, DC: Air Force History and Museums Program, 2004.

Interceptor Body Armor

A form of body armor employed by U.S. military forces, first introduced in 1998. It has been used extensively in Operations ENDURING FREEDOM and IRAQI FREEDOM. Manufactured by Point Blank Body Armor, Inc., Interceptor body armor replaced the Personnel Armor System for Ground Troops (PASGT) and is considerably more effective in protecting troops than traditional bulletproof outerwear. Interceptor body armor is considered a personnel protection "system," the individual parts of which work together to provide superior protection from bullets, shrapnel, and other projectiles.

The system is comprised of an outer tactical vest (OTV) and two small-arms protective inserts (SAPI). The outer vest and the inserts are made of finely woven Kevlar KM2 fibers, which are both heat and bullet resistant. The armor was tested to be able to withstand and stop a 9-millimeter (mm) 124-grain full metal jacket bullet (FMJ) traveling at a velocity of 1,400 feet per second. The system will stop a variety of slower-moving bullets and shrapnel fragments, and it features removable inserts for shoulder, neck, throat, and groin protection. The two SAPIs that may be added to the front or back of the outer vest significantly increase the system's protective capacity. Made of boron carbide ceramic, the inserts can stop 7.62-mm NATO rifle round with a muzzle velocity of 2,750 feet per second.

Interceptor body armor also features numerous configurations that mimic existing backpacks and carrying systems, so soldiers can tailor their body armor for specific tasks or missions. The body armor system is available in several exterior patterns, including coyote brown, traditional woodland camouflage, three-color desert camouflage, and the newer universal camouflage pattern. When worn with the two inserts, the total weight of the armor system is 16.4 pounds (the outer vest weighs 8.4 pounds, while the two inserts weigh 4 pounds each). This is markedly less than the Interceptor's predecessor, the PSAGT, which weighed in at a hefty 25.1 pounds. Nearly 10 pounds lighter, Interceptor body armor also allows soldiers considerably more freedom to maneuver. More recently, SAPIs designed for side protection have also been introduced. Heavier than the standard inserts, they weigh in at 7.1 pounds each. A complete armor system costs $1,585.

During the Iraq War, many infantry soldiers complained that Interceptor body armor was too cumbersome and too stout for the generally lightly-armed Iraqi insurgents they were battling. Some argued that they were unable to pursue the enemy with the full armor system and the many supplies and arms they had to carry. On the other hand, U.S. troops who principally rode in vehicles praised the system for its ability to protect against improvised explosive devices (IEDs) and ambushes.

Interceptor body armor has not been without its problems and detractors, however. In May 2005, the U.S. Marine Corps ordered the recall of more than 5,000 OTVs because they allegedly were unable to stop a 9-mm bullet, which was the requirement upon manufacture. The problems soon received press attention, and in November 2005 the Marines recalled an additional 10,342 OTVs because ballistics tests had proven their inadequacy against 9-mm bullets. The problems with the armor system led a sizable number of American troops to purchase their own civilian body armor, a development that deeply troubled the Pentagon. Furthermore, many soldiers and Marines refused to wear the additional side inserts because of their added weight, making them more vulnerable to injury or death. One Marine Corps study has suggested that 43 percent of those marines killed by torso wounds may have been saved had Interceptor body armor been more effective.

The problems with Interceptor armor received high-profile media coverage, and the U.S. Congress launched several investigations into its manufacturing and deployment. In May 2006, the U.S. Army announced that it would be sponsoring a competition for a new body-armor system that would replace the Interceptor body armor. In the meantime, numerous improvements and additions have been made to the existing body armor, including the use of an entirely new and improved outer tactical vest. In September 2006, the Marine Corps announced that its personnel would begin receiving modular tactical vests in lieu of the Interceptor OTV, made by Protective Products International. The controversies surrounding Interceptor body armor proved to be a public-relations fiasco for the Pentagon, raising claims that the Department of Defense was not adequately protecting U.S. soldiers.

PAUL G. PIERPAOLI JR.

See also

Improvised Explosive Devices

References

Savage, Robert C. Woosnam. *Brassey's Book of Body Armor.* Dulles, VA: Potomac Books, 2002.

Solis, William M. *Defense Logistics: Army and Marine Corps Individual Body Armor System Issues.* Washington, DC: U.S. Government Printing Office, 2007.

International Atomic Energy Agency

International organization first established in 1957 under the aegis of the United Nations (UN) and charged with harnessing and controlling the use of atomic energy and technology throughout the world. The mission of the International Atomic Energy Agency (IAEA) includes the control of nuclear proliferation. The IAEA is headquartered in Vienna, Austria, although it maintains laboratories and research centers in Monaco, Italy, and Seibersdorf, Austria. With a total budget of more than 285 million euros ($443 million), the IAEA's secretariat is composed of more than 2,200 professionals, in many different fields, representing some 90 nations.

Closely affiliated with the UN, the agency is an independent, stand-alone organization, although it does provide the UN with annual reports on its activities and consults with the organization on an ad hoc basis as need arises. After the 1986 disaster at the Soviet-built Chernobyl nuclear reactor, the IAEA broadened its programs to include more safety measures aimed at civilian-oriented nuclear facilities.

The IAEA played a significant role in weapons inspections in Iraq, particularly after the 1991 Persian Gulf War and prior to the March 2003 operation, IRAQI FREEDOM. After Swedish diplomat Hans Blix became head of the IAEA in 1981, he led several inspections of Iraq's nuclear facility at Osiraq, which was destroyed in an Israeli bombing raid later that year. Blix had contended that the reactor was being developed for peaceful purposes. After that time, the agency made numerous trips into Iraq to search for illegal nuclear weapons programs. Blix complimented the Iraqis on their cooperation, but also condemned them when they refused to allow access to sites and records. Blix left the IAEA in 1997 but came out of retirement in 2000 to lead the ill-fated United Nations Monitoring, Verification and Inspection Commission (UNMOVIC), which was charged with determining the extent of Iraq's development of weapons of mass destruction (WMDs), including nuclear weapons, prior to the March 2003 Iraq War.

In 1997, Egyptian diplomat Mohamed ElBaradei became director-general of the IAEA. ElBaradei's tenure has not been without controversy, especially in the lead up to the invasion of Iraq in March 2003, which was ostensibly launched to rid Iraq of WMDs. In 2002, ElBaradei, working in tandem with Blix's commission, visited Iraq with weapons inspectors to hunt for signs of an Iraqi nuclear weapons program. The results of the inspections were inconclusive and did not unearth any hard evidence of an Iraqi nuclear program. ElBaradei strongly opposed an invasion of Iraq based on the presumed presence of WMDs. Just prior to the coalition invasion, ElBaredei informed the UN Security Council that Anglo-American claims that Iraq had tried to purchase enriched uranium from Niger were not credible; indeed, many experts believed that a forged document was involved. The story had been used by both President George W. Bush and Secretary of State Colin L. Powell as a justification for the Iraq War.

In 2005, when ElBaradei's second term was set to expire, he received sufficient support among IAEA members nations to begin a third term, which the United States vigorously protested. Washington argued that it had always favored a two-term limit for heads of any international agency or organization. Many have

posited, however, that the American resistance to a third ElBaradei term stemmed from his unwillingness to support the American line against Iraq and, later, Iran. Despite the American opposition, ElBaradei began a third term in December 2005.

Since then, ElBaradei and the IAEA have been criticized for their handling of Iran's emerging nuclear program. Tehran insists that its program is aimed only at the development of nuclear energy. Numerous Western nations, including the United States, however, believe that Tehran intends to produce nuclear weapons, and Washington has repeatedly charged ElBaradei with being far too lenient toward the Iranians. In his defense, ElBaradei has stated that the IAEA is closely monitoring the situation in Iran and will step up its efforts to ascertain the true nature and extent of the Iranian nuclear program. In October 2007, the IAEA and ElBaradei were named corecipients of the Nobel Peace Prize for their work.

PAUL G. PIERPAOLI JR.

See also

Blix, Hans; ElBaradei, Muhammad Mustafa; Nuclear Weapons, Iraq's Potential for Building; United Nations Special Commission; United Nations Weapons Inspectors; Weapons of Mass Destruction

References

Pearson, Graham S. *The Search for Iraq's Weapons of Mass Destruction: Inspection, Verification, and Non-Proliferation.* London: Palgrave Macmillan, 2005.

Sagan, Scott, and Kenneth Waltz. *The Spread of Nuclear Weapons: A Debate.* New York: Norton, 1997.

International Emergency Economic Powers Act

Federal law that grants presidents the power to identify and respond to any unusual or extraordinary threat originating outside the United States by confiscating property and prohibiting fiscal transactions under Title 50, Chapter 35, Sections 1701–1707, United States. These confiscations and controls can be applied to individuals, groups, organizations, and foreign nations.

Congress passed the International Emergency Economic Powers Act (IEEPA) on October 28, 1977. As Public Law 95-223, 91 Stat. 1626, this act falls under the provisions of the National Emergencies Act (NEA), passed in 1976, which means that an emergency declared under the act is subject to annual renewal and may be repealed at any time by a joint congressional resolution. The act is a further clarification of the Trading with the Enemy Act, which had provided a source of both presidential emergency authority and wartime authority.

There are two specific provisions contained in Section 1701 of the IEEPA. First, it authorizes the president to address "any unusual and extraordinary threat, either in whole or substantial part outside the nation, to the national security, foreign policy, or economy of the United States, if the President declares a national emergency with respect to such threat." This means that a president can block financial transactions and freeze assets to deal with the threat. If the country is attacked, the president can also confiscate property connected with a country, group, or person that has been accused of aiding in the attack. Second, presidential authority "to which a national emergency has been declared may not be exercised for any other purpose" and "any exercise of such authorities to deal with any new threat shall be based on a new declaration of national emergency which must be with respect to such threat."

The origins and evolution of IEEPA date back to the Great Depression. In 1933, when President Franklin D. Roosevelt assumed office, his New Deal legislation implied that the president had the power to declare emergencies without limiting their scope and length of time. The Roosevelt administration claimed that there was no need to cite pertinent statutes and that it did not have to report to Congress. Subsequent presidents followed this line of thinking, including President Harry S. Truman in his response to the nationwide steel strike during the Korean War, until the U.S. Supreme Court in *Youngstown Sheet & Tube Co. v. Sawyer* (1952) limited what a president could do in such an emergency. The court did not, however, limit the power of emergency declaration itself. Shortly after the Vietnam War, a 1973 Senate investigation revealed that four declared emergencies were still in existence: the 1933 gold issue; the 1950 Korean War emergency; the 1970 postal workers strike; and the 1971 response to rampant inflation. The NEA officially terminated these emergencies in 1976, and the IEEPA was passed the next year to restore executive emergency powers, albeit in a limited fashion and with oversight by Congress.

The first time the IEEPA was used was during the Jimmy Carter administration in reaction to the Iranian hostage crisis of 1979–1981. Since then, the IEEPA has been invoked by presidents against Iraq (1990–2004), for its invasion of Kuwait; Libya (1986–2004), for sponsoring terrorism; Liberia (2001–2004), for human rights violations; Panama (1988–1990), for the military coup by Manuel Noriega; South Africa (1985–1991), for its apartheid policy; Zimbabwe (since 2003), for undermining democratic institutions; North Korea (since 2008), for the risk of the proliferation of weapon-usable fission material, and other countries for supporting terrorism, including the former Taliban regime in Afghanistan.

Some of the terror organizations and terrorists targeted by the IEEPA are the Egyptian Islamic Jihad, Al Qaeda, the Abu Sayyaf group, the Taliban, Ayman al-Zawahiri, Abu Abdullah, and Osama bin Laden. One of the more notable cases involving an American was in 1983, when financier Marc Rich was accused and convicted of violating the act by trading in Iranian oil during the Iranian hostage crisis. Rich was later pardoned by President Bill Clinton.

Over the years, new restrictions on certain powers have amended the IEEPA. Presidents no longer have the authority to regulate or prohibit personal communications that do not involve the transfer of items of value. Presidents cannot regulate or prohibit the transfer of articles for humanitarian aid unless it is deemed such transfers would interfere with the ability to deal with the emergency or endanger U.S. military forces. Nor can a president regulate or prohibit the importation from any country or exportation to any country informational materials such as records, photographs, compact discs, CD-ROMs, artworks, and publications.

When the act was first passed, presidents used it to order sanctions directed at specific nations. Since then, presidents have used the IEEPA to shut down terrorist organizations and to cut off aid and support to individuals. One recent case occurred in 2006, when Javed Iqbal was arrested and charged with conspiracy for violating the act by airing material produced by Al-Manar Television in New York City during the Israel-Lebanon conflict that summer. The IEEPA has taken on greater importance as well as more scrutiny in light of the Global War on Terror.

CHARLES F. HOWLETT

See also
Al-Manar Television; Al Qaeda; Bin Laden, Osama; Global War on Terror; Iraq, Sanctions on; Taliban

References
Carter, Barry E. *International Economic Sanctions.* Cambridge: Cambridge University Press, 1988.
Malloy, Michael P. *United States Economic Sanctions: Theory and Practice.* Netherlands: Kluwer Law International, 2001.
Patterson, Thomas G., et al. *A History of American Foreign Relations since 1895.* Boston: Houghton Mifflin, 2005.

International Security Assistance Force

Multinational military security and assistance mission to Afghanistan, currently led by the North Atlantic Treaty Organization (NATO) and formed by the United Nations (UN) Security Council on December 20, 2001. The International Security Assistance Force (ISAF) is composed of a military headquarters, an air task force, regional commands, forward support bases, and Provincial Reconstruction Teams (PRTs). Its mission is to help the Afghan central government extend its authority throughout the provinces, mentor and train the Afghan National Army and Afghan National Police, conduct military operations in coordination with Afghan security forces to stabilize and secure the country, assist the Afghan government in disarming illegal militias, support Afghan counternarcotics programs, and provide humanitarian assistance when needed.

In December 2001, two months after the United States and coalition forces began Operation ENDURING FREEDOM to destroy Al Qaeda and topple the Taliban government in Afghanistan, the international community held a conference in Bonn, Germany, to assist Afghanistan in creating a stable government and reconstructing the country. This international effort, known as the Bonn Agreement, included a military component. On December 20, 2001, the United Nations Security Council authorized the deployment of an International Security Assistance Force to operate in the Afghan capital at Kabul. Its mission was to assist with

Afghan National Army major Gul Akbar gives a cash payment to an Afghan farmer on November 17, 2009, at Forward Operating Base Wolverine in Zabul, Afghanistan. The International Security Assistance Force was compensating farmers for using their land in support of Operation ENDURING FREEDOM. (U.S. Department of Defense)

stabilizing the country and to create conditions for the establishment of peace. The ISAF was not a United Nations force but rather an organization created by volunteer countries acting under the authority of the United Nations Security Council.

The United Kingdom headed the first ISAF rotation, from December 2001 to July 2002. Eighteen additional countries contributed troops, equipment, and other assets, bringing the initial number of troops to 5,000. According to the United Nations Security Council mandate, this force could only operate in Kabul. Turkey commanded ISAF II from July 2002 to January 2003. Germany, Canada, France, Turkey, and Italy each led a subsequent ISAF rotation, with each rotation lasting six months. In addition, the United Kingdom led a 10-month rotation from May 2006 to February 2007. U.S. lieutenant general Dan K. McNeill served as ISAF commander from February 2007 to May 2008, followed by General David D. McKiernan, another American, who took over as ISAF commander in June 2008. ISAF commanders coordinate their activities with the United Nations Assistance Mission in Afghanistan and other top coalition leaders.

One problem of the ISAF command arrangement was that each rotation lasted only six months, which required a constant search for another coalition partner to volunteer to lead the organization. Even with briefings and coordinated handovers from one command to the next, the new, incoming staff usually lacked sufficient knowledge or understanding of conditions in Afghanistan. This inexperience led to uneven transitions in programs and operations.

NATO finally provided the solution to the rotating ISAF headquarters problem. In April 2003, the North Atlantic Council authorized a peacekeeping force in Afghanistan, which would be responsible for the command, coordination, planning, and headquarters for ISAF. A permanent NATO command also allowed smaller coalition nations to participate more fully in what would become a multinational headquarters, since it was too difficult for them to lead a 1,700-strong ISAF staff on their own. NATO formally assumed command of the ISAF on August 11, 2003. Its primary mission was to focus on stabilization, reconstruction, and maintaining security in relatively quiet areas of Afghanistan, while U.S. forces concentrated on combat operations against insurgent forces as well as training the Afghan National Army.

In 2003, ISAF headquarters and coalition troops consisted of 5,882 personnel from 32 nations and still operated exclusively in Kabul. In October 2003, however, the UN Security Council approved the expansion of ISAF into other areas of Afghanistan.

Estimated International Security Assistance Force (ISAF) Troop Strength (as of April 2009)

Country	Organization Affiliation	Troop Strength
Albania	NATO	140
Australia	None	1,090
Austria	EAPC	2
Azerbaijan	EAPC	90
Belgium	NATO	450
Bosnia and Herzegovina	None	2
Bulgaria	NATO	820
Canada	NATO	2,830
Croatia	NATO	280
Czech Republic	NATO	580
Denmark	NATO	700
Estonia	NATO	140
Finland	EAPC	110
France	NATO	2,780
Georgia	EAPC	1
Germany	NATO	3,465
Greece	NATO	140
Hungary	NATO	370
Iceland	NATO	8
Ireland	EAPC	7
Italy	NATO	2,350
Jordan	None	7
Latvia	NATO	160
Lithuania	NATO	200
Luxembourg	NATO	9
Macedonia	EAPC	170
Netherlands	NATO	1,770
New Zealand	None	150
Norway	NATO	490
Poland	NATO	1,590
Portugal	NATO	30
Romania	NATO	860
Singapore	None	20
Slovakia	NATO	230
Slovenia	NATO	70
Spain	NATO	780
Sweden	EAPC	290
Turkey	NATO	660
Ukraine	EAPC	10
United Arab Emirates	None	25
United Kingdom	NATO	8,300
United States	NATO	26,215
Total		58,391

The first extension was into the northern provinces. The joint civil-military Provincial Reconstruction Teams, which conducted reconstruction efforts and supported the expansion of the central Afghan government's authority into the provinces, provided the means to begin the expansion. The ISAF took control of the Kondoz PRT from Germany in December 2003. Soon after, the ISAF assumed control of four additional PRTs—in Mazar-e Sharif, Meymaneh, Fayzabad, and Baghlan. By October 2004, the ISAF became responsible for operations in the nine northern provinces.

Stage two of the expansion occurred in the western provinces in May 2006. The ISAF took control of the Herat and Farah PRTs as well as a forward support base in Herat. The ISAF opened new PRTs in Chaghcharan and Qala-i Now in September 2006. The northern and western provinces constituted about half of Afghanistan's territory, and were the most stable and secure areas. The expansion of the ISAF into the violent southern and eastern provinces proved more difficult. Beginning in July 2006, the ISAF took responsibility for the volatile southern provinces, including the heart of the Taliban-led insurgency in the Helmand, Kandahar, and Uruzgan provinces. At this time, the number of ISAF forces increased from 10,000 to 20,000 troops. The ISAF completed the final phase of the expansion in October 2006. As of August 2008, the ISAF commands 52,700 troops in Afghanistan, including troops from the United States; operates 26 PRTs; and represents the contributions of 40 nations. An additional 19,000 U.S. troops operate independently from the ISAF along the Afghan-Pakistan border.

While the ISAF commander is headquartered in Kabul, his chain of command extends back through multiple headquarters in Europe. The ISAF commander reports to the Allied Joint Force Command Headquarters Brunssum (JFC HQ Brunssum) in the Netherlands and the joint force commander, currently in Germany. The joint force commander reports to the Supreme Headquarters Allied Powers Europe (SHAPE), located in Mons, Belgium. The distance of the chain of command and the differing rules governing how each of the various nations can engage in combat has often limited the effectiveness of ISAF operations. Some nations limit the kinds of engagements their troops may engage in, and some do not allow their troops to engage in combat operations at all. These national caveats hamper the effective use of coalition troops and shift the burden of heavy fighting to those nations with more freedom to conduct military operations, such as Canada, the United Kingdom, and the United States, among others. The constraints have been a constant source of tension between the NATO-led ISAF and the United States.

In addition to supplying headquarters personnel and combat forces for operations in Afghanistan, ISAF member nations contribute funding and equipment for the Afghan security forces. Slovenia, Hungary, and Latvia have provided small arms, mortars, and ammunition, while others, including Poland, Germany, and Romania, have donated uniforms and spare parts for weapons systems. Other nations have donated such military equipment as howitzers, tanks, aircraft, and helicopters. The ISAF currently participates in Task Force Phoenix, the military organization whose mission is to train the Afghan National Army and Afghan National Police by providing personnel for the headquarters and for the embedded mentoring and training teams that deploy with Afghan army units.

Since the ISAF has taken control of most military operations in Afghanistan, the level of violence has risen considerably in the southern and eastern provinces, while areas in the north and west remain stable. The Taliban and other enemy forces have adopted such guerrilla and terrorist tactics as ambushes, roadside bombs, and suicide bombs in the south and east. For example, roadside bombs increased from 60 detonations in 2003 to 1,256 in 2007. Since 2006, the worst fighting has taken place in the southern province of Helmand, where British and Canadian troops serve.

In December 2007, the Afghan National Army, supported by ISAF troops, engaged in several days of hard fighting to liberate Musa Qala from Taliban control.

In more stable areas, ISAF has contributed to reconstruction efforts, building infrastructure such as roads and bridges as well as supporting provincial and local governments. As of April 2008, over 5,600 civil-military reconstruction projects have been completed. While the economy is improving in Afghanistan, the population's reliance on growing poppy for the illegal narcotic drug trade in opium and for heroin production continues to be one of the more difficult problems to solve. There is ample evidence that illegal drug money is helping to fund the Taliban insurgency, but other evidence shows deep involvement in the drug trade by associates and relatives of the current Afghan government. The initial American strategy in Afghanistan of the Barack Obama administration was to target individuals higher up in the drug trade as well as to destroy crops.

While some Afghans do support the Taliban, a December 2007 poll suggested that the population supports international involvement in Afghanistan, including the presence of international military forces and the reconstruction efforts of the coalition.

LISA M. MUNDEY

See also

Afghan National Army; Afghanistan; Bonn Agreement; North Atlantic Treaty Organization; Provincial Reconstruction Teams, Afghanistan; Taliban Insurgency, Afghanistan; Task Force Phoenix

References

Combat Studies Institute Contemporary Operations Study Group. *A Different Kind of War: The United States Army Operation Enduring Freedom (OEF), September 2001–September 2005.* Fort Leavenworth, KS: Combat Studies Institute Press, 2009.

Jalali, Ali A. "The Future of Afghanistan." *Parameters* (Spring 2006): 4–19.

Maloney, Sean M. "Afghanistan Four Years On: An Assessment." *Parameters* (Autumn 2005): 21–32.

———. *Enduring the Freedom: A Rogue Historian in Afghanistan.* Washington, DC: Potomac Books, 2007.

Sundquist, Leah R. *NATO in Afghanistan: A Progress Report.* Carlisle Barracks, PA: U.S. Army War College, 2008.

Interrogation, Coercive

See Coercive Interrogation

Intifada, First

Start Date: December 1987
End Date: September 1993

A spontaneous protest movement by Palestinians against Israeli rule and an effort to establish a Palestinian state through a series of demonstrations, improvised attacks, and riots. The First Intifada (literally meaning "shaking off") began in December 1987 and ended in September 1993 with the signing of the Oslo Accords and the creation of the Palestinian National Authority (PNA).

The founding of Israel in 1948 created a situation in which Palestinians and citizens of the new Israeli state were attacked and evicted from their homes, and able to resettle only where the Israeli military permitted. Others were forced to become refugees. This basic reality would remain the most contentious issue in the region for decades to come. Palestinians hoped for a return to their land and property, but their rights were not recognized by Israel. Those active politically at first thought they could bring about the *awda,* or the return to their land, through armed struggle. They realized, however, that they could never defeat Israel by themselves and needed other Arab states to assist them. Pro-Palestinian sentiment was generally shared by other Arab nations and by the Arab world at large, and material and military support often followed. Palestinians had resisted the repressive measures of the 1950s and 1960s, but they were unable to change their circumstances. Israel's treatment of them became even worse later, especially with the ascendance of the Likud Party in Israel. Some Palestinians joined what was called the Movement of the Camps in the refugee areas in 1969 when, after the great Arab failure in the 1967 Six-Day War, it was believed that Palestinians must defend themselves through any means necessary. In the early 1970s and 1980s, as Palestinians experienced even poorer treatment, more property encroachment, and more difficulties, their leadership moved toward negotiation as a strategy. By the time of the intifada, most Palestinians had experienced or knew those who had experienced Israel's de jure or de facto draconian civil and criminal enforcement practices, including torture, summary executions, mass detentions, and the destruction of property and homes.

In 1987, strained relations between Palestinians and Israelis were pushed to the limit when, on October 1, Israeli soldiers ambushed and killed seven Palestinian men from Gaza alleged to have been members of the Palestinian terrorist organization Islamic Jihad. A few days later, an Israeli settler shot a Palestinian schoolgirl in the back. With violence against Israelis by Palestinians also on the increase elsewhere, a wider conflict may have been inevitable.

The tension only mounted as the year drew to a close. On December 4, an Israeli salesman was found murdered in Gaza. On December 6, a truck driven by the Israel Defense Forces (IDF) struck a van, killing its four Palestinian occupants. That same day, sustained and heavy violence involving several hundred Palestinians took place in the Jabalya refugee camp, where the four Palestinians who died in the traffic accident had lived. The unrest spread quickly and eventually involved other refugee camps. By the end of December, the violence had made its way to Jerusalem. The Israelis reacted with a heavy hand, firing at unarmed protesters, which only fanned the fires of Palestinian outrage. On December 22, 1987, the United Nations (UN) Security Council officially denounced the Israeli reaction to the unrest, which had taken the lives of scores of Palestinians.

Ignoring a pouring rain, Palestinian protesters, some with their faces covered in the traditional keffiyeh headdress, hurl rocks at Israel Defense Forces soldiers, not seen in this photograph. The confrontation took place in Nablus in the occupied West Bank on January 12, 1988. (AP/Wide World Photos)

The result of the escalating spiral of violence was the intifada, a series of Palestinian protests, demonstrations, and ad hoc attacks whose manifestations ranged from youths throwing rocks at Israeli troops to demonstrations by women's organizations. While the movement was quite spontaneous at first, a shadowy organization, the Unified Leadership of the Intifada, emerged, issuing directives via numbered statements. Along with a series of general strikes and boycotts, the demonstrations caused such disruption to the Israeli state that the government responded with military force. Heated tensions proved a hotbed for further violence, which led to increasingly violent reprisals on both sides. Some Palestinian boys and young men advanced from throwing rocks to throwing Molotov cocktails. Others simply burned tires and used spray paint to write graffiti of the intifada; merchants closed their stores, and Palestinians boycotted some Israeli goods and tried to produce their own. Israeli rules were such that the Palestinian flag and its colors were banned, so these were displayed by the demonstrators. In the meantime, Israeli defense minister Yitzhak Rabin exhorted the IDF to "break the bones" of demonstrators. Rabin's tactics resulted in more international condemnation and a worsening relationship with Washington, which had already been on the skids. Moshe Arens, who succeeded Rabin in the Ministry of Defense in 1990, seemed better able to understand both the root of

the uprising and the best ways of subduing it. Indeed, the number of Palestinians and Israelis killed declined during the period from 1990 to 1993. However, the intifada itself seemed to be running out of steam after 1990, perhaps because so many Palestinian men were in prison by then.

Despite continued violence on the part of Hamas (Islamic Resistance Movement), on September 13, 1993, Rabin, now prime minister, and Palestine Liberation Organization (PLO) chairman Yasser Arafat signed the historic Oslo Accords on the White House lawn. The accords, which brought both Rabin and Arafat the Nobel Peace Prize, called for a five-year transition period during which the Gaza Strip and the West Bank would be jointly controlled by Israel and the PNA, after which power would be turned over to the Palestinian people.

The First Intifada caused both civil destruction and humanitarian suffering, but it also produced gains for the Palestinian people before it was brought to an end. First, it solidified and brought into focus a clear national consciousness for the Palestinian people and made statehood a clear national objective. Second, it cast Israeli policies toward the Palestinian people, especially the killing of Palestinian children, in a very negative light on the world stage. Third, it was seen by some Israelis to clearly indicate that their primary struggle was with Palestinians and not all Arabs. Thus, it rekindled public and political dialogue on the Arab-Israeli conflict across Europe, in the United States, in other Middle Eastern states, and in efforts to conclude additional separate peace agreements, as it would with Jordan. Fourth, the First Intifada threatened the leadership role of the PLO in Tunis, illustrating the self-mobilization of the population in the territories and leading eventually to friction between the old guard in Tunis and younger leadership in the occupied territories. Finally, it cost Israel hundreds of millions of dollars in lost imports and tourism.

At the time the Oslo Accords were signed in September 1993, the six-year-long intifada had resulted in well over 1,000 deaths, most of them Palestinian. It is believed that approximately 1,160 Palestinians died in the uprising, of which 241 were children. On the Israeli side, 160 died, 5 of whom were children. Clearly, the IDF's inexperience in widespread riot control had contributed to the high death toll, for in the first 13 months of the intifada alone, more than 330 Palestinians were killed. Indeed, the policies and performance of the IDF split Israeli public opinion on the handling of the intifada and also invited international scrutiny.

In more recent years, continued terrorist attacks by pro-Palestinian interests, Israeli control of the Palestinian territories long beyond the time line set by the Oslo Accords, and the failure of the accords to proceed have caused unrest both in the international community and in Palestinian-Israeli relations. In 2000, a new wave of violent Palestinian protest broke out and would eventually become known as the Second (al-Aqsa) Intifada.

PAUL G. PIERPAOLI JR.

See also

Arafat, Yasser; Hamas; Intifada, Second; Islamic Jihad, Palestinian; Palestine Liberation Organization; Rabin, Yitzhak

References

Brynen, Rex, ed. *Echoes of the Intifada: Regional Repercussions of the Palestinian-Israeli Conflict.* Boulder, CO: Westview, 1991.

Farsoum, Samih K., and Naseer H. Aruri. *Palestine and the Palestinians: A Social and Political History.* 2nd ed. Jackson, TN: Westview, 2006.

Hunter, F. Robert. *The Palestinian Uprising: A War by Other Means.* Berkeley: University of California Press, 1991.

Peretz, Don. *Intifada: The Palestinian Uprising.* Boulder, CO: Westview, 1990.

Said, W. Edward. *Intifada: The Palestinian Uprising against Israeli Occupation.* Boston: South End, 1989.

Schiff, Ze'ev, and Ehud Ya'ari. *Intifada: The Palestinian Uprising—Israel's Third Front.* New York: Simon and Schuster, 1990.

Intifada, Second

Start Date: September 28, 2000
End Date: 2004

A popular Palestinian uprising and period of enhanced Israeli-Palestinian hostilities that broke out on September 28, 2000, following the collapse of the Camp David peace talks that summer, and came to an unofficial end in 2004 (later, according to some). The Second (al-Aqsa) Intifada is so-named because it began at the al-Aqsa Mosque in the Old City of Jerusalem. On September 28, 2000, Israel's Likud Party leader Ariel Sharon, accompanied by a Likud Party delegation and 1,500 police and security forces, entered and moved through the Haram al-Sharif complex, where Muslim holy sites are located in Jerusalem's Old City. The area is termed the Temple Mount by Israelis and is the location of the al-Aqsa Mosque and the Dome of the Rock. The enclave is one of Islam's three most holy sites and is sacred to Jews as well. The area had been closed to non-Muslims during prayer times and controlled by the Palestinian National Authority (PNA). Many observant Jews will not walk on the Temple Mount for fear of desecrating the remnants of the temple underneath it. Some Jewish and Christian organizations have called for the destruction of the Dome of the Rock or its relocation to an Arab country so that Jews can reclaim the site.

Sharon said that he was investigating Israeli complaints that Muslims were damaging archaeological remains below the surface of the Temple Mount. He declared Israeli control over the area, despite the understanding that even Israeli tour guides would hand over their charges to their Arab counterparts because the area was under the supervision of the PNA.

Palestinians believed that Sharon's actions and statements in the show of Israeli control over the Haram al-Sharif demonstrated Israeli contempt for limited Palestinian sovereignty and for Muslims in general. Anger built as a result, and demonstrations and riots soon erupted. Israeli troops launched attacks in Gaza, and on September 30, 2000, television footage showed the shooting of an unarmed 12-year-old boy, Muhammad Durrah, hiding behind his father as Israeli forces attacked. Protests grew more violent, involving Israeli Arabs as well as Palestinians. For the first time, stores and banks were burned in Arab Israeli communities. Thousands of Israelis also attacked Arabs and destroyed Arab property in Tel Aviv and Nazareth during the Jewish holiday of Yom Kippur. On October 12, two Israeli reservists were lynched by a mob at the Ramallah police station, further inflaming Israeli public opinion. In retaliation, Israel launched a series of air strikes against Palestinians.

On October 17, Israeli and Palestinian officials signed the Sharm al-Sheikh agreement to end the violence, but it continued nevertheless. Sharon's election as prime minister in February 2001 heightened Israel's hard-line tactics toward the Palestinians, which included the use of F-16 aircraft for the first time. Both Palestinians and Israelis admitted that the Oslo period had failed. Some Palestinians characterized their response as the warranted resistance of an embittered population that had received no positive assurances of sovereignty from years of negotiations. Others began or encouraged suicide attacks, as in the June 1, 2001, attack on Israelis waiting to enter a Tel Aviv discotheque and another attack on a Jerusalem restaurant on August 9, 2001. While some attacks were claimed by various Palestinian organizations, the degree of organizational control over the bombers and issues such as payments made to the so-called martyrs' families remain disputed.

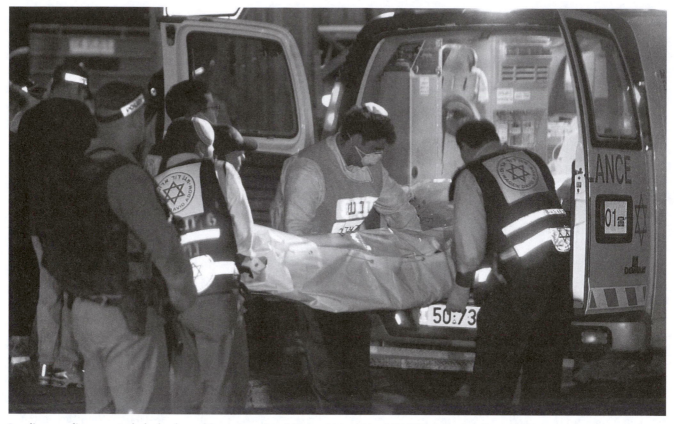

Israeli paramedics evacuate the body of one of the victims of a suicide bombing on March 27, 2002, in the Israeli resort of Netanya, where guests had gathered for a Passover Seder, the ritual meal ushering in the Jewish holiday. At least 16 people were killed and more than 100 wounded in the attack. (AP/Wide World Photos)

These attacks in public places terrified Israelis. Those in modest economic circumstances had to use public transportation, but most malls, movie theaters, stores, and day care centers hired security guards. Israeli authorities soon began a heightened campaign of targeted killings, or assassinations, of Palestinian leaders. Some political figures began to call for complete segregation of Arabs and Israelis, even within the Green Line (the 1967 border). This would be enforced by a security wall and even population transfers, which would involve evicting Arab villagers and urban residents from Israel in some areas and forcing them to move to the West Bank.

A virulent campaign against Palestine Liberation Organization (PLO) chairman and Palestinian National Authority (PNA) president Yasser Arafat's leadership began in Israel with American assent, complicating any negotiations between the two sides. Arafat was charged with corruption and with supporting the intifada. Israelis argued that he had actually planned it, a less than credible idea to most professional observers. However, the anti-Arafat campaign increased after the Israel Defense Forces (IDF) captured the ship *Santorini* filled with weapons purchased by Ahmad Jibril, head of the Popular Front for the Liberation of Palestine (PFLP) General Command (a PLO faction that did not accept the Oslo Accords) in May of 2001, and captured the *Karine-A,* a vessel carrying weapons allegedly from Iran, in January 2002.

The regional response to the Second Intifada consisted of cautious condemnation by Egypt and Jordan, which had concluded peace agreements with Israel and calls of outrage from other more hard-line states, including Syria. In February 2002, Crown Prince Abdullah of Saudi Arabia called for Arabs to fully normalize relations with Israel in return for Israeli withdrawal from the occupied territories. This plan was formally endorsed at an Arab League Summit in Beirut in March, although Israeli authorities prohibited Arafat from attending the summit. The proposal was never acknowledged by Israel.

Instead, in response to a suicide bomber's attack on the Netanya Hotel on March 28, 2002, in which 30 Israeli civilians died, the Israeli military began a major military assault on the West Bank. The PNA headquarters was besieged and international negotiations became necessary when militants took refuge in the Church of the Nativity in Bethlehem. A major attack took place at the large refugee camp at Jenin. Charges of a massacre in the IDF's onslaught there were investigated, revealing a death count of 55, smaller than had been claimed. However, the campaign ruined much of the building and the restoration that had taken place since Oslo.

The Israeli military response to the intifada did not successfully convince Palestinians to relinquish their aims of sovereignty and seemed to spark more suicide attacks rather than discourage them. In contrast, political measures and diplomacy produced some short interruptions in the violence, which gradually lengthened on the part of some Palestinian organizations and actors. In March 2003, Mahmoud Abbas, under pressure from Israel and the United States, became the first Palestinian prime minister of the PNA because the United States and Israel refused to recognize or deal with Arafat. On April 30, 2003, the European Union (EU), the United States, Russia, and the United Nations (UN) announced the so-called Road Map to Peace that was to culminate in an independent Palestinian state.

The plan did not unfold as designed, however, and in response to an Israeli air strike intended to kill Abd al-Aziz Rantisi, the leader of Hamas, militants launched a bus bombing in Jerusalem. At the end of June 2003, Palestinian militants agreed to a *hudna* (truce), which lasted for seven weeks and longer on the part of certain groups. There was no formal declaration that the intifada had ceased, and additional Israeli assassinations of Palestinian leaders as well as suicide attacks continued. Nevertheless, Hamas respected a cease-fire from 2004 for a lengthy period. Following the Second Intifada, several other issues temporarily took center stage: Arafat's November 2004 death, the Israeli unilateral withdrawal from Gaza (without negotiations or agreement with the Palestinians), and the Palestinian elections in 2006, resulting in the negative Israeli response to Hamas's electoral victory.

Casualty numbers for the Second Intifada are disputed. By September 2004, approximately 1,000 Israelis had died, and 6,700 more had been wounded. By 2003 the Israelis reported that 2,124 Palestinians had been killed, but a U.S. source reported 4,099 Palestinians killed and 30,527 wounded by 2005. Israel's tourism sector suffered a considerable decline at a time in which inflation and unemployment were already problematic.

An outcome of the Second Intifada in the global context of the September 11, 2001, terror attacks on the United States was that Israeli officials began branding all Palestinian resistance—indeed all activity on behalf of Palestinians—as terrorism. This discourse and the heightened violence have lent credence to those who call for separation rather than integration of Israelis with Arabs, such as the anti-Arab politician Avigdor Lieberman. Therefore, the building of the security barrier known as the Israeli Security Fence, which effectively cuts thousands of Palestinians off from their daily routes to work or school, was widely supported by Israelis. Similarly, Sharon's idea of unilateral withdrawal from Gaza was essentially funded by this idea, but his government had to confront those who were unwilling to relinquish settlements in that area.

The intifada resulted in crisis and despair among some Israeli peace activists and discouraged many independent efforts by Israelis and Palestinians to engage and meet with the other side. A 2004 survey showed that the numbers of Israelis in general who believed that the 1993 Oslo Peace Accords would lead to settlements declined during the intifada, and greater numbers believed that Israel should impose a military solution on the Palestinians.

Such opinions may well have shifted, however, since Israeli attacks on Lebanon in the summer of 2006.

The intifada also had deleterious effects on Palestinians who had hoped for the blossoming of normalcy in the West Bank, particularly as 85 percent of those in Gaza and 58 percent in the West Bank live in poverty. Since the outbreak of the intifada, the IDF demolished 628 housing units in which 3,983 people had lived. Less than 10 percent of these individuals were implicated in any violence or illegal activity.

Another outcome of the intifada was its highlighting of intra-Palestinian conflict. This includes that between the Tunis PLO elements of the PNA and the younger leaders who emerged within the occupied territories, between Fatah and Hamas, and between Fatah and the al-Aqsa Martyrs Brigades. Also evident were the difficulties of responding to Israeli demands for security when security for Palestinian citizens was not in force. Some Palestinian Israeli citizens have asserted their Palestinian identity for the very first time as a result of the intifada. The conflict most certainly caused discord in the Arab world as well.

SHERIFA ZUHUR

See also

Arafat, Yasser; Fatah; Hamas; Intifada, First; Palestine Liberation Organization; September 11 Attacks; September 11 Attacks, International Reactions to; Sharon, Ariel; Terrorism; United States Coordinating and Monitoring Mission

References

Baroud, Ramzy, et al. *The Second Palestinian Intifada: A Chronicle of a People's Struggle.* London: Pluto, 2006.

Khalidi, Walid. "The Prospects of Peace in the Middle East." *Journal of Palestine Studies* 32 (Winter 2003): 50–63.

Reinhart, Tanya. *The Road Map to Nowhere: Israel/Palestine since 2003.* London: Verso, 2006.

Shulz, Helena Lindholm. "The al-Aqsa Intifada as a Result of Politics of Transition." *Arab Studies Quarterly* 24 (Fall 2002): 21–47.

Stork, Joe. "Erased in a Moment: Suicide Bombing Attacks against Israeli Civilians." *Human Rights Watch* (2002): 1–160.

Iran

Iran is a Middle Eastern nation of 636,293 square miles, slightly larger than the U.S. state of Alaska, with a population in 2007 of 70.473 million. Iran is bordered by the Persian Gulf and the Gulf of Oman to the south; Turkey, Azerbaijan, the Caspian Sea, and Armenia to the north; Afghanistan and Pakistan to the east; and Iraq to the west. Iran has long been important because of its strategic location at the geographic nexus of the Middle East, Europe, and Southwest Asia. Its location captured the attention of both Britain and Russia in the 19th century, with each nation seeking to control the area. Rivalry over Iran continued in the early years of the Cold War as both the United States and the Soviet Union sought to control its oil resources.

A view of Tehran, Iran's capital and its largest city. (iStockphoto)

Iran is predominantly a Shia Islam nation. However, Shiism did not become identified with the state until the Safavid Empire formed. The Shia were found in a variety of locations in the Middle East and Southern Asia, having originated in the Arabian Peninsula before the sect actually coalesced as such. Sunni Muslims comprise the great majority of Muslims in the Middle East and around the world, and Shia Iranians have periodically viewed the actions of Sunni-dominated governments as a direct threat to their economic, political, religious, and social well-being and independence. Iran has a Sunni minority, and had a sizable Bahai and Jewish population, although members of the latter two groups have been persecuted and forced out.

In 1921, the Pahlavi dynasty was established in Iran by Shah Reza Pahlavi I, a military officer known first as Reza Khan, who led a coup against the last Qajar shah. A reformer and modernizer, Reza Pahlavi instituted agricultural, economic, and educational reforms and began the modernization of the country's transportation system. In the end, these and other reforms threatened the status of the Shia clerics in Iran, who began to oppose the shah and his reforms that tightened control over their areas of authority. Desiring to stress the country's lengthy and imperial pre-Islamic tradition and so as to include Iranians who were not from Fars (the central province), Reza Pahlavi changed the country's name from Persia to Iran in 1935.

Reza Pahlavi's lack of cooperation with the Allies during World War II led to his forced abdication in 1941 in favor of his son, Mohammad Reza Pahlavi. During the war, Iran was occupied by Soviet and British forces in the north and south of the country, respectively, and was a key conduit for Lend-Lease supplies. The shah's strong ties to the West over the next four decades often meant economic difficulty for Iran. For example, during World War II the British-controlled Anglo-Iranian Oil Company (AIOC) artificially deflated the price of oil to reduce the cost of the war to the British economy. Certainly, the shah's popularity declined because of his ties to the West.

Mohammad Mosaddeq, a member of the National Front Party (NFP), became prime minister in 1951 and soon became the shah's most prominent critic. Mosaddeq's persistent criticism of the regime's weak position vis-à-vis Britain led him to nationalize the British-owned AIOC in 1951, which Washington chose to see as a clear example of his communist tendencies. Britain responded by imposing an embargo on Iranian oil and blocking the export of products from the formerly British properties. Because Britain was Iran's primary oil consumer, this had a considerable impact on Iran. Mosaddeq then asked the shah to grant him emergency powers that included direct control of the military. The shah refused, precipitating a domestic political crisis.

Mosaddeq understood the power of his popularity. He promptly resigned, causing widespread protests and demands that he be returned to power. Unnerved, in 1952 the shah reappointed Mosaddeq, who then took steps to consolidate his power. This included the implementation of land reforms and other measures, which to the West seemed socialist. Although Mosaddeq had not had any direct contact with the Soviets, the events in Iran were nevertheless of great concern to the United States, which feared a Soviet takeover (based on Soviet efforts to annex northern Iran at the end of World War II).

The United States refused Mosaddeq's repeated requests for financial aid because he refused to reverse the nationalization of the AIOC. By the summer of 1953, Mosaddeq's intransigence and his legalization of the leftist Tudeh Party led the United States to join Britain and the temporarily exiled shah in a covert August 1953 plot to overthrow Mosaddeq. Known as Operation AJAX the coup against Mosaddeq was successful, and the shah was back in power by the end of August 1953. While the British were correct in viewing Mosaddeq as a threat to their position in Iran, the United States was incorrect in presuming that he was a communist. Rather, he was an Iranian nationalist who saw the income of Iranian farmers drop to $110 a year and witnessed many Iranians fall into abject poverty. He sought to ameliorate these conditions and establish a more independent foreign policy.

The decade that followed was marked by the creation in 1957 of the Sazeman-e Ettelaat va Amniyat-e Keshvar (SAVAK, National Information and Security Organization), the shah's dreaded secret police, and a number of failed or overly ambitious economic reforms. Iranian economic policy was similar to that of many other developing nations in its preference to large state projects over a true free-market economy. Predictably, the largely state-run economy failed to perform as promised. This and pressure by the United States finally led the shah to propose the White Revolution, which called for land reform, privatization of government-owned firms, electoral reform, women's suffrage, the nationalization of forests, rural literacy programs, and profit sharing for industrial workers. The shah hoped that such ambitious measures would spark economic growth and mitigate growing criticism of his regime. The White Revolution proved far less than revolutionary. That same year also witnessed a brutal crackdown on Iranian dissidents and fundamentalist clerics, which did nothing to endear the shah to his own people.

Ayatollah Ruhollah Khomeini, a conservative Muslim cleric, became the shah's most prominent opponent in the early 1960s, berating the regime for its secular focus and the shah for his elaborate and regal Western lifestyle. Khomeini was critical of Iran's close relationships with the United States and Israel. From Khomeini's perspective, the Americans provided arms, training, and technical assistance to their key anticommunist ally in the Middle East. And Israel provided training to SAVAK, which included intelligence-gathering, interrogation, and counterterrorism techniques. Thus, when SAVAK arrested, tortured, and killed antiregime activists, the United States and Israel were blamed along with the shah.

Khomeini's popularity prevented the shah from eliminating him but not from exiling him. Forced to leave Iran in 1964, Khomeini set himself apart from other quietist Iranian clerics, who sought to separate politics from religion, by refusing to compromise with the shah. While in exile Khomeini continued to denounce the shah, Zionism, and the United States in his many sermons.

As the shah's reforms failed to bring about the desired effects, leftist groups such as the Mujahideen-e Khalq and Fidiyann-e Islami Khalq joined the National Front Party and religious conservatives in unified opposition. The increase in oil revenue after the 1973–1974 oil crisis was insufficient to compensate for an Iranian economy teetering on insolvency and lacking clear private property rights.

During the 1970s, opposition to the regime often took the form of overt acts of defiance, such as the wearing of the *hijab* by Iranian women, the attendance of mosques whose imams openly criticized the shah, performance of religious plays during holidays, and demonstrations convened on the memorial days of slain protesters. When an article critical of Khomeini ran in a Tehran newspaper in January 1978, the city's streets filled with Khomeini supporters and regime opponents. The shah's failure to quell the riots that followed only emboldened his opponents, and each demonstration led to another riot and a new set of martyrs.

U.S. president Jimmy Carter's administration was repeatedly given false information by SAVAK, which misrepresented the level of civil unrest in Iran. In the end, after massive general strikes in the autumn of 1978, the shah lost control of the country in January 1979 and fled. This was followed by the triumphal return of Khomeini from exile on February 1, 1979, and the establishment of a transitional government composed of the various opposition groups.

Such relative moderates as Mehdi Bazargan and Abolhasan Bani-Sadr, the first prime minister and president, respectively, after the Pahlavi collapse, were soon forced out of power by Khomeini's supporters, who firmly held the reins of power by 1980. Iran was transformed into an Islamic government, with Khomeini as supreme *faqih* (expert in Islamic law), the de facto national leader. Angered by the U.S. government's decision to admit the Shah of Iran, who was ill with cancer but reportedly had left Iran with his immense fortune, Iranian students attacked the United States and its representatives. It was with the support of the Revolutionary Guards—and the tacit support of Khomeini himself—that Iranian students were able to seize the U.S. embassy in Tehran on November 4, 1979, and take the Americans there hostage. The crisis endured for 444 days, paralyzing the Carter administration.

The incoming Ronald Reagan administration (1981–1989) viewed the new Iranian regime as a threat to American interests in the Middle East and to its closest ally, Israel. This led the United States to support Iraqi dictator Saddam Hussein's September 22, 1980, invasion of Iran. Initially, the Iraqi Army had great success against the poorly led, disorganized, and surprised

Ayatollah Ruhollah Khomeini is thronged by supporters after delivering a speech at the Tehran airport, February 1, 1979, the day of his return from 14 years in exile. (AP/Wide World Photos)

Iranians. However, Iranian zeal led to counteroffensives in 1982 that pushed the Iraqis back. The war then settled into a bloody stalemate during which the Iraqis for the most part fought from prepared defensive positions in the fashion of World War I and the Iranians endured huge casualties while staging unsophisticated human wave attacks against prepared Iraqi positions. Khomeini viewed the war as a jihad (holy war) and rejected any end to the fighting before the destruction of Hussein's secular government. After almost a decade of war and more than a million casualties, the Iran-Iraq War ended in 1988 with no clear victor.

Khomeini died in 1989, but a movement promoting reform did not begin until the late 1990s. Following Khomeini's death, his Islamic Religious Party continued to dominate the government bureaucracy and the policy-making apparatus. It also eliminated many political or religious rivals.

According to the United States government, Iran was the single most important state sponsor of terrorism in the 1980s, although Middle Eastern states do not necessarily agree with Washington's definition or list of "terrorist" groups. Actually, Iran's regional influence dates back only to a few years of active efforts to "internationalize" Iran's Islamic revolution. After the Iran-Iraq War sapped Iranian resources, funding actions throughout the region became less important than focusing on Iran's domestic issues.

In these years, Iranian leaders who had been sheltered by the Left, Palestinians, and Lebanese wanted to help the Lebanese defend themselves against Israel control over South Lebanon.

Hezbollah, actually founded by Shia clerics trained in Iraq, benefited from Iranian support in the form of funds and military training. Iran also supported Hezbollah's efforts to modernize and mobilize the Shia community of Lebanon because of their backwardness and lack of representation. Israel possesses nuclear weapons and has long regarded Iran as a threat. Israel's superior military and nuclear capacity would make a direct Iranian strike against the Jewish state suicidal, and such an attack would kill Palestinians. Israeli leaders have, however, argued that Israel might need to mount a preemptive strike against Iran's nuclear facilities. It has also accused Iran of supporting Hamas and Hezbollah. When Israel finally withdrew from southern Lebanon in May 2000, Iran continued, in its statements and media, to support Hezbollah's struggle against Israeli encroachment of Lebanon, and against Saudi- and U.S.-backed elements within Lebanon.

The Islamic Republic of Iran has also strongly supported the Palestinian struggle against Israel and criticized the United States for its blind support of Israel. One reason for that stance is to differentiate itself from the former shah, who was an ally of Israel and an even stronger ally of the United States.

During the 1990s, U.S. president Bill Clinton attempted to pursue détente with Iran and sought to restore economic relations with that country. More recently, however, the United States has accused Iran of being a key supporter of the insurgency in Iraq following the Anglo-American invasion of that nation in 2003.

In 2007, the United States grudgingly agreed to talks with Iranian officials, the first of their kind since the 1979 Iranian Revolution, in an attempt to discuss key issues between neighbors, including Iranian pilgrim traffic into Iraq and the alleged Iranian aid to anti-American elements in that country.

In recent years, the U.S. government has demonsrated great concern that Iran has been seeking to develop nuclear weapons and acquire the long-range missile technology needed to deliver nuclear warheads to Israel and Europe. The United States government has also accused Iran, along with Syria, of linkages with the resistance in Iraq, and in supporting groups that continue to promote political resistance against Israel. However, the Iranians point to the Israeli-Palestinian issue as a Muslim concern and one of social justice. Iranian reformers have also stressed the need to deal with pressing economic issues at home, where increased oil revenues have expanded the funds available to the clerics and the government. Electoral support for the hard-liners has stayed relatively firm. A student-led reform movement called Doh-e Khordad, which seemed to argue for a more moderate approach in the early 2000s, is no longer attracting a broad range of support. Nevertheless, during the George W. Bush administration, U.S. secretary of state Condoleezza Rice announced that the government would try to spur regime change through "soft approaches" and dedicated $74 million to that project. This, together with threats against Iran over its nuclear development program, has tended to galvanize Iranian sentiment against external interference.

ADAM LOWTHER, LOUIS A. DIMARCO,
PAUL G. PIERPAOLI JR., AND SHERIFA ZUHUR

See also

Hamas; Hezbollah; Hussein, Saddam; Iran-Iraq War; Iranian Revolution; Jihad; Katyusha Rocket; Khomeini, Ruhollah; Reza Pahlavi, Mohammad; Shia Islam; Sunni Islam; Terrorism; United States, Middle East Policy, 1945–Present

References

Ansari, Ali. *Confronting Iran*. New York: Basic Books, 2006.
———. *A History of Modern Iran since 1921: The Pahlavis and After*. Boston: Longman, 2003.
Daniel, Elton. *The History of Iran*. Westport, CT: Greenwood, 2001.
Keddie, Nikki R. *Modern Iran: Roots and Results of Revolution*. New Haven, CT: Yale University Press, 2003.
Kinzer, Stephen. *All the Shah's Men: An American Coup and the Roots of Middle East Terror*. Hoboken, NJ: Wiley, 2003.
Pappas, Theodore, ed. *Iran*. New York: Wiley, 2006.
Zuhur, Sherifa. *Iran, Iraq, and the United States: The New Triangle's Impact on Sectarianism and the Nuclear Threat*. Carlisle, PA: Strategic Studies Institute, 2006.

Iran, Armed Forces

Iran's armed forces, which during much of the Cold War were heavily equipped with U.S. weaponry and hardware, served as a symbol of modernism until the 1979 Iranian Revolution, which overthrew Mohammad Reza Shah Pahlavi. After that, Iranian armed forces tended to reflect the new Islamic regime's inability—and even unwillingness—to maintain and upgrade technical capabilities as well as the state's emphasis on the personal zeal of military personnel rather than their training and leadership abilities.

From the earliest days of the shah's reign, indeed as early as 1941, Iran's armed forces were vitally important to his rule. Iran's strategic geographical position and the shah's constitutional authority that gave him direct control over the armed forces (but not over other matters of state) made military expansion and modernization his single most important program. After the 1953 coup led by the U.S. Central Intelligence Agency (CIA) that solidified his position, the shah increasingly turned to the United States for matériel and technical support.

Although the shah was a much-welcomed customer, U.S. officials up until 1969 expressed concerns that he should channel more efforts toward internal reforms, including land and economic restructuring. Washington often did not have complete confidence in the shah's ability to retain control over his nation, and his placing of military objectives above other national interests did not ease this apprehension.

There were caps on both the quantity and types of weapons systems available to Iran, but that changed during Richard Nixon's presidency, which began in January 1969. By 1972, the shah could order virtually any type of military technology in whatever quantities he wished. This set a significant new precedent, as both the U.S. Defense and State departments had previously sought to limit Iranian weapons purchases. The Nixon administration, in an attempt to pull back from worldwide military and defense commitments, hoped to use the shah as a bulwark against communist and Pan-Arab advances in the Middle East.

The results were immediate and dramatic. Iranian military purchases from the United States skyrocketed from $500 million per year in 1972 to $2.5 billion in 1973. By 1976, Iran had purchased $11 billion in new weaponry from American suppliers. Weapons acquisitions included helicopters, jet fighters, antiaircraft missiles, submarines, and destroyers. These acquisitions continued until 1977, when President Jimmy Carter reimposed limits on such sales.

The 1970s also brought significant importations of Western technical assistance. Large numbers of military advisers, technicians, and logistics and maintenance personnel arrived in Iran, primarily from the United States. As long as military matériel and spare parts arrived from the West, to be used by native and nonnative technicians, the military functioned smoothly. If that flow of goods and expertise were to be halted, as it was after 1979, the Iranian military's ability to function would be seriously compromised.

In early 1979, the shah was forced to abdicate and depart the country, and the monarchy was taken over by the conservative Islamic Republic. Less than two years later, in September 1980, Iraq attacked Iran, sparking the Iran-Iraq War (1980–1988). The

A ballistic missile on display in front of a picture of revolutionary founder of the Islamic Republic of Iran Ayatollah Ruhollah Khomeini at his mausoleum during a military parade ceremony marking the 29th anniversary of the start of the 1980–1988 Iran-Iraq War, September 22, 2009. (AP/Wide World Photos)

Iraqis faced a diminished Iranian military, augmented by and sometimes competing with nonprofessional Revolutionary Guard units that met the first assaults and performed poorly.

When the Islamic Republic of Iran was created, the officer corps of all three Iranian armed services had been purged, followed by a rash of desertions. According to one estimate, 60 percent of the army deserted in 1979 alone. The numbers of qualified pilots and technicians in the air force plummeted, as did the number of naval personnel. One significant exception was an increase in the number of marines, at least up until the mid-1980s.

In August 1980 just prior to the Iraqi attack, the Iranian Air Force operated 447 first-line combat aircraft, including 66 U.S.-built Grumman F-14 Tomcats. The Iranian Navy had 7 guided-missile destroyers and frigates and 7 guided-missile corvettes. The Iranian Army stood at 150,000 troops equipped with 1,700 tanks and 1,000 artillery pieces, many of them self-propelled. The country also reportedly had more than 100,000 Revolutionary Guards, or Pasadran. Armed primarily with light infantry weapons, they were a highly motivated but very poorly trained combat force.

The departure from Iran of foreign advisers and technicians who had serviced aircraft, radar, missile, and ground systems had a dramatic effect on the Iranian armed forces. One example of the dangers of relying on technology created and supported by outsiders was the air force's computer-based logistics system. Without the proper technical support, the system was unusable. Procuring spare parts, which grew increasingly scarce, was a slow and laborious process. As the war progressed, the multinational boycott on Iranian oil, which depleted government funds, forced the Iranians to continually cannibalize their own equipment. This took a heavy toll on effectiveness and readiness.

The Iraqi invasion caught the Iranian military divided and decimated. Iraqi aircraft roamed over the battlefield almost unchallenged, as the Iranian air defense system was overwhelmed and lay in disarray. Iraqi armored units were able to engage and defeat individual Iranian armored and mechanized infantry units. However, at the tactical level, Iranian units enjoyed superior combat cohesion and tactical direction. Moreover, the Revolutionary Guard units proved fanatical in their defense of cities and fixed positions, and the Iraqi offensive bogged down within two weeks. Iranian Air Force units struck back at targets in Iraq and along the battlefield, and individual Iranian pilots proved superior to their Iraqi counterparts, but shortages of spare parts suppressed aircraft readiness rates, which declined rapidly over time.

The war entered a period of stalemate after October 1980 as the Iraqis shifted to the defensive. Heavy losses in seizing Khorramshahr forced the Iraqis to reconsider assaulting the oil center of

Abadan, and they settled on a siege instead. The Iranians used the period of relative calm to reorganize and restructure their forces. Armored and artillery units were concentrated, and the infantry reorganized into combat brigades. A working relationship was established with the Revolutionary Guards. Combined arms tactics with specialized units (engineers, armor, and artillery) were practiced with the units designated to conduct an attack. Revolutionary Guards were to provide the initial shock and exploitation force in any offensive.

These new tactics were first employed in a series of small-scale offensives near Susangerd and then Abadan. By the autumn of 1981 the tactics began to prove effective, slowly driving back the Iraqi forces. By early 1982 the Iraqis had been driven completely from Iran. The tactics were then expanded to follow a repetitive pattern. Short, sharp artillery barrages were directed at Iraqi trenches, which were then subjected to massive human wave attacks by Revolutionary Guard units. Iranian Army mechanized units followed.

This was a costly approach to ground operations. The Iraqis, lacking the combat cohesion of their Iranian counterparts, resorted to using chemical weapons and massive artillery barrages to destroy Iranian forces' concentrations. Over time, the losses began to take a horrific toll, although this was partially the result of employing untrained civilians who volunteered or were forced to volunteer, including young boys. Some analysts claim that Iran lost more than 1 million people killed in the eight-year war. Certainly, the Iranians suffered at the very least several hundred thousand wounded, killed, and missing. By 1988, even Revolutionary Guard units began to suffer morale breakdowns. Ultimately, that is what drove Iran to reach a peace agreement with the Iraqis.

During the 1980–1988 war with Iraq, Iran was forced to seek weapons from sources other than the United States and Western Europe. Thus, Iran received war matériel from the People's Republic of China (PRC), Brazil, North Korea, and Israel. It also secured some Soviet equipment, usually purchased through third parties. Reflecting the reliance on Chinese weapons, the Iranian armed forces possessed Silkworm antiship cruise missiles and Chinese-built armored personnel carriers. Most bizarre was the supply of some American equipment, especially air-to-surface and antitank missiles. These weapons systems were furnished by the United States in return for cash used to finance U.S. government actions against the Sandinistas in Nicaragua in what came to be known as the Iran-Contra Affair.

Following the Iran-Iraq War, the Iranians moved to improve their military, which meant procuring matériel from abroad. By 2000, increased oil revenues and Russian frustration with U.S. policies in the Middle East had enabled Iran to purchase limited numbers of weapons and equipment from Russia. Iran has long had a missile program in development as well as other weapons programs. In addition, it has a nuclear development program that dates back to the 1970s. Iranian efforts at enriching uranium, which reportedly began in 2006, have brought much international concern over Iranian intentions and a widespread belief that they intend to produce nuclear weapons.

Only the future will tell for certain the direction of the Iranian military establishment, but the efficiency and effectiveness of the armed forces is probably inhibited by the political aspect of the leadership-selection process, and limited access to high-tech weapons systems and training opportunities. While the effectiveness of the Iranian armed forces remains in question, Iran's pursuit of nuclear weapons and ballistic missile programs remain one the thorniest security issues in the Middle East. Also, given the weakness and instability of the Iraqi regime, some have exploited fears of the Iranian military overrunning at least part of Iraq in the future, although it is clear from Iranian statements that the government has reassured Iraq that it is not seeking a war with that country.

ROBERT N. STACY AND CARL OTIS SCHUSTER

See also

Arms Sales, International; Iran; Iran-Iraq War; Khomeini, Ruhollah; Reza Pahlavi, Mohammad; United States, Middle East Policy, 1945–Present

References

Hickman, William F. *Ravaged and Reborn: The Iranian Army 1982.* Washington, DC: Brookings Institute Press, 1983.

Karsh, Efraim. *The Iran-Iraq War, 1980–1988.* Oxford, UK: Osprey, 2002.

Krosney, Herbert. *Deadly Business: Legal Deals and Outlaw Weapons; The Arming of Iran and Iraq, 1975 to the Present.* New York: Four Walls Eight Windows, 1993.

Rubin, Barry, and Thomas A. Keaney, eds. *Armed Forces in the Middle East: Politics and Strategy.* Portland, OR: Frank Cass, 2002.

Schahgaldian, Nikola. *The Iranian Military under the Islamic Republic.* Santa Monica, CA: RAND Corporation, 1987.

Iran Air Flight 655
Event Date: July 3, 1988

Iran Air Flight 655 (IR655) was an Iranian passenger jetliner mistakenly shot down by a U.S. naval warship in the Persian Gulf on July 3, 1988. The event occurred during the highly destructive Iran-Iraq War of 1980–1988 and came on the heels of incidents in 1987 and 1988 that had seen engagements of both Iranian and Iraqi forces with U.S. warships operating in the Persian Gulf. They had occurred after the Ronald Reagan administration had vowed to keep vital shipping lanes open by providing U.S. Navy warship escorts for neutral ships through the perilous waters of the Persian Gulf in Operation EARNEST WILL (1987–1988). At the time, both Iranian and Iraqi forces were targeting civilian cargo and tanker ships in the region in an effort to deprive the other of commerce and supplies.

At the time of the tragedy of Flight 655, tensions were running very high in the Persian Gulf. On March 17, 1987, an Iraqi Mirage F-1 jet fighter mistakenly fired two air-to-surface missiles at the U.S. Navy Perry-class guided-missile frigate *Stark,* which was on routine duty in the Persian Gulf. The attack resulted in the deaths of 37 crewmen and heavy damage to the ship. Little more than a year later, in April 1988, another U.S. guided-missile frigate, the Oliver Hazard Perry–class *Samuel P. Roberts,* hit an Iranian-laid mine in the Persian Gulf, which almost sank the ship. No lives were lost, but the ship underwent almost $90 million in repairs. This incident prompted American retaliation against Iranian assets via Operation PRAYING MANTIS on April 18, 1988. With tensions running dangerously high in the Persian Gulf by the summer of 1988, other violent incidents were almost inevitable.

At 10:17 a.m. local time on July 3, 1988, Iran Air Flight 655 (IR655) took off from Bandar Abbas, Iran bound for Dubai, United Arab Emirates. There were 290 people, including the crew, on board the Airbus A300, a medium-range, wide-body passenger jetliner. It began to fly over the Strait of Hormuz shortly after take-off during the short 30-minute flight. At the same time, the U.S. Navy Aegis-class guided missile cruiser *Vincennes* was steaming through the strait returning from escort duty in the Persian Gulf. Earlier that morning, a helicopter from the *Vincennes* had received warning fire from several Iranian patrol boats. The *Vincennes* subsequently exchanged fire with the Iranian vessels, which then promptly withdrew.

Only minutes later, radar on board the *Vincennes* picked up IR655, and radar operators mistook it for an American-made Grumman F-14 Tomcat fighter. The Airbus's radar profile closely resembled that of the F-14. Also, the *Vincennes* crew members knew that the plane had taken off from Bandar Abbas, from which Iran operated not only commercial aircraft but also F-14 fighters and other military aircraft. Crew members also believed that the plane was descending as it was approaching the ship, which was later discounted as inaccurate. In fact, the aircraft was turning away from the ship as it was fired upon.

The *Vincennes* attempted seven times (three times on the civilian military frequency and four times on the military emergency frequency) to contact the crew of IR655, which did not respond. However, the U.S. warship failed to use air traffic control frequencies, so it is likely that the Airbus's crew members did not receive the radio messages or did not know that the messages were directed at them.

Believing that the ship was under attack, when the airplane was about 11 nautical miles from the *Vincennes,* the ship's crew fired two SM-2MR medium-range surface-to-air missiles at 10:24 a.m. Both missiles hit their target, sending the airliner plunging into the Strait of Hormuz. There were no survivors.

The downing of the aircraft caused international consternation and greatly embarrassed the Ronald Reagan administration. The events surrounding the tragedy were immediately contested by the Iranian government, which claimed that Flight 655 was doing nothing wrong or illegal. It also voiced great skepticism that experienced radar operators could mistake a passenger jetliner for an F-14 fighter. Furthermore, Tehran asserted that even if the aircraft had been a military fighter, the *Vincennes* had no reason to shoot it down because it was still technically in Iranian airspace, had not

followed an attack pattern, and indeed had not taken any hostile actions at all. Iran concluded that the *Vincennes* crew had acted impetuously and improperly and was quick to point out that when Iraq attacked the *Stark* the year before, Washington concluded that the Iraqi pilot realized—or should have realized—that his target was an American warship. The very same thing, Tehran argued, could be said of the *Vincennes* crew.

U.S. Navy officials found no wrongdoing on the part of the *Vincennes* crew, who were in fact awarded Combat Action Ribbons. Although the U.S. government issued a "note of regret" about the loss of innocent lives, it neither admitted responsibility nor apologized for the incident. The affair plunged Iranian-American relations further into the deep freeze, although some assert that it may have convinced Iran's leader, Ayatollah Ruhollah Khomeini, to finally end the Iran-Iraq War, realizing that it could not prevail so long as the United States was working against him. Indeed, the war ended little more than a month later. In 1989, Iran took its case to the International Court of Justice, but not until 1996 did the U.S. government agree on a payment settlement, which was $131.8 million. About half that amount went to the families of those killed in the crash; the remainder went to the Iranian government in reimbursement for the lost jetliner.

PAUL G. PIERPAOLI JR.

See also

Iran; Iran-Iraq War; Iraq, History of, Pre-1990; PRAYING MANTIS, Operation; *Stark* Incident

References

Hiro, Dilip. *The Longest War: The Iran-Iraq Military Conflict.* London: Routledge, 1991.

Karsh, Efraim. *The Iran-Iraq War, 1980–1988.* Oxford, UK: Osprey, 2002.

Rogers, Will, Sharon Rogers, and Gene Gregston. *Storm Center: The USS Vincennes and Iran Flight 655; A Personal Account of Tragedy and Heroism.* Annapolis, MD: Naval Institute Press, 1992.

Iran-Contra Affair

Start Date: August 1985
End Date: March 1987

Political scandal of President Ronald Reagan's administration involving the illegal sale of weapons to Iran, the proceeds of which were used to illegally fund Nicaraguan Contra rebels. As its name implies, Iran-Contra was the linkage of two otherwise vastly different foreign policy problems that bedeviled the Reagan administration at the beginning of its second term in 1985: how to secure the release of American hostages held by Iranian-backed kidnappers in Lebanon and how to support the Contra rebels fighting against Nicaragua's Cuban-style Sandinista government. In both cases Reagan's public options were limited, for he had explicitly ruled out the possibility of negotiating directly with hostage takers, and Congress had refused to allow military aid to be sent to the Contras.

In August 1985 Reagan approved a plan by Robert McFarlane, national security adviser (NSA) to the president, to sell more than 500 TOW antitank missiles to Iran, via the Israelis, in exchange for the release of Americans held by terrorists in Lebanon (Reagan later denied that he was aware of an explicit link between the sale and the hostage crisis). The deal went through, and as a follow-up, in November 1985, there was a proposal to sell HAWK antiaircraft missiles to Iran. Lieutenant Colonel Oliver North, a decorated marine attached to the National Security Council's staff, was put in charge of these and subsequent negotiations. A number of Reagan's senior cabinet members, including Secretary of State George Shultz, Secretary of Defense Caspar Weinberger, and White House Chief of Staff Donald Regan, began to express reservations about this trade with Iran, for it was not only diametrically opposed to the administration's stated policy, but was also illegal under U.S. and international law.

Nevertheless, Reagan continued to endorse arms shipments throughout 1986, and in all more than 100 tons of missiles and spare parts were exported to Iran by the end of the year. Meanwhile, North had begun secretly funneling the funds from the missile sales to Swiss bank accounts owned by the Nicaraguan Contra rebels, who used the money in part to set up guerrilla training camps run by agents of the Central Intelligence Agency (CIA). All this was in direct violation of the Second Boland Amendment, a congressional law passed in October 1984 that specifically forbade the U.S. government from supporting any paramilitary group in Nicaragua. To what extent North's superiors knew of the Contra connection at this stage remains unclear, as is the final amount of money supplied to the Nicaraguans, although it is thought to have been on the order of tens of millions of dollars. Later investigations suggested numerous accounting irregularities by North, but these were never proven.

On November 3, 1986, the affair became public when a Lebanese magazine, *Al-Shira'a*, revealed that the Americans had been selling missiles to the Iranians. Reagan responded with a televised statement in which he denied any arms-for-hostages deal, and U.S. attorney general Edwin Meese was ordered to conduct an internal inquiry. North and his secretary, Fawn Hall, immediately began shredding incriminating documents, but on November 22, Meese's staff discovered material in North's office that linked the Iranian shipments directly to the Contras. Meese informed Reagan, and on November 25 the U.S. Justice Department announced its preliminary findings to the press. North was fired, and national security adviser Vice Admiral John Poindexter, who had replaced McFarlane, promptly resigned.

The following month, Reagan appointed an independent commission to investigate the affair, chaired by former Texas senator John Tower. The commission's March 1987 report severely criticized the White House for failing to control its NSA subordinates, which led to the resignation of Regan. An apparently contrite President Reagan admitted to having misled the public in his earlier statements, although he pled sins of ignorance rather than design.

Marine lieutenant colonel Oliver North testifies before the joint House-Senate panels investigating the Iran-Contra affair on Capitol Hill on July 7, 1987. North served as an aide to the National Security Council (NSC) during the Reagan administration and was a key figure in the Iran-Contra scandal that erupted in 1986. (AP/Wide World Photos)

A subsequent congressional inquiry lambasted the president for failings of leadership but decided that he had not known about the transfers of money to the Contras.

In 1988 independent prosecutor Lawrence Walsh indicted North, Poindexter, and 12 other persons on a variety of felony counts. Eleven were convicted, but North and Poindexter were later acquitted on Fifth Amendment technicalities. At the end of his term in office in December 1992, President George H. W. Bush, who had claimed ignorance of the Iran-Contra connection and avoided close scrutiny in the affair, pardoned six other persons implicated in the Iran-Contra scandal, including Weinberger and McFarlane.

ALAN ALLPORT

See also

Arms Sales, International; Bush, George Herbert Walker; Iran; Reagan, Ronald Wilson; Shultz, George Pratt; Weinberger, Caspar Willard

References

Chang, Laurence, et al., eds. *The Chronology: The Documented Day-by-Day Account of the Secret Military Assistance to Iran and the Contras.* New York: Warner Books, 1987.

Draper, Theodore. *A Very Thin Line: The Iran-Contra Affairs.* New York: Hill and Wang, 1991.

Walsh, Lawrence. *Iran-Contra: The Final Report.* New York: Times Books, 1994.

Wroe, Ann. *Lives, Lies and the Iran-Contra Affair.* New York: I. B. Tauris, 1991.

Iran Hostage Rescue Mission

See EAGLE CLAW, Operation

Iranian Revolution

Event Date: 1979

The 1979 Iranian Revolution precipitated the overthrow of Mohammad Reza Shah Pahlavi, a staunch U.S. ally whose government had ruled the country since 1941. Replacing the shah's dictatorship was the Islamic Republic of Iran, a conservative Shiite Islamic regime led by the religious cleric Ayatollah Ruhollah Khomeini, who ruled the country until his death in 1989. The Islamic Republic of Iran remained at great odds with much of the West, especially the United States, and the two nations have not enjoyed diplomatic relations since 1979. Today, power in Iran remains in the hands of clerics who favored Khomeini's party and have supported an Islamic government for nearly three decades.

Many factors contributed to the demise of the shah's repressive regime. His government's suppression of dissent through his secret police, the SAVAK (short for Sazeman-e Ettelaat va Amniyat-e Keshvar, or National Information and Security Organization) alienated large segments of Iran's population, particularly Iran's powerful Shiite religious community, university students, and many intellectuals. Furthermore, the shah's close ties to the United States, which included huge military equipment sales and the importation of American products and culture, alienated and offended many conservative and traditional Iranians who regarded these developments as having corrupted Iran and its Islamic culture and traditions.

Iran's burgeoning population also produced strains on the Iranian economy and aggravated class and social conflicts, particularly between the impoverished countryside and the cities. The shah sought to develop and modernize both the economy and society, believing that this would secure his rule. In part, his economic plans were too ambitious. At the same time, modernization and rural-urban emigration failed to improve living conditions for ordinary Iranians. Simultaneously, the shah attacked the traditional merchant sectors, accusing them of corruption. Therefore, many of the shah's reforms only aggravated existing national problems and worsened tensions within the population, thus increasing resentment and opposition to his rule. This in turn led to increasing repression by the SAVAK against dissidents and opponents of the shah. By the early 1960s, Islamic clerics had begun preaching against the shah's government because of his changes in education, law, and land tenure. Demonstrations and protests commenced, many of which were put down by brute force.

In addition, because many of the expensive modernization projects had little overall effect on the economy and standard of living, they only highlighted the corruption and incompetence of the shah's regime. Over time, land reform measures intended to increase land ownership among Iran's poor peasants actually worsened their situation by giving them too little land to earn an effective living, thereby increasing rural poverty and unemployment. At the same time, the failed program attracted opposition from the country's Islamic community, which regarded the reform initiative as an attempt by the shah to divest the clerics of their control over income through the system of religious endowments (*vaqf*). Changes in land tenure, which included experiments in agricultural collectives, excluded many agricultural laborers and sharecroppers, who now found themselves unemployed.

At the same time, the shah's investment in heavy industry and the mechanization of agriculture served only to increase rural unemployment, forcing many workers to migrate from the villages to the cities, especially Tehran, in search of jobs, creating massive shanty towns and breeding grounds for urban unrest. Finally, such beneficial reforms as heavy investment in literacy and education, health care, and female suffrage (despite rigged elections) proved unable to counteract and overcome the negative effects of the shah's ineffective and failed reforms. In sum, the rural areas and urban slums continued to lag behind the prosperous areas where expatriates lived in Tehran. The rise of an urban middle class with decidedly Western values dramatized the one-sided nature of the shah's reforms, which widened the social, economic, and political gulfs in Iran.

In 1963, from his home in Qom, Ayatollah Ruhollah Khomeini, a respected and erudite cleric, began to preach against the shah's rule, attacking its corruption, neglect of the rural poor, sale of oil to Israel, and failure to defend the country's sovereignty and independence against what he saw as American domination. Khomeini regarded the shah as a puppet of the West and believed that the United States was imposing anti-Islamic policies on Iran, such that Khomeini and his growing group of followers came to regard anything Western and American as corrupt, immoral, and evil. The persecution of Khomeini by the shah only served to legitimize him in the eyes of many Shia Muslims. Despite the fact that Khomeini was briefly arrested several times (which invariably led to deaths when the SAVAK raided his madrasah, or religious school, and mosque) his continued attacks on the shah endeared him to the Shiite community.

In 1964 the shah deported and exiled Khomeini from Iran. Khomeini eventually settled in the Shia town of Najaf in southern Iraq until pressure from the shah convinced the Iraqi government to deport him in 1978. Khomeini then took up residence in Paris, where he remained until returning to Iran on February 1, 1979, at which time he presided over the Iranian Revolution, already in progress. While in exile, Khomeini continued his attacks on the shah, and his sermons were frequently smuggled into Iran on audiotapes.

By the late 1970s, the flood of wealth into Iran from rising oil prices had led to high inflation, which affected the entire country, including, for the first time, the urban middle class. Attempts by the shah to reduce unemployment through reductions in government spending only led to a rise in unemployment, and all the while the number of rural poor migrating into Iran's cities, particularly Tehran, increased dramatically.

An effigy of the deposed shah of Iran is burned during a demonstration outside the U.S. Embassy in Tehran in late 1979. Iran's Islamic revolution of that year began as an uprising against Shah Mohammad Reza Pahlavi, whose autocratic rule and ties to the West were extremely unpopular in his country. (AP/Wide World Photos)

Pressure by newly elected American president Jimmy Carter (1977–1981) and awareness of the new president's commitment to human rights compelled the shah to relax his repression by releasing some political prisoners. He also promised to improve prison conditions, meet with representatives of Amnesty International, and promote such legal reforms as the right of the accused to an attorney and to be tried in a civilian rather than a military court, but none of this silenced resistance to his regime. A state visit to Washington, D.C., in late 1977, which featured the shah toasting champagne with President Carter, angered many Iranians, and the shah's embattled regime became symbolized by images of him near the White House wiping his eyes in reaction to tear gas from a nearby demonstration against his visit.

On January 7, 1978, an ill-advised article accusing Khomeini of being a homosexual and a British agent sparked massive protests by religious students and worshipers in Qom, Iran, and clashes with the police led to a number of casualties. From Paris, Khomeini praised the protests and urged them to continue. By then, the demonstrations and protests had exploded, growing to include urban merchants and factory workers protesting economic conditions. Facing a decline in their living standards, the urban, educated middle class no longer tolerated the shah's regime and joined the chorus of protests against him. In early September 1978 the shah imposed martial law, but the protests and violent confrontations with the police and SAVAK increased throughout the fall. As desertions increased among the military, the shah left the country on January 16, 1979, ostensibly for a vacation but in reality for exile, never to return to Iran. He died from cancer on July 27, 1980, in Cairo, Egypt, where he was granted asylum and is buried.

Khomeini made a triumphant return to Iran on February 1, 1979. He immediately set about restoring the country's Islamic heritage. Within two weeks of Khomeini's return, the military announced its intention to remain neutral and thus avoided being persecuted by local Islamic Revolutionary Committees, or Komitehs, composed of armed, militant Shia organized around local mosques who acted as vigilantes, enforcing Islamic values and laws. Senior officials of the shah's regime were arrested by Komitehs, tried by a revolutionary court, and executed, including the former head of the SAVAK. In March 1979, a referendum ratified Khomeini's decision to establish an Islamic republic by a 97 percent majority. Khomeini went on to create a separate paramilitary force, the Revolutionary Guard Corps, which served as secret police.

Over the summer, loyalists to Khomeini crafted a new constitution and a nominally democratic government with an elected parliament, elected municipal councils, and an elected president, but they also established a Council of Guardians composed of twelve clerics and jurists who approved candidates seeking elected office and also approved of or vetoed legislation passed by the parliament. This council, in which the real power of the government was vested, was tasked with assuring that legislation and politics remained strictly Islamic. The constitution also confirmed Khomeini and his successors as the supreme leaders of the government, with the right to appoint the heads of the armed forces, the head of the Revolutionary Guard Corps, and half of the members of the Council of Guardians. The Tudeh Party, liberal groups, and even moderate Islamist groups that had supported the revolution and Khomeini now found themselves marginalized and excluded from the new government, and some members were even executed for allegedly being anti-Islamic.

In November 1979, after President Carter reluctantly allowed the shah to enter the United States for cancer treatments, enraged Iranian students stormed the U.S. embassy in Tehran, seizing diplomatic personnel as hostages and thereby creating an international crisis that lasted for over a year. The American hostages were released only after the inauguration of President Ronald Reagan on January 20, 1981. Khomeini had supported the students and their demands that the United States turn over the shah for trial in exchange for releasing the hostages.

In September 1980, Iraqi dictator Saddam Hussein, in an attempt to take advantage of the still chaotic situation in Iran, launched an invasion of the country that precipitated a bloody and destructive eight-year war. Iraq's invasion turned Khomeini's regime toward fighting Iran's archenemy, and for the next eight years the conflict preoccupied the regime's attention and absorbed much of its resources. In the meantime, Khomeini and the Islamic clerics consolidated their power and imposed a regime in Iran that was every bit as repressive as that of the Shah. Following Khomeini's death in 1989, the government elevated another senior Shiite cleric, Sayyid Ali Khamenei, to the post of the supreme guide of Iran and the rank of ayatollah. He remains in that position today.

STEFAN M. BROOKS

See also

Iran; Iran, Armed Forces; Iran-Iraq War; Khomeini, Ruhollah; Reza Pahlavi, Mohammad

References

Axworthy, Michael. *A History of Iran.* New York: Basic Books, 2008.
Keddie, Nikki R. *Modern Iran: Roots and Results of Revolution.* New Haven, CT: Yale University Press, 2003.
Mackey, Sandra. *The Iranians: Persians, Islam, and the Soul of a Nation.* New York: Penguin, 1998.

Iran-Iraq War

Start Date: September 22, 1980
End Date: August 20, 1988

Protracted and costly Middle Eastern military conflict that began on September 22, 1980, with a surprise Iraqi invasion of western Iran along their common border. The war was in many ways a continuation of the ancient Persian-Arab rivalry fueled by 20th-century border disputes and competition for hegemony in the Persian Gulf and Middle East regions. In the late 1970s, the long-standing rivalry between these two nations was abetted by a collision between the Pan-Islamism and revolutionary Shia Islamism of Iran and the Pan-Arab nationalism of Iraq.

The border between the two states had been contested for some time, and in 1969 Iran had abrogated its treaty with Iraq on the navigation of the Shatt al-Arab waterway, Iraq's only outlet to the Persian Gulf. In 1971 Iran had seized islands in the Persian Gulf, and there had been border clashes between the two states in mid-decade. The rivalry between the two states was also complicated by minorities issues. Both states, especially Iraq, have large Kurdish populations in their northern regions, while an Arab minority inhabits the oil-rich Iranian province of Khuzestan.

Given their long-standing rivalry and ambitions, it was natural that the leaders of both states would seek to exploit any perceived weakness in the other. Thus, Iraqi president Saddam Hussein sought to take advantage of the upheaval following the fall of Mohammad Reza Shah Pahlavi and the establishment of Ayatollah Ruhollah Khomeini's Islamic Republic after the Iranian or Islamic Revolution of 1978–1979. This event had been precipitated by the disbandment of the shah's military establishment and an end to U.S. military assistance to Iran, which meant a shortage of spare parts. Hussein saw in this situation an opportunity to punish Iran for its support of Kurdish and Shia opposition to Sunni Muslim domination in Iraq. More important, it was a chance for Iraq to reclaim both banks of the Shatt al-Arab as well as Khuzestan, to acquire the islands of Abu Musa, Greater Tunb, and Lesser Tunb on behalf of the United Arab Emirates, and to overthrow the militant Islamic regime in Iran.

On the eve of the war, Iraq enjoyed an advantage in ground forces, while Iran had the edge in the air. Iraq had a regular army of some 300,000 men, 1,000 artillery pieces, 2,700 tanks, 332 fighter aircraft, and 40 helicopters. Iran had a regular army of 200,000 men, somewhat more than 1,000 artillery pieces, 1,740 tanks, 445 fighter aircraft, and 500 helicopters.

The Iraqi attack of September 22, 1988, came as a complete surprise to Iran. Hussein justified it as a response to an alleged assassination attempt sponsored by Iran on Iraqi foreign minister Tariq Aziz. Striking on a 300-mile front, Iraqi troops were initially successful against the disorganized Iranian defenders. The Iraqis drove into southwestern Iran, securing the far side of the Shatt al-Arab. In November they captured Khorramshahr in Khuzestan Province. In places, the Iraqis penetrated as much as 30 miles into Iran, but Iran is a large country, and the Iraqi forces moved too cautiously, throwing away the opportunity for a quick and decisive victory. Another factor in their stalled offensive was certainly the rapid Iranian mobilization of resources, especially the largely untrained but fanatical Pasdaran (Revolutionary Guard Corps) militia.

A Soviet-built tank of Iraq's army prepares to cross the Karoun River in October 1980 as Iraqi troops celebrate a success in their war against Iran. The smoke in the background is from an Iranian oil pipeline. (AP/Wide World Photos)

Recovering from the initial shock of the Iraqi invasion, the Iranians soon established strong defensive positions. Their navy also carried out an effective blockade of Iraq. On the first day of the war, Iraqi air strikes destroyed much of the Iranian Air Force infrastructure, but most of the Iranian aircraft survived, and Iraq lacked the long-range bomber aircraft to be truly effective strategically against a country as large as Iran. Indeed, Iranian pilots flying U.S.-manufactured aircraft soon secured air superiority over the Iraqi Air Force's Soviet-built airplanes. The Iranians were then able to carry out ground-support missions utilizing both airplanes and helicopters that played an important role in checking the Iraqi advance.

Far from breaking Iranian morale as Hussein has hoped, the Iraqi attack served to rally public opinion around the Islamic regime. Ideologically committed Iranians flocked to join the Pasdaran and the army. By March 1981, the war had settled into a protracted stalemate. With both sides having constructed extensive defensive positions, much of the combat came to resemble the trench warfare of World War I.

In January 1982, Jordanian volunteers began arriving to assist the Iraqis, but this addition had little impact on the fighting. Then on March 22, the Iranians launched a major counteroffensive. Their forces included large numbers of ill-trained but fanatical Pasdaran fighters. Lasting until March 30, the offensive enjoyed considerable success, driving the Iraqis back up to 24 miles in places.

During April 30–May 20, the Iranians renewed their attacks, again pushing the Iraqis back. Then on the night of May 22–23, the Iranians encircled the city of Khorramshahr, which the Iraqis had captured at the beginning of the war, forcing its surrender on May 24. There the Iranians captured large quantities of Soviet-manufactured weapons. Flush with victory, the Iranians now proclaimed as their war aim the overthrow of Saddam Hussein.

With the war now going badly for his country, Hussein proposed a truce and the withdrawal of all Iraqi troops from Iranian soil within two weeks of a truce agreement. Iraq also declared a unilateral cease-fire. Sensing victory, Iran rejected the proposal and reiterated its demand for the ouster of Hussein.

Given the Iranian rebuff and realizing that he had no legitimate hope of retaining his forces in Iran, Hussein now withdrew them back into well-prepared static defenses in Iraq, reasoning that Iraqis would rally to his regime in a fight to defend their homeland. For political reasons, Hussein announced that the purpose of the withdrawal was to allow Iraqi forces to assist Lebanon, which had been invaded by Israeli forces on June 6, 1982.

Meanwhile, Iranian leaders rejected a Saudi Arabian–brokered deal that would have witnessed the payment of $70 billion in war reparations by the Arab states to Iran and complete Iraqi withdrawal from Iranian territory, in return for a peace agreement. Iranian leaders, however, insisted that Hussein be removed from power, that some 100,000 Shiites expelled from Iraq before the war be permitted to return home, and that the reparations figure be set at $150 billion. There is some suggestion that Iran did not expect these terms to be accepted and hoped to use this as justification to continue the war with an invasion of Iraq. Indeed, Iranian leader Ayatollah Khomeini announced, "The only condition is that the regime in Baghdad must fall and must be replaced by an Islamic Republic," a scenario that was extremely unlikely.

The Iranians now sought to utilize their numerical advantage in a new offensive, which was launched on July 20, 1982. They directed it against Shiite-dominated southern Iraq, with the objective being the capture of Iraq's second-largest city of Basra. Iranian human-wave assaults, occasioned by a shortage of ammunition, encountered well-prepared Iraqi static defenses, supported by artillery. Hussein had also managed to increase substantially the number of Iraqis under arms.

Although the Iranians did manage to register some modest gains, these came at heavy human cost. In the five human-wave assaults of their Basra offensive (Operation RAMADAN), the Iranians sustained tens of thousands of casualties. Particularly hard-hit were the untrained and poorly armed units of boy-soldiers who volunteered to march into Iraqi minefields to clear them with their bodies for the trained Iranian soldiers who would follow them. The Iraqis also employed poison gas against the Iranians, inflicting many casualties. On July 21, Iranian aircraft struck Baghdad.

A young Iranian soldier shouts "Allahu Akhbar" (God is Great), the battle cry from the trenches during the Iran-Iraq War. (AP/Wide World Photos)

Iraq retaliated in August with attacks on the vital Iranian oil shipping facilities at Khargh Island, which also sank several ships.

During September–November, the Iranians launched new offensives in the northern part of the front, securing some territory near the border town of Samar, which Iraq had taken at the beginning of the war. The Iranians also struck west of Dezful and, in early November, drove several miles into Iraq near Mandali. Iraqi counterattacks forced the Iranians back into their own territory. In the southern part of the front, on November 17, the Iranians advanced to within artillery range of the vital Baghdad-Basra Highway.

Iran was now receiving supplies from such nations as the People's Republic of China, the Democratic People's Republic of Korea (North Korea), and Albania. Iraq was securing supplies from the Soviet Union and other Warsaw Pact states, France, Great Britain, Spain, Egypt, Saudi Arabia, and the United States. Iraq's chief financial backers were Saudi Arabia, Kuwait, and the United Arab Emirates.

In the course of 1983, Iran launched five major offensives against Iraq. Before the first of these, however, during February 2–March 9, the Iraqi Air Force carried out large-scale air attacks against Iranian coastal oil-production facilities, producing the largest oil spill in the history of the Persian Gulf region. Again seeking to utilize their advantage in troop strength, during February 7–16 Iranian leaders launched the first of their ground offensives. The Iranians hoped to isolate Basra by cutting the Baghdad-Basra Highway at Kut. They drove to within 30 miles of their objective but were then halted and thrown back. In the fighting, the Iraqis claimed to have destroyed upward of 1,000 Iranian tanks.

During April 11–14, the Iranians attacked west of Dezful but failed to make meaningful gains. On July 20, Iraqi aircraft again struck Iranian oil production facilities. Three days later, the Iranians attacked in northern Iraq but again registered few gains. The Iranians mounted a major offensive west of Dezful on July 30 but failed to break through. In the second week in August, however, the Iranians blunted an Iraqi counterattack. In this fighting, both sides suffered heavy casualties.

In late October the Iranians launched yet another attack in the north to close a salient there opened by Iranian Kurdish rebels. Iraqi leader Hussein was disappointed in his hope that the failed Iranian ground offensives and ensuing heavy casualties would make that regime more amenable to peace talks. Indeed, Iranian leader Ayatollah Khomeini restated his determination to overthrow the Baath regime in Iraq.

Determined to prevent the spread of militant Islamism in the Middle East, the Ronald Reagan administration in the United States made a firm commitment to support Iraq. Washington supplied Baghdad with intelligence information in the form of satellite photography, as well as furnishing economic aid and weapons. In a National Security Decision Directive of June 1982, Reagan determined that the United States must do whatever necessary to prevent Iraq from losing the war.

Believing that more aggressive tactics were necessary to induce Iran to talk peace, Hussein announced that unless Iran agreed to halt offensive action against Iraq by February 7, 1984, he would order major attacks against 11 Iranian cities. In answer, Iran mounted a ground attack in the northern part of the front, and Hussein then ordered the air and missile attacks against the cities to proceed. These lasted until February 22. Iran retaliated, in what became known as the "War of the Cities." There were five such air campaigns in the course of the war.

On February 15, 1984, the Iranians launched the first in a series of ground offensives. It fell in the central part of the front and pitted 250,000 Iranian troops against an equal number of Iraqi defenders. During February 15–22 in Operation DAWN 5, and during February 22–24 in Operation DAWN 6, the Iranians attempted to take the city of Kut to cut the vital Baghdad-Basra Highway there. The Iranians came within 15 miles of the city but were then halted.

The Iranians enjoyed more success in Operation KHANIBAR, during February 24–March 19. This renewed drive against the southern city of Basra came close to breaking through the stretched Iraqi defenders. The Iranians did capture part of the Majnoon Islands, with their undeveloped oil fields, then held them against an Iraqi counterattack supported by poison gas. The Iranians occupied these islands until near the end of the war.

With his forces having benefited from substantial arms purchases financed by the oil-rich Persian Gulf states, on January 18, 1985, Hussein launched the first Iraqi ground offensive since late 1980. It failed to register significant gains, and the Iranians responded with an offensive of their own, Operation BADR, beginning on March 11. Having become better trained, the Iranians eschewed the costly human-wave tactics of the past, and their more effective tactics brought the capture of a portion of the Baghdad-Basra Highway. Hussein responded to this considerable strategic emergency with desperate chemical weapons attacks and renewed air and missile strikes against 20 Iranian cities, including Tehran.

On February 17, 1986, in a surprise offensive employing commandoes, Iranian forces captured the strategically important Iraqi port of Faw, southeast of Basra at the southeast end of the Faw peninsula on the Shatt al-Arab waterway. In January 1987, Iran launched Operation KARBALA-5, a renewed effort to capture the city of Basra in southern Iraq. When the operation ground to a halt in mid-February, the Iranians launched NASR-4 in northern Iraq, which threatened the Iraqi city of Kirkuk during May–June.

On March 7, 1987, the United States initiated Operation EARNEST WILL to protect oil tankers and shipping lanes in the Persian Gulf. The so-called Tanker War had begun in March 1984 with the Iraqi air attack on strategic Kharg Island and nearby oil installations. Iran had then retaliated with attacks, including the use of mines, against tankers carrying Iraqi oil from Kuwait and on any tankers of the Persian Gulf states supporting Iraq. On November 1, 1986, the Kuwaiti government petitioned the international community to protect its tankers. The Soviet Union agreed to charter tankers, and on March 7, 1987, the United States announced that it would provide protection for any U.S.-flagged tankers. This would protect neutral tankers proceeding to or from Iraqi ports, ensuring that Iraq would have the economic means to continue the war.

On the night of May 17, 1987, an Iraqi French-manufactured Mirage F-1 fighter aircraft on antiship patrol fired two AM-39 Exocet antiship cruise missiles at a radar contact, apparently not knowing that it was the U.S. Navy frigate *Stark* (FFG-31). Although only one of the missiles detonated, both struck home and crippled the frigate, killing 37 crewmen and injuring another 50. The crew managed to save their ship, which then made port under its own power.

On July 20, 1987, the United Nations (UN) Security Council passed unanimously U.S.-sponsored Resolution 598. It deplored attacks on neutral shipping and called for an immediate cease-fire and withdrawal of armed forces to internationally recognized boundaries.

Acting in retaliation for Iranian ground offensives, during February 1988, the Iraqis launched a renewed wave of attacks against Iranian population centers, and the Iranians reciprocated. These attacks included not only aircraft but also surface-to-surface missiles, principally the Soviet-built Scud type. Iraq fired many more missiles than did Iran (reportedly some 520 as opposed to 177). Also during February and extending into September, the Iraqi Army carried out a massacre of Kurds in northern Iraq, known as the al-Anfal ("Spoils of War") Campaign, claiming as many as 300,000 civilian lives and the destroying some 4,000 villages.

On April 14, 1988, meanwhile, the U.S. Navy frigate *Samuel B. Roberts,* involved in Operation EARNEST WILL, was badly damaged when it struck an Iranian mine in the Persian Gulf. No one was killed, but the ship nearly sank. Four days later, the navy responded with Operation PRAYING MANTIS, the U.S. Navy's largest battle involving surface warships since World War II. This one-sided battle also saw the first surface-to-surface missile engagement in the navy's history. U.S. forces damaged two Iranian offshore oil platforms, sank one of the Iranian frigates and a gunboat, damaged another frigate, and sank three Iranian speedboats. The United States lost one helicopter.

By the spring of 1988, Iraqi forces had been sufficiently regrouped to enable them to launch major operations. By contrast, Iran was now desperately short of spare parts, especially for its largely U.S.-built aircraft. The Iranians had also lost a large number of airplanes in combat. As a result, by late 1987 Iran was less able to mount an effective defense against the resupplied Iraqi Air Force, let alone carry out aerial counterattacks against a ground attack.

The Iraqis mounted four separate offensives. In the process they were able to recapture the strategically important Faw peninsula, which had been lost in 1986, drive the Iranians away from Basra, and make progress in the northern part of the front. The Iraqi victories came at little cost to themselves, while the Iranians suffered heavy personnel and equipment losses. These setbacks were the chief factor behind Khomeini's decision to agree to a cease-fire as called for in United Nations Security Council Resolution 598.

On July 3, 1988, the crew of the U.S. Navy cruiser *Vincennes,* patrolling in the Persian Gulf and believing that they were under attack by an Iranian jet fighter, shot down Iran Air Flight 655, a civilian airliner carrying 290 passengers and crew. There were no survivors. The United States government subsequently agreed to pay $131.8 million in compensation for the incident. It expressed regret only for the loss of innocent life and did not apologize to the Iranian government. The incident may have served to convince Iranian leader Ayatollah Khomeini of the dangers of the United States actively entering the conflict against Iran and thus made him more amenable to ending the war.

War weariness and pressure from other governments induced both sides to accept a cease-fire agreement on August 20, 1988, bringing the eight-year war to a close. Total Iraqi casualties, including 60,000 men taken prisoner by Iran, numbered about 375,000 people (perhaps 200,000 of these killed). This figure does not include those killed in the Iraqi government campaign against its Kurdish population. Iran announced a death toll of nearly 300,000 people, but some estimates place this figure as high as 1 million or more. The war ended with a status quo antebellum, with none of the outstanding issues resolved. The UN-arranged cease-fire merely ended the fighting, leaving these two isolated states to pursue an arms race with each other and with the other states in the region.

Negotiations between Iraq and Iran remained deadlocked for two years after the cease-fire. In 1990, concerned with securing its forcible annexation of Kuwait, Iraq reestablished diplomatic relations with Iran and agreed to the withdrawal of Iraqi troops from occupied Iranian territory, the division of sovereignty over the Shatt al-Arab, and a prisoner-of-war exchange.

Iraqi leader Saddam Hussein, despite having led his nation into a disastrous war, emerged from it with the strongest military in the Middle East, second only to Israel. His power unchallenged in Iraq, he trumpeted a great national victory. The war, however, put Iraq deeply in debt to its Persian Gulf Arab neighbors, and this played a strong role in the coming of the Persian Gulf War (the $14 billion debt owed to Kuwait was a key factor in Iraq's decision to invade that nation in 1990). In Iran, the war helped consolidate popular support behind the Islamic Revolution.

SPENCER C. TUCKER

See also

Aziz, Tariq; EARNEST WILL, Operation; Hussein, Saddam; Iran; Iran Air Flight 655; Iranian Revolution; Iraq, History of, Pre-1990; Iraq, History of, 1990–Present; Khomeini, Ruhollah; PRAYING MANTIS, Operation; *Stark* Incident

References

Ansari, Ali. *A History of Modern Iran since 1921: The Pahlavis and After.* Boston, MA: Longman, 2003.
Cordesman, Anthony H., and Abraham R. Wagner. *The Lessons of Modern War,* Vol. 4, *The Gulf War.* Boulder, CO: Westview, 1996.
Rajaee, Farhang. *The Iran-Iraq War: The Politics of Aggression.* Gainesville: University Press of Florida, 1993.
Karsh, Efraim. *The Iran-Iraq War, 1980–1988.* Oxford, UK: Osprey, 2002.
Marr, Phebe. *The Modern History of Iraq.* 2nd ed. Boulder, CO: Westview, 2003.
Willet, Edward C. *The Iran-Iraq War.* New York: Rosen, 2004.
Wright, Robin. *In the Name of God: The Khomeini Decade.* New York: Simon and Schuster, 1989.

Iraq, Air Force

The Iraqi Air Force, initially created under the direction and guidance of the British Mandate government in 1931, grew steadily through six decades by importing technology and hardware from multiple sources, most notably Great Britain, France, and the Soviet Union. Its expansion was largely driven by the aftermath of unsuccessful attacks on Israel, which often led to the destruction of significant numbers of Iraqi warplanes. In 1991, it was virtually destroyed by the combined air forces of the international coalition formed to evict Iraqi occupation units from Kuwait (Operation DESERT STORM). Just prior to the 1991 Persian Gulf War, much of the pre-1991 Iraqi air fleet was flown to Iran, in the hope of preserving the airplanes for future use. The government of Iran seized control of the warplanes, however, further degrading Iraq's aerial defense capability. In the years after the Persian Gulf War, Iraq's remaining warplanes slowly degenerated due to poor maintenance, a lack of trained aircraft technicians, and a shortage of vital repair parts.

During the 2003 Anglo-American–led invasion of Iraq (Operation IRAQI FREEDOM), coalition forces reported virtually no aerial activity by the Iraqi military.

In 1931, the air arm of the Iraqi Army was created, primarily using obsolete British equipment. Throughout the next four decades, the growing Iraqi Air Force continued to use equipment considered obsolete by Western standards, but of sufficient quality to become one of the most powerful Arab air forces in the Middle East. Regionally, only the Israeli and Egyptian air forces were of superior size and quality. When Iraq became an independent nation in 1947, it continued to pursue surplus equipment from Great Britain, France, and the Soviet Union. By using cast-off warplanes, the fledgling Iraqi government kept the purchase and maintenance costs of its air force manageable.

In 1948, the Iraqi Air Force saw its first significant action outside of the national borders. When the state of Israel proclaimed its independence on May 14, 1948, it was immediately invaded by the armies of Egypt, Iraq, Lebanon, Syria, and Transjordan. Because Israel had no warplanes at the start of the Israeli-Arab War of 1948–1949, Iraqi attack aircraft held complete air superiority and could attack Israeli ground forces with impunity. They proved largely ineffective, however, and over the course of the war the nascent Israeli Air Force proved equal to the task of driving back the Iraqi warplanes. In June 1967, Israel launched preemptive strikes against Egypt, Jordan, and Syria, fearing an attack from the Arab nations was imminent. This prompted the Six-Day War. After the initial assaults, the Israeli Air Force turned its attention to Iraq, launching massive raids against Iraqi airfields and destroying much of the Iraqi Air Force on the ground. The few warplanes that survived the attacks remained grounded at airfields in eastern Iraq, presumably outside the range of Israeli raids. In the October 1973 Yom Kippur (Ramadan) War, elements of the Iraqi Air Force joined the conflict in support of the Syrian Army, and performed well enough against the Israeli Air Force that Iraq exited the war with its aerial fleet largely intact.

Throughout the 1970s and 1980s, Iraq used France and the Soviet Union as its primary warplane suppliers. Over 100 French Mirage F1 jets replaced the obsolete fleet of British Hawker Hunters. These were supplemented by approximately 100 French-built Gazelle, Super-Frelon, and Alouette helicopters. The most advanced Soviet fighter in the Iraqi arsenal was the MiG-29 Fulcrum; 24 joined a fleet of more than 200 MiG-21 Fishbed aircraft in 1987. Air transport capacity was primarily supplied by the Il-76 Candid transport and aerial tanker. During the Iran-Iraq War (1980–1988), the Iraqi Air Force served primarily in support of Iraqi ground forces. Iraq was able to maintain local air superiority over the primary battle zone of the war, but could not withstand the numerically superior Iranian Army. Soon the Iraqi Air Force began to deploy chemical weapons in a desperate attempt to hold off massive Iranian offensives.

After only two years of peace, the Iraqi Air Force was again committed to combat. On August 2, 1990, Iraqi president Saddam

Hussein ordered an invasion of Kuwait in the form of an overwhelming combined-arms assault on the small Persian Gulf nation. The world reaction was outrage, as American and Saudi Arabian military units scrambled into position to prevent further aggression. The United Nations (UN) imposed economic sanctions and threatened the use of force to drive Iraq from Kuwait. When Hussein refused to withdraw his troops, a U.S.-led multinational invasion of Kuwait and Iraq ensued (Operation DESERT STORM). The invasion began on January 17, 1991, and lasted several weeks, involving massive air strikes against Iraqi command and control centers, airfields, and antiair defenses.

Despite the fact that Iraq owned the sixth-largest air fleet in the world, including as many as 750 warplanes in 1990–1991, the Iraqi Air Force offered minimal resistance to the coalition's establishment of complete air superiority. During the entire aerial campaign, Iraqi fighters did not shoot down a single coalition aircraft, and rarely attempted to intercept coalition warplanes. Coalition forces downed 42 Iraqi aircraft, including 9 Mirage F1s and 5 MiG-29s, and reported that Iraqi pilots were poorly trained and ineffective in aerial combat. Rather than face annihilation, approximately 130 Iraqi combat pilots flew to Iran, where they were interned by the Iranian government for the duration of the war. When the conflict ended, the pilots were released, but the aircraft were integrated into the Iranian military. According to American estimates, more than 200 Iraqi aircraft were destroyed on the ground during DESERT STORM. By the end of the war, the air force contained only 50 Mirage F1s, 15 MiG-29s, and less than 100 older aircraft models.

In the period after the Persian Gulf War, coalition forces established a pair of "no-fly" zones over Iraq, prohibiting Iraqi warplanes from overflying all but the central third of the nation. Coalition aircraft frequently bombed targets in Iraq to enforce compliance with the terms of the 1991 cease-fire. From 1991 until 2003, the Iraqi Air Force rapidly deteriorated due to massive shortages of spare aircraft parts and trained mechanics. As of 2002, Iraq owned only 5 serviceable MiG-29 fighters and less than 40 serviceable Mirage F1s, supplemented by less than 100 older warplanes. By the beginning of the Anglo-American–led coalition invasion of

U.S. forces pull an Iraqi Air Force MiG-25R Foxbat-B from beneath the sands of Iraq on July 6, 2003. While U.S. and coalition forces discovered a great deal of secreted military equipment, no weapons of mass destruction, a pretext for going to war with Iraq, have ever been found. (U.S. Department of Defense)

Iraq in March 2003 (Operation IRAQI FREEDOM), the Iraqi Air Force had virtually ceased to exist. Coalition forces routinely found derelict aircraft as they captured Iraqi airfields. Some advanced Iraqi warplanes were found literally buried in the desert in an attempt to preserve them from enemy air strikes. After Iraqi president Saddam Hussein was deposed in April 2003, coalition forces began to slowly rebuild the Iraqi military as a key component of the establishment of a democratic Iraqi government. The resurgent air force now serves primarily in a transport capacity, and it has been outfitted with American-built C-130 Hercules transport planes and UH-1 helicopters. Iraq has not been able to import new aircraft since the 1991 Persian Gulf War, and thus its few remaining aircraft have become increasingly obsolete.

In August 2009 the Iraqi Defense Ministry revealed that Iraq owns 19 MiG-21 and MiG-23 fighter jets in storage in Serbia. Saddam Hussein had sent the aircraft to Serbia for repairs in the late 1980s during the Iran-Iraq War. The aircraft could not be returned to Iraq because of the subsequent international sanctions. Upon learning of the existence of the aircraft in 2009, the Iraqi government arranged with the Serbs to refurnish and return the aircraft on a priority basis.

The United States has agreed to provide Iraq with propeller-driven Hawker Beechcraft T-6A aircraft that would be used to train Iraqi jet pilots to fly the Lockheed Martin F-16 Fighting Falcon. Discussions over Iraqi purchases of the F-16 from the United States are still ongoing, however.

PAUL J. SPRINGER

See also

Aircraft, Attack; Aircraft, Fighters; Air Defenses in Iraq, Iraq War; Air Defenses in Iraq, Persian Gulf War; Chemical Weapons and Warfare; DESERT STORM, Operation; Iraq, Army; IRAQI FREEDOM, Operation

References

Butler, Richard. *The Greatest Threat: Iraq, Weapons of Mass Destruction and the Growing Crisis in Global Security*. New York: PublicAffairs, 2000.

Herzog, Chaim. *The Arab-Israeli Wars: War and Peace in the Middle East from the War of Independence to Lebanon*. Westminster, MD: Random House, 1984.

Hiro, Dilip. *The Longest War: The Iran-Iraq Military Conflict*. London: Routledge, 1991.

Murray, Williamson, and Robert H. Scales Jr. *The Iraq War: A Military History*. Cambridge, MA: Belknap, 2005.

Rubin, Barry, and Thomas A. Keaney, eds. *Armed Forces in the Middle East: Politics and Strategy*. Portland, OR: Frank Cass, 2002.

Iraq, Army

The Iraqi Army has historically been one of the most technologically advanced and aggressive military forces in the modern Middle East. Since the end of World War II, Iraq has joined three wars against Israel, launched invasions of Iran and Kuwait, and been attacked by two multinational forces under American leadership. The Iraqi Army has also frequently engaged in internal strife, fighting to put down repeated Kurdish and Shiite revolts against the government. In addition, the Iraqi Army has played a fundamental role in the Iraqi government, having participated in a series of coups d'état against the existing government beginning in the late 1950s. After the most recent invasion and occupation of Iraq, which began in 2003 with Operation IRAQI FREEDOM, the Iraqi Army was declared dissolved by the Coalition Provisional Authority (CPA), the interim occupation government. The CPA then began to rebuild the Iraqi military from the ground up, including its complete retraining.

The military history of Iraq stretches back several thousand years. The region of Mesopotamia, situated astride the Tigris and Euphrates rivers, is often considered the "cradle of civilization." The ancient Sumerian, Akkadian, and Babylonian empires each dominated the region. By the ninth century AD, Baghdad was an economic and cultural center for the entire the Muslim world. In 1638, the region was assimilated into the Ottoman Empire through military conquest. Iraq remained a part of Ottoman Turkey until World War I, when it was invaded and occupied by a British expeditionary force that landed at Basra and gradually moved northward. The British troops were assisted by Iraqi Arabs, emboldened by promises of independence at the end of the war. When World War I ended, the Ottoman Empire was dissolved, but the modern state of Iraq was largely controlled by the British and remained a British Mandate until 1947.

In the interwar period, a series of rebellions against British rule erupted in Iraq. The first began in May 1920, when Iraqi nationalists, angered at the creation of the British Mandate, led a general Arab insurrection against the newly constituted government. In addition to feeling frustrated by their failure to obtain independence, the rebels also resented the actual composition of the mandate government. It consisted almost entirely of foreign bureaucrats, particularly British colonial officials transplanted from India. By February 1921, British military forces had successfully quelled the rebellion, only to see a Kurdish revolt begin the following year. The Kurdish attempt to form an independent Kurdish state was primarily stymied through the use of airpower, against which the Kurds had no defense. Iraqi Army units under British control assisted in the suppression of the Kurdish revolt. In the 1930s, two more major uprisings occurred. In August 1933, Assyrian Christians rebelled against the government, provoking a harsh retaliation by the Iraqi Army that left 600 dead. A religious-based revolt occurred again in 1935, when Shiite Muslims attempted to overthrow the reigning government and were brutally suppressed by British and Iraqi troops.

In 1941, with World War II raging in Europe, Iraqi politician Rashid Ali al-Gaylani and his military colleagues known as the Golden Square perceived an opportunity to overthrow British control. After they seized power, Ali proclaimed an independent Iraq. The Allied powers feared that he would align his government with the Axis nations of Germany and Italy because Germany had been directing propaganda efforts in neighboring Syria and Iraq. British residents and officials took refuge in the British legation, and to rescue them, the British sent in forces that quickly defeated the Iraqi Army and reestablished the mandate government. Three separate Kurdish revolts broke out in the 1940s, each led by Mullah Mustafa Barzani. All were quickly suppressed by the Iraqi Army, bolstered by British air power.

On May 14, 1948, Jews in Palestine led by David Ben-Gurion proclaimed the State of Israel. The announcement provoked an immediate invasion by Egypt, Iraq, Lebanon, Syria, and Transjordan; thus began the Israeli-Arab War of 1948–1949. Iraqi forces operated in conjunction with Syrian and Transjordanian troops and were occasionally aided by members of the Palestinian Arab Liberation Army. The Arab forces did not have a technological advantage as had been claimed, and the Arab coalition was incapable of overrunning the new nation. The Iraqi expeditionary force made small initial gains but could not withstand the eventual Israeli counterattack. The Iraqi Army in 1948 included more than 20,000 troops, of which 5,000 were initially committed to the war effort. The Iraqi troops were supported by an armored battalion and 100 warplanes. After initial rapid advances on the central front, Iraqi general Nur ad-Din Mahmud ceded the operational initiative and shifted to a defensive stance. The Iraqi troop contingent grew to over 20,000 men during the war, including thousands of poorly trained recruits who volunteered for service in Palestine. Despite maintaining numerical superiority for the entire war, Iraqi troops made no progress in Israel after June 1948. By mid-1949, Iraqi troops had withdrawn from Israel, although the formal state of war remained through 2006.

In 1956, the Suez Crisis threatened to expand into a larger regional conflict. While Egyptian and Israeli units sparred for control of the Sinai peninsula, Iraqi Army troops crossed into Jordan to prevent an Israeli attack there. Shortly after Iraqi troops returned home, Brigadier General Abd al-Karim al-Qasim led the Iraqi military in a coup against King Faisal II's government. Faisal had been installed as monarch in 1947, with British support. During the seizure of power, the king and Prime Minister Nuri al-Said were both killed. Qasim then consolidated his power and put down repeated counterrevolutions, including an attempted coup by Sunni officers of the army and another Kurdish revolt. In 1961, Britain relinquished control of Kuwait, which was immediately claimed by the Iraqi government. In response, Britain deployed troops to Kuwait to defend it from a potential Iraqi invasion.

The longest and most successful Kurdish revolt against Iraqi rule commenced in 1961. Mustafa Barzani led yet another uprising

Heavily armed soldiers in the streets of Baghdad, Iraq, on July 14, 1958, a few hours after the military seized control, overthrowing the monarchy and declaring a republic. (AP/Wide World Photos)

in the hope of gaining autonomy for the Kurdish people. The Iraqi Army proved incapable of quelling the rebellion, however, even when assisted by the Iraqi Air Force. By 1963, Syrian military forces moved into Iraq to assist in ending the rebellion, hoping to prevent an expansion of the uprising. With the exception of a one-year cease-fire that ended in April 1965, the conflict continued until 1970, when the Iraqi government finally admitted defeat and granted Kurdish autonomy without full independence.

In 1967, the June Six-Day War erupted between Israel and an Arab coalition. Israeli intelligence, detecting a massive Arab military buildup on its borders, compelled Israel to launch a series of preemptive strikes to prevent or delay the invasion. The majority of the Egyptian Air Force was destroyed in the first raids, and a similar raid against Iraqi airfields achieved modest success, destroying some aircraft and driving the rest to airfields in eastern Iraq, beyond the reach of Israeli attack aircraft. Although Iraq did not formally participate in the 1967 war, Iraqi troops again moved into defensive positions in Jordan, helping to deter a major Israeli advance across the Jordan River.

On October 6, 1973, Arab armies surprised Israel with a massive invasion on three fronts, sparking the Kom Kippur or Ramadan War. Although the Iraqi Army did not participate in the first days of the conflict, within a week Iraqi armor units were fighting the Israelis on the Golan Heights. Over 60,000 Iraqi troops were deployed in the war, supplemented by 700 tanks. The decision to attack Israel proved to be a debacle for the Iraqi Army, however. On October 13, an Israeli ambush destroyed 80 Iraqi tanks in a single day without the loss of any Israeli tanks. Iraqi military performance improved little throughout the war. The Iraqi military coordinated poorly with its Arab allies and was repeatedly mauled by the aggressive tactics of Israeli commanders. Although Iraq itself was never threatened with invasion, the Iraqi Army at the conclusion of the war showed the effects of devastating battlefield losses. During the spring of 1974, Barzani led another Kurdish revolt, this time supported by Mohammad Reza Shah Pahlavi of Iran. This rebellion was brutally put down by the Iraqi Army, forcing Pahlavi to withdraw his support. For the remainder of the decade, Iraq attempted to rebuild its army, relying primarily upon the Soviet Union for the supply of heavy weapons.

After five years of border disputes with Iran, Iraqi president Saddam Hussein ordered an invasion of Iran, beginning on September 22, 1980. At the time of the invasion, the Iraqi Army had grown to almost 200,000 troops, supplemented by 4,500 tanks, mostly of Soviet design. By gradually increasing tank imports while maintaining older designs in service, the Iraqi armored divisions fielded a very mixed force of vehicles, ranging from the T-55, designed in 1947, to the T-80 model of 1976. Initially, the army managed to advance into Iranian territory. However, the advance was soon halted by stronger-than-expected Iranian resistance. Eight years of bloody stalemate ensued, costing almost 1 million total casualties. In an effort to end the stalemate, Hussein ordered the use of chemical weapons on Iranian troops and the Iranian civilian population. The use of chemical weapons alarmed

the entire region, particularly because the Iraqi government had a well-established nuclear weapons program in place and was actively seeking atomic weapons. On June 7, 1981, Israel launched an air raid to destroy Iraq's Osiraq nuclear reactor, destroying the bulk of the nuclear program in a single strike.

After eight years of combat, Iran and Iraq agreed to an armistice returning to the status quo antebellum. In 1988, Iraq possessed the largest army in the Middle East, capable of fielding 1 million troops from a population of only 17 million. In addition, imports of Soviet hardware made the Iraqi Army the most advanced in the region. Iraqi armored divisions relied on the Soviet T-80 main battle tank. The army contained 70 divisions of veteran troops, with a large number of artillery pieces. The Soviet Union also provided Iraq with tactical and strategic missiles capable of delivering biological and chemical weapons to Israel.

The Iraqi military did not remain idle for long after the Iran-Iraq War. Following two years of rebuilding, Iraq again looked to expand its territory along the Persian Gulf coast. After renewing claims that Kuwait was a renegade province of Iraq, the Iraqi government accused Kuwait of stealing oil reserves through illegal slant-drilling techniques and manipulating the price of oil. When Kuwait refused a series of Iraqi demands, Hussein ordered the invasion of Kuwait, beginning on August 2, 1990. The invasion quickly overwhelmed the small Kuwaiti military. The United States immediately deployed forces to Saudi Arabia to prevent further Iraqi aggression, and within four months, 500,000 American troops defended Saudi Arabia, bolstered by detachments from dozens of nations (Operation DESERT SHIELD). Included in the defensive forces were units from many of Iraq's Arabic neighbors. When Hussein ignored United Nations (UN) resolutions demanding the evacuation of Kuwait, the coalition forces launched a series of air strikes against targets in Iraq and Kuwait beginning in January 2001. Eventually, during Operation DESERT STORM, a massive ground assault forced Iraqi units to retreat from Kuwait.

Although Hussein threatened that coalition forces would face "the mother of all battles" if they dared to invade Iraq, the coalition ground attack quickly overwhelmed Iraqi units entrenched in prepared positions. The Iraqi military had no defense against coalition air supremacy, and thousands of destroyed Iraqi tanks and armored vehicles littered the retreat route. The vaunted Republican Guard divisions, elite units of the Iraqi Army, were eviscerated by coalition aircraft and tanks. Although the exact number of Iraqi soldiers killed remains unknown, estimates put the number at between 15,000 and 100,000, with a further 300,000 wounded in the fighting.

Even after Iraqi forces were driven from Kuwaiti soil, Iraq remained under tight economic sanctions in the decade after the Persian Gulf War. Because Hussein refused to account for the entire Iraqi biological and chemical weapons arsenal, UN weapons inspectors roamed the nation. Restrictions on imports into Iraq prevented Hussein from rebuilding the devastated Iraqi Army, and even vehicles that survived the coalition onslaught could not be maintained for want of spare parts.

On March 20, 2003, the United States led a thin coalition in a new invasion of Iraq (Operation IRAQI FREEDOM). Ostensibly, the invasion was triggered by Iraqi refusals to comply with UN weapons inspections. However, the new coalition did not include any of Iraq's Middle Eastern neighbors. Regardless of the much smaller size of the invading forces, the 2003 invasion conquered Iraq in only three weeks, deposing Hussein in April. Weapons inspectors did not find the expected stockpiles of chemical and biological weapons, although some small caches of illegal weapons were discovered in the aftermath of the fighting. At the time of the invasion, the Iraqi Army was a mere shadow of its 1990 size, with less than 400,000 poorly trained troops using obsolete equipment. Estimates for total Iraqi casualties in the 2003 war vary greatly, but U.S. general Tommy Franks reported in April 2003 that approximately 30,000 Iraqi soldiers died during the invasion.

After conquering Iraq, the Anglo-American–led forces established a provisional government. One its earliest directives, proposed by Paul Bremer, head of the Coalition Provisional Authority (CPA), and announced on May 23, 2003, dissolved the Iraqi military, a move that in retrospect proved to be a disaster because occupying and pacifying the nation without the army proved impossible, especially considering that American forces in theater were only a fraction of what would have been needed. Rather, the provisional government planned to completely rebuild and retrain the Iraqi Army. This decision created a massive power vacuum in Iraqi society, and contributed to the high unemployment, lawlessness, and insurgency that have characterized occupied Iraq. The Iraqi Army continues to operate Soviet-built tanks, but the vast majority of Iraq's top-quality armored vehicles were destroyed in 1991 and 2003, ensuring that most remaining Iraqi tanks are of long-obsolete designs, such as the T-62 and T-55. From the 70 divisions of 1988, the Iraqi Army was down to only 10 divisions by 2006. One division is currently mechanized; the remainder is composed of motorized infantry units. Many analysts fear that the Iraqi Army would be incapable of defending the nation from a determined assault from one of its stronger neighbors. As of this writing, coalition forces remain in occupation of Iraq, attempting to rebuild the Iraqi Army into an effective force capable of

Iraqi and American soldiers exit a U.S. Marine Corps helicopter during partnered air assault training at Camp Ramadi, Iraq, November 15, 2009. (U.S. Department of Defense)

maintaining internal and external security. These efforts have been hindered by a continuing insurrection bolstered by foreign fighters attempting to defeat the occupation and destroy the newly formed Iraqi Army. The army has proven unwilling or unable to halt the insurrection and protect the civilian population, and the Iraqi government has likewise been unable to effectively mobilize its military and security forces to stanch the insurgency.

PAUL J. SPRINGER

See also

Biological Weapons and Warfare; Chemical Weapons and Warfare; DESERT SHIELD, Operation; DESERT STORM, Operation; Faisal II, King of Iraq; Hussein, Saddam; Iran-Iraq War; Iraq, Air Force; Iraq, History of, Pre-1990; Iraq, History of, 1990–Present; Iraq, Sanctions on; Iraqi Forces, Postwar U.S. Training of; IRAQI FREEDOM, Operation; Iraqi Insurgency; Kurds; Shia Islam; Sunni Islam

References

Butler, Richard. *The Greatest Threat: Iraq, Weapons of Mass Destruction and the Growing Crisis in Global Security*. New York: PublicAffairs, 2000.

Finnie, David H. *Shifting Lines in the Sand: Kuwait's Elusive Frontier with Iraq*. Cambridge: Harvard University Press, 1992.

Herzog, Chaim. *The Arab-Israeli Wars: War and Peace in the Middle East from the War of Independence to Lebanon*. Westminster, MD: Random House, 1984.

Hiro, Dilip. *The Longest War: The Iran-Iraq Military Conflict*. London: Routledge, 1991.

Murray, Williamson, and Robert H. Scales Jr. *The Iraq War: A Military History*. Cambridge, MA: Belknap, 2005.

Rubin, Barry, and Thomas A. Keaney, eds. *Armed Forces in the Middle East: Politics and Strategy*. Portland, OR: Frank Cass, 2002.

Iraq, History of, Pre-1990

Iraq is a Middle Eastern nation covering 168,753 square miles, slightly smaller than the U.S. state of California. It borders Saudi Arabia to the west and south, Kuwait and the Persian Gulf to the south, Iran to the east, and Syria and Turkey to the north. Most important to a modern understanding of Iraq is the Arab conquest of the region (633–644 CE), which was responsible for making Iraq the culturally, ethnically, linguistically, and religiously diverse country it is today. As the capital of the Muslim Abbasid Empire shifted from Damascus to Baghdad, Iraq rose to renewed prominence with a new culture and religion. The synthesis of this empire and subsequent Muslim states with the influence of Iraq's numerous tribes remains a powerful historical aspect of life in Iraq.

The Ottoman defeat in World War I left Great Britain the new master of the former Ottoman provinces of Mosul, Baghdad, and Basra, which now form the modern state of Iraq. Independence in 1932, however, was far less than the salvation many Iraqis assumed it would be. Iraq was split between Sunni and Shia; among Arab, Kurd, and Turcoman; and between urban and rural, and deep cleavages tore at the fabric of Iraqi society.

While it lasted, the Hashimite monarchy (1921–1958) attempted to build a unified sense of identity in Iraq. Following the

1958 coup that toppled the monarchy and brought General Abd al-Karim Qasim to power, Iraqi governments fell in rapid succession.

In 1940, Prime Minister Rashid Ali al-Gaylani offered to support Britain in World War II if Palestine were to be established as a state. Winston Churchill's refusal caused a split between the nationalists, who thought that Axis support would help them, and such moderates as former prime minister Nuri al-Said. The crisis led to a British and Transjordan Arab Legion occupation of Baghdad and the flight of Gaylani and his allies from Iraq, and it lent support to the later Baathist anti-imperialist stance.

When Israel declared its independence on May 14, 1948, a new dimension was added to an already unstable regional situation. In the Israeli-Arab War of 1948–1949, Iraq provided 3,000 troops in May 1948, adding 15,000 troops during the months that followed. Iraqi forces successfully held the Jenin-Nablus-Tulkaram triangle but singularly failed to launch an attack on Jewish forces. The failure of the allied Arab forces to succeed on the battlefield left Arab leaders with little choice but to negotiate the 1948 cease-fire.

Arab failure, as in the past, led to the persecution of Iraqi Jews, whose loyalty was suspect. The focus on internal deficiencies of the regime was replaced by charges that the small number of Iraqi Jews had spied for Israel and were responsible for Iraq's military failure. This pattern of behavior repeated itself during the 1967 Six-Day War and the 1973 Yom Kippur (Ramadan) War. Later, Iraqi dictator Saddam Hussein would perfect this ploy and use it on a number of occasions against other enemies to deflect attention away from his own economic, military, and political failures.

In 1955 Iraq joined the pro-Western Baghdad Pact, allying itself with Turkey, Iran, and Pakistan in a mutual defense agreement sponsored by the United States. The pact was a direct affront to the long-simmering nationalist sentiments within the Iraqi Army officer corps. Indeed, the pact became the catalyst that ignited the 1958 revolution, the first in a string of coups and countercoups that would plague Iraq until the Baathists finally consolidated power in 1968. The 1958 coup was led by a secret nationalist organization known as the Free Officers Movement. On July 14, 1958, its members seized control of Baghdad and executed King Faisal II and Prime Minister Said. The revolutionaries then abolished the monarchy, proclaimed Iraq a republic, and sought closer ties to the Soviet Union. Colonel Qasim had led the coup, but his policies ultimately created a great many internal and external enemies.

The republican period of Iraqi history (1958–1968) was marked by internal conflict in which the antimonarchist factions fought among themselves. Qasim's rule of Iraq was short-lived, and he was overthrown in 1963 by a coalition of anticommunist military officers and secular Arab nationalists and Baathists who installed Colonel Abd al-Salam Arif as president and Hasan al-Bakr as prime minister. Allies in the National Council of the Revolutionary Command, which took the reins of government in February 1963, soon turned against one another, as it became clear that the military and the Baath Party fundamentally disagreed on the path that Iraq should pursue. President Arif's tenure in office ended abruptly when he was killed in a helicopter crash in

1966. His more pliable brother, Abdal-Rahman Arif, took over and served as president until 1968.

Iraq's failure to support fellow Arab states in the Six-Day War led to massive riots in Baghdad, which the regime was ineffective in suppressing. On July 17, 1968, the Baathists seized radio stations, the Ministry of Defense, and the headquarters of the Republican Guard. The Baath Party thus came to power with Hasan al-Bakr taking the posts of president, prime minister, and secretary general of the party. His cousin, Saddam Hussein, worked in the background to eliminate adversaries of the new regime.

Over time, Hussein proved to be a ruthless operator whose patronage system broke down the historic bonds in Iraqi society. His network of security organizations so thoroughly penetrated government, the military, and society that he was able to remove Bakr from power without a challenge. Security operatives also settled old scores with the communists and Free Officers on Hussein's behalf.

The Baath regime did, however, pursue numerous needed reforms. These included land reform, agricultural investment, the renegotiation of oil contracts, hospital and school construction, and a number of other reforms in a continuing effort to bring the society into the regime's broader network of patronage. This task was also accomplished through the activities of the large Baath Party itself. Iraqi society was dependent on a patronage network in which

association with party, military, or government officials was necessary and in which bribes were used. For this and other reasons, such as rural-urban migration, economic reforms did not succeed, and from 1973 onward Iraq was largely dependent on oil revenues.

When the Yom Kippur (Ramadan) War began in October 1973, a recently attempted coup by the brutal head of state security services, Nadhim Kzar, was still at the forefront of government efforts to purge the Baath Party. This led to Iraq playing only a minor role in the war in the form of an armored division sent to Syria. The Iraqis fought alongside the Syrians as they sought to retake the Golan Heights. The effort failed.

Defeat in the war was the third consecutive defeat for the Arabs at the hands of Israel, and it led the Iraqi regime to turn inward. This meant that the Kurds, Shiites, and communists suffered the brunt of the regime's onslaught throughout the 1970s. Survival became the focus of existence for these three groups. With the establishment of the Islamic Republic of Iran in 1979, the Iraqi regime saw a looming threat from Ayatollah Ruhollah Khomeini's Shiite-fundamentalist regime.

After Hussein assumed the presidency in 1979, his consolidation of power was complete. He launched an offensive against the southern Iranian city of Khorramshahr on September 17, 1980, sparking the Iran-Iraq War, which would drag on until 1988 and would witness more than 1 million combined casualties. Neither

Saddam Hussein waves to cheering crowds during a visit to the holy Muslim shrines in Samara on August 9, 1988. The Iraqi president visited the site for prayers and to give thanks following an agreement on a cease-fire in the eight-year long Iran-Iraq War. (AP/Wide World Photos)

side achieved a clear victory, and both countries saw their economies dramatically decline during the war. For Israel, however, the Iran-Iraq War was a respite that reduced foreign threats.

Exhausted, Iran and Iraq reached a cease-fire agreement in July 1988. In the aftermath of the war, Hussein turned to Saudi Arabia and Kuwait for financial assistance but was rebuffed. Under Ottoman rule, Kuwait had been part of Basra Province and only became an independent emirate during the British Mandate. This historical quirk provided Hussein with an excuse to invade Kuwait.

But Hussein had other reasons to attack Kuwait. He accused the Kuwaitis of manipulating the price of oil to the detriment of Iraq and asserted that Kuwait was illegally tapping Iraqi oil reserves by slant-drilling into Iraqi oil fields. Hussein also fumed that the Kuwaitis would not accede to debt reduction to help a struggling Iraqi economy. To Hussein's way of thinking, if the Kuwaiti emir would not provide financial relief to Iraq, then the Iraqi Army would simply conquer Kuwait.

In the days leading up to the 1990 Iraqi invasion of Kuwait, the United States failed to clearly communicate its disapproval of an Iraqi invasion, and instead led the Iraqis to believe that they were free to invade Kuwait. After the invasion began on August 2, 1990, the United Nations (UN) quickly condemned Iraq, and U.S. president George H. W. Bush began deploying American troops to Saudi Arabia. Although the Iraqi regime was convinced that the United States would not attack, the Iraqi high command began planning for such a contingency. Part of the plan called for a massive air strike that would see Israel's major cities hit by devastating chemical weapons attacks designed to bring Israel into the war and cause other Arab nations to terminate their support of the U.S.-led coalition. The attack never materialized, but Iraq did manage to strike Israel with approximately two dozen Scud missiles in January 1991. The United States responded by deploying two Patriot missile batteries to Israel.

In the wake of a resounding coalition victory in February 1991, Iraq was reduced economically and politically by the sanctions placed on Hussein's regime and the presence of UN weapons inspectors who scoured the country for weapons of mass destruction (WMDs). Average Iraqis suffered intensely under the sanctions. The UN's Oil-for-Food Programme was designed to bring needed medicine and food to Iraq while preventing the regime from rebuilding its WMD capabilities. Instead, Hussein built lavish palaces and exported the medical supplies and food intended for Iraqis to foreign countries. He also ruthlessly suppressed uprisings by both the Kurds and Shiites.

Iraq's link to international terrorism had begun as early as the 1980s. It was in fact the Iraqi regime that provided Abu Abbas, mastermind of the *Achille Lauro* ocean liner hijacking, safe haven in 1985. In the years that followed the Persian Gulf War, Hussein dramatically stepped up his support for terrorist organizations.

ADAM LOWTHER, LOUIS A. DiMARCO,
AND PAUL G. PIERPAOLI JR.

See also

Abbas, Abu; *Achille Lauro* Hijacking; Arif, Abd al-Salam; Baath Party; Baghdad Pact; Bakr, Ahmad Hassan al-; Bush, George Herbert Walker; DESERT STORM, Operation; Faisal II, King of Iraq; Hussein, Saddam; Iran-Iraq War; Iranian Revolution; Iraq, Air Force; Iraq, Army; Iraq, History of, 1990–Present; Iraq, Navy; Iraqi Claims on Kuwait; Kurds; Kurds, Massacres of; Nuri al-Said; Qasim, Abd al-Karim; Terrorism; United Kingdom, Middle East Policy

References

Abdullah, Thabit. *A Short History of Iraq*. London: Pearson, 2003.

Dodge, Toby. *Inventing Iraq: The Failure of Nation-Building and a History Denied*. New York: Columbia University Press, 2003.

Karsh, Efraim. *Islamic Imperialism*. New Haven, CT: Yale University Press, 2006.

Makiya, Kanan. *Republic of Fear: The Politics of Modern Iraq*. Berkeley: University of California Press, 1998.

Murray, Williamson, and Robert H. Scales Jr. *The Iraq War: A Military History*. Cambridge, MA: Belknap, 2005.

Oren, Michael B. *Six Days of War: June 1967 and the Making of the Modern Middle East*. Novato, CA: Presidio, 2003.

Pelletiere, Stephen. *The Iran-Iraq War: Chaos in a Vacuum*. New York: Praeger, 1992.

Polk, William R. *Understanding Iraq: The Whole Sweep of Iraqi History, from Genghis Khan's Mongols to the Ottoman Turks to the British Mandate to the American Occupation*. New York: Harper Perennial, 2006.

Tripp, Charles. *A History of Iraq*. Cambridge: Cambridge University Press, 2007.

Iraq, History of, 1990–Present

From 1990 until the U.S.-led coalition invasion of Iraq on March 20, 2003, which overthrew the government of President Saddam Hussein, Iraq was in perpetual crisis, and many of its citizens suffered from severe economic and military hardships. To make matters worse, Iraqi government policies during that period only exacerbated the chaos that defined the nation between 1990 and 2003. After Hussein was overthrown, Iraq was convulsed by violence due to sectarian strife and a potent Iraqi insurgency, and occupation forces have had mixed success in dealing with the unrest. Reconstruction has proceeded slowly, and, with no long-standing tradition of a freely elected democratic government, the new Iraqi government has proven to be not very adept at managing the nation's affairs.

During much of the time period, Iraq was ruled by Saddam Hussein, who was president of Iraq from July 16, 1979, until April 9, 2003. On April 9, 2003, coalition forces captured Baghdad and established the Coalition Provisional Authority (CPA) to govern Iraq, which was later formed into the Iraqi Interim Government. The permanent government was elected in 2005. Large numbers of coalition forces—most of them American—remained in the country as part of an effort to quell the violence and help the government gain control of the country.

Demolished vehicles and equipment on Al Mutla Pass, north of Kuwait City. They were destroyed by U.S. Air Force and Army Tiger Brigade forces engaging Iraqi troops fleeing Kuwait City during Operation DESERT STORM in 1991. (U.S. Department of Defense)

Following the conclusion of the eight-year Iran-Iraq War in 1988, Iraq faced economic disaster. The nation's foreign debt was estimated to be between $100 billion and $120 billion, with recovery costs estimated at more than $450 billion. Iraq's estimated 100-billion-barrel oil reserve, however, continued to be a viable asset. Nevertheless, Iraq's economy was incapable of absorbing most of the nearly 500,000 soldiers who were still in active service in the Iraqi military. Hussein had hoped that neighboring Saudi Arabia or Kuwait would write off Iraq's war debts or even offer funds for reconstruction. When this did not occur, he became angry and accused Kuwait of deliberately keeping oil prices low by overproducing in an effort to further injure the Iraqi economy. He also accused the Kuwaitis of illegally slant-drilling oil from the Rumaila Oil Field, located in southeastern Iraq.

On August 2, 1990, Iraqi troops invaded Kuwait and quickly occupied it. Immediately following the invasion, Kuwaiti officials and much of the international community condemned the action and demanded the withdrawal of Iraqi troops. The United Nations (UN) also denounced the act and immediately passed UN Resolution 661, which imposed wide-ranging sanctions on Iraq. These sanctions provided for a trade embargo that excluded only medical supplies, food, and other essential items. The embargo further depressed the Iraq economy. The UN also authorized a naval blockade of Iraq. The United States, meanwhile, was deeply concerned about the occupation of Kuwait, a potential Iraqi incursion into Saudi Arabia, and a potential disruption to world oil supplies; what is more, it worried over Iraqi programs that had called for the production of weapons of mass destruction (WMDs). U.S. officials feared that these developments would upset the balance of power in the region and might imperil Israel.

The United States and Great Britain soon spearheaded a military coalition of 34 countries, including many Arab nations, to face down the Iraqi aggression. When diplomatic negotiations yielded no progress, coalition forces began a massive aerial campaign against Iraq on January 17, 1991. Nearly a month of aerial attacks against Iraq destroyed much of the entire infrastructure of Iraq and killed an estimated 12,000 to 15,000 Iraqi soldiers and civilians. The aerial bombardment was followed by a quick ground assault in February 1991 in which coalition forces advanced into Kuwait and southern Iraq. Kuwait was liberated and Iraq resoundingly defeated in just 100 hours of ground combat. Some 60,000 Iraqi troops surrendered without a fight. On February 27, 1991, U.S. president George H. W. Bush ordered coalition forces to stand down. Estimates of Iraqi deaths during Operation DESERT STORM, including civilian casualties, range anywhere from 20,000 to 281,000 people. Meanwhile, Iraq's military had been badly mauled, the economy was in tatters, and the nation's infrastructure was badly damaged.

Despite the destruction caused by the Persian Gulf War, Hussein's government survived. Bush called for the Iraqi people to force Hussein to step aside, and uprisings occurred among various groups, including Iraqi Army troops returning from their defeat. These began in March 1991 and soon engulfed much of the country. Shiite Muslims in southern Iraq and Kurds in northern Iraq, two religious sects that had been violently persecuted throughout Hussein's presidency, also rebelled against the Iraqi government. The refusal of the coalition governments to support the insurgents, however, allowed the government to suppress the rebellions with brutal force. Unfortunately for the opponents of Hussein, the Iraqi government was allowed under the terms of the agreements ending the war to employ helicopters, which it used with devastating effectiveness against the insurgents. Many Kurds fled north to Turkey to avoid the violent suppression that followed, and Shiite Muslims and Kurds continued to face persecution throughout the rest of Hussein's presidency.

The brutal campaigns against the Shiites and Kurds—especially those against the Kurds in the north—received wide-ranging media coverage and garnered much sympathy for the Kurdish population. Partly because of such coverage, a "no-fly zone," an area over which the Iraqi Air Force had to relinquish its control, was established in northern Iraq, followed by a similar zone in southern Iraq.

Following the successful suppression of the uprisings, the Iraqi government set out to strengthen its hold on power. Hussein favored his most loyal supporters, Arab Sunnis from the area of his hometown of Tikrit. With the economy in shambles, many Iraqi people had begun seeking old institutions, such as Arab tribes, for support. At the same time, Hussein shrewdly sought backing from tribal leaders within Iraq. The government thus established an Assembly of Tribes, and Hussein made a public apology for past land reforms that had hurt tribal leaders. Tribalism and favoritism soon led to violence and ruthless competition among the various groups, however. In 1994, in order to quell such unrest, the government responded by implementing harsh new laws designed to limit the power of tribal groups. However, because of selective enforcement of such laws, there was little reduction in violence.

At the same time, UN sanctions devastated the Iraqi economy. Also, government policies supported large military and internal security forces at the expense of other sectors. The sanctions had declared that 30 percent of Iraqi oil exports had to be set aside for war reparations, but the Iraqi economy had grown to depend on its oil exports at the expense of other industries, especially agriculture. Thus, when money from the oil trade was diminished, many Iraqis suffered from malnourishment and grinding poverty. The effects of the sanctions, combined with the large debts incurred during the war with Iran, brought on hyperinflation, which nearly wiped out the Iraqi middle class. The value of the Iraqi currency, the dinar, plummeted, and food prices rose rapidly after the war. Cancer rates also increased, reportedly a result of the 300 to 800 tons of depleted uranium used in Iraq during the war.

Medical supplies were scarce in Iraq as a result of the sanctions, and the government hoarded them. Mortality rates in children under the age of five increased steeply. The Iraqi government implemented food rationing, but that did little to improve the situation. Illiteracy rates in Iraq also rose because many roads and schools had been damaged or destroyed. To add to the problem, the government withdrew much of its support for teachers and other salaried professionals. Power shortages caused widespread problems in homes and industries throughout Iraq, and many modern manufacturing facilities were forced to shut down.

In 1991, the Iraqi government had rejected UN proposals to trade its oil for food and other humanitarian supplies. On May 20, 1996, however, a Memorandum of Understanding was signed between the United Nations and the Iraqi government. The memorandum stated that the Iraqi government could sell oil to purchase food and other humanitarian supplies. The first shipments of food arrived in Iraq in March 1997. Unfortunately, the program suffered from rampant corruption, and did little to improve the lot of average Iraqis, who continued to suffer from extreme poverty. By the late 1990s, the People's Republic of China and Russia were calling for a significant easing of UN sanctions. Such calls went unheeded, however, as the United States and other Western powers refused to grant any leniency to the Iraqi regime. By 2000, as many as 16 million Iraqis depended on some form of government assistance for survival.

Following the Persian Gulf War, the United States and its allies continued to limit Hussein's power through numerous punitive military operations. These operations, mostly air and missile strikes, damaged infrastructure and put even more of a strain on the Iraqi economy. On October 8, 1994, Operation VIGILANT WARRIOR began as a response to the deployment of Iraqi troops toward the Kuwaiti border. After some 170 aircraft and 6,500 military personnel were deployed to southern Iraq, Hussein recalled his troops and the crisis passed. On September 3, 1996, Operation DESERT STRIKE was launched in response to the movement of 40,000 Iraqi troops into northern Iraq, which threatened the Kurdish population. More than two years later, on December 16, 1998, the United States and Great Britain began Operation DESERT FOX, a four-day bombing campaign against select Iraqi targets. It was in response to the Iraqi government's refusal to comply with UN Security Council (UNSC) resolutions that called for the dismantling of certain weapons and the government's interference with UN weapons inspectors, whose goal was to ensure that the Iraqi government was complying with UN resolutions. The stated goal of DESERT FOX was to destroy any hidden weapons of mass destruction and the Iraqi government's ability to produce and deploy them. The bombing targeted research and development installations.

On February 16, 2001, the United States and Great Britain launched a bombing campaign to damage Iraq's air defense network. Throughout the interwar period, bombing efforts meant to force Iraq's compliance with UN mandates caused much destruction while doing little to weaken Hussein's hold on power.

GOVERNORATES OF IRAQ

TURKEY

SYRIA

IRAN

JORDAN

SAUDI
ARABIA

KUWAIT

Caspian Sea

Persian
Gulf

Zakho • DAHUK
Dahuk ★
Akre •
Rayat •
Mosul ★
Sinjar •
ARBIL
Arbil ★
NINAWA
Hatra •
Kirkuk ★
KIRKUK
Sulaymaniyah ★
SULAYMANIYAH
Bayji •
Tikrit •
SALAHUDDIN
Samarra ★
DIYALA
Qaim •
Anah •
Haditha •
Baquba ★
IRAQ
Akashat •
Lake Tharthar
Euphrates R.
Baghdad ⊛
BAGHDAD
Ramadi ★
Fallujah •
WASIT
Trebil •
Lake Razzaza
Karbala ★
Hillah ★
Kut ★
ANBAR
KARBALA
BABIL
Nukhayb •
Najaf ★
Diwaniya ★
Amarah ★
QADISIYA
MAYSAN
Shatra •
Uzair •
Samawah ★
Nasiriyah ★
NAJAF
THI QAR
BASRA
Basra ★
Salman •
Zubair •
Umm Qasr
MUTHANNA
KUWAIT
Kuwait ⊛

Tigris R.

NAJAF   Governorate
★   Governorate capital
⊛   National capital

0   100   200 mi
0   100   200 km

Iraqis at work near a giant mural depicting Iraqi president Saddam Hussein on horseback fighting a mythical creature whose three heads are representations of U.S. president George W. Bush, center, Israeli prime minister Ariel Sharon, bottom, and British prime minister Tony Blair, bottom. Baghdad, Iraq, September 18, 2002. (AP/Wide World Photos)

In response to such attacks, the Iraqi government, which had essentially been controlled by the decidedly secular Baath Party, began using Islam as way to rally its citizens. The struggle against the United States was depicted as a jihad, or holy war, against the Western world. In 1994, the government encouraged the building of mosques as part of a new "faith campaign." Large murals portraying Hussein in prayer were exhibited, and government money was set aside to construct the largest mosque in the world. Hussein and his government also encouraged loyalty to the regime, and Hussein was depicted as a hero in his conflict against the United States.

In northern Iraq, the Kurds were now separated from the rest of the country, and self-rule was largely implemented. Kurdish political parties allowed cable television from outside Iraq to be broadcast into their region. The UN and international aid groups with access to the north were able to distribute aid to the region. On the eve of the March 2003 invasion of Iraq, the Kurdish economy was performing much better than the rest of the country. Many Kurdish villages had been resettled, medical facilities were restored, and the infant mortality rate had improved dramatically.

Following the terror attacks on the United States of September 11, 2001, the George W. Bush administration took a more assertive stance with Iraq. Bush and his closest advisers believed that Iraq posed a threat to the United States and its allies, including Israel. Many of Bush's advisers mistakenly believed that Iraq possessed weapons of mass destruction and suggested an attack against Iraq, which would at once remove Hussein from power, secure the alleged WMDs, and serve as a warning to other rogue states. Beyond that, they hoped that a democratic Iraq might be a force for change in the entire region.

Bush hoped to secure approval from the UN before proceeding with an attack. On September 12, 2002, Bush addressed the UN Security Council and attempted to make his case for an invasion of Iraq. Much of the international community was critical of such a move, however. Other world leaders did not believe that Iraq posed a threat or had links to such terrorist organizations as Al Qaeda, which the Bush administration alleged. On November 8, 2002, the UN Security Council passed Resolution 1441, which offered Iraq a final chance to comply with its disarmament agreements. The resolution required that the Iraqi government destroy all chemical, biological, and nuclear weapons as well as the means to deliver them, and to provide complete documentation of such.

On February 5, 2003, U.S. secretary of state Colin Powell addressed the UN General Assembly and presented evidence, some of which was later proven to be false, that Iraqi officials were impeding the work of the weapons inspectors, continuing to develop weapons of mass destruction, and directly supporting Al Qaeda, which had carried out the 9/11 attacks. Following the presentation, the United States and Great Britain, among others, proposed a UN resolution calling for the use of force against Iraq. Other countries, such as Canada, France, Germany, and Russia, urged continued diplomacy. Although the American effort failed, the United States decided to pursue an invasion without UN authorization.

On March 20, 2003, a U.S.-led coalition invaded Iraq with the objectives of disarming Iraq, ending Hussein's reign as president, and freeing the Iraqi people. Coalition forces were able to advance quickly through Iraq. On April 9, they captured Baghdad and officially toppled the Iraqi government, forcing Hussein to go into hiding.

On May 1, 2003, Bush declared that major combat operations in Iraq were over and that the postinvasion reconstruction phase had begun. However, the postinvasion period would prove very difficult for coalition forces. With the absence of government authority and social order, the country soon experienced widespread civil disorder, with many people looting palaces, museums, and even armories that the Iraqi government had once controlled. To complicate things, the coalition did not have enough troops on the ground to prevent such disorder and keep an insurgency at bay.

In an attempt to bring order in Iraq, the United States established the Coalition Provisional Authority to govern Iraq, and put it in place on April 20, 2003. While many of Hussein's palaces were looted, their physical structures remained intact. It was from these palaces that the CPA governed Iraq. On May 11, 2003, President Bush selected diplomat Lewis Paul Bremer III to head the CPA. On June 3, 2003, as part of the first act of the CPA, Bremer ordered the de-Baathification of Iraq. Senior officials within the Baath Party were removed from their positions and banned from future employment in the public sector. In all, about 30,000 party members became instantly unemployed. The next day, Bremer dissolved Iraq's 500,000-member army. This order left Iraq without a military or police force to stop the widespread looting. It also ensured a huge number of disgruntled, unemployed dissidents who viewed the CPA with great enmity. Violence against the occupation armies steadily increased. Notwithstanding the apparent early successes of the coalition forces, individuals opposed to the coalition presence in Iraq engaged in acts of violence, such as the use of ambush tactics, improvised explosive devices, and suicide bombings against coalition forces. Despite a quick military victory, coalition forces faced a long battle with Iraqi insurgents in their attempt to bring peace to Iraq.

Sectarian strife was also increasing, and by mid-2004, some analysts claimed that Iraq was perched on the edge of a full-blown civil war. The Arab Sunni leadership capitalized on Sunni fear of Shiite dominance of a new government. Sunnis extremists routinely employed bombing and suicide-bombing attacks against Shiite civilians. Also, Shiite members of the new Iraqi Army used extralegal means to execute Sunni civilians. Shiites organized death squads, which killed many Iraqi civilians.

In the face of such violence, on June 28, 2004, governing authority was transferred to the Iraqi Interim Government, which was led by Prime Minister Iyad Allawi. The generally pro-Western Allawi launched a campaign to weaken the rebel forces of Muqtada al-Sadr, who had spoken out against the CPA. On September 1, 2004, Allawi pulled out of peace negotiations with Sadr. Eventually, however, Sadr agreed to a cease-fire and took part in the legislative elections, which were held on January 30, 2005.

As part of the January 2005 elections, the Iraqi people chose representatives for the 275-member Iraqi National Assembly. With 58.4 percent voter turnout, a total of 8.4 million people cast their ballots. At least every third candidate on the candidate lists was female. There were nine separate attacks in Iraq on election day that killed 44 people, although these numbers were less than most experts had expected.

Two parties supported largely by Shiite Muslims won a majority of the seats, and 85 of the 275 members were women. Many Sunni Arabs, who had largely supported Hussein and held power in the previous government, boycotted the elections, leading some observers to challenge the legitimacy of the elections. The assembly was immediately charged with writing a constitution for Iraq and approved an Iraqi Transitional Government on April 28, 2005. The transitional government gained authority on May 3, 2005. The Iraqi Constitution was approved on October 15, 2005, and described Iraq as a democratic, federal, representative republic.

On December 15, 2005, a second general election was held to elect a permanent Iraqi Council of Representatives. Following approval from the members of the National Assembly, a permanent government of Iraq was formed on May 16, 2006. Turnout for this election was high, at 79.4 percent, and the level of violence was lower than during the previous election. The United Iraqi Alliance, a coalition of Arab Shiite parties, won the most votes with 41.2 percent. Ibrahim al-Jafari was nominated for the post of prime minister, but he was passed over after growing criticism by Nuri al-Maliki, a member of the Islamic Dawa Party, a conservative Shiite group. As prime minister, Maliki successfully negotiated a peace treaty with Sadr's rebel forces in August 2007.

Meanwhile, on December 13, 2003, U.S. forces captured Saddam Hussein in Dawr, a small town north of Baghdad and near Tikrit, his birthplace. An Iraqi Special Tribunal charged Hussein with crimes committed against the inhabitants of the town of Dujail in 1982. Dujail had been the site of an unsuccessful assassination attempt against Hussein. The former Iraqi president was charged with the murder of 148 people, with having ordered the torture of women and children, and with illegally arresting 399 others. On November 5, 2006, he was found guilty and sentenced to death by hanging. On December 30, Hussein was executed by Iraqi authorities.

In January 2007, President Bush presented his plan for "A New Way Forward" in Iraq. This was a new U.S. military strategy whose stated goal was to reduce the sectarian violence in Iraq and

An Iraqi woman voting in Baghdad in the elections for a permanent national parliamentary government, December 15, 2005. (U.S. Department of Defense)

help the Iraqi people provide security and stability for themselves. Five additional U.S. Army brigades were deployed to Iraq between January and May 2007, totaling about 40,000 troops. Operations to secure Baghdad began immediately. The U.S. troop surge, as many commentators called the plan, continued into 2009.

The interpretations of the results of the surge were mixed. Many U.S. media outlets, including CNN, reported that violence had dropped anywhere from 40 to 80 percent in Iraq following the surge. ABC ran many reports on its nightly news show that highlighted the progress in Iraq. *New York Times* writer David Brooks argued that even President Bush's harshest critics would have to concede that he finally got one right. Barack Obama, who was elected president of the United States in November 2008 and was once a harsh critic of the surge, later asserted that the new military strategy had led to an improved security situation in Iraq, although he was quick to point out that the war should not have been launched in the first place.

Critics have argued that while violence may have fallen in Iraq following the surge, such evidence did not indicate that the surge was truly successful. A 2008 study of satellite imagery suggested that Shiite ethnic cleansing of Sunni neighborhoods had been

largely responsible for the decrease in violence in Sunni areas. Some independent journalists argued that violence was down because the Shiites had won the battles of Baghdad in 2006–2007 and had controlled nearly three-fourths of the capital city. Others praised Maliki's government, not the U.S. government, for its efforts to stop the violence. Still others attributed it to deals struck by the occupying troops with the Sunnis to turn against Al Qaeda and other extremists.

Public opinion in Iraq seemed to suggest that Iraqis did not believe that the surge had led to any reduction in violence. A multi–news agency poll conducted in March 2008 showed that only 4 percent of Iraqis gave the U.S. surge any credit for any reduction in violence following the surge. Instead, many Iraqi people gave Iraqi institutions credit for the lowering of violence. Despite the reduction in violence, 50 percent of Iraqis still view security as the nation's main concern. In 2007 the Iraqi population was 29.267 million.

On December 4, 2008, the U.S. and Iraqi governments concluded the Status of Forces Agreement, which stipulated that U.S. troops would depart from all Iraqi cities by June 30, 2009, and would leave Iraq entirely by December 31, 2011. U.S. forces were no longer allowed to hold Iraqi citizens without charges for more than 24 hours. Also, immunity from prosecution in Iraqi courts was taken away from U.S. contractors. Maliki, however, was faced by detractors who called for the immediate removal of foreign troops from Iraq. They believed the agreement only prolonged an illegal occupation. Iraq's grand ayatollah, Sayyid Ali Husayn al-Sistani, led many of these protests and contended that Maliki was ceding too much control to the Americans. Such dissent forced the government to promise to hold a referendum on the agreement no later than June 20, 2009. If Iraqi citizens vote down the agreement, the Iraqi government would inform the U.S. that its troops would have to leave by June 2010, and the U.S. would be forced to accept the referendum. The referendum was not held by the June 2009 deadline and was put off until sometime in 2010.

Despite the effect of two wars and a continued insurgency against coalition forces in the country, the Iraqi economy has improved largely due to an influx of money pouring in from abroad. Wages rose over 100 percent between 2003 and 2008, and taxes were cut by 15–45 percent, allowing many Iraqi citizens to increase their spending power. However, despite such successes, Iraq faced many economic problems as well. Unemployment remained high; the Iraq government estimated that unemployment was between 60 and 70 percent in 2008. At the same time, the Iraqi foreign debt rose as high as $125 billion. Internal fragmentation and acts of sectarian violence continued to pose a large problem in Iraq, and U.S. and Iraqi forces have been unable to completely stop the violence.

GREGORY W. MORGAN

See also

Allawi, Iyad; Bremer, Jerry; DESERT STORM, Operation; Hussein, Saddam; Maliki, Nuri Muhammed Kamil Hasan al-; Iran-Iraq War; Iraq,

History of, Pre-1990; IRAQI FREEDOM, Operation; Iraqi Insurgency; Sadr, Muqtada al-; Sistani, Sayyid Ali Husayn al-; Surge, U.S. Troop Deployment, Iraq War

References

Abdullah, Thabit. *A Short History of Iraq.* London: Pearson, 2003.

Allawi, Ali A. *The Occupation of Iraq: Winning the War, Losing the Peace.* New Haven, CT: Yale University Press, 2007.

Inati, Shams Constantine. *Iraq: Its History, People, and Politics.* Amherst, MA: Humanity Books, 2003.

Marr, Phebe. *The Modern History of Iraq.* 2nd ed. Boulder, CO: Westview, 2003.

Tripp, Charles. *A History of Iraq.* Cambridge: Cambridge University Press, 2007.

Iraq, Navy

Prior to the 1991 Persian Gulf War, the Iraqi Navy was primarily a coastal defense force that could not operate far beyond its territorial waters. The United States Central Command (CENTCOM) estimated that the Iraqi Navy had poor overall operational capabilities. The force's readiness and training levels were low, and its ships were aging and in disrepair after the 1980–1988 Iran-Iraq War; it also suffered from poor maintenance programs. The main Iraqi naval base was in Basra, but access to the Persian Gulf was essentially blocked by remnants from the war with Iran. Other naval facilities were located in Az-Zubayr and Umm Qasr.

At the beginning of Operation DESERT STORM, the Iraqi Navy comprised 13 missile boats, 9 mine warfare ships, 6 amphibious warfare ships, 4 Exocet-armed helicopters, and several patrol boats and auxiliary vessels. The missile boats included one FPB-57 missile boat armed with Exocet missiles, 5 TNC-45 missile boats with Exocet missiles, 5 Osa IIs with Styx missiles, and 2 Osa Is with Styx missiles. Of mine warfare ships, the Iraqis had 2 Soviet T-43 fleet minesweepers, 3 Yevgenya-class inshore minesweepers, and 4 Nestin-class river minesweepers. Of amphibious warfare ships, it had 3 Polnocny-class tank landing ships and 3 Zahraa-class ships. The Iraqi Navy also operated a training frigate and had 4 operational (and 3 nonoperational) French-made Aérospatiale Super Frelon naval helicopters armed with Exocet antisurface missiles (AM-39). These helicopters posed a threat to shipping in the Persian Gulf as well as to allied warships.

The most serious threat posed by the Iraqi Navy came from its missile boats armed with Styx and Exocet missiles; these were the primary concern for coalition forces. In addition, mines laid by the mine warfare ships posed a threat to coalition ships in the Persian Gulf, while the smaller patrol boats had the ability to harass coalition warships. The Iraqi Navy's cache of various types of mines, and its ability to deploy them covertly was thought to be a serious threat to allied naval forces and shipping within the Gulf.

Because of these perceived military threats, U.S. Navy ships in the Persian Gulf area had orders to sink every Iraqi ship in sight. On the first night of the war, January 17, coalition air forces launched a strike on Umm Qasr Naval Base. Three days later, coalition forces again struck Umm Qasr. Coalition naval forces devastated the Iraqi Navy; the few ships that survived did so by fleeing to Iran. On January 29, 1991, U.S. Navy pilots sank an FBP-57 and two TNC-45s that were headed toward Iranian waters. The next day, under orders from Iraqi leader Saddam Hussein, more Iraqi vessels tried to escape to Iran. Coalition forces attacked the fleeing vessels and shattered the Iraqi Navy. Coalition forces destroyed or damaged seven missile boats, three amphibious warfare ships, one minesweeper, and nine other Iraqi vessels in the same area. Only one missile boat and one amphibious ship managed to escape to Iranian waters, where they were seized by the Iranians.

By February 2, 1991, any threat posed by the Iraqi Navy had been removed. The Iraqi Navy lost 19 ships sunk and 6 others damaged. In all more than 100 Iraqi vessels of all types were destroyed in the war. The few Iraqi ships that survived the war were in poor condition and were thereafter rarely operated.

By 1993, the Iraqi Navy had only 1 operational Osa II missile patrol boat, 1 torpedo boat, a few small boats, and a few Silkworm missiles. In 1995, the navy comprised 2,000 personnel, 1 former Yugoslav frigate, 2 Assad-class corvettes, 1 Osa I missile fast patrol boat, and 11 patrol boats (3 Thornycroft types, 2 Bogomol-class, 1 Poluchat I–class, 2 Zhuk-class, and 3 PB-90–class). After 1991, the subsequent United Nations (UN)-imposed arms, trade, and economic sanctions crippled the Iraqis' ability to repair their fleet and rebuild their naval force.

In 2002, Iraqi general Ali Hassan al-Majid al Tikriti (also known as "Chemical Ali") commanded military forces in the southern region of Iraq (one of four military commands), including the Iraqi Navy. The navy operated from bases at Basra, Umm Qasr, and Az-Zubayr. Personnel still numbered about 2,000 men.

Just prior to the start of the 2003 Iraq War, the Iraqi Navy consisted of seven patrol and coastal combat vessels, as well as other auxiliary ships and small boats. It included one Bogomol-class large patrol craft (PCF); one Osa I–class fast-attack missile craft (PTFG) equipped with Styx missiles; two 90-class inshore coastal patrol craft (PC); and three mine warfare craft (one Soviet Yevgenya-class and two Nestin-class minesweepers). The navy also operated a yacht with a helicopter deck for President Saddam Hussein.

There were many nonoperational craft in the Iraqi Navy, including an Osa I–class fast-attack missile boat and 3 mine warfare craft reportedly nonoperational since 1991. The presidential yacht was also nonoperational. There were many small patrol boats that were not heavily armed but could be used for mining or raiding missions. By some estimates, Iraq had more than 150 of these vessels.

The Iraqi Navy played little role in Operation IRAQI FREEDOM. On March 20, 2003, the first day of the war, coalition forces conducted an air and amphibious assault on the Faw peninsula to secure oil wells located nearby. The Iraqi Navy had sent forces to guard the oil terminals, but coalition forces quickly took control of them. British forces took Umm Qasr and moved to Basra within the first two weeks of the war. The Iraqi Navy was decimated by coalition air strikes during the first days of the invasion. The Iraqi Navy is now in the process of being reconstituted.

ALISON LAWLOR

See also

DESERT STORM, Operation; Faw Peninsula; IRAQI FREEDOM, Operation; Majid al Tikriti, Ali Hassan al-; Umm Qasr; Umm Qasr, Battle of

References

Marolda, Edward, and Robert Schneller. *Shield and Sword: The United States Navy and the Persian Gulf War.* Annapolis, MD: U.S. Naval Institute Press, 2001.

Pokrant, Marvin. *Desert Shield at Sea: What the Navy Really Did.* Westport, CT: Greenwood, 1999.

———. *Desert Storm at Sea: What the Navy Really Did.* Westport, CT: Greenwood, 1999.

Iraq, Sanctions on

The international community imposed sanctions on Iraq beginning on August 6, 1990, four days after the Iraqi invasion of Kuwait. Various sanctions remained in place until May 22, 2003, at which time the Saddam Hussein government had been overthrown by the Anglo-American–led invasion of Iraq in March 2003. This was one of the longest and hardest sanction regimes ever imposed by the international community and the United Nations (UN) on one of its member states.

An Iraqi woman and her son carry their monthly food ration, distributed by the government under the Oil-For-Food Programme, Baghdad, August 12, 2002. (AP/Wide World Photos)

On August 2, 1990, Iraq's armed forces occupied Kuwait. Four days later UN Security Council Resolution 661 imposed comprehensive trade sanctions on Iraq. The sanctions prohibited the importation of any Iraqi commodities or products into all UN member states as well as the sale or supply of any products to Iraq. The resolution excluded the sale of medical supplies to Iraq as well as foodstuffs for humanitarian purposes.

Although the Persian Gulf War officially ended on February 28, 1991, the Security Council continued to employ sanctions against Iraq. Security Council Resolution 687 of April 3, 1991, instructed the government of Iraq to destroy, remove, and render harmless all its weapons of mass destruction (WMDs) and medium-range missiles. The UN also decided to send to Iraq a team of international inspectors to supervise the implementation of the resolution. Continuing economic sanctions were supposed to maintain international pressure on Iraq to cooperate with the inspectors.

Because the 1991 war caused major damage to Iraq's infrastructure, including power plants, oil refineries, pumping stations, and water treatment facilities, the sanctions crippled Iraqi efforts to revive the economy and created a humanitarian crisis. In response to the plight of Iraqi civilians, UN secretary-general Javier Pérez de Cuéllar submitted a report to the Security Council on March 20, 1991, describing in detail the humanitarian crisis existing in Iraq after the war. In its conclusions, the report recommended that the international community work rapidly to reconstruct Iraq to improve the humanitarian situation there.

As a means of improving the humanitarian situation in Iraq, the Security Council passed Resolutions 706 and 712 in August and September of 1991, respectively. These resolutions allowed for the limited sale of Iraqi crude oil for the strict purpose of purchasing basic humanitarian goods for the Iraqi population. The government of Iraq rejected the offer, however, and demanded that all sanctions be immediately abolished.

The sanctions inflicted much more damage on Iraqi society during the 1990s. United Nations Children's Fund (UNICEF) surveys revealed that in the southern and central regions of Iraq, home to approximately 85 percent of the country's population, the mortality rate of children under the age of five had nearly tripled, from 56 deaths per 1,000 live births during 1984–1989 to 131 deaths per 1,000 live births during 1994–1999. Infant mortality (defined as children in their first year) increased from 47 per 1,000 live births to 108 per 1,000 live births within the same time frame.

The harsh conditions in Iraq soon caused a rift among the Security Council's permanent members. The United States and the United Kingdom advocated continuing the sanctions until the Iraqi government fulfilled all its obligations in compliance with Security Council Resolution 687. Their stance, however, was challenged by China, France, and Russia, which claimed that the sanctions only enhanced the suffering of the Iraqi people without influencing the Iraqi government to comply with Resolution 687.

On April 14, 1995, the UN Security Council suggested in Resolution 986 that the Iraqi government accept international supervision of the sale of Iraq's crude oil in return for humanitarian aid and basic needs such as food, medicine, and other essential civilian supplies. This diplomatic initiative finally bore fruit in May 1996 when the UN and Iraq signed a Memorandum of Understanding (MOU). Iraq began exporting crude oil under UN supervision in December 1996.

The MOU began the Oil-for-Food Programme, which operated until the invasion of Iraq by American- and British-led forces on March 20, 2003. The program was officially terminated on November 21, 2003, when authority was handed to the Coalition Provisional Authority, the entity that assumed the governance of Iraq headed by an American. On May 22, 2003, the Security Council abolished all sanctions against Iraq.

When the Oil-for-Food Programme began, Iraq was permitted to sell $2 billion of oil every six months. Two-thirds of the profits were channeled to humanitarian needs. In 1999 the Security Council decided to abolish the ceiling.

Under the program, the government of Iraq sold oil worth $64.2 billion. Of that amount, $38.7 billion was spent on humanitarian aid. Another $18 billion was given as compensation for lawsuits stemming from the occupation of Kuwait by Iraq. Finally, $1.2 billion was used to fund the program itself.

A total of $31 billion in humanitarian aid and equipment was transferred to Iraq under the program. Additional supplies and equipment totaling $8.2 billion were planned to be delivered to Iraq when the war broke out in March 2003. The program also helped to minimize the damage wrought by severe droughts in Iraq during 1999–2001.

During its seven years of operation, the program had a positive impact on civilian nutrition and health. It raised the average daily caloric intake for every Iraqi from 1,200 calories to 2,200 calories per day. The spread of contagious diseases such as cholera was also contained. The sewage system improved slowly during the 1990s, as did the delivery of medicine, particularly after the Oil-for-Food Programme was launched.

While the Oil-for-Food Programme succeeded in improving humanitarian conditions in Iraq, the diet quality was still poor. This caused malnutrition because of deficiencies in vitamins and minerals, which led to the spread of anemia, diarrhea, and respiratory infections, especially among young children. Furthermore, the program was criticized for restricting aid to food rather than also allowing the repair of infrastructure and the generation of employment. Because the aid was distributed through the government of Iraq, it actually helped the government maintain its hold over the people.

The full deficiencies of the aid plan became known after the occupation of Iraq began in 2003. In 2004 following complaints from U.S. senators and congressional representatives regarding irregularities in the UN-managed Oil-for-Food Programme, the UN created an independent inquiry committee (IIC) led by American banker Paul A. Volcker. The IIC completed its work at the end of 2005. The committee report pointed to mismanagement by the UN, corruption and bribery by top UN officials, and manipulation of the aid scheme by the government of Iraq, which received $1.8 billion in illegal aid. Also, IIC experts estimated that the government of Iraq was able to illicitly smuggle approximately $11 billion of oil outside Iraq, thereby circumventing the Oil-for-Food Programme.

CHEN KERTCHER

See also

DESERT STORM, Operation; Economic Effects of the Persian Gulf War on Iraq; Iraq, History of, 1990–Present; IRAQI FREEDOM, Operation; United Nations Security Council Resolution 661; United Nations Security Council Resolution 687; United Nations Weapons Inspectors

References

Arnove, Anthony. *Iraq under Siege: The Deadly Impact of Sanctions and War.* London: Pluto, 2000.
Lopez George A., and David Cortright. "Containing Iraq: the Sanctions Worked." *Foreign Affairs* 83(4) (2004): 90–103.
Malone, David M. *The International Struggle over Iraq: Politics in the UN Security Council, 1980–2005.* Oxford: Oxford University Press, 2006.

Iraqi Claims on Kuwait

Iraq made numerous claims to Kuwait before its invasion of August 2, 1990. Since the seventeenth century, the Ottoman Empire had ruled present-day Kuwait, which was then part of the Basra Province. Following World War I, much of Basra Province became part of the British-administered League of Nations mandate of Iraq.

In 1756 the al-Sabah family established an autonomous sheikhdom in Kuwait, and thereafter the Ottoman Empire exercised only nominal rule. In order to prevent the possibility of the Ottomans increasing both their control and taxation, Kuwaiti sheik Mubarak al-Sabah sought British protection. The British were concerned about the area, as Kuwait had been mentioned as the possible terminus of the German-backed Berlin to Baghdad railroad project. The Ottoman government did make an effort to exert more control over Kuwait in 1898, which the British then protested. On January 23, 1899, Kuwait and Great Britain signed an agreement in which Britain assumed control over Kuwait's foreign affairs and defense and agreed not to conclude alliances with other powers and make any concessions—economic or military—to any other nation. Kuwait thus became a British protectorate.

In 1904 Kuwaiti territory was formally drawn as a 40-mile radius around its center at Kuwait City. The Anglo-Ottoman Convention of 1913 defined Kuwait as an "autonomous caza" of the Ottoman Empire. The sheikhs of Kuwait were regarded as provincial sub-governors of the Ottoman Empire. The convention thus provided British recognition of Ottoman interests in Kuwait in return for the promise of Ottoman non-interference in Kuwaiti internal affairs. The later claims by Iraq that this constituted British recognition of Iraqi jurisdiction in Kuwait is a weak one.

During World War I the British kept some troops in Kuwait, its importance dramatically increasing with oil production.

Following the war the British had to deal with Wahhabi attacks into Kuwait, which were repulsed by the British in 1919 and 1927–1928. The boundaries of Kuwait and the Nejd were fixed in a treaty in 1921. Later a small neutral zone was established. In any case, in the Treaty of Lausanne of 1923, Turkey renounced all claims to its former possessions in the Arabian Peninsula. In 1934 Kuwait granted an oil concession to a company half owned by the American Gulf Oil Company and half owned by the British Anglo-Iranian Oil Company. Soon Kuwait was a major oil supplier.

Following the Allied victory in World War I, Britain secured a League of Nations mandate over Iraq, with King Faisal I, of the Hashemite dynasty, as its ruler. Faisal and his son, Ghazi, eventually criticized British occupation of Arab lands, including Kuwait. After Iraq secured its independence from Britain in 1932, Ghazi demanded the incorporation of the whole of Kuwait into Iraq, asserting that Kuwait was an artificial—and therefore illegitimate—political entity and in fact part of Iraq. Ghazi became king in 1933, but he died in 1939, failing to achieve his goal of annexing Kuwait. The British occupied Iraq from 1941 to 1947, and the issue of Iraqi sovereignty over Kuwait was not seriously raised again until 1961.

In July 1958 Abd al-Karim Qasim overthrew the Hashemite monarchy that had ruled Iraq since 1921. King Faisal II, who had ruled from 1939 to 1958, was pro-British and had not pushed Iraqi claims to Kuwait. On June 25, 1961, six days after Kuwait gained its independence from Britain, however, Qasim claimed that Kuwait had always been a part of Basra and therefore belonged to Iraq. Qasim deployed troops across the border in an attempt to take back Kuwait. On July 1, at the Kuwaitis' urging and to protect its oil interests, Britain sent troops to protect Kuwait from an Iraqi invasion.

In February 1963 the Iraqi Baath Party overthrew Qasim. Later that year, seeing that attacks against Kuwait had brought Iraq only isolation in the Arab world, Iraq changed policy and recognized Kuwait's independence in October 1963. However, following more political turmoil and the Baath Party's return to power in 1968 under the leadership of Ahmad Hassan al-Bakr and his deputy, Saddam Hussein, Iraq now insisted on deploying troops along Kuwaiti territory to protect itself from Iranian attack. Although Kuwait did not agree with the deployment, Iraqi troops nevertheless remained in Kuwaiti territory for nearly a decade.

Following the Iran-Iraq War (1980–1988), Iraq was deeply in debt, and Hussein, who had become president of Iraq in July 1979, was angered by the lack of Kuwaiti financial support. Among other assertions, Iraq claimed that Kuwait should have written off the war loans, amounting to some $13 billion, arguing that it had helped protect Kuwait from an Iranian invasion at the cost of many thousands of Iraqi lives. Iraq also accused Kuwait of manipulating the price of oil by purposefully overproducing the commodity. This, Hussein charged, was preventing Iraq from using its own oil revenues to pay back its debts and jump-start its economy. Finally, the Iraqis accused Kuwait of slant drilling into its oil fields near and along the border. Hussein, like many Iraqi leaders before

him, also claimed that Kuwait was a part of Iraq and was separated from Iraq only because of earlier British influence. Indeed, the Iraqi regime on the eve of the invasion of Kuwait referred to it as its "19th province."

Hussein, in his attempt to eliminate this "trace of Western colonialism," invaded Kuwait on August 2, 1990, sparking the Persian Gulf War. While there was certainly historical precedent to back up Hussein's assertions of Kuwaiti sovereignty, his other charges against the Kuwaitis were either inaccurate or without basis in fact.

GREGORY W. MORGAN

See also

Baath Party; Bakr, Ahmad Hassan al-; Faisal II, King of Iraq; Hussein, Saddam; Iran-Iraq War; Iraq, History of, Pre-1990; Iraq, History of, 1990–Present; Kuwait; Kuwait, Iraqi Invasion of; Kuwait-Iraq Diplomacy; Qasim, Abd al-Karim; United Kingdom, Middle East Policy

References

Khadduri, Majid, and Edmund Ghareeb. *War in the Gulf, 1990–91: The Iraq-Kuwait Conflict and Its Implications.* Oxford: Oxford University Press, 2001.
Schofield, Richard. *Kuwait and Iraq: Historical Claims and Historical Disputes.* London: Royal Institute of International Affairs, 1991.

Iraqi Forces, Postwar U.S. Training of

Since the Anglo-American–led invasion of Iraq and the overthrow of President Saddam Hussein's government in April 2003, the United States and coalition forces have sought to rebuild, equip, and train the Iraqi Security Forces (ISF)—both the military and police—to assume responsibility for providing security and defending the country. The ISF was ultimately to assume these responsibilities from the U.S. troops and multinational coalition forces stationed in Iraq. The effectiveness of the training efforts and the ability of the ISF to fight insurgents and terrorists have been the subject of much dispute and controversy. During 2006 there violence rose sharply throughout Iraq, including an increase in the number of U.S. troops killed, which in turn produced growing opposition to the war among the American public. This led to increased political pressure on President George W. Bush's administration to turn over combat and security responsibilities to the ISF and to begin withdrawing U.S. troops from Iraq.

According to the White House's National Strategy for Victory in Iraq, the ultimate goal of training the ISF is for it to be able to take the lead in defeating insurgents and terrorists. In a speech given on June 28, 2005, President Bush explained, "The U.S. military is helping to train Iraqi security forces so that they can defend their people and fight the enemy on their own. Our strategy can be summed up this way: As the Iraqis stand up, we will stand down."

According to the U.S. State Department, as of October 25, 2006, the United States had appropriated $5 billion for security and law enforcement efforts in Iraq. However, the precise number of combat-effective ISF personnel has long been subject to much debate. According to the same report, there were 312,400 trained and equipped ISF members, including 129,700 army troops and 128,000 policemen. Many of these troops were judged not capable of conducting combat operations independent of U.S. troops, however, and even those units that were capable remained dependent on U.S. forces for intelligence and logistics as well as artillery and air support.

According to an October 2006 statement by General George Casey, commander of U.S. forces in Iraq, it would be another 12 to 18 months before the ISF was completely capable of taking over responsibility for Iraqi security. Yet even then, he acknowledged that some unspecified level of U.S. support would be required. He estimated that the current progress of U.S. efforts to train and equip the ISF was about 75 percent complete. Critics, however, noted that Casey had made such predictions before. In July 2005 he had predicted major U.S. troop withdrawals by summer 2006, but because of the inability of the ISF to cope with the rise of sectarian violence in Iraq that year, no U.S. troops had yet been withdrawn.

According to a U.S. State Department report dated October 4, 2006, 88 battalions, 27 brigades, and 6 divisions of the ISF were in "the lead" in counterinsurgency operations, and ISF troops controlled more than 60 percent of Iraq. Yet in that same month, 16 of 18 Iraqi provinces remained under U.S. military control. With respect to the mounting sectarian violence plaguing Iraq, Casey stated that 90 percent of sectarian attacks between Sunni and Shiites occurred in or near Baghdad and that a like percentage of all violence in Iraq was limited to 5 of the country's 18 provinces.

On May 23, 2003, one month after the fall of Saddam Hussein's government, then-U.S. Administrator of Iraq L. Paul Bremer dissolved all of Iraq's armed forces, except for the Iraqi police, in order to build a new military that would exclude members of Saddam's Baath Party. Critics charged that this was a major mistake, as it forced the United States to create a new military from scratch, thereby delaying not only the process of recruiting, training, and equipping but also the deployment of this new force for combat.

The heavy casualties suffered by the ISF—double those of U.S. and coalition forces—have adversely impacted recruiting for the ISF. From the overthrow of Hussein until October 2006, nearly 6,000 ISF had been killed and another 40,000 wounded. In October 2006 alone, 300 Iraqi army soldiers were killed. The police suffered the greatest toll. According to the Iraqi Ministry of the Interior, there were 6,000 deaths in a three-year span, partly because the police force was more poorly equipped than the army and partly because the force was infiltrated by sectarian militias.

Corruption in arms procurement was also cited as another problem frustrating the training and equipping of the ISF. Iraq has been identified as one of the most corrupt nations on earth, and the Iraqi government has investigated more than 1,000 cases of corruption involving billions of dollars.

Much of what remained of Iraq's military equipment after the end of the Persian Gulf War in 1991 was destroyed in the 2003 invasion of Iraq. Consequently, the ISF was badly equipped, particularly with regard to vehicles, artillery, armor, communication equipment, heavy weapons, air transport, and aircraft support. U.S. commanders have been reluctant to give the inexperienced ISF sophisticated equipment that could end up in the hands of insurgents or terrorists.

The ethnic composition of the ISF is yet another problem, with comparatively fewer Sunnis enlisting in the ISF than Shiites and Kurds. There have been reports of Iraqi units refusing to deploy to provinces outside their ethnic home or region. Neighboring Iran and Syria have also worked to undermine U.S. efforts to stabilize Iraq. The two states have supplied arms, equipment, and training to insurgents. Iran has been especially active in arming Shiite militias.

With the beginning of the U.S. troop surge in early 2007, and as security improved and violence declined dramatically, the training of ISF personnel has accelerated and greatly improved, so much so that the ISF assumed responsibility for providing security during the January 31, 2009, provincial elections held nationwide. Coupled with an improving economy, national political reconciliation, and an increasingly stable government, the prospects for the ISF to assume responsibility for defending the country and enforcing law and order have improved, but challenges remain.

According to a December 2008 U.S. Department of Defense report titled "Measuring Security and Stability in Iraq," the ISF currently numbers 600,000 in the ministries of Interior, Defense, and National Counter-Terrorism Force. Although recruitment goals are currently on track, difficulties do remain, which, if unresolved, could undermine short-term gains and the long-term effectiveness of the ISF. Because of the limited number of training facilities, the Ministry of the Interior faces training difficulties and delays, while the Ministry of Defense faces a hiring freeze due to budget constraints. Budget allocation is also an issue; money appropriated for the ISF is slowly distributed, delaying training as well as weapons and equipment procurement. Despite improvements, budget coordination and cooperation among Iraq's various governmental ministries remains a problem, but military and security coordination is improving.

Recent and ongoing operations against militants and insurgents have demonstrated not only a willingness by the ISF to confront enemies of the regime but also an improvement in the skill and ability of the ISF in planning missions and deploying and commanding units. As revealed during operations in the southern city of Basra, the ISF, however, remain dependent on U.S. forces for logistics, close air support, fire support, communications, explosive ordnance, and intelligence and surveillance. The December 2008 Defense Department report notes that U.S. "mentorship and partnership [with the ISF] will be necessary for several [more] years to overcome." The Iraqi Interior ministry is developing a national supply and distribution network to overcome logistics dependence on U.S. forces. The same U.S. report noted that insufficient capacity to train civilian managers and staff, inadequate training personnel, deteriorating and insufficient facilities (poor housing and living conditions), and an inability to fill positions with trained personnel are challenges that also hinder the Iraqi governmental ministries.

For these reasons, many civilians working for the Interior and Defense ministries are not only unqualified but, owing to cumbersome management and decision-making procedures, 40 percent of civilian positions in the Defense ministry remain unstaffed. In sum, the Iraqi Ministry of Defense is not able to effectively support the ISF. Also hampering the effectiveness of the ISF, particularly the military, is the Iraqi government's poorly defined national security strategy, which inhibits planning, decision-making, and the execution of coordinated operations among different military units.

By early 2009 the Iraqi Army numbered 13 infantry divisions and 1 mechanized division. The Iraqi military remains an infantry army with little armor and artillery, however. Current combat strength is 165 of 208 planned battalions, but as of October 31, 2008, only 110 (or 67 percent) of the battalions were able to plan and execute operations with minimal or limited U.S. military support. The Iraqi Army suffers from insufficient numbers of officers (currently at 70 percent of strength) and noncommissioned officers (68 percent of strength), and the 80 percent graduation rate from basic combat training in 2008 was insufficient to meet the Iraqi government's desired army strength. The reasons for shortages stem from budget constraints and from the Iraqi government's mandated Transition and Reintegration Program (TNR), which reintegrates certain military and security members of Hussein's government as well as insurgents and militants into the new Iraqi government of Prime Minister Nuri al-Maliki. Those subject to the TNR, however, are not allowed to share the same training base with other recruits. Currently, 8 of 11 planned army divisional training centers are complete, with 3 more nearing completion and 1 unfunded. Lack of electricity is a problem, because few military bases are connected to the national power grid or a functional centralized power plant.

As of October 2008, 165 Iraqi Army battalions were conducting operations, including 9 newly formed battalions. Another 9 Iraqi Army battalions are expected to be deployed by the end of 2009. Five Iraqi Special Forces Operationsbattalions are conducting operations, but all 5 remain dependent on U.S. support

Although there are 1,300 local police stations throughout Iraq, professionalization of the police force remains incomplete, particularly among officers. A police officer training program is near completion, with the first pilot class scheduled to begin in late 2008 and a full program beginning in 2009, but the Ministry of the Interior still faces police recruitment, training, and equipment problems.

The National Police, tasked with supporting the local police and providing a national-level rapid-response police capability to counter large-scale civil disobedience activities, is beginning to deploy outside of Baghdad. As with the local police, the National Police lacks officers (its current officer strength is at 48 percent) but continues to achieve an ethnic-sectarian balance reflective of Iraqi society. Additionally, the National Police suffers from infrastructure problems, including a lack of housing, unit headquarters, motor pools, warehouse storage, and maintenance facilities.

Grounded from 1991 to 2005, the Iraqi Air Force faces many challenges. The air force aims to reach 7,000 personnel by 2010 and currently has 35 officers and enlisted personnel. Unlike army soldiers, it takes much longer to train pilots, and among the few pilots who have flying experience, more than half will reach retirement age by 2020; there is also a shortage of senior officers. The Iraqi Air Force added 25 aircraft in the first nine months of 2008 for a total of 77 aircraft, with delivery of an additional 42 aircraft in 2009, but procurement problems remain, thereby delaying delivery of new aircraft and equipment. In August 2009 the Iraq Defense Ministry revealed that it had discovered 19 Soviet MiG-21 and MiG-23 aircraft stored in Serbia. These aircraft had been sent to the former Yugoslavia for repairs in the 1980s, but Iraq was not able to bring them back because of international sanctions. Although the number of sorties flown has increased and flight-training programs have accelerated, the absence of aircrews capable of servicing the aircraft and the lack of English-language proficiency among pilots and ground crew remain distinct challenges.

Because Iraq has very little coastline, developing the Iraqi Navy has been a less urgent priority and poses fewer problems. Comprising 2,000 personnel and operating from a single base at Umm Qasr, the navy consists of five 24-meter fast assault boats and two marine battalions. In 2009 the first of four 54-meter patrol ships were delivered, increasing the range and strength of the navy. The long-term effectiveness of the navy, however, will require additional housing, a command headquarters, warehouses, and improved training facilities.

With respect to arms sales, the average time to process such orders by the Iraqi government has improved, and as of November 2008 $4.5 billion worth of arms, equipment, and services has been paid for by the Iraqi government. Owing to management procedures in the Ministry of Defense, procurement procedures remain cumbersome within that ministry, thereby delaying arms and equipment for the Iraqi military.

The postwar training of Iraqi Security Forces (ISF) by the United States has continued throughout 2009 and into 2010, with continued progress being made such that on June 30, 2009, per the Status of Forces Agreement, U.S. forces formally handed over the responsibility for security to Iraqi forces and withdrew from Iraqi cities and towns. According to the Status of Forces Agreement signed between former president George W. Bush and Iraqi prime minister Nuri al-Maliki, all U.S. forces are to leave Iraq by December 31, 2011. This deadline, however, is dependent on the security situation in Iraq, and a December 2009 report by the U.S. Defense Department titled "Measuring Security and Stability in Iraq" notes that "the pace of the drawdown of U.S. forces in Iraq will be commensurate with Iraq's improving security while providing U.S. commanders sufficient flexibility to assist the Iraqis with emerging challenges." The same report states that "by August 31, 2010, U.S. forces will have transitioned from a combat and

A member of the Iraqi Security Force, armed with a rocket-propelled grenade (RPG) launcher, on patrol at Camp Cooley, Iraq, April 28, 2005. (U.S. Department of Defense)

counterinsurgency (COIN) mission to a focus on training, advising, and assisting Iraqi Security Forces, protecting U.S. military and civilian personnel and facilities, assisting and conducting targeted counter-terrorism operations, and supporting civilian agencies and international organizations."

With the end of sectarian violence between Shiite and Sunni Muslims and Al Qaeda in Iraq (AQI) and its affiliates (such as the Islamic State of Iraq) no longer controlling areas of Iraq, U.S. casualties in Iraq have continued to decline over the last two years. In 2008, 314 U.S. soldiers were killed in Iraq compared to 149 in 2009, and as of March, 31, 2010, 16 soldiers have been killed.

With its ability to inflict casualties on U.S. and Iraqi forces significantly weakened, violence in Iraq has declined over the last two years. From September to November 2009, the average number of monthly incidents of violence throughout Iraq dropped by 50 percent compared to the same period in 2008—a decline of an average of 10 Iraqi civilians being killed each day to 5 killed each day—but Al Qaeda and its affiliates have increasingly resorted to high-profile attacks, particularly through the use of car bombings and assassinations. For example, on the day that U.S. forces formally handed over security duties to Iraqi forces, a car bomb killed 27 people in the northern city of Kirkuk; four days later a car bomb exploded in Baghdad, killing 69 people; and on August 19 a series

of car bombs throughout Baghdad killed more than 100 people and injured more than 200. Historically car bombings have been the hallmark of Al Qaeda and its affiliates, and although Al Qaeda's power and popular support have eroded, the organization continues to be the most active and violent group in Iraq and responsible for the most high-profile attacks. On October 25, 2009, Al Qaeda once again demonstrated its ability to inflict mass casualties when it exploded two car bombs near several Iraqi government buildings, killing 151 people and injuring hundreds. Due to the troop surge strategy implemented by President Bush in 2006–2008, Al Qaeda and its affiliates have lost most of their sanctuaries and popular support, given that they have increasingly relied on car bombings to inflict mass casualties. Despite the recurrence of car bombings and assassinations, the Iraqi parliamentary election was held on March 7, 2010, but more than 200 people were killed in the four weeks leading up to the election.

Since June 30, 2009, Iraqi Security Forces are no longer supporting American forces in military operations but instead are conducting their own operations. According to a December 2009 U.S. Department of Defense report, as of November 30, 2009, there were approximately 664,000 personnel in the Ministry of Defense, Ministry of the Interior, and the Iraqi National Counter-Terrorism Force. The Iraqi Army currently consists of 14 divisions (189 battalions and 6 Special Forces battalions), and the Iraqi government has shifted its emphasis from manpower and recruitment of the army to the development of logistics and combat support units that provide engineering, bomb disposal, medical evacuation, signal, and intelligence, surveillance, and reconnaissance (ISR) capabilities. Delays in equipping and deploying forces along with budget and procurement problems continue to plague the Ministry of the Interior, which includes the Iraqi police. Although the Interior Ministry has improved training capability, it still suffers from poor facilities and budget shortfalls. The Interior Ministry is tasked with the primary responsibility for maintaining security at the local level, but security in Iraq will not improve until problems with the Interior Ministry and the Iraqi police are corrected. As of November 2009, the Iraqi government has spent $5.2 billion in purchasing weapons, with another $4.3 billion spent on sales and development. Corruption remains a significant problem in the Iraqi government, particularly in the Ministry of the Interior. The inspector general of the Interior Ministry has identified more than $80 million in fiscal improprieties, and 223 cases of financial misconduct have been referred to the Iraqi Central Criminal Court for prosecution.

STEFAN M. BROOKS

See also

Bremer, Jerry; Bush, George Walker; Iraq, History of, 1990–Present; IRAQI FREEDOM, Operation; Iraqi Insurgency; Kurds; Maliki, Nuri Muhammed Kamil Hasan al-; Shia Islam; Sunni Islam; Surge, U.S. Troop Deployment, Iraq War

References

Cordesman, Anthony. *Iraqi Security Forces: A Strategy for Success.* Westport, CT: Praeger Security International, 2005.

Hashim, Ammed S. *Insurgency and Counter-insurgency in Iraq.* Ithaca, NY: Cornell University Press, 2006.

Rathmell, Andrew. *Developing Iraq's Security Sector.* Santa Monica, CA: RAND Corporation, 2006.

IRAQI FREEDOM, **Operation**
Start Date: March 20, 2003
End Date: May 1, 2003

Those who take the long view of history may be inclined to blame British prime minister David Lloyd George as much as U.S. president George W. Bush for the current situation in Iraq. British and French actions after World War I to fill the Middle Eastern void left by the collapse of the Ottoman Empire created modern Iraq and other Arab nations without regard for traditional ethnic and religious boundaries. Conditions in the European-created, artificial country of Iraq (especially the long-held animosity between the country's three major ethnic and religious populations of Kurds, Sunni, and Shia) made it a perfect breeding ground for such strong-arm dictators as Saddam Hussein to seize and hold power over a divided population, while incubating simmering ethnic and religious rivalries.

Iraq, compared with Afghanistan, the other major theater of combat operations for President Bush's Global War on Terror, played out with mixed success in two very different campaigns: a stunning conventional assault that rapidly destroyed the Iraqi army, captured Baghdad, ousted Saddam Hussein, and paved the way for a U.S.-led occupation of the country, and a smoldering insurgency conducted by Al Qaeda fighters and both Sunni and Shia faction Iraqi militia groups that began shortly after Hussein's defeat.

Although the two Iraq campaigns bear a superficial similarity to what transpired in Afghanistan (large-scale conventional combat operations to defeat the enemy's main forces followed by an insurgency), the Iraq War and occupation have shown striking differences in scope, intensity, and even in the justification U.S. leaders gave for invading the country. While Operation ENDURING FREEDOM was launched to strike directly at those presumed responsible for masterminding the September 11, 2001, terror attacks and the Afghan Taliban regime that harbored them, no such justification can be claimed for the Bush administration's decision to launch the March 2003 invasion of Iraq. Despite Iraqi president Saddam Hussein's track record of general support for terrorist organizations hostile to the United States and the West, no direct link to Al Qaeda has ever been proven. And while U.S. strategy regarding Afghanistan might be classified as *reactive,* the decision of America's leaders to invade Iraq can only be termed *proactive,* a surprising and controversial preemptive action.

In the wake of the 1990–1991 Persian Gulf War, Hussein used chemical weapons on Iraq's Kurdish minority. Subsequently, Hussein was often vilified for using chemical weapons on "his own people," but he did not consider the Kurds to be "his people"; his loyalty lay only with his Baathist Party cronies and his own tribe. What is perhaps surprising about his use of chemical weapons is that he did not use them more extensively. Iraqi officials were recalcitrant to inspections by the United Nations (UN) and failed, by late 2002, to produce an adequate accounting of the disposition of the weapons of mass destruction the country was known to possess (and use) in 1991. Further, the Iraqis failed to provide a full and open disclosure of the status of its suspected nuclear weapons program. If Iraq had added nuclear weapons to its 1991 chemical arsenal, as was charged by Iraqi émigrés (such as Khidhir Hamza, self-proclaimed "Saddam's Bombmaker," who toured U.S. college campuses in the autumn of 2002 trumpeting his "insider" knowledge of Iraq's alleged nuclear program), it would be foolish to ignore the threat such weapons posed. By failing to cooperate promptly, fully, and openly with UN weapons inspectors, Hussein had almost literally signed his own death warrant.

Opting for a preemptive strategy instead of risking a potential repeat of the September 11 terror attacks—with the added specter of chemical, biological, or nuclear weapons—Bush and his advisers (principally Vice President Dick Cheney and Deputy Secretary of Defense Paul Wolfowitz, described as "a major architect of Bush's Iraq policy . . . and its most passionate and compelling advocate") decided to act, unilaterally if necessary. Armed chiefly with what would later be exposed as an egregiously inaccurate Central Intelligence Agency (CIA) report about Iraq's possession of nuclear and other weapons of mass destruction, Bush obtained a legal justification for invading Iraq when the Senate approved the Joint Resolution "Authorization for Use of Military Force Against Iraq Resolution of 2002" in October 2002. In February 2003 Secretary of State Colin Powell addressed the UN Security Council with information based largely on the same flawed CIA report, but action was blocked by France, Germany, and Russia. Although the three powers bolstered their opposition with claims that military action against Iraq would threaten "international security," their true motives were suspect to some who supported military action (France and Germany, for example, already had made billions of dollars by illegally circumventing the UN Oil-for-Food Programme with Iraq). Regardless of their motives, all three countries had a vested interest in maintaining the status quo in Iraq and little motivation to participate in an American-led pre-emptive strike. Although Britain joined Bush's "coalition of the willing" (from 2003, 75 countries contributed troops, matériel, or services to the U.S.-led effort), the absence of France and Germany left his administration open to strong criticism for stubbornly proceeding without broad-based European support.

Bush's proactive rather than reactive strategy was heavily criticized by administration opponents as a sea-change departure from that of past U.S. presidents and slammed for its unilateralism. Yet, as historian John Lewis Gaddis points out in *Surprise, Security and the American Experience,* it was not without historical precedent. He cites the preemptive, unilateral actions of presidents John Adams, James K. Polk, William McKinley, Woodrow Wilson, and even Franklin D. Roosevelt. Yet, with U.S. ground forces already stretched thin by Operation ENDURING FREEDOM, mounting a major, preemptive invasion of Iraq was considered by many—particularly U.S. military leaders—as risky. Military drawdowns during Clinton's presidency, for example, had reduced U.S. Army active duty strength from 780,000 to about 480,000.

Even in the years before the 2003 Iraq invasion, Army Chief of Staff general Eric Shinseki had clashed with Secretary of Defense Donald Rumsfeld over Department of Defense proposals to reduce army end strength even further. Rumsfeld had taken office in 2001, firmly convinced that technology could replace large numbers of ground combat forces, and he doggedly clung to that conviction. Moreover, Rumsfeld, who had previously served as president Gerald Ford's secretary of defense in 1975–1977, often acted as if he were unaware of how profoundly the 1986 Goldwater-Nichols Act had affected U.S. military culture by eliminating much of the petty, interservice bickering that he had earlier witnessed. Shinseki further provoked Rumsfeld's ire when he told the Senate Armed Services Committee on the eve of the Iraq invasion that an occupation of that country would require "several hundred thousand" troops, an estimate that, in hindsight, seemed prescient indeed, but which was sharply criticized in 2003 by Rumsfeld and Paul Wolfowitz as "wildly off the mark."

On March 20, 2003, U.S. and British forces (plus smaller contingents from Australia and Poland) invaded Iraq in Operation IRAQI FREEDOM. The 297,000-strong force faced an Iraqi army numbering approximately 375,000, plus an unknown number of poorly trained citizens' militias. U.S. combat strength was about half of that deployed during the 1990–1991 Persian Gulf War. With U.S. Central Command general Tommy Franks in overall command, the U.S. ground forces prosecuting the invasion were led by U.S. V Corps commander Lieutenant General William Scott Wallace.

Preceded by a shock-and-awe air campaign reminiscent of the one that blasted Hussein's forces and Iraqi infrastructure in the Persian Gulf War, ground forces (including U.S. Marines and British combat units) executed another "desert blitzkrieg" that quickly smashed the Iraqi army. Despite the failure of the Turkish government at the last minute to allow the United States to mount a major invasion of northern Iraq from its soil, two ground prongs struck north from Kuwait, while Special Forces and airborne forces worked with the Kurds in the north in a limited second front. The ground advance north was rapid. Baghdad fell on April 10, and Hussein went into hiding. (He was captured in December 2003, brought to trial, found guilty, and executed on December 30, 2006.)

President Bush declared the "mission accomplished" and the end of major combat operations while aboard the U.S. aircraft carrier *Abraham Lincoln* on May 1, 2003. Subsequent events during the postinvasion occupation of Iraq would prove Bush's dramatic statement to be wildly premature: although only 139 U.S. personnel and 33 British soldiers died during the invasion, more than 4,000 Americans were to die thereafter in the insurgency that accompanied the occupation. Bush administration decisions to include the dismissal of Baathist Party officials (essentially, Iraq's only trained administrators), and the disbanding of the Iraqi Army (that, at one stroke, dumped nearly 400,000 trained soldiers and potential insurgent recruits into the Iraqi general population) contributed to the insurgency.

JERRY D. MORELOCK

See also

Bush, George Walker; Cheney, Richard Bruce; Franks, Tommy Ray; Goldwater-Nichols Defense Reorganization Act; Powell, Colin Luther; Rumsfeld, Donald Henry; Shinseki, Eric Ken; Wallace, William Scott; Wolfowitz, Paul Dundes

References

Atkinson, Rick. *In the Company of Soldiers: A Chronicle of Combat.* New York: Henry Holt, 2005.

Cavaleri, David. *Easier Said Than Done: Making the Transition between Combat Operations and Stability Operations.* Fort Leavenworth, KS: Combat Studies Institute Press, 2005.

DiMarco, Louis A. *Traditions, Changes and Challenges: Military Operations and the Middle Eastern City.* Fort Leavenworth, KS: Combat Studies Institute Press, 2004.

Franks, Tommy, with Malcolm McConnell. *American Soldier.* New York: Regan Books, 2004.

Gaddis, John Lewis. *Surprise, Security and the American Experience.* Cambridge: Harvard University Press, 2005.

Iraqis walk past U.S. marines who have taken positions on the road east of Nasiriyah leading to the Iraqi capital of Baghdad in an attempt to secure the road for use by military convoys, March 31, 2003. (AFP/Getty Images)

Gordon, Michael R., and General Bernard E. Trainor. *Cobra II: The Inside Story of the Invasion and Occupation of Iraq.* New York: Pantheon Books, 2006.

Murray, Williamson, and Robert H. Scales Jr. *The Iraq War: A Military History.* Cambridge, MA: Belknap, 2005.

Ricks, Thomas E. *Fiasco: The American Military Adventure in Iraq.* New York: Penguin, 2006.

Sanchez, Ricardo S., and Donald T. Phillips. *Wiser in Battle: A Soldier's Story.* New York: Harper, 2008.

Woodward, Bob. *Bush at War.* New York: Simon and Schuster, 2002.

———. *Plan of Attack.* New York: Simon and Schuster, 2004.

———. *State of Denial: Bush at War, Part III.* New York: Simon and Schuster, 2006.

Zinmeister, Karl. *Boots on the Ground: A Month with the 82d Airborne Division in the Battle for Iraq.* New York: St. Martin's, 2004.

———. *Dawn over Baghdad: How the U.S. Military Is Using Bullets and Ballots to Remake Iraq.* New York: Encounter Books, 2004.

IRAQI FREEDOM, Operation, Air Campaign
Start Date: March 20, 2003
End Date: April 7, 2003

The air campaign was an important part of the Anglo-American invasion of Iraq (Operation IRAQI FREEDOM) and contributed enormously to its rapid success. For IRAQI FREEDOM, the U.S.-led coalition assembled a formidable array of air power. The United States contributed 64,246 air personnel, including reserve and National Guard, and 1,663 aircraft. The latter included 293 fighters, 51 bombers, 182 tankers, and 337 aircraft of other types operated by the U.S. Air Force; 232 fighters, 52 tankers, and 124 aircraft of other types operated by the U.S. Navy; 130 fighters, 22 tankers, and 220 aircraft of other types operated by the U.S. Marine Corps; and 20 aircraft operated by the U.S. Army.

Aircraft participating in the operation included almost all models in the U.S. inventory: the North American/Rockwell/Boeing B-1B Lancer, Northrop Grumman B-2 Spirit, and Boeing B-52H Stratofortress bombers; Fairchild Republic A-10A Thunderbolt II and Lockheed AC-130 Spectre combat support aircraft; Boeing F-15 Eagle, Lockheed Martin F-16 Fighting Falcon, McDonnell Douglas (now Boeing) F/A-18 Hornet, and Lockheed F-117 Nighthawk fighters; Lockheed KC-130 Hercules transports; and McDonnell Douglas KC-10 Extender and Boeing KC-135 Stratotanker tankers.

The Royal Air Force contributed some 8,000 personnel and 113 aircraft, including 66 fighters, 12 tankers, and 35 aircraft of other types. The Royal Australian Air Force contributed 22 aircraft, including 14 fighters, and 250 airmen. Canada contributed 3 transport aircraft.

The Iraqi side at the beginning of the hostilities had 20,000 air force personnel, 325 combat aircraft, and 210 surface-to-air missiles.

The air campaign was designed as an integral part of a joint military operation, serving as a force multiplier to supplement the

A U.S. Navy F-14B Tomcat landing on the flight deck of the aircraft carrier *Harry S. Truman* in the Persian Gulf on March 17, 2005. (U.S. Department of Defense)

firepower of a relatively light land component. The allied air campaign was able to take advantage of operations NORTHERN WATCH and SOUTHERN WATCH, which the U.S. Air Force and Royal Air Force had been conducting since 1991, effectively transforming the United Nations–sanctioned policing of "no-fly zones" over northern and southern Iraq into a de facto sustained air campaign to conduct reconnaissance and suppress Iraqi air defenses. Thus, the coalition was able to prepare for battle well before the start of Operation IRAQI FREEDOM.

The air campaign of Operation IRAQI FREEDOM began early in the morning of March 20, 2003, with an unsuccessful air strike near Baghdad, involving two F-117A stealth fighter-bombers, aimed at killing top Iraqi leaders, including President Saddam Hussein. The strike was followed by massive cruise-missile attacks on key Iraqi command and control centers in and around Baghdad. By March 23–25, the air assault developed into the strategic phase of a so-called shock-and-awe campaign aimed to prevent the use of weapons of mass destruction by the Iraqis and to disorganize the enemy, forcing its rapid defeat.

Afterward, the coalition air campaign changed its focus to aiding ground forces moving into Iraq from Kuwait; at this point,

more than half of the new targets were not preplanned targets of opportunity. The Iraqis returned fire with sporadic and highly ineffective antiaircraft fire and random launches of surface-to-air missiles. They also managed to launch seven Ababil-100 tactical ballistic missiles, five of which were destroyed by U.S. Patriot batteries; two others missed their targets.

The growing flexibility of allied targeting reflected the proliferation of precision-guided munitions (PGM, smart bombs) in the coalition air force, which allowed more options in strike capabilities, redirecting of aircraft, performing close air support, and striking targets of opportunity. The air campaign also demonstrated the impressive global-reach capabilities of allied air power. Indeed, bombers were flying in from bases as far away as Missouri, Diego Garcia in the Indian Ocean, and Great Britain. Others were operating from aircraft carriers in the Persian Gulf and the Mediterranean, and from bases across the Middle East. The allies enjoyed uncontested air supremacy, as the remnants of the Iraqi air defense system were unable to operate effectively, and the enemy was unable to master a single sortie during the war. The coalition also benefited from the use of unmanned aerial vehicles (UAVs) as sensors and decoys to confuse the Iraqis.

The arrival of a major sandstorm on March 25–26 canceled about 65 percent of all sorties. Nevertheless, the coalition was able to adjust its reconnaissance and surveillance missions to harsh weather using the Joint Surveillance and Target Reader System (JSTARS) aircraft and long-range UAVs, which provided high-flying bombers with necessary information and data.

With the resumption of the ground march toward Baghdad, the allied air campaign shifted its focus to providing ground support, particularly targeting Iraqi Republican Guard units and militia formations, which were defending road approaches to the Iraqi capital. Finally, the air and ground assault on Baghdad merged into one coordinated effort.

Coalition air power was able to destroy or significantly degrade the Republican Guard formations and to open a new dimension in the urban warfare, providing constant surveillance, reconnaissance, intelligence, and fire support to allied ground forces. Coalition air power was also instrumental in the opening of the second front in northern Iraq. Major air operations in Iraq effectively ended with one final unsuccessful attempt on April 7 to eliminate Hussein when a B-1 bomber attacked a palace in Baghdad where the dictator was allegedly staying.

The aerial campaign during the Iraq War again demonstrated that there is no substitute for air dominance in modern warfare, a lesson that was gleaned from the 1990–1991 Persian Gulf War. Additionally, the technological superiority and application of air power in joint warfare operation allowed the coalition to enjoy unprecedented efficiency in reconnaissance, surveillance, and flexible, real-time targeting, while combining centralized control with decentralized execution of air operations. This also provided the coalition air force with almost instant capability to evaluate its performance as ground forces rapidly advanced into Iraq.

At the same time, however, the operation also witnessed an insufficiency in allied intelligence, particularly in regard to "decapitation" air strikes. Some observers have noted that the planners of the operation displayed overconfidence that a massive initial air assault on limited command and control targets would lead to the quick collapse of the regime. The campaign also revealed a shortage of aerial tankers, as the prosecution of combat missions deep inside Iraq put serious pressure on the allied tanker fleet.

Overall, coalition air forces conducted 41,404 sorties in the skies over Iraq. The U.S. Air Force contributed 24,196 sorties of those sorties; the U.S. Navy conducted 8,945 sorties; the U.S. Marine Corps contributed 4,948 sorties; the U.S. Army contributed 269 sorties; the Royal Air Force conducted 2,481 sorties; and the Royal Australian Air Force flew 565 sorties. Of 29,199 munitions used, 68 percent were precision-guided. The coalition lost just seven aircraft to enemy fire (six helicopters and one combat/support aircraft A-10A, and two pilots). One Royal Air Force fighter was lost due to friendly fire.

PETER J. RAINOW

See also

Aircraft, Helicopters; Bombs, Precision-Guided; Cruise Missiles, Employment of, Persian Gulf and Iraq Wars; IRAQI FREEDOM, Operation; NORTHERN WATCH, Operation; SOUTHERN WATCH, Operation; United Kingdom, Air Force, Iraq War; United States Air Force, Iraq War; United States Air Force Air Combat Command

References

Boyne, Walter J. *Operation Iraqi Freedom: What Went Right, What Went Wrong and Why.* New York: Forge Books, 2003.

Keegan, John. *The Iraq War: The Military Offensive, from Victory in 21 Days to the Insurgent Aftermath.* New York: Vintage, 2005.

Murray, Williamson, and Robert H. Scales Jr. *The Iraq War: A Military History.* Cambridge, MA: Belknap, 2005.

IRAQI FREEDOM, Operation, Coalition Ground Forces

During Operation IRAQI FREEDOM, the 2003 invasion of Iraq, U.S. forces led a small coalition of allied states to overthrow the regime of Saddam Hussein. The coalition was officially designated as Combined and Joint Task Force 7 (CJTF-7), with "combined" meaning more than one nation and "joint" meaning more than one military service.

In an effort to avoid past problems in coalition warfare including political interference and a lack of unity in the chain of command and in light of limited potential contributions to the invading force, the United States developed an invasion plan that emphasized U.S. forces and those of the nation's close ally, the United Kingdom. When the government of Turkey refused to grant the United States permission to launch a second front from its territory, the invasion plan was revised to call for the major ground assault to occur from Kuwait, supported by airborne assaults and action by special operations forces in the north.

The coalition consisted of 248,000 U.S. personnel along with 45,000 British, 2,000 Australian, 1,300 Spanish, and 200 Polish troops. The majority of the Australian and Polish troops were special operations forces. The main British ground unit was the 1st Armoured Division. Prior to the invasion, the U.S. Army provided command and control gear to some of the British units to facilitate interoperability (the U.S. Army had to provide similar equipment to U.S. Marine Corps units). The equipment allowed the allied forces to communicate and exchange information through satellite systems and to employ tactical Internet capabilities. Nonetheless, national liaison officers had to be stationed among the units to coordinate air support and ground fire.

Coalition units were under the overall operational command of U.S. Army lieutenant general David McKiernan, who was appointed as the head of Coalition Forces Land Component Command. McKiernan was second-in-command to the overall operation commander, U.S. general Tommy Franks. The senior British military officer was Air Chief Marshal Brian Burridge.

Prior to the onset of hostilities, coalition special operations forces crossed into Iraqi territory to gather intelligence and identify targets. On March 20 the invasion began. The majority of non-U.S. coalition forces were placed under the operational umbrella of the U.S. I Marine Expeditionary Force (I MEF). The southern area of Iraq was the main target of the British-led forces, which included most of the Australian and Polish troops. British and Polish commandos and U.S. marines attacked and captured the port city of Umm Qasr, including the majority of the area's oil wells, and gradually took control of the Faw peninsula. The British then secured Basra and worked to open the port to coalition shipping and humanitarian supplies. The British then moved northward and linked with U.S. forces at Amarah. The Spanish troops did not take part in offensive combat operations and instead provided engineering and support for the coalition from Kuwait. In the north, Polish and U.S. special operations units, along with the U.S. 173rd Airborne Brigade, collaborated with anti-Hussein Kurdish militias to create a second front in Operation NORTHERN DELAY. The coalition forces were able to capture the strategic city of Kirkuk in April 2003.

The coalition's main offensive was a two-pronged advance on Baghdad conducted mainly by U.S. forces. The western advance was led by the U.S. V Corps, in turn led by the 3rd Infantry Division, while the eastern attack was undertaken by the I MEF as the British forces continued operations in the south. The 3rd Infantry Division reached the Iraqi capital on April 4 and had control by April 10. On May 2, U.S. president George W. Bush announced an end to major combat operations. However, an insurgency arose with former Hussein loyalists and foreign fighters fighting against coalition forces.

Additional countries meanwhile contributed troops to the coalition war effort. In September 2003 Iraq was divided into zones of occupation. The British took charge of the multinational forces in the four southern provinces, designated the South Zone. Coalition forces in the South Central Zone, consisting of four provinces and parts of two others, came under Polish command. Poland maintained elements of either an armored or mechanized division as its core contribution, rotating units such as the 12th Mechanized Division or the 11th Lubusz Armored Cavalry Division through multiple tours in Iraq beginning in May 2003. Poland's peak contribution to the coalition was 2,500 troops, but the country withdrew its forces in October 2008.

A number of other countries also had significant deployments of more than 1,000 troops. In 2004 South Korea dispatched 3,600 troops, mainly medical, construction, and engineering units, but all forces were withdrawn in December 2008. The South Korean units were formed into the Zaytun Division (*zaytun* is Arabic for "olive"). Italy deployed 3,200 soldiers in 2003; however, these troops were withdrawn in November 2006. Georgia contributed 2,000 troops but withdrew the bulk of its forces during the brief Soviet-Georgian War of August 2008. Ukraine deployed the 5th, 6th, and 7th Mechanized brigades in succession, beginning in 2003, with a top commitment of about 1,800 troops. Ukraine withdrew its troops in December 2005. Australia deployed about 1,400 ground troops, including units from the Royal Australian Regiment, the 2nd Cavalry Regiment, and the Light Horse Regiment (Queensland Mounted Infantry). The Netherlands provided approximately 1,350 troops in July 2003 and withdrew its forces two years later. Spain contributed 1,300 troops in 2003 but withdrew the forces in 2004.

By 2008, 40 countries had deployed forces at some point to support CJTF-7, which was renamed the Multi-National Force–Iraq (MNF-Iraq) on May 15, 2004. However, the cost in both economic terms and loss of life led to growing antiwar sentiment in coalition states, leading many to draw down or completely withdraw their forces. As of the end of 2008, there were approximately 6,100 non-U.S. coalition troops in Iraq, the bulk of which (4,100) were British. By then, 314 non-U.S. coalition soldiers had been killed in Iraq. As of August 2009, all non-U.S. coalition forces had withdrawn from Iraq.

In addition to the larger contingents, the following countries contributed at least 100 soldiers (mostly support, medical, or engineering units): Albania, Azerbaijan, Bulgaria, the Czech Republic, Denmark, the Dominican Republic, El Salvador, Honduras, Hungary, Japan, Latvia, Lithuania, Mongolia, Norway, Nicaragua, Portugal, Romania, Slovakia, and Thailand.

The following countries contributed fewer than 100 troops: Armenia, Bosnia-Herzegovina, Estonia, Iceland, Kazakhstan, Macedonia, Moldova, New Zealand, the Philippines, Singapore, and Tonga. Several of these deployments were symbolic; for instance, Iceland deployed only 2 soldiers. In addition, Fiji deployed 150 troops in support of the United Nations (UN) mission in Iraq.

TOM LANSFORD

See also

IRAQI FREEDOM, Operation, Coalition Naval Forces; Hungary, Role in Persian Gulf, Afghanistan, and Iraq Wars; Multi-National Force–Iraq; New Zealand, Role in Persian Gulf, Afghanistan, and Iraq Wars; Norway, Role in Persian Gulf, Afghanistan, and Iraq Wars; Poland, Forces in Iraq; Special Air Service, United Kingdom; Special Boat Service, United Kingdom; United Kingdom, Army, Iraq War; United Kingdom, Marines, Iraq War

References

Cockburn, Patrick. *The Occupation: War and Resistance in Iraq*. New York: Verso, 2007.

Keegan, John. *The Iraq War: The Military Offensive, from Victory in 21 Days to the Insurgent Aftermath*. New York: Vintage, 2005.

Murray, Williamson, and Robert H. Scales Jr. *The Iraq War: A Military History*. Cambridge, MA: Belknap, 2005.

IRAQI FREEDOM, **Operation, Coalition Naval Forces**

Naval forces from the United States and other nations played an important role in Operation IRAQI FREEDOM. Military operations opened on March 20, 2003, with the firing of 40 Tomahawk cruise missiles by British and American warships and air strikes by both U.S. Air Force and U.S. Navy fixed-wing aircraft; meanwhile, U.S. Navy Grumman EA-6 Prowlers jammed Iraqi radar systems. This was followed by the seizure of two offshore gas and oil platforms by Navy SEALs.

When coalition ground forces invaded Iraq, carrier aircraft provided close air support and struck targets in support of the bombing campaigns. The five U.S. Navy carrier battle groups operating in the Persian Gulf, the Indian Ocean, and the eastern Mediterranean Sea flew more than 7,000 sorties during the first three weeks of operations. Marines landed from two amphibious ready groups and joined army troops in the invasion of Iraq. The campaign was swift, and only a week after the Iraqi capital at Baghdad fell on April 10, 2003, Vice Admiral Timothy Keating, commander of the 140 U.S. warships in the region, suggested the return home or redeployment elsewhere of naval units. By the end of operations on April 30, 35 coalition ships had fired 1,900 Tomahawks, one-third of them from submarines.

There were no significant naval surface engagements because Iraqi leader Saddam Hussein did not possess naval forces capable of posing a credible threat to coalition naval operations. After British and American marines captured the Iraqi port of Umm Qasr 30 miles south of Basra on March 30, four U.S. and six British minesweepers (operating with the mother ship RFA *Sir Belvedere*) began clearing the narrow Khor Abd Allah waterway that linked the port to the Persian Gulf. Working with unmanned underwater vehicles (UUVs) and with more than 20 trained dolphins of the navy's Marine Mammals System (MMS), a Navy Very Shallow Water (VSW) detachment consisting of Navy SEALs, Marine Force Reconnaissance divers, and Explosive Ordnance Disposal divers opened the waterway so that supplies could be funneled through the city to troops advancing inland.

President George W. Bush consistently referred to the Iraq War as "the central front in the War on Terror," contributing to the difficulty in distinguishing between naval forces involved in operations in Operation IRAQI FREEDOM (OIF), Operation ENDURING FREEDOM–Afghanistan (OEF-A), and Operation ENDURING FREEDOM–Horn of Africa (OEF-HOA). Warships of Great Britain's Royal Navy joined U.S. Navy forces in OIF, and the two navies often shifted forces between bilateral operations in the Persian Gulf and multinational operations farther afield. The invasion phase of the war was declared over on April 30, 2003, after which time the line between operations was further blurred with the establishment of Combined Task Force 150 (CTF-150) to support OIF, OEF-A, and OEF-HOA by monitoring shipping and countering piracy in the northern Persian Gulf.

Australia, Canada, Denmark, France, Germany, Italy, the Netherlands, New Zealand, Pakistan, Turkey, the United Kingdom, and the United States assigned warships to CTF-150 at varying times. CTF-150 usually contains about 15 ships, the command of which rotates among the participating navies in four- to six-month intervals. Commanders have included Spanish rear admiral Juan Moreno, British commodore Tony Rix, French vice admiral Jacques Mazars, Dutch commodore Hank Ort, Pakistani rear admiral Shahid Iqbal, German rear admiral Heinrich Lange, and British commodore Bruce Williams.

In 2003, Combined Task Force 158 (CTF-158) was formed by U.S., British, Australian, and Iraqi naval forces to operate jointly with units of the Iraqi armed forces to train Iraqi naval personnel, protect Iraqi assets such as the Khawr al Amayah and Al Basrah oil terminals (KAAOT and ABOT, respectively) located on platforms off the coast of the Faw (Fao) peninsula in southern Iraq, operate jointly with Kuwaiti naval patrol boats, and patrol international waters in a cone-shaped area extending into the Persian Gulf beyond the territorial waters of Iraq. Its commanders have included British commodore Duncan Potts and U.S. rear admiral Kendall Card.

JAMES C. BRADFORD

See also

Iraq, Navy; IRAQI FREEDOM, Operation; Mines, Sea, and Naval Mine Warfare, Persian Gulf and Iraq Wars; SEAL Teams, U.S. Navy; United States Navy, Iraq War

References

Boyne, Walter J. *Operation Iraqi Freedom: What Went Right, What Went Wrong and Why.* New York: Forge Books, 2003.

Holmes, Tony. *US Navy Hornet Units in Operation Iraqi Freedom.* 2 vols. Oxford, UK: Osprey, 2004–2005.

Lambeth, Benjamin S. *American Carrier Air Power at the Dawn of a New Century.* Santa Monica, CA: RAND Corporation, 2005.

Miller, Richard F. *A Carrier at War: On Board the USS Kitty Hawk in the Iraq War.* Washington, DC: Potomac Books, 2003.

IRAQI FREEDOM, **Operation, Ground Campaign**
Start Date: March 20, 2003
End Date: May 1, 2003

For some time the United States and its coalition partners had been building up their forces in Kuwait. More than 300,000 personnel were deployed in the theater under U.S. Army Central Command (CENTCOM) commander General Tommy Franks. Actual coalition combat strength on the ground to implement COBRA II, the ground invasion of Iraq, numbered some 125,000 U.S. troops; 45,000 British troops; 2,000 Australian troops; and 200 Polish troops. Other nations supplied support or occupation troops. Unlike the 1990–1991 Persian Gulf War, there was no broad-based coalition helping to bear the cost of the war. Although Kuwait and Qatar supported the United States, Saudi Arabia refused the use of its bases for air strikes against Iraq. The United States also experienced a major setback when the Turkish Parliament, despite pledges of up to $30 billion in financial assistance, refused to allow the United States to use its territory to open up a northern front, a key component of the U.S. military plan. Three dozen ships laden with equipment for the 30,000-man U.S. 4th Infantry Division lay off Turkish ports. Only after the war began were they redirected through the Suez Canal and around the Arabian Peninsula to Kuwait. The Turkish government's decision meant that the 4th Infantry Division would have to be part of the follow-on force and that Iraq could concentrate its military efforts to the south.

Although some air strikes were launched on the night of March 19 (one—the Dora Farms Strike—was an unsuccessful effort to kill Saddam Hussein and his sons, but most strikes were directed

A British royal marine fires a Milan wire-guided missile at an Iraqi position on the Faw Peninsula of southern Iraq on March 21, 2003. (AP/Wide World Photos)

against Iraqi air defense and missile systems threatening coalition forces in Kuwait as well as leaflet drops with capitulation instructions), the Iraq War began at 5:34 a.m. Baghdad time on March 20, 2003 (9:34 p.m., March 19 EST). Initially known as Operation IRAQI LIBERATION, it was later renamed Operation IRAQI FREEDOM (the British code name was Operation TELIC, while the Australian forces knew it as Operation FALCONER). The war commenced just hours after the expiration of U.S. president George W. Bush's 48-hour ultimatum to Saddam Hussein to step aside.

Baghdad was repeatedly hit with cruise missile attacks and air strikes by B-1, B-2, and B-52 bombers against key headquarters and command and control targets. This shock-and-awe campaign did not appear to be on the massive scale that CENTCOM had suggested. Part of this was the use of 70 percent smart bombs (guided) and 30 percent dumb aerial munitions (unguided), as opposed to only 10 percent smart weapons during the 1990–1991 Persian Gulf War. Also, a good many of the air strikes occurred away from the capital.

As the air attacks unfolded, the ground war also began. The coalition advance from Kuwait was along two main axes northwest toward Baghdad by U.S. Army and marine units, and one supporting thrust due north toward Basra. British forces on the far right under 1st Armoured Divison commander Major General Robin Brims were assigned the task of securing the Shatt al-Arab

waterway and important Shiite city of Basra, Iraq's second largest. At the same time, Lieutenant General James Conway's I Marine Expeditionary Force in the center and Lieutenant General William Scott Wallace's U.S. Army's V Corps to the west would drive on the Iraqi capital of Baghdad, 300 miles to the north. Major General Buford Blount's 3rd ID, with the 7th Armored Cavalry Regiment leading, made the most rapid progress, largely because it moved through more sparsely populated areas.

In the center part of the front, the I Marine Expeditionary Force, carrying out the longest march in its storied history, skirted to the west of the Euphrates River, through the cities of Nasiriyah and on to Najaf and Karbala. Key factors in the allied success were coalition air power (Iraqi aircraft and helicopters never got off the ground), including Apache helicopter gunships and the highly resilient tank-busting A-10 Thunderbolt, the rapidity of the advance, and the ability of coalition troops to fight at night.

The marines were successful in seizing by coup de main the oil fields north of Basra, some 60 percent of the nation's total, including key refineries. Having secured the Shatt al-Arab, and wishing to spare civilians, the British were hopeful of an internal uprising and did not move into Basra itself. They were not actually encamped in the city until the night of April 2. In the meantime they imposed a loose blockade and carried out a series of raids into Basra to destroy symbols of the regime in an effort to demoralize

DRIVE ON BAGHDAD, MARCH 20–APRIL 12, 2003

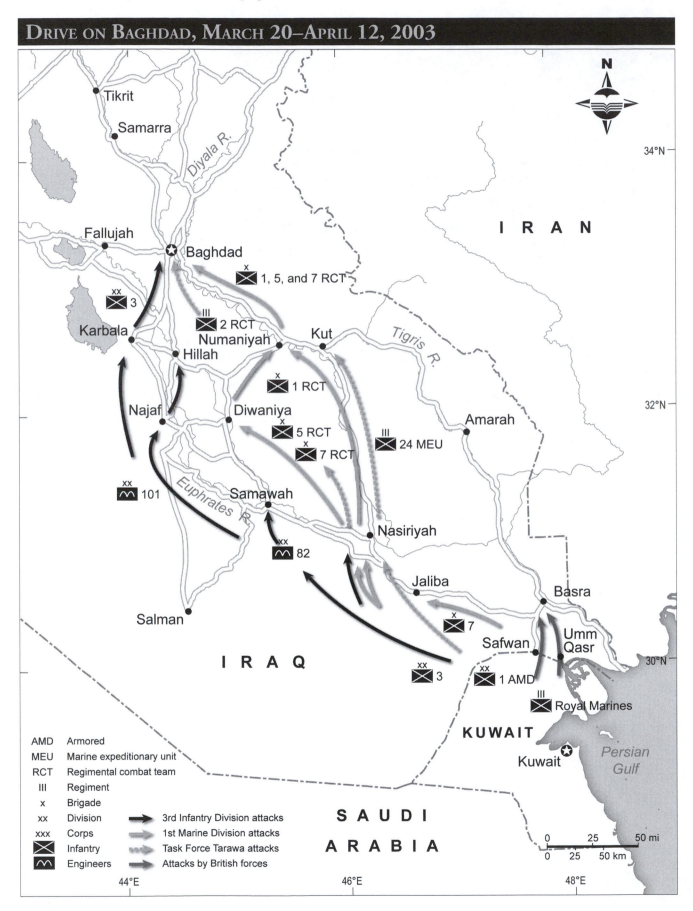

the defenders and to convince them that coalition forces could move at will. At the same time, British forces distributed food and water to convince the inhabitants that they came as liberators rather than conquerors.

U.S. Special Forces secured airfields in western Iraq, and on the night of March 26, 1,000 members of the 173rd Airborne Brigade dropped into Kurdish-held territory in northern Iraq. Working in conjunction with lightly armed Kurdish forces, the brigade opened a northern front and secured the key oil production center of Mosul. U.S. Special Forces also directed air strikes against the Islamic Ansar al-Islam camp in far northeastern Iraq, on the Iranian border.

A number of Iraqi divisions moved into position to block the coalition drive north. These troops largely evaporated, however, with many of their personnel simply deserting. Meanwhile, so-called Saddam Fedayeen, or "technicals"—irregulars often wearing civilian clothes—carried out attacks using civilian vehicles with mounted machine guns and rocket-propelled grenades on supply convoys along the lines of communication from Kuwait north, which came to be dubbed "Ambush Alley." Indeed, on March 23, the 507th Maintenance Company, part of a convoy moving north near the Euphrates, took a wrong turn, was ambushed, and in an ensuing firefight lost nine killed, five wounded, and six captured.

On March 26 U.S. 7th Cavalry regiment and 3rd Infantry Division elements defeated an Iraqi force near Najaf in the largest battle of the war thus far, killing some 450 Iraqis. On March 28, with U.S. forces some 100 miles south of Baghdad, there was an operational pause because of a fierce sandstorm extending over March 25–26 and the need for some army units to resupply.

The Iraqi leadership, meanwhile, repositioned its six Republican Guard divisions around Baghdad for a defense of the capital. As some of these divisions moved to take up new positions south of the city, they came under heavy air attack and lost much of their equipment. The coalition advance quickened again during April 1–2, following the serious degrading of the Baghdad and Medina divisions.

On April 3 U.S. forces reached the outskirts of Baghdad and over the next two days secured Saddam International Airport, some 12 miles from the city center. The speed of their advance allowed U.S. forces to take the airport with minimal damage to its facilities, and it soon became a staging area. By that date, too, the Iraqi people sensed the shift of momentum and an imminent coalition victory. Advancing U.S. troops reported friendly receptions from civilians and increasing surrenders of Iraqi troops, including a reported 2,500 Republican Guards north of Kut on April 4.

By April 5 the 3rd Infantry Division was closing on Baghdad from the southwest, the marines from the southeast, and the 101st Airborne Division was preparing to move in from the north. Baghdad was in effect under a loose blockade, with civilians allowed to depart. On that day also, the 3rd Infantry Division's 2nd Brigade, commanded by Colonel David Perkins, pushed through downtown Baghdad in a three-hour-long operation, called a "Thunder Run," inflicting an estimated 1,000 Iraqi casualties. This proved a powerful psychological blow to the Iraqi regime, which had claimed U.S. forces were nowhere near the city and that it still controlled the international airport. It also led to an exodus of many Baath Party officials and Iraqi military personnel.

This process was repeated on April 6 and 7. In a fierce firefight on April 6, U.S. forces killed an estimated 2,000 to 3,000 Iraqi soldiers for 1 killed of their own. On April 7, 3 battalions of the 3rd Infantry Division remained in the city. The next day marine elements moved into southeastern Baghdad. With the 101st Airborne closing on the city from the northwest and the 3rd Infantry Division from the southeast, the ring around the capital was closed. On April 9 resistance collapsed in Baghdad as Iraqi civilians assisted by U.S. Marines toppled a large statue of Saddam Hussein. There was still fighting in parts of the city as diehard Baath loyalists sniped at U.S. troops, but Iraqi government central command and control had collapsed by April 10.

Elsewhere on April 10, following the collapse of resistance in Baghdad, a small number of Kurdish fighters, U.S. Special Forces, and the 173rd Airborne Brigade liberated Kirkuk. The next day, Mosul, Iraq's third largest city, fell when the Iraqi V Corps commander surrendered some 30,000 men. Apart from some sporadic shooting in Baghdad and massive looting there and in other cities, the one remaining center of resistance was Hussein's ancestral home of Tikrit.

On April 12 the 101st Airborne relieved the marines and 3rd Infantry Division in Baghdad, allowing them to deploy northwest to Tikrit. Meanwhile, the 173rd Airborne Brigade took control of the northern oil fields from the Kurds in order to prevent any possibility of Turkish intervention. The battle for Tikrit failed to materialize. Hussein's stronghold collapsed, and on April 14 allied forces entered the city. That same day the Pentagon announced that major military operations in Iraq were at an end; all that remained was mopping up. Through the end of April, the coalition suffered 139 U.S. and 31 British dead. The coalition reported that 9,200 Iraqi military personnel had also been slain, along with 7,299 civilians, the latter figure believed by many critics of the war to be far too low.

On May 1, 2003, President Bush visited the U.S. aircraft carrier *Abraham Lincoln* off San Diego, the carrier having just returned from a deployment to the Persian Gulf. There the president delivered his "Mission Accomplished" speech, broadcast live to the American public. Bush's characterization that the war was won proved premature. The administration had given insufficient thought to the postwar occupation of Iraq, and long-simmering tensions between Sunni, Shiite, and Kurds erupted into sectarian violence. A series of ill-considered policy decisions, including disbanding the Iraqi Army, abetted the poor security situation, as angry Sunnis, supported by volunteers from other Arab states, took up arms and launched suicide attacks against Iraqi civilians and the U.S. occupiers. Unguarded ammunition dumps provided plentiful supplies for the improvised explosive devices (IEDs) that claimed growing numbers of allied troops.

SPENCER C. TUCKER

See also

Ansar al-Islam; Baghdad, Battle for; Basra, Battle for; Blount, Buford, III; Brims, Robin; Bush, George Walker; Conway, James Terry; Franks, Tommy Ray; Hussein, Saddam; Improvised Explosive Devices; Najaf, First Battle of; Nasiriyah, Battle of; Wallace, William Scott

References

Atkinson, Rick. *In the Company of Soldiers: A Chronicle of Combat.* New York: Henry Holt, 2005.

Franks, Tommy, with Malcolm McConnell. *American Soldier.* New York: Regan Books, 2004.

Murray, Williamson, and Robert H. Scales Jr. *The Iraq War: A Military History.* Cambridge, MA: Belknap, 2005.

Purdum, Todd S., and the Staff of *The New York Times. A Time of Our Choosing: America's War in Iraq.* New York: Times Books/Henry Holt, 2003.

West, Bing, and Ray L. Smith. *The March Up: Taking Baghdad with the 1st Marine Division.* New York: Bantam, 2003.

IRAQI FREEDOM, **Operation, Planning for**

On September 15, 2001, U.S. president George W. Bush and his national security team met to discuss how to respond to the September 11 terrorist attacks on the United States. Secretary of Defense Donald Rumsfeld and his aides offered three targets for retaliation: Al Qaeda, Afghanistan's Taliban regime, and Iraq. In November Pentagon planners began to ponder formally how to attack Iraq. From the outset Rumsfeld and his circle of civilian planners argued with senior military officers over whether to attack Iraq and how many ground troops to employ. As pressure built for a U.S. invasion, based on the premise that Iraq possessed weapons of mass destruction (WMD), the U.S. Central Command (CENTCOM), commanded by General Tommy Franks, assumed responsibility for planning and executing the invasion of Iraq. For a variety of reasons, particularly civilian pressure from Rumsfeld and his aides, a perceived urgency that imposed undue haste, an overburdened staff that also had to address Afghanistan, and Franks's command style that squashed dissent, war planners focused on the relatively easy task of defeating the Iraqi military. They gave little thought to what would come afterward.

During the years following the 1990–1991 Persian Gulf War, military planners had prepared a plan for a second war against Iraq. Dubbed Operation DESERT CROSSING, it envisioned a large invasion force of about 350,000 men, with some variants involving a force of upwards of 500,000 men. The Rumsfeld circle argued that this was far too many ground forces. They pointed to the tremendous improvement in the U.S. military's ability to deliver precision-guided weapons as well as technical advances in reconnaissance systems and command and control networks and asserted that the military was now more mobile and more lethal than during the Persian Gulf War. Proponents of a smaller invasion force argued that these changes, coupled with the deterioration of the Iraqi military that had begun during the Persian Gulf War, implied that a second

war against Iraq would not be a difficult undertaking. The Rumsfeld circle also wanted the flexibility to launch the ground invasion without a long, prewar buildup of forces.

The demand for a lean force that could attack without a long logistical buildup constrained military planners. CENTCOM created a list of things that it wanted to be able to affect or influence, including the Iraqi leadership, internal security, its WMD, and the Republican Guard. They then matched this list against such U.S. military capabilities as Special Operations Forces, air power, and conventional ground forces.

Meanwhile, a group of military planners, notably Secretary of State (and retired four-star general) Colin Powell, warned the Bush administration that the Iraqi Army was the glue holding Iraq together. If the United States dissolved that bond by destroying the army, it would inherit the responsibility for occupying and governing Iraq for a very long time. However, this minority viewpoint had little influence on the development of war plans.

During his 2002 State of the Union address President Bush identified Iraq, Iran, and North Korea as hostile nations, part of an "axis of evil." He asserted that the United States would not stand idle while these nations threatened American interests with WMD. In June 2002 Bush spoke at the U.S. Military Academy, West Point, and formally announced the adoption of a strategy of preemption, known as the Bush Doctrine. These two speeches provided the intellectual rationale for the March 2003 invasion of Iraq.

In August 2002 the Bush administration drafted a secret document titled "Iraq: Goals, Objectives and Strategy." It was an ambitious statement that sought to eliminate the Iraqi WMD threat once and for all, end the Iraqi threat to its neighbors, liberate the Iraqi people from Saddam Hussein's tyranny, and end Iraqi support for international terrorism. The intention was that a stable democracy would be planted in Iraq that would grow and spread throughout the Middle East. In addition, the stupendous show of U.S. force would overawe potential future adversaries.

In its final form, the war plan called for army Special Operations helicopters and air force aircraft to begin operations on the evening of March 19 against Iraqi observation posts along the Saudi and Jordanian borders. Then, coalition special operations units would infiltrate western Iraq to eliminate missile sites that threatened Israel. Two days later, at 9:00 p.m. on March 21, Tomahawk cruise missiles, Lockheed F-117 Nighthawk stealth fighters, and Northrop Grumman B-2 Spirit stealth bombers would strike targets in and around Baghdad. The next morning, COBRA II, the ground invasion, would begin. The army's V Corps, built around the tank-heavy 3rd Infantry Division, along with the 101st Airborne Division, would conduct the main thrust toward Baghdad. Simultaneously, the 1st Marine Division would seize the Rumaila oil fields, drive north across the Euphrates River, and protect the V Corps' flank. The converging army and marine units would then form a cordon around Baghdad to prevent senior Iraqi leaders or WMD from escaping. British forces would seize the largely Shiite city of Basra in southeastern Iraq.

Plans had also called for an attack south from Turkey, mounted by the 4th Infantry Division. Last-minute Turkish obstinacy, despite financial incentives offered by the United States, blocked this part of the plan, forcing the 4th Infantry Division to become a follow-on force and allowing the Iraqis to concentrate their forces to the south. The northern front consisted of the 173rd Airborne Brigade working with lightly armed Kurdish forces to secure the key oil production center of Mosul. In total, the invading ground force was to number about 145,000 men, which was enough to provide a breakthrough force but insufficient to pacify conquered territory.

Planners thought that the ground invasion coming so soon after the air strike would surprise Iraqi military leaders. Air attacks began ahead of schedule, however, when intelligence reports indicated a meeting of Hussein and his senior leaders. The intelligence proved wrong.

COBRA II began on March 21 (local time), 2003. Conventional operations proceeded relatively smoothly, reaching an apparent high-water mark on April 9, when a live television broadcast showed U.S. troops helping a jubilant Iraqi crowd topple a giant statue of Saddam Hussein in downtown Baghdad. Thereafter, the failure to plan adequately for the subsequent occupation led to an insurgency that has persisted for years.

JAMES ARNOLD

See also

IRAQI FREEDOM, Operation; IRAQI FREEDOM, Operation, Air Campaign; IRAQI FREEDOM, Operation, Coalition Ground Forces; IRAQI FREEDOM, Operation, Coalition Naval Forces; IRAQI FREEDOM, Operation, Ground Campaign

References

Cordesman, Anthony H. *The Iraq War: Strategy, Tactics, and Military Lessons.* Westport, CT: Praeger, 2003.

Gordon, Michael R., and General Bernard E. Trainor. *Cobra II: The Inside Story of the Invasion and Occupation of Iraq.* New York: Pantheon Books, 2006.

Record, Jeffrey. *Wanting War: Why the Bush Administration Invaded Iraq.* Dulles, VA: Potomac Books, 2009.

Ricks, Thomas E. *Fiasco: The American Military Adventure in Iraq.* New York: Penguin, 2006.

Iraqi Front for National Dialogue

A Sunni-led Iraqi political list that was formed to contest the December 2005 elections, the Iraqi Front for National Dialogue (al-Jabha al-Iraqiyya li al-Hiwar al-Watani, IFND) describes itself as a nonsectarian political coalition that seeks to end the presence of foreign troops in Iraq and to rebuild government institutions. Saleh al-Mutlaq, former Iraqi minister of state, is a key figure in the IFND. He campaigned against the constitution during the October 2005 referendum and refused to join the other main Sunni Arab–led list, the Iraqi Accord Front, because that group's largest component, the Iraqi Islamic Party, had backed the new constitution. The IFND coalition also includes Kurds, Arabs, Assyrians, and Shabaks.

The IFND's main components include the Iraqi National Front, led by Mutlaq; the National Front for a Free and United Iraq, led by Hassan Zaydan; the Iraqi Christian Democratic Party, led by Minas al-Yusufi; the Democratic Arab Front, led by Farhan al-Sudayd; and the Sons of Iraq Movement, led by Ali al-Suhayri. The IFND is distinct from the Iraqi National Dialogue Council, headed by Khalaf al-Ulayyan, which is a component of the Iraqi Accord Front.

Although it won 11 seats in the December 2005 election, the IFND complained of widespread election fraud.

The IFND's platform has emphasized ending the foreign occupation; reconciliation among Iraq's political, religious, and ethnic groups; rebuilding government institutions; and improving the economic and security situation within Iraq. According to an October 2008 poll, however, only 3.6 percent of the public supports the INDF. Mutlaq has disagreed with Prime Minister Nuri al-Maliki's management of the Iraqi government and has stated publicly that he believes that Maliki is not serious about national reconciliation and coalition building. Mutlaq also decried a law passed by the Iraqi parliament in early 2008 that upheld the earlier decision to ban Baathism in any form in Iraq. He termed the legislation unrealistic and difficult to enforce.

RICHARD M. EDWARDS AND PAUL G. PIERPAOLI JR.

See also

Iraq, History of, 1990–Present; Maliki, Nuri Muhammed Kamil Hasan al-

References

Packer, George. *The Assassins' Gate: America in Iraq.* New York: Farrar, Straus and Giroux, 2005.

Stansfield, Gareth. *Iraq: People, History, Politics.* Cambridge, UK: Polity, 2007.

Iraqi Insurgency
Event Date: 2003–Present

A violent resistance by segments of the Iraqi population against the foreign occupation powers deployed in Iraq and the new Iraqi government set up after the fall of the Baathist state. The term "insurgency" is employed in U.S. governmental circles and by coalition forces but is not used in the Arab media, except in discussions with U.S. spokespersons. The term was not initially employed by the U.S. government, but its appearance in 2004 onward led to a major emphasis on insurgency theory and new approaches to counterinsurgency.

The Iraqi insurgency commenced soon after the official end of hostilities that followed the overthrow of Iraqi president Saddam Hussein in the spring of 2003. Until the U.S. military gained control of Iraq and President George W. Bush declared "mission accomplished" on May 1, 2003, Operation IRAQI FREEDOM was essentially a war between the Iraqi government and military and the coalition powers that overthrew it. Since then, IRAQI FREEDOM has morphed into a battle between coalition and allied Iraqi forces and

STRUGGLE AGAINST THE INSURGENCY, AUGUST 31–SEPTEMBER 29, 2004

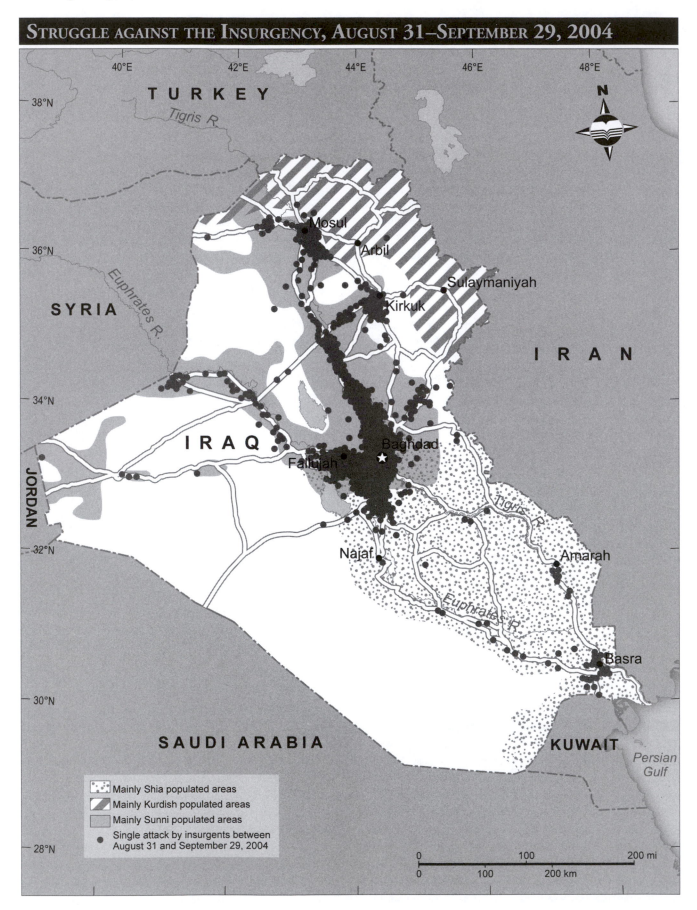

Mainly Shia populated areas

Mainly Kurdish populated areas

Mainly Sunni populated areas

• Single attack by insurgents between August 31 and September 29, 2004

Iraqi firefighters extinguish flames resulting from a car bomb explosion in southern Baghdad, April 14, 2005. (U.S. Department of Defense)

a wide array of insurgent groups, now characterized as an insurgency war.

A number of factors led to the insurgency, but the chief cause was the power vacuum created by the sudden collapse of the highly centralized Iraqi government and by the failure of the U.S. armed forces to properly fill that void in a timely manner with a power structure acceptable to those governed. Many Iraqis did not welcome a change in government, or feared the opposition elements who assumed power. Coalition forces have sometimes argued that the lack of electricity, fuel, potable water, and basic social services created daily personal grievances among many Iraqis, but far more resentment was engendered by attacks, arrests, and detentions, and later, by Iraqi-on-Iraqi campaigns that led those who could afford or were able to flee Iraq to do so. The Iraqi people expected the occupying American forces to provide for their security, but the latter either had insufficient numbers to do so effectively or were not assigned to protect Iraqis, their property, or their state institutions.

The U.S.-led invasion of Iraq and subsequent fall of the country's dictator, Saddam Hussein, made conditions ripe for power struggles to emerge among various sectarian and political groups. Even though Iraqis had a history of intermarriage and mixed communities, many had been suppressed and mistreated by Hussein's government and had scores to settle.

The U.S. government hoped that the period immediately following the overthrow of Hussein would see the installation of a broadly based Iraqi government led by those who had opposed Saddam. However, the Iraqi people viewed many of the new leaders as pursuing their own narrow interests or those of their parties.

Also, the initial U.S. governmental appointees in the Interim Authority were intent on wiping out all vestiges of the previous government and institutions through de-Baathification. This led many Sunni Iraqis to conclude that they had absolutely nothing to gain and could possibly force the occupying troops to leave Iraq if they took up arms and established control in those areas of the country where they were a majority. Initially, the coalition refused to accept both the severity of this fighting and its toll on Iraqis, but a virtual civil war began to engulf Iraq in 2006.

A telling feature of the Iraqi insurgency has been its decentralized nature. It is conducted by a large number of disparate groups, many of which are ideologically different, although temporary alliances are not uncommon. For example, there were at least 40 different Sunni Muslim insurgent factions, although the coalition primarily focused on the threat presented by Al Qaeda in Iraq. Others were local nationalists, made up of former Iraqi security service members and soldiers of the old Iraqi armed forces, some of whom aligned with new Islamist groups. Their goal, broadly speaking, was to drive the United States and its allies from Iraq and regain the power that they once had enjoyed, or at least, sufficient power to force the central Shia-dominated Iraqi government to grant them autonomy in certain areas. This segment of the resistance was motivated by a mixture of nationalism, opposition to occupation, loss of status and income, fear of future discrimination, and the lure of financial incentives provided by various groups. These predominantly Sunni groups had valid reasons to fear that the new security services dominated by Shia and Kurds would oppress them. Some of these insurgents were believed to be trained and equipped soldiers with previous combat experience and knowledge of the local terrain.

A second element within the Sunni Iraqi community consisted of jihadist salafiyya (or salafis) whose ultimate goal was the establishment of an Islamic state in Iraq while excluding the Shia and/or non-Islamists from power altogether. The U.S. government identified this group as consisting primarily of foreign volunteer fighters, who indeed traveled to Iraq from Saudi Arabia, Jordan, Syria, Egypt, and Libya. Actually, there were far fewer of these foreign volunteers than was claimed, and a far larger number of salafist or jihadi salafists were Iraqis who adopted this role in desperation, or who had become salafist in the Saddam Hussein era. These groups targeted coalition forces as well as Iraqi military, police, government, and civilians in suicide attacks. Among these groups was Al Qaeda in Iraq, which was originally the Tawhid wal-Jihad group headed by now-deceased Abu Musab al-Zarqawi.

Although Al Qaeda leaders in Afghanistan warned the Iraqi group, which had sworn allegiance to them, that attacking Iraqi Shia was a dubious policy, they went on doing so. The leaders of Al Qaeda in Iraq considered the Shia to be renegades (and apostates) and held them accountable for collaborating with the occupying forces.

In 2008 the coalition began to claim that many insurgents were not ideologically committed (perhaps because efforts to convince Iraqis that they were un-Islamic were failing). They asserted that many fighters were motivated by the need for a source of income because of the economic collapse of Iraq and the general state of lawlessness. This claim appears to have been true in some limited areas where kidnapping rings operated just after the initial defeat of Hussein's government. It is the type of claim that can be made in civil wars generally, but is demonstrably untrue, for most of the insurgent statements claim religious convictions.

The insurgents have employed a wide array of tactics against their targets. Some rely on sabotage of electric stations, oil pipelines and facilities, and coalition reconstruction projects. Others use small-arms gunfire against coalition forces and attempt assassinations of public officials and private citizens. Firing rockets and mortar shells at fixed coalition positions has also been an insurgent tactic. The use of improvised roadside bombs and improvised explosive devices (IEDs) has proven especially lethal to coalition troops. Suicide bombers, car bombs, and truck bombs have also been used to great effect by the insurgents.

Insurgents have deployed ambushes that involve the simultaneous use of mines, grenades, and rocket-propelled grenades.

Insurgents also engage in the kidnapping of local citizens and foreigners to exchange them for ransom, or simply to execute them. Initially, insurgent violence was primarily directed at coalition forces. As the occupation has persisted, however, attacks by various insurgency groups have begun shifting toward the Iraqi police and security forces as well as opposing militias representing the various warring sects. Attacks on Iraqi civilians, especially those associated with the government or seeking employment with the police force, also escalated after 2004.

The United States accused Syria and Iran of aiding various insurgency groups in the funding and planning of their activities. There was evidence that some former Baathists, including the acknowledged leader of the resistance, Ibrahim al-Duri, were in Syria. Both Syria and Iran oppose the establishment of a pro-American democracy in Iraq, and fear that their influence in the region would be jeopardized by the long-term stationing of U.S. troops in Iraq.

The United States has employed several strategies to squelch the insurgency in Iraq. The initial phase of counterinsurgency efforts in late 2003 and early 2004 consisted mainly of occupation forces engaging in indiscriminate and sometimes culturally insensitive tactics that alienated many Iraqis, such as mass arrests, night searches, heavy-handed interrogations, and blanket incarcerations. Such actions enraged and embittered formerly friendly or neutral Iraqis. The United States then responded to insurgents by engaging in a variety of counterinsurgency measures, including Operation DESERT THRUST, Operation PHANTOM FURY in Fallujah, Operation TOGETHER FORWARD, and Operation PHANTOM THRUST, just to name a few. These full-scale assaults on insurgency bases have had only a temporary and limited effect, however.

The most notable counterinsurgency effort was mounted during 2007. The so-called troop surge accounted for an increase in U.S. troop size by about 30,000 additional soldiers. The move has been hailed a success by U.S. officials for bringing down the levels of violence in Iraq. Critics, however, contend that the levels of violence have gone down only in some areas of the country, and only through methods that have cordoned off and imposed barriers around neighborhoods that have been cleansed on a sectarian basis. In spring 2009 there was, for example, an upsurge of bombings targeting both Shia and Sunni areas in Baghdad. While most insurgent activity involved only Sunnis, other groups have also been involved. Thus, there was also armed resistance by members of Muqtada al-Sadr's Mahdi Army when Iraqi government forces engaged them. They had not been a part of the insurgency but rather sought to enhance their power within the body politic.

Another reason for a drop in the violence was the fact that the U.S. military struck a bargain with various Sunni groups, some of them jihadist salafists. This permitted coalition forces to concentrate on fighting Al Qaeda in Iraq in these areas. However, these so-called Awakening Councils were subject to numerous attacks and have been clashing with the government. Since their support rested on financial incentives, their continued compliance is unclear. It remains uncertain if the reduction in the Iraq insurgency will survive the withdrawal of U.S. troops from Iraq.

KRISTIAN P. ALEXANDER AND SHERIFA ZUHUR

See also

Al Qaeda in Iraq; Baath Party; Fedayeen; Iran; Iraq, History of, 1990–Present; IRAQI FREEDOM, Operation; Jihad; Mahdi Army; Salafism; Shia Islam; Sunni Islam; Surge, U.S. Troop Deployment, Iraq War; Syria

References

Chehab, Zaki. *Iraq Ablaze: Inside the Insurgency.* New York: I. B. Tauris, 2006.

Cordesman, Anthony. *Iraqi Security Forces: A Strategy for Success.* Westport, CT: Praeger Security International, 2005.

Hafez, Mohammed. *Suicide Bombers in Iraq: The Strategy and Ideology of Martyrdom.* Washington, DC: United States Institute of Peace Press, 2007.

Hashim, Ammed S. *Insurgency and Counter-insurgency in Iraq.* Ithaca, NY: Cornell University Press, 2006.

Pelletiere, Stephen. *Losing Iraq: Insurgency and Politics.* Westport, CT: Praeger Security International, 2007.

Iraqi Occupation of Kuwait, Atrocities
Start Date: 1990
End Date: 1991

On August 2, 1990, some 100,000 Iraqi soldiers crossed the Iraq-Kuwait border, and within five hours the Iraqi military had successfully occupied the entire country of Kuwait. On August 28, 1990, Iraqi dictator Saddam Hussein announced the annexation of Kuwait as the 19th governorate of Iraq. Beginning with the initial invasion and continuing throughout the occupation period, which lasted until February 1991, the Iraqis pursued a brutal policy of torture, plunder, and destruction against the nation and peoples of Kuwait.

Initial Kuwaiti protests over the occupation were met with brutal reprisal. Iraqi soldiers fired indiscriminately into unarmed crowds of Kuwaiti civilians demonstrating against the occupation of their country. Houses from which snipers fired on Iraqis were promptly demolished, along with surrounding properties. Thousands of injured Kuwaitis were denied medical services and left to die.

Arbitrary and mass arrests became commonplace. Under the Iraqi secret police, the Mukhabarat, led by Ali Hassan al-Majid Tikriti, 22 torture centers were established throughout Kuwait City. Key Kuwaiti opponents to the occupation were arrested and summarily executed, an estimated 1,000 people in the first week alone. Simply denying the legitimacy of the occupation, flying the Kuwaiti flag, or voicing support for the exiled government became justification for arrest and torture. Entire families were arrested together and forced to witness the interrogation and torture of individual members. Torture methods ranged from simple beatings to electroshocks, dismemberment, and the use of hot irons.

Kuwaiti women were routinely raped by Iraqi occupiers; young girls and women were especially targeted by Iraqi soldiers. Also, an estimated 20,000 Kuwaitis were transported to Iraq to be used as slave labor. An additional 3,000 to 5,000 Kuwaitis were taken as hostages and used as human shields.

During the occupation, Iraq systematically plundered Kuwait's resources and infrastructure. The Kuwaiti Central Bank, for example, was robbed of some $2 billion. Electronic, communications, and industrial equipment was dismantled and shipped to Iraq, while equipment and spare parts were looted from Kuwaiti oil fields. Iraqi soldiers plundered museums, homes, stores, and markets as well.

A November 1992 U.S. Pentagon report titled "Report on Iraqi War Crimes: Desert Shield/Desert Storm" charged Hussein and his army with 16 violations of the law of war as enumerated by The Hague and Geneva conventions. The 199th Judge Advocate General International Law Detachment, tasked with investigating Iraqi war crimes, confirmed the many atrocities committed against Kuwaitis citizens and residents. The report details documents collected by the 199th that showed that the Iraqi leadership had intended to use chemical weapons against Kuwaiti citizens. The evidence in the report included accounts of rape and torture, photographs of murdered Kuwaitis, and videotapes of mass burial sites and torture implements. It also detailed shocking violations of human rights that included amputations, dismemberments, forced self-cannibalism, the use of electric drills, acid baths, repeated rapes, and many other horrific acts. The Pentagon's report concluded that 1,082 Kuwaiti deaths were "directly attributed to Iraqi criminal conduct." The Pentagon report also stated that the violations were so widespread that they could not have happened "without the explicit knowledge or authorization of Saddam [Hussein]."

According to the same report, Iraq also sabotaged Kuwait's ability to manufacture oil, the backbone of the Kuwaiti economy. Documents show quite clearly Iraq's premeditated plans for the destruction of the Kuwaiti oil fields. The International Affairs Division of the War Crimes Documentation Center revealed that, following coalition military action against Iraq, Iraqi forces released Kuwaiti oil into the Persian Gulf from ships and from the Mina al-Ahmadi facility in Kuwait. In the desert, 590 oil wellheads were damaged or destroyed and another 82 were sufficiently damaged, with millions of barrels of oil freely flowing into the desert.

In the period before the war, there were accusations that the United States had embellished the Iraqi atrocities in order to secure Middle Eastern oil. Critics charged President George H. W. Bush with exaggerating the atrocities in order to help sell the American people on the value of invading Kuwait. Even those who originally supported the war effort developed a skepticism regarding the atrocities. Jimmy Hayes, a Louisiana congressman who initially defended Bush's decision to go to war, asserted that the Kuwaiti government had paid many public relations firms to support their cause in an effort to rally American opinion against Hussein and his forces.

The world's largest public relations firm at the time, Hill & Knowlton, was active in influencing American public opinion. Hill

& Knowlton ran a $10 million public relations campaign to build support in the United States. In October 1990, a young woman identified as "Nayirah" appeared in front of Congress and described the Iraqis taking newborn babies out of their incubators. Hill & Knowlton was accused of having orchestrated Nayirah's testimony. "Citizens for a Free Kuwait," a front organization for Kuwait's ruling royal family, was believed to have paid Nayirah for her testimony. Despite the accusations of exaggeration and fabrication, American officials maintained that the atrocities taking place in Kuwait warranted an invasion force to oust Hussein's forces from Kuwait. In the end, the specificity and sheer number of documented Iraqi atrocities in Kuwait make it all but certain that Hussein had conducted nefarious deeds throughout the occupation period.

ROBERT W. MALICK AND GREGORY W. MORGAN

See also

Bush, George Herbert Walker; DESERT SHIELD, Operation; DESERT STORM, Operation; Hussein, Saddam; Kuwait; Kuwait, Iraqi Invasion of; Kuwait, Occupation of by Iraq; Oil Well Fires, Persian Gulf War

References

Al-Damkhi, Ali Mohamed. *Invasion: Saddam Hussein's Reign of Terror in Kuwait.* London: Kuwait Research and Advertising, 1992.

Hawley, T. M. *Against the Fires of Hell: The Environmental Disaster of the Gulf War.* New York: Harcourt Brace Jovanovich, 1992.

McNeill, John H. *Report on Iraqi War Crimes (Desert Shield/Desert Storm).* Department of Defense, Office of General Counsel. Washington, DC: U.S. Government Printing Office, November 19, 1992.

Pimlott, John, and Stephen Badsey, eds. *The Gulf War Assessed.* London: Arms and Armour, 1992.

Stevens, Richard P. *The Iraqi Invasion of Kuwait: American Reflections.* Washington, DC: International Education and Communications Group, 1993.

Iraqi-Russian Relations, 1992–Present

The Anglo-American–led invasion of Iraq and overthrow of Iraqi dictator Saddam Hussein in 2003 deprived Russia of a key source of influence in the Middle East. Indeed, close Russian (and Soviet) ties to Iraq go back at least to the 1960s. The Soviet Union had been a major supplier of weapons to Saddam Hussein's regime and had enjoyed friendly relations with that government. The Soviets had been eager to foster friendly relations with Iraq to counter U.S. influence in the Persian Gulf region and especially to offset the close U.S. relationships with Mohammad Reza Shah Pahlavi of Iran and the Saudi Arabian monarchy. Hussein proved receptive to Soviet overtures and increased offers of military aid, but was nevertheless careful to maintain his country's independence and not become a puppet or satellite of the Soviets.

In the final years of the Soviet Union, its imploding economy turned that once militarily powerful country into a mere spectator of world affairs. The Soviet Union supported American and world condemnation of Iraq's August 2, 1990, invasion of Kuwait, but it lacked the influence to forestall Operation DESERT STORM and

thus save Hussein from ensuing military defeat in February 1991. Soviet leader Mikhail Gorbachev neither sought to block the international military coalition that invaded Iraq nor sent troops to the fight, a scenario that would have been unthinkable at the height of the Cold War. In December 1991 the Soviet Union ceased to exist, and Gorbachev was no longer in power, their places taken by the Russian Federation and President Boris Yeltsin.

Throughout much of the 1990s, Russia was preoccupied with domestic affairs, especially a flagging economy. Under the leadership of the largely pro-American Yeltsin, Russia played only a negligible role in the long confrontation between Iraq and the United States and United Nations (UN) weapons inspectors who were charged with dismantling Hussein's stocks of weapons of mass destruction (WMD). By the late 1990s, however, Yeltsin's health had deteriorated and decision-making increasingly fell into the hands of other officials. At the same time, much of world opinion was tiring of the international sanctions imposed on Iraq. Although it was Hussein's own policies that were making life miserable for the Iraqi population, he succeeded in convincing outsiders that their suffering was a direct result of the sanctions, which continued to receive the strong support of both the United States and Great Britain.

At the same time that Yeltsin's influence was fading, that of nationalist Vladimir Putin, who would become prime minister in 1999 and president in 2000, was sharply increasing. Russia's economy was also improving rapidly, thanks in larger part to exports of oil and natural gas. Russia began the new century in a quest to assert a more independent foreign policy, and in the final year of the U.S. president Bill Clinton's administration proved less compliant to U.S. wishes. By 2001 Russia, along with France, began to question the utility of continuing sanctions against Iraq.

After the terror attacks of September 11, 2001, the administration of President George W. Bush sought to invade Iraq not only to deny Hussein the opportunity to rebuild his stockpiles of WMD and form alliances with Islamic terrorist groups but also to create a democratic regime that senior administration officials hoped would reshape the entire Middle East. Russian president Putin strenuously objected to the U.S.-led invasion of Iraq without authorization by the UN. Putin undoubtedly regarded Bush's invasion of Iraq as nothing more than an excuse to extend U.S. influence in the Middle East. With U.S. troops occupying Iraq beginning in March 2003, Russia sought closer ties with Iran, and it has been providing weapons to that nation as well as assisting in developing Iran's nuclear program, ostensibly for energy uses only.

Despite the dominating influence of the United States in Iraq, Russia has sought to gain influence there and will continue to do so, particularly in the years to come, when U.S. military presence in the country is expected to decline. Although the Iraqi government of Prime Minister Nuri al-Maliki is understandably wary of Russia, owing to the Soviet ties with Saddam Hussein, Russia's opposition to the 2003 Iraq War, and Russia's closer ties with its

Soviet defense minister General Andrei Grechko, left, confers with Iraqi minister of the interior Saddam Hussein, right, in Baghdad, December 15, 1971. (AP/Wide World Photos)

arch-rival, Iran, Russia has redoubled its efforts to benefit from Iraq's newly increasing prosperity by becoming involved in reconstructing and upgrading the country's decaying infrastructure.

Russia has written off most of Iraq's $12.9 billion debt (much of it dating back to Soviet-era supplies of military equipment), and on February 11, 2008, the British Broadcasting Corporation (BBC) reported that Russia had signed a deal with Iraqi foreign minister Hoshiyar Zebari in Moscow that would grant Russia permission to invest $4 billion from Russian companies, including oil producer Lukoil, to upgrade Iraq's oil infrastructure and to tap Iraq's vast oil deposits.

Russia clearly seeks to benefit from Iraq's vast wealth in oil and hopes to regain its 1997 Hussein-era West Qurna oil field deal, worth $3.7 billion, to tap one of Iraq's biggest oil deposits. Absolving Iraq of the entirety of its Soviet-era debt had been delayed because Russia sought preferential access to Iraqi oil, revival of the 1997 West Qurna oil deal, and access to the Rumaila field. Iraq refused to accede to these requests. Iraqi officials held that the Russian Lukoil oil company would have to renegotiate the West Qurna deal. On February 11, 2008, however, Russian finance minister Alexei Kudrin announced that Russia had agreed to write off $11.1 billion of Iraqi debt immediately, another $900 million in the next few years, and restructure another $900 million for 17 years.

On March 28, 2008, Fox News reported that in a message to Prime Minister Maliki, Putin lobbied on behalf of Russian companies seeking to be awarded contracts for rebuilding Iraq's infrastructure, particularly in the oil and gas sector. Putin once again raised Russia's interest in the huge West Qurna oil field and announced that Russia had expanded its diplomatic presence in the city of Erbil, in northern Iraq, and was also expected to restore a consular mission in the south in the city of Basra. However, Russia has yet to establish an embassy in Baghdad, which no doubt reveals Moscow's ongoing concern for security in the capital. Putin's efforts came two days after Iraq's Oil Ministry had invited local and international oil companies to bid for contracts providing technical support for the development of two major oil fields in the country. Putin stated that he hoped that this Russian overture would receive a positive Iraqi response. Iraqi leaders, however, apparently remain wary of Russia.

STEFAN M. BROOKS

See also

Iraq, History of, 1990–Present; Maliki, Nuri Muhammed Kamil Hasan al-; Putin, Vladimir Vladimirovich; Russia, Middle East Policy, 1991–Present; Yeltsin, Boris Nikolayevich

References

Covarrubia, Jack, et al. *Strategic Interests in the Middle East.* Aldershot, UK: Ashgate, 2007.

Melville, Andrew. *Russian Foreign Policy in Transition: Concepts and Realities.* Budapest: Central European University Press, 2005.

Iraqi-Soviet Relations

During the Cold War, leaders of the Soviet Union viewed Iraq as a nation vital to their strategic and security interests. Iraqi-Soviet ties were long-standing yet at times difficult. Diplomatic relations between the two states were first established during World War II, on September 9, 1944, but they were severed in 1955 when Iraq joined the U.S.-sponsored Baghdad Pact, a military alliance designed to contain Soviet expansionism in the Middle East.

The coup d'état of July 14, 1958, led by Iraqi general colonel Abd al-Karim Qasim, brought an end to the monarchy and established a republic. It also brought close ties between the new Iraqi government and the Soviet Union. Qasim quickly restored diplomatic relations with Moscow and arranged for the purchase of Soviet arms. During the next several years, the Soviet Union extended significant economic and military aid to Qasim's government.

By late 1959, however, relations became strained with the persecution of members of the Iraqi Communist Party (ICP). While Soviet propaganda outlets denounced the execution of Iraqi Communist Party members, Moscow was careful not to attack Qasim openly for fear of alienating his anti-Western government. No doubt, Moscow welcomed Qasim's assassination on February 8, 1963, with cautious optimism.

The Baath Party coup against Qasim did not, however, lead to an improvement in Iraqi-Soviet relations, which rather only worsened under the leadership of Iraq's new ruler, President Abd al-Salam Arif. To Moscow's dismay, the Arif government continued, if not increased, a policy of persecuting the ICP and even murdered the head of the party, Hussein al-Radi. Moscow publicly condemned what it called the "bloody terror" against communists in Iraq, including Radi's murder, and even labeled the Baath regime "fascist." Moscow also publicly denounced a military campaign against Iraqi Kurds as "genocide," issued a formal complaint to Iraq's ambassador in Moscow, and protested Iraq's actions to its neighbors, including Iran, Turkey, and Syria. In response to Iraqi actions against both the ICP and its Kurdish community, the Soviet Union reduced economic and military assistance to Baghdad. In retaliation, Iraqi prime minister Ahmad Hassan al-Bakr attacked what he characterized as a "foreign propaganda campaign" and, while indicating a desire to maintain friendly relations with the Soviet Union, denounced what he regarded as attempts by Moscow to interfere in Iraq's domestic affairs.

This war of words between the Soviet Union and Iraq was indicative of the nature of their relationship. While Iraq welcomed Soviet economic and military support and assistance, it was determined to maintain complete independence from Moscow. Indeed, it never sought to become a close ally, or client, of the Soviet Union. As such, Iraq consistently refused to establish binding ties with the Soviet Union, such as the establishment of Soviet bases in the country or signing a mutual defense treaty. The Soviet Union, for its part, likely never had any illusions regarding its ability to influence, much less control, Iraq, and despite providing significant economic and military aid, it never regarded Iraq as a stable ally or in the same vein as it did Syria or Egypt.

As the military campaign against the Kurds stalled and the persecution of the ICP subsided, relations between the Soviet Union and Iraq improved, as evinced by the first visit to Moscow by Iraqi government officials in 1966 and the warm Soviet response to Iraq's recognition of Kurdish national and linguistic rights. But Arif died in a helicopter crash in 1966, and his brother Abd al-Rahman Arif's ascension to power was short-lived. He was overthrown by the Baath Party on July 17, 1968, which had earlier split with Arif's regime when Arif ended his support and alliance with the Baath Party and by 1963 had removed all Baath officials from the government.

It was not until the Socialist Baath Party seized power in 1968 that Soviet-Iraq relations became closer. Indeed, the period 1968–1975 can be regarded as the high point of Iraqi-Soviet relations. In 1972 the two powers signed a Treaty of Friendship and Cooperation but, reflective of Iraq's desire to retain its independence, the treaty did not include any military obligations, nor was it a military alliance. In any case, seeking to modernize and also increase its military power, Iraq received considerable quantities of weapons from the Soviet Union. By the late 1970s, however, relations cooled again as Iraq's economic wealth increased, owing to the sharp rise in oil prices. That in turn allowed Iraq to be less dependent on the Soviet Union and brought closer relations with the West, particularly France. Iraq's ties to France soon eclipsed those with Moscow, and Iraq began placing substantial arms orders with the French.

Relations between Moscow and Baghdad became increasingly strained because of renewed suppression of the ICP, Iraqi denunciation of the Soviet Union's recognition of Israel, and disputes over the larger Arab-Israeli conflict. The 1979 Soviet invasion of Afghanistan was another cause of friction between the two governments.

Iraqi-Soviet ties did not markedly improve after Vice President Saddam Hussein assumed the presidency of Iraq in 1979. When Hussein took Iraq into war with Iran on September 22, 1980, Moscow did not denounce the invasion, but it did suspend military aid until 1982. At that point, with the war turning against Iraq, Baghdad promised to withdraw to its international border, but Moscow continued to call for a peaceful settlement of the conflict and offered to mediate an end to the war. At the same time, presumably disappointed with the poor level of Soviet support in its war with Iran, Iraq sought closer ties with the United States and even resumed diplomatic relations with Washington, D.C., in 1984, which had been suspended by Iraq as a consequence of the 1967 Six-Day War. For its part, alarmed at the possibility of an Iranian victory, the United States had begun providing covert military and intelligence support to Iraq as early as 1982.

After the end of the Iran-Iraq War in 1988, Iraqi-Soviet ties continued to deteriorate as the Soviet Union, preoccupied with its myriad economic and political problems, largely ignored Iraq and concentrated instead on domestic political and economic reforms. The Soviet Union condemned Iraq's August 2, 1990, invasion of Kuwait, and Moscow voted for United Nations (UN) Resolution 678, which authorized the employment of "all necessary means" to end the Iraqi occupation of Kuwait. To appease Communist hard-liners, embattled Soviet president Mikhail Gorbachev tried to negotiate a last-minute settlement to save Iraq from being invaded by a U.S.-led international military force, but the United States rejected the Soviet proposal. Moscow then watched as the U.S.-led international coalition routed Iraq's army in early 1991. On December 25, 1991, the Soviet Union dissolved.

STEFAN M. BROOKS

See also

Arif, Abd al-Salam; Baath Party; Baghdad Pact; Bakr, Ahmad Hassan al-; Hussein, Saddam; Iran-Iraq War; Iraq, History of, Pre-1990; Iraq, History of, 1990–Present; Qasim, Abd al-Karim; Soviet-Afghanistan War; Soviet Union, Middle East Policy

References

Golan, Galia. *Soviet Policies in the Middle East: From World War Two to Gorbachev.* Cambridge: Cambridge University Press, 1990.
Shemesh, Haim. *Soviet-Iraqi Relations, 1968–1988.* Boulder, CO: Lynne Rienner, 1992.
Smolansky, Oleg. *The USSR and Iraq: The Soviet Quest for Influence.* Durham, NC: Duke University Press, 1991.

Iraq-Kuwait Diplomacy

See Kuwait-Iraq Diplomacy

Iraq Liberation Act

Legislation passed by the United States Congress to establish a program to support a transition to democracy in Iraq. The act was sponsored by Representative Benjamin A. Gilman (R-N.Y.) and passed by Congress on October 7, 1998. President William Jefferson Clinton signed the act into law on October 31, 1998.

The Iraq Liberation Act of 1998 (ILA) encapsulated sentiment on the part of Congress that the United States should support efforts to remove Iraqi dictator Saddam Hussein from power and replace his regime with a democratic government. Enactment of the ILA coincided with growing tensions and frustrations within the international community during 1997–1998 over Iraq's continued failure to comply with United Nations (UN) resolutions mandating United Nations Special Commission (UNSCOM) inspections of suspected Iraqi nuclear, biological, and chemical weapons sites. Residual concerns and mistrust stemming from the 1991 Persian Gulf War and the Iraqi suppression of Kurdish and Shiite opposition factions within the country also contributed to the rising tensions.

The ILA evolved from two prior pieces of legislation, the Emergency Supplemental Appropriations Act for Fiscal Year 1998, and the Omnibus Consolidated and Emergency Supplemental Appropriations Act for Fiscal Year 1999. Both acts provided monetary assistance to identified democratic opposition groups in Iraq. Pursuant to the Fiscal Year 1998 act, the U.S. Department of State also submitted a report to Congress detailing plans to establish a program of assistance for Iraqi democratic opposition groups. In spite of doubts over democratic opposition capabilities, the ILA provided additional assistance and, more importantly, encapsulated Congress's wishes for Iraq's future.

The ILA first delineated the historical chronology of Iraqi actions from its invasion of Iran on September 22, 1980, to Iraqi obstruction of UNSCOM inspection efforts in 1998 and the U.S. response of financial assistance to democratic opposition groups. The descriptive chronology provided a supportive framework for the third section, and core, of the ILA: the articulation of Congress's sentiment that U.S. policy toward Iraq should entail the removal of President Saddam Hussein's regime and support of democratic tendencies within the country. To that end, the ILA authorized the president to grant broadcasting, military, and humanitarian assistance to certain Iraqi democratic opposition groups. Seed money in the amount of $2 million for Fiscal Year 1999 was provided for television and radio broadcasting. Military assistance included up to $97 million in defense material and services from the Department of Defense, as well as military education and training for these groups. However, a separate but significant section made it clear that beyond providing materials, services, and training, the ILA should not be considered as authorizing direct U.S. military force to effectuate regime change in Iraq. Finally, the ILA authorized humanitarian assistance for individuals living in areas of Iraq controlled by democratic opposition groups. A particular emphasis was placed on providing humanitarian assistance to refugees fleeing from areas controlled by the Hussein regime.

A restrictive clause in the ILA prohibited the provision of such assistance to any group actively cooperating with Hussein's regime at the time when such assistance was to be provided, but Congress proceeded further in a separate section to clearly set out criteria to determine which opposition groups were eligible to receive assistance under the ILA. A number of religious and secular opposition groups had emerged in Iraq, and Congress wished to ensure assistance was provided to appropriate groups in accordance with congressional intent. Thus, Congress restricted presidential authorization of assistance to only those organizations composed of a diverse array of Iraqi individuals or groups opposed to Hussein's regime, with a corresponding commitment to democratic values, human rights, peace within the region, Iraq's territorial integrity, and the cultivation of cooperation among all democratic opposition groups. The ILA further urged the president to make an appeal to the United Nations to establish a war crimes tribunal for Iraq. Finally, the ILA contemplated additional U.S. support and assistance for democratic Iraqi parties when Hussein lost power in Iraq.

President Clinton signed the ILA into law the same day Iraq ceased all cooperation with UNSCOM. Six weeks later, beginning on December 16, 1998, the United States and Great Britain responded by launching Operation DESERT FOX, an air-strike campaign to degrade Iraqi command centers, airfields, and missile installations. The ILA and DESERT FOX served as further steps in the evolving U.S. policy toward Iraq. It took only a short step from there to reach a revised policy of active and direct regime change in Iraq after the terrorist attacks of September 11, 2001.

MARK F. LEEP

See also

Clinton, William Jefferson; DESERT FOX, Operation; United Nations Special Commission; United Nations Weapons Inspectors

References

Condron, Captain Sean M. "Justification for Unilateral Action in Response to the Iraqi Threat: A Critical Analysis of Operation Desert Fox." *Military Law Review* 161 (1999): 115–180.

Katzman, Kenneth. *Iraq: U.S. Regime Change Efforts and Post-Saddam Governance.* Washington, DC: Congressional Research Office, March 2006.

Paulus, Andreas. "The War against Iraq and the Future of International Law: Hegemony or Pluralism?" *Michigan Journal of International Law* 25 (2004): 691–733.

Iraq National Museum

The Iraq National Museum is the nation's premier museum of archaeological holdings and perhaps one of the largest collections of antiquities in the Middle East. It is located in Baghdad. The Iraq National Museum's most notable and valuable holdings involve collections from the Mesopotamian period (ca. 5000 BCE to 600 BCE). The museum, first known as the Baghdad Archaeological Museum, originated about 1926, when noted British author and archaeologist Gertrude Bell began assembling artifacts in Baghdad at the royal palace. The actual museum was not opened to the public until 1932.

Over the years, the British and Iraqis continued to add to the museum's collections. By the 1980s, it boasted the largest collection of Mesopotamian artifacts in the world, spread out among 28 vaults and galleries. Just prior to the Persian Gulf War, Iraqi president Saddam Hussein ordered the museum closed in order to protect it from the pending invasion. In reality, however, Hussein for years had restricted museum visitations to his personal friends and others who had been vetted by his security apparatus. The facility was finally "reopened" in April 2000 in celebration of Hussein's birthday, but access continued to be severely restricted. Many Iraqis cynically referred to the museum as "Saddam's personal treasure chest."

During both Operation DESERT STORM (1991) and Operation IRAQI FREEDOM (2003), allied war planes assiduously avoided bombing too close to the Iraq National Museum. However, in the immediate aftermath of the March 2003 invasion, the museum fell victim to looters, who carted off thousands of priceless relics and artifacts. The trouble began in early April, when Iraqi troops engaged allied forces from within the museum compound. Reluctant to go after the Iraqis for fear of damaging or destroying the museum, U.S. and coalition forces essentially left the museum in the hands of the Iraqis.

The looting and burglaries took place sometime between April 8 and April 12, 2003, during which time there were no museum staff members on hand. The looters took priceless objects and manuscripts from common areas, galleries, storage areas, and vaults. The looting was likely perpetrated by, or at least took advantage of, individuals with some in-depth knowledge of the collections and their worth, but more than 3,100 archaeological site pieces (vessels, jars, pottery remnants, etc.) went missing. Because of the artifacts' uniqueness, any looters who attempted to sell them would have quickly been identified as thieves. In total, an astounding 17,000 items had been taken in just four days. Some were large items, such as friezes, busts, and statues, but most were much smaller, although no less noteworthy or valuable. Thousands of manuscripts were also stolen.

Many other Iraqi institutions were looted as well, including the National Archives (Dar al-Kutub); the Ministry of Awqaf (religious endowments), the collections of which had been packed up for safety but were promptly looted upon their return; and the Iraqi Academy of Sciences.

The reaction to the museum looting was one of lament and outrage. The United States was heavily criticized around the world for failing to prevent the looting by simply providing protection. Museum curators and archaeologists from virtually every corner of the globe argued that the thefts represented a great and incalculable loss of the world's historical heritage and hastened to try to reconstruct lists of the museum's holdings. The museum looting was one of the earliest adverse effects of the decision by Secretary of Defense Donald Rumsfeld, which ran contrary to every time-tested rule of sound military planning, to restrict U.S. troop levels to the minimum levels possible and to ignore completely post-conflict tasks and requirements. The Pentagon dismissed such criticism, arguing that such events are often uncontrollable in a wartime situation. Rumsfeld shrugged off the Baghdad looting as "untidiness." When pressed, he claimed that the museum looting did not indicate any "deficit" in the U.S. plan to overthrow Hussein and occupy Iraq. Subsequent events have proved otherwise.

In the immediate aftermath of the museum looting, the U.S. Federal Bureau of Investigation (FBI) sent agents to Iraq to try to track down the stolen objects. In Paris on April 17, 2003, archaeological and museum experts from around the world met in an emergency meeting convened by the United Nations Educational, Scientific, and Cultural Organization (UNESCO) to assess the damage and devise ways to track down the missing treasures.

The director of the Iraqi National Museum rummages through papers with the hope of recovering museum documents following the 2003 looting of the museum by Iraqis in the wake of the overthrow of Saddam Hussein by U.S.-led forces. (U.S. Department of Defense)

The following day, the Baghdad Museum Project was established in the United States. Still in operation today, the organization is dedicated to locating and retrieving the looted museum pieces.

By mid-May 2003, American officials announced that some 700 objects and 40,000 manuscript pages had been recovered. Some looters returned the objects themselves, encouraged by monetary rewards and promises that they would not be prosecuted. While a fair portion of the thousands of items looted from the Iraqi museum has now been recovered, a great many are still unaccounted for. The Iraqi Academy of Sciences lost about 80 percent of its holdings, while libraries and universities all over the country have been destroyed or divested of their holdings, laboratories, and other equipment. The international condemnation of this destruction remains a powerful symbol of the inadequacy of American war planning during the Iraq War.

PAUL G. PIERPAOLI JR.

See also
Baghdad; Iraq, History of, Pre-1990; Iraq, History of, 1990–Present; Mesopotamia; Rumsfeld, Donald Henry

References
Allawi, Ali A. *The Occupation of Iraq: Winning the War, Losing the Peace.* New Haven, CT: Yale University Press, 2007.
Al-Tikriti, Nabil. Iraq Manuscript Collections, Archives and Libraries Situation Report, University of Chicago, June 8, 2003.
Reddy, Jairam. "The Current Status and Future Prespects for the Transformation and Reconstrution of the Higher Education System in Iraq." United Nations University, May 1, 2005.
Ricks, Thomas E. *Fiasco: The American Military Adventure in Iraq.* New York: Penguin, 2006.

Iraq Sanctions Act of 1990

On November 5, 1990, the United States enacted the Iraq Sanctions Act of 1990 (Public Law 101-513; H.R. 5114) in response to the invasion and occupation of Kuwait by Iraq that began on August 2, 1990. Among other things, the act imposed on the government of Iraq sweeping economic sanctions and a trade embargo on most imports and exports.

In the Iraq Sanctions Act, the U.S. Congress supported the actions taken by the president in response to the invasion of Kuwait, called for the immediate and unconditional withdrawal of Iraqi forces from that country, supported the efforts of the United Nations Security Council (UNSC) to end the violation of international law and threat to peace, supported the imposition and enforcement of multinational sanctions against Iraq, called upon allies and other countries to support the UNSC resolutions to help bring about the end of the Iraqi occupation of Kuwait, and condemned the Iraqi violations of Kuwaiti human rights associated with the occupation, including mass arrests, torture, summary executions, rapes, pillaging, and mass extrajudicial killings.

The Iraq Sanctions Act also continued the trade embargo and economic sanctions that were imposed upon Iraq and Kuwait following Iraq's invasion of Kuwait on August 2, 1990 (as they were enumerated in Executive Orders 12722 and 12723 [August 2, 1990] and 12724 and 12725 [August 9, 1990]). Consistent with UNSC Resolution 666, foodstuffs or payment for foodstuffs for humanitarian assistance were exempt from the embargo.

The sanctions applied to Iraq included the following goods and services: foreign military sales; commercial arms sales; exports of certain goods and technology; nuclear equipment, materials, and technology; assistance from international financial institutions; assistance through the Import-Export Bank; assistance through the commodity credit corporation; and all forms of foreign assistance other than emergency humanitarian assistance.

Two members of a boarding team from the U.S. Navy guided-missile destroyer *Goldsborough* disembark from the Iraqi merchant vessel *Zanoobia* after a preliminary inspection of the ship's cargo, December 1991. The *Goldsborough* was part of the Maritime Interdiction Force (MIF), a multinational force organized at the start of Operation DESERT SHIELD in 1990 to enforce U.S. trade sanctions against Iraq. (U.S. Department of Defense)

Under the Iraq Sanctions Act, the United States denied funds from the Foreign Assistance Act of 1961 and Arms Export Control Act to any country that did not comply with UNSC sanctions against Iraq, unless those funds promoted the interest of the United States, assisted needy people in Iraq, or helped foreign nationals who were fleeing Iraq and Kuwait. In addition, the Iraq Sanctions Act authorized penalties of $25,000 to $1,000,000 on individuals or corporations who deliberately evaded Executive Orders 12722, 12723, 12724, and 12725.

The Iraq Sanctions Act stated that Iraq violated the charter of the United Nations and other international treaties. It described Iraq's abysmal human rights record and referenced Iraq's history of summary executions, mass political killings, disappearances, widespread use of torture, arbitrary arrests, prolonged detention, deportation, and denial of nearly all civil and human rights. In addition, it highlighted Iraq's repression of the Kurdish people, cited its use of chemical weapons, and named it a state sponsor of terrorism. Congress sought multilateral cooperation to deny potentially dangerous technology transfers to Iraq and to encourage the country to improve its human rights record.

Under the act, the president retained the right to waive the sanctions if there were fundamental changes to Iraqi policies and

actions, or if there were fundamental changes in Iraqi leadership and policies. The president was also required to consult fully with, and report periodically to, Congress, to transmit new regulations before they went into effect, and to advise Congress of his intentions at least 15 days before terminating the embargo.

The sanctions were originally viewed as a nonviolent, diplomatic mechanism to apply pressure to the regime in Iraq. The sanctions achieved some, but not all, of the intended policy goals, but they also negatively affected the civilian population of Iraq. Over the next decade, members of the international community questioned the legitimacy and purpose of the sanctions, given the widespread human suffering in Iraq. According to some, the sanctions were the most damaging part of the Persian Gulf War.

As part of the Iraq Sanctions Act, the United States also supported the UN sanctions on Iraq. Indeed, the U.S. and UN sanctions resulted in a near-total embargo on Iraq, but they did not succeed in creating fundamental change in Iraq's policies, removing Saddam Hussein from power, or ending Iraq's weapons of mass destruction (WMD) programs.

The main criticism of the sanctions is that they had little impact on regime behavior, yet the civilian population suffered immensely. Under the sanctions, Iraq could not export oil (its primary source of wealth), and its imports were dramatically reduced. Food and medicine were permissible imports, but fertilizer, pesticide, livestock, seeds, dual-use chemicals (including many medicines and vaccines), agricultural machinery, books, journals, and parts for electrical and water purification systems were banned. As a result, there was widespread malnutrition and disease in Iraq. Infant mortality rates increased dramatically to the highest levels in over 40 years. Estimated numbers of deaths related to the sanctions are disputed, but the UN estimates that over 1 million Iraqis died because of the sanctions. Children were disproportionately affected.

The devastating humanitarian suffering led the United Nations to create the Oil-for-Food Programme (UNSC Resolution 986), which allowed Iraq to sell limited quantities of oil in order to meet the population's humanitarian needs. The program was established in April 1995, but oil was not exported until December 1996, and the first shipment of food did not arrive in Iraq until March 1997. The Oil-for-Food Programme eased, but did not eliminate, the human suffering in Iraq, a good bit of which, however, was the direct result of President Saddam Hussein's policies.

The U.S.-imposed sanctions continued until the 2003 U.S.-led invasion of Iraq. On May 7, 2003, after the Hussein regime had been toppled, President George W. Bush suspended the Iraq Sanctions Act of 1990. On May 22, 2003, the United Nations passed UNSC Resolution 1483, which lifted its sanctions on Iraq.

ALISON LAWLOR

See also

Bush, George Herbert Walker; Bush, George Walker; Hussein, Saddam; Iraq, History of, Pre-1990; Iraq, History of, 1990–Present; Iraq, Sanctions on; Oil; United Nations

References

Haass, Richard N., ed. *Economic Sanctions and American Diplomacy.* Washington, DC: Council on Foreign Relations, 1998.

Katzman, Kenneth. *Iraq: Oil for Food Program, International Sanctions, and Illicit Trade.* Washington, DC: Congressional Research Services, Library of Congress, April 16, 2003.

Tripp, Charles. *A History of Iraq.* Cambridge: Cambridge University Press, 2007.

Iraq Study Group

A bipartisan commission empowered by the United States Congress on March 15, 2006, to examine and analyze the situation in Iraq following the March 2003 invasion of that country and to recommend courses of action to curb the insurgency and end sectarian strife there. The Iraq Study Group was chaired by former secretary of state James Baker III and former U.S. representative Lee Hamilton. Also known as the Baker-Hamilton Commission, the group consisted of five Democrats and five Republicans and

was aided in its work by the United States Institute of Peace. In addition to Baker, the other Republicans on the commission included Edwin Meese III (former U.S. attorney general); Lawrence Eagleburger (former secretary of state); Sandra Day O'Connor (former U.S. Supreme Court justice); and Alan K. Simpson (former U.S. senator from Wyoming). The Democrats, in addition to Hamilton, included Leon Panetta (former chief of staff to President Bill Clinton); Charles Robb (former U.S. senator from Virginia); Vernon Jordan (informal adviser to Bill Clinton); and William J. Perry (former secretary of defense). The group's final report was issued on December 6, 2006. During its deliberations, however, it maintained contact with the George W. Bush administration, and in particular with National Security Advisor Stephen Hadley.

Creation of the Baker-Hamilton Commission was prompted by the steadily increasing violence in Iraq, which had continued to result in casualties and deaths to U.S. soldiers and Iraqi military personnel as well as civilians. By early 2006, the situation on the ground was growing ever more dire, and it was clear that U.S. public support for the war was eroding at an alarming rate. Although much congressional disapproval toward the war came from the Democratic ranks, an increasing number of Republicans were also questioning the conflict and the Bush administration's handling of it. With critical midterm congressional elections in the offing, many in Congress believed the time had come to reassess the situation in Iraq and assert congressional authority over the conduct of the war there. In public, the Bush White House voiced its approval of the commission, welcoming its bipartisanship, and appeared reassured that the group was being cochaired by James Baker. At the same time, the White House stated that it would not be beholden to the commission's recommendations if these were deemed antithetical to American interests. Privately, however, there was considerably more consternation about the Iraq Study Group, and on several occasions White House officials allegedly clashed with commission members over their recommendations. In mid-November, about three weeks before the commission's report was released, President Bush and key members of his national security team met with the group so that it could question them about specific details and give them a preview of the report to come. Just prior to that, the commission had also met with British prime minister Tony Blair, the Bush administration's primary ally in the war in Iraq.

Several U.S. news magazines and other media outlets reported that there was considerable contention among the members of the Baker-Hamilton Commission. Some of these conflicts centered on different philosophies toward national security policy and the implementation of Middle East policy, while others involved the Bush administration's opposition to key recommendations. Among the recommendations was the group's position that the United States should engage in discussions with Iran and Syria to stem the external influences on the Iraqi insurgency. The White

House was adamantly opposed to this idea, and squabbling among the commission's members on this point nearly led to a deadlocked conclusion. Nevertheless, consensus was reached, and the commission's report was issued on December 6, 2006. It offered 79 specific recommendations. The timing was crucial, as the Republicans had just lost control of Congress in the November elections, and Secretary of Defense Donald Rumsfeld, a chief architect of the Iraq War, had been recently forced to resign. The White House stated, for the first time, that new approaches to the war were needed, but it also let it be known that it would not implement all of the commission's recommendations.

The report stated clearly that the situation in Iraq was grave and deteriorating rapidly. It also criticized the Pentagon for having underreported the sectarian violence in Iraq and underreporting the number of Iraqi casualties. It went on to suggest that the Iraqi government must quickly ramp up the number of Iraqi soldiers and accelerate their training. During this time, the United States should increase significantly its troop presence in Iraq to enable the Iraqis to take over their own affairs. Once that was accomplished, U.S. troops should be withdrawn rapidly from the country. The report was careful not to suggest a timetable for these developments, however, which the Bush administration had been on record as strongly opposing. The report also called for the United States to engage in a dialogue with the Syrians, Iranians, and other regional groups that might lead to their assistance in curbing the Iraqi insurgency. The commission hoped to see gradual, phased U.S. troop withdrawals beginning in 2007 and a complete withdrawal by the end of 2008. Overall, the commission's report was well received, both in the United States and abroad.

In the end, the Bush administration did not follow many of the report's prescriptions. In early 2007, the White House announced its surge strategy, which saw the insertion of as many as 30,000 additional U.S. troops in Iraq.

PAUL G. PIERPAOLI JR.

See also

Baker, James Addison, III; Bush, George Walker; Iraqi Insurgency; United States Congress and the Iraq War

References

Baker, James A., III, and Lee Hamilton. *The Iraq Study Group: The Way Forward, a New Approach.* New York: Vintage Books, USA, 2006.
Stiglitz, Joseph E., and Linda J. Bilmes. *The Three Trillion Dollar War: The True Cost of the Iraq Conflict.* New York: Norton, 2008.

Irhabi 007
Birth Date: 1984

Al Qaeda Internet propagandist and terrorist Yunis Tsouli was born in 1984 in Morocco, the son of a low-level diplomat; little is known about the circumstances of his birth or early years. About 2003 he was a student in London, studying information technology. Irhabi (meaning "terrorist" in Arabic) 007 was one of Tsouli's numerous aliases, and one that he often favored while conducting Internet transactions. It is believed that the "007" is a reference to the code name of Ian Fleming's fictitious British spy James Bond.

In 2003 Tsouli began posting graphic images on the Internet designed to glorify terrorist extremists and denigrate Westerners. He also published an online "how-to" book on computer hacking and began to plan cyber attacks on high-profile Web sites in Great Britain. Gradually, he became well known among international terrorist organizations, including Al Qaeda, and began posting film clips of assassinations and murders recorded by various groups involved in the Iraqi insurgency. His Internet work, funded in part by Al Qaeda, was seen increasingly as a powerful propaganda tool for terrorist groups.

By 2005 Tsouli's Internet handiwork included the posting of how-to guides for assembling suicide bombs and other explosive devices. By the summer of 2005, Tsouli was openly taunting the U.S. Central Intelligence Agency (CIA), Britain's M16, and other law enforcement and intelligence services, positing that they would "never" be able to apprehend him.

Following the July 2005 London terrorist bombings, Tsouli reveled in the mayhem they caused, writing on his Web site "I am very happy." By the end of that summer, Tsouli was essentially running Muntada al-Ansar al-Islami, a computer Web forum used by more than 4,000 Islamic extremists around the world to communicate with one another and share information. Through the forum he also disseminated Al Qaeda propaganda and recruited suicide bombers. By the autumn of 2005, the CIA and M16 were well familiar with Tsouli's work but as yet were unable to track him down or learn his true identity.

Meanwhile, Tsouli had also begun stealing identities and credit card numbers online by hacking Web sites and using the stolen card numbers to purchase Web-hosting services. It is estimated that he used at least 72 stolen credit card numbers to buy such products. The CIA and M16 expended hundreds of hours tracking Tsouli and his jihadist accomplices online.

In mid-October 2005 a known terrorist with ties to Tsouli was arrested in Sarajevo. When authorities searched the man's computer, they found links to Tsouli, which for the first time provided a firm identity for him. Further analysis showed that the arrested terrorist had called Tsouli numerous times on his cell phone, which helped M16 locate Tsouli. British officials finally arrested him in his home in Shepherds Bush, in London, on October 21, 2005.

Following several weeks' worth of investigation and analysis of Tsouli's computers, they discovered the full extent of his involvement in cyberspace terrorism. He was soon charged under the Terrorism Act of 2000 for conspiracy to murder by explosion, conspiracy to receive money by deception, and fund-raising for known terrorist organizations.

Tsouli's high-profile trial began in May 2007. Prosecutors emphasized Tsouli's great ability to use and manipulate computer technology, his "flair for marketing," and his skill in posting images and information on the Internet that were at once easily accessed but difficult to get rid of. Tried with two co-conspirators, Tsouli was found guilty in July 2007. He received 10 years' imprisonment for his crimes, but upon an appellate review, a British court increased his sentence in December 2007 to 16 years in prison. Tsouli's actions showcased the ability of terrorist organizations to use the Internet to further their own causes with relative impunity, and with minimal expense. They also proved that the Global War on Terror would have to take into account virtual, as well as actual, terrorism.

PAUL G. PIERPAOLI JR.

See also

Al Qaeda; Global War on Terror; Iraqi Insurgency; Terrorism

References

Atwan, Abdel Bari. *The Secret History of Al-Qaeda.* Berkeley: University of California Press, 2006.

Gerges, Fawaz A. *The Far Enemy: Why Jihad Went Global.* Cambridge: Cambridge University Press, 2005.

Labi, Nadya. "Jihad 2.0." *Atlantic,* July/August, 2006.

Islamic Dawa Party

Iraqi Shia political party founded in 1958 by junior Islamic clerics (*ulama*), merchants, and religious intellectuals in the Shiite holy city of Najaf. The party sought to achieve a staged implementation of an Islamic governing system based on Islamic law. The party's name in Arabic, Hizb al-Da'wah al-Islamiyyah, translates roughly as the "Islamic Call Party." The Arabic word *dawa* in this context refers to "call" or "invitation" in the religious missionary sense. The party's founding council included several Shiite clerics who would rise to prominence in later decades, including Muhammad Mahdi al-Hakim and Muhammad Baqir al-Hakim, sons of Grand Ayatollah Muhsin al-Hakim, the preeminent Shiite religious scholar in Iraq from 1955 until his death in 1970.

Baqir al-Hakim founded the Supreme Council for Islamic Revolution in Iraq (recently renamed the Supreme Islamic Iraqi Council) in 1982 while in exile in Tehran, Iran, with the support of Grand Ayatollah Ruhollah Khomeini and the Iranian revolutionary government. The Dawa Party's unofficial religious guide was Ayatollah Muhammad Baqir al-Sadr (1935–1980), an activist Iraqi cleric, a noted Islamic thinker and author, and a student of Muhsin al-Hakim. Subsequently, many Dawa Party members were arrested, imprisoned, and killed by Iraqi Baathists, and hundreds of others went into self-imposed exile in Iran, the Persian Gulf states, and Europe. Some returned to Iraq in 2003 following the overthrow of Iraqi dictator Saddam Hussein and his Baath Party in the spring of 2003.

Baqir al-Sadr was a prolific writer who penned numerous books on subjects ranging from Islamic economics and philosophy to the establishment of an Islamic state and is probably best known for an early two-volume work on Islamic economics. His ideas influenced the formation of the Islamic state in Iran, and he was known as the "Khomeini of Iraq." He also wrote several textbooks on Islamic jurisprudence and Qur'anic hermeneutics, which remain classics in modern Shiite thought and are still used in Shiite and even Sunni seminaries today. His theory of *wilayat al-ummah* (governance or authority of the people) and proposals for a four-stage implementation of an Islamic system of governance were the basis of the Dawa Party's founding political platform.

In the first stage of this process, Islamic principles and ideas would be spread by Dawa members to build party membership and create a viable political constituency. In the second stage, once it had laid this groundwork, the party would enter the political realm and seek to build up its power and influence. The third stage would witness the party removing the ruling secular elite from power. In the final stage, triumphant Dawa members would establish an Islamic system of government in which clerics would play a substantial role but would not govern day-to-day affairs.

Baqir al-Sadr broke formal ties with the party in 1961 at the insistence of his teacher, Grand Ayatollah Hakim, because affiliation with the party would have compromised Sadr's scholarly status; clerics were to remain at least somewhat separate from political parties. However, he reportedly maintained ties to the party and continued to serve as a *marja,* or spiritual leader, to Dawa members. Sadr was executed because of his political activism in April 1980, along with his sister Amina bint Haydar al-Sadr (also known as Bint al-Huda), on the direct orders of Saddam Hussein.

The Dawa Party expanded its membership between 1958 and 1963, taking advantage of a series of military coups beginning with the overthrow of the Hashemite monarchy in 1958 by Abd al-Karim Qasim. During his tenure of office, the Dawa Party competed with secular Iraqi political parties, such as the Iraqi Communist Party, that were gaining ground among Iraqi youths, including many Shia. The growing number of Iraqi Shiite activists came under increasing pressure during the 1960s, and the detachment of the senior Shiite *ulama* from politics convinced these activists that an alternative to the religious elite was needed to achieve their political goals. The party recruited in Najaf, at Baghdad University, and in the Thawra slum of Baghdad, later known as Saddam City (and now Sadr City).

The Baath Party's seizure of power in July 1968 marked a new chapter in the relationship between the Dawa Party and the central Iraqi government. In April 1969 Grand Ayatollah Hakim refused to issue a fatwa (juridical opinion) in support of Iraqi president and Baath Party chief Ahmad Hassan al-Bakr in his dispute with Mohammad Reza Shah Pahlavi of Iran over control of the Shatt al-Arab waterway. Angered, Bakr cracked down on Shiite political, social, and religious institutions. In response, Hakim issued a fatwa prohibiting Muslims from joining the Baath Party. Hakim's death in 1970 led to a split within the Iraqi Shia, with political activists looking to Baqir al-Sadr and political quietists following Ayatollah Abu al-Qasim al-Khoi, another student of Hakim's.

Baath suppression of the Dawa Party continued in the 1970s. Hundreds of party members were arrested, imprisoned, tortured, and even executed. Despite increasing government pressure, Baqir al-Sadr continued to call for activism against the ruling Baath regime. In 1977 the government banned religious processions commemorating Ashura, a 10-day period of mourning that commemorates the martyrdom of the third Shiite imam, Hussein bin Ali, and his companions at Karbala in October 680 during the Islamic month of Muharram. Hundreds of Shia were arrested for ignoring the ban. Shortly before the arrest of Baqir al-Sadr and his sister Amina, a decree was issued by new Iraqi president Saddam Hussein that sentenced all members of the Dawa Party to death for treason. Following Baqir al-Sadr's execution, hundreds of Dawa members fled abroad to escape Baathist suppression. During their two decades in exile, party members participated in the Committee for Collection Action and the Iraqi National Congress, two major Iraqi exile political coalitions.

The exiled Dawa Party leadership and many members returned to Iraq following the U.S.- and British-led invasion during the spring of 2003. Along with the Supreme Islamic Iraqi Council, the Dawa Party was a key ally of the American, British, and coalition forces and it held seats on the Iraqi Governing Council, an advisory body set up following the collapse of the Baath Party government. Dawa Party secretary-general Ibrahim al-Jafari served as the interim prime minister from April 2005 to May 2006.

After losing the political backing of the U.S. government and, more importantly, key Iraqi Shia leaders including Grand Ayatollah Ali al-Sistani, Jafari was replaced as prime minister and Dawa secretary-general by Nuri (Jawad) al-Maliki, also a Dawa adherent, in May 2006.

CHRISTOPHER ANZALONE

See also

Baath Party; Hakim, Muhammad Baqir al-; Iraq, History of, Pre-1990; Iraq, History of, 1990–Present; Jafari, Ibrahim al-; Khomeini, Ruhollah; Qasim, Abd al-Karim; Shia Islam; Sistani, Sayyid Ali Husayn al-; Sunni Islam; Supreme Iraqi Islamic Council

References

Aziz, T. M. "The Role of Muhammad Baqir al-Sadr in Shii Political Activism in Iraq from 1958 to 1980." *International Journal of Middle East Studies* 25 (May 1993): 207–222.

Baram, Amatzia. "Two Roads to Revolutionary Shi'i Fundamentalism in Iraq: Hizb al-Da'wa Islamiyya and the Supreme Council of the Islamic Revolution of Iraq." In *Accounting for Fundamentalisms*, edited by Martin E. Marty and R. Schott Appleby, 531–588. Chicago: University of Chicago Press, 1994.

Jabar, Faleh A. *The Shi'ite Movement in Iraq.* London: Saqi Books, 2003.

Mallat, Chibli. *The Renewal of Islamic Law: Muhammad Baqer as-Sadr, Najaf, and the Shi'i International.* Cambridge: Cambridge University Press, 2004.

Nakash, Yitzhak. *Reaching for Power: The Shi'a in the Modern Arab World.* Princeton, NJ: Princeton University Press, 2006.

al-Ruhaimi, Abdul-Halim. "The Da'wa Islamic Party: Origins, Actors and Ideology." In *Ayatollahs, Sufis and Ideologues: State, Religion, and Social Movements in Iraq,* edited by Faleh A. Jabar, 149–155. London: Saqi Books, 2002.

Shanahan, Rodger. "Shi'a Political Development in Iraq: The Case of the Islamic Da'wa Party." *Third World Quarterly* 25 (2004): 943–954.

Islamic Jihad, Palestinian

A militant nationalist Palestinian group, Harakat al-Jihad al-Islami fi Filastin, known as the Palestinian Islamic Jihad (PIJ), was established by Fathi Shiqaqi, Sheikh Abd al-Aziz al-Awda, and others in the Gaza Strip during the 1970s. Several different factions identified with the name Islamic Jihad, including the Usrat al-Jihad (founded in 1948); the Detachment of Islamic Jihad, associated with the Abu Jihad contingent of Fatah; the Islamic Jihad Organization al-Aqsa Battalions, founded by Sheikh Asad Bayyud al-Tamimi in Jordan in 1982; Tanzim al-Jihad al-Islami, led by Ahmad Muhanna; and several non-Palestinian groups. This has caused much confusion over the years. Also, the PIJ movement portrayed itself as being a part of a jihadi continuum rather than a distinct entity.

While in Egypt in the 1970s, Shiqaqi, al-Awda, and the current director-general of the PIJ, Ramadan Abdullah Shallah, embraced an Islamist vision similar to the Muslim Brotherhood in Egypt. But they rejected the moderation forced on that organization by the Egyptian government's aim of political participation in tandem with *dawa* (proselytizing and education). The Palestinian group distinguished itself from secular nationalists and antinationalist Islamists in calling for grassroots organization and armed struggle to liberate Palestine as part of the Islamic solution.

Shiqaqi returned to Palestinian territory, and the PIJ began to express its intent to wage jihad (holy war) against Israel. Israeli sources claim that the PIJ developed the military apparatus known as the Jerusalem Brigades (Saraya al-Quds) by 1985, and this organization carried out attacks against the Israeli military, including an attack known as Operation GATE OF MOORS at an induction ceremony in 1986. The PIJ also claimed responsibility for the suicide bombing in Beit Led, near Netanya, Israel, on January 22, 1994. In the attack, 19 Israelis were killed and another 60 injured.

Shiqaqi spent a year in jail in the early 1980s and then in 1986 was jailed for two more years. He was deported to Lebanon along with al-Awda in April 1988. The PIJ established an office in Damascus, Syria, and began support and services in Palestinian refugee camps in Lebanon.

Shallah had meanwhile completed a doctorate at the University of Durham, served as the editor of a journal of the World and Islam Studies Enterprise, and taught briefly at the University of South Florida. When Shiqaqi was assassinated by unidentified agents (allegedly from Mossad, Israel's intelligence agency) in Malta in 1995, Shallah returned to lead the PIJ. His Florida associations led to the trials of Sami Al-Arian, Imam Fawaz Damra, and others who allegedly supported the PIJ in the United States.

The PIJ emerged prior to Hamas. The organizations were rivals, despite the commonality of their nationalist perspectives, but Hamas gained a much larger popular following than the PIJ, whose estimated support is only 4–5 percent of the Palestinian population in the territories. The PIJ has a following among university students at the Islamic University in Gaza and other colleges and became very active in the Second (al-Aqsa) Intifada, or Second Intifada, which began in September 2000.

In Lebanon, the organization competes with Fatah, the primary and largest political faction in the Palestine Liberation Organization (PLO). Like Hamas and secular nationalist groups known as the Palestinian National Alliance, the PIJ rejected the 1993 Oslo Accords and demanded a full Israeli withdrawal from Palestinian lands. The group has a following among Palestinian refugees and at Ain Hilweh, a Palestinian camp in Lebanon, but also suffers from the political fragmentation of Palestinian and Islamist organizations there.

The Palestinian National Authority (PNA) closed down a publication sympathetic to the PIJ but eventually allowed it to reopen. In June 2003, under significant international pressure, Syria closed PIJ and Hamas offices in Damascus, and Shallah left for Lebanon. He later returned to Syria.

In the Palestinian territories, the PIJ continues to differ with Hamas. Hamas ceased attacks against Israel beginning in 2004 and successfully captured a majority in the Palestinian elections of January 2006. Hamas moderates are also considering the recognition of Israel and a two-state solution. The PIJ, in contrast, called for Palestinians to boycott the 2006 elections and refused any accommodation with Israel. It continued to sponsor suicide attacks after 2004 in retaliation for Israel's military offensives and targeted killings of PIJ leaders, including Louay Saadi in October 2005. The PIJ claimed responsibility for two suicide attacks in that year.

Israeli authorities continue to highlight Iranian-PIJ links. They cite Shiqaqi's early publication of a pamphlet that praised Ayatollah Ruhollah Khomeini for the 1979 Islamic revolution based on Sharia (Islamic law) and for recognizing the Palestinian cause. And an intercepted PNA security briefing has led the Israelis to assert that the PIJ continues to rely on Syrian support and Iranian funding.

SHERIFA ZUHUR

See also

Fatah; Hamas; Intifada, Second; Jihad; Muslim Brotherhood; Palestine Liberation Organization

References

Abu-Amr, Ziad. *Islamic Fundamentalisms in the West Bank and Gaza: Muslim Brotherhood and Islamic Jihad.* Bloomington: Indiana University Press, 1994.

Journal of Palestine Studies. "The Movement of Islamic Jihad and the Oslo Process: An Interview with Ramadan Abdullah Shallah." *Journal of Palestine Studies* 28 (1999): 61–73.

Knudsen, Are. "Islamism in the Diaspora: Palestinian Refugees in Lebanon." *Journal of Refugee Studies* 18(2) (2005): 216–234.

Islamic Radicalism

This term is used to describe radical movements, organizations, and parties that, regardless of doctrinal and political differences, promote and legitimize their political objectives by invoking Islam. A radical is an individual who espouses extreme views and seeks major, if not revolutionary, change in government and society and often favors illegal means, including violence, to promote such change.

Islamic radicals, also known as Islamic fundamentalists, espouse a literal interpretation of Islam and Sharia (Islamic law) and favor the establishment of an Islamic state based on that law. They share these goals with Islamists, who are sometimes incorrectly deemed radicals, since not all support revolutionary means for Islamization. Some claim that Islamic radicals eschew Western ideas and values, including secularism, democracy, and religious tolerance and pluralism. However, this is untrue of many who value Western ideas but not existing morals in Western society. To certain extreme Islamic radicals, governments and laws that are based on anything but their interpretation of Islam are considered heretical. These radicals feel bound to impose their values on others, and even, if possible, to overthrow heretical governments.

Al Qaeda, the Taliban, the Armed Islamic Group of Algeria, the Salafist Group for Preaching and Combat of Algeria, Laskar Jihad, and Egyptian Islamic Jihad are some of the better-known radical Islamic groups. Others, such as the Muslim Brotherhood in Egypt have forsworn violence and imposing change on others, and are thus less radical. Hezbollah and Hamas have employed violence against Israelis.

Some Islamic radical groups are Shia, and some are Sunni movements. Iran, one of the few countries with a majority Shia population, is an example of a radical Islamic state, but radical Shia movements also exist in Iraq, Yemen, and the Gulf States.

The origins of Islamic radicalism are threefold. First, although the Islamic world was once a great and powerful civilization, beginning in the eleventh century with the Crusades, followed by Ottoman rule and then European colonial rule after World War I, it has been in decline, eclipsed, and in its own view, dominated and exploited by the West. This view is also shared by Bernard Lewis and other such Western thinkers as Samuel Huntington, but many Muslims argue that the reason for the domination and exploitation is their own fault—that Muslims abandoned jihad in its fighting form and must now return to it. Second, other movements, like nationalism and socialism, failed to bring about a better political solution, and Muslims sought out Islamist or radical Islamic groups as an alternative. Third, many Muslims have come to regard the West, and particularly the United States, with contempt for its alleged social, moral, and economic decadence. They also see that while preaching democracy, the Western powers have supported the very authoritarian governments that oppress them.

To Islamic radicals, the Islamic world has lost its way because it has forsaken Islamic values, amalgamated Western and Islamic law, and transposed foreign cultures onto its own peoples. Accordingly, the solution for the revival of Islamic civilization is a return to an allegedly authentic or purified Islamic way of life. Islamic radicalism is thus, in many ways, an explicit rejection of the current ills of Muslim society. Certain, but not all, Islamic radicals thus seek to overthrow the regimes and rulers they regard as un-Islamic, and some of these are supported by the West and the United States, such as those in Saudi Arabia, Egypt, Jordan, and Kuwait. Islamic radicals were responsible for the overthrow in 1979 of the pro-American Mohammad Reza Shah Pahlavi Iran and the assassination two years later of President Anwar Sadat of Egypt. They have also been responsible for myriad terror attacks against Western interests, including the September 11, 2001, attacks in the United States that killed some 3,000 people.

STEFAN M. BROOKS

See also

Al Qaeda; Global War on Terror; Hamas; Hezbollah; Iran; Jihad; Muslim Brotherhood; Reza Pahlavi, Mohammad; Shia Islam; Sunni Islam; Taliban; Terrorism

References

Choueri, Youssef. *Islamic Fundamentalism.* New York: Continuum Publishing Group, 2002.

Esposito, John. *What Everyone Needs to Know About Islam.* New, York: Oxford University Press, 2002.

———. *Unholy War: Terror in the Name of Islam.* New York: Oxford University Press USA, 2003.

Lewis, Bernard. *What Went Wrong? The Clash between Islam and Modernity in the Middle East.* New York: Oxford University Press, 2002.

———. *The Crisis of Islam: Holy War and Unholy Terror.* New York: Random House, 2003.

Milton-Edwards, Beverly. *Islamic Fundamentalism since 1945.* New York: Routledge, 2002.

Sidahmed, Abdel Salam. *Islamic Fundamentalism.* Boulder, CO: Westview, 1996.

Tibi, Bassam. *The Challenge of Fundamentalism: Political Islam and the New World Disorder.* Berkeley: University of California Press, 1998.

Islamic Virtue Party of Iraq

See Fadhila Party

Israel

Israel, the world's only Jewish nation, has an area of some 8,019 square miles and a 2008 population of about 7.1 million people. It is bordered by the Mediterranean Sea to the west, Lebanon to the north, Jordan and Syria to the east, and Egypt to the southwest. Its government is a parliamentary-style democracy, and the country boasts an advanced Western-style economy.

During World War I, in order to secure Jewish support for the war, the British government in 1917 issued the Balfour Declaration. Named for Foreign Secretary Arthur Balfour, it announced British support for the "establishment in Palestine of a national home for the Jewish people." At the same time, however, in order to secure Arab support against the Turks, the British government promised support for establishment of an Arab state.

In 1920 Britain and France divided up the Middle Eastern possessions of the Ottoman Empire as League of Nations mandates. Great Britain secured Palestine and Iraq. In 1922 Britain split Palestine into two; the area east of the Jordan River became Trans-Jordan, and the land west of the river retained the name Palestine.

A number of Jews had already arrived in Palestine and settled there, purchasing Arab lands. Following World War I, the number of Jews grew substantially, and the Arabs saw themselves becoming a marginalized minority in their own land. In response to continuing Jewish immigration, sporadic Arab attacks against Jews as well as British officials in Palestine occurred, escalating into the so-called Arab Revolt of 1936–1939.

At the same time, militant Jewish groups began to agitate against what they saw as restrictive British immigration policies for Jews in Palestine. Armed Zionist groups carried out actions against the British administration in Palestine, and a three-way struggle emerged that pitted the British against both militant Arabs and Jews. Amid sharply increased violence, the British government attempted a delicate balancing act, made more difficult by the need to secure Arab (and Jewish) support against Germany and Italy in World War II.

The Holocaust, the Nazi scheme to exterminate the Jews during World War II, resulted in the deaths of some 6 million Jews in Europe. During the war and immediately afterward, many of the survivors sought to immigrate to Israel. The Holocaust also created in the West a sense of moral obligation for the creation of a Jewish state, and it brought pressure on the British government to relax the prewar restrictive policies it had instituted regarding Jewish immigration into Palestine. At the same time, however, the Arabs of Palestine were adamantly opposed to an increase in the number of Jews in Palestine, or the creation there of a Jewish state.

Following World War II, as Jewish refugees sought to gain access to Palestine, many were forcibly turned away by the British. At the same time, the British government wrestled with partitioning Palestine into Arab and Jewish states. Unable to resolve these differences, in February 1947 Britain announced that it would turn the problem over to the United Nations (UN).

The UN developed a plan for partitioning Palestine into separate Arab and Jewish states. The city of Jerusalem was to be internationalized under the UN. Although at the time the Arab population in Palestine was 1.2 million people and the Jews numbered just 600,000, the UN plan approved by the General Assembly on November 29, 1947, granted the proposed Jewish state some 55 percent of the land and the Arab state only 45 percent. The Arab states rejected the partition plan, while the Jewish Agency in Palestine accepted it.

Immediately following the UN vote, militant Palestinian Arabs and foreign Arab fighters began attacks against Jewish communities in Palestine, beginning the Arab-Jewish Communal War (November 30, 1947–May 14, 1948). The United States, with the world's largest Jewish population, became the chief champion and most reliable ally of a Jewish state, a position that cost it dearly in its relations with the Arab world and greatly impacted subsequent geopolitics in the Middle East.

The British completed their pullout on May 14, 1948. That same day David Ben-Gurion, executive chairman and defense minister of the Jewish Agency, declared independence for the State of Israel. Ben-Gurion became the new state's first prime minister, a post he held during 1948–1953 and 1955–1963.

At first, the interests of the United States and those of the Soviet Union regarding the Jewish state converged. U.S. recognition of Israel came only shortly before that of the Soviet Union. Moscow found common ground with the Jews in their suffering at the hands of the Nazis in World War II and identified with the socialism espoused by the early Jewish settlers in Palestine, as well as their anti-British stance. The Cold War, the reemergence of official anti-Semitism in the Soviet Union, and Moscow's desire to court the Arab states by supporting Arab nationalism against the West soon changed all that.

Immediately following the Israeli declaration of independence, the Arab armies of Egypt, Lebanon, Jordan, Syria, and Iraq invaded, sparking the Israeli-Arab War (1948–1949), also known as the Israeli War of Independence. Jewish forces defeated the Arab armies, and a series of armistices in 1949 ended the war with Israel left in control of an additional 26 percent of the land of Mandate Palestine west of the Jordan River. Jordan, however, controlled large portions of Judea and Samaria, later known as the

Aftermath of the explosion of two trucks on Ben Yehuda Street, in the heart of the Jewish business district of Jerusalem, on February 2, 1948. The blasts killed 27 people and injured more than 100. (AP/Wide World Photos)

West Bank. The establishment of Israel and subsequent war also produced 600,000–700,000 Palestinian Arab refugees. Meanwhile, the Israelis set up the machinery of state. Israel's early years were dominated by the challenge of absorbing and integrating into society hundreds of thousands of Jewish immigrants from different parts of the world.

The 1949 cease-fires that ended the 1948–1949 war were not followed by peace agreements. The Arab states refused not only to recognize the existence of Israel but also to concede defeat in the war. Throughout most of the 1950s Israel suffered from repeated attacks and raids from neighboring Arab states as well as Palestinian Arab paramilitary and terrorist groups. Aggressive Israeli retaliation failed to stop them. Egyptian leader Gamal Abdel Nasser further increased tension between Israel and Egypt. Nasser built up the Egyptian military, supported cross-border raids into Israeli territory by so-called fedayeen (guerrilla fighters) from the Gaza Strip, and formed alliances with other Arab states.

In 1956 Nasser nationalized the Suez Canal. Israel joined France and Britain to develop a secret plan to topple Nasser and secure control of the canal. On October 29, 1956, Israeli forces invaded the Sinai peninsula and headed for the Suez Canal, providing the excuse for the British and the French to intervene. The U.S. government applied considerable pressure, and all three states agreed to withdraw. Israel was the clear winner. It secured the right to free navigation through the Suez Canal and on the waterways through the Straits of Tiran and Gulf of Aqaba. The UN also deployed a peacekeeping force along the border between Egypt and Israel.

Throughout the spring of 1967, Israel faced increasing attacks along its borders from Syria and the Palestine Liberation Organization (PLO), a quasi-terrorist organization created in 1964 to represent the Palestinian Arabs and coordinate efforts with Arab states to liberate Palestine. The PLO mounted cross-border attacks from Jordan. By May, war seemed imminent. With the Arab states mobilizing, on May 23 Egypt closed the Straits of Tiran and blockaded the Gulf of Aqaba, thereby cutting off the Israeli port of Eilat.

Fearing an imminent coordinated Arab attack, Israel launched a preemptive strike on June 5, 1967, which crippled the air forces of Egypt, Syria, Jordan, and Iraq. Having achieved air supremacy, Israel then easily defeated the armies of Egypt, Jordan, and Syria as well as Iraqi units. Five days later Israel occupied the Sinai and Gaza Strip from Egypt, the West Bank and East Jerusalem from Jordan, and the Golan Heights from Syria, doubling the size of the Jewish state and providing buffer zones in the new territories. In the wake of its military victory, Israel announced it would not withdraw from these captured territories until negotiations with the Arab states took place, leading to recognition of Israel's right to exist. Israel's military victory did not bring peace with its Arab neighbors, however. Humiliated by their defeat, the Arab states refused to negotiate with, recognize, or make peace with Israel.

In 1969 the War of Attrition began with Egypt shelling Israeli targets in the Sinai along the Suez Canal and Israel responding by launching retaliatory raids and air strikes. Nasser sought Soviet military aid and support, including surface-to-air missiles (SAMs). Israel's euphoria from its decisive 1967 victory had turned into disillusionment over rising Israeli casualties.

Following Nasser's death in September 1970, Anwar Sadat, Nasser's successor, became frustrated by the lack of progress in peace talks and initiated a new war. On October 6, 1973, during Yom Kippur, Egypt and Syria launched a surprise attack on Israel. Although both attacking powers enjoyed initial success and inflicted heavy casualties on Israeli forces, after regrouping and being resupplied by the United States, the Israeli Defense Forces (IDF) turned back the Egyptians and Syrians and secured control of the Sinai and Golan Heights. Israel thus won the Yom Kippur (Ramadan) War but only after heavy losses. Nevertheless, although Israel remained the dominant military power in the Middle East, the notion of Israeli invincibility had ended. The Yom Kippur War shook Israel's confidence and morale and proved costly in terms of lives. It also made Israel more economically dependent on the United States. Meanwhile, increasing acts of terrorism by the PLO focused world attention on the Arab-Israeli conflict and the Palestinian cause.

In May 1977 Israel's Likud Party ended the 29-year political reign of the Labor Party, and Menachem Begin became prime minister. Egyptian president Sadat shocked the world by announcing on November 9, 1977, his willingness to go to Jerusalem and meet with the Israelis face-to-face to negotiate peace. Accepting an invitation by Begin to visit, Sadat arrived in Israel on November 19, the first Arab head of state to do so, effectively recognizing Israel's right to exist. Although every other Arab state refused to negotiate with Israel, after two years of negotiations mediated by U.S. president Jimmy Carter, Egypt and Israel made peace on March 26, 1979. Per the Camp David Accords, Israel withdrew from the Sinai in exchange for Egypt's recognition of Israel. Discussions about the status of the Palestinians took place, but the parties never achieved any common ground.

On July 7 1981, the Israeli Air Force bombed the Iraqi nuclear reactor at Osiraq, thwarting Iraqi efforts to acquire nuclear weapons. The next year Israel reinvaded Lebanon, which had been experiencing a civil war since 1975, ostensibly to defend its northern border from terrorist attacks but also to expel the PLO from Lebanon, which it did by capturing the capital of Beirut and forcing the PLO to relocate to Tunisia. This had come at terrible human cost to Lebanese civilians, as well as great material destruction, and Israel failed to achieve its broad policy objectives of creating a stable, pro-Israeli government in Lebanon. In 1983 Begin resigned and was replaced by fellow Likud member Yitzhak Shamir. Israel withdrew from most of Lebanon in 1986 but maintained a buffer zone there until May 2000, when it surrendered that territory as well.

A major Palestinian uprising—the First Intifada—erupted in 1987 in the Israeli-occupied territories of the West Bank and Gaza Strip and consumed much of Israel's military resources. In

Debris in the city of Tel Aviv following an Iraqi Scud missile attack. Eight Scuds were fired into Israel on January 18, 1991, injuring at least 10 people. In firing the Scuds at Israel, the Iraqis hoped to bring the Jewish state into the war, alienating the Arab coalition members. (AP/Wide World Photos)

1991, during the Persian Gulf War, Iraq targeted Israel with Scud intermediary-range missiles in an attempt to provoke an Israeli counterattack of Iraq and cause the Arab states to withdraw from the multinational U.S.-led coalition force. However, heavy U.S. pressure and the dispatch of U.S. Patriot anti-missile batteries to Israeli kept the Jewish state from retaliating.

The collapse of the Soviet Union in December 1991 and end of the Cold War resulted in an influx into Israel of more than 1 million Jews from the Soviet Union and its former satellites over the next 13 to 14 years. It also left many Arab states, previously allied with Moscow, isolated and gave the United States much more influence and leverage in the region. Accordingly, peace talks were held in 1991 and 1992 among Israel and Syria, Lebanon, Jordan, and the Palestinians. Those talks paved the way for the 1993 Oslo Accords between Israel and the PLO, stipulating the beginning of Palestinian self-rule in the West Bank and Gaza Strip, and peace between Israel and Jordan in 1994.

Initial Israeli support for the Oslo Accords waned following a series of terrorist attacks by Hamas—a Palestinian terrorist group founded in 1987 at the beginning of the First Intifada—and other groups that opposed peace with Israel. On November 4, 1995, a right-wing Jewish nationalist assassinated Prime Minister Yitzhak Rabin for his peace efforts with the Palestinians and willingness to cede occupied territory in the West Bank to the Palestinians.

Continued Hamas terrorism led to the election as prime minister of hard-liner Benjamin Netanyahu of Likud. Netanyahu refused to pursue the "land for peace" dialogue with the Palestinians, and thus the peace process stalled. In 1999 Labor's Ehud Barak defeated Netanyahu, and in 2000 talks between Barak and Yasser Arafat, mediated by U.S. president Bill Clinton, failed to produce agreement on a Palestinian state. The collapse of these talks and the visit of Likud's Ariel Sharon to the contested religious site known to Jews as the Temple Mount and to Muslims as the Haram al-Sharif, where the al-Aqsa Mosque is located, sparked the Second Intifada. Relations between the Israelis and Palestinians tumbled downward.

Sharon was elected prime minister in March 2001 and reelected in 2003. In the face of stalled peace talks with the Palestinians, by September 2005 Israel had withdrawn from the Gaza Strip, although it controlled its borders, coast, and airspace. Under Sharon, the Israeli government also began building a system of barriers to separate Israel from most of the West Bank. This so-called security fence barrier is designed to defend Israel from repeated Palestinian terrorist attacks, but its construction has been criticized as a violation of international law and as an impediment to the establishment of any viable, independent Palestinian state. Sharon suffered a massive stroke on January 4, 2006, and Ehud Olmert became prime minister.

In June 2006, after a Hamas raid killed two Israeli soldiers and led to the capture of another, Israel launched a series of attacks on Hamas targets and infrastructure in the Gaza Strip. The next month the Olmert government became involved in a conflict in Lebanon following an attack on Israel by Hezbollah—an Iranian and Syrian-backed terrorist and political group—that killed three Israeli soldiers and captured two others. This month-long conflict, which devastated much of southern Lebanon, seemed to many observers a repeat of 1982, with Israel having failed to achieve its broad policy objectives and leaving Hezbollah stronger than ever.

Meanwhile, Israeli voters remained keenly interested in such issues as the role of the Orthodox minority, the rights of Israeli Arabs, the fate of Israeli settlements in the West Bank, and the ups and downs of the economy. Currently, the two nearest and direct threats to Israel remain Hamas and Hezbollah, although Israel regards Iran's desire to acquire nuclear weapons—a charge denied by Iran—as a palpable threat. With respect to peace with the Palestinians, the presence of several hundred thousand Israeli settlers in the West Bank, the ongoing terrorism campaign by Hamas and Hezbollah, and disputes over the precise borders of any future Palestinian state remain the principal outstanding issues of contention. In addition, the surprising victory of Hamas in the January 2006 legislative elections for the Palestinian government was regarded as a major setback for the cause of peace.

In September 2007 the Israeli Air Force launched a surprise raid on a suspected nuclear facility in Syria, drawing a sharp rebuke from Damascus. Yet, in early 2008, Syrian president Bashar al-Asad revealed that Israel and Syria had been engaged in secret peace discussions, with Turkey as mediator. Israel confirmed his revelation. In December 2008 the shaky Hamas-Israeli cease-fire ended when Hamas fighters began launching rocket attacks on Israel from the Hamas-controlled Gaza Strip. Israel responded with heavy air strikes, and on January 3, 2009, sent troops into Gaza. The resulting conflict wrought much damage and killed many Palestinian civilians living in Gaza. Israel declared a cease-fire on January 17 and began a troop pullback. Hamas followed suit with its own cease-fire, but tensions remained very high. In February 2009, after Olmert declared his intention to resign the premiership, parliamentary elections were held, but they resulted in an unclear mandate. With Israeli political sentiment having shifted to the right, President Shimon Peres called on Likud Party leader Benjamin Netanyahu to form a coalition government. When the moderate Kadima Party rejected his overtures, Netanyahu formed a coalition with the right-wing Yisrael Beiteinu Party; its leader, Avigdor Lieberman, became foreign minister. The new government took office on April 1.

STEFAN M. BROOKS, DANIEL E. SPECTOR, AND SPENCER C. TUCKER

See also

Arab-Israeli Conflict, Overview; Begin, Menachem; Hamas; Hezbollah; Intifada, First; Intifada, Second; Israel, Armed Forces; Israel-Egypt Peace Treaty; Israel-Jordan Peace Treaty; Lebanon; Lebanon, Israeli Invasion of; Netanyahu, Benjamin; Palestine Liberation Organization; Rabin, Yitzhak; Sharon, Ariel; Suez Crisis

References

Dowty, Alan. *Israel/Palestine*. Malden, MA: Polity, 2005.

Gilbert, Martin. *Israel*. New York: William Morrow, 1999.

Reich, Bernard. *A Brief History of Israel*. New York: Checkmark Books, 2005.

Sachar, Howard M. *A History of Israel: From the Rise of Zionism to Our Time*. New York: Knopf, 1976.

Israel, Armed Forces

Tzava Haganah l-Yisra'il is the official name of the State of Israel's military establishment known as the Israel Defense Forces (IDF). In the relatively short period of its existence, the IDF has become one of the most battle-tested, effective, and simultaneously respected and reviled military forces in the world. Israel claims to have no territorial ambitions. Its strategy is defensive, supported by offensive tactics. The IDF consists of a regular tactical air force, a regular coastal navy, and a small standing army with a large and well-trained reserve, an early warning capability, and efficient mobilization and transportation systems.

The IDF's approach to fighting wars is based on the premise that Israel cannot afford to lose a single war. Given the State of Israel's experience and the long-stated intentions of some of its more hostile neighbors, there can be little doubt of the validity of that assumption. Israel tries to avoid war through a combination of political means and the maintenance of a very credible military deterrent.

Once fighting starts, Israel's lack of territorial depth makes it imperative that the IDF take the war to the enemy's territory and determine the outcome as quickly and decisively as possible. In seven major wars, beginning with the Israeli War of Independence (1948–1949) and continuing through the seemingly never-ending occupation duty and counterterrorism actions into 2006, more than 22,000 Israeli military personnel have been killed in the line of duty. During that same time period, the IDF, usually fighting outnumbered, has inflicted many times more that number of casualties on its enemies. The IDF strives to maintain a broad, qualitative advantage in advanced weapons systems, many of which are now developed and manufactured in Israel. The IDF's major strategic advantage, however, has always been the high quality, motivation, and discipline of its soldiers.

The IDF is the backbone of Israel. With the exception of most Muslim Israelis, all Israeli citizens are required to serve in the armed forces for some length of time, and that experience forms the most fundamental common denominator of Israeli society. For most new immigrants to Israel the IDF is the primary social integrator, providing educational opportunities and Hebrew-language training that might not have been available to immigrants in their countries of origin.

Part of the Israel Defense Forces honor guard welcomes U.S. secretary of defense Robert M. Gates during his visit to Tel Aviv on April 18, 2007. (U.S. Department of Defense)

Most Israelis are inducted into the IDF at age 18. Unmarried women serve for two years, and men serve for three years. Following initial service, the men remain in the reserves until age 51 and single women until age 24. Reservists with direct combat experience may qualify for discharge at age 45. Most reservists serve for 39 days a year, although that period can be extended during emergencies. Because older reservists in particular may have considerable mismatch between their military ranks and their positions in the civilian world, the IDF pays a reservist on active duty what he was making in his civilian position. The IDF is one of the very few militaries in the world with such an expensive policy. Indeed, more than 9 percent of Israel's gross domestic product (GDP) goes to military expenditures.

There are some exceptions to IDF service. Older immigrants may serve shorter periods or be deferred completely. Most religiously Orthodox women receive deferments, as do ultraorthodox men who pursue Torah studies or are enrolled in other religious studies programs. Although Bedouin Arabs, Christian Arabs, Druze, Circassians, and some other Arab Israelis are permitted to serve in the IDF, most Arab Israelis are not. Because military service qualifies Israelis for particular benefits, this constitutes one of the principal fault lines of Israeli society.

Conscripts who have performed their initial IDF service successfully may apply to become career officers or noncommissioned officers (NCOs). The recruitment process is highly selective, and the training is rigorous. There is no Israeli military academy or reserve officers' training corps (ROTC). Once an officer completes initial training, the IDF provides him or her with multiple opportunities to pursue advanced civilian education at IDF expense. IDF officers who retire or otherwise leave active duty retain reserve commissions and are subject to recall in time of war. The most famous example is Ariel Sharon, who commanded a division in the 1967 Six-Day War, retired as a major general in 1973, and was recalled only a few months later and placed in command of a division in the Yom Kippur War.

IDF general officers are a major force in Israeli society. Many go into politics when they leave active duty. In fact, many Israeli prime ministers have been IDF generals, as have most Israeli defense ministers. Lieutenant general (*rav aluf*) is the highest rank in the Israeli military, held only by the IDF chief of staff. Until recently, all IDF chiefs of staff had come from the army. In 2005 Lieutenant General Dan Halutz became the first air officer to head the IDF. He resigned in January 2007 after coming under widespread criticism for his handling of the 2006 war in Lebanon.

Although Israel has never formally admitted to having nuclear weapons, Mordecai Vanunu revealed the program to the world, becoming an enemy of the state as a result. The Jewish experience in the Holocaust is often cited as the justification for Israel to take any measures necessary, including nuclear weapons, to ensure its survival. With French support, Israel constructed its first nuclear reactor at Dimona in 1960. The IDF most probably acquired a nuclear weapons capability in the late 1960s. Most estimates today place Israel's nuclear stockpile at between 100 and 200 weapons, including warheads for the Jericho-1 and Jericho-2 mobile missiles and bombs for longer-range delivery by Israeli aircraft.

The IDF is the direct successor of the Haganah, the secret Jewish self-defense organization whose roots go back to the 1907 formation of the Bar Giora organization, established to protect Jewish towns and settlements in Palestine. During World War I many Jews acquired military training and experience in the British Army, which formed the Zion Mule Corps in 1915 and the all-Jewish 38th, 39th, and 40th King's Fusiliers near the end of the war.

With Palestine becoming a British mandate after World War I, Haganah was formed in 1920 as a local self-defense force, although the British considered it an illegal militia. In 1931 a group of Haganah members broke away to form the far more aggressive Irgun Tsvai Leumi (National Military Organization). During the Arab Revolt of 1936–1939, the British cooperated unofficially with Haganah, and Captain Orde C. Wingate formed and trained the Special Night Squads, one of Israel's first special operating forces.

In 1941 Haganah formed the Palmach as its strike force. The same year, an even more radical group broke away from Irgun to form the Lohamei Herut Israel (Lehi), also called the Stern Gang. During the course of World War II more than 30,000 Palestinian Jews served in the British Army. The Jewish Brigade served with distinction against the Germans in northern Italy during the final stages of the World War II.

Following World War II Haganah defied British rule in Palestine by smuggling in Holocaust survivors and other Jewish refugees, all the while conducting clandestine military training and defending Jewish settlements. Irgun and Lehi, which many considered little more than terrorist organizations, launched an all-out armed rebellion against the British. Under the orders of future prime minister Menachem Begin, Irgun bombed the King David Hotel, Britain's military headquarters in Jerusalem, on July 22, 1946.

Immediately following the establishment of the State of Israel, the provisional government on May 28, 1948, issued Defense Army of Israel Ordinance No. 4 establishing the IDF and merging all Jewish fighting organizations under it. Immediately thereafter David Marcus, a U.S. Army Reserve colonel and World War II veteran, received a commission as Israel's first general (*aluf*), making him the first Jewish soldier to hold that rank since Judas Maccabeus 2,100 years earlier. Marcus was killed near Jerusalem less than two weeks later.

Although the IDF essentially absorbed the general staff and combat units of Haganah, the integration of the other units was difficult and protracted. Lehi dissolved itself, and its members joined the IDF individually. Some battalions of Irgun joined the IDF, while others fought on independently. The turning point came when Prime Minister David Ben-Gurion ordered the IDF to sink Irgun's arms ship *Altalena* as it approached Tel Aviv in June 1948. It was a defining moment for the new State of Israel and established the authority of the central government. The remaining Irgun battalions finally disbanded on September 20, 1948.

The IDF is organized administratively into traditional branches of service, with the army, navy, and air force all having their own career tracks and distinctive uniforms. Operationally, the IDF is organized into four joint regional commands. The Northern Command is responsible for the occupation of the Golan Heights and the security of Israel's northern border with Lebanon and Syria. The Southern Command is responsible for the occupation of Gaza and for securing the porous southern border through the trackless Negev desert. The Central Command is responsible for the occupation of the West Bank and the security of the Israeli settlements there. The Home Front Command's main role is to provide security to civilians during wars and mass disasters.

The Israeli standing ground force consists of four infantry brigades (Givati, Nahal, Golani, and Paratroopers) plus several mixed-unit battalions and several special forces and counterterrorism units, including Sayeret. The armor force has three brigades: the Barak Armored Brigade (the 188th Brigade), the Ga'ash Brigade (the 7th Brigade), and the Ikvot Habarzel Brigade (the 401st Brigade). The artillery also has three brigades, the engineers have one brigade, and each infantry brigade has an engineer company.

The Israeli Air Force (IAF) is one of the strongest in the Middle East, and with much justification its pilots are considered the best in the world. Since the IAF began in 1948, its pilots have shot down 687 enemy aircraft in air-to-air combat. Only 23 Israeli aircraft have been shot down in air-to-air combat, giving the IAF an incredible 30-to-1 victory ratio. Thirty-nine IAF pilots have achieved ace status by shooting down 5 or more enemy aircraft. The leading Israeli ace is Major General Giora Epstein with 17 kills, all against jet aircraft, making him the world's record holder for number of jets shot down.

Two Israeli Air Force F-16 Fighting Falcons from Ramon Air Base, Israel, head to the Nevada Test and Training Range on July 17, 2009, during Training Exercise Red Flag 09-4. (U.S. Department of Defense)

The Israeli Navy was also formed in 1948. Its predecessor was Haganah's Palyam (Sea Company). The Palyam's primary mission had been smuggling Jewish refugees from Europe to Palestine. Today the navy operates in two unconnected bodies of water. Its main base on the Mediterranean Sea is at Haifa, and its main base on the Red Sea is at Eilat. The three principal operating units of the Israeli Navy are the Missile Boats Flotilla, the Submarine Flotilla, and Shayetet 13, a naval special operations force similar to the U.S. Navy SEALs.

The IDF's Directorate of Main Intelligence (Aman) is a separate branch of service on the same level as the army, navy, and air force. The head of Aman is also a coequal to the heads of Shin Bet (internal security and counterintelligence) and Mossad (foreign intelligence), and together they direct all Israeli intelligence operations. The army itself has an Intelligence Corps (Ha-Aman) that is responsible for tactical-level intelligence but also comes under the overall jurisdiction of Aman.

The IDF recognizes seven major wars for which it awards campaign ribbons: the 1948 Israeli War of Independence, the 1956 Sinai Campaign, the 1967 Six-Day War, the 1967–1970 War of Attrition, the 1973 Yom Kippur (Ramadan) War, the 1982 Lebanon War, and the 2006 Second Lebanon War. The 1948–1949 Israeli War of Independence began immediately after the declaration of statehood, as Egypt attacked from the south, Syria and Lebanon attacked from

the north, and Jordan backed by Iraqi and Saudi troops attacked from the east. Outnumbered almost 60 to 1 in population, the new Jewish state's prospects for survival looked bleak. By the time of the cease-fire on July 20, 1949, however, the IDF had managed to secure all of its major objectives, with the exceptions of East Jerusalem and the Arab Legion fortress at Latrun.

Immediately following the war, the sectors of Palestine not under Israeli control were occupied by the other Arab states, with Jordan occupying the West Bank and Egypt occupying Gaza. Plagued throughout the early 1950s by continual Palestinian infiltration and terror raids, the IDF in 1953 formed Unit 101. Under the command of Sharon, the special operations unit carried out retaliatory strikes into Jordanian territory. Criticized for its ruthless tactics, Unit 101 was disbanded in late 1955.

The 1956 Sinai Campaign, the second of Israel's major wars, commenced after Egypt nationalized the Suez Canal. Simultaneously, the IDF launched a full-scale attack into the Sinai peninsula to eliminate Egyptian and Palestinian irregular forces known as the fedayeen that had been conducting terror attacks against Israeli civilians in the south. The IDF captured Gaza and the entire Sinai peninsula as well as the canal but later withdrew under international pressure.

In 1967 Egypt massed 100,000 troops in the Sinai and closed the Straits of Tiran to Israeli ships. In response, the IDF launched a massive preemptive strike on the morning of June 5, virtually destroying the Egyptian Air Force on the ground. By noon that day the IAF had also annihilated the Syrian and Jordanian air forces. During the Six-Day War the IDF again captured the Sinai and Gaza and came within striking distance of Alexandria. The Egyptians lost some 15,000 soldiers killed, while only 338 Israelis died. The IDF also captured the strategic Golan Heights from Syria, and East Jerusalem and the rest of the West Bank from Jordan. Following the Six-Day War, the War of Attrition ground on with the Egyptians along the Suez Canal and with the Syrians along the northern borders, ending in 1970.

The Yom Kippur (Ramadan) War began on October 6, 1973, when Egypt and Syria launched a surprise attack on the holiest Jewish holiday of the year. Initially the IDF took heavy losses, but after U.S. airlifted weapons and supplies began to arrive on October 14, the tide turned, and the IDF pushed the Egyptians and Syrians back to their original lines. On the Golan Heights some 177 Israeli tanks stopped more than 1,500 Syrian tanks. In the critical Valley of Tears Pass, 8 tanks from the 77th Tank Battalion launched a counterattack against hundreds of Syrian tanks and armored personnel carriers and won. In the Sinai an Israeli armored division started to cross the Suez Canal on October 15 and was only some 65 miles away from Cairo by October 24. By the time the war ended under international pressure, the IDF had suffered 2,700 dead while inflicting more than 15,000 deaths on its enemies.

The IDF's most famous special operation came during July 3–4, 1976, when the elite Sayeret Matkal (also known as General Staff Reconnaissance Unit 269) rescued Israeli passengers held hostage at the Entebbe airport in Uganda after their plane was hijacked by Palestinian terrorists. The complex operation managed to save 80 of the 83 passengers. The only IDF casualty was the operational commander, Colonel Jonathan Netanyahu, brother of future prime minister Benjamin Netanyahu.

On June 7, 1981, IAF F-15s and F-16s destroyed Iraq's Osiraq nuclear reactor. Although almost universally condemned in international circles at the time, the preemptive strike almost certainly neutralized Saddam Hussein's nuclear weapons program.

During Operation PEACE FOR GALILEE, the IDF invaded southern Lebanon on June 6, 1982, in retaliation for Palestinian terrorist and rocket attacks launched from Lebanon's territory against Israeli civilian targets in the north. Although the IDF neutralized the Palestinian threat, it became bogged down in a long and grinding occupation of southern Lebanon that ended only in September 2000. The reputation of the IDF also suffered severely from the September 16, 1982, massacre at the Sabra and Shatilia refugee camps, with many international figures branding then-defense minister Sharon as a war criminal.

The IDF performed stability operations during the First Intifada in the Palestinian territories, which lasted from 1987 to 1993. The Second Intifada, which began in September 2000, was far more violent than the first, and the resulting security demands have placed a heavy and seemingly endless burden on the IDF, with most reservists having to perform far more than the standard annual duty. The constant strain of occupation duty in the territories has resulted in morale and discipline problems.

Following Israel's withdrawal from its settlements in Gaza in the summer of 2005, Palestinian militant groups continued to conduct cross-border raids and even increased the rate of Qassam rocket attacks. On June 28, 2006, the IDF mounted a major incursion into Gaza under the justification of rescuing a recently captured Israeli soldier. Hezbollah protested the campaign in Gaza, as did many Arab states. On July 12 Hezbollah crossed the border and killed 3 IDF soldiers and captured 2. In response, Israel launched a series of massive air attacks against not only Hezbollah installations but also Lebanese infrastructure nodes in Beirut and elsewhere in the country. Hezbollah responded with Katyusha rocket attacks and even longer-range missile attacks. Wary of getting drawn into another quagmire on the ground in Lebanon, the Israeli strategy was apparently to drive a wedge between Hezbollah and the rest of the Lebanese population. The air campaign did not work, however, and IDF ground forces started crossing the border on July 23. By the time a UN-brokered cease-fire went into effect on August 14, 2006, the IDF had lost 119 killed and more than 400 wounded. Israel finally lifted its blockade of Lebanon on September 8.

The 2006 Lebanon conflict was different in many ways from any of Israel's previous wars. For the first time, Israel suffered a large number of civilian casualties on its own soil as Hezbollah rockets hit locations in Haifa, Tiberias, Nazareth, and other major cities in the north. Forty-four Israeli civilians were killed, and more than 1,350 were injured. The IDF also inflicted many more civilian than military casualties on its enemy. Only 250–600 Hezbollah fighters were killed, while 1,187 Lebanese civilians died, some 3,600 were injured, and more than 250,000 were internally displaced. The IDF reported 119 Israeli soldiers killed, 400–450 wounded, and 2 taken prisoner. IDF chief of staff Halutz came under severe criticism for the failure of the initial air campaign as well as for the halting and poorly organized ground campaign that followed. Rather than undermining its popular support among the Lebanese people, Hezbollah appeared to increase its support. Many observers proclaimed that by merely surviving the Israeli pounding, Hezbollah emerged the victor of the conflict. The myth of the IDF's invincibility had been shattered once and for all. That claim, however, has been made before, especially following the Yom Kippur War.

DAVID T. ZABECKI

See also

Arab-Israeli Conflict, Overview; Begin, Menachem; Intifada, First; Intifada, Second; Hezbollah; Israel; Lebanon; Netanyahu, Benjamin; Sharon, Ariel; Suez Crisis

References

Heller, Charles E. *Economy of Force: A Total Army, the Israel Defense Force Model.* Carlisle, PA: Strategic Studies Institute, 1992.

Hersh, Seymour. *The Sampson Option: Israel's Nuclear Arsenal and American Foreign Policy.* New York: Random House, 1991.

Kahalani, Avigdor. *The Heights of Courage: A Tank Leader's War on the Golan.* Westport, CT: Praeger, 1992.

Van Creveld, Martin. *The Sword and the Olive: A Critical History of the Israeli Defense Force.* New York: PublicAffairs, 2002.

Williams, Louis. *The Israel Defense Forces: A People's Army.* Lincoln, NE: Authors Choice, 2000.

Israel-Egypt Peace Treaty

A landmark peace accord signed between Egypt and the State of Israel on March 26, 1979, in Washington, D.C. The Israel-Egypt Peace Treaty was the culmination of an ongoing peace process between the Israelis and Egyptians that dated to November 1977. It was also the result of the Camp David Accords, signed by Egyptian president Anwar Sadat and Israeli prime minister Menachem Begin on September 17, 1978.

The peace treaty stipulated that the two nations would officially recognize the sovereignty of the other and end the state of war that had existed between them since 1948. It also stipulated that Israel would withdraw from the Sinai peninsula. Finally, it guaranteed Israel the right of passage through the Suez Canal and recognized that both the Straits of Tiran and the Gulf of Aqaba

were international waterways subject to international law and maritime guidelines. The Israel-Egypt Peace Treaty was the first such treaty between an Arab state and Israel.

The Camp David Accords of 1978 had emerged from 13 days of intensive negotiations at the U.S. presidential retreat at Camp David. President Jimmy Carter had mediated the talks between Sadat and Begin. But it was President Sadat's unprecedented move in November 1977 that had made the historic Israeli-Egyptian peace process possible. On November 19, 1977, Sadat became the first Arab leader in history to visit Israel in an official capacity. He went at the invitation of Prime Minister Begin and addressed the Knesset (Israeli parliament). Sadat's speech offered conciliatory words and a genuine desire to end the conflict between Israel and Egypt, and laid out specific steps that might be taken to broker an enduring peace. Specifically, he called for the implementation of United Nations (UN) Resolutions 242 and 338, which among other things called for the withdrawal of Israeli forces from land captured in the 1967 Six-Day War. Sadat's visit stunned many Israelis as well as much of the world.

Most Arab nations, however, were outraged that Sadat would choose to negotiate with the Israelis. Not only did this go against the prevailing Arab philosophy that viewed Israel as a threat and a tool of Western hegemony, but it also meant that Sadat was

President Jimmy Carter shakes hands with Egyptian president Anwar Sadat and Israeli prime minister Menachem Begin at the signing of the Israel-Egypt Peace Treaty on the grounds of the White House on March 26, 1979. (Library of Congress)

essentially recognizing the legitimacy of the State of Israel, something that no Arab state had been willing to do. A separate peace treaty also negated any prospect of a comprehensive peace solution favored by some. Equally troubling to Arab states was that this peace overture was coming from Egypt, at the time the most powerful Arab military force in the region and the birthplace of modern Arab nationalism under Gamal Abdel Nasser.

When the Camp David Accords were signed, there was no clear consensus or binding agreement that a formal, comprehensive peace treaty would be signed. Indeed, between September 1978 and March 1979, both parties to the accords had considerable hesitations about signing a formal treaty. Sadat had come under intense pressure from other Arab leaders not to sign a peace agreement. He also encountered resistance within his own country. For his part, Begin was under enormous pressure not to allow the issue of Palestinian independence to enter into any formal discussions or accords with the Egyptians. Indeed, Begin's refusal to do so nearly torpedoed the peace settlement.

Although Sadat lost the support of most Arab leaders (and Egypt was expelled from the Arab League after the treaty was signed), his government did gain the support of the United States, both diplomatically and economically. In fact, the United States gave Egypt and Israel subsidies worth billion of dollars as a result of the rapprochement. These subsidies continue to the present day. From the Israeli perspective, the peace treaty was a coup, because Egypt had now been separated from its Arab neighbors. Yet from a geopolitical perspective, the Israeli-Egyptian peace process led to the breakdown of the united Arab front against Israel, creating a power vacuum of sorts once Egypt fell out of that orbit. This allowed such nations as Iran and Iraq to fill in the gap, with disastrous consequences. Only months after the Israel-Egypt Peace Treaty was signed the Iran-Iraq War (1980–1988) broke out, which demonstrated Iraqi president Saddam Hussein's ambitions to become the undisputed Arab leader of the Middle East.

The peace treaty has not brought the expected economic cooperation, travel, and exchange of views between Egyptians and Israelis, because it has been informally boycotted since about 1982, leading to the term "cold peace." While there has been an exchange of diplomats and meetings between representatives of both Egypt and Israel, few Egyptians will travel to Israel; if they do so, they are ousted by professional associations.

On the other hand, the Camp David process and the resultant peace treaty demonstrated that fruitful negotiations between Arabs and Israelis are indeed possible. Furthermore, it showed that progress toward peace can come only with meaningful dialogue, mutual cooperation, and strong leadership. Nevertheless, it would take another 15 years for a second Arab-Israeli peace treaty to come about, this time between the Jordanians and Israelis. Currently, only Egypt and Jordan have concluded such agreements.

PAUL G. PIERPAOLI JR.

See also

Arab League; Arab Nationalism; Begin, Menachem; Camp David Accords; Egypt; Israel; Israel-Jordan Peace Treaty; Nasser, Gamal Abdel; Sadat, Muhammad Anwar; Suez Crisis

References

Carter, Jimmy. *Keeping Faith: Memoirs of a President.* Fayetteville: University of Arkansas Press, 1982.

Kamel, Mohamed Ibrahim. *The Camp David Accords: A Testimony.* London: Kegan Paul International, 1986.

Lenczowski, George. *The Middle East in World Affairs.* 4th ed. Ithaca, NY: Cornell University Press, 1980.

Quandt, William. *Camp David: Peacemaking and Politics.* Washington, DC: Brookings Institution, 1986.

Israel-Jordan Peace Treaty

A comprehensive peace accord between Israel and Jordan signed on October 26, 1994, at the border settlement of Wadi Arabah. Officially titled the "Treaty of Peace between the State of Israel and the Hashemite Kingdom of Jordan," the agreement settled long-standing territorial conflicts and fully normalized diplomatic and economic relations between the two states. It was intended as part of the larger Arab-Israeli peace process that had begun in 1991 at the Madrid Conference and had continued in the Oslo Accords, agreed to and signed by the Israelis and Palestinians the previous summer. The treaty was only the second one of its kind signed between the Israelis and an Arab nation, the first one having been negotiated with Egypt in 1979.

Over the years relations between Jordan and Israel had been complex and sometimes hostile. Be that as it may, Israel's relations with Jordan were generally not as difficult as those with the other Arab states. Jordan's King Hussein, while cleaving to anti-Israeli stances alongside his Arab neighbors because a large proportion of Jordan's population was Palestinian, was also a pragmatist. Thus, his actions did not always match his anti-Zionist rhetoric. He was also reliably pro-Western in orientation, which surely tempered his anti-Israeli policies. Also, his relatively modest territorial demands and Jordan's proximity to Israel worked as a moderating force in the Israeli-Jordanian relationship.

This does not mean, however, that Jordanian-Israeli relations were not without serious tensions. Indeed, in the run-up to the 1967 Six-Day War, Israeli leaders implored King Hussein not to join the Egyptian-led coalition arrayed against Israel. King Hussein ignored the forewarning, and Jordan suffered the consequences. By war's end the Israelis had seized control of East Jerusalem and the strategically and economically crucial West Bank, which had been an economic lifeline to the Kingdom of Jordan. The Israeli occupation of the West Bank would also significantly complicate future peace negotiations with the Palestinians, who believe that the West Bank must be at the heart of any future Palestinian state. Indeed, the Jordanians conferred their claim to the West Bank to the Palestine Liberation Organization (PLO) in 1988.

In 1970, as the Jordanians prepared to expel the PLO from their country in what came to be called Black September, Israel tacitly aided them in the struggle by dispatching fighter jets to menace Syrian forces that had begun to intervene in Jordan on the side of the PLO.

In 1973, although King Hussein was caught off guard by the Egyptian and Syrian attack on Israel in the Yom Kippur War, he was soon under pressure from these two Arab states to join the conflict. He tried to avoid involvement but was nevertheless drawn in, ironically to stave off a crushing Syrian defeat. He did not commit his air force, realizing that this would bring a crushing Israeli retaliation, as in 1967, but on October 13 he sent the crack 40th Armored Brigade, equipped with British-made Centurion tanks, into Syria, to save that nation from the threat posed by the Israeli invasion to Damascus and the survival of the Syrian Army. The 40th Brigade came into battle with the Israelis on October 16 and fought bravely, holding until the Syrians were told by their Soviet advisers to withdraw.

In 1987 Israeli foreign minister Shimon Peres undertook a tentative attempt to arrive at a Jordanian-Israeli peace settlement. In secret deliberations he and King Hussein agreed that the West Bank would be ceded back to Jordan in exchange for mutual peace and security guarantees. The deal was never consummated because internal Israeli politics prevented such a sweeping move. The peace attempt did strengthen relations between the two nations, however, and a year later Jordan abandoned its claim to the West Bank and agreed to help settle the Palestinian-Israeli impasse without violence.

It was really the 1993 Oslo Accords that set the stage for the Israel-Jordan Peace Treaty. In light of what appeared at the time to be a historic period in Arab-Israeli peacemaking, King Hussein was more receptive to a peace deal with Israel. U.S. president Bill Clinton and Secretary of State Warren Christopher had also begun to nudge King Hussein toward a peace agreement, even promising to reduce or eliminate Jordan's foreign aid debts to the United States. Perhaps what clinched the deal for the king was Egyptian president Hosni Mubarak's support of an Israeli-Jordanian peace accord, although Syrian president Hafiz al-Asad opposed the agreement. The diplomacy worked, and King Hussein, ever the pragmatist, agreed to a nonbelligerency treaty with the Israelis. The Washington Declaration, signed in Washington, D.C., on July 25, 1994, ultimately led to the signing of the formal peace treaty on October 24, 1994.

The provisions of the treaty included the establishment of the Jordan River as the boundary between the two nations, the full normalization of diplomatic and economic relations, cooperation in antiterrorism, respect for each other's territory, a more equitable distribution of Jordan River water and other joint water supplies, and a joint effort at alleviating the Palestinian refugee problem. Soon thereafter, the Israeli-Jordanian border became an open one, and

Israelis and Jordanians embarked on tourist and business excursions in each other's countries. These have been interrupted by Israel's campaigns against Palestinians and, as in Egypt, boycotted by many Jordanian groups. Jordanian Islamists strongly opposed the peace treaty, and they continue to block widened cooperation between the two countries. Unfortunately, the Israeli-Jordanian peace settlement has not led to a wider peace in the region.

PAUL G. PIERPAOLI JR.

See also

Arab-Israeli Conflict, Overview; Asad, Hafiz al-; Clinton, William Jefferson; Hussein ibn Talal, King of Jordan; Israel; Israel-Egypt Peace Treaty; Jordan; Mubarak, Hosni; Oslo Accords; Palestine Liberation Organization

References

Freedman, Robert Owen, ed. *The Middle East and the Peace Process: The Impact of the Oslo Accords.* Gainesville: University Press of Florida, 1998.

Majali, Abdul Salam, et al. *Peacemaking: An Inside Story of the 1994 Jordanian-Israeli Treaty.* Norman: University of Oklahoma Press, 2006.

Peres, Shimon. *The New Middle East.* New York: Henry Holt, 1993.

Weinberger, Peter. *Co-opting the PLO: A Critical Reconstruction of the Oslo Accords, 1993–1995.* New York: Rowman and Littlefield, 2006.

Italy

A southern European nation located on the Italian Peninsula, Italy is officially known as the Italian Republic. Italy is bordered by Slovenia to the northeast, Austria and Switzerland to the north, and France to the northwest. Its remaining boundaries consist of the Adriatic Sea along its eastern coast, the Ionian Sea along the southeastern coast, the Mediterranean Sea along the southern coast, the Tyrrhenian Sea along the western coast, and the Ligurian Sea along its northwest coast. Additionally, Italy's borders completely surround two autonomous enclaves: the Holy See (Vatican City) and the Republic of San Marino. Switzerland completely surrounds the Italian exclave of Campione d'Italia. Italy also has numerous small islands along its coastline as well as two major islands, Sicily, located just to the south of the peninsula, and Sardinia, located off the west coast. Italy comprises 116,346 square miles, and its population in 2008 was 58 million.

Italy's armed forces include an army, navy, and air force, as well as the Carabinieri, a separate branch of the armed forces that functions as both a military and civilian police force. In addition to its participation in the North Atlantic Treaty Organization (NATO), the Italian government has also agreed, if needed, to provide military support staff or forces to the Eurocorps. U.S. military forces are located at various installations in Italy. Major U.S. bases are located in Vicenza, Livorno, Aviano, Sigonella, and Naples.

Italian forces have jointly participated in various NATO and other bilateral operations since the 1990s. During the Persian Gulf

War of 1990–1991, Italy deployed eight Panavia Tornado Inter-dictor Strike (IDS) bombers to Saudi Arabia. Italian troops went into the Kurdish region in northern Iraq after the war. Between December 9, 1992, and May 4, 1994, Italian forces, including men from the Folgore Parachute Brigade participated in humanitarian efforts sanctioned by the United Nations (UN).

Al Qaeda's attack against the United States on September 11, 2001, resulted in NATO invoking Article 5 of its charter (the mutual defense clause), and provided justification for Italian troops to be used against Al Qaeda and the Taliban in Afghani-stan. Italian troops are currently part of the International Secu-rity Assistance Force, tasked with control over NATO's Regional Command–West in Herat, Afghanistan. Italy's refusal to partici-pate militarily in Operation IRAQI FREEDOM did not apply to peace-keeping operations after major combat operations ended. Italian prime minister Silvio Berlusconi allowed his country's military forces to take part in the UN-sanctioned Multi-National Force–Iraq. Italy initially deployed 3,200 military personnel to Iraq, including forces from the Folgore Parachute Brigade and the Car-binieri. Italian forces' operational areas were located in southern Iraq. In addition to peacekeeping operations, Italian forces also participated in training elements of the new Iraqi Army and the Iraqi police. In July 2005 Italy began reducing troop levels in Iraq; the last of its forces were withdrawn in September 2006. The Iraq War proved quite unpopular among Italians.

WYNDHAM WHYNOT

See also

International Security Assistance Force; Italy, Armed Forces in Iraq and Afghanistan; North Atlantic Treaty Organization

References

Hearder, Harry. *Italy: A Short History.* 2nd ed., revised and updated by Jack Morris. Cambridge: University of Cambridge Press, 2002.

Killinger, Charles L. *Italy.* Edited by Frank W. Thackeray and John E. Findling. Westport, CT: Greenwood, 2007.

Italy, Armed Forces in Iraq and Afghanistan

Italian ground forces did not participate in Operation DESERT STORM in Iraq, however, the Italian Air Force deployed eight Panavia Tor-nado Interdictor Strike (IDS) bomber jets to Saudi Arabia, and Italian pilots flew combat missions during that short war. One Italian pilot was shot down in January 1991 and was taken pris-oner by the Iraqis. Later in 1991, after the war, Italian Army troops deployed to northern Iraq to assist Kurdish refugees who were under attack by Iraqi forces loyal to President Saddam Hussein, in Operation PROVIDE COMFORT.

In Afghanistan, Italian military forces were early participants in Operation ENDURING FREEDOM, the allied effort to oust the Tal-iban from power and rid the country of Al Qaeda, which began in October 2001. A navy battle group, including the aircraft

carrier *Giuseppe Garibaldi,* patrolled the Indian Ocean, and Ital-ian McDonnell Douglas Harrier AV-8B aircraft provided close air support for ground operations. From March to September 2003 the Italian Army Task Force Nibbio, whose primary element was the elite mountain warfare 2nd Alpini Regiment, provided base security at the Salerno Forward Operating Base at Khost in south-eastern Afghanistan.

During this time, Italian forces conducted the first air assault in the history of the Italian Army. They also participated in Opera-tions HAVEN DENIAL and WARRIOR SWEEP with the U.S. 82nd Airborne, the Afghan National Army (ANA), and Special Forces units. The Italian Army also made more than 2,000 conventional patrols that led to the capture and disposal of many weapons caches.

Consistent with the policy of rotating commanding officers every six months, Italian lieutenant general Mauro Del Vecchio commanded the International Security Assistance Force–Afghan-istan (ISAF) from August 2005 through January 2006. During their tenure in the country, Italian army forces included an infan-try unit; special forces, an engineer company and command of a multinational engineer task force, a chemical-biological-radiation platoon, military police, and logistic, liaison, and staff elements.

Italy also supplied three Italian-built CH-47 Chinook helicop-ters. The CH-47s and their army aviation crews, known as Task Force Eracle, arrived in August 2005. Originally stationed at Herat, which was also the site of Italy's Provisional Reconstruction Team (PRT), Eracle's first operation was to fly protection missions dur-ing the Afghan parliamentary elections on September 18, 2005. Shortly after their arrival, the CH-47s took part in a high-altitude rescue operation of a Dutch Chinook that was disabled from a hard landing high in the mountains.

Beginning in November 2005, the CH-47 and other smaller Italian helicopters, including the Bell AB 212 Twin Huey and Bell AB 412 Twin Huey aircraft, were dispatched at various times and were part of the ISAF Quick Reaction Force (QRF) stationed at Kabul International Airport.

With periodic small increases in troops and equipment, Ital-ian forces numbered 2,350 men by the end of 2008, and Italy headed the Regional Command West. In the original deployment of its forces, the Italian parliament had forbidden the assignment of Italian ground forces to direct, sustained front-line combat. Controversy over Italian participation in Afghanistan continued throughout the military's tenure in the country. Parliament con-stantly debated the recall of all forces, and Italian political leaders were extremely sensitive to any casualties. Not until July 2008 did the Italian government relax the restriction against direct combat, but the Italian defense minister explained that Italian forces had engaged in limited combat operations, as noted above, as early as 2003 and more recently in 2007 in the Fara area.

With the loosening of restrictions, some Italian army units moved south to participate in direct combat against the Taliban. In late September 2008 Italy sent four Panavia Tornado jet aircraft to be used in surveillance missions. Two Alenia C-27J Spartan tactical transport aircraft also supported military operations in the country.

By October 2008 Italy had suffered 13 deaths, 2 by hostile fire, 4 by roadside bombs, 1 kidnapped soldier slain during a rescue operation (undetermined whether killed by the kidnappers or the rescuers), and the others by non-hostile fire accidents. In 2007 2 other kidnapped Italian soldiers were successfully rescued by British and Italian forces; in 2006 the Italian government paid a $2 million ransom for a kidnapped Italian photographer; and in 2007 Italy arranged the release of 5 Taliban captives to retrieve a kidnapped Italian journalist. Italy remains a cautious, risk-averse ally in Operation ENDURING FREEDOM.

Italy did not participate in the initial period of combat operations during Operation IRAQI FREEDOM, which began in March 2003. The Italian government was opposed to preemptive war in Iraq without an explicit authorization by the United Nations (UN) Security Council. However, in May 2003, after what turned out to be a premature declaration of victory, the Italians did commit forces for peacekeeping and reconstruction purposes. The deployment, codenamed Operation ANTICA BABILONIA, consisting of land forces and a joint air task force of two helicopter squadrons, dispatched to Iraq in July 2003. The army worked in the vicinity of Nasiriyah and ultimately assumed responsibility for the entire Thi Qar Province. At its height, Italy maintained 3,200 forces in Iraq, the fourth-largest contingent in southern Iraq. The Italian army engaged in elimination of ordnance operations, various small combat operations, support of coalition allies, and security and humanitarian activities. The largest number of Italian forces, however, was composed of the Carabinieri, the famous Italian military police, which is a separate branch of the Italian armed forces. One of Italy's special responsibilities involved protection of Iraq's archaeological treasures. As a nation with countless historical treasures and with much experience in dealing with thieves looking for invaluable archaeological artifacts, Italy brought particular expertise to southern Iraq. The Italian army captured archaeological looters, recovered ancient artifacts, and trained Iraqis to fulfill these duties in the future.

The two major combat operations in which the Italian army participated were the 2004 battles around Nasiriyah. The first engagement unfolded on April 5, 2004, when Mahdi Army forces loyal to Muqtada al-Sadr seized three undefended bridges. The Italian government authorized Italian forces to retake the bridges. A force of 600 Italian soldiers and 68 mechanized and motorized vehicles carried out the operation. By the end of the day, Italian soldiers had expended 30,000 rounds of ammunition and had been resupplied five times. The Mahdi forces withdrew into the civilian population of Nasiriyah and asked for a truce to conduct

Italian Army personnel on convoy duty depart Tallil Air Base, Iraq, in a light truck armed with a Browning M2 .50-caliber heavy machine gun, 2005. (U.S. Department of Defense)

negotiations. In the negotiations, it was agreed that Italian forces would patrol the south side of the city's bridges and Iraqi policemen would patrol the north side. Official casualties stood at 15 Italian and 14 Sadrists killed in action, but the Iraqi death toll might have been as high as 150 to 200. In mid-May 2004, more heavily armed Mahdi forces attacked the bridges again, as well as a Coalition Provisional Authority building and military base. The assault was beaten back at the cost of 1 Italian death and 15 wounded. Again, a cease-fire was negotiated, but it was continually broken as tensions remained high in and around Nasiriyah.

In June 2005 the Italian air force deployed four RQ-1 Predator unmanned aerial vehicles to Iraq. The Italians had recently acquired the weapons system, and they had not yet fully defined the rationale for its use. For the most part the Predators were successful, but command and control problems and other operation issues surfaced, leading Italian commanders to call for a better plan for the deployment and usage of the unmanned vehicles.

Extremely sensitive to casualties, Italian politicians, especially those on the Left, have threatened to remove forces from Iraq since 2005. Indeed, 1,000 forces were withdrawn in June and July 2006, and on September 21, 2006, Italy declared that its mission was completed as it handed over Thi Qar Province to the Iraqis. The remaining Italian forces departed in November 2006. The Italian withdrawal occurred during some of the worst insurgency-related violence in Iraq and before the U.S.-announced troop surge in January 2007. In total, from 2003 to 2006, Italian forces suffered 34 deaths in Iraq. Several hundred others were wounded. The largest loss of life came on November 12, 2004, when a suicide car bombing at the Carabinieri Corps headquarters killed 12 Carabinieri, 4 army officers, 2 Italian civilians, and 10 Iraqis. Another 80 people were wounded. In December 2008 an Italian military court convicted General Bruno Stano, commanding officer of Italian forces in Iraq, of failing to provide proper security at the base.

On March 5, 2005, Italian intelligence officer Nicola Calipari was mistakenly shot and killed as his car approached an American checkpoint at high speed. He had just secured the release of captured Italian journalist Giuliana Screna.

In November 2007 the Iraqi government contracted with Italy for the construction of four modified Diciotti-class 400-ton Saettia MK4 missile patrol boats. The first was delivered in June 2009, with the remainder to be delivered in 2010. The Iraqi crews are being trained in Italy.

JOE P. DUNN

See also

Afghan National Army; Al Qaeda; DESERT STORM, Operation; ENDURING FREEDOM, Operation; International Security Assistance Force; IRAQI FREEDOM, Operation; Iraqi Insurgency; Mahdi Army; PROVIDE COMFORT, Operation; Provincial Reconstruction Teams, Afghanistan; Sadr, Muqtada al-; Taliban

References

Cappelli, Riccardo. "Iraq: Italian Lessons Learned." *Military Review* (March–April 2005): 58–61.

Earling, David C. *Italy and the Gulf War.* Los Alamos National Laboratory, September 1991. Document call number M-U 43813-15.

Isikoff, Michael, and David Corn. *Hubris: The Inside Story of Spin, Scandal, and the Selling of the Iraq War.* New York: Three Rivers/Random House, 2007.

Jalali, Ali A. "The Future of Afghanistan." *Parameters* (Spring 2006): 4–19.

Maloney, Sean M. "Afghanistan Four Years On: An Assessment." *Parameters* (Autumn 2005): 21–32.

Williams, Garland H. *Engineering Peace: The Military Role in Postconflict Reconstruction.* Washington, DC: United States Institute of Peace, 2005.

IVORY JUSTICE, **Operation**
Start Date: July 24, 1990
End Date: August 1990

U.S. military operation launched on July 24, 1990, to demonstrate to Iraq the U.S. ability to protect the United Arab Emirates (UAE) and other American allies in the Persian Gulf. The operation failed to dissuade Iraqi president Saddam Hussein from invading Kuwait on August 2, 1990, possibly because the scale of the military forces involved in the operation was too small. The unwillingness of Kuwait or the UAE to fully support the U.S. demonstration was also problematic.

With the recent fall of communism in Eastern Europe and the diminution of Soviet military and political power, many Middle Eastern rulers were concerned that their positions might be in peril. The loss of the Soviet-U.S. balance of power in the region caused them to fear possible U.S. and Israeli domination, radical elements in their own countries that might attempt to overthrow them, or exertion of control by a regional power like Iran or Iraq. Hussein in particular had reason to be concerned, for Iraq had purchased most of its weaponry from the Soviet bloc. During the 1980s some of Hussein's Soviet ties had been offset by aid from Western nations, especially France and the United States, which favored an Iraqi victory in the Iran-Iraq War (1980–1988).

During the first half of 1990, however, the West's relationship with Hussein soured. Hussein began to agitate for war against Israel, and even more ominously, he revived old Iraqi claims on Kuwait and its oil resources. Hussein was incensed with Kuwait and the UAE for their part in driving down the price of oil since the late 1980s, as most of Iraq's income came from the export of oil. Both Kuwait and the UAE continued to prosper when oil prices went down, because they controlled oil distribution points and refining. Iraq, in contrast, depended almost solely on the sale of crude oil, and with low oil prices, it was unable to service the huge debt from the Iran-Iraq War.

On July 16, 1990, Iraqi foreign minister Tariq Aziz delivered a memorandum to the secretary-general of the Arab League laying out Iraq's charges against Kuwait and the UAE. Among other things, he accused them of a scheme to drive down the price of oil, depriving Iraq of $89 billion of potential income. He also accused Kuwait of slant drilling into Iraq's Rumaila oil field. Further, Kuwait had moved some of its military posts and other installations into disputed territory claimed by Iraq. The sum total of the charges, according to the document, amounted to military aggression against Iraq by the two nations.

The Kuwaiti government believed the memorandum was basically a bluff by Hussein to obtain money or loan cancellations. Although Kuwait put its armed forces on alert, it also offered to negotiate a settlement. At the same time, however, U.S. analysts reported that Iraqi Republican Guard divisions were advancing toward the border with Kuwait, and by July 19, 35,000 men in three Republican Guard divisions were within 30 miles of the Kuwaiti border.

Although the Kuwaiti government was not overly concerned about invasion, the UAE believed it had reason to fear military attack. During the Iran-Iraq War, Hussein had charged that the UAE was not supporting Iraq enough, and in 1986 he ordered aircraft to fly more than 600 miles down the Persian Gulf to bomb two oil rigs belonging to the UAE. Although the Iraqi Foreign Ministry later claimed it was a mistake, most observers believed that the attack had been intended to intimidate the UAE. To protect its oil rigs and other facilities, the UAE decided to mount a standing patrol of Dassault Mirage 2000 fighters. On July 22 the UAE requested assistance from the United States.

The U.S. government immediately approved the request and launched Operation IVORY JUSTICE on July 24. Two Boeing KC-135 Stratotankers, along with a Lockheed C-141 Starlifter and support equipment and personnel, arrived in the Persian Gulf that same day. The plan was for the tankers to refuel UAE fighters in flight, allowing them to loiter above UAE airspace and intercept any incoming Iraqi aircraft. The emirates also requested a ground link to the U.S. Airborne Warning and Control System (AWACS) and Northrop Grumman E-2C Hawkeye radar aircraft that flew above the Persian Gulf. Such a link would allow the emirates to monitor reports of air traffic over the Gulf, and the UAE would therefore be able to receive information about possible Iraqi attackers long before they arrived. The U.S. Navy's Central Command was also involved in the operation. Rear Admiral William Fogarty ordered two frigates into the northern half of the Persian Gulf. Their radar would search for incoming Iraqi bombers, providing more warning to UAE fighters.

Operation IVORY JUSTICE did not go smoothly. The Mirage 2000's refueling probes were found to be incompatible with the KC-135's drogues, rendering aerial refueling impossible. The UAE's fighter pilots had not been trained in aerial refueling in any case, and would not likely have been able to carry out midair refueling. The operation could have been more impressive if additional forces had been committed. The *Independence* carrier battle group was nearby and could have been ordered to the Strait of Hormuz for a greater show of force, if required. The U.S. Navy, however, was convinced that the shallow waters and restricted area in the Persian Gulf were not suitable to carrier operations and was reluctant to commit them to the region.

Even though the U.S. force in Operation IVORY JUSTICE was small, it did raise concerns in Baghdad. When word of an increased U.S. presence in the area became known, some Arab countries protested. Even the UAE presented it as nothing more than routine training. Iraqi ministers complained to U.S. ambassador to Iraq April Glaspie, who reassured the Iraqis that the United States wanted improved relations with their country. During her only meeting with Hussein, Glaspie tried to strike a conciliatory tone with the Iraqi leader, which was in line with official policy. Some critics believe that Glaspie's failure to suggest a U.S. military response to an invasion of Kuwait encouraged Hussein to invade Kuwait. In retrospect, she had no authority to do so, and the very limited show of force of IVORY JUSTICE may have led Hussein to believe that a Kuwaiti invasion would not be challenged.

Iraqi talks with Kuwait subsequently collapsed, and on August 2, 1990, eight Iraqi divisions crossed into Kuwait and swiftly occupied the country. IVORY JUSTICE essentially dissolved with the buildup of coalition forces during Operation DESERT SHIELD.

TIM J. WATTS

See also

Arab League; DESERT SHIELD, Operation; DESERT STORM, Operation; Glaspie, April; Iraq, History of, Pre-1990; Kuwait; United Arab Emirates

References

Freedman, Lawrence, and Efraim Karsh. *The Gulf Conflict, 1990–1991: Diplomacy and War in the New World Order.* Princeton, NJ: Princeton University Press, 1993.

Gordon, Michael R., and General Bernard E. Trainor. *The Generals' War: The Inside Story of the Conflict in the Gulf.* New York: Little, Brown, 1995.

J

JACANA, Operation
Start Date: April 2002
End Date: July 2002

A series of military operations intended to be a "mopping up" exercise by United Kingdom Royal Marine commandos (45th Commando) in the aftermath of Operation ANACONDA against the Taliban in Afghanistan. Operation JACANA took place between April and July 2002. The commandos were specifically requested by the U.S. government because their reputation and training seemed appropriate to conditions in Afghanistan at the time. The commandos were withdrawn after less than four months, amid reports of failure and after drawing criticism from U.S. officials.

After the U.S.-assisted Northern Front forces in Afghanistan overthrew the Taliban and its Al Qaeda terrorist organization allies in late 2001, operations continued in an effort to destroy the remaining Taliban fighters and to capture Al Qaeda leader Osama Bin Laden. Although most operations were undertaken by U.S. Special Forces, the United States requested assistance from allies around the world. Some allied units provided manpower for security throughout the country, while Great Britain and others supplied instructors to train Afghan army units. The British-led International Security Assistance Force (ISAF) units were lightly armed and not expected to become involved in combat operations. For combat, U.S. leaders requested units that were specially trained for the cold and the high altitudes encountered in much of Afghanistan, the areas favored by the Taliban and Al Qaeda fighters.

Along with Norwegian Special Forces and Australian Special Air Service (SAS), U.S. military commanders selected the British 45th Commando of the Royal Marines as being especially suitable for service in Afghanistan. A formal request for assistance was issued in March 2002. The British government had resisted earlier requests for combat troops, but it acceded to this request. The Pentagon announced the deployment on March 18, surprising many members of the British Parliament. Secretary of State for Defence Geoff Hoon emphasized that the commandos were being sent in a combat role and warned the country to expect casualties. It was Britain's largest deployment of a combat force overseas since the end of the 1991 Persian Gulf War.

The 45th Royal Marine Commando was a battalion-sized unit with 690 Royal Marines augmented by a number of specialists attached from the Royal Navy. It was supported by 7th Battery, 29th Artillery Commando, equipped with 105-mm howitzers. The 59th Independent Commando of the Royal Engineers and members of the Royal Logistics Regiment were included for support. Mobility was provided by the 27th Squadron of the Royal Air Force, with Boeing CH-47 Chinook helicopters. The entire unit was flown to Bagram Airfield in Afghanistan for deployment and was in place by the beginning of April 2002.

The deployment of 45th Commando was known as Operation JACANA. The entire operation included four suboperations. The first was Operation PTARMIGAN, which occurred in April. It consisted of sweeps through high mountain valleys in southern Afghanistan to seek out Taliban fighters. No combat occurred.

The second was Operation SNIPE, in early May. With the assistance of Afghan forces, the commandos swept through parts of southeast Afghanistan. They seized a number of weapons and explosives, but no major contact with Taliban or Al Qaeda forces occurred.

The next operation was code-named CONDOR. It began on May 17, following an ambush against an Australian SAS patrol by Taliban fighters. The patrol called in air strikes that killed 10 rebels.

The commandos were then sent in to try to catch the Taliban forces before they could withdraw from the area. In a series of sweeps and gun battles, the commandos killed at least 11 members of the Taliban and captured another 9. They also secured weapons and explosives. Between the end of May and July 2002, the commandos cooperated with Afghan army units to patrol the Khost region of southeast Afghanistan in the fourth suboperation. During that time, they had no contact with rebel forces.

The results of Operation JACANA were somewhat disappointing. Few enemy fighters were killed or captured, and some critics charged that most of the weapons and explosives captured had belonged to friendly warlords. Despite their training, a number of commandos suffered from altitude sickness and had to be evacuated. The tactics the commandos used were criticized as ineffective, and some critics charged that they suffered from low morale. Much of the blame was placed on their commander. On May 20, 2002, the Defence Ministry announced that Brigadier Roger Lane would be relieved when the unit returned to Great Britain in July. Although explained as a normal command change, the announcement during Operation CONDOR was seen by many as significant. In fact, Lane had angered U.S. officials during his time in Afghanistan, and he contradicted Secretary of Defense Donald Rumsfeld by publicly stating that the war in Afghanistan would be over in several weeks. Other critics have contended that the commando effort suffered from a lack of clear objectives.

TIM J. WATTS

See also

ENDURING FREEDOM, Operation; International Security Assistance Force; United Kingdom Forces in Afghanistan

References

Harclerode, Peter. *Commando: The Illustrated History of Britain's Green Berets from Dieppe to Afghanistan.* Stroud, UK: Sutton, 2003.

Micheletti, Eric. *Special Forces in Afghanistan: 2001–2003: War against Terrorism.* Paris: Histoire and Collections, 2003.

Jafari, Ibrahim al-
Birth Date: March 25, 1947

Iraqi politician and prime minister of Iraq in the transitional government from 2005 to 2006 before being ousted under intense pressure from the U.S. government. Jafari is a former member of the Party of Islamic Call (Hizb al-Da'wa al-Islamiyya) but was reportedly expelled in June 2008 for his vocal public criticisms of his successor and fellow Dawa official, Nuri al-Maliki, and for forming a rival faction within the party. Ibrahim al-Jafari, an Arab Shia, is a *sayyid* (descendant of the Prophet Muhammad) and was born on March 25, 1947, in the southern Iraqi shrine city of Karbala to the prominent al-Ishayker family.

Jafari received his university education in medicine at the University of Mosul and is a medical doctor. He subsequently joined the Dawa Party, an Iraqi Shia political party founded in 1958.

Some reports say that he joined in 1966; others claim 1968. The party sought to achieve the staged implementation of an Islamic governing system and received guidance from one of its founding members, Ayatollah Muhammad Baqir al-Sadr, who was tortured and executed by the Iraqi Baath Party in April 1980. Jafari, along with many other Dawa Party members, left Iraq following the execution of Sadr. In 1989 Jafari took up residence in London after living in Iran for a time and became one of the party's chief spokespeople in Great Britain. The party was a key member of the coalition of opposition parties active against the Iraqi government during the 1980s and 1990s.

Jafari and the Dawa Party leadership were publicly opposed to the U.S.- and British-led invasion and subsequent occupation of Iraq in 2003, but they returned en masse to the country shortly after Saddam Hussein's regime collapsed in April of that year. Jafari was one of those selected to serve on the Iraqi Governing Council, an interim governing body formed by the U.S.-dominated Coalition Provisional Authority (CPA), that exercised limited political control over Iraq from 2003 until the transfer of power from the CPA to the Iraqi government in June 2004. Following the transfer of power, Jafari served as one of the two vice presidents in the interim government until the January 2005 elections.

The United Iraqi Alliance (UIA), a loose coalition of mainly Shia Arab political parties of which the Dawa Party is a member, dominated the January 2005 elections, and it became clear that a member of one of the UIA's two largest parties, Dawa or the Supreme Islamic Iraqi Council (SIIC), would most likely become prime minister. On April 7, 2005, Jafari formally became Iraq's first post-Hussein prime minister after his chief rival for the post, the Iraqi exile Ahmad Chalabi, who had fallen from the good graces of the United States and many of his Iraqi colleagues because of his duplicity and corruption, withdrew his name from consideration. Jafari is a strong supporter of the idea that Islamic law should play a key role in Iraq's legal code but is opposed to the formation of an Iranian-style governmental system in Iraq and does not support the formation of a clerically run Islamic state.

Jafari enjoyed widespread support and popularity initially, with some 2004 polls indicating that his popularity among Iraqis was second only to Grand Ayatollah Ali al-Husayni al-Sistani, Iraq's senior resident Shia religious scholar, and the militant Iraqi Shia nationalist Muqtada al-Sadr. Despite this popularity, Jafari's tenure as Iraq's first postinterim government prime minister (April 7, 2005–May 20, 2006) was marked with a noticeable increase in politically motivated sectarian tensions. The SIIC, unlike the Dawa Party, has a large paramilitary wing (the 10,000-man Badr Organization, also commonly called the Badr Corps). During Jafari's premiership, the SIIC leader, Abd al-Aziz al-Hakim, gained control over several key ministries, including the Ministry of the Interior, which controls the Iraqi police and internal security forces. The ministry, police, and internal security forces, including elite commando units, were staffed with Badr Corps officers and paramilitaries who were more loyal to Hakim than to Iraq as a nation-state.

Hakim used these units against political and communal rivals, both Shia, namely the Sadr Movement led by Muqtada al-Sadr, and Sunni insurgents and civilians.

Jafari's inability or unwillingness, or both, to address such issues lost him the support of U.S. president George W. Bush, who began to pressure Iraq's chief political leaders to choose a replacement. The UIA again dominated the December 2005 parliamentary elections, winning the right to select the next prime minister. Jafari narrowly defeated, by one vote, Adil Abd al-Mahdi, a senior SIIC official. This victory was largely due to the support of members of parliament loyal to Muqtada al-Sadr, who vocally opposed U.S. pressure on the Iraqi parliament and political elite to replace Jafari. President Bush bluntly remarked in early 2006 that his administration, which designed and launched the invasion and occupation of Iraq, "doesn't want, doesn't support, doesn't accept" the continuation of Jafari's premiership. Although Jafari initially refused to bow to U.S. pressure and domestic pressure from Sunni and Kurdish political rivals as well as pressure from Iraqi secular parties, he finally succumbed to pressure from Grand Ayatollah al-Sistani and the *marjaiyya,* the informal council of Iraq's senior resident Shia scholars sitting in the southern shrine city of Najaf, and stepped down. Jafari was replaced as Iraqi prime minister by a fellow Dawa Party official, Nuri al-Maliki, who also took over from Jafari as the party's secretary-general in May 2007.

In late May 2008 Jafari announced the formation of a new political party, the National Reform Party, which led to his public expulsion from the Dawa Party.

CHRISTOPHER ANZALONE

See also

Badr Organization; Chalabi, Ahmed Abd al-Hadi; Iraq, History of, 1990–Present; Iraqi Insurgency; Islamic Dawa Party; Maliki, Nuri Muhammed Kamil Hasan al-; Sadr, Muqtada al-; Supreme Iraqi Islamic Council; United Iraqi Alliance

References

Ghosh, Bobby. "The Doctor of Politics." *Time,* February 22, 2005.
Seattle Times News Services. "Al-Maliki Aims to Smooth Ties with Iran." *Seattle Times,* June 8, 2008.
Wong, Edward. "Shiites Say U.S. Is Pressuring Iraqi Leader to Step Aside." *New York Times,* March 28, 2006.

Japan

Both of the wars in Iraq (Operations DESERT STORM and IRAQI FREEDOM) have had major repercussions across the globe, and that includes Japan. Prior to the 1990 Iraqi invasion of Kuwait, Japan was fully cognizant of the military limitations imposed by Article 9 of its constitution. Put in place during the U.S. occupation of Japan after World War II, Article 9 prohibits the Japanese from maintaining "land, sea, and air forces, as well as other war potential." In 1954, under the Self-Defense Forces Law, the Japanese made tentative steps toward creating a military, but it was clearly for defensive purposes only. Divided into the Japanese Ground Self-Defense Force (JGSDF), Japanese Maritime Self-Defense Force (JMSDF), and Japanese Air Self-Defense Force (JASDF), the military was committed to limited missions to preserve the home islands. This commitment extended beyond the military, to public policymakers as well. Since 1976 the Japanese government has maintained a military spending limit of 1 percent of Japan's gross national product (GNP). There have been long-standing desires to amend the status of the Japanese military by right-leaning candidates, but the public by and large has been content with the status quo.

Because of these restrictions, the Japanese Self-Defense Force (JSDF) was not permitted to undertake operations in support of Operation DESERT SHIELD or, initially, DESERT STORM. Although Japan committed $10 billion to the international coalition dedicated to driving Iraqi forces from Kuwait, none of the money could be used to purchase weapons. Japan provided the third-largest monetary contribution to the war, but the Japanese public outcry against "checkbook diplomacy" was strong and pronounced. In response to public criticism, Japan sent three minesweepers but provided them only after combat operations had ceased. Despite these limitations and concerns, the 1990–1991 Persian Gulf War was a watershed event for Japan, as it began a period of serious reconsideration of its military policy.

Increasingly, the 1990s saw a more active role for the Japanese military. In June 1992 the National Diet (parliament) passed the United Nations (UN) Peacekeeping Cooperation Law, which gave the JSDF the ability to participate in overseas peacekeeping operations under limited conditions. For example, in 1993 the JSDF sent 53 members to Mozambique to participate in peacekeeping operations there.

A particular turning point for Japan's military policy was the non–UN-sanctioned deployment of Japanese troops to Iraq in 2004. Prime Minister Junichiro Koizumi, at the behest of the United States, pushed the Humanitarian Relief and Iraqi Reconstruction Special Measures Law through the Diet on December 9, 2003. This allowed a small deployment of Japanese troops to Iraq beginning in 2004. Called the Japanese Iraq Reconstruction and Support Group, the 600 troops were sent to Samawah to facilitate reconstruction efforts and keep the peace. Because of constitutional restraints, the soldiers of the JSDF were sent unarmed and placed under the protection of Australian forces. The troops were withdrawn in July 2006.

The Japanese Air Force has also been assisting coalition forces in Iraq since 2004 by helping airlift supplies and personnel to and from Kuwait. Although there is continuing debate in Japan concerning the length of the air mission, the operation was renewed until July 31, 2007, and then extended for an additional two years. The Iraqi operations have caused considerable debate in Japan, with many Japanese regarding them as illegal. In April 2008 Japan's Nagoya High Court ruled the Japanese air mission in Iraq as partly unconstitutional, although the Japanese government has stated that it will not be bound by the court's decision.

ROBERT H. CLEMM

See also

DESERT SHIELD, Operation; DESERT STORM, Operation; DESERT STORM, Operation, Coalition Nations' Contributions to; IRAQI FREEDOM, Operation

References

Blair, Arthur. *At War in the Gulf.* College Station: Texas A&M University Press, 1992.

Bouissou, Jean-Marie. *Japan: The Burden of Success.* Boulder, CO: Lynne Rienner, 2002.

Hutchinson, Kevin Don. *Operation Desert Shield/Desert Storm: Chronology and Fact Book.* Westport, CT: Greenwood, 1995.

Katzenstein, Peter J. *Cultural Norms and National Security: Police and Military in Postwar Japan.* Ithaca, NY: Cornell University Press, 1996.

Kawashima, Yutaka. *Japanese Foreign Policy at the Crossroads: Challenges and Options for the Twenty-first Century.* Washington, DC: Brookings Institution Press, 2003.

Jarrah, Ziyad al-

Birth Date: May 11, 1975
Death Date: September 11, 2001

Individual alleged to have been one of the 19 terrorists who carried out the September 11, 2001, attacks in the United States, although his family, girlfriend, and others contend that he was merely a passenger aboard United Airlines Flight 93, which crashed in southwestern Pennsylvania. The Federal Bureau of Investigation (FBI) alleged he was the pilot of the aircraft. It is believed that the hijackers had planned to crash the Boeing 757 into the U.S. Capitol or the White House in Washington, D.C. From a prosperous and influential Lebanese family, Ziyad Samir al-Jarrah was born on May 11, 1975, in Beirut, Lebanon. His father held a high-ranking post in the Lebanese social security system, and his mother taught school.

Jarrah attended Christian schools in Lebanon. After Jarrah completed his schooling, the family sent him to study biochemistry in Greifswald, Germany, in the spring of 1996. There, he met Aysel Sengün, a young Turkish student, and they lived together as a couple from 1999.

Jarrah had little in common with the other hijackers. He never evinced beliefs similar to the others in the group and had no connection with the mosque attended by others in Hamburg, Germany; indeed, he rarely attended the mosque, and friends could not remember seeing him pray. He apparently had no connection with Muhammad Atta, one of the better-known hijackers, but did appear in a photograph at a wedding of someone who Atta knew.

Jarrah decided to study aeronautical engineering at Hamburg University at the Institute of Applied Science, which was located in a different area of the city from the Hamburg cell members' residences or places of study. He had a serious relationship with his girlfriend, and his family assumed they would marry.

According to the official accounts of the hijackers, Jarrah traveled to Las Vegas at the same time as others in the plot and enrolled in flight school, supposedly because his major in aeronautical engineering would last two years. He is also alleged to have traveled to Afghanistan, based on videotape evidence, which some doubters believe was doctored to include images of the hijackers.

Allegedly, Jarrah trained at an Al Qaeda camp beginning in November 1999. He entered the United States on June 27, 2000, and trained at the Florida Flight Training Center in Venice, Florida. His flight instructor considered him an average pilot, and he received a license to fly a single-engine plane after about six months of study; it was issued on July 30, 2001.

In January 2001 Jarrah returned to Germany. In April he was back in the United States, living in Hollywood, Florida, and taking martial arts lessons. Jarrah made a trip to Germany to visit his girlfriend, leaving on July 25 and returning on August 4. While still in Germany, he received word that he had qualified for a commercial license to fly single-engine aircraft. Upon his return to Florida, Jarrah began to study the manuals for flying Boeing 757 and 767 aircraft. Later that month, he moved to an apartment in Lauderdale-by-the-Sea with Ahmed al-Haznawi. Throughout late August and September, Jarrah traveled frequently from south Florida to the Washington, D.C., area. On September 7 he traveled from Fort Lauderdale to Newark, New Jersey, on a Continental Airlines flight with Haznawi. Jarrah reappeared in the Washington, D.C., area, receiving a speeding ticket on Interstate 95 in Maryland. He and two of his fellow conspirators finally checked in at the Newark Airport Marriott soon after midnight on September 11. Before boarding United Airlines Flight 93, Jarrah made a phone call to Sengün in Germany.

The FBI asserts that Jarrah was the pilot of the hijacked United Airlines Flight 93, although his family asserts he was merely a passenger unlucky enough to be aboard. Once in the air, the hijackers seized control of the aircraft; the new pilot headed the plane toward Washington. There were only three hijackers to control the crew and passengers.

Soon passengers learned through cell phone calls that the aircraft was to be used as a flying bomb. They rose up and attempted to regain control of the plane. When it became apparent that they were about to overpower the hijackers, the pilot apparently crashed the aircraft into the ground near Shanksville, Pennsylvania. Jarrah and three other hijackers died in the crash, as did the 40 passengers and crew members.

STEPHEN A. ATKINS

See also

Al Qaeda; Atta, Muhammad; Bin Laden, Osama; Hamburg Cell; September 11 Attacks

References

Bernstein, Richard. *Out of the Blue: The Story of September 11, 2001, from Jihad to Ground Zero.* New York: Times Books, 2002.

Longman, Jere. *Among the Heroes: United Flight 93 and the Passengers and Crew Who Fought Back.* New York: Perennial, 2003.

McDermott, Terry. *Perfect Soldiers: The 9/11 Hijackers: Who They Were, Why They Did It.* New York: HarperCollins, 2005.

Jihad

The term "jihad" (*jehad*) is often translated as "holy war." It means "striving" or "to exert the utmost effort" and refers both to a religious duty to spread and defend Islam by waging war (lesser jihad) and an inward spiritual struggle to attain perfect faith (greater jihad.) The distinction between lesser and greater is not accepted by all Muslims in all circumstances. Many distinguish between jihad as an individual versus a collective duty, as when Muslims face attack or cannot practice their faith (individual duty) or when led by an appropriate Muslim authority (collective duty). In general, mainstream modern Islam emphasizes the greater jihad, the struggle to be a good Muslim, while recognizing the lesser jihad, the struggle through war as a historical necessity.

Within the spectrum of Islamic belief, definitions of jihad have also rested on historical circumstances. Nineteenth-century Indian reformer Sayyid Ahmad Khan argued for a more limited interpretation of jihad whereby believers could perform acts of piety or charity in place of armed struggle and that it was incumbent only if Muslims could not practice their faith. But others held that Khan's ideas were innovative and thus false. The reform movement of Muhammad ibn abd al-Wahhab in 18th-century Arabia, in contrast, reasserted the incumbency of jihad as armed struggle for all believers. As the Qur'an contains verses that promote mercy and urge peacemaking but also verses (referred to as the Sword Verses) that more ardently require jihad of believers, there is a scriptural basis for both sides of this argument.

Interpretations of the Qur'anic statements about the nature of jihad began when the early Muslims at Medina created an Islamic state in 622 CE. but faced the armed warriors of Mecca. The initial mention of jihad in the Qur'an (22:39) deals with defensive warfare only, and the statement "those who stay at home" could be taken as a condemnation of those who abstained from an early key battle of the Muslims against the Meccan forces. Many Muslim scholars believed that the admonition to pursue an aggressive jihad "with their wealth and their persons" (Qur'an 4:95) overrode verses revealed earlier on. Fighting and warfare (*qital*) are, however, differentiated from jihad, which is always accompanied by the phrase "*ala sabil Allah*" ("on the path of God"), similar to the way that just war is differentiated from other forms of conflict in the Christian tradition.

Some scholars differentiate the fulfilling of jihad by the heart, the tongue, or the sword as a means of preserving the Muslim community, but such teachings have by and large been contradicted by the revival of activist jihad, first in response to European 19th-century colonialism and then again in the 20th century.

Mainstream Islam considers foreign military intervention; foreign occupation; economic oppression; non-Islamic cultural realignment; colonialism; and the oppression of a domestic government, either secular or Islamic, of an Islamic people or country to be a sufficient reason, if not a Qur'anic mandate, to participate in a defensive jihad. The more militant and fundamental end of the Islamic spectrum asserts that a social, economic, and military defensive jihad is justifiable and necessary. A widespread discussion of jihad is ongoing in the Muslim world today in response to the rise of militancy, however, and there is a concerted effort to separate the concepts of jihad and martyrdom when they are the rallying call of such irresponsible extremists as Osama bin Laden.

Notable defensive jihads in the more recent history of Islam include the resistance of the Afghan (1979) and Chechnyan (ongoing) mujahideen against their respective Soviet and Russian occupations, and the struggle of Algerians to gain independence from France in the Algerian War (1954–1962). Some Islamic religious scholars, such as Abdullah Yusuf Azzam, a former professor of bin Laden, have argued for jihad against the West. Numerous clerics and scholars have held, along with the views of their communities, that the Palestinian struggle against Israel is a defensive jihad because of the infringements on life and liberty, the use of collective punishment, and the seizure by Israel of *waqf* (endowment) lands.

Essentially, the early Muslim community adopted offensive jihad because no defensive action would have protected them against the allied tribal forces determined to exterminate them. In such a jihad, the Peoples of the Book (*dhimma*), meaning other monotheistic traditions like Judaism and Christianity, must be treated differently than enemies who are unbelievers (*kuffar*). The Peoples of the Book must submit to Islamic rule, however, including the paying of poll and land taxes. Rules of engagement, truces, and treatment of prisoners and non-Muslims were all specified in medieval texts concerned with *siyar*, or Islamic international law.

Classical Islamic law and tradition asserts that a jihad that is a collective duty (simplified in Western texts as an offensive jihad) can be declared only by the caliph, the successor to the prophet Muhammad and the lawful temporal and spiritual authority for the entire Islamic community. On the other hand, no authority other than conscience or the awareness of an oppression targeting Islam or Islamic peoples is necessary to participate in an individually incumbent jihad.

When the Mongols attacked Baghdad in 1258, the caliphate, long since a divided patchwork of sultanates and emirates, ceased to exist. It was the only political structure recognized by the classical interpretation of Islamic doctrine as being capable of leading a (offensive) jihad. That did not prevent the Ottoman sultans from declaring themselves caliphs and calling for jihad, but the Muslim world did not recognize them as such. Other jihads were declared in the early modern period, for instance by the Mahdiyya of the Sudan, the Wahhabi in Arabia, and the Sanusiyya in present-day Libya.

Leaders of such movements, like contemporary jihadists, have sometimes proclaimed jihads by issuing a fatwa, or statement. Although a fatwa is supposed to be a legal response issued by a qualified jurist, self-proclaimed leaders and clerics sometimes say that the traditional *ulema*, or mullahs, crushed by modern state governments, have failed in their duty and therefore claim the right to speak in their stead.

Although many Muslims recognize their respective governments and political leaders as worthy of defining and declaring

Pakistani demonstrator with a placard reading "Jihad is Not Terrorism, Jihad is our Life," October 15, 2001. (Pascal Le Segretain/Corbis Sygma)

defensive jihads, many others perceive their governments as illegitimate Islamic states or their leaders as illegitimate Islamic leaders. Turkey, Egypt, and Pakistan, for example, are quasi-democratic states that grant secular political parties and politicians the same rights as Islamic political parties and politicians. Islamic militant groups in all three countries see these governments and their leaders as heretical and illegitimate under Sharia (Islamic law). In a similar vein, some Muslims, most notably the Takfiri (apostates), declare jihad against Muslim governments perceived as oppressive, anti-Islamic, or corrupt (that is, being "non-Muslim," in their eyes). Additionally, many of the Islamic theocratic monarchies, such as Saudi Arabia, are deemed illegitimate by fundamentalist Muslims. This perception is due in part to the willingness of some of these monarchies and democracies to cooperate and form alliances with non-Islamic nations or with nations that wage economic, cultural, or military war against Islam and Muslims. Some of these monarchies and democracies also limit the power of the clerics within their countries.

Various Islamic movements, most notably Al Qaeda, have stepped into the void created by the disappearance of the caliphate and the resultant fractured Islamic political and religious world. These movements have interpreted Islam as they wish and declared jihad as they desire, although often with the assistance and support of some clerics as well as leaders with a degree of

religious knowledge. Because early Muslims killed in jihad were considered martyrs, there is an extensive tradition that exalts martyrdom. The possibility of martyrdom appeals to modern jihadists, particularly younger or more desperate followers. Defensive jihad, inclusive of martyrdom, is deemed appropriate in order to end Israel's occupation of the perceived Islamic territories of the West Bank, East Jerusalem, and Gaza Strip, if not all of Palestine.

A martyr secures a place in paradise and may intercede for other Muslims. Antiterrorist campaigns in the Muslim world have argued, against the weight of literature and popular belief, that modern jihadists are not martyrs if they set out to martyr themselves, because suicide is forbidden in Islam. Noncombatant Muslims who perish in a jihad are also considered martyrs. Jihadists thus excuse the deaths of innocents caught in their crossfire with targets or authorities. They explain the deaths of non-Muslim civilians as being deserved for their failure to submit to Islam or for their open oppression of Islam or Islamic peoples. In the case of Israeli civilians, the fact that all provide military service to their country means that they are not really considered civilians by the jihadists.

The term "jihad" is incorporated into the organizational names of numerous militant groups, including the Egyptian Islamic Jihad, the Egyptian and former Iraqi Tawhid wal-Jihad, and the Palestinian Islamic Jihad.

The struggle in contemporary Islam to redefine jihad and detach its meaning from adventurism, martyrdom, and attacks on Muslim governments as well as Westerners is one of the most significant challenges at this time in history.

RICHARD EDWARDS AND SHERIFA ZUHUR

See also

Al Qaeda; Fatwa; Hamas; Islamic Jihad, Palestinian; Martyrdom; Qur'an; Sharia; Terrorism; Wahhabism

References

Bostrom, Andrew G., ed. *The Legacy of Jihad: Islamic Holy War and the Fate of Non-Muslims.* Amherst, NY: Prometheus, 2005.

Delong-Bas, Natana. *Wahhabi Islam: From Revival and Reform to Global Jihad.* Oxford: Oxford University Press, 2004.

Esposito, John. *Unholy War: Terror in the Name of Islam.* New York: Oxford University Press USA, 2003.

Fregosi, Paul. *Jihad in the West: Muslim Conquests from the 7th to the 21st Centuries.* Amherst, NY: Prometheus, 1998.

Kepel, Gilles. *Jihad: The Trail of Political Islam.* Cambridge, MA: Belknap, 2003.

John Paul II, Pope
Birth Date: May 18, 1920
Death Date: April 2, 2005

Roman Catholic prelate and pope (1978–2005). Born in Wadowice, Poland, on May 18, 1920, Karol Jósef Wojtyła grew up in humble circumstances and knew hardship as a youth. His mother died when he was just nine years old, and three years later his only sibling, a brother, also died. An engaging young man who was an exemplary student, Wojtyła enrolled in the faculty of philosophy at Jagellonian University in Krakow in 1938.

To avoid imprisonment under the German occupation during World War II after September 1939, Wojtyła was forced to work first in a stone quarry and then in a chemical plant. In 1942 he clandestinely entered an underground seminary in Krakow and enrolled in the faculty of theology at Jagellonian University.

Wojtyła transferred to the archbishop of Krakow's residence in August 1944, where he remained until Poland was liberated in 1945. In 1946 Wojtyła completed his fourth year of studies, was ordained a priest, and left for Rome for postgraduate studies. In 1947 he earned his licentiate in theology. The following year he earned a master's degree and doctorate in sacred theology from Jagellonian University.

In the late 1940s and into the mid-1950s Wojtyła served in a variety of pastoral positions in Poland, began to publish, and ultimately held the chair of ethics at Poland's Catholic University in Lublin in 1956. He was named auxiliary bishop in the archbishopric of Krakow in 1958, becoming its archbishop in 1964. All the while he labored under the considerable restrictions of communist-controlled Poland, which was openly hostile toward the Catholic Church. Wojtyła became a cardinal in 1967. During the early

to mid-1970s he continued to publish prolifically on a wide range of scholarly and theological topics. He also traveled extensively.

On October 16, 1978, following the sudden death of Pope John Paul I, Wojtyła was elected pope on the eighth balloting, astounding many pundits. In honor of his immediate predecessor, he took the name John Paul II and became the first non-Italian pope in 455 years. At 58 years old, he was also an unusually youthful pontiff who was an avid skier, swimmer, and hiker.

From the very beginning of his pontificate, John Paul II, who spoke eight languages, eschewed many of the trappings of his office. Instead, he became known as a master communicator who relished personal contacts, often wading into huge crowds. Just eight months into his pontificate, he paid an emotional nine-day visit to his native Poland, the first pope to visit the nation. His sojourn caused great consternation among communist officials, who feared that the pope's strong anticommunist sentiments would result in popular unrest. Although this did not immediately happen, communist officials had much to worry about. By the early 1980s John Paul II had tacitly aligned himself with Poland's Solidarity movement, and by the early 1990s he was credited with being a key force behind the events of 1989 that swept away communist rule in Eastern Europe and hastened the end of the Cold War.

The pope's attitude toward the Middle East was in many ways a radical departure from that of his predecessors. He was a tireless proponent of peace in the region, and he championed both Muslim and Jewish causes. Although he decried the violence of radical Palestinians, he was nonetheless supportive of Palestinian statehood. Instead of highlighting the differences between Christianity and Islam, he viewed them as complementary religions, sharing many of the same tenets and historical figures. This was a far different path than those of his predecessors, who saw Islam in an antipathetic light. Indeed, the pope helped narrow the chasm between the Muslim and Christian worlds. At the same time, he was a supporter of Israel and tried to bridge the considerable and centuries-long gap between Jews and the Catholic Church.

Throughout his long papacy, the pope sought to build bridges with both the Jewish and Muslim communities. His explicit admissions of wrongdoing toward both groups by the Catholic Church of the past earned him a good number of supporters in each camp. Clearly, he was unable to heal the rift between Israelis and Palestinians or between Jews and Muslims. What he did do, however, was to identify with the injustices of all.

In 2001 John Paul II became the first pontiff in the 2,000-year history of the Catholic Church to make an official visit to a mosque. The dramatic gesture, which took place in an ancient mosque in Damascus, Syria, was heightened when the pope urged Christians and Muslims to forgive one another and work toward common goals of peace and justice.

In 1979 John Paul II visited the Auschwitz concentration camp, and in 2001 he traveled to Israel and prayed for forgiveness at Yad Vashem, which deeply moved many Jews. In 1986 he became the first pope to officially visit a synagogue, another hugely important act of symbolism. His approaches to the Jewish and Arab worlds were not without their detractors. Some hard-line Muslims savaged him for his attempts to heal the rift with the Jews. Many Israelis, on the other hand, criticized his failure to support the Iraq War (2003). John Paul II was also critical of the U.S. war in Afghanistan, believing that too many innocent civilians were being killed or wounded, and he signaled only tepid acceptance of the Persian Gulf War of 1991. Indeed, before that conflict he had urged both the Iraqis and the international coalition to exhibit restraint and avoid military confrontation, but to no avail.

Pope John Paul II was the most visible and well-traveled pontiff in history. During his reign he completed 104 foreign pastoral visits. He was also the first pontiff to visit a predominantly Orthodox nation (Romania in 1999). It is hard to overstate the impact that John Paul II had on world politics, as he reached out in an unprecedented way to the world's Jews as well as Muslims and non-Catholic Christians.

In affairs of social justice, faith, and Church governance, John Paul II was at once liberal and conservative. On most social issues he was considered liberal and was a vocal critic of both communism and the excesses of capitalism. He frequently decried the gap between rich and poor nations and was a champion of the world's impoverished and downtrodden. He had little use for political oppression of any stripe and was also an ardent foe of the death penalty and abortion. These stances made him popular with both liberals and conservatives around the world. Yet in terms of Catholic doctrine, the pope was conservative if not orthodox. He steadfastly refused to consider the ordination of women, the abandonment of celibacy for Catholic clergy, or the lifting of the Church's ban on contraception.

John Paul II died in Rome on April 2, 2005, after battling a series of debilitating ailments, some of which were the result of a near-mortal gunshot wound he received at the hands of a Turkish extremist during a May 1981 assassination attempt in St. Peter's Square.

PAUL G. PIERPAOLI JR. AND LUC STENGER

See also
Arab-Israeli Conflict, Overview

References
Ascherson, Neal. *The Struggles for Poland*. London: M. Joseph, 1987.
John Paul II, Pope. *In My Own Words*. New York: Gramercy, 2002.
McBrien, Richard P. *Lives of the Popes: The Pontiffs from St. Peter to John Paul II*. San Francisco: Harper San Francisco, 1997.
Szulc, Tad. *Pope John Paul II: The Biography*. New York: Scribner, 1995.
Weigel, George. *Witness to Hope: The Biography of John Paul II*. New York: HarperCollins, 1999.

Joint Chiefs of Staff

The principal military advisory group to the president of the United States and the secretary of defense, composed of the chiefs of staff of the U.S. Army and the U.S. Air Force, the chief of U.S. Navy operations, the commandant of the U.S. Marine Corps, and the chairman and vice chairman of the Joint Chiefs of Staff (JCS). The National Security Act of 1947 changed the JCS from executive agents dealing with theater and area commanders to planners and advisers.

The JCS originally consisted of only the service chiefs of the U.S. Army, U.S. Navy, and U.S. Air Force and the chairman. The commandant of the U.S. Marine Corps became a member later, and even later the position of vice chairman was established by the Goldwater-Nichols Act. The chairman and vice chairman can be appointed from any of the four services.

Responsibilities as members of the JCS took precedence over duties as the chiefs of military services. The president nominated the chairman for appointment, and the U.S. Senate confirmed him. By statute, the chairman was either a full (four-star) general or a full admiral and served a two-year tour of duty. The president had discretionary power to renominate the chairman for additional two-year terms.

The 1986 Goldwater-Nichols Department of Defense Reorganization Act identified the chairman of the JCS as the senior-ranking member of the armed forces. As such, the chairman of the JCS serves as the principal military adviser to the president, the secretary of defense, and the National Security Council (NSC). In carrying out his duties, the chairman of the JCS consults with and seeks the advice of the other members of the JCS and the combatant commanders, as he considers appropriate.

All JCS members are by law military advisers, and they can respond to a request or voluntarily submit, through the chairman, advice or opinions to the president, the secretary of defense, or the NSC. The modern JCS has no executive authority to command combatant forces. In fact, the JCS members are bypassed in the chain of command so that responsibilities for conducting military operations flows from the president to the secretary of defense directly to the commanders of the Unified Combatant Commands. However, the JCS members have authority over personnel assignments, equipment, training, operational doctrine, and resource management of their respective services as well as oversight of resources and personnel allocated by their services to the combatant commands.

Collectively, the JCS serves as the second-highest deliberative body for military policy behind the NSC. The chairman of the JCS is also a member of the NSC. As of 2008, there were eight directorates of the JCS: J1 Personnel and Manpower; J2 Intelligence; J3 Operations; J4 Logistics; J5 Strategic Plans and Policy; J6 Command, Control, Communications and Computer Systems; J7 Operational Plans and Joint Force Development; and J8 Force Structure, Resources, and Assessment.

When Iraq invaded Kuwait on August, 2 1990, the members of the JCS were General Colin L. Powell, chairman; Admiral David Jeremiah, vice chairman; General Michael J. Dugan, U.S. Air Force chief of staff; General Carl Vuono, U.S. Army chief of staff; Admiral Frank B. Kelso II, chief of U.S. Navy operations; and General Alfred Gray, U.S. Marine Corps commandant. At a time when most senior military men were uneasy about the defense of Saudi Arabia and wanted to avoid giving Iraqi leader Saddam Hussein an additional incentive to invade, Dugan promoted the notion that strategic airpower provided a near-term offensive option. His public promotion of this idea included comments about targeting Hussein and his family. Dugan's comments made newspaper headlines and infuriated Powell, who accused Dugan of leaking secret information and misrepresenting the war plans. In September 1990 General Merrill McPeak replaced Dugan.

The JCS participated in all the important decisions regarding Operations DESERT SHIELD and DESERT STORM. Once the ground invasion began in February 1991, the JCS proved particularly wary of what might go wrong and sensitive to avoiding needless American casualties. This attitude frequently put the JCS at odds with White House officials who were eager to teach Hussein a lesson by seriously degrading Iraq's military. Chairman Powell was a particular voice of caution and restraint, and he played a pivotal role in the controversial decision recommending a quick end to the war that did not include the toppling of Hussein's regime.

After the Persian Gulf War ended, U.S. Army general John M. D. Shalikashvili served as chairman of the JCS, replacing Powell in 1993. Shalikashvili stayed on until 1997. During his tenure, the JCS examined the lessons from the Persian Gulf War and focused on the long lead times required to move substantial forces and their

logistical backing to the Gulf region. A result of this examination was the prepositioning of equipment and supplies in the Gulf. U.S. Army general Henry H. Shelton was JCS chairman during the September 11, 2001, terrorist attacks on the United States. He retired on October 1, 2001.

Having served as vice chairman of the JCS from March 2000 to September 2001, U.S. Air Force general Richard B. Myers became the chairman of the JCS on October 1, 2001. He served in that capacity during the earliest planning stages for the Global War on Terror, including Operations ENDURING FREEDOM and IRAQI FREEDOM. As such, Myers served as the military's public face by conducting high-level media briefings. His air force experience as commander in chief of the U.S. Space Command clearly informed his keen understanding of the role that command, control, communications, and computers played in the battlefield. He also acknowledged the necessity for networked joint interagency computers and the need to link sensor and reconnaissance platforms with shooting platforms. Also, Myers promoted enhanced joint warfighting capabilities.

Upon Meyer's retirement in 2005, U.S. Marine Corps general Peter Pace, who had become vice chairman of the JCS on September 30, 2001, became chairman. Pace was the first marine officer to hold either the vice chairman or the chairman positions. Pace's tenure coincided with a major escalation in the Iraqi insurgency.

Chairman of the U.S. Joint Chiefs of Staff Navy admiral Mike Mullen testifies before the U.S. Senate Committee on Foreign Relations on December 3, 2009, about President Barack Obama's decision to send an additional 30,000 troops to Afghanistan. (U.S. Department of Defense)

However, his comments in 2007 concerning homosexuals (he termed homosexual acts "immoral") and gays in the military caused an uproar that turned many against him. In 2005 Pace also publicly disagreed with Secretary of Defense Donald Rumsfeld concerning torture, and in 2007 Pace contradicted the White House's contention that Iran was supplying arms to Iraqi insurgents. In June 2008 Secretary of Defense Robert Gates recommended that Pace not be renominated for another term, fearing that he would be the object of protracted grilling by a Democratically controlled Congress upset with the progress of the war.

In turn, Admiral Mike Mullen became chairman on October 1, 2007. With considerable reluctance, the JCS endorsed the George W. Bush administration's troop surge strategy in Iraq, which began in the late winter of 2007. Likewise, the JCS acquiesced to President Barrack Obama's intentions to drawn down forces in Iraq and send reinforcements to Afghanistan. On January 27, 2009, JCS chairman Admiral Mullen stated that America's most challenging security threat was centered in Afghanistan and Pakistan, which seemed to confirm the new president's military focus.

JAMES ARNOLD

See also

Bush, George Herbert Walker; Bush, George Walker; Gates, Robert Michael; Mullen, Michael Glenn; Obama, Barack Hussein, II; Pace, Peter; Powell, Colin Luther; Rumsfeld, Donald Henry; Shalikashvili, John Malchese David

References

Burton, James G. *The Pentagon Wars.* Annapolis, MD: Naval Institute Press, 1993.

Gordon, Michael R., and General Bernard E. Trainor. *The Generals' War: The Inside Story of the Conflict in the Gulf.* New York: Little, Brown, 1995.

Scales, Robert H. *Certain Victory: The U.S. Army in the Gulf War.* Washington, DC: Brassey's, 1994.

Joint Direct Attack Munition and Small Diameter Bomb

Two highly accurate, all-weather, autonomous air-delivered weapons developed by the U.S. Air Force that utilize the precise timing signal of the Navigation Signal Timing and Ranging (NAVSTAR) Global Positioning System (GPS) satellites for all-weather precision attacks of ground targets. The Joint Direct Attack Munition (JDAM) is a tail kit that attaches to the rear of conventional 500-pound, 1,000-pound, or 2,000-pound gravity bombs. The carrying aircraft can launch the weapon up to 15 miles from the target and program each weapon it carries to strike separate targets. Once released, the bomb's Inertial Navigation System (INS)/GPS guides the bomb to its target regardless of weather conditions. The weapon can impact within 5 yards of the target in the GPS-aided INS mode or within 10 yards in INS-only mode.

The U.S. Air Force began developing the JDAM in the late 1980s but shelved it in 1989. During the Persian Gulf War, however, the air force discovered that clouds and smoke adversely affected the accuracy of its laser-guided bombs. Chief of staff of the air force General Merrill A. McPeak subsequently directed the development of an all-weather, low-cost, and highly accurate air-delivered weapon. In 1995 McDonnell Douglas (now Boeing) began producing the JDAM tail kits at a cost of $18,000 each. Today, every strike aircraft in the U.S. Air Force, the U.S. Navy, and the U.S. Marine Corps and many strike aircraft of U.S. allies can carry the JDAM.

The JDAM, launched from the B-2 Spirit bomber, first saw combat during Operation ALLIED FORCE, the North Atlantic Treaty Organization (NATO) 1999 bombing campaign against the Federal Republic of Serbia. Flying nonstop from Whiteman Air Force Base, Missouri, the B-2s, equipped with 16 2,000-pound JDAMs, each delivered more than 650 JDAMs with 96 percent reliability and hit 87 percent of their intended targets during the campaign. The bombers could launch the JDAMs individually or in groups, each programmed to hit a separate target.

During Operation ENDURING FREEDOM that began in October 2001, the JDAM quickly became the air-delivered weapon of choice to attack enemy forces in close proximity to friendly forces or civilian centers. Using laser range-finding binoculars and GPS receivers, special operations ground controllers with Northern Alliance forces identified targets and relayed the coordinates to the Air Operations Center in Kuwait or to aircraft over the battlefield.

The venerable Boeing B-52 Stratofortress and the 20-year-old Rockwell International B-1B Lancer, carrying up to 24 2,000-pound JDAMs each, loitered over the battlefield up to eight hours a day with air refueling, waiting for new targeting data, until they expended their ordnance. These strategic bombers had essentially become on-call aerial artillery. Many carrier-based aircraft took off without knowing the location of their targets, receiving this data only as they entered the combat zone.

After the Anglo-American–led invasion of Iraq in March 2003 and during the continuing combat in Afghanistan and in Iraq, U.S. and coalition aircraft continued to refine procedures to hit targets of opportunity with JDAMs in near real time. As combat operations continued, the war fighters in the Middle East identified the need for two additional capabilities: a JDAM capable of striking moving targets and a precise weapon with a smaller blast and fragmentation pattern than the 500-pound JDAM. By mid-2007 the Air Armament Center, Eglin Air Force Base, Florida, had developed the Laser JDAM with a laser seeker in the nose that tracks and hits a target moving up to 50 miles per hour and awarded the production contract to Boeing.

The U.S. Air Force began development of the Small Diameter Bomb (SDB) in 2003. It is only six feet long and weighs 285 pounds. It comes in two variants, one with GPS/INS guidance only and one with GPS/INS guidance and a laser seeker to hit moving targets. Its special bomb carriage system can carry four SDBs on one weapons station. The weapon can be launched up to 60 miles from the target. Because of its smaller size, strike aircraft can carry more individual weapons, giving the fliers increased kills per mission.

U.S. Air Force F-15E Strike Eagle aircraft from the 335th Fighter Squadron drop Joint Direct Attack Munitions (JDAMs) on a cave in eastern Afghanistan on November 26, 2009. (U.S. Department of Defense)

It also provides reduced collateral damage in urban areas (such as those in Iraq) in which the military struggles at times to find a weapon with the desired kill effect but without excessive blast or fragmentation effects.

The U.S. Air Force declared the SDB operational in September 2006 with initial integration with the F-15E Strike Eagle with follow-on integration on other air force strike aircraft. Because of its capabilities, the SDB system is an important air-delivered weapon in the ongoing Global War on Terror.

ROBERT B. KANE

See also

B-52 Stratofortress; Bombs, Gravity; Bombs, Precision-Guided; ENDURING FREEDOM, Operation, U.S. Air Campaign; IRAQI FREEDOM, Operation, Air Campaign; Navigation Satellite Timing and Ranging Global Positioning System

References

History Office. *History of the Air Armament Center, 1 October 2006–30 September 2007.* Eglin Air Force Base, FL: Air Armament Center, 2008.

Lambeth, Benjamin S. *Air Power against Terror: America's Conduct of Operation Enduring Freedom.* Santa Monica, CA: RAND Corporation, 2005.

———. *NATO's Air War for Kosovo: A Strategic and Operational Assessment.* Project Air Force Series on Operation Allied Force. Washington, DC: RAND Corporation, 2001.

Joint Surveillance and Target Radar System Aircraft

A Joint U.S. Air Force–U.S. Army airborne surveillance and target acquisition radar/command and control system built on a Boeing 707-300 airframe. There are currently 17 aircraft outfitted as Joint Surveillance and Target Radar System (JSTARS) aircraft, which are operated by the 116th Air Control Wing based at Robins Air Force Base, Georgia. The 116th is a joint wing staffed by both air force and army National Guard personnel. Each aircraft, when configured for JSTARS, cost approximately $250 million. The developer/builder of the system was Northrop Grumman. After an airframe was completed, it was shipped to Northrop-Grumman's Battle Management Systems Division in Melbourne, Florida, where the specialized electronics were installed and tested.

JSTARS was used in a limited capacity during the 1991 Persian Gulf War, flying 49 sorties, but it was still in its developmental phase. Nevertheless, in some 500 hours of flying, its success rate was held to be 100 percent. It was able to accurately detect Iraq's mobile forces, including tanks and mobile Scud missile launchers. The first fully deployable JSTARS aircraft was delivered in September 1996; since then, the aircraft have been deployed for peacekeeping missions in Bosnia-Herzegovina and in Kosovo. JSTARS have also been deployed to Afghanistan since 2001, and during March–April 2003 (Operation IRAQI FREEDOM) eight JSTARS flew some 50 missions over Iraq.

JSTARS aircraft provide information on ground situations via secure data links connected to mobile army stations, air force command posts, and far-removed command and information-gathering posts so that military analysts can properly interpret data being relayed. JSTARS give a complete picture of ground information, similar in nature to the information about air situations provided by the Airborne Warning and Control System (AWACS). JSTARS has the ability to determine the direction, number, and speed of all ground vehicles and other patterns of military activity. It can also provide similar information on helicopters. This allows air force and army commanders to make important decisions and to fine-tune attack plans and battle tactics on the fly in real time.

JSTARS aircraft employ four turbojet engines with 18,000 pounds of thrust each. The plane has an air endurance of 11 hours (20 hours with in-flight refueling). The aircraft is 152 feet 11 inches in length and 42 feet 6 inches high. It has a wing span of 145 feet 9 inches. Weight fully fueled is 155,000 pounds; it has a maximum gross weight of 336,000 pounds. Cruising speed is 448–586.8 miles per hour at a maximum ceiling of 42,000 feet. On a standard mission, JSTARS aircraft carry 21 personnel (3 flight crew and 19 systems operators). On longer missions, the crew can number as many as 34 people (6 flight crew and 28 systems operators). Beginning in 2006, Northrop-Grumman began upgrading JSTARS aircraft with more powerful engines and improved electronics. The first of the retrofitted aircraft are to be delivered in late 2010; the upgrades will likely continue into 2013. Perhaps the most recognizable part of the JSTARS is the huge 24-foot-long antenna mounted under the front of the aircraft, which can be swiveled into numerous configurations by operators during flight. By 2007, JSTARS aircraft had accrued 10,000 hours of combat missions, and their performance was hailed by both army and air force commanders.

The JSTARS aircraft features 17 operations consoles and 1 navigation/self-defense console. Each console is assigned to a specific operator with expertise in that specific area of data collection. To enhance its communications capabilities, JSTARS aircraft have 12 encrypted UHF radios, 2 encrypted HF radios, 3 encrypted VHF radios, and multiple intercom networks.

PAUL G. PIERPAOLI JR.

See also

Airborne Warning and Control System; Scud Missiles, U.S. Search for during the Persian Gulf War; United States Air Force, Afghanistan War; United States Air Force, Iraq War; United States Air Force, Persian Gulf War

References

Boyne, Walter J. *Beyond the Wild Blue: A History of the U.S. Air Force, 1947–2007.* 2nd ed. New York: Thomas Dunne Books, 2007.

Daso, Dik Alan. *The U.S. Air Force: A Complete History.* New York: Hugh Lauter Levin Associates, 2006.

Jordan

Middle Eastern nation covering 35,637 square miles, about the size of the U.S. state of Indiana. Jordan, officially known as the Hashimite Kingdom of Jordan, borders Israel and the West Bank to the west, Syria and the Golan Heights to the north, Iraq to the east, and Saudi Arabia to the east and south. Its current population is estimated at 6.05 million people. From 1516 to 1919 Jordan was part of the Ottoman Empire. With the end of World War I and the collapse of the Ottoman Empire, Transjordan (as it was then known) became part of Britain's League of Nations mandate over Palestine in 1920. In 1921 Abdullah ibn Hussein, a member of the Hashimite dynasty, became the de facto king of Transjordan. Transjordan became a constitutional monarchy under Abdullah I, who was formally placed on the throne by the British in 1928. Nevertheless, Transjordan was still considered part of the British Mandate. That changed in May 1946 when Transjordan secured its independence.

Because Transjordan was a member of the Arab League when the State of Israel was created in May 1948, Abdullah was obliged to fight alongside his Arab neighbors against the Israelis. As with most Arabs, he flatly rejected Zionist ambitions. Jordan gained legal authority over the West Bank in 1949 as a result of the Israeli War of Independence (1948–1949). Abdullah strongly supported Palestinian rights and officially changed his country's name to Jordan to differentiate the new territories west of the Jordan River from the broader Transjordan. Months later he was accused of trying to permanently annex the West Bank, although the charges might have arisen due to his proposal 10 years earlier arguing for the creation of a united Arab kingdom of Transjordan and Palestine. Jordan, unlike other Arab states, allowed Palestinians to take Jordanian citizenship.

A large number of displaced Palestinians, about 70,000 by 1949, fled to Jordan, and 280,000 Palestinians were already residing in or fled to the West Bank. The Palestinian population outnumbered the Jordanian population, and although these people received citizenship, their identity and aspirations were a point of tension within Jordan. In 1951 a Palestinian assassinated Abdullah in Jerusalem, and the following year he was succeeded by his grandson, King Hussein I. Hussein ruled Jordan for the next 47 years.

A series of anti-Western uprisings in Jordan, combined with the 1956 Suez Crisis, compelled Hussein to sever military ties to Britain. The British government had taken part in a covert scheme with the French and Israeli governments to topple Egyptian president Gamal Abdel Nasser and wrest back control of the Suez Canal from the Egyptians.

In February 1958 Hussein formed the Arab Federation with Iraq. The king viewed this as a needed countermeasure to the newly established United Arab Republic (UAR), formed between Egypt and Syria and dominated by Nasser, Egypt's Pan-Arab nationalist president. The Arab Federation fell apart by the autumn of 1958, however, after the Iraqi king was overthrown in a coup. Later that same year, leaders of the UAR called for the overthrow of governments in Beirut and Amman. Hussein fought back by requesting help from the British, who dispatched troops to Jordan to quell antigovernment protests. The Americans had simultaneously sent troops to Lebanon to bolster its besieged Christian-led government.

Jordan's relations with the UAR remained tense. Indeed, in 1963 when a rival Jordanian government-in-exile was set up in Damascus, Syria, King Hussein declared a state of emergency. The crisis subsided when the United States and Britain publicly endorsed Hussein's rule. For good measure, the United States placed its Sixth Fleet on alert in the Mediterranean.

After the mid-1960s and more than a decade of crises and regional conflicts, Hussein turned his attention to domestic issues. He was devoted to improving the welfare of his people and launched major programs to improve literacy rates (which were very low), increase educational opportunities, bolster public health initiatives, and lower infant mortality rates. In these endeavors he was quite successful. By the late 1980s literacy rates approached 100 percent, and infant deaths were down dramatically. Jordan's economy also began to expand as the nation engaged in more trade with the outside world and as its relations with Egypt improved. Hussein also began to erect a modern and reliable transportation system and moved to modernize the country's infrastructure. Notable in all of this was that he accomplished much without resorting to overly repressive tactics. Indeed, throughout the Cold War most Jordanians enjoyed a level of freedom virtually unrivaled in the Middle East. However, the government undertook sharp responses to antiregime elements and tensions with the Palestinian population.

By the late 1960s another Arab-Israeli conflict was in the making. After Egypt blockaded Israeli shipping in the Gulf of Aqaba in 1967, King Hussein signed a mutual defense pact with Egypt, setting aside his former differences with Nasser's government. Normally a moderating force in volatile Middle East politics, Hussein reluctantly entered the war on the side of Egypt, even as Tel Aviv was imploring him though diplomatic channels not to do so. When the June 1967 Six-Day War ended, Israel took from Jordan the entire West Bank and all of Jerusalem.

As a result of the war, thousands of Palestinians fled to Jordan from the West Bank, now controlled by Israel. Indeed, it is estimated that as many as 300,000 Palestinians poured into Jordan after June 1967, swelling the Palestinian refugee population there to almost 1 million. This massive influx severely taxed Jordanian infrastructure as well as schools, health care, and other services and engendered considerable resentment among some Jordanians. The number of Palestinians in Jordan by 1968 meant that Palestinian groups—especially resistance groups such as the fedayeen—increased their power and clout considerably within Jordan. These groups were well armed (receiving significant assistance from Syria and Egypt) and posed a serious threat to Hussein's rule. By 1970 it appeared as if the Palestinian resistance fighters were in the process of creating a Palestinian state within a state, much as they would do in Lebanon. This situation greatly alarmed King Hussein.

In early 1970 Palestinian guerrilla groups and the Palestine Liberation Organization (PLO) were already skirmishing with Jordanian troops. Open warfare erupted in June. Heretofore the Jordanian Army had been unsuccessful in its attempts to stop Palestinian attacks on Israel from taking place on Jordanian soil. Hussein also opposed the Palestinian aims of creating a Palestinian state in the West Bank, which he hoped to regain in the future.

In September 1970 following 10 days of bloody conflict, thousands of Palestinians, including the leadership of the PLO, fled Jordan for Syria and Lebanon. Hussein and his government were deeply troubled by this conflict, as were many of the Jordanians of Palestinian origin. From the Palestinian perspective, the fighting and forced expulsion in September were seen as a great betrayal. Indeed, the Palestinians referred to the events of September 1970 as Black September.

The early 1970s saw continued unrest. In 1972 King Hussein tried to create a new Arab federation, which would have included the West Bank. Israel as well as most of the Arab states flatly rejected the idea. In December 1972, Hussein was nearly assassinated by a Palestinian.

During the 1973 Yom Kippur (Ramadan) War Hussein played only a minor role, ordering a limited troop deployment (one brigade) to fight in Syria. In 1974 he finally agreed to recognize the Arab League's position that the PLO was the sole representative of the Palestinian people.

Beginning in the late 1970s Hussein strengthened relations with neighboring Syria, and he vigorously opposed the 1979 Israeli-Egyptian peace treaty. Jordan backed Iraq in the Iran-Iraq War (1980–1988). The 1980s was a period of economic chaos for the Jordanian people. Job creation did not keep pace with the expanding population, resulting in high unemployment. Inflation became a problem, foreign investment fell off, and exports declined. In 1989 riots occurred in southern Jordan over the lack of jobs and a government-mandated increase in basic commodities, including electricity and water. These severe economic dislocations led Hussein to seek U.S. financial aid in the late 1980s, and the nation's foreign debt burden grew substantially.

When King Hussein refused to condemn Iraqi dictator Saddam Hussein in the 1991 Persian Gulf War, U.S. assistance and much general Western aid was curtailed. Saudi Arabia and later Kuwait also withheld financial support, and Jordan's economy went from bad to worse. When some 700,000 Jordanians returned to Jordan because they were now unwelcome in Kuwait and Saudi Arabia, the economic situation became truly dire. Jordan's tourism declined precipitously after 1991, oil came at a very high premium, and exports suffered enormously. By 1995 unemployment stood at 14 percent (as stated by the government), although other measures estimated that it may have been twice that. Not until 2001 did the economy begin to regain its footing. Hussein's decision to back Iraq put Jordanian-U.S. relations in a holding pattern, and Jordanian relations with other major Western powers were little better.

By 1993–1994, however, Jordanian-U.S. relations were on an upswing. The Jordanians decided to become an active partner in the Arab-Israeli peace process, and King Hussein actively supported United Nations (UN) sanctions on the Iraqi regime. On July 25, 1994, Hussein signed a historic nonbelligerent agreement with the Israelis (the Washington Declaration), which was soon followed up by the October 26, 1994, signing of the Israel-Jordan Peace Treaty.

King Hussein died in February 1999 and was succeeded by his son, King Abdullah II. Following the outbreak of the Second (al-Aqsa) Intifada in 2000, Abdullah has tried to continue Jordan's role as the force of moderation in the Middle East. He has attempted to keep avenues of dialogue open between the Israelis and the Palestinians and continues to counsel both sides that discussions and agreements are far preferable to conflict and war. Nevertheless, in a show of Arab solidarity, Jordan recalled its ambassador from Israel. This lasted until 2005. Although Abdullah publicly criticized the Iraq War that began in March 2003, he quietly provided assistance to the United States and Britain and has partnered with the West in an attempt to bring a semblance of control to war-torn Iraq. Jordan itself has not been immune to terrorism, and in November 2005 a group calling itself Al Qaeda in Iraq, led by a native Jordanian, detonated three bombs in Amman, killing 57 people and wounding at least 100 others.

PAUL G. PIERPAOLI JR.

See also

Al Qaeda in Iraq; Arab-Israeli Conflict, Overview; Arab League; DESERT STORM, Operation; Fedayeen; Hussein ibn Talal, King of Jordan; Israel-Jordan Peace Treaty; Jordan, Armed Forces; Nasser, Gamal Abdel; Palestine Liberation Organization; Suez Crisis; United Arab Republic

References

Abdullah ibn al-Husayn, King. *King 'Abdallah of Jordan: My Memoirs Completed (al-Takmilah)*. Translated by Harold W. Glidden. Washington, DC: American Council of Learned Societies, 1954.

Lunt, James D. *Hussein of Jordan: Searching for a Just and Lasting Peace*. New York: William Morrow, 1989.

Salibi, Kamal S. *The History of Modern Jordan*. New York: William Morrow, 1993.

Wilson, Mary C. *King Abdullah, Britain and the Making of Jordan*. Cambridge and New York: Cambridge University Press, 1988.

Jordan, Armed Forces

The Jordanian armed forces, and especially the Jordanian Army, are highly professional organizations with a heritage dating to the formation of the Transjordan (officially changed to Jordan in 1949) Arab Legion, which was initially led by British officers. Organized in 1920, the Arab Legion was at first a small police force led by Captain (later Major General) Frederick Gerard Peake, known to Transjordanians as Peake Pasha. In 1930 Captain (later

Lieutenant General) John Bagot Glubb became second-in-command of the Arab Legion and a close personal friend and trusted political adviser of Transjordan's King Abdullah. Glubb Pasha, as the Jordanians called him, organized a Bedouin desert patrol consisting of mobile detachments based at strategic desert forts and equipped with communications facilities. On Peake's retirement in 1939, Glubb took command of the Arab Legion and made it into the best-trained military force in the Arab world. The Arab Legion participated in the Iraqi and Syrian campaigns in 1941.

By Transjordan's independence in 1946, the Arab Legion numbered some 8,000 soldiers in 3 mechanized regiments along with 16 infantry companies and included a civil police force of about 2,000 men. The Jordanian ground force officially changed its name in 1956 from the Arab Legion to the Jordanian Army, but the older name remained in popular usage for some time afterward. General Glubb was dismissed in March 1956, a consequence of King Hussein's desire to show political independence from the United Kingdom and to Arabize the Jordanian officer corps. By 1956 the Jordanian military had grown to around 25,000 troops, with well-trained Arab officers replacing the British. This expansion was nonetheless supported by the continuation of British aid.

Jordan's most significant actual and potential military adversary from 1948 to 1994 was Israel. Jordanian forces fought in the 1948–1949 Israeli War of Independence and were certainly the most effective of the Arab militaries in that war. Jordanian forces (with some Iraqi military help) managed to retain control of the territory subsequently known as the West Bank as well as East Jerusalem and the entire Old City and especially control of the Jerusalem–Tel Aviv Road at Latrun, thus winning the only significant Arab victories of the war.

During the 1948–1949 war the Jordanians had no tanks, although they did possess some light artillery, around 50 armored cars, and mortars to support the infantry. Jordan received its first tanks, which were British manufactured, in 1953. Jordanian forces did not fight in the 1956 Sinai Campaign stemming from the Suez Crisis. Jordanian military forces occasionally became involved in border skirmishing with the Israelis throughout the 1950s and 1960s, and Israeli forces conducted several major reprisal raids into Jordan during this period in response to Palestinian terrorism.

By the early 1960s Jordan was receiving limited military assistance from the United States in addition to support from the United Kingdom. The relationship with the United States expanded dramatically in August 1964 when Washington agreed to supply M-48 Patton tanks and armored personnel carriers. Later, in February 1966, the United States added fighter aircraft in the form of Lockheed F-104 Starfighters, aging systems that were being phased out of the U.S. Air Force inventory. The United States agreed to this expanded military relationship with Jordan out of fear that Amman might seek and receive Soviet aid in the absence of continuing Western supplies of arms. By early 1967 the United States and the United Kingdom had become Jordan's primary arms suppliers.

In the June 1967 Six-Day War with Israel, Jordanian forces suffered a massive defeat along with the militaries of Egypt and Syria. On the eve of the war, Jordan had about 55,000 troops and 350 tanks as well as a fledgling air force. Some thought that because Jordan had been under political attack by the republican and Arab socialist regimes of Egypt and Syria, it might be reluctant to engage Israel. Indeed, the Israelis hoped that Jordan would remain neutral, but the Israel Defense Forces (IDF) also planned for a full-scale Jordanian offensive. King Hussein indeed supported Egypt and Syria and tried to defend Jordan and the West Bank. The Jordanians fought well, but the army's performance suffered as a result of Israeli air supremacy. As a result of the 1967 war, Jordan lost all of the Palestinian territory that it had previously secured in the 1948–1949 war. The Israelis destroyed Jordan's entire small air force of 21 subsonic British-made Hawker Hunters, and Jordan also lost 179 tanks and 700 troops with large numbers wounded, missing, or taken prisoner. The four F-104 Starfighters then in Jordanian possession had not been fully integrated into the air force and were sent to Turkey before the war to escape destruction. By 1968 Jordan's military strength was somewhat restored by the U.S. transfer of 100 M-48 tanks. Then in 1969 and 1970, the Americans released 36 additional F-104 aircraft for transfer to Jordan.

The Jordanian military fought effectively against the Israelis in the March 1968 Battle of Karameh, when a large Israeli force crossed into Jordan to destroy Palestinian guerrilla forces operating from the kingdom. The Jordanians also defeated Palestinian guerrillas in September 1970 and again in July 1971 when these forces attempted to create a state within a state in Jordan. Additionally, Amman sent the Jordanian 40th Armored Brigade as an expeditionary force to aid the Syrians and protect their withdrawal during the 1973 Yom Kippur (Ramadan) War.

King Hussein chose not to open an additional front with Israel in 1973, mistakenly believing (or at least claiming) that the mere presence of his army on the Jordanian-Israeli border would tie down large numbers of Israeli troops. Jordan also sent a limited number of Special Forces troops to fight in support of royalist forces in Oman in the 1970s. During the 1980–1988 Iran-Iraq War, Jordan supported the Iraqis and sent a token military force of volunteers to support the war effort against Iran. They apparently did not see combat in that war.

During the 1970s and 1980s Jordan supplemented its military assistance from Western countries with financial support for military modernization from Arab oil-producing states. Such support allowed Jordan to make a number of major purchases, including U.S.-made Northrop F-5 Freedom Fighter aircraft to replace the aging F-104s, U.S.-made M-60 tanks, and a Hawk missile defense system to protect Amman. Nevertheless, in an abrupt turnabout, military procurement was disrupted in the 1990s as a result of difficulties in relations with the United States, Saudi Arabia, and Kuwait following King Hussein's decision not to join the U.S.-led coalition in the Persian Gulf War of 1991. These problems severely disrupted the flow of outside aid necessary for the Jordanian military to make key purchases and carry out military modernization.

The Israel-Jordan Peace Treaty of 1994 ended the state of war between Jordan and Israel and brought about a major reorientation of the Jordanian Army to deal with other regional threats. The Jordanian military officially ended conscription in 1994 as a response to the peace treaty, although young men had only been drafted sporadically before then in response to variations in manpower needs and financial resources. Some Western military aid programs were restored by the mid-1990s, and in November 1996 Jordan was designated as a major non–North Atlantic Treaty Organization (NATO) ally.

Currently, the Jordanian armed forces comprise about 100,000 active duty personnel and 30,000 reservists. The most important branch of the service is the army. The Jordanian Army is a highly professional force with top-notch officers and noncommissioned officers. Its chief maneuver combat units are two armored divisions, two mechanized divisions, and two separate brigades. Its combat doctrine is almost entirely defensive, as Jordan does not have the resources to conduct large-scale offensive operations. Jordanian forces are organized into four regionally based commands with a strategic reserve and a Special Operations Command. In addition to their self-defense role, Jordanian troops are called upon to secure the Jordanian border with Israel and prevent terrorist infiltration from Jordanian soil.

The Jordanian ground forces are in the process of converting to a lighter force structure that has smaller combat formations and greater mobility. Such a force is expected to have fewer tank battalions and is both cheaper and better equipped to deal with internal security problems than are armor-heavy units. Nevertheless, Jordan retains more than 1,000 tanks in active service, all of which are of U.S. or British manufacture. Since 2004, Jordan has undertaken a major upgrade program for its U.S.-made M-60 tanks. Some of Jordan's British-made Challenger tanks have been subject to either British or domestic Jordanian updating and modification. Some older tanks, including the M-48s and Centurions, are not operational or are in storage. The Jordanian Army has approximately 400 self-propelled artillery pieces (a significant number for a force its size) as well as about 100 older towed artillery pieces. It also has large numbers of modern and effective antitank weapons, such as the U.S.-made Javelin and upgraded Dragon.

Jordan's Special Forces troops are among the best in the region and in recent years have emerged as an especially important component of the Jordanian force structure. The Special Operations Command was formerly led by Abdullah when he served as a brigadier general prior to becoming king in 1999. In the years just prior to the 2003 Iraq War, Jordanian Special Forces troops played a leading role in securing the Iraqi border, where almost nightly clashes took place between Jordanian forces and Iraqi smugglers. In April 2002 Jordan sent a Special Forces training unit to Yemen to assist American forces training the Yemeni military to fight terrorist groups.

Royal Jordanian Air Force F-16 Fighting Falcon aircraft flying over Jordan, 2009. (U.S. Department of Defense)

The Royal Jordanian Air Force is led by King Abdullah's brother, Prince Faisal, and has about 15,000 personnel. It has approximately 100 fixed-wing combat aircraft with 85 fighter aircraft including U.S.-made General Dynamics F-16 Fighting Falcons and French Mirage F-1s. Jordan also retains some of its older F-5 aircraft, which are increasingly obsolete. The air force also has 14 transport aircraft, including 4 American-made C-130 Hercules aircraft. Jordan also has more than 40 attack helicopters that are included within its air force. About 22 of these helicopters are equipped with TOW antiarmor missiles. While the Royal Jordanian Air Force has excellent pilots and good levels of training, its modernization efforts have been significantly restricted by long-term Jordanian resource constraints.

Jordanian air defense forces have likewise suffered from a period of neglect following the 1991 Persian Gulf War as well as other episodes of budgetary shortfalls. Jordanian air defense systems, including its improved Hawk missile batteries, have a number of limitations, although some upgrading has been taking place. The Jordanian military also has three Patriot missile batteries that include a limited antimissile capability.

The Royal Jordanian Coast Guard (sometimes called the Royal Jordanian Navy) is extremely small and operates out of Jordan's only port, at Aqaba. The coast guard has a few small patrol boats in the Dead Sea. There are approximately 500 personnel assigned to the coast guard and fewer than 20 coastal defense craft and patrol vessels. This service is nevertheless scheduled to expand in the future with the planned development of a special organization within the coast guard for counterterrorism and to help support planned upgrades in coastal and port security.

Jordanian military personnel have served during recent years in a range of multinational peace support missions and regional military exercises. Jordanian units have supported peacekeeping operations in the Balkans and Africa through the provision of infantry units, field hospitals, international monitors, and military staff officers in international missions. The peacekeeping missions that were most extensively supported were in Croatia in the 1990s (3,200 Jordanian troops deployed) and in Sierra Leone (where Jordan had a peak of about 1,800 troops in 2000). Jordan has also provided field hospitals to support the reconstruction of postwar Iraq and post-Taliban Afghanistan. The Jordanians also train Arab officers from friendly countries at their own facilities, including the Jordanian National Defense University. In coordination with the United States, Jordan has further supported an extensive effort to train army officers and police forces in postwar Iraq (after 2003).

The Jordanian military retains strong ties to the militaries of the United States and the United Kingdom. Leading male members of the royal family have a tradition of attending the United

Kingdom's Royal Military Academy, Sandhurst. Jordanian officers and noncommissioned officers also participate in a variety of military education and training programs offered by the United States and other Western powers. A joint U.S.-Jordanian military commission has coordinated a number of important military concerns since 1974, and Jordanian cooperation with the West usually includes at least one major U.S.-Jordanian military exercise per year as well as Jordanian participation in multilateral exercises organized by the United States.

W. ANDREW TERRILL

See also

Arab-Israeli Conflict, Overview; Arms Sales, International; Hussein ibn Talal, King of Jordan; Jordan; Suez Crisis

References

Cordesman, Anthony H. *The Military Balance in the Middle East.* Westport, CT: Praeger, 2004.

El Edross, Syed Ali. *The Hashemite Arab Army, 1908–1979.* Amman, Jordan: Central Publishing House, 1986.

International Institute for Strategic Studies. *The Military Balance.* London: IISS, 2005.

Nevo, Joseph, and Illan Pappe, eds. *Jordan in the Middle East: The Making of a Pivotal State.* London: Frank Cass, 1994.

JUST CAUSE, **Operation**
Start Date: December 20, 1989
End Date: January 31, 1990

U.S. military intervention in Panama designed to remove Panamanian dictator Manuel Noriega from power and protect U.S. citizens. Operation JUST CAUSE had considerable impact on planning for the Persian Gulf War, which occurred less than a year later. Throughout much of the 1980s U.S.-Panamanian relations steadily deteriorated because of Noriega's involvement with drug trafficking, his repressive political activities, and numerous treaty violations and provocations of U.S. military personnel in Panama. In 1987 one of Noriega's principal lieutenants charged the dictator with drug trafficking, election fraud, and murder. Riots ensued in Panama City, and the situation grew more serious as the country's economy deteriorated. To deflect the attention of the Panamanian public, Noriega increasingly resorted to anti-American rhetoric and directed the Panamanian Defense Force (PDF) to increase the harassment of U.S. military personnel in the country.

The situation continued to worsen. The Ronald Reagan administration responded by sending a company of marines and several military police units to bolster American forces already in Panama. On April 12, 1988, gunfire was exchanged between U.S. marine guards and several armed intruders at a fuel farm near Howard Air Force Base. By the end of 1988 there had been more than 300 incidents of Panamanian forces harassing or intimidating U.S. military personnel and their families.

Tensions continued throughout the following year. There were a number of significant incidents, including the detainment of a U.S. Navy civilian employee, the beating of an off-duty U.S. Navy lieutenant, and the seizure of nine Department of Defense school buses loaded with 100 children. The buses and children were released after three hours, but the incident demonstrated the new level of harassment faced by Americans in Panama.

In early May 1988 Panama held national elections. When Noriega's handpicked candidate lost decisively at the polls, the dictator declared the elections invalid. Two days later the victorious opposition candidates were attacked at a postelection rally, and one of their personal bodyguards was killed. The PDF also abducted, beat, and robbed a U.S. Navy sailor. In response, President George H. W. Bush dispatched 1,900 combat troops and military police to augment American security.

This deployment, which was called Operation NIMROD DANCER, was intended as a show of force to enhance the security of U.S. citizens and property in the Panama Canal Zone. To demonstrate U.S. resolve, these units initiated a number of exercises that were permitted under previous treaty arrangements.

Tensions remained at a high level throughout the summer. In response, hundreds of family members of U.S. servicemen were evacuated from Panama, and tighter restrictions were imposed on access to U.S. military installations. Within days of General Maxwell Thurman assuming command of U.S. Southern Command (SOUTHCOM), one of Noriega's senior commanders attempted a coup against the dictator. The coup failed, however, and its leader was executed.

On December 15, 1988, the pro-Noriega legislative assembly appointed him "Maximum Leader" of the country. In his acceptance speech, Noriega announced that "the Republic of Panama is declared to be in a state of war" with the United States. Late the next day, four off-duty U.S. military officers driving through Panama City were stopped at a PDF roadblock. When the PDF guards demanded that the officers get out of their vehicle, the officers refused and drove off. The guards fired at the car, fatally wounding one of the occupants, a marine lieutenant. A navy lieutenant and his wife who had witnessed the incident were then seized by the PDF and taken to Noriega's headquarters. There the lieutenant was questioned and beaten while his wife was assaulted. The couple was released four hours later.

General Thurman, in northern Virginia, was notified of the incident and immediately returned to Panama after conferring with General Colin Powell, chairman of the Joint Chiefs of Staff (JCS). Shortly thereafter, President Bush authorized contingency plans for a military intervention in Panama "to safeguard the lives of Americans, to defend democracy in Panama, to combat drug trafficking, and to protect the integrity of the Panama Canal Treaty." Later Bush ordered the immediate apprehension and extradition of Noriega.

Planning for a military intervention in Panama had begun in 1987 and sought to rectify some of the military failures revealed in

U.S. marines stand guard with their LAV-25 light armored vehicles outside a destroyed Panamanian Defense Force building on December 20, 1989, the first day of the U.S. invasion of Panama, Operation JUST CAUSE. (U.S. Department of Defense)

the U.S. invasion of Grenada (Operation URGENT FURY) in October 1983. The original plan, code-named BLUE SPOON, had been built on an assumption that a gradual buildup of U.S. military forces in the Panama Canal Zone along with increased economic and diplomatic pressure on the Panamanian government would prevail and that the Panamanian electorate would vote the dictator out of office. By early 1989, however, it had become clear that these assumptions were no longer valid. The contingency plan was thus revised, and the failure of the October coup precipitated additional changes. The new plan, calling for the insertion of combat forces from both the 82nd Airborne and 7th Infantry divisions along with selected special operations forces, was based on swift and decisive action to ensure adequate security for American personnel and the Panama Canal Zone while minimizing Panamanian casualties and avoiding excessive damage to the country's infrastructure.

As the plan was being refined, only a small number of senior commanders and staff officers were aware that an armed intervention in Panama was being planned. However, units at military installations in the United States and Panama were directed to alter their training schedules and tempo of activities to prepare for an unknown contingency operation. In Panama, under provisions of the 1978 Canal Treaty, which authorized U.S. military personnel unrestricted movement within the Panama Canal Zone for

training exercises, U.S. military forces were able to practice movement to preselected targets potentially critical to a military operation in the country. These exercises, code-named SAND FLEA, and the arrival and departure of aircraft carrying troops to and from the United States served to desensitize the PDF to the increasingly frequent troop movements and ground maneuvers that were in preparation for the coming operation.

Meanwhile, back in the United States units from the 82nd Airborne Division, 75th Ranger Regiment, and the Joint Special Operations Command (JSOC) practiced the kinds of missions called for in the contingency plans for Panama. The XVIII Airborne Corps commander, Lieutenant General Carl Steiner, was designated the operational commander for the planned intervention.

On December 17, 1989, President Bush made the decision to launch the military invasion of Panama. General Steiner selected 1:00 a.m. on Wednesday December 20 for H-Hour. On December 19 the 7th Infantry Division, stationed at Fort Ord, California, boarded aircraft at Travis Air Force Base and flew to Panama. Meanwhile, paratroopers from the 82nd Airborne Division departed Pope Air Force Base in North Carolina.

The initial strike force included about 7,000 troops, including a composite brigade from the 82nd Airborne Division, the 75th Rangers, and the equivalent of five battalions of special operations forces. The second wave would include about 7,000 additional soldiers from the 7th Infantry Division and the 16th Military Police Brigade. These forces would join about 13,000 troops stationed in Panama, to include the 193rd Infantry Brigade, a battalion from the 7th Infantry Division, a battalion from the 5th Infantry Division, two companies of marines, an assortment of military police, and other army, air force, and navy personnel.

The tactical command headquarters of the XVIII Airborne Corps, operating directly under SOUTHCOM, divided these forces into four conventional ground task forces—Atlantic (centered around the 3rd Brigade, 7th Infantry Division), Pacific (comprised largely of the 1st Brigade, 82nd Airborne Division), Bayonet (under control of the 193rd Infantry Brigade), and Semper Fi (centered around the 6th Marine Expeditionary Brigade)—as well as an aviation task force and five unconventional task forces: Green (Army Delta Force), Black (3rd Battalion, 7th Special Forces), Red (the Rangers), and Blue and White (SEAL units).

The plan for the operation was built around surprise and the use of a nighttime attack. The first objective was to isolate Noriega from his military forces and to neutralize the PDF as a viable threat to the security of the Panama Canal Zone, U.S. citizens, and Panamanian civilians. To accomplish this, U.S. forces would simultaneously strike almost two dozen targets within a 24-hour period of time.

The operation began with an assault of strategic installations including an attack by SEALs on the civilian Punta Paitilla Airport in Panama City; a Ranger parachute assault on the PDF garrison and the airfield at Rio Hato, where Noriega also maintained a residence; the seizure of the Omar Torrijos International Airport by paratroopers from the 82nd Airborne Division; and attacks by other units on other military command centers throughout the country.

The attack on the central headquarters of the PDF, La Comandancia, touched off several fires, one of which destroyed most of the adjoining and heavily populated El Chorrillo neighborhood in downtown Panama City.

Fort Amador, at the Pacific entrance to the Panama Canal, was a major objective because of its relationship to the large oil farms adjacent to the canal and the Bridge of the Americas over the canal. Additionally, there were key command and control elements of the PDF stationed on the installation. Furthermore, Fort Amador also had a large U.S. housing area that needed to be secured to prevent the PDF from taking U.S. citizens hostage. This objective was secured by elements of the 508th Airborne Infantry and 59th Engineer Company (sappers), who conducted a nighttime helicopter-borne air assault that quickly overwhelmed the PDF defenders.

A few hours after the invasion began, Guillermo Endara was sworn in as president of Panama at Rodman Naval Base. It is generally agreed that Endara was the victor in the presidential election, which had been held earlier that year.

In fewer than five days all military objectives were secured and ground combat operations ceased, but the hunt for Noriega continued. However, he remained at large for several days. Realizing that he had few options in the face of a massive manhunt and with a $1 million reward for his capture, Noriega sought refuge in the Vatican diplomatic mission in Panama City. The U.S. military's psychological pressure on him and diplomatic pressure on the Vatican mission, however, were relentless, and Noriega finally surrendered to U.S. military forces on January 3, 1990. He was immediately extradited to the United States to stand trial on drug trafficking charges.

During the operation, U.S. forces sustained 23 killed in action and 322 wounded. The total U.S. casualties included friendly fire incidents and injuries sustained in drop zones. The PDF, numbering more than 15,000 personnel of all ranks and duty assignments, had 314 killed in action, 124 wounded, and more than 5,300 detained by U.S. forces. There has been considerable controversy over the number of Panamanian civilian casualties resulting from the invasion, but the SOUTHCOM estimated the number at 200. The quick and relatively uncomplicated victory for the United States proved a great morale booster for U.S. armed forces, served as proof that combined operations could indeed work seamlessly, and greatly assisted in the planning and execution of Operation DESERT STORM, which unfolded only slightly more than a year later.

JAMES H. WILLBANKS

See also

Bush, George Herbert Walker; Powell, Colin Luther

References

Donnelly, Thomas, Margaret Roth, and Caleb Baker. *Operation Just Cause: The Storming of Panama.* New York: Lexington Books, 1991.

McConnell, Malcolm. *Just Cause: The Real Story of America's High-Tech Invasion of Panama.* New York: St. Martin's, 1991.

Woodward, Bob. *The Commanders.* New York: Simon and Schuster, 1991.

Yates, Lawrence A. *The U.S. Military Intervention in Panama.* Washington, DC: Center of Military History, United States Army, 2008.

K

Kakar, Mullah
Birth Date: ca. 1966
Death Date: May 13, 2007

A leading figure in the Taliban movement in Afghanistan from 1995 until his death in 2007. Mullah Dadullah (aka Mullah Dadullah Akhund), born probably in 1966, was a member of the Kakar tribe from Uruzgan Province. He fought in the Afghanistan-Soviet War and reportedly lost a leg in that war in the 1980s. Little is known of his activities prior to the late 1990s.

Dadullah emerged as a key figure in Taliban leadership circles beginning in the late 1990s. He was reportedly responsible for the brutal repression of the religious minority Shia population throughout Afghanistan and the ethnic minority Hazara population near Bamyan in 2000. In 2001 he was engaged in fighting against the Northern Alliance in northern Afghanistan. A leading military commander on the northern front, he escaped encirclement in the city of Kunduz, returning to Kandahar on foot and becoming a local hero to Taliban sympathizers in the Pashtun-controlled southern provinces of Afghanistan.

Following the U.S.-assisted ouster of the Taliban government, Dadullah became one of the early leaders of the Taliban insurgency. In 2002–2003 he was engaged in recruiting fresh Pashtun volunteers from madrasahs in Baluchistan and Karachi. In 2004 he traveled to Pakistan's Federally Administered Tribal Areas to coordinate activity with Taliban fighters in that region. Mullah Mohammed Omar, the Taliban's leader, selected Dadullah as one of the original 10 members of the 2003 Rahbari Shura (leadership council), and Dadullah was retained as one of the 12 members when the Rahbari Shura expanded in 2004. Dadullah was initially appointed 1 of 3 military leaders of the Taliban southern front in 2003, sharing command with Abd al-Razzaq Akhund and Akhtar Osmani.

Although Dadullah was a powerful and innovative leader, many of his cohorts considered him an extremist. He reportedly had significant disagreements, including a physical confrontation, with fellow Rahbari Shura member Akhtar Osmani, a conflict that ended with Osmani's death in late 2006. Some Taliban sources claim that Osmani's death resulted from a Dadullah tip-off to North Atlantic Treaty Organization (NATO) forces in Afghanistan.

By 2004 Dadullah had full command of the Taliban southern front, and his influence in the movement expanded as he began innovative new practices. Dadullah initiated the tactic of launching repeated attacks, regardless of casualties, against the same targets in remote districts. This demonstrated Taliban commitment to success whatever the cost and encouraged local officials to either leave their posts or cooperate with local Taliban cadres. In early 2006 Dadullah announced the creation of Taliban political representatives in all districts, facilitating the establishment of a Taliban shadow government throughout southern and southeastern Afghanistan in particular. By the end of that year he was negotiating to win tribal loyalties in the countryside, promising to share power and resources with tribal leaders in return for their support.

These efforts were all aimed at sustaining the Taliban's so-called final offensive in 2006. It began in the first week of February, with attacks in Helmand. By early summer, thousands of Taliban forces were engaged throughout the south and southeast, sometimes operating in battalion-sized units of up to 400 men each. The offensive surprised many analysts but eventually proved too difficult to sustain, and Dadullah called an end to the campaign in November 2006.

Dadullah was a great innovator, at least in the context of the very conservative Taliban movement. He deliberately chose a flamboyant lifestyle, which became a useful propaganda tool. His extended family lived openly just outside Quetta, and in September 2003 he held a spectacular family wedding that was attended by local Pakistani political leaders and military officers. He encouraged the creation and distribution of a series of brutal videos depicting execution of prisoners, and he advocated Taliban atrocities against Westerners and humanitarian aid workers. He was also one of the few leaders willing to be photographed and even agreed to interviews with the Al Jazeera news network.

In 2005 Dadullah announced that he was accepting assistance from Al Qaeda in Iraq, which may account for the increased emphasis on and effectiveness of suicide bombings. This shift reflected not only access to expertise from the international extremist community but also an interest in generating greater publicity for the upcoming final offensive. Suicide bombings increased from just 6 in 2004 to an average of more than 10 per month in 2006 and 2007. These bombings were carried out primarily by foreign volunteers; through 2007 most suicide bombers came from Afghan refugee camps or madrasahs in Pakistan. Dadullah was involved in recruitment efforts in Pakistan, and he took credit for having "hundreds" of suicide bombers ready by mid-2006.

On May 13, 2007, Dadullah was killed in a firefight with NATO and Afghan government forces outside the town of Garmser in Helmand Province. Reportedly, he had traveled there from Quetta and had been tracked by units of the British Special Boat Service, which had spearheaded the effort to track him down.

TIMOTHY D. HOYT

See also

Afghanistan; Al Qaeda in Iraq; Madrasahs; Omar, Mohammed; Special Boat Service, United Kingdom; Taliban; Taliban Insurgency, Afghanistan

References

Giustozzi, Antonio. *Koran, Kalashnikov, and Laptop: The Neo-Taliban Insurgency in Afghanistan.* New York: Columbia University Press, 2008.

Rashid, Ahmed. *Descent into Chaos: The United States and the Failure of Nation-building in Pakistan, Afghanistan, and Central Asia.* New York: Viking, 2008.

Kamiya, Jason K.
Birth Date: 1954

U.S. Army general who commanded the joint American force (Combined Joint Task Force 76) in Afghanistan during Operation ENDURING FREEDOM from 2005 to 2006. Jason K. Kamiya was born in 1954 in Honolulu, Hawaii. He graduated from Gonzaga University in Spokane, Washington, in 1976, and as a member of the U.S. Army Reserve Officers' Training Corps (ROTC) program he was commissioned a second lieutenant on May 15, 1976. His first assignment was to U.S. forces in the Republic of Korea (ROK, South Korea) as a rifle platoon leader.

Posts of increasing responsibility followed, and Kamiya eventually commanded at the company, battalion, and brigade levels. He earned his paratrooper wings and attended the Naval Postgraduate School, the Armed Forces Staff College, and the U.S. Army War College. He then held a mix of staff and line positions. A Japanese linguist, Kamiya served as aide-de-camp to the commanding general at Camp Zama, Japan, and was also a special assistant to the commander, U.S. Southern Command. Kamiya served in Operations DESERT SHIELD and DESERT STORM and commanded a battalion in the 101st Airborne Division before becoming chief of staff for that division.

In December 2000 Kamiya was promoted to brigadier general. He assumed command of Fort Polk, Louisiana, a year later and helped prepare troops for peacekeeping service in Bosnia. In September 2002 he began a tour of duty in Afghanistan as U.S. security coordinator and chief of the Office of Military Cooperation. A year later he assumed command of the Southern European Task Force (Airborne), headquartered in Vicenza, Italy. On January 5, 2005, Kamiya was promoted to major general.

In March 2005 Kamiya assumed command of Combined Joint Task Force 76, which included both soldiers and marines and, with about 18,000 troops, was the largest combat command in Afghanistan. Its efforts were centered in southern Afghanistan, where the Taliban insurgency was strongest. Kamiya was also charged with helping to create the Afghan National Army and remove individual warlords who were in competition with the central government supported by the United States. He also oversaw the protection of aid, such as school construction and providing medical care for the Afghan people. Planners in Washington hoped that the humanitarian projects would win support for the new central government.

Kamiya's tour as commander of Combined Joint Task Force 76 included a significant milestone: the first democratic elections for a National Assembly in Afghanistan since before the Soviet invasion in 1979. These elections of September 18, 2005, were seen by international observers as a significant measure of the North Atlantic Treaty Organization (NATO) success in creating a stable government. The Afghan National Army and the Afghan National Police provided primary responsibility. To help make the task easier for the Afghan security forces, Kamiya ordered a series of operations that summer that reportedly killed between 450 and 500 Taliban fighters.

Kamiya's tour, however, was also marked by friction with the Afghan government. Afghan president Hamid Karzai criticized the use of air strikes in battles with Taliban fighters that killed innocent civilians. American troops also came under criticism for breaking down doors of Afghan houses when searching for Taliban fighters. Kamiya then ordered that Afghan soldiers accompany American patrols and that the former take the responsibility of securing the homeowners' permission to enter in accordance with Muslim culture.

The most serious charge against American troops during Kamiya's tenure involved the cremation of slain Taliban fighters. On October 1, 2005, American soldiers were filmed burning the bodies of fighters killed the day before. Because the Americans planned to stay in the area for several days, they believed that the bodies posed a health risk. Unfortunately, cremation is viewed as desecration by Muslims. Worse, two American soldiers were filmed taunting the Taliban while the bodies were burning. Television clips of the video outraged Muslims around the world. The soldiers involved received administrative disciplinary punishments, but the Afghan government was upset over what it considered to be lenient treatment.

When Kamiya learned of this incident, he ordered all operations in Afghanistan to stand down on October 19 and also ordered the institution of training in Muslim culture for all troops under his command. Wallet-sized laminated cards were issued to soldiers to carry and refer to when dealing with Afghanis. Kamiya pointed out that failure to observe Muslim traditions threatened to erase gains in building a democratic and pro-Western society in Afghanistan.

Kamiya's tour in Afghanistan ended in March 2006. On July 25, 2006, he assumed command of the Joint Warfighting Center in Suffolk, Virginia.

TIM J. WATTS

See also

Afghanistan; Afghanistan, Coalition Combat Operations in, 2002–Present; ENDURING FREEDOM, Operation; Karzai, Hamid; Taliban; Taliban Insurgency, Afghanistan

References

Heinatz, Stephanie. "War Center Receives New Commander: Army Maj. Gen. Jason K. Kamiya now leads the Suffolk Site." *Daily Press* [Newport News, Virginia], July 26, 2006.

Schmitt, Eric. "A Man Does Not Ask a Man about His Wife." *New York Times*, January 8, 2006, 7.

Kandahar, Battle for
Start Date: October 29, 1994
End Date: November 5, 1994

The capture of Kandahar in southern Afghanistan in November 1994 was a pivotal moment in the Taliban's rise to power. Between October 29 and November 5, 1994, Taliban forces engaged in heavy fighting to capture the city. Loosely organized on a regional basis, the Taliban had emerged following the destruction and chaos of the Afghan Civil War (1989–1992). The Taliban ("students," meaning Islamic students) was one of the many mujahideen groups formed during the Afghan-Soviet War (1979–1989). In the aftermath of the withdrawal of Soviet forces, the Soviet-backed government fought a brutal civil war against a coalition of mujahideen groups.

Following the end of the Afghan-Soviet War, Afghanistan descended into civil war as rival mujahideen factions fought for control. In Kandahar, rival militias loyal to Naquib Ullah, Mullah Haji Bashir, Hamid Karzai, and Gulbuddin Hekmatyar fought each other for control. The interfactional fighting descended into chaos as militias killed civilians and plundered indiscriminately. Hostage taking, rape, murder, and lawlessness became commonplace as mujahideen commanders turned on the local population. As the traditionalists and Islamists fought for control, the traditional tribal structure disintegrated, allowing the emergence of a puritanical Islamic movement.

The origins of the Taliban's rise to power are shrouded in mystery. One scenario is that in the spring of 1994 neighbors from Mullah Mohammed Omar's village of Singesar told him that a local mujahideen commander had abducted 2 teenage girls and taken them to a military camp, where there were raped. In response, Omar gathered 30 Talibs (local fighters) and attacked the base, where they freed the girls and hanged the commander from the barrel of an old Soviet tank. In addition, the Taliban fighters captured small quantities of arms and ammunition. A second incident during the summer of 1994 bolstered Taliban credentials. Two mujahideen commanders confronted each other in a Kandahar bazaar. In the ensuing battle, civilians shopping or trading in the bazaar were killed. Again, Omar and the Talibs intervened. Following these two incidents, Omar left for the neighboring Baluchistan Province of Pakistan.

A mitigating factor leading to the Battle for Kandahar was control of the lucrative trade routes to Turkmenistan. Sensing an opportunity in the shifting terrain of Afghan politics, the Pakistani leadership saw domestic political gain in supporting the Taliban, which they commenced immediately.

The fight for Kandahar began on October 12, 1994, when 200 Taliban soldiers and Pakistani militants arrived at the Afghan border town of Spin Baldak controlled by a militia loyal to Gulbuddin Hekmatyar. After a short battle, the Taliban dislodged Hekmatyar's forces from this vital border town. As a result of the skirmish at Spin Boldak, 7 of Hekmatyar's men died and several were wounded, while only 1 Taliban member died. The Taliban fighters then captured a large arms depot at Spin Baldak, which included dozens of artillery pieces and tanks.

On October 29, 1994, a Pakistani trade convoy was stopped by Amir Lalai, Mansur Achakzai, and Ustad Halim, three local mujahideen commanders, 12 miles outside of Kandahar at Takht-e-Pul. The warlords demanded money and a share of the goods and also demanded that Pakistan cease support of the Taliban. On November 3, 1994, the Taliban attacked the militia in Takht-e Pul, quickly defeating the local commanders and killing Mansur Achakzai and 10 of his men in the process. That same evening the Taliban moved into Kandahar, where after two days of heavy fighting they defeated the forces of Lalai and Halim. Mullah Naqib, the last remaining prominent mujahideen commander inside Kandahar, negotiated his personal surrender. His forces, which consisted of 20,000 men, were then absorbed into the Taliban ranks. As a result of this victory, the Taliban captured dozens of tanks, armored cars, and military vehicles along with many individual weapons, six MiG-21 fighters, six transport helicopters, all at a cost of only a dozen men.

KEITH A. LEITICH

See also

Afghanistan; Karzai, Hamid; Madrasahs; Mujahideen, Soviet-Afghanistan War; Omar, Mohammed; Taliban

References

Coll, Steve. *Ghost Wars: The Secret History of the CIA, Afghanistan, and Bin Laden, from the Soviet Invasion to September 10, 2001.* New York: Penguin, 2004.

Rashid, Ahmed. *Taliban: Militant Islam, Oil, and Fundamentalism in Central Asia.* New Haven, CT: Yale University Press, 2001.

Karbala, First Battle of
Start Date: March 31, 2003
End Date: April 6, 2003

Karbala is located in central Iraq some 60 miles southwest of Baghdad and is regarded as one of the holiest cities in Shia Islam. Three notable battles have occurred there: one in October 680 CE among Islamic factions, one during Operation IRAQI FREEDOM in 2003, and one between Iraqi factions in 2007. The March 31–April 6, 2003, battle occurred during the Iraq War when U.S. forces attempted to evict Iraqi forces from Karbala. Units involved in the fight included those from the U.S. 3rd Infantry Division, the 1st Armored Division, and the 101st Airborne Division; Iraqi forces consisted of members of the Fedayeen Saddam and Syrian mercenaries.

During the initial phase of the 2003 invasion of Iraq, advance units of the U.S. 3rd Infantry Division, having pushed their way through Republican Guard forces southeast of Karbala, arrived in the area on March 31. While some troops kept a watchful eye on the Iraqis in Karbala, the main body bypassed the city and attacked Baghdad through the Karbala Gap. This meant that U.S. forces would have to clear the Iraqis out of Karbala later.

This task fell principally to the 101st Airborne Division, supported by the 2nd Battalion, 70th Armored Regiment, 1st Armored Division. On April 2, 2003, a U.S. Army Sikorsky UH-60 Black Hawk helicopter was shot down near Karbala, killing seven soldiers and wounding four others. This event appeared to indicate a significant enemy presence in the city.

The 101st Airborne Division decided to insert three battalions via helicopter at three landing zones (LZs) on the outskirts of the city, designated LZ Sparrow, LZ Finch, and LZ Robin. M-1 Abrams tanks and M-2 Bradley fighting vehicles of the 2nd Battalion, 70th Armored Regiment, were to support these forces.

On the morning of April 5, 23 UH-60 Black Hawks escorted 5 CH-47 Boeing Chinook helicopters ferrying three battalions of the 502nd Infantry Regiment to their LZs. The 3rd Battalion landed at LZ Sparrow and met heavy but uncoordinated resistance. The 2nd Battalion landed to the south at LZ Robin and found numerous arms caches hidden in schools as well as a suspected terrorist training camp. As night fell, the battalion had cleared 13 of its 30 assigned sectors.

The 1st Battalion landed at LZ Finch in the southeast, where it captured a large store of weapons. As the infantry moved forward, it was constantly supported by helicopters and artillery. While the soldiers went house to house, armored vehicles from the 2nd Battalion, 70th Armored Regiment, arrived and engaged the enemy.

The following morning, April 6, the Americans continued operations until 5:00 p.m., when all sectors were secured. Symbolic of the victory, members of the 2nd Battalion, 70th Armored Regiment, tore down a large statue of Iraqi dictator Saddam Hussein in the middle of the city. Reported casualties were as many as 260 for the Iraqis; the Americans suffered 8 killed. One UH-60 helicopter was also lost. One U.S. M1 Abrams tank was disabled but not destroyed.

WILLIAM P. HEAD

See also

IRAQI FREEDOM, Operation; Karbala, Second Battle of; Karbala Gap

References

Atkinson, Rick. *In the Company of Soldiers: A Chronicle of Combat.* New York: Henry Holt, 2005.

NBC Enterprises. *Operation Iraqi Freedom: The Insider Story.* Kansas City, MO: Andrews McMeel, 2003.

Karbala, Second Battle of
Start Date: August 27, 2007
End Date: August 29, 2007

Karbala is located in central Iraq some 60 miles southwest of Baghdad and is one of the holiest cities in Shia Islam. There have been three notable battles there: one in October 680 CE among Islamic factions, one during Operation IRAQI FREEDOM in 2003, and one between Iraqi factions in 2007. The Second Battle of Karbala (August 27–29, 2007) began as thousands of Shia pilgrims gathered in the city for the annual festival of Nisf Sha'ban (Laylat al-Barat). The fighting occurred between members of the Mahdi Army, charged with providing security for the pilgrims, and Iraqi Security Forces (police), most of whom belonged to the Badr Brigades.

By August 27, 2007, a large security force was present in the city because pilgrims had been killed during previous pilgrimages. Early that evening, small-arms fire broke out between the Mahdi Army and local police. The number of forces on each side has not been determined.

The Mahdi Army is a militia force loyal to Iraqi leader Muqtada al-Sadr. Senior members of Iraq's Interior Ministry soon accused the Mahdi Army of attacking government forces in Karbala who were guarding two shrines under the control of the Supreme Islamic Iraqi Council.

"Iraqi PM Orders Curfew in Karbala." BBC News, August 29, 2007, http://news.bbc.co.uk/2/hi/middle_east/6968236.stm.

"Toll Rises in Karbala Fighting." Al Jazeera, August 28, 2007, http://english.aljazeera.net/news/middleeast/2007/08/2008525141014347965.html.

Karbala Gap

A sandy 20-mile-wide plain located in central Iraq's Karbala Province, some 55 miles south-southwest of the Iraqi capital of Baghdad. Situated between Lake Buhayrat al-Razzazah to the west and the Euphrates River to the east, the Karbala Gap is an area of marshes and rich farmland; it is also the location of the city of Karbala, with a population of some 500,000 people. Given its location, geographical constraints, and proximity to Baghdad, the Karbala Gap is a major choke point and last natural obstacle for an invading force moving from the south against Baghdad. A major battle had been fought there in 680 CE.

The importance of the Karbala Gap was well known and had been the object of pre-2003 Iraq War U.S. war-gaming exercises. During the Iraq War, both U.S. Army 3rd Infantry Division commander Major General Buford Blount and Iraqi Army corps commander Lieutenant General Raad al-Hamdani, who had charge of the area, recognized that passage by the gap was the only rapid way for mechanized forces to reach Baghdad. The major concerns for Blount were the potential Iraqi use of chemical weapons and the Iraqi destruction of the bridges crossing the Euphrates. Hamdani's major concern was the lack of manpower to block the U.S. drive northward. The Iraqi high command had positioned the Medina and Nebuchadnezzar Republican Guard divisions to block the Karbala Gap, but Hamdani argued for reinforcements. The Iraqi leadership ignored his appeals, however, because it feared going against President Saddam Hussein's orders and having troops cut off from the defense of Baghdad.

On April 1, 2003, following a delay imposed by a massive *shamal* (sandstorm), units of the 3rd Infantry Division attacked through the Karbala Gap. That day the 3rd Brigade, strongly supported by the divisional artillery and helicopters, secured control of the eastern outskirts of Karbala, while its 1st Brigade attacked from the other side. On April 2 U.S. forces moved against the al-Qaid Bridge over the Euphrates River (Objective Peach), east of Karbala and near Hindiyah. The bridge had been marked for demolition, but this had not yet been carried out when, on the afternoon of April 2, three U.S. tanks got across the span. Although Iraqi engineers then detonated some charges, the bridge survived, and the Americans quickly cut other detonation lines and rooted out the Iraqi engineers to prevent further damage. U.S. engineers then used the bridging trains following the 3rd Infantry Division to throw several other spans across the river. Iraqi counterattacks on April 2, including what was for all intents and purposes a suicide attempt to explode charges on the main bridge, were turned back

Pilgrims in the street as smoke rises in the background following clashes in the Shiite holy city of Karbala, August 27, 2007. (AP/Wide World Photos)

On August 28 the Iraqi government deployed more troops to the city. On August 29 Prime Minister Nuri al-Maliki imposed a curfew that directed pilgrims to end their devotions early. Although he claimed that the situation was then under control, sporadic shooting continued. Only after additional Iraqi security forces had arrived and most of the pilgrims had departed did the violence end. Casualties in this factional struggle were estimated at 30–40 killed and more than 100 wounded. It is believed that 10 Iraqi policemen died in the confrontation.

In the aftermath of this fighting, the head of the Mahdi Army in Karbala, Ali Sharia, was arrested and tried for inciting the violence at Karbala. In August 2008 he was convicted and sentenced to death.

WILLIAM P. HEAD

See also

Badr Organization; Karbala, First Battle of; Mahdi Army; Maliki, Nuri Muhammed Kamil Hasan al-; Sadr, Muqtada al-; Supreme Iraqi Islamic Council

References

Craig, Charles. "Iraq Militias Fighting for Supremacy." *Time,* August 29, 2007, http://www.time.com/time/world/article/0,8599,1657449,00.html.

by American armor and highly effective close air support. Two divisions of the Iraqi Republican Guard were effectively destroyed, and the way to Baghdad was now open.

SHAWN LIVINGSTON AND SPENCER C. TUCKER

See also

Blount, Buford, III; IRAQI FREEDOM, Operation; Karbala, Second Battle of; Shia Islam; Sunni Islam

References

Brown, Todd S. *Battleground Iraq: Journal of Company Commander.* Washington, DC: Department of the Army, 2007.

Hodierne, Robert, and Riad Kahwaji. "History Explains Stiff Iraqi Resistance at Karbala Gap." *Navy Times* 52(28) (2003): 21.

Zimmerman, Dwight Jon, and John Gresham. *Beyond Hell and Back: How America's Special Operations Forces Became the World's Greatest Fighting Unit.* New York: St. Martin's, 2007.

Kari Air Defense System

French-built Iraqi integrated air defense system (IADS) intended to defeat air attacks on key targets in Iraq. The system was state of the art when it was designed in the late 1970s and early 1980s, but its weaknesses were exploited by coalition air forces during the 1991 Persian Gulf War. The hierarchical nature of the Kari system made it possible for coalition planners to determine how to remove centralized control from local defenses. After only a few days of air operations, Iraqi air defenses were in ruins, and coalition aircraft were largely free to operate at medium to high altitudes without excessive danger.

Two factors during the 1980s prompted the Iraqi government to purchase and implement an integrated air defense system. The first was the ease with which Iranian aircraft operated over Iraqi territory during the 1980–1988 Iran-Iraq War. Iranian aircraft were largely able to carry out their missions without fear of interception by Iraqi fighters or missiles. The second event was the Israeli air attack that destroyed the Osiraq nuclear reactor in 1981. This raid was intended to prevent Iraq from developing nuclear weapons. The Iraqis not only lost an important research and possible weapons development site, but the government was greatly embarrassed by the failure of its air defenses to prevent the attack.

To implement a new IADS, the Iraqis turned to two sources. The first was the Soviet Union, which had developed outstanding air defense technology during the Cold War. The Iraqis purchased large numbers of Soviet surface-to-air missiles (SAMs) along with thousands of antiaircraft artillery (AAA) pieces. Soviet experts also advised the Iraqis on how to integrate the equipment into a system of layered defenses. The Soviet system was attractive to President Saddam Hussein because it highly valued centralized control.

The second source to which Hussein turned was France. French companies had been important sources of military equipment for Iraq before and during the war with Iran. The Thomson-CSF company developed an integrated computer system for Iraq that promised to gather information from radars and use it to determine how to intercept incoming air raids most efficiently. The system was completed and largely deployed by 1987. Displaying some humor, the French called it "Kari," which was the French spelling of "Iraq" backwards.

The computer system was the core of Iraq's air defense, and on paper it looked very effective. Kari is a fully integrated command, control, and communications system. Under Kari, a national air defense operations center (ADOC) was established in downtown Baghdad.

Iraq was divided into four sectors. Each sector was controlled by a Sector Operations Center (SOC), which reported information to the ADOC and then received orders from that source. The 1st SOC was also known as the Central Air Defense Sector. The SOC headquarters were at Taji Airfield and covered Baghdad and surrounding areas. The 2nd SOC was also known as the Western Air Defense Sector. It was headquartered at H-3 airfield. The 3rd SOC covered the southern area of Iraq and was headquartered at Talil. The 4th SOC was the Northern Air Defense Sector and covered the oil fields of northern Iraq.

Each SOC controlled a number of interception operation centers (IOC) in its geographical area. The IOCs received information from different radar installations in their areas and passed the information along to the SOCs, which passed it up the line to the ADOC. In theory, Kari allowed central command to receive all information available, evaluate the threat, and decide what course of action should be taken. Missile batteries could be brought to readiness, AAA batteries prepared, or fighters launched. SOCs and IOCs were sited in locations that had good telecommunications.

Both voice and data communications were used to report incoming raids and to pass orders to subordinates. The system utilized both land lines and microwave communications. The French designers had planned that each node could switch from either form of communication without delay or interruption. All SOCs, all IOCs, and the ADOC were placed in hardened shelters, specially buried bunkers.

The Kari IADS controlled large numbers of resources to defend Iraq. Most of its equipment came from the Soviet Union, but sizable portions came from France. Iraqi air defense weapons were a mixture of state-of-the-art and obsolete systems.

First, information was fed to the ADOC from more than 500 different radars from more than 100 different sites around the country. These radars included a range of early warning and surveillance to target acquisition and fire control that were connected to individual batteries and weapons. Kari also controlled approximately 7,000 SAMs. Most were Soviet-produced weapons. For area defense, each SOC controlled one or more brigades of SA-2 and SA-3 missiles to cope with higher-flying aircraft. Low- to medium-level aircraft were countered with batteries of SA-6 missiles from the Soviet Union. Key strategic targets, especially those near Baghdad, were defended by shorter-range missiles, such as the 250 French-made Roland missiles and the Soviet SA-8 SAMs.

Many mobile SAMs, such as the SA-9 and the SA-13, were also deployed but were most often used to protect Republican Guard divisions. They were not usually controlled by the Kari system.

Kari also controlled the AAA batteries. Approximately 10,000 weapons were available. Once again, many were grouped around Baghdad to protect the key industrial, communications, and governmental installations. These batteries received information from the Kari system but were more often expected to fire in barrages, without more specific targeting information. Key weapons included 37-millimeter (mm) and 57-mm guns. Some were on self-propelled mountings, while others were located on top of buildings throughout Baghdad. Light AAA batteries included 14.5-mm and 23-mm weapons that were most effective at low altitudes. Below 10,000 feet, Iraq's AAAs were expected to be lethal, especially in daylight when aircraft could be tracked visually.

Finally, Kari also controlled jet fighters that could be scrambled and vectored to intercept incoming aircraft. Aircraft available included Soviet-made MiG-25s and MiG-29s along with French-made Mirage F-1s. The Iraqis adopted many of the Soviet procedures regarding air interceptions, requiring pilots to closely follow the orders of ground controllers. Because the Iraqi Air Force put a greater emphasis on ground attack, most of the best pilots were in those units. The ones who remained in the air defense squadrons were not as well trained. The Iraqis also planned to keep most fighters in hardened defenses when attacked. After the SAMs and AAAs had weakened enemy attackers, fighters could be scrambled to complete the job. Aggressiveness and initiative were not expected from the pilots.

Although Kari appeared impressive, it suffered from a number of weaknesses. The first was that the system could be overloaded. It was designed to deal with attacks by regional rivals of Iraq, especially Israel and Iran. Raids by those two states were expected to consist of 20 to 40 aircraft at a maximum. Each SOC had a theoretical capacity of tracking up to 120 aircraft at a time, but the reality was somewhat less. The system could be easily overloaded, as it was by coalition air forces in 1991. The use of many decoy targets confused and misled the Iraqi controllers and tended to paralyze the system. Because of Kari's centralized control and hierarchical structure, local controllers were not likely to act on their own initiative.

Because Kari was intended to deal mostly with Israeli and Iranian attacks, the defenses and most complete coverage were concentrated to the east and west of Baghdad. Less attention was paid regarding the south, where Saudi Arabia was an unlikely threat. Although the Iraqis did try to improve their radar coverage of the southern approaches to Baghdad, it was not possible to integrate new sites into Kari in the time prior to the Persian Gulf War.

The hierarchical structure of Kari was also a weakness that the coalition was able to exploit. Because information flowed upward to a centralized decision-making body and orders flowed down, an interruption in communications would cause disorder and paralyze the system. Although the French designers had included redundancy in their system, coalition planners were able to

overcome it. Priority targets in the first hours of Operation DESERT STORM included key communication centers. Cruise missile and stealth aircraft strikes were able to take out many land-line communications, while jamming procedures prevented microwave links from working. Direct attacks on the ADOC and SOC headquarters were also effective in disrupting communications.

The coalition also concentrated on suppression of enemy air defenses (SEAD) early in the war. Decoys caused Iraqi controllers to turn on their radars, allowing SEAD aircraft to take them out with high-speed antiradiation missiles (HARMs). Other known radar sites were attacked directly with Hellfire missiles or U.S. Army long-range tactical missile systems. By identifying key parts of the Kari system and their weaknesses, coalition planners developed a comprehensive plan to take Kari out within hours. Although 17 coalition aircraft were lost in the first week of the war, Iraq's IADS was effectively destroyed within the first 24 hours of the war.

After DESERT STORM, Iraq retained and upgraded Kari. One of the most important upgrades was the use of Chinese fiber optic systems to improve the speed and reliability of communications between different levels of operations. Kari was finally eliminated during the March 2003 invasion of Iraq, when the country was overrun and occupied in short order. Kari posed little threat to coalition forces during Operation IRAQI FREEDOM.

TIM J. WATTS

See also

Air Defenses in Iraq, Persian Gulf War; Antiaircraft Guns; Antiaircraft Missiles, Iraqi; Antiradiation Missiles, Coalition; Artillery; DESERT STORM, Operation, Coalition Air Campaign; Missiles, Surface-to-Air

References

Hallion, Richard P. *Storm over Iraq: Air Power and the Gulf War*. Washington, DC: Smithsonian Institution Press, 1997.

Murray, Williamson. *Air War in the Persian Gulf*. Baltimore: Nautical and Aviation Publishing Company of America, 1995.

Watson, Bruce W., ed. *Military Lessons of the Gulf War*. Novato, CA: Presidio, 1991.

Karpinski, Janis
Birth Date: May 25, 1953

U.S. Army officer who was in charge of the Abu Ghraib Prison in Abu Ghraib, Iraq, some 20 miles west of Baghdad, when allegations of prisoner mistreatment and torture surfaced. Born on May 25, 1953, in Rahway, New Jersey, Janis Leigh Karpinski graduated from Kean College. She received her commission as a second lieutenant in 1977 and attended the Military Police Officer Basic Course at Fort McClellan, Alabama, and the Airborne School at Fort Benning, Georgia. Karpinski served primarily as a military intelligence and military police officer until 1987, when she left active duty and joined the reserves. She worked as an intelligence officer at Fort Bragg, North Carolina, and during Operation DESERT

Army brigadier general Janis Karpinski, commander of the 899th Military Police Brigade at Abu Ghraib prison, the largest prison in Iraq. Karpinski commanded Abu Ghraib during the abuse of Iraqi prisoners, which became public knowledge on April 28, 2004. Karpinski, who claimed she had been made a scapegoat, was forced to retire in July 2005. (Chris Helgren/Reuters/Corbis)

STORM in 1991 she deployed to Saudi Arabia, where she was a targeting officer.

Immediately following this brief assignment in the Persian Gulf, Karpinski spent six years as a reservist and adviser, developing and implementing a military training program for women in the United Arab Emirates. After 1997 Karpinski continued as a reservist while also pursuing a civilian career in business.

In 2003 Karpinski was promoted to brigadier general. That June she took command of the 800th Military Police Brigade, which gave her charge of operations that included 3,400 army reservists and several battalions of active duty soldiers at 16 detention facilities in southern and central Iraq, including Abu Ghraib, and in the city of Mosul in the north.

While Karpinski was commanding the 800th Military Police Brigade, reports began to surface charging the unit with incidences of prisoner abuse and torture. While the army investigated the charges, in January 2004 Karpinski's superior, Lieutenant General Ricardo Sanchez, suspended her and 16 others from duty. In April 2005 after the Taguba Investigation, spearheaded by Major

General Antonio Taguba, substantiated details of prisoner abuse by some soldiers under her command, the army relieved Karpinski of her duties and command. In May 2005 President George W. Bush approved her demotion to colonel.

Subsequently the army accused Karpinski of dereliction of duty, making a material misrepresentation to investigators, and failure to obey a lawful order. Later, however, army officials cleared Karpinski of the latter two charges. Karpinski mounted a spirited defense, claiming that she had no knowledge of the abuse until the investigation began, that the particular cellblock in question (1A) was under the control of the military intelligence command at the time, and that the army had used her as a scapegoat for the aberrations that occurred at Abu Ghraib. Yet as the commander responsible for the facility, it was her duty to know what was taking place within her command, which she failed to do.

In 2005 Karpinski published an account of her life, career, and involvement in the controversial events at the prison titled *One Woman's Army: The Commanding General of Abu Ghraib Tells Her Story*. In it she attributes the abuses at Abu Ghraib to "conflicting orders and confused standards extending from the military commanders in Iraq all the way to the summit of civilian leadership in Washington. . . . Anyone fighting the counterterrorist war in the Middle East had a clear mandate . . . but only fuzzy rules of engagement." Karpinski retired from military service in July 2005. She lives on Hilton Head, South Carolina, and works as a business consultant.

The Abu Ghraib Scandal had ramifications far greater than the negative impact on Karpinski's career. It added fuel to critics who condemn the Bush administration's decision to go to war in Iraq in 2003 and compounded similar charges of abuse at Bagram in Afghanistan and in other prisons of Iraq as well as attacks on civilians in Iraq. The handling of the incident and the poor treatment of General Taguba showed a consistent effort by the military to pass off responsibility on others and also demonstrated inappropriate decisions made by intelligence, contractors, the military, and the civilian leadership in the hopes of breaking the insurgency, which amounted to promotion of dehumanizing practices. Internationally, the scandal was a considerable embarrassment to the United States, and many believed that it put Americans at greater risk due to the demonstrated lack of respect for prisoner's rights.

DEBORAH KIDWELL

See also

Abu Ghraib; IRAQI FREEDOM, Operation; Taguba, Antonio Mario

References

Greenberg, Karen J., and Joshua L. Dratel, eds. *The Torture Papers: The Road to Abu Ghraib.* Cambridge: Cambridge University Press, 2005.

Karpinski, Janis L., and Steven Strasser. *One Woman's Army: The Commanding General of Abu Ghraib Tells Her Story.* New York: Hyperion, 2005.

Schlesinger, James R. *Final Report of the Independent Panel to Review DOD Detention Operations.* Buffalo, NY: William S. Hein, 2005.

Karzai, Hamid
Birth Date: December 24, 1957

Afghan politician, supporter of the mujahideen, and leader of Afghanistan since the demise of the Taliban regime in December 2001. Hamid Karzai was born into a politically prominent family on December 24, 1957, in Karz, not far from Kandahar, Afghanistan. A Sunni Muslim, Karzai is an ethnic Pashtun from the Popalzai tribe. His grandfather was a high-ranking Afghan official, and his father, Abdul Ahad Karzai, was a tribal elder and served as deputy speaker of the Afghan parliament in the 1960s. In 1976 Hamid Karzai went to India as an exchange student. He later studied international relations and political science at Simla University, from which he earned an MA degree in 1983. During his stay in India, his nation was invaded and occupied by Soviet troops in December 1979, prompting a hard-fought struggle against the Soviets that lasted until 1989.

Beginning in 1984, Karzai dedicated himself fully to the ouster of Soviet forces from his homeland by helping to raise money to support the mujahideen fighters, who had begun to wage an increasingly effective guerrilla war against Soviet occupation troops. He also served as director of information for the National Liberation Front, located in neighboring Pakistan, and later served as deputy director of its political operations. Karzai reportedly became a key contact for the U.S. Central Intelligence Agency (CIA), which was helping to funnel money and weapons to the mujahideen.

Before long, Karzai had cultivated close ties with CIA director William Casey and Vice President George H. W. Bush. For a time Karzai was in the United States, but he returned to Afghanistan in 1989 at which time the Soviets had withdrawn their troops from the country. At the same time, the mujahideen were attempting to form a new government.

In late 1989 Karzai began serving the provisional Afghan government as director of foreign relations for the interim president. In 1992 a permanent government was inaugurated, and Karsai began serving as Afghanistan's deputy foreign minister. By 1994 civil war had broken out among numerous mujahideen groups and the ascendant Taliban, an extreme right-wing fundamentalist movement. Initially Karzai supported the Taliban, but he quickly withdrew his support when he saw for himself its real agenda. Resigning his government post in 1994, he began working to form a national Grand Council (Loya Jirga) that would eventually, he hoped, oust the Taliban from power. He exiled himself to Quetta, Pakistan, and there worked with his father to bring down the Taliban. In 1999 his father was assassinated presumably by agents of the Taliban, an event that served to strengthen Karzai's resolve.

When Operation ENDURING FREEDOM began in October 2001, Karzai returned to Afghanistan and organized local support in Kandahar to aid coalition forces and the Northern Alliance in their drive to topple the Taliban. This was accomplished in December 2001. On December 5 he became chairman of the Interim

Thrust into the role of interim leader of a country devastated by war and world events, Hamid Karzai was sworn in as chairperson of Afghanistan's coalition government on December 22, 2001. In presidential elections held on October 9, 2004, Karzai received a majority of votes cast and was subsequently confirmed as president. (NATO)

Administration of Afghanistan. Less than three weeks later he was sworn in as interim chairman.

Karzai's job was a difficult one, attempting to rule over a nation exhausted and ravaged by years of war and unrest. Indeed, he found it nearly impossible to travel outside the confines of Kabul, the capital city. In June 2002 Karzai became president of the interim government. In the meantime, he and other Afghan leaders had convened the Loya Jirga.

In October 2004 Karzai was formally elected president in nationwide elections. He began serving his five-year term in December 2004 in an inauguration that received much worldwide attention. Since then, Karzai has found it almost impossible to implement needed reforms on a countrywide basis. He has also witnessed a rise in activity by Taliban fighters and members of Al Qaeda. The nation remains desperately poor, and he rejected U.S. demands that he put an end to poppy production, fearing that doing so would further impoverish Afghans. Nevertheless, Karzai has tried to be a uniting force in a fractious country and has enjoyed some success in forging alliances with tribal and regional leaders. He remains committed to championing human rights in his country, and he has attempted to empower Afghan women. Toward this end, he has appointed several women to high-ranking government posts. This has met with much resistance among conservatives.

In recent years Karzai has made some headway in the economic sphere and has even reached out to moderate Taliban members, claiming that the Taliban is welcome in Afghanistan so long as it does not include militants or terrorists. Karzai has frequently criticized the United States and the North Atlantic Treaty Organization (NATO) for air strikes aimed at eradicating militants in rural Afghanistan. Numerous attacks have injured or killed innocent civilians. Karzai also pointed out in 2006 that the billions of dollars going to the Iraq War could have easily reconstructed Afghanistan, putting that nation on a much firmer footing. Despite his criticisms, he remains deeply appreciative of American efforts in his nation since 2001 and remains an important ally in the Global War on Terror. In 2006 he pledged to end poppy cultivation in Afghanistan as soon as practical, acknowledging that the crop was helping to feed the continued insurgency there. Between 2002 and 2008 Karzai was been the target of four assassination attempts, at least two of which were blamed on radical Taliban insurgents.

In the waning years of the George W. Bush administration relations between Washington and Kabul deteriorated, especially after Karzai publicly criticized the U.S. war in Iraq, claiming that it was siphoning badly needed funds from the reconstruction effort in Afghanistan. He also rankled U.S. policy makers by proclaiming his close ties to Iran. During 2008 and into 2009, U.S. attacks on Taliban strongholds that inadvertently killed civilians angered the Afghan president. In turn, the Barack Obama administration has criticized Karzai for being ineffective and unsteady and has argued that his regime has done too little to stop the poppy and narcotics trade. Nevertheless, Karzai announced his intention to run for reelection in August 2009 despite U.S. signals that it preferred an alternative candidate and despite rampant Afghan corruption.

Karzai won the 2009 election, amid cries of corruption, intimidation, and vote rigging, when his opponent in the second runoff election bowed out. Throughout 2009, many Western leaders, including Obama, tried to distance themselves from the Karzai regime. In particular, the United States rebuked Karzai for the continued vast corruption and drug trade in Afghanistan and his failure to address security concerns of his people. In January 2010 Karzai reached out to the Taliban, asking them to join a *loya jirga* in an attempt to reach a peace settlement. Karzai was reportedly not much enthused with the Obama administration's decision to send thousands of additional troops to Afghanistan beginning in early 2010.

PAUL G. PIERPAOLI JR.

See also

Afghanistan; Al Qaeda; Central Intelligence Agency; Mujahideen, Soviet-Afghanistan War; Soviet-Afghanistan War; Taliban

References

Abrams, Dennis. *Hamid Karzai.* Langhorne, PA: Chelsea House, 2007.

Wolny, Philip. *Hamid Karzai: President of Afghanistan.* New York: Rosen, 2007.

Katyusha Rocket

The Soviet Union's Katyusha multiple rocket launcher was developed by a design team headed by Gregory E. Langemak at the Leningrad Gas Dynamics Laboratory beginning in 1938 and was in direct response to German development in 1936 of the six-barrel Nebelwerfer rocket launcher. The Soviet rocket was at first intended for aircraft use and was approved on June 21, 1941, on the eve of the German invasion of the Soviet Union. It was first employed in combat in a truck-mounted mode by the Red Army against the Germans in July 1941. The rockets were unofficially named for the title of a popular Russian wartime song, with "Katyusha" a diminutive for Ekaterina (Catherine). The Germans knew the weapon as the Stalinorgel (Stalin's Organpipes) for its distinctive sound.

The unguided Katyusha rocket appeared in a variety of sizes. The first was the BM-8 (BM for *boyevaya mashina*, or combat vehicle) 82-millimeter (mm), but by the end of the war the Soviets were using BM-13 132-mm rockets. The BM-13 was nearly six feet in length, weighed 92 pounds, and had a range of about three miles. Such rockets could be armed with high-explosive, incendiary, or chemical warheads. Although not an accurate weapon, the Katyusha could be extremely effective in saturation bombardment when large numbers of launch trucks were deployed side by side.

The launch system consisted of a series of parallel rails with a folding frame that was raised in order to bring the rockets into firing position. Katyushas were mounted on a variety of truck beds to fire forward over the cab. Each truck mounted between 14 and 48 launchers. Trucks included the Soviet ZiS-6 and the Lend-Lease–supplied and U.S.-manufactured Studebaker US6 2.5-ton. Katyushas were also mounted on T-40 and T-60 tanks and on aircraft for use against German tanks and also appeared on ships and riverine vessels in a ground-support role. Artillerists were not fond of the multiple launch system because it took up to 50 minutes to load and fired only 24 rounds, whereas a conventional howitzer could fire four to six times as many rounds in a comparable time period.

Katyushas continued to undergo refinement. During the Cold War, Soviet forces were equipped with the BM-24 240-mm Katyusha, which had a range of about six miles. Each truck mounted 12 rockets. Two racks, one on top of the other, contained 6 rockets each. In 1963 the Soviets introduced the 122-mm BM-21. It was exported to more than 50 countries. Larger 220-mm and 300-mm Katyushas were also developed.

Over time, the name "Katyusha" has become a generic term applied to all small artillery rockets, even those developed by Israel and based on Katyushas captured during the June 1967 Six-Day War. The Israeli Light Artillery Rocket (LAR) has a range of some

A Katyusha rocket launcher, captured by Israeli forces in southern Lebanon during Operation PEACE FOR GALILEE, shown here on June 29, 1982. (Baruch Rimon/Israeli Government Press Office)

27 miles and can be loaded with a variety of different munitions. It was employed in the October 1973 Yom Kippur (Ramadan) War and in the 1982 invasion of Lebanon.

Katyushas have also been employed by Hezbollah and Islamic Jihad against Israel and by Iraqi insurgents against U.S. and coalition forces. In March 2006 a BM-21 122-mm Katyusha was fired into Israel from the Gaza Strip, the first time a Katyusha had been sent into Israel from Palestinian-controlled territory. The 9-foot, 2-inch BM-21 has a range of nearly 13 miles and a warhead of nearly 35 pounds. Katyushas are much more a worry to Israel than the short-range home-made Qassam rocket, fired by Hamas into Israel from the Gaza Strip.

It has been estimated that in the fighting between Israel and Hezbollah in Lebanon during July–August 2006, Hezbollah launched as many as 4,000 Katyusha rockets against the Jewish state, with about one-quarter of them hitting densely populated civilian areas. While the rockets were not at first a major problem for U.S. forces in the Iraq War, the use of Katyushas has undergone an increase, probably in response to Syrian and Iranian support of the Iraq Insurgency. In March 2008 Katyusha rockets were reportedly launched against Baghdad's heavily fortified Green Zone. The United States developed the Tactical High Energy Laser (THEL) system specifically to defeat the Katyusha during flight.

The U.S. counterpart to the Katyusha is the Multiple Launch Rocket System (MLRS) M270. The tracked M270 vehicle fires 12 8.9-inch (227-mm) 13-foot long unguided rockets from two self-contained six-round pods.

SPENCER C. TUCKER

See also

Green Zone in Iraq; Hezbollah; Iraqi Insurgency; Islamic Jihad, Palestinian; Israel; Lebanon; Lebanon, Israeli Invasion of

References

Bellamy, Chris. *Red God of War: Soviet Artillery and Rocket Forces.* Herdon, VA: Potomac Books, 1986.

O'Malley, T. J. *Artillery: Guns and Rocket Systems.* Mechanicsburg, PA: Stackpole, 1994.

Kazakhstan and the Afghanistan and Iraq Wars

Eurasian country that straddles central Asia and eastern Europe. Kazakhstan covers 1.052 million square miles and had a 2008 population of 15.341 million people. A former Soviet republic that declared its independence in 1991, Kazakhstan borders Russia, Kyrgyzstan, Turkmenistan, Uzbekistan, China, and the Caspian

Sea. Kazakhstan is a presidential republic with a parliamentary-style legislative process. The president holds significant power, as he is both head of state and commander in chief of the armed forces. The prime minister is head of government. There are several political parties in the country. The Fatherland (Otan) Party is by far the largest, followed by the coalition of a Just Kazakhstan, the Democratic Party of Kazakhstan Bright Path, the Social Democratic Party, and the People's Communist Party of Kazakhstan. Kazakhstan has been pro-Western in orientation since the mid-1990s.

Kazakhstan supported the U.S.-led coalitions during Operations ENDURING FREEDOM and IRAQI FREEDOM as part of a broader effort to bolster ties with the United States and the West. Specifically, Kazakhstan sought to improve its security relations with the United States and the North Atlantic Treaty Organization (NATO) as a means to counter Russian influence in the Caspian region. Concurrently, the United States endeavored to enhance its relationship with oil- and gas-rich Kazakhstan in order to gain increased access to energy supplies.

Following the terrorist attacks on the United States on September 11, 2001, Kazakhstan emerged as an important geostrategic U.S. partner because of its proximity to Afghanistan and the potential for expanded terrorist activities in the region. Kazakhstan granted the United States and its allies use of Kazakh airspace, and increased intelligence cooperation was initiated between the government and the coalition in Afghanistan. The Kazakh government also offered the coalition the use of an air base, but the United States instead chose to use bases in Uzbekistan and Kyrgyzstan because of their closer proximity to Afghanistan. To provide support for Kazakhstan, the United States increased foreign aid to the country. Between 2001 and 2008 the United States provided Kazakhstan with more than $200 million in direct government aid and economic development assistance.

During the buildup to the 2003 Iraq War, Kazakhstan became concerned over the possibility that any conflict might escalate and spread into the Caspian region. The government was also concerned that energy prices could drop dramatically if the war was short and if Iraq quickly restored its production capabilities beyond the limits imposed at the time by international sanctions. The country redeployed forces, including antiaircraft batteries, to protect infrastructure and energy fields.

The Kazakh government officially supported a resolution of the conflict under the auspices of the Untied Nations (UN). However, when the invasion of Iraq began in March 2003, the Kazakh government issued a statement of support for the U.S.-led coalition. Kazakhstan also agreed to send a small number of troops to Iraq and deployed engineering elements of KAZBAT (for Kazakhstan Battalion) in September 2003. The Kazakh contingent numbered about 30 troops, who engaged in de-mining operations and ordnance disposal tasks. The Kazakhs operated in the Wasit Province in southwestern Iraq within the Polish area of operations. The deployment was viewed by the Kazakh government as a manifestation of its growing ties with the United States and the West and as a means of providing its peacekeeping battalion with practical experience. Soldiers rotated through Iraq on 6- to 12-month deployments. The government also announced that it sought greater participation in multilateral peacekeeping operations in the future.

Kazakhstan withdrew its forces from Iraq in October 2008 in line with the general drawdown of international troops. Kazakh forces lost one soldier killed in Iraq when ordnance unexpectedly detonated during a loading operation. Concurrent with the withdrawal of Kazakh forces from Iraq, the government initiated discussions with NATO for the deployment of peacekeepers as part of the alliance's operations in Afghanistan.

TOM LANSFORD

See also

Afghanistan, Coalition Combat Operations in, 2002–Present; IRAQI FREEDOM, Operation, Coalition Ground Forces; Multi-National Force–Iraq; North Atlantic Treaty Organization in Afghanistan

References

Cockburn, Patrick. *The Occupation: War and Resistance in Iraq.* New York: Verso, 2007.
Keegan, John. *The Iraq War: The Military Offensive, from Victory in 21 Days to the Insurgent Aftermath.* New York: Vintage, 2005.

Kelly, David Christopher
Birth Date: May 17, 1944
Death Date: July 17, 2003

British biological weapons expert, official in the Ministry of Defence, and United Nations (UN) weapons inspector whose actions and mysterious death in 2003 provoked a political scandal in Great Britain. David Christopher Kelly was born on May 17, 1944, in Rhondda, Wales, United Kingdom. He earned an undergraduate degree from the University of Leeds, a master of science degree from the University of Birmingham, and a doctorate in microbiology from Linacre College, Oxford University, in 1971.

After working in the private sector for a number of years, in 1984 Kelly entered the civil service and became chairman of the United Kingdom's Defence Microbiology Division. He worked on a wide variety of government and international projects dealing with biological weapons, and he twice visited Russia in the 1990s as a weapons inspector. He also worked with the UN in the aftermath of the 1991 Persian Gulf War and was among the weapons inspectors sent to Iraq to ensure that the nation was complying with the postwar disarmament agreements.

Between 1991 and 1999 Kelly made some 37 trips to Iraq as a member of the United Nations Special Commission (UNSCOM), and during several of those trips he uncovered evidence of Iraq's biological weapons program. He was lauded both at home and abroad for his work, and more than one colleague nominated him for a Nobel Peace Prize for his findings.

In 2002 Kelly was peripherally involved with the compilation of a top-secret but very controversial dossier assembled by the British Defence Intelligence Staff. The dossier was designed to provide intelligence on Iraq's weapons programs to British prime minister Tony Blair, who at the time was considering an Anglo-American–led invasion of Iraq ostensibly to rid the nation of weapons of mass destruction (WMDs). Because of his vast experience in Iraq and his familiarity with Iraqi weapons programs, Kelly was asked to review the report before it was presented to Blair. What Kelly found troubled him, particularly the claim that Iraq was capable of firing chemical and/or biological weapons on the battlefield within 45 minutes of their order for use. Kelly's findings did not support such a claim, but his superiors prevailed, and the information was left in the dossier.

Kelley continued to believe, however, that Iraq may have had some semblance of a biological weapons program, right up to the April 2003 invasion that toppled Iraqi dictator Saddam Hussein. As such, in June 2003 Kelly joined an international weapons inspection team charged with looking for Iraq's alleged WMDs. When the media triumphantly announced that inspectors had found two mobile laboratories designed to produce biological weapons, Kelly ridiculed the idea, speaking to a reporter off the record and asserting that they in fact were not biological weapons labs. *The Observer*, a British newspaper, ran the story, but it created little stir because the source was anonymous.

A month prior, in May 2003, Kelly had agreed to meet with Andrew Gilligan, an investigative reporter for the British Broadcasting Company (BBC). The two men agreed that Kelly would discuss strictly off the record the content of the intelligence dossier used by Tony Blair and especially the claim that Iraq could have fired biological or chemical weapons within 45 minutes of first order, an assertion that Kelly believed to be entirely false. On May 29 Gilligan broadcast his findings but attributed the bogus claim in the dossier to Alastair Campbell, Blair's communications director. In fact, certain claims in the dossier were copied from a journal article without attribution, but putting the blame on those responsible for the dossier's publication set off a firestorm at Number 10 Downing Street, as the Blair government vigorously denied any involvement in the compilation of the dossier. Now panicked and perturbed that Gilligan had made claims that he himself had never made, Kelly told his superiors of his contact with Gilligan, and soon the news had leaked out that Kelly had been the true source of Gilligan's story. In the meantime, the Blair government continued to deal with the fallout from the incident.

In July 2003 Kelly, anguished over the unintended results of his actions and mortified by all the publicity, was forced to testify before the House of Commons Foreign Affairs Select Committee, which had been charged with investigating the dossier incident. On July 15 he appeared, visibly shaken, before the committee. After grueling questions, he left under duress and was bombarded by reporters. The next day he was similarly grilled by members of the Intelligence and Security Committee. On July 17 Kelley left

his Oxfordshire home to take a walk. Instead, he went to a heavily wooded area about a mile from his home, swallowed as many as 30 painkillers, slashed his left wrist, and later died. His body was found by the police the next morning.

The strange circumstances of Kelly's death and his role in the political scandal involving faulty prewar intelligence led many Britons to fear that he had been murdered in an attempt to keep the scandal from snowballing. Because of this, the British government assembled a judicial inquiry to look into the matter, including the circumstances of Kelly's death. On August 1, 2003, the Hutton Inquiry, named after James Brian Edward, Lord Hutton, began its work. On January 28, 2004, the Hutton Inquiry issued its report.

The report, which was met with some skepticism, unequivocally stated that Kelly had taken his own life, that nobody had aided him in any way, and that none of the other people involved in the dossier incident had threatened him or made him believe that taking his life was a solution to the problem. During the investigation, however, a British foreign service official recalled a conversation he had with Kelly in Geneva in February 2003. Allegedly, Kelly had told the unnamed person that he had told the Iraqis that they would not be invaded if they cooperated with weapons inspectors. When pressed, Kelly reportedly said to the man that if war did come, he would "probably be found dead in the woods." Skeptics and critics claimed that there was not enough blood found at the death scene to square with the coroner's report that listed loss of blood as the chief cause of death. In 2006 another investigation was launched into Kelly's death, but no definitive conclusions could be drawn. Some continue to believe that Kelly was a scapegoat for the false claims made to justify the invasion of Iraq and the subsequent war and that someone within the Blair government had ordered him silenced.

Paul G. Pierpaoli Jr.

See also

Biological Weapons and Warfare; Blair, Tony; United Nations Special Commission; United Nations Weapons Inspectors; Weapons of Mass Destruction

References

Baker, Norman. *The Strange Death of David Kelly*. London: Methuen, 2007.
Stephens, Philip. *Tony Blair: The Making of a World Leader*. New York: Viking Books, 2004.

Kennedy, John Fitzgerald
Birth Date: May 29, 1917
Death Date: November 22, 1963

U.S. congressman (1946–1952), senator (1953–1961), and president of the United States (1961–1963). John Fitzgerald Kennedy was born in Brookline, Massachusetts, on May 29, 1917, into a large and wealthy Irish Catholic family. He earned his bachelor's degree from Harvard University in 1940 and served four years in

Democrat John F. Kennedy, elected president in November 1960, ushered in a new period in U.S. history. Kennedy was assassinated in Dallas, Texas, on November 22, 1963. (John F. Kennedy Presidential Library)

the U.S. Navy during World War II. He was awarded the Navy and Marine Corps Medal and the Purple Heart for action as commander of *PT-109,* which was rammed and sunk by a Japanese destroyer in the South Pacific.

After the war Kennedy worked for a brief time as a newspaper reporter before entering national politics at the age of 29, winning election as Democratic congressman from Massachusetts in 1946. In Congress he backed social legislation that benefited his largely working-class constituents and criticized what he considered to be President Harry S. Truman's weak stand against communist China. Throughout his career, in fact, Kennedy was known for his vehement anticommunist sentiments.

Kennedy won election to the U.S. Senate in 1952, although he had a relatively undistinguished career in that body. Never a well man, he suffered from several serious health problems, including a back operation in 1955 that nearly killed him. Despite his fragile health and lackluster performance in the Senate, he won reelection in 1958. After losing a close contest for the vice presidential nomination at the 1956 Democratic National Convention, he now set his sights on the presidency. Four years later he won the Democratic nomination for president on the first ballot.

Candidate Kennedy promised more aggressive defense policies, health care reform, and housing and civil rights programs. He also proposed his New Frontier agenda, designed to revitalize the

flagging U.S. economy and to bring young people into government and humanitarian service. Winning election by the narrowest of margins, he became the nation's first Roman Catholic president. Only 42 years old, he was also the youngest man ever to be elected to that office.

As president, Kennedy set out to fulfill his campaign pledges. Once in office, he was forced to respond to the increasingly urgent demands of civil rights advocates, although he did so rather reluctantly and tardily. By establishing both the Alliance for Progress and the Peace Corps, he delivered American idealism and goodwill to aid developing countries.

Despite Kennedy's idealism, no amount of enthusiasm could blunt the growing tensions in the U.S.-Soviet Cold War rivalry. One of Kennedy's first attempts to stanch the perceived communist threat was to authorize a band of U.S.-supported Cuban exiles to invade the communist island in an attempt to overthrow Fidel Castro in April 1961. The Bay of Pigs invasion, which turned into a disaster for the president, had been planned by the Central Intelligence Agency (CIA) under President Dwight D. Eisenhower. Although Kennedy harbored reservations about the operation, he nonetheless approved it. The failure further heightened Cold War tensions with the Soviets and ultimately set the stage for the Cuban Missile Crisis of 1962.

Cold War confrontation was not limited to Cuba. In the spring of 1961 the Soviet Union renewed its campaign to control West Berlin. Kennedy spent two days in Vienna in June 1961 discussing the hot-button issue with Soviet premier Nikita Khrushchev. In the months that followed, the crisis over Berlin was further intensified by the construction of the Berlin Wall, which prevented East Berliners from escaping to the West. Kennedy responded to the provocation by reinforcing U.S. troops in West Germany and increasing the nation's military strength. In the meantime, he had begun deploying what would be some 16,000 U.S. military advisers to prop up Ngo Dinh Diem's regime in South Vietnam. In so doing, Kennedy had put the United States on the path to full-scale military intervention in Vietnam.

With the focus now directed away from Europe, the Soviets began to clandestinely install nuclear missiles in Cuba. On October 14, 1962, U.S. spy planes photographed the construction of missile-launching sites in Cuba. The placement of nuclear missiles only 90 miles from U.S. shores threatened to destabilize the Western Hemisphere and undermine the uneasy Cold War nuclear deterrent. Kennedy imposed a naval quarantine on Cuba that was designed to interdict any offensive weapons bound for the island. The world held its collective breath as the two Cold War superpowers appeared perched on the abyss of thermonuclear war. But after 13 harrowing days the Soviet Union agreed to remove the missiles. In return the United States pledged not to preemptively invade Cuba and to secretly remove its obsolete nuclear missiles from Turkey.

Both Kennedy and Khrushchev had been sobered by the Cuban Missile Crisis, realizing that the world had come as close as it ever had to a full-scale nuclear war. Cold War tensions were diminished when the Soviet Union, Britain, and the United States signed the Limited Nuclear Test-Ban Treaty on August 5, 1963, forbidding atmospheric testing of nuclear weapons. To avoid potential misunderstandings and miscalculations in a future crisis, a hot line was installed that directly linked the Oval Office with the Kremlin.

As a congressman in 1951, Kennedy had visited the Middle East. Even then he voiced his opposition to colonialism in the region, urging that Middle Eastern nations should govern their own affairs. He specifically called upon the French to give independence to Algeria. Despite these early remonstrations, he nevertheless became the first U.S. president to agree to a major weapons sale to the Israelis, which gave the impression that his administration was pro-Israeli and, by definition, anti-Arab.

Such was not the case. While the Kennedy administration did support Israel, it was not because it was anti-Arab. The president approved the sale of U.S.-made Hawk air defense missiles to Israel chiefly because the Soviets, the French, and even the British had supplied arms to Arab states. Kennedy hoped to readjust the balance of power in the Middle East by bolstering Israeli defenses. The administration made numerous commitments to and statements of support for Arab nations in the Middle East and exhibited compassion toward the Palestinian refugee issue.

In the end, President Kennedy refused to enter into a binding military alliance with the Israelis and was reluctant to sell large caches of armaments and weapons to them. To do so, he believed, would have placed the United States in a vulnerable position in a future Middle East crisis. He did not want a new world war to erupt in the Middle East, which was not out of the realm of possibility given the tense state of superpower relations. He did, however, accede to regularly scheduled consultations between Israeli and American military officials. The Kennedy administration's Middle East policies were guided more by pragmatism than ideology.

At the same time that Kennedy agreed to send antiaircraft missiles to Israel, he was also engaging in quiet diplomacy with Egyptian president Gamal Abdel Nasser. Recognizing Nasser's importance and popularity in the Middle East, Kennedy sought rapprochement with Egypt. Indeed, he and Nasser exchanged personal letters many times. But Nasser's decision to intervene in the civil war in Yemen soured the growing relationship between the two leaders. Kennedy dispatched U.S. fighter aircraft to Saudi Arabia to protect it and to serve as a warning to the Egyptians not to increase their role in Yemen. Although Kennedy did not have to contend with any major crises in the Middle East, he nonetheless engaged in a delicate game of diplomatic chess by which he sought to aid the Israelis, engage the Arabs, limit Soviet influence, and keep the region's rich oil supplies flowing.

Following the nerve-wracking Cuban Missile Crisis, Kennedy looked toward 1963 with considerable enthusiasm. He was also buoyed by his successful efforts to reduce Cold War tensions. In an effort to mediate between warring conservative and liberal Democratic Party factions in Texas, a state that was vital to his reelection, in November 1963 Kennedy embarked on a whirlwind tour there with his wife and vice president. While riding in an open car in Dallas, Texas, on November 22, 1963, Kennedy was assassinated. In a great national and international outpouring of grief the slain president was laid to rest in Arlington National Cemetery on November 25, 1963.

LACIE A. BALLINGER

See also

Arms Sales, International; Nasser, Gamal Abdel; Soviet Union, Middle East Policy; United States, Middle East Policy, 1945–Present

References

Bass, Warren. *Support Any Friend: Kennedy's Middle East and the Making of the U.S.-Israel Alliance.* New York: Oxford University Press, 2003.

Dallek, Robert. *An Unfinished Life: John F. Kennedy, 1917–1963.* Boston: Little, Brown, 2003.

Druks, Herbert M. *John F. Kennedy and Israel.* New York: Greenwood, 2006.

Schlesinger, Arthur M. *A Thousand Days: John F. Kennedy in the White House.* New York: Houghton Mifflin, 1965.

Kerry, John Forbes
Birth Date: December 11, 1943

Vietnam War veteran, U.S. senator (1985–), and 2004 Democratic presidential nominee. John Forbes Kerry was born in Aurora, Colorado, on December 11, 1943, the son of a World War II Army Air Corps test pilot, foreign service officer, and attorney. His mother, a nurse, was a member of the distinguished and wealthy Forbes family of Boston. As a child Kerry lived abroad for a time and also attended an exclusive college preparatory school in New Hampshire.

Kerry attended Yale University, graduating in 1966. That same year he joined the U.S. Navy, serving on a destroyer off the coast of Vietnam. During 1968–1969 he volunteered to command a swift (navy patrol) boat; he was stationed first at Cam Ranh Bay and then on the island of Phu Quoc. He received three Purple Heart medals for combat wounds, returned to the United States in the spring of 1969, and left the service on March 1, 1970.

Results of the 2004 U.S. Presidential Election

Name	Party	% of Popular Vote	Electoral Votes
George W. Bush	Republican	50.74%	286
John Kerry	Democratic	48.27%	251
Ralph Nader	None	0.38%	0
Michael Badnarik	Libertarian	0.32%	0
Michael Peroutka	Constitution	0.12%	0
John Edwards	Democratic	0.01%	1
Other	—	0.16%	0

Democrat John Forbes Kerry has been a U.S. senator from Massachusetts since 1985. In the election of 2004, Kerry lost his bid to become president of the United States to Republican incumbent George W. Bush. (U.S. Senate)

Upon his return Kerry, who was proud of his service in the war, nevertheless dedicated much energy to opposing the war and speaking out on policies that he believed had failed the U.S. mission in Vietnam. Some of his actions were not without controversy. His antiwar activity included membership in several antiwar organizations, writings against the war, testimony to the U.S. Senate Foreign Relations Committee, the publicizing of alleged war crimes committed by American and Vietnamese soldiers, and participation in numerous demonstrations, including a famous one in which he and nearly 1,000 fellow Vietnam veterans threw down their service medals on the steps of the U.S. Capitol before television cameras.

In 1972 Kerry decided to run for a U.S. House of Representatives seat, representing northeastern Massachusetts as a Democrat. He lost the race and decided to attend law school at Boston College, from which he earned a degree in 1976. He then became a full-time prosecutor in Middlesex County. He left that post in 1979 to establish his own law firm, which was a modest success. In 1982 he successfully ran for the post of lieutenant governor in Massachusetts and served under Governor Michael Dukakis. Two years later Kerry ran for a U.S. Senate seat and won. He has remained in the Senate since January 1985.

In the Senate, Kerry earned a reputation for his earnestness, deep grasp of national issues, and ability to reach across the aisle when necessary to effect bipartisan legislative compromises. He is considered a moderate to left-leaning Democrat. In 2000 he was on Vice President Al Gore's short list of potential running mates for the autumn 2000 presidential election.

Kerry decided to run for president in 2004 and soon established himself as one of the front runners in an unusually crowded slate of Democratic hopefuls. After winning the January 2004 Iowa Caucus, Kerry went on to win a string of state primaries, and by the early spring he was the presumptive Democratic presidential nominee. After choosing North Carolina senator John Edwards as his vice presidential running mate, Kerry was formally nominated at the Democratic National Convention that summer and began a hard-fought campaign to unseat the incumbent George W. Bush.

Kerry's main platform in the election was his opposition to the war in Iraq and Bush's handling of the Global War on Terror after the September 11, 2001, terror attacks. Kerry also scoffed at Bush's economic policies, which had caused huge budget deficits and an uneven economy and had skewed income toward those who already possessed the vast majority of wealth in the country. Kerry also made vague promises of health care reform. Without a doubt, however, the Iraq War was the most important subject of debate in 2004. In this, Kerry's past voting record did not serve him particularly well, as he strongly backed the October 2002 joint congressional resolution authorizing the use of force against Iraq. After the March 2003 invasion of Iraq and the subsequent revelation that Iraq did not have weapons of mass destruction (WMDs), Kerry turned sharply against the war and became an outspoken critic of the Bush administration.

Not surprisingly, the Bush campaign jumped on Kerry's position vis-à-vis the Iraq War, particularly Kerry's ill-considered comment that he "first voted for it before he voted against it," opening himself up to charges of flip-flopping on the war. Over the course of the late summer and into the autumn, seeds of doubt were planted in the electorate's mind as to Kerry's competence, decisiveness, and ability to handle national security issues. Indeed, Kerry was portrayed as a weak and effete Massachusetts liberal who was out of step with American voters. The Kerry campaign was sometimes slow and tepid in its reactions to these attacks, which only compounded the damage. A series of searing television ads by the Swift Boat Veterans for Truth group also hobbled Kerry's campaign. Among other things, the group accused Kerry of dishonorable conduct during and after his Vietnam War service and charged that he had lied or greatly exaggerated his role in the war.

Kerry went on to lose the 2004 election by a close margin (Bush won 31 states to Kerry's 19 plus the District of Columbia but bested him by less than 3 percent of the popular vote and 35 electoral college votes). Remaining in the U.S. Senate, Kerry continued to criticize the Bush administration's policies, especially those toward the Iraq War.

PAUL G. PIERPAOLI JR.

See also
Bush, George Walker; Swift Boat Veterans for Truth; United States, National Elections of 2004

References
Kerry, John. *A Call to Service: My Vision for a Better America*. New York: Viking Books, 2003.
Kranish, Michael, Brian C. Mooney, and Nina J. Easton. *John F. Kerry: The Complete Biography*. New York: PublicAffairs, 2004.

Keys, William Morgan
Birth Date: 1937

U.S. Marine Corps general who commanded the 2nd Marine Division during the 1991 Persian Gulf War. William Morgan Keys was born in 1937 in Fredericktown, Pennsylvania. He was commissioned a second lieutenant in the U.S. Marine Corps in 1960 upon graduation from the U.S. Naval Academy, Annapolis. He subsequently attended various U.S. Marine Corps schools, including the Amphibious Warfare School and the Command and Staff College at Quantico, Virginia, and he earned a master's degree from American University. Keys also served two tours in Vietnam, and on March 2, 1967, he earned the Navy Cross for action against North Vietnamese forces.

By September 1989 Keys was a major general and commander of the 2nd Marine Division at Camp Lejeune, North Carolina. In August 1990 Iraqi forces overran Kuwait, triggering Operation DESERT SHIELD, a buildup of U.S. and coalition forces in Saudi Arabia. At first the division's contribution to the effort was support of the 4th Marine Expeditionary Brigade in the Persian Gulf. In November 1990 the division was alerted for likely deployment to Saudi Arabia in case force was necessary to remove the Iraqis from Kuwait. Much of the equipment needed by the division was provided by prepositioned merchant ships already in the area. To fill out the division, a number of marine reservists were called to active duty. The armor battalions assigned to the division were also equipped with M1-A1 Abrams tanks, giving them state-of-the-art armor. The division was still short one regiment, however, so an armor brigade from the 2nd Armored Division was attached to the 2nd Marine Division. Known as the Tiger Brigade, this U.S. Army unit added significant firepower to the marine division.

Keys arrived in Saudi Arabia on December 14, 1990, and immediately joined in the planning for offensive operations. Initially the marines were ordered to attack near the Persian Gulf coast, with the 1st Marine Division breaking through the Iraqi defenses. Keys's 2nd Marine Division was then supposed to advance through the 1st Marine Division. Later the plan called for the 1st Marine Division to pass through the 2nd Marine Division. The passage of one division through another was a difficult undertaking, and the marines had never tried such a maneuver. Keys was understandably unhappy with the plan.

On January 29, 1991, Iraqi armored forces crossed into Saudi Arabia after the air campaign had begun on January 17, reaching the Saudi town of Khafji. Marine light armor and antitank missiles, along with attack helicopters, helped stop the incursion. Arab forces then drove the Iraqis out of Khafji with support from marine artillery and aircraft. Keys observed the Iraqis carefully and was not impressed with their fighting abilities; he believed that they would not fight against stiff opposition and that their overall coordination was poor. He then approached his commander, Lieutenant General Walter Boomer, about changing the marine plan of attack. Instead of using both divisions to make only one breach in Iraqi defenses, Keys wanted to have the marine divisions attack side by side, breaking through the defending Iraqis more quickly. Boomer, who deeply respected Keys, amended the plan accordingly.

The 2nd Marine Division then shifted to the west. On February 24, the day the ground offensive began, the division quickly broke through Iraqi minefields and drove 20 miles into Kuwait. Thousands of Iraqis were taken prisoner. The marines were so successful that the main attack farther west was moved up from February 25 to the afternoon of February 24. The next morning an Iraqi armored counterattack failed to stop the marine advance. Army and marine tanks destroyed some 70 Iraqi tanks before continuing toward Kuwait City. On February 26 the marines and the Army's Tiger Brigade captured Mutla Ridge and the suburb of Jahrah, west of Kuwait City. The main road to Iraq ran across Mutla Ridge, creating a bottleneck that the division plugged. Along with air force, navy, and marine aircraft, the 2nd Marine Division destroyed hundreds of Iraqi vehicles trying to escape. The division finished the war in place, accepting the surrender of Iraqis soldiers who were unable to escape northward.

Following the war, Keys was promoted to lieutenant general and served as commander of U.S. Marine Corps Forces, Atlantic. He retired on September 1, 1994. Keys later became the chief executive officer of the Colt Manufacturing Company.

TIM J. WATTS

See also
DESERT STORM, Operation; DESERT STORM, Operation, Ground Operations; Khafji, Battle of; Mutla Ridge; United States Marine Corps, Persian Gulf War

References
Gordon, Michael R., and General Bernard E. Trainor. *The Generals' War: The Inside Story of the Conflict in the Gulf*. New York: Little, Brown, 1995.
Mroczkowski, Dennis P. *U.S. Marines in the Persian Gulf, 1990–1991: With the 2d Marine Division in Desert Shield and Desert Storm*. Washington, DC: History and Museums Division, U.S. Marine Corps, 1993.

Khafji, Battle of
Start Date: January 29, 1991
End Date: February 1, 1991

First major land battle of the Persian Gulf War (Operation DESERT STORM) that occurred from January 29 to February 1, 1991. The fight unfolded after units of the Iraqi Army crossed the border from Kuwait into Saudi Arabia, where they occupied the town of Ras al-Khafji. The Iraqis were forced out of Khafji after heavy fighting with American, Saudi Arabian, and Qatari forces.

Since January 17, 1991, the Iraqi army occupying Kuwait had been bombarded relentlessly by coalition aircraft, which commenced the air campaign. With casualties and material losses mounting and morale plummeting, the Iraqi high command decided on a bold plan to regain the initiative in the war. Three Iraqi divisions would launch a ground attack into Saudi Arabian territory, inflict a humiliating defeat on the Saudis, and provoke a coalition counterattack. The Iraqis hoped that they could inflict such heavy casualties on the counterattacking Americans that public opinion in the United States would turn against the war.

In order to carry out the plan, the Iraqi 5th Mechanized Division pushed down the coastal highway from Kuwait toward Khafji. The 5th Division attack was supported by several hundred Iraqi commandoes who sailed along the coast in small boats, landed behind Saudi lines, and raided communication links. To the right of the 5th Division, the Iraqi 3rd Armored Division was to overwhelm the border posts held by the Saudis and American marines before swinging left to attack the port city of Al Mishab, south of Khafji. Farther inland, the 1st Iraqi Mechanized Division would cover the flank of the other two attacking divisions.

The attacks of the Iraqi 1st and 3rd divisions were stalled on the evening of January 31, however, by determined U.S. marine resistance at the frontier border posts, followed by devastating American air attacks that caught Iraqi vehicles out in the open. The coastal commando raids were intercepted and destroyed by U.S. and British Royal Navy warships. However, elements of the Iraqi 5th Division succeeded in scattering Saudi frontier defenses and storming into Khafji.

The civilian population of Khafji, which normally numbered about 10,000, had been evacuated at the start of the war. A 12-man U.S. marine reconnaissance detachment was left stranded behind Iraqi lines in Khafji, from where they began calling in air strikes.

Frantic to liberate Khafji from the invaders, the Saudi government ordered immediate counterattacks. Two poorly coordinated Saudi attacks, backed up by a detachment of Qatari tanks, failed on the evening of January 30 and the morning of January 31. The Saudis were fortunate to escape with light casualties, thanks largely to the wild inaccuracy of Iraqi fire. However, massive American air strikes ensured that the Iraqis would be unable to reinforce their troops in Khafji. The Iraqi defenders in the town were also worn down by the nonstop air attacks. A third Saudi attack on February 1 finally succeeded in overwhelming the demoralized Iraqis in Khafji, who had been abandoned to their fate by the Iraqi high command.

The estimated Saudi and Qatari losses in the fighting for Khafji numbered 18 dead and 50 wounded. Seven to 10 Saudi V-150 armored personnel carriers and 2 Qatari AMX tanks were destroyed. The Iraqis lost anywhere from 60 to 100 killed and 400 taken prisoner plus at least 50 tanks destroyed in Khafji itself. But further heavy losses to coalition air strikes among Iraqi units to the north of Khafji may have resulted in a total of more than 2,000 Iraqi casualties plus 300 vehicles.

The success of American airpower in the Battle of Khafji led some theorists to claim that airpower was now the decisive factor in modern warfare, although that claim has not been widely accepted. The battle also revealed the serious shortcomings in the Saudi armed forces and in the command and control capabilities of the Iraqi Army.

PAUL W. DOERR

See also

DESERT STORM, Operation; Kuwait, Occupation of by Iraq; Qatar; Saudi Arabia, Armed Forces

References

Gordon, Michael R., and General Bernard E. Trainor. *The Generals' War: The Inside Story of the Conflict in the Gulf.* New York: Little, Brown, 1995.

Pollack, Kenneth M. *Arabs at War: Military Effectiveness, 1948–1991.* Lincoln: University of Nebraska Press, 2002.

Warden, John. "Employing Air Power in the Twenty-first Century." In *The Future of Air Power in the Aftermath of the Gulf War,* edited Robert L. Pfalzgraff Jr. and Richard H. Schultz, 125–157. Maxwell Air Force Base, AL: Air University Press, 1992.

Khalifa, Isa bin Salman al-
Birth Date: June 3, 1933
Death Date: March 6, 1999

Emir of Bahrain from 1961 to 1999 and a member of the ruling family of Khalifa. Born in Manama, Bahrain, on June 3, 1933, Sheikh Isa bin Salman al-Khalifa grew up in the Khalifa family that had ruled Bahrain since 1783. He was educated at the royal court by British and Arab tutors. Sheikh Isa became heir apparent to the throne of Bahrain in 1958 and succeeded his father, Sheikh Salman bin Hamad al-Khalifa, as head of state in December 1961. It was not until August 15, 1971, that the younger Khalifa assumed the title of emir (prince), after Bahrain established itself as a fully independent state from Britain.

In an important speech made after independence, Sheikh Isa promised that the people of Bahrain would be able to participate in governing their nation. To keep his promise, in June 1972 he agreed to establish a Constitutional Assembly and enact a new constitution. The promise proved short-lived, however, after he suspended the Constituent Assembly and the constitution itself in 1975.

The influence of external forces dominated Sheikh Isa's rule, and the emir had to contend with potential threats from Arab radicals in Iran and those within Bahrain, allegedly inspired by Iran. Tensions between Bahrain and Iran reached a crisis point in December 1981 after it became apparent that Iran was supporting an attempted coup in Bahrain. The plan called for the assassination of Sheikh Isa and members of the Khalifa family by the Islamic

Front for the Liberation of Bahrain, which was supported by the Iranian government. In response to these threats, Sheikh Isa forged several formal alliances with Saudi Arabia and the United States.

Although those alliances wavered throughout the 1970s and the early part of the 1980s, cooperation between Bahrain and the United States increased steadily in the run-up to the 1991 Persian Gulf War. During the Persian Gulf War, Bahrain fully supported the United Nations (UN)–backed coalition that liberated neighboring Kuwait from Iraqi occupation, and Sheikh Isa dispatched a small military force that was part of the coalition. Bahrain was also employed as a forward base of operations for Western troops. After the war, in 1992, Bahrain and the United States reached a 10-year bilateral defense agreement that restored a formal U.S. presence in Bahrain.

Under Sheikh Isa's leadership, Bahrain's economy was transformed through the expansion of its banking industry and the development of its industries, especially the petroleum industry. Indeed, oil revenues have made Bahrain a wealthy nation since the 1970s. Sheikh Isa has also been credited for his role in the creation of the Cooperation Council for the Arab States of the Gulf (also known as the Gulf Cooperation Council, GCC) in 1981, a council comprised of Bahrain, Kuwait, Saudi Arabia, Qatar, Oman, and the United Arab Emirates. The GCC provided vital support to coalition forces during the Iraqi occupation of Kuwait.

In the 1990s Sheikh Isa undertook modest government reforms, producing a mixed public response. In 1993 he appointed a 30-member Consultative Council, and in 1995 he changed Bahrain's cabinet, for the first time in 20 years. Sheikh Isa died on March 6, 1999, in Manama, Bahrain. He was succeeded by his son, Crown Prince Sheikh Hamad bin Isa Salman al-Khalifa.

KIRSTY MONTGOMERY

See also

Bahrain; DESERT STORM, Operation; Gulf Cooperation Council

References

Cordesman, Anthony H. *Bahrain, Oman, Qatar, and the UAE: Challenges of Security.* Boulder, CO: Westview, 1997.

Countrywatch. *Bahrain: 2006 Country Review.* Houston, TX: Countrywatch, 2006.

Metz, Helen Chapin. *Persian Gulf States: Country Studies.* 3rd ed. Washington, DC: Federal Research Division, Library of Congress, 1994.

Zahlan, Rosemarie Said. *The Making of the Modern Gulf States: Kuwait, Bahrain, Qatar, The United Arab Emirates, and Oman.* London: Unwin Hyman, 1989.

Khalil, Samir al-

Birth Date: 1949

Iraqi-born British architect and academic who made a case for regime change in Iraq based on charges of human rights abuses. Samir al-Khalil is the pseudonym used by Kanan Makiya, now a professor at Brandeis University, who was born in Baghdad in 1949 and is the son of renowned architect Mohammed Makiya. He attended the Massachusetts Institute of Technology (MIT), earning an undergraduate degree in architecture in 1971 and a master's degree in architecture in 1974. He also studied planning at the London School of Economics. In 1975 he wrote about his father's architectural legacy in transforming Abbasid structures into modern forms in *Post-Islamic Classicism.* Beginning in 1975, he was managing director of Makiya Associates in London, the family-owned firm, which built various major projects in Iraq and elsewhere in the Arab world.

In 1981 Khalil left architecture to write a harsh judgment of President Saddam Hussein's Iraqi regime. The book, titled *Republic of Fear: The Politics of Modern Iraq* (1990), traces the extreme violence in Iraq and the prominent role of the military in the nation back to the massacre of 3,000 Assyrians in 1933; hostility to the enemies of Pan-Arabism as iterated by Sati al-Husri, Iraqi director-general of education; and the bloody wars among political factions in post-1958 Iraq. The book indicts Hussein's government for flagrant human rights violations. Seventy publishers rejected Khalil's manuscript before it was finally published. It became a best seller during the 1991 Persian Gulf War.

In 1992 Khalil established the Iraq Research and Documentation Project at Harvard University, where a large number of Iraqi government documents captured by the Kurds during the Persian Gulf War were housed. In 2003 this project transitioned into the Iraq Memory Foundation, now headquartered in Baghdad. The Foundation has since amassed a much larger collection, which documents the legacy of state violence in Iraq, and has released videos about victims, which were broadcast on Iraqi television in 2007.

With Khalil's sudden prominence as a dissident and the challenges to Arabism during the 1991 Persian Gulf War, a war of words soon emerged between Palestinian-American intellectual Edward Said and Khalil, and between Said and Khalil's ex-wife, Afsaneh Najmabadi. Said's attacks on Khalil were far stronger a decade later because of Said's distress over the American-led 2003 invasion of Iraq, and because Khalil had attacked Said and the poet Mahmud Darwish in his *Cruelty and Silence: War, Tyranny, Uprising and the Arab World* (1994). A pervasive theme in Khalil's work is the failure of Arab intellectuals to respond to crises in their societies, especially in Iraq. The book chronicles the genocidal Iraqi government's Anfal Campaign, which witnessed the deaths of more than 100,000 people.

In 2002 Khalil joined the U.S. Department of State's Future of Iraq Project in its Democratic Principles Working Group, which proposed the democratization and de-Baathification of Iraq following demilitarization. It also proposed war crimes tribunals. Khalil returned to Iraq in 2003 and was appointed an adviser to the Iraq Interim Governing Council by the Coalition Provisional Authority. Khalil, who was close to Ahmad Chalabi, collected thousands of documents for his foundation during 2003–2006 and was among the drafters of the Iraqi constitution. He returned to Brandeis University in 2006.

Khalil has also published a novel, *The Rock: A Tale of Seventh-Century Jerusalem* (2001), controversial in that its hero is a Yemenite Jewish adviser to the Caliph Umar, conqueror of Jerusalem, and in its claim that the Dome of the Rock was constructed to be the Third Temple, implying that Islam is the continuation of Judaism.

SHERIFA ZUHUR

See also

Chalabi, Ahmed Abd al-Hadi; Iraq, History of, Pre-1990; Iraq, History of, 1990–Present; Said, Edward

References

Khalil, Samir al-. *Cruelty and Silence: War, Tyranny, Uprising, and the Arab World.* New York: Norton, 1994.

———. *Republic of Fear: The Inside Story of Saddam's Iraq.* New York: Pantheon Books, 1990.

Packer, George. "Dreaming of Democracy." *Sunday New York Times Magazine,* March 2, 2003.

Khalilzad, Zalmay Mamozy
Birth Date: March 22, 1951

Afghani-born diplomat who served as the U.S. ambassador to Afghanistan (2003–2005), U.S. ambassador to Iraq (2005–2007), and U.S. ambassador to the United Nations (UN) (2007–2009). Zalmay Khalilzad was born in Mazar-e Sharif, Afghanistan, on March 22, 1951, a member of the Pashtun ethnic group. His family was among the elites of Afghanistan, and his father had served in the government of the last king, Mohammed Zahir Shah. Growing instability in Afghanistan contributed to Khalilzad's desire to emigrate. He first went to the United States as an exchange student in high school. He subsequently attended the American University in Beirut, Lebanon, then a major educational center for the Middle East. He then returned to the United States for graduate training in political science at the University of Chicago, where he earned his PhD before going on to teach political science at Columbia University, where he taught from 1979 to 1989.

In 1984 the Council on Foreign Relations awarded Khalilzad a fellowship with the U.S. State Department. There he worked under Paul Wolfowitz, the director of Policy Planning and an Allan Bloom student who would loom large in neoconservative circles within the George H. W. Bush and George W. Bush administrations. When his fellowship ended, Khalilzad stayed on with the State Department, serving as an adviser on Afghanistan and the Middle East; given his background, he was particularly active in American policy vis-à-vis the arming of the mujahideen. In the George H. W. Bush administration, Khalilzad was made deputy undersecretary of Policy Planning at the Department of Defense.

Upon the election of President Bill Clinton in 1992, Khalilzad returned to the private sector, working for the RAND Corporation.

Khalilzad continued to teach and to participate in foreign affairs, writing on the role of the United States in international relations, as well as potential challenges posed by the People's Republic of China (PRC) for the United States. He also took consulting jobs with energy consortiums, advising them on the politics of the Middle East and Central Asia. Khalilzad also became one of the first members of the Project for the New American Century, which included numerous neoconservatives. The Project for the New American Century argued for the continuation of American preeminence within international relations that had existed since the end of the Cold War in 1991. In addition, the group strongly urged the maintenance of U.S. military strength as the foundation for American hegemony.

Upon the election of George W. Bush in 2000, Khalilzad returned to public service, heading the Bush transition team for personnel in the State and Defense departments. Once the administration was in office, he became director for Southwest Asia, Middle East, and North Africa for the National Security Council (NSC). After the attacks of September 11, 2001, Khalilzad, given his background and training, was deeply involved in planning for the war in Afghanistan. On December 31, 2001, he became the president's special envoy to Afghanistan, which post he held until November 2003, when he began serving as the U.S. ambassador to Afghanistan, a position he held until June 2005. In these positions, Khalilzad played a major role in guiding the new Afghanistan government and President Hamid Karzai in the successful oversight of democratic elections and in the first meeting of Afghanistan's legislative body, the Loya Jirga. He was also influential in overseeing relief and recovery efforts in Afghanistan.

In addition to his role in Afghanistan, Khalilzad also became in 2002 the ambassador at large for the free Iraqis, a key position in the run-up to the 2003 Iraq War. This post required Khalilzad to help expatriate Iraqis who wished to return to their nation and be active in a new regime, although his many duties in Afghanistan largely removed him from the bureaucratic battles over planning that took place within the Bush administration. In June 2005 Khalilzad succeeded John Negroponte as the U.S. ambassador to Iraq. In Iraq, Khalilzad oversaw the ratification of the Iraqi constitution, the 2005 Iraqi elections, and the formation of a national government, among other duties. During Khalilzad's tenure in Iraq, the insurgency continued to grow, however. In addition, intersectarian violence became an increasing problem, so much so that Khalilzad warned the Bush administration that these intersectarian conflicts might ultimately destroy the Iraqi state.

In February 2007 President Bush nominated Khalilzad to be the U.S. representative to the UN, and the U.S. Senate unanimously confirmed him in the post. He replaced the polarizing John R. Bolton, whose nomination had forced a showdown between the Democratically controlled Congress and the Bush White House. In the UN, Khalilzad continued to pursue the administration's stance toward Iran, which called for an immediate halt to its nuclear program and sanctions against Iran for failing to comply with the

International Atomic Energy Agency (IAEA), and support for a tribunal to be held in Lebanon to determine whether or not Syria was culpable in the assassination of former Lebanese prime minister Rafic al-Hariri. In general, however, Khalilzad struck a far more conciliatory tone than his predecessor. Khalilzad remains an active and influential figure in Republican foreign policy circles, particularly on issues involving southwest Asia and the Middle East.

Michael K. Beauchamp

See also

Afghanistan; Bolton, John Robert, II; Bush, George Walker; Iraq, History of, 1990–Present; Karzai, Hamid; Loya Jirga, Afghanistan; Mujahideen, Soviet-Afghanistan War; Negroponte, John Dimitri; Neoconservatism; Wolfowitz, Paul Dundes

References

Crews, Robert D., and Amin Tarzi, eds. *The Taliban and the Crisis of Afghanistan.* Cambridge: Harvard University Press, 2008.

Khalilzad, Zalmay. *From Containment to Global Leadership? America and the World after the Cold War.* Santa Monica: RAND Corporation, 1995.

———. *Prospects for the Afghan Interim Government.* Santa Monica: RAND Corporation, 1991.

Khomeini, Ruhollah
Birth Date: May 17, 1900
Death Date: June 3, 1989

Shiite cleric, leader of the 1979 revolution that overthrew Mohammad Reza Shah Pahlavi, and religious and political head of the Islamic Republic of Iran (1979–1989). Born Ruhollah Mustafa al-Musavi on May 17, 1900, in Khomayn (Khumayn), some 180 miles south of the Iranian capital of Tehran, he was the son and grandson of Shiite religious scholars and leaders (*fuqaha*). Musavi, whose father was murdered when he was seven months old, was instructed in Islam and the Qur'an by his elder brother Ayatollah Pasandideh, following the death of his mother. Musavi studied Islamic law at Arak and moved with his teacher in the 1920s to Qum, where he was recognized as a *mujtahid* (a male Islamic scholar competent to interpret Sharia, or Islamic law) and gave lectures at the Faziye Seminary. By the 1950s, and in response to Pahlavi's actions in the 1960s, he began to express views on the need to Islamicize politics. In the 1950s he was proclaimed an ayatollah (gift of God). At that time he changed his surname to that of his birthplace. In 1962 Burujerdi, the last Grand Ayatollah to be recognized as the ultimate authority, died, and Khomeini's views became more important.

Khomeini detested liberalizing foreign influences and governments that he believed were leading Iran away from true Islam. The primary Iranian force in this Westernizing and modernizing trend was the shah and his family. In 1921 the Russians had helped Reza Shah Pahlavi overthrow Iran's first constitutional government, and his son, Mohammad Reza Shah Pahlavi, rose to power

in 1941 with the aid of Great Britain, France, and the United States. In 1953, aided by the U.S. Central Intelligence Agency (CIA), the shah led a coup that deposed Prime Minister Mohammad Mosaddeq. This event solidified the shah's hold on power. Khomeini, who publicly denounced the new regime, was arrested and imprisoned for eight months. He was released and exiled from Iran to Turkey in November 1964 after challenging the emancipation of women and the shah's reduction of religious estates through land reforms.

Seemingly a permanent exile, Khomeini eventually settled in the Shia holy city of Najaf in northern Iraq. There he developed the doctrine that an Islamic state should be ruled by the clergy (*vilayet-e faqih,* or rule of the jurist). When Iraqi president Saddam Hussein forced Khomeini from Najaf, he and his followers moved to France in 1978 and from there urged the ouster of the shah and his U.S. allies. Khomeini also published numerous statements and books, among them *Islamic Government* (*Hukumah Islamiyyah*), a series of lectures delivered at Najaf in 1970. These lectures laid out his principal beliefs in an Islamic state in which the *fuqaha,* or clergy, should play a guiding and political role. With the Iranian revolution and the flight of the shah on January 16, 1979, Khomeini returned to the country. He arrived from France on February 1, acknowledged by millions of Iranians as the leader of the revolution. Mahdi Bazargan was appointed prime minister of an interim government, but he became critical of Khomeini's Islamic Republican Party (IRP), and the IRP eliminated its civilian rivals and some clerics.

On November 4, 1979, Khomeini's followers, most of them young, zealous Iranian students, stormed the U.S. embassy in Tehran and took 70 Americans hostage in blatant defiance of international law. Bazargan resigned. Over the course of the next 14 months, the U.S. government attempted without success to secure the release of the hostages through sanctions against Iran and the freezing of Iranian assets. Seemingly encouraged by Khomeini, the hostage takers refused to intervene and bring an end to the standoff. U.S. president Jimmy Carter's failure to resolve the Iranian hostage crisis brought with it great frustration and embarrassment. A disastrous aborted hostage rescue attempt on April 24, 1980, only added to American frustration over the situation. The hostage crisis was a major cause of Ronald W. Reagan's victory over Carter in the U.S. presidential election of November 1980. Only minutes after Reagan took the oath of office on January 20, 1981, the hostages were released.

In December 1980 Khomeini secured his goal of a new constitution in which Iran was officially declared an Islamic republic. Within several years, hundreds of Khomeini's opponents had been executed. The clergy in Iran were still committed to their traditional roles in education and law. Part of the task of the Islamic revolution was then to transform Iran's laws and prevailing practice to conform with Sharia. Rather than leave this up to individuals, committees and guards imposed dress rules that included wearing the *hijab* in addition to the traditional *chador.* The legislature imposed a new criminal code based on Islamic law. Alcohol was banned, and for many years Western and Persian music was banned, until some revival of the latter was permitted. Khomeini's Iran remained rather insular on the international stage and became a vociferous opponent of Israel. Although Iran was not itself an active participant in fighting against Israel, it separated itself from the former shah's pro-Israeli positions and sent aid and training to organizations that fought Israel, including Hezbollah in Lebanon.

As Khomeini's revolution progressed, Iraq's Saddam Hussein attempted to take advantage of the turmoil of the revolution and the weakened state of the Iranian military by invading Iran on September 22, 1980. This sparked the devastating Iran-Iraq War, which lasted for eight long years (1980–1988) before both sides accepted a truce brokered by the United Nations (UN). Just as Khomeini had been headstrong about not bringing a quick end to the 1979–1981 hostage crisis, so too was he unwilling to end the war expeditiously. Only after Iran had suffered devastating human losses (some sources estimate more than a million dead) did Khomeini realize that nothing further could be gained by prolonging the war, which featured chemical and biological attacks by the Iraqis. As Khomeini's health declined and a clerical power struggle ensued, Khomeini attempted to preserve the revolution and the Islamic state by strengthening the authority of the presidency, the parliament, and other institutions. In so doing, he further entrenched the power of religious conservatives, who more often than not pursued counterproductive foreign policies that further isolated their country. The long war severely strained the Iranian economy. Khomeini died on June 3, 1989, in Tehran. His legacy was a country bound by Islamic rules and practice and enmity with the United States.

RICHARD EDWARDS

See also

Carter, James Earl, Jr.; Hezbollah; Hussein, Saddam; Iran; Iran-Iraq War; Iranian Revolution; Reza Pahlavi, Mohammad; Terrorism

References

Bill, James A. *The Shah, the Ayatollah, and the United States.* New York: Foreign Policy Association, 1988.

Heikal, Mohamed. *Iran, the Untold Story: An Insider's Account, from the Rise of the Shah to the Reign of the Ayatollah.* New York: Pantheon, 1982.

Hoveyda, Fereydoun. *The Shah and the Ayatollah: Iranian Mythology and Islamic Revolution.* Westport, CT: Praeger, 2003.

Khomeini, Imam. *Islam and Revolution.* Translated by Hamid Algar. Berkeley, CA: Mizan, 1981.

Marshcall, Christin. *Iran's Persian Gulf Policy: From Khomeni to Khatami.* Oxford: Routledge/Curzon, 2003.

Kimmitt, Robert Michael
Birth Date: December 19, 1947

U.S. attorney, presidential adviser, and deputy secretary of the Treasury (2005–2009). Robert Michael Kimmitt was born in Logan, Utah, on December 19, 1947, and graduated with

distinction from the United States Military Academy, West Point, in 1969. He served with the 173rd Airborne Brigade in Vietnam (April 1970–August 1971), earning three Bronze Star medals, the Purple Heart, and the Vietnamese Cross of Gallantry. After leaving the regular army, Kimmitt remained with the reserves until his retirement in November 2004 as a major general. In 1977 Kimmitt earned a law degree from Georgetown University.

Kimmitt was twice a member of the National Security Council (NSC) staff, once from 1976 to 1977 and again from 1978 to 1983. During 1977–1978 he was a law clerk to Judge Edward A. Tamm of the U.S. Court of Appeals for the District of Columbia Circuit. He then served the White House as the NSC executive secretary and general counsel (1983–1985) with the rank of deputy assistant to the president for national security affairs.

From 1985 to 1987 Kimmitt served as general counsel to the U.S. Treasury Department, before leaving to become a partner in a private law firm (1987–1989). Kimmitt returned to government as undersecretary of state for political affairs (1989–1991), where he was instrumental in creating the coalition of 34 Western and Muslim nations that defeated Saddam Hussein's Iraqi forces during the 1991 Persian Gulf War. U.S. president George H. W. Bush awarded Kimmitt the Presidential Citizen's Medal, the nation's second-highest civilian award, for his accomplishments.

Kimmitt served as the ambassador to Germany (1991–1993) before returning again to the private sector. During 1993–1997 Kimmitt was a managing director of Lehman Brothers. He was also a partner in the law firm of Wilmer, Cutler & Pickering (1997–2000); vice chairman and president of Commerce One, a software company (2000–2001); and executive vice president of global public policy for Time Warner, Inc. (2001–2005). Just prior to joining the George W. Bush administration, Kimmitt again served as a partner in a law firm. Kimmitt continued his public service during his private sector tenure as a member of the National Defense Panel (1997), as a member of the Director of Central Intelligence's National Security Advisory Panel (1998–2005), and as a member of the Panel of Arbitrators of the World Bank's International Center for the Settlement of Investment Disputes.

As the deputy secretary of Treasury, a post he began in August 2005, Kimmitt appeared before the Treasury Committee House Financial Services Subcommittee on Domestic and International Monetary Policy in March 2006. At the hearing, he supported Trade and Technology DP (Dubai Ports) World's purchase of the Peninsular and Oriental (P&O) Steam Navigation Company of the United Kingdom, then the fourth-largest ports operator in the world. This would have placed numerous U.S. ports under the nominal control of Dubai, a move that elicited considerable opposition. The bid was soon dropped.

Kimmitt also served as the Bush administration's envoy to the International Compact With Iraq (ICI), an international conference at the United Nations (UN). The goal of the meeting was to develop a framework that would transform the Iraqi economy into a self-sustaining economy within five years. The ICI was an initiative of the Iraqi government with assistance from the United States and the UN Assistance Mission in Iraq (UNAMI). In this capacity, Kimmitt traveled to Iraq, the United Arab Emirates (UAE), and Kuwait. He also attended the January 2008 Davos World Economic Forum and there warned against a trend toward protectionism in the United States, Europe, and Asia regarding sovereign wealth funds (SWFs) that use state wealth to invest in the assets of other sovereign nations, or businesses based in other sovereign nations. He is thought to have been a candidate for the presidency of the World Bank in May 2007.

RICHARD M. EDWARDS

See also

Bush, George Walker; Iraq, History of, 1990–Present

References

Carter, Ralph G. *Contemporary Cases in U.S. Foreign Policy: From Terrorism to Trade.* 3rd ed. Washington, DC: CQ Press, 2007.

Coll, Steven. *Ghost Wars: The Secret History of the CIA, Afghanistan, and Bin Laden, from the Soviet Invasion to September 10, 2001.* New York: Penguin, 2004.

Oliphant, Thomas. *Utter Incompetents: Ego and Ideology in the Age of Bush.* New York: Thomas Dunne Books, 2007.

United States. *Nominations of Robert M. Kimmitt, Randal Quarles, Sandra L. Pack, and Kevin I. Fromer: Hearing Before the Committee on Finance, United States Senate.* Washington, DC: U.S. Government Printing Office, 2005.

King Khalid Military City

American-built military base located in northeastern Saudi Arabia, about two hours from the Kuwaiti border. Construction of the U.S.-designed base began in 1974 and ended in 1987. King Khalid Military City (KKMC) was named in honor of Saudi King Khalid ibn Abd al-Aziz and was designed to accommodate as many as 65,000 people, or an army division of three brigades. It was part of a joint Saudi-American effort beginning in the 1950s to build several military facilities throughout Saudi Arabia. The Saudis funded the construction of the facilities, which were designed by U.S. Army and Air Force engineers. The KKMC facility was the single largest project ever undertaken by the U.S. Army Corps of Engineers.

Located in a fairly remote and sparsely populated region of Saudi Arabia, the self-contained city has a large, fully functioning airport and runways capable of handling the largest commercial and military aircraft. The cost of the airfields alone was $700 million. KKMC hosted thousands of U.S. and coalition soldiers and airmen during Operation DESERT SHIELD and Operation DESERT STORM.

The construction cost of the KKMC has been variously estimated to be as little as $1.3 billion and as high as $20 billion—the Saudi government has never divulged the precise cost. To erect the mammoth facility, the Saudis created a new port on the Persian Gulf designed specifically to receive supplies for the KKMC. The largest pre-cast concrete plant in the world was constructed on the building site, and 21 deep-water wells were drilled to supply the city with ample water supplies. Utility tunnels run between most major structures, and there are 3,398 two-story family housing units within the city's confines. Also included in the city are five multidomed mosques and several large stores.

Since it commenced operations in the late 1980s, a contingent of the U.S. Military Training Mission (USMTM) in Saudi Arabia has been stationed at the KKMC, although in the years after the Persian Gulf War the U.S. presence has been significantly diminished. During Operation DESERT SHIELD and Operation DESERT STORM, thousands of U.S. and coalition troops were housed at the KKMC, and it was one of three major debarkation points for the war effort (the other two being Dhahran and Riyadh). By January 1991, on the eve of DESERT STORM, the KKMC was at or even a bit above capacity in terms of personnel stationed there. The Saudi government does not release figures relating to troop strength within the military city. Clearly, the construction of the facility was meant to facilitate a military endeavor very much like the one that unfolded in 1990–1991.

Without such a large and self-sustaining base of operations, the United States and coalition forces would have had a much more difficult time preparing to wage war against Iraq. Saudi and U.S. officials have over the years tried to segregate their respective armed forces personnel in the KKMC because of cultural and religious differences. Nevertheless, the large U.S. and Western presence there in 1990–1991 saw the emergence of an American-dominated sector within the KKMC.

In 1990–1991 U.S. forces undertook numerous construction projects to make the KKMC more amenable to the war effort. These included the construction of more storage facilities, the erection of a forward operating base, and improvements and additions to runways and air hangars. During the ground phase of DESERT STORM, on February 21, 1991, Iraqi forces fired three Scud missiles at KKMC, which were deflected by the nearby Patriot missile batteries surrounding the facilities.

Sensitive to the Saudis' desire not to host large numbers of foreign troops on their soil after the war was won, the U.S. military and allied forces began a large troop drawdown at the KKMC in the spring of 1991. The U.S. government hoped to place a large amount of its supplies and equipment in storage in Saudi Arabia, but the Saudi government balked. Thus, most American equipment and nonperishable supplies had to be removed from the KKMC and other Saudi facilities. Some of the equipment was relocated to neighboring Kuwait. Thereafter, the Saudis made other infrastructure improvements to the site, including the addition of 149 more living quarters and the completion of a presidential complex where Saudi officials and dignitaries can stay and work.

In the aftermath of DESERT STORM, the U.S. presence at the KKMC has been small, and there are currently fewer than 50 U.S. personnel located there. The city did not play a role in Operation IRAQI FREEDOM.

PAUL G. PIERPAOLI JR.

See also

DESERT SHIELD, Operation; DESERT STORM, Operation; Saudi Arabia; Saudi Arabia, Armed Forces

References

Bronson, Rachel. *Thicker Than Oil: America's Uneasy Partnership with Saudi Arabia.* New York: Oxford University Press, 2008.

Safran, Nadav. *Saudi Arabia: The Ceaseless Quest for Security.* Ithaca, NY: Cornell University Press, 1988.

Kirkuk

The oldest site of continuous human occupation in Iraq, Kirkuk is located approximately 142 miles north of Baghdad and rests along the Hasa River, atop the remains of the 11th century BCE Assyrian capital city of Arrapha, in Iraqi Kurdistan. Kirkuk is a city of some 710,000 people (according to 2005 estimates). Its predominant population of Iraqi Kurds and Turkomen, along with the city's position as a hub of the Iraqi petroleum industry, has made Kirkuk a critically strategic center during all of Iraq's political turmoil since World War I. The city played a significant political and geostrategic role during the run-up to the 2003 Iraq War.

In its early incarnation, Kirkuk was a bloody battleground for at least three empires—the Assyrian, the Babylonian, and the Median—for whom the city on the banks of the Hasa was a strategic stronghold. Under the Babylonians, the city was called Kurkura, while under the Greeks it was known as Karkha D-Bet Slokh, which translates as "citadel of the house of Selucid." By the seventh century CE, following the Arab invasion of the Sassanid Empire, Muslim Arabs were calling the city Kirkheni, or "citadel."

With the discovery of oil in 1927 at Bab Gurgur, near Kirkuk, the city became the center of petroleum production in northern Iraq. The oil rush led to the Iraqi annexation of the former Ottoman Mosul wilayah, of which Kirkuk was a part. From 1963 onward the Iraqi Arabs attempted to transform the ethnic makeup of the entire region to take power away from the Kurds and ensure that Iraqi Arabs stayed in control of the oil fields. In 1975 the Iraqi Baath Party, under Ahmad Hassan al-Bakr, began to "Arabize" the Kirkuk area by imposing restrictions on Kurds and Turkomen who lived there, while trying to replace them with Arabs from central or southern Iraq. As many as 1,400 Kurdish villages were razed, and more than half a million Kurds were forcibly relocated. The Arabization process intensified following the failed Kirkuk/Kurdish uprising after the Persian Gulf War in 1991, and between 1991 and 2003 an estimated 120,000 Kurds and Turkomen were forcibly relocated out of Kirkuk.

In the lead-up to the Iraq War (2003), Kirkuk, along with Mosul, proved to be a sticking point that prevented the United States from being able to launch a prong of its assault into Iraq from bases in Turkey. The Turkish Parliament wanted guarantees that Kurdish fighters would not be allowed to capture Kirkuk or Mosul. Because the United States would not, or could not, make such a promise, Turkey refused to grant the Americans and their allies permission to launch attacks from Turkish soil. The Turks also saw this move as a means of squelching the Iraqi Kurds' nationalism, since many of the Kurds view Kirkuk as the "Kurdish Jerusalem."

On April 11, 2003, after days of heated battles, the U.S.-led coalition forces and Kurdish Peshmerga fighters secured Kirkuk from Saddam Hussein's Baath Party loyalists. Victims of the Kirkuk's Arabization attempted to return once the area was free of the Baath Party, yet the new postwar Iraqi government has done little to resolve this crisis, leaving most returning Kurds in a refugee limbo.

B. KEITH MURPHY

See also

Baath Party; Bakr, Ahmad Hassan al-; Kurds; Mosul; Peshmerga; Turkey, Role in Persian Gulf and Afghanistan Wars

References

Astarjian, Henry D. *The Struggle for Kirkuk: The Rise of Hussein, Oil, and the Death of Tolerance in Iraq.* Westport, CT: Praeger Security International, 2007.

Polk, William R. *Understanding Iraq: The Whole Sweep of Iraqi History, from Genghis Khan's Mongols to the Ottoman Turks to the British Mandate to the American Occupation.* New York: Harper Perennial, 2006.

Kissinger, Henry Alfred
Birth Date: May 27, 1923

U.S. national security adviser (1969–1975) and secretary of state (1973–1977) who, together with President Richard M. Nixon, devised and implemented a major reorientation of U.S. foreign policy. Of German Jewish extraction, Henry Kissinger was born on May 27, 1923, in Fürth, Germany. He left Adolf Hitler's Germany for New York in 1938 and became an American citizen five years later. After serving in the U.S. Army as a sergeant in civil affairs, Kissinger became a professor of government at Harvard University, publishing his doctoral dissertation, *A World Restored,* in 1955. The book focuses particularly on Austria's Prince Klemens Wenzel von Metternich, whom Kissinger admired and in some ways modeled himself upon. Kissinger also published a study of U.S. atomic policy for the prestigious Council on Foreign Relations.

Although his intellectual capabilities were highly respected, Kissinger's real ambitions lay in the practice, not the study, of international relations. He used his Harvard position to meet major political figures and served as an adviser to leading Republicans, including New York governor Nelson A. Rockefeller and former vice president Nixon. Kissinger's efforts won him only minor assignments under President John F. Kennedy, but when Nixon became president he appointed Kissinger his national security adviser. Kissinger greatly overshadowed William P. Rogers, who was the nominal secretary of state until August 1973, when Kissinger succeeded him and took virtual control of U.S. foreign policy.

Henry Alfred Kissinger, U.S. national security adviser (1969–1975) and secretary of state (1973–1977). (Library of Congress)

Kissinger's undoubted abilities included an immense capacity for hard work, a talent for grand designs and broad conceptualization, and the imagination to reformulate the international system to accommodate the relative weakness of the United States. He deemphasized ideology in favor of a balance of power and the pursuit of closer relations with the communist People's Republic of China (PRC) and detente with the Soviet Union. This strategy resulted in the 1972 Strategic Arms Limitation Treaty (SALT I) and the Anti-Ballistic Missile (ABM) Treaty, which imposed limits on Soviet and American nuclear arsenals and delivery systems; the 1975 Helsinki Accords, which normalized relations between Eastern and Western Europe; the creation of the permanent Conference on Security and Cooperation in Europe (CSCE); and a rapprochement between communist China and the United States that Kissinger pioneered with a secret personal visit to Beijing in 1971.

Initially Nixon and Kissinger left Secretary of State William Rogers to handle Middle Eastern policy while they concentrated on big-power diplomacy. In 1969, seeking to resolve outstanding issues from the 1967 Six-Day War, Rogers and Joseph Sisco, assistant secretary of state for Near Eastern and South Asian affairs,

developed a peace plan envisaging Israeli withdrawal from occupied territories in return for evenhanded Soviet and U.S. policies toward both Arabs and Israel in the Middle East, and a brokered peace settlement guaranteed by both big powers. Kissinger privately informed Soviet ambassador Anatoly Dobrynin that the White House had no interest in this scheme, thereby effectively sabotaging the Rogers Plan, which the Soviet Union in any case rejected in October 1969.

U.S. Middle Eastern policy thereafter remained largely static until the October 1973 Yom Kippur (Ramadan) War, when Egypt and Syria launched a surprise attack on Israel intended to regain the territories they had lost in the previous war. When the Israelis rallied and then counterattacked, threatening to wipe out the Egyptian Third Army, President Anwar Sadat of Egypt, who had tilted toward the United States the previous year in the hope of enabling Egypt to regain the Sinai, appealed to the Soviet Union for aid. To prevent Soviet intervention, Nixon ordered military forces to a DefCon 3 military alert, two levels below outright war, while successfully pressuring the Israelis not to destroy the Egyptian Third Army in return for shipments of U.S. arms to resupply Israel's depleted arsenals. Oil-producing Arab states reacted by imposing an oil embargo on the United States and other Western powers that had supported Israel, while greatly enhancing the international clout of the Organization of Petroleum Exporting Countries (OPEC) by raising oil prices fourfold.

The October 1973 war and its aftermath diverted Kissinger from his previous preoccupation with triangular U.S.-Soviet-Chinese relations. The oil embargo marked the beginning of a decade of economic difficulties for all the Western powers. European powers quickly responded by adopting more pro-Arab policies, a shift that Nixon and Kissinger strongly resented and characterized as craven. Kissinger embarked on several months of high-profile shuttle diplomacy with Israel, Syria, and Egypt, showing himself an excellent negotiator and eventually brokering an armistice. Under both Nixon and President Gerald Ford, Kissinger continued to mediate among the contending Middle Eastern powers for the next two years, eventually negotiating the Sinai Accords of September 1975, whereby Israel returned part of the Sinai to Egypt, a settlement that probably contributed to the more extensive Camp David Accords that President Jimmy Carter negotiated in 1978.

Critics claim Kissinger's weaknesses include a penchant for secrecy and intrigue, vanity, and unseemly personal ambition; an overriding concern to maintain international stability that often led him to endorse brutal right- or left-wing regimes; and an exclusive focus upon realism in foreign policy. Kissinger has also been criticized for his involvement in the controversial bombing of Cambodia and U.S. incursion into the country to wipe out Viet Cong and North Vietnamese sanctuaries there during the Vietnam War; his endorsement of Indonesia's military takeover of Portuguese East Timor in December 1975; and his readiness to authorize wiretapping against American bureaucrats suspected of leaking official information to the press. These aspects of Kissinger made him the bête noire of many American liberals.

Conservative Republicans found equally opprobrious Kissinger's willingness to accommodate the communist Soviet Union and China and, if Sino-American rapprochement required, to jettison China on Taiwan, a longtime U.S. ally. Under Ford, who became president in August 1974 when the Watergate Scandal forced Nixon's resignation, both the 1972 SALT I Treaty and the 1975 Helsinki Accords on Europe became targets for attack by such conservatives as California governor and presidential hopeful Ronald W. Reagan, who assailed the Soviet human rights record. The fall of Vietnam to communist forces in April 1975, little more than two years after Kissinger had negotiated the Paris Peace Accords supposedly ending the war, also damaged his credibility. On November 3, 1975, Ford replaced Kissinger as national security adviser, although Kissinger remained secretary of state until Ford left office in January 1977.

Upon leaving government Kissinger established an influential business consultancy firm. He continued to provide unofficial advice to successive administrations, wrote and spoke extensively on international affairs, and published three weighty volumes of memoirs. Kissinger has also advised the George W. Bush administration on the War on Terror and the Iraq War. By late 2006, however, he had concluded publicly that a U.S. military victory in Iraq was "not possible." At the same time, however, he warned that a precipitous withdrawal from Iraq could prove disastrous and provoke a wider Middle East conflict.

Kissinger remains a perennially controversial figure. Liberals still denigrate his foreign policy accomplishments, and even decades later journalists including Seymour Hersh and, most notably, Christopher Hitchens have argued that Kissinger's past behavior makes him liable to trial and conviction for war crimes. Pointing out discrepancies between Kissinger's own account of his time in office and the increasingly available documentary record became almost an academic parlor game for these journalists. Outside the United States, Kissinger is a less-polarizing figure, and many in Europe and Asia still admire his achievements.

PRISCILLA ROBERTS

See also

Arab-Israeli Conflict, Overview; Nixon, Richard Milhous; Reagan, Ronald Wilson; Sadat, Muhammad Anwar; United States, Middle East Policy, 1945–Present

References

Hanhimaki, Jussi. *The Flawed Architect: Henry Kissinger and American Foreign Policy.* New York: Oxford University Press, 2004.

Hersh, Seymour. *The Price of Power: Kissinger in the Nixon White House.* New York: Simon and Schuster, 1983.

Isaacson, Walter. *Kissinger: A Biography.* New York: Simon and Schuster, 1992.

Kissinger, Henry A. *White House Years.* Boston: Little, Brown, 1979.

———. *Years of Renewal.* New York: Simon and Schuster, 1999.

———. *Years of Upheaval.* Boston: Little, Brown, 1982.

Koran

See Qur'an

Korea, Republic of, Role in Persian Gulf and Iraq Wars

East Asian nation located on the southern half of the Korean Peninsula, with a 2008 population of 48.380 million people. The Republic of Korea (ROK, South Korea) covers 38,023 square miles and is bordered by the Democratic People's Republic of Korea (DPRK, North Korea) to the north, the Sea of Japan to the east, the Korea Strait to the south, and the Yellow Sea to the west. South Korea is a multiparty representative democracy in which the president holds the reins of executive power. Since the 1980s South Korea's economic development has placed it among the world's major economic powers.

South Korea's military is highly advanced, large, and well trained; it has been the beneficiary of U.S. weapons systems and military hardware since the early 1950s, and it has maintained a high level of readiness because of ongoing tensions with its neighbor, North Korea. Since the end of the Korean War in 1953, the United States has permanently garrisoned troops in South Korea, with as many as 37,000 in place at any one time. Not surprisingly, South Korea has been a strong supporter of U.S. foreign policy, and it provided material contributions to the Vietnam War, Persian Gulf War, and Iraq War.

The South Korean government championed U.S. president George H. W. Bush's tough approach to Iraqi dictator Saddam Hussein's invasion of Kuwait in August 1990. It also fully supported the various United Nations (UN) resolutions that sought to pressure Hussein into withdrawing prior to the beginning of hostilities in January 1991. When Operation DESERT STORM began, South Korea had already promised material support to the coalition. Ultimately, South Korea dispatched about 350 troops to serve alongside coalition forces, although not in a combat capacity. South Korean forces consisted of medical and transportation support personnel.

South Korea also supported the 2003 invasion of Iraq, orchestrated by the United States. South Korea deployed 3,600 troops to Iraq in May 2003, at which time major combat operations were declared complete. This was the largest foreign troop deployment after those of the United States and Britain, and consisted mostly of engineers and medical personnel. The first contingent of troops, numbering about 670 men, was dispatched to the southern city of Nasiriyah in May 2003; in February 2004 the troops were redeployed to the northern city of Irbil to join another South Korean unit, nicknamed "Zaytun" (Arabic for "olive"), which had arrived in that city in September 2004. Another South Korean unit, the 48th Expeditionary Airlift Wing, consisting of four Lockheed C-130 Hercules cargo planes and 150 airmen, was based in

Kuwait and provided logistics and air support for South Korean troops in Iraq.

Besides providing the community of Irbil with millions of dollars worth of humanitarian supplies, South Korean troops rebuilt schools, repaved roads, repaired water treatment and sewage plants, and provided humanitarian aid and medical care. After Islamic militants kidnapped and beheaded a South Korean civilian working in Iraq in 2004, South Korea's military deployment to Iraq became unpopular among a number of South Koreans. Many South Koreans viewed the American invasion of Iraq as unjust and also questioned the relevance of Iraq to South Korea's interests and security. Others believed, however, that participating in Iraq was a way to express gratitude to the United States for defending and protecting South Korea since the beginning of the Korean War in 1950; they also believed that South Korean participation could strengthen that country's ties with the United States.

Despite public opposition to the deployment, South Korean troops were generally spared from attack because of their deployment in the generally peaceful and stable Kurdish region of northern Iraq. Indeed, the country's only military casualty came in Irbil when a soldier was murdered in a military base barbershop in May 2007.

Over the next several years, South Korea gradually reduced its troop strength in Iraq by about a third. On November 21, 2005, President Roh Moo-hyun's cabinet endorsed the withdrawal of 1,000 troops during the first half of 2006. By 2007 only about 1,200 troops remained in Iraq, and the next year that number had declined to about 600. Nonetheless, despite public opposition to the deployment, the United States requested that South Korea extend its Iraq deployment, and in December 2007 the South Korean parliament voted 146–104 to extend the country's mission in Iraq for another year. President Moo-hyun announced the planned one-year extension in October, saying that it would solidify South Korea's military alliance with the United States—particularly at a time when North Korea was pursuing nuclear weapons and renewing threats toward South Korea.

On December 1, 2008, the day South Korea's remaining 600 troops left Iraq, a South Korean Defense Ministry spokesman announced that the country's mission in Irbil had provided medical services for 88,805 local residents and vocational training to almost 2,500 people. He also reported that all medical facilities, as well as 36,472 articles of medical equipment, would be left for the benefit of the Iraqi people.

STEFAN M. BROOKS

See also

DESERT STORM, Operation; DESERT STORM, Operation, Coalition Nations' Contributions to; IRAQI FREEDOM, Operation

References

Fawn, Rick, and Raymond A. Hinnebusch, eds. *The Iraq War: Causes and Consequence.* Boulder, CO: Lynne Rienner, 2006.

Murray, Williamson, and Robert H. Scales Jr. *The Iraq War: A Military History.* Cambridge, MA: Belknap, 2005.

Kristol, William
Birth Date: December 23, 1952

Prominent conservative author, pundit, strategist, and intellectual whose views helped shape the modern neoconservatism that influenced the George W. Bush administration. William Kristol was born on December 23, 1952, in New York City to Irving Kristol, who is considered the father of neoconservatism, and Gertrude Himmelfarb, a well-known intellectual historian of the Victorian era. Kristol graduated from Harvard University in 1973 before going on to graduate school in government at the same institution. After receiving his PhD in 1979, Kristol taught at the University of Pennsylvania and the John F. Kennedy School of Government at Harvard.

In 1985 Kristol entered government service as chief of staff to William J. Bennett, President Ronald W. Reagan's secretary of education. With the election of George H. W. Bush to the presidency in 1988, Kristol became chief of staff to Vice President Dan Quayle. After President Bill Clinton's election in 1992, Kristol served in a series of Republican think tanks and foundations. Most notably, he chaired the Project for a Republican Future, which urged Republicans to oppose Clinton administration initiatives rather than pursue compromise measures, in particular when it came to the Clinton health care plan of 1993. The strategy Kristol advocated ultimately paid handsome dividends, as the health plan failed miserably, and Republicans won control of both the House and the Senate in 1994, gaining control of the House for the first time since 1954.

In 1994 Kristol and another prominent neoconservative, John Podhoretz, son of neoconservative Norman Podhoretz, launched the *Weekly Standard*, a conservative opinion-making journal. The *Weekly Standard* differs from such other conservative organs as the *National Review* in that it advocates a far more muscular American foreign policy. In addition, the *Weekly Standard* has a far more practical political approach than does the *National Review*, which is more philosophically conservative. In 2000 the *Weekly Standard* supported Arizona senator John McCain in the Republican primaries but was quite supportive of George W. Bush after he won the nomination, and maintained strong ties to the Bush administration once it was in office.

In 1997 Kristol and Robert Kagan, another prominent foreign policy expert, founded The Project for the New American Century, a conservative think tank whose members include many prominent conservative intellectuals and elected officials. The Project for the New American Century seeks to extend into the 21st century the preeminent international position that the United States enjoyed in the aftermath of the Cold War. In essence, Kristol and others believe that the United States, in a role of global leadership, is a source for good in the world and that, in certain circumstances, such leadership requires the use of armed force. The Project explicitly promotes a sort of American hegemony as preferable to a scenario in which international politics reverts back to a balance of power. In addition, The Project for the New American Century calls for continued investment to sustain American military preeminence in the world as the basis for American leadership, something its critics contend promotes conflicts over soft power. Kristol and other so-called neoconservatives called for and were supportive of the Clinton administration's eventual use of air strikes to stop Serbian aggression in Bosnia and later Kosovo, despite the opposition of many more traditional Republicans, and Democrats as well.

Given Kristol's political philosophy and that of the *Weekly Standard* and The Project for the New American Century, he was a strong proponent of the 2003 invasion of Iraq. In Kristol's view, the beliefs that Iraq might possess weapons of mass destruction (WMDs) and support terrorism were compelling reasons enough for invasion, but the very nature of the regime and the threat it posed to its neighbors were also valid reasons for the use of force against Iraq. Consequently, Kristol strongly supported an invasion of Iraq well before the attacks on September 11, 2001, or even the advent of the George W. Bush administration. Indeed, in 1998 the Project for the New American Century sent a letter to President Clinton urging an invasion of Iraq, which was ignored.

With the George W. Bush administration in office in January 2001, Kristol and The Project for the New American Century, as well as many *Weekly Standard* writers, continued to urge this military course in Iraq and found themselves with a far more receptive audience. Even so, Kristol and others, while supportive of the goals in invading Iraq, were often critical of the invasion's implementation. In particular, once they recognized the nature of the Iraqi insurgency, Kristol and other commentators were critical of Secretary of Defense Donald Rumsfeld for inadequate planning regarding the occupation of Iraq.

Kristol remains a supporter of the American war effort in Iraq and is a staunch proponent for a firm American partnership with Israel that opposes terrorist groups of all sorts. As a consequence, Kristol favored the Israeli incursion into Lebanon in the summer of 2006 and Israeli actions in the West Bank and Gaza Strip. Kristol continues to be an editor at the *Weekly Standard,* a columnist for the *New York Times,* a Fox News commentator, and an influential conservative opinion maker. In addition, he serves on a host of conservative boards, organizations, and think tanks.

MICHAEL K. BEAUCHAMP

See also

Bush, George Walker; Bush Doctrine; Neoconservatism; Rumsfeld, Donald Henry

References

Kristol, Irving. *Neo-conservatism: The Autobiography of an Idea.* New York: Free Press, 1995.

Kristol, William, ed. *The Weekly Standard Reader: 1995–2005.* New York: HarperCollins, 2005.

Kristol, William, and Lawrence F. Kaplan. *The War over Iraq: Saddam's Tyranny and America's Mission.* New York: Encounter Books, 2003.

Kurdistan Democratic Party

Kurdish political party operating in Kurdish-dominated northern Iraq. The Kurdistan Democratic Party (KDP) was founded in Baghdad in 1946. Mustafa Barzani, tribal chief, fervent Kurdish nationalist, and Naqshbandi sheikh, was its elected president in exile. The KDP, which generally embraces a social democratic ideology and has consistently fought for a Kurdish state, finds its support base in northern Kurdistan (i.e., Irbil, about 50 miles east of Mosul). Most members belong to the Naqshbandi Sufi order and speak the Kurmanji dialect. There are also KDPs in Iran, Syria, and Armenia as well as a KDP-Bakur in Turkey. This entry describes only the KDP operating in and around Iraq.

In 1958 Barzani returned to Iraq from exile in the Soviet Union, claiming that he could unify all Kurdish groups under his control. His return coincided with the overthrow of the Iraqi monarchy that same year. When Iraqi prime minister Abd al-Karim Qasim began forcibly deporting Kurds from Kirkuk, Barzani responded in 1961 by leading a rebellion against the Iraqi regime that lasted on and off until 1975. The Baathists controlling Iraq committed the full strength of their army and air force to destroy the Kurds and drive them into the Zagros and Taurus mountains.

Barzani along with thousands of Kurds fled to neighboring Iran, for Iran provided the KDP with weapons, supplies, and sanctuary. Barzani and the KDP would thus become a permanent enemy of successive Iraqi governments. In 1979 on the death of Mustafa Barzani, his son, Masud Barzani, became the leader of the KDP. He is currently the president of the Kurdistan Regional Government (KRG).

In the late 1980s Iraqi dictator Saddam Hussein tried to eradicate the Kurds during the Anfal Campaign. As many as 4,000 Kurdish villages were destroyed, and more than 100,000 Kurds were killed. A number of members of the Barzani family, tribe, and associated relatives were among those murdered. This campaign caused the Kurds to change their strategy prior to Operation DESERT STORM, which included union with competing political groups.

The KDP, the Patriotic Union of Kurdistan (PUK), and other Kurdish groups now formed the Iraqi Kurdistan Front (IKF) to combine forces to fight Hussein. Once DESERT STORM began in January 1991, 50 percent of the Kurdish soldiers in the Iraqi Army deserted, and some fought in conjunction with coalition troops. After Iraq's defeat in the Persian Gulf War, Kurds from all walks of life joined the IKF. Barzani and Jalal Talabani, leader of the PUK, jointly directed IKF attacks, using Peshmerga (Kurdish fighters). They seized Kirkuk and 75 percent of Kurdistan, and added many Iraqi army deserters to their ranks, thereby obtaining large numbers of heavy weapons. However, immediately after the Persian Gulf War cease-fire, the Iraqi Republican Guards destroyed many Kurdish irregular units, and by March 1991 nearly 1.5 million Kurds had become refugees.

On April 5, 1991, the United Nations (UN) passed Resolution 688, which codified the no-fly zones in northern and southern Iraq and provided for the airdropping of food and medicine to the Kurds. At the same time, the United States and several of its allies implemented Operation PROVIDE COMFORT, a major humanitarian mission to help the embattled Kurds. On April 10, 1991, the United States established the northern no-fly zone at the 36th Parallel. On April 18, 1991, the UN created a Kurdish-controlled enclave in northern Iraq. However, because there was no political support for a long-term occupation of the region, the UN withdrew all forces on July 5, 1991.

The KDP and PUK now established control in the UN-mandated Kurdish zone. In May 1992 the Kurds founded the KRG, which is composed of, among other groups, the KDP, the PUK, and the Iraqi Communist Party. The Kurds held elections and established a joint legislative assembly with a cabinet. However, the KDP and PUK each tried to seize control of the autonomous region. Amnesty International later reported that in 1994 and 1995 both groups committed scores of killings during their battle for power.

In August 1996, 2,000 Iranian Revolutionary Guard Corps (IRGC) soldiers entered Iraq and attacked the KDP on behalf of the PUK. Barzani turned to Hussein for help. Soon a force of as many as 60,000 Iraqi Republican Guards entered the autonomous Kurdish region and drove the PUK from Irbil. The KDP then pushed the remnants of the PUK to the Iranian border. Hussein and the KDP now controlled all of northern Iraq.

On February 5, 1999, U.S. president Bill Clinton issued Presidential Decision Directive 99-13, which authorized the KDP and the PUK to receive U.S. military assistance through the Iraq Liberation Act (Public Law 105-338). During the 2003 invasion of Iraq, the PUK and KDP cooperated with the Anglo-American–led coalition and sent soldiers into the fight. They also removed Ansar al-Islam from the Kurdish region.

Most recently, the Kurdistan Brigades, led by Dilshad Kalari (Dilshad Garmyani), have publicly called for jihad against the KDP and PUK. The Kurdistan Brigades considers both Masud and PUK leader Talabani apostate politicians. Among other things, the Kurdistan Brigades decries the cooperation between the Peshmerga and the Nuri al-Maliki administration in Baghdad and has criticized the loss of control over certain areas in Kurdistan.

Many Iraqi Kurds have fully assimilated into Iraq and do not support Kurdish separatism. The Kurdish region has few resources with which to develop a viable economy, which is one reason why Kurdish nationalists want control of the Kirkuk oil fields. Since 2003 the KDP and PUK have once again united to form the Democratic Patriotic Alliance of Kurdistan in an attempt to realize a Kurdish state. The parties hotly contested the 2005 Iraqi elections, but continued infighting among them has led some to believe that a truly unified and effective Kurdish popular front may be very difficult to achieve.

DONALD R. DUNNE

See also

Kurdistan Workers' Party; Kurds; Kurds, Massacres of; Patriotic Union of Kurdistan; Peshmerga

References

Batatu, Hanna. *The Old Social Classes and the Revolutionary Movement of Iraq: A Study of Iraq's Old Landed and Commercial Classes and of Its Communists, Ba'athists, and Free Officers.* Princeton, NJ: Princeton University Press, 1978.

Bengio, Ofra. *Saddam's Word: Political Discourse in Iraq.* New York: Oxford University Press USA, 1998.

Marcus, Aliza. *Blood and Belief: The PKK and the Kurdish Fight for Independence.* New York: New York University Press, 2007.

Natali, Denise. *International Aid, Regional Politics, and the Kurdish Issue in Iraq after the Gulf War.* Abu Dhabi: Emirates Center for Strategic Studies and Research, 1999.

O'Leary, Brendan, John McGarry, and Khaled Smith. *The Future of Kurdistan in Iraq.* Philadelphia: University of Pennsylvania Press, 2005.

Stansfield, Gareth R. V. *Iraqi Kurdistan: Political Development and Emergent Democracy.* New York: Routledge, 2003.

Kurdistan Workers' Party

Militant Kurdish separatist group that operates in both northern Iraq and southern Turkey and has been labeled a terrorist organization by numerous nations, including the United States. The Kurdistan Workers' Party (Parti Karkerani Kurdistan, PKK) was founded by Turkish-born Abdullah Ocalan on October 27, 1978. From 1966 to 1978 Ocalan attended the Faculty of Political Science in Ankara, Turkey, where he immersed himself in Marxist-Leninist ideologies. The Turkish government had long suppressed the Kurds, refusing to recognize their ethnicity, language, and culture or to permit Kurdish to be taught in schools. The government employs euphemisms for the conflict and the Kurds, such as the "troubles in the southeast," or deems them all terrorists. It has even prosecuted non-Kurds, such as Nobel Prize–winner Orhan Pamuk, for writing about the issue. Beginning in May 1979, Ocalan directed the PKK from Damascus, Syria.

The PKK desires a wholly independent Kurdistan nation defined by borders that encompass both Turkish and Iraqi Kurds. It would then incorporate Iranian and Syrian Kurds into a regional federation. In addition to seeking Kurdish separatism and nationalism, the PKK also seeks to create a Marxist-Leninist political and economic system for Kurdistan. Historically, the PKK's strategy has included terrorist tactics against Turkish military and security service personnel as well as against Kurds who are believed to collaborate with Turkish officials. From 1980 to 1990 the PKK sought to establish guerrilla cells across Turkey, but many of its members were killed in clashes with the Turkish Army. In the late 1980s PKK terrorists began fleeing into northern Iraq after attacking targets in Turkey. They were often abetted by Iran and Iraq and received safe haven from them. After Operation DESERT STORM, however, the level of Iraqi support to the PKK was a matter of speculation. Nevertheless, open-source reports claimed that the PKK maintained training camps in Iraq after 1991.

In 1991 the number of Kurdish refugees became an issue of global interest, especially after Iraqi dictator Saddam Hussein's brutal crackdown against the Kurds in northern Iraq in the aftermath of the Persian Gulf War. The PKK used this heightened awareness to garner more support for its agenda. At the time, its strength was estimated at about 3,000 members, but some sources claim that its active supporters ranged in number from 2,000 to 5,000. This increased support enabled the PKK to dramatically increase attacks across Turkey. As part of its attack plan against the Turkish government, the PKK sought to drive tourists away from Turkey by bombing hotels and restaurants. Some of its operations included grenade attacks at beaches and suicide bombing attacks. The party's ranks soon swelled to 10,000 to 15,000 guerrillas. At least 5,000 to 6,000 of them were located in Turkey.

Iran's continued support for the PKK may be due in large part to a PKK pledge that it would not foment insurrectionist and separatist causes among the Iranian (Persian) Kurds. In October 1995, however, Iran and Turkey agreed to conduct a joint operation to remove the PKK from their shared border. Nothing substantive resulted, probably because Osman Ocalan, Abdullah's brother, resided in Iran for a time.

The PKK continues to use its safe havens in northern Iraq and northwestern Iran to wage war against Turkey, and Turkey has adamantly refused to enter into negotiations or even shift its policies to permit expressions of Kurdish culture. Turkey has come under significant criticism for its Kurdish policies during the course of its quest to be admitted to membership in the European Union (EU).

Meanwhile, Turkey has conducted offensive military operations into Iraq and Iran. In 1998, Turkish officials captured Semdin Sakik, Ocalan's deputy commander. Turkey threatened to invade Syria if it continued harboring Ocalan, and Damascus quickly expelled him. Turkish agents arrested Ocalan as he left the Greek embassy in Nairobi, Kenya, in 1999, and he was extradited to Turkey to stand trial. Ocalan's arrest prompted Kurdish demonstrations in many nations, and some Kurds stormed Greek embassies in protest. After Ocalan's arrest, Syria expelled many PKK operatives, many of whom relocated to northern Iraq.

On May 31, 1999, the day his trial began, Ocalan apologized for PKK violence that had claimed the lives of more than 30,000 people. He was convicted on June 29, 1999, of violating Article 125 of the Turkish penal code: seeking to separate a portion of Turkey to create another polity. His death sentence was commuted on October 3, 2002, however, out of concern for Turkey's EU membership requirements, which forbid death penalties. Ocalan is serving his life sentence in Imrali Island Prison in the Sea of Marmara, Turkey.

In April 2002 at its Eighth Party Congress, the PKK changed its name to the Kurdistan Freedom and Democracy Congress (KADEK) and declared that it would pursue Kurdish rights using political processes instead of armed violence. Nevertheless, it stands accused of having armed 8,000 Kurdish guerrillas across Turkey. Since then, the United States and Turkey have begun exploring ways to eliminate KADEK. KADEK responded by changing its name to the Kurdistan People's Congress (Kongra-Gel, KGK), to give it the appearance of a political party. In the summer of 2004 the KGK began attacking Turkish security forces. It is believed that it maintains 500 militants in Turkey and 3,000–5,000 militants in northern Iraq.

Because Turkey has been unable to induce the new Iraqi government to take military action against the KGK/PKK in Iraq, Turkey began conducting cross-border operations using U.S. intelligence reports. Those operations are ongoing. To date, the conflict between Kurdish separatists in Turkey, including the PKK and Turkish military and security forces, has resulted in the destruction of some 3,000 villages and has created more than 1 million refugees. It has also brought about the deaths of at least 35,000 people. Currently, some 15,000 KGK/PKK members are incarcerated.

DONALD R. DUNNE

See also
Kurds; Kurds, Massacres of

References

Barkey, Henri J., and Graham E. Fuller. *Turkey's Kurdish Question.* Lanham, MD: Rowman and Littlefield, 1998.

Marcus, Aliza. *Blood and Belief: The PKK and the Kurdish Fight for Independence.* New York: New York University Press, 2007.

O'Leary, Brendan, John McGarry, and Khaled Smith. *The Future of Kurdistan in Iraq.* Philadelphia: University of Pennsylvania Press, 2005.

Stansfield, Gareth R. V. *Iraqi Kurdistan: Political Development and Emergent Democracy.* New York: Routledge, 2003.

Kurds

People of Indo-European origin who inhabit the upcountry and mountainous areas chiefly in Iran, Iraq, Syria, and Turkey. Their primary area of concentration in southern Turkey, and northern parts of Iran and Iraq, is known as Kurdistan, although this is not an autonomous region. There are also small enclaves of Kurds in southwestern Armenia, Azerbaijan, and Lebanon. The total Kurdish population worldwide is estimated to number between 30 million and 35 million people, making the Kurds one of the biggest ethnic groups in the world who do not enjoy their own autonomous homeland. The Kurds, whose language is of Indo-European background, are not Arabs. However, numerous Kurds have intermarried with Arabs and have played an important role in Arab and Muslim history. Salah al-Din al-Ayyubi (Saladin, one of the greatest of Muslim leaders) was of Kurdish origin. There have also been numerous Kurdish dynasties, such as the Ziyarids, the Jastanids, and the Kakuyids.

The great majority of Kurds are Sunni Muslims, and their language is related to Persian (which is spoken chiefly in Iran, Afghanistan, and Tajikistan). There are numerous dialects of Kurdish divided into two primary dialect groups: Sorani and

An Iraqi Kurd father carries the body of his dead child in a Turkish refugee camp in May 1991. Ethnic Kurds fled their homes in Iraq for the relative safety of the mountains along the Turkish-Iraqi border when fighting intensified between the Iraqi Army and Kurdish Peshmerga guerrillas. (Joel Robine/AFP/Getty Images)

Kumanji. Just as they have their own language, the Kurds maintain their own unique culture and traditions.

Until the first few decades of the 20th century, most Kurds lived a pastoral, nomadic existence and divided themselves into tribes. For centuries, they led a somewhat isolated lifestyle that clung to tradition and was well ordered by tribal hierarchy and customs. The mountain Kurds' principal avocation was goat and sheep herding, which was migratory in nature. In this sense, they were not unlike the Bedouins to the south. However, when the Ottoman Empire broke apart as a result of World War I, the Kurds found themselves circumscribed within newly created states, none of which was interested in allowing them to continue their centuries-old lifestyle and customs.

As new nations such as Iraq and Turkey (where the bulk of Kurds live) organized themselves into nationalistic nation states, the Kurds came under great pressure to abandon their tribal ways and assimilate into the majority culture. They were also greatly limited in their migratory patterns, which served only to further marginalize them.

Soon after World War I, Kurds began to call for their own nation, Kurdistan. They expected support in this endeavor from the United States. But as an Associated Power in World War I, rather than an Entente Power, the United States had not declared war on the Ottoman Empire and therefore after the war had no voice in its dismemberment and the subsequent League of Nations Mandates. Beyond that, however, the American public had little interest in such a course of action.

While the British gave some lip service to the establishment of a Kurdish state, the Turks effectively quashed the idea, with Iraq and Iran agreeing that they would recognize no Kurdish state encompassing any part of their territory. The Kurds were now subjected to discrimination and oppression in general. This situation was particularly bad in Turkey. The Turkish government refused to recognize the Kurds as a distinct ethnic group (a state of affairs that continues today), forced them to abandon their language, banned their traditional garb, and lured them into urban areas to curtail their pastoral life. This, of course, only brought more discrimination and resulted in high unemployment and poverty rates for urbanized Kurds.

In Turkey the Kurds have periodically risen up in rebellions that have been promptly crushed by the Turkish government. However, an underground Kurdish guerrilla group, formed out of the Kurdish Workers' Party (PKK) in the 1980s, continues to pursue the dream of an independent Kurdish state and has engaged Turkish, Iranian, and Syrian troops in an ongoing military struggle. In the late 1940s and again in the late 1970s, Kurds attempted

Kurds at a refugee camp near the Turkish-Iraqi border wait in line near a German army helicopter to receive an allotment of water from coalition troops, who have come to the camp to distribute aid and prepare the refugees for a move to organized camps within Iraq as part of Operation PROVIDE COMFORT. Thousands of Kurds fled into Turkey after fighting between Kurdish groups and Iraqi government forces erupted following Operation DESERT STORM. (U.S. Department of Defense)

to form their own autonomous region in Iran. These efforts were both put down by the Iranians.

For decades, Kurds have been subjected to brutal oppression by the Iraqi government. From 1960 to 1975, Iraqi Kurds under the leadership of Mustafa Barzani waged a guerrilla-style war with Iraqi regular forces. This brought significant casualties to the Iraqis and forced them in 1970 to enter into talks with the rebelling Kurds. That same year, the Iraqi government offered a peace deal to the Kurds that would have brought them their own autonomous region (but not sovereignty) by 1974. Meanwhile, Barzani continued his campaign, and the peace offer never took hold. In 1975 the Iraqis began moving thousands of people into northern Iraq in an attempt to Arabize the region while simultaneously exiling close to 200,000 Kurds.

The Iran-Iraq War (1980–1988) brought great misery and many fatalities to Iraqi Kurds. Saddam Hussein's government was brutal in its treatment of the minority, and in 1988 Hussein launched his so-called Anfal ("spoils of war") Campaign. Over a period of several months, Iraqi forces killed perhaps as many as 100,000 Kurds and destroyed some 2,000 villages, often employing chemical weapons. In 1991, in the immediate aftermath of the

Persian Gulf War, Iraqi Kurds rebelled again, and they were again crushed.

The Kurdish region of northern Iraq, comprising three provinces, is roughly divided in two by two competing political parties—the Kurdistan Democratic Party, headed by Massoud Barzani, and the Patriotic Union of Kurdistan, led by Jalal Talabani. Although there is much political infighting between the two groups, their goals and programs are remarkably similar, and they have been able to work together effectively, especially in post-Hussein Iraq. Indeed, the Kurdish fighting groups known as the Peshmerga have fought for decades in Iraq, Iran, and Turkey. Some have fought alongside U.S. troops in a joint effort to defeat Kurdish Islamic extremist groups, such as Ansar al-Islam.

After the 2003 Anglo-American invasion of Iraq and Hussein's overthrow, Kurds took control of Kirkuk and most of Mosul. Ironically, while the United States and its allies have been unable to build a stable, democratic regime in central and southern Iraq, the Kurds in the north have been more successful in creating a stable environment in their sphere of influence. The Kurds are strongly pro-democratic, and somewhat more pro-American than other Iraqis. Northern Iraq has experienced some attacks and bombings, and Mosul and Kirkuk remain key problem areas as of 2009, but other areas of historic Iraqi Kurdistan have been less dangerous for coalition forces.

The major Kurdish political parties decry Islamic extremism and do not support a theocratic government, although many smaller Kurdish groups do. There is still a great deal of support for the creation of a separate Kurdish nation among Kurds. Such a move, however, would be vociferously opposed by the Turks and Iranians. There is as yet no resolution over the status of Kirkuk, where Arabs and Turkomen dispute Kurdish claims. However, if this issue and some other matters can be resolved, and the Kurds exercise autonomy over their region, they will have a nation in everything but name.

PAUL G. PIERPAOLI JR.

See also

Hussein, Saddam; Iran; Iran-Iraq War; Iraq, History of, Pre-1990; Iraq, History of, 1990–Present; Kurdistan Democratic Party; Kurds, Massacres of; Patriotic Union of Kurdistan; Peshmerga

References

Bulloch, John, and Harvey Morris. *No Friends but the Mountains: The Tragic History of the Kurds.* New York: Oxford University Press, 1993.

Ciment, James. *The Kurds: State and Minority in Turkey, Iraq, and Iran.* New York: Facts on File, 1996.

Izady, Mehrdad R. *The Kurds: A Concise Handbook.* Washington, DC: Crane Russak, Taylor and Francis, 1992.

Lawrence, Quil. *Invisible Nation: How the Kurds' Quest for Statehood Is Shaping Iraq and the Middle East.* New York: Walker, 2008.

McDowall, David. *A Modern History of the Kurds.* New York: I. B. Tauris, 2000.

Kurds, Massacres of

The Kurdish people are spread across a number of countries in the Middle East, including Turkey, Iraq, Syria, and Iran. Kurds have campaigned for their own homeland for many years and have suffered persecution throughout their history. During recent times, the Kurds have been subjected to repeated repressions and massacres.

Following an uprising led by Mustafa Barzani from 1961 to 1963, the Kurds were given some representation in the Iraqi government. However, following the outbreak of the Iran-Iraq War in September 1980, the Kurdish leadership tended to side with Iran, and as a result Iraqi dictator Saddam Hussein began a program of systematic persecution against the Kurds. Iraqi attacks increased dramatically from 1986 on. The lead figure directing these attacks was Ali Hasan al-Majid, a cousin of President Hussein. The use of chemical weapons during the attacks on the Kurds would earn Majid the sobriquet "Chemical Ali."

During the campaign as a whole, the Iraqi army deployed more than 200,000 troops against the Kurds. The campaign, launched by Majid himself, was split into seven phases between February and September 1988. This campaign against the Kurds became known as the Anfal Campaign, meaning "the spoils of war." In each phase, an area of Kurdish-dominated territory was sealed off and then attacked. Tactics against the Kurds included the employment of aircraft to bomb the Kurdish villages, as well as ground forces to secure Kurdish settlements and detain and interrogate all males between the ages of 15 and 70. It was then official Iraqi policy either to execute these men immediately or transport them, along with their families, to the Topzawa Camp just outside the northern Iraqi town of Kirkuk. Here the men of proscribed age were segregated and summarily shot; the bodies were then bulldozed into shallow burial pits.

This deliberate plan of genocide grew as the campaign progressed. In the first stage (between February 23 and March 19, 1988), there was no official policy calling for the killing of all adult males; however, by the last phase (August 25–September 6, 1988) Majid did promulgate such a policy. Within Kirkuk, there was mass deportation of Kurdish families. The Baath Party then built large-scale housing projects and encouraged poor Arabs from the south of Iraq to settle in them. This policy of "Arabization" allowed Baghdad to better control the oil-rich area around Kirkuk.

Perhaps the most infamous incident during the Anfal operation was the chemical attack that took place against the Kurdish town of Halabja. Although there were a total of 40 separate chemical attacks in the entire six-month campaign against the Kurds, the one against Halabja was by far the most significant. Halabja, located 150 miles northeast of Baghdad, had an estimated population of 80,000 people. Eight Iraqi Air Force aircraft struck the town on the evening of March 16, 1988, and the attacks continued throughout the night. Chemical agents employed in the attack included mustard gas and nerve agents such as sarin and tabun. During this one attack, more than 5,000 civilians were killed and many thousands of others were injured.

Initially, Baghdad claimed that the attack had been intended to strike Iranian troops, but between 1992 and 1994 the organization Human Rights Watch effectively proved Iraqi culpability in the Halabja massacre. In total, the Anfal Campaign claimed perhaps as many as 50,000 civilian lives and destroyed some 2,000 villages, 1,750 schools, and 2,500 mosques.

Following the outbreak of the 1991 Persian Gulf War, the Kurds in Iraq rose up against the Hussein regime, and under the protection of an allied air umbrella were able to establish their own governments in so-called safe havens established by the United Nations (UN). In 2003 the Kurdish leadership supported the American-led invasion of Iraq and has now established effective control over Kirkuk and the surrounding areas. Thus far, it has prevented any further atrocities against the Kurdish people in Iraq.

Yet Iraq is not the only place where the Kurds have recently suffered. Within Turkey, Turkish security forces have leveled more than 3,000 Kurdish villages and displaced some 378,000 Kurds since 1982. In Iran, during the revolutionary period from 1979 to 1982, Islamic Revolutionary Guards campaigned against the Kurds, killing some 10,000 civilians. And attacks on Kurdish settlements continue. The most recent incidents occurred on July 9, 2005, following the murder of a Kurdish activist. In Syria, too, there have been incidents. On March 12, 2004, 180 Kurdish civilians were killed or injured in clashes with Syrian forces in Qamishli, a Kurdish city in the northeastern part of the country.

Former Iraqi dictator Saddam Hussein and Ali Hasan al-Majid were both tried and convicted by the Iraqi Special Tribunal of crimes against humanity for their role in the Anfal Campaign.

RALPH BAKER

See also

Biological Weapons and Warfare; Chemical Weapons and Warfare; Hussein, Saddam; Iran-Iraq War; Iraq, History of, Pre-1990; Iraq, History of, 1990–Present; Kurds; Majid al Tikriti, Ali Hassan al-; No-Fly Zones

References

Lawrence, Quil. *Invisible Nation: How the Kurds' Quest for Statehood Is Shaping Iraq and the Middle East.* New York: Walker, 2008.

McDowall, David. *The Kurds: A Nation Denied.* Austin, TX: Harry Ransom Humanities Research Center, 1992.

Potter, Lawrence G., and Gary G. Sick, eds. *Iran, Iraq, and the Legacies of War.* New York: Palgrave Macmillan, 2004.

Rudd, Gordon W. *Humanitarian Intervention: Assisting the Iraqi Kurds in Operation Provide Comfort, 1991.* Washington, DC: Department of the Army, 2004.

Yildiz, Kerim, and Tom Blass. *The Kurds in Iraq: The Past, Present and Future.* London: Pluto, 2004.

Kuwait

Middle Eastern monarchy. The state of Kuwait, with a 2007 population of approximately 2.39 million, occupies 6,880 square miles, including the Kuwaiti share of the Neutral Zone defined by agreement with Saudi Arabia in 1922 and partitioned by mutual agreement in 1966. Kuwait is thus about the size of the U.S. state of Hawaii. More than half of Kuwait's population is made up of noncitizen workers attracted by job opportunities in this oil-rich Persian Gulf nation.

Kuwait is strategically located at the northern end of the Persian Gulf and is bordered by Saudi Arabia to the south, Iraq to the west and north, and the Persian Gulf to the east. The topography is flat, low desert, and the climate is very hot and dry. More than 95 percent of the Kuwaiti people live in urban areas, mostly along the coast. The nation's major natural resources are oil and natural gas, comprising an estimated 10 percent of the world's known reserves. There is a minor fishing industry, but oil sales make up half of Kuwait's gross domestic product (GDP) and provide 80 percent of the government's yearly revenues. The large oil reserves have sustained a relatively high per capita GDP annually and allow for extensive social services for Kuwaiti citizens.

Oil and geographic location have made Kuwait a crucial strategic state, far beyond what might be expected of a country its size and population. Kuwait has been a key to British imperial interests in the Middle East, a major player in regional affairs, a staunch

The Liberation Tower in Kuwait City, named in commemoration of the expulsion of Iraqi forces from Kuwait in 1991. (iStockPhoto)

Cold War ally of the United States, the focus of the 1990 Persian Gulf War, and an important staging area for subsequent American-led operations in Iraq beginning in 2003.

In contrast to its current prominence, Kuwait was a remote part of the Ottoman Empire in the 18th century, largely left to manage its own affairs. This earlier insignificance is manifest in the fact that the Utub tribes that settled in the area early in the 18th century called their central town Kuwait, the Arabic diminutive for *kut,* meaning a fortress built near water. By mid-century the Utub's al-Sabah tribe, whose descendants rule Kuwait to this day, had emerged as the most prominent in the area. The al-Sabah focused on developing the local pearl beds and taking advantage of location to promote regional trade.

Recognizing the fact that any increase in the wealth of Kuwait and the al-Sabah family would attract Ottoman attention and invite closer imperial control and higher taxation, Sheikh Mubarak al-Sabah sought the protection of Britain, the major European power in the region. The result was an 1899 agreement in which Kuwait ceded control over its foreign affairs and defense to the British. In return, Kuwait agreed to eschew alliances with other powers and promised not to cede any concessions—economic or military—to any other nation. Kuwait thus became a British protectorate. This situation remained fairly stable until Britain reduced its imperial commitments after World War II. Kuwait became fully independent in June 1961.

Kuwait then aligned itself with the West—the United States in particular—in regional and international affairs. The 1979 Iranian Revolution served to further strengthen this alliance, and Kuwait became a staunch supporter of Iraq during the Iran-Iraq War, which began in 1980. That support included nearly $35 billion in grants, loans, and other assistance to the Iraqi government. After the war, which ended in 1988, Iraqi leader Saddam Hussein demanded that Kuwait forgive Iraq's loans, reasoning that Iraq had been the bulwark in the Arab world against Iran and was thus owed monetary concessions. Iraq also accused the Kuwaitis of slant drilling for oil into Iraqi fields and claimed, as it had in the past, that Kuwait was an Iraqi province, as parts of Kuwait had been in the province of Basra under the Ottoman Empire.

Angry with Kuwait's refusal to forgive the Iraqi debt and convinced that the kingdom was keeping oil prices artificially low by pumping too much oil, Hussein launched an invasion of Kuwait on August 2, 1990. The international response, which was divided into two stages, was strong and swift. The U.S.-led Operation DESERT SHIELD saw a large-scale military buildup in Saudi Arabia. Then in January 1991, when Hussein steadfastly refused to withdraw from Kuwait, Operation DESERT STORM began, during which the United States led a large international military coalition, including other Arab nations, to drive Iraqi forces from Kuwait. The brief war ended on February 27, 1991, with Iraq compelled to recognize Kuwaiti independence. Kuwait was heavily damaged during the Iraqi occupation and subsequent war, but the nation's immense oil wealth and small size allowed it to rebuild quickly and efficiently.

Thereafter, Kuwait remained a firm ally of the United States, backing it after the September 11, 2001, terror attacks and the subsequent campaign in Afghanistan that unseated the Taliban regime. The Kuwaitis also allowed their territory to be used as a staging area for the U.S.-led effort to oust Hussein from power in the spring of 2003. Kuwait has served as a primary forwarding point for U.S. troops deployed to Iraq, and has hosted a major administrative center for humanitarian aid in Iraq after the March 2003 invasion. In return, the United States has been restrained in its criticism of Kuwaiti internal affairs. In May 2005 Kuwait's parliament did grant full political rights to women, although in the May 2008 elections no women were elected to office. The United States maintains a significant military and naval presence in the region that protects the al-Sabah ruling family of Kuwait, which has had long experience in maintaining its position from the 19th century to the present.

Kuwait has not been a major military force in the Arab-Israeli conflict, but it has strongly supported the Palestinian movement. Numerous Palestinian refugees and students have lived in Kuwait, and branches of both the Fatah and Hamas organizations have been established there. Kuwait did not participate in the 1948 and 1956 wars in and around Israel. After its independence from Britain in 1961, Kuwait sent small numbers of troops to fight in the 1967 and 1973 wars. These were token forces, and Kuwait focused on internal development of its oil resources. The Kuwaiti government taxed the large proportion of Palestinians in the Kuwaiti workforce, and these funds were then used to support Palestinian causes. Yet there was a suspicion of Palestinians as a possible source of political dissidence, such as had occurred in Jordan and Lebanon in the 1970s and 1980s. Palestine Liberation Organization (PLO) support for Iraq in the 1990 conflict with Iraq enraged Kuwaitis, who then evicted the Palestinians after the conflict. Kuwait has an active Islamist opposition and is wary of Shia-dominated Iran.

DANIEL E. SPECTOR

See also

DESERT STORM, Operation; Hussein, Saddam; Iran-Iraq War; Iraq, History of, Pre-1990; Iraq, History of, 1990–Present; IRAQI FREEDOM, Operation; Palestine Liberation Organization; Saudi Arabia

References

Assiri, Abdul-Reda. *Kuwait's Foreign Policy: City-State in World Politics.* Boulder, CO: Westview, 1990.

Cordesman, Anthony J. *Kuwait: Recovery and Security after the Gulf War.* Boulder, CO: Westview, 1997.

Daniels, John. *Kuwait Journey.* Luton, UK: White Crescent, 1971.

United States Army. *Area Handbook Series: Persian Gulf States.* Washington, DC: U.S. Government Printing Office, 1984.

Kuwait, Armed Forces

Prior to the 1991 Persian Gulf War, the small Persian Gulf nation of Kuwait, with a population of 2.597 million people, maintained a small military force of only about 12,500 personnel. Most of its armaments had been purchased from Great Britain, with which it had long-standing military and political ties, and the United States. Kuwaiti armed forces were in no position to resist an Iraqi invasion.

Within hours on August 2, 1990, Iraq's vastly superior and exponentially larger forces overwhelmed the modest Kuwaiti defenses and began a nearly seven-month occupation of the nation. Sheikh Jabir al-Ahmad al-Jabir al-Sabah, Kuwait's 13th emir, promptly fled to neighboring Saudi Arabia, where he established a government in exile. What remained of the Kuwaiti armed force's equipment was either taken by the Iraqis or destroyed.

Only the Kuwaiti air force escaped complete destruction, as many of its airplanes were able to fly to fields in Saudi Arabia during the initial assault. Many military personnel also managed to escape, most of them to Saudi Arabia. Some 9,900 of them were integrated into coalition forces to fight against Iraq when the Persian Gulf War began.

The Kuwaiti military falls under the general command of the ruling emir and is composed of six components: army, navy, air force, national police, national guard, and coast guard. Prior to the 1990 Iraqi invasion, it is believed that the Kuwaiti government spent about $2.1 billion per year on national defense, or about 4.2 percent of gross domestic product (GDP). Kuwait has gradually

Kuwaiti soldiers stand at attention during a multinational military exercise in Egypt in 2001. (U.S. Department of Defense)

increased military spending since then, and is estimated to now be spending about $3.01 billion per year, or 5.1 percent of GDP, making its per capita military spending among the highest in the world.

Currently, Kuwait's army has about 11,000 active and reserve, combat-ready personnel. The air force has 2,500 men, and the navy has about 1,800 personnel. The coast guard numbers about 400 people. There are thus some 15,000 military personnel in all, not counting the national police or national guard.

In 2002, the last year for which reliable figures are available, Kuwait's military arsenal included 368 main battle tanks (including some 200 M-84 tanks) and 18 self-propelled 150-mm guns purchased from France. The air force had 81 combat aircraft of various types and capabilities. The Kuwaiti navy had 16 ships. It is not clear how many vessels the coast guard possessed.

Although Kuwait did not participate directly in either Operation ENDURING FREEDOM or Operation IRAQI FREEDOM, it continues to expand both the size and capabilities of its armed forces. In this it has received considerable help from the United States. Indeed, in September 1991 Kuwait agreed to a multiyear defense cooperation agreement with the Americans that promised arms and technology transfers, advanced training for Kuwaiti troops, and periodic joint military exercises. In return, the United States was granted access to Kuwaiti ports and air bases, as well as storage areas for military hardware.

In 1996, in response to Iraqi provocations, the United States agreed to permanently station a U.S. battalion-sized military unit in Kuwait. As many as 5,000 troops—mostly army and marine units—have been in place in Kuwait since that time, the largest portion being a part of the U.S. Army Central Command (ARCENT), which is part of the U.S. Central Command (CENTCOM). Kuwait was a primary staging area for the 2003 Anglo-American–led invasion of Iraq, although no Kuwaiti troops have participated in that conflict.

U.S. troops and equipment are located in 16 bases and facilities throughout the country, including the Kuwait International Airport. Since 1996 American sales of military equipment to Kuwait have exceeded $5.9 billion. The most noteworthy Kuwaiti acquisitions have been the Patriot missile system, McDonnell Douglas/ Boeing F-18 Hornet aircraft, and Abrams M-1A2 main battle tanks. These purchases, combined with continued close cooperation with U.S. forces, have resulted in a Kuwaiti military establishment considerably more robust than the one that faced the Iraqi invasion of August 1990.

PAUL G. PIERPAOLI JR.

See also

Kuwait; Kuwait, Iraqi Invasion of; United States Central Command

References

Assiri, Abdul-Reda. *Kuwait's Foreign Policy: City-State in World Politics.* Boulder, CO: Westview, 1990.

Cordesman, Anthony J. *Kuwait: Recovery and Security after the Gulf War.* Boulder, CO: Westview, 1997.

Finnie, David H. *Shifting Lines in the Sand: Kuwait's Elusive Frontier with Iraq.* Cambridge: Harvard University Press, 1992.

Isiorho, S. A. *Kuwait.* Philadelphia: Chelsea House, 2002.

Kuwait, Iraqi Atrocities in

See Iraqi Occupation of Kuwait, Atrocities

Kuwait, Iraqi Claims on

See Iraqi Claims on Kuwait

Kuwait, Iraqi Invasion of
Event Date: August 2, 1990

At 2:00 a.m. on August 2, 1990, Iraqi forces invaded Kuwait. Two weeks before, on July 17, 1990, Iraqi dictator Saddam Hussein had threatened military action against that small Persian Gulf nation for exceeding production limits set by Organization of Petroleum

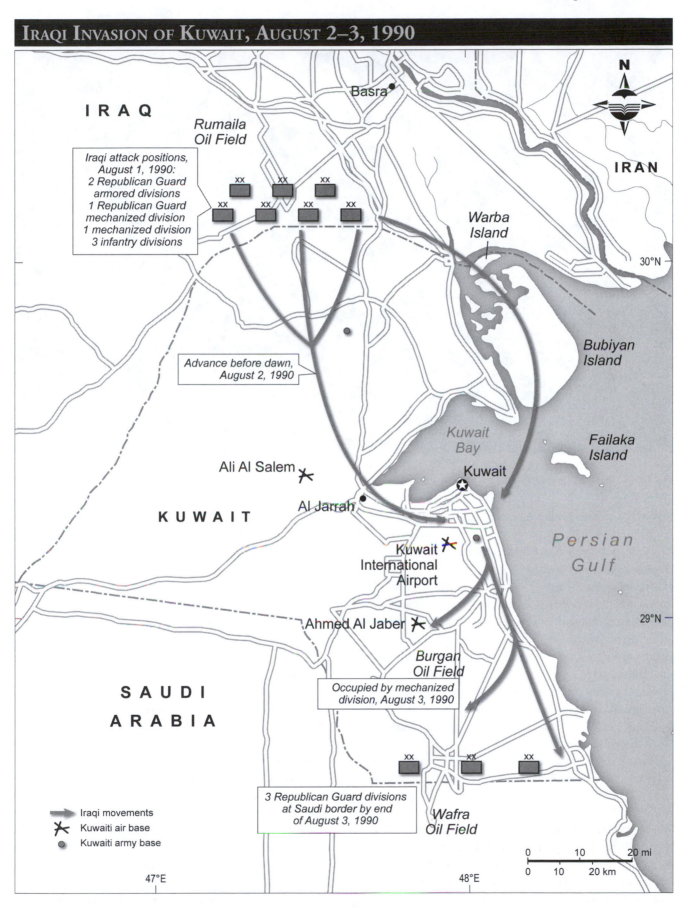

Iraqi Invasion of Kuwait, August 2–3, 1990

IRAQ

Basra

Rumaila
Oil Field

Iraqi attack positions,
August 1, 1990:
2 Republican Guard
armored divisions
1 Republican Guard
mechanized division
1 mechanized division
3 infantry divisions

Warba
Island

IRAN

30°N

Bubiyan
Island

Advance before dawn,
August 2, 1990

Kuwait
Bay

Failaka
Island

Ali Al Salem ✈

Kuwait ★

Persian
Gulf

KUWAIT

Al Jarrah

Kuwait
International
Airport ✈

29°N

Ahmed Al Jaber ✈

Burgan
Oil Field

SAUDI

Occupied by mechanized
division, August 3, 1990

ARABIA

3 Republican Guard divisions
at Saudi border by end
of August 3, 1990

Wafra
Oil Field

➤ Iraqi movements
✈ Kuwaiti air base
● Kuwaiti army base

47°E

48°E

0   10   20 mi

0   10   20 km

Iraqi Army troops in Baghdad celebrate their country's successful invasion and occupation of Kuwait in August 1990. (David Turnley/Corbis)

Exporting Counties (OPEC) oil quotas, which had helped drive down the price of oil.

Relations between the two countries had previously been close. In 1979 a radical regime had come to power in Iran, and Kuwait subsequently proved a staunch ally during Iraq's protracted war (1980–1988) with Iran. Hundreds of thousands of people died on both sides in the war, and Iraq had accumulated a considerable war debt of some $80 billion. Hussein was thus anxious that oil prices be as high as possible, and Kuwaiti excess production worked against this. Kuwait was also the major creditor for the Iraqi war effort, to the tune of some $35 billion. Hussein demanded that these loans be forgiven, reasoning that Iraq had borne the brunt of the fight in defense of Arab interests and deserved monetary concessions.

Hussein was also angry over Kuwaiti slant drilling into Iraqi oil fields along their common border. Finally, Iraq had long claimed Kuwait as a province dating back to the arbitrary administrative boundaries during the period of the Ottoman Empire. Iraq's desire to gobble up its small neighbor certainly did not begin with Hussein. When Britain granted Kuwait its independence in 1961, Iraqi strongman Abd al-Karim Qasim had immediately asserted Iraq's claim to sovereignty. This was a matter of securing not only Kuwaiti oil but also that nation's long coastline. Iraq's sole access

to the Persian Gulf was the Shatt al-Arab waterway, sovereignty over which was a point of contention with its enemy Iran. Securing Kuwait would mean easy Iraqi access into the Persian Gulf.

The war with Iran had left Iraq with one of the world's largest military establishments, and Hussein was determined to employ it to advantage. For some time Washington had been concerned over Iraq's expanding nuclear industry and a chemical and biological capability that Hussein had used in the war against Iran as well as against some of his own people, the Kurds. Then, in mid-July 1990, American intelligence satellites detected Iraqi forces massing near the Kuwait border.

Yet U.S. policy was unclear. Fearful of radical Islam in Iran, both the Soviet Union and the United States had assisted Iraq in its war with Iran. Washington had provided valuable satellite intelligence. Up until the invasion of Kuwait, moreover, Washington assumed that Hussein was weary of war and would in any case need a protracted period of peace to rebuild. At the same time, U.S. ambassador to Iraq April Glaspie had followed the George H. W. Bush administration's policy of delivering "mixed messages," which seemed to allow Hussein operational freedom in the Persian Gulf. Hussein probably believed that his moves against Kuwait would not be challenged by the United States. On its part, the State Department did not believe that Hussein would actually mount a full-scale invasion. If military action occurred, Washington expected only a limited offensive to force the Kuwaitis to accede to Iraqi's demands of bringing the cost of oil in line. Clearly Washington underestimated Hussein's ambitions. The intelligence was there, but the administration failed to act on a Pentagon call for a show of force to deter possible Iraqi aggression. Indeed, the Bush administration did not draw a firm line in the sand until Hussein had already crossed it.

Commander of the Republican Guards, Lieutenant General Ayad Futahih al-Rawi, had charge of the invasion force. It consisted of the Iraqi Hammurabi Armored Division and Tawakalna Mechanized Division, supported by Iraqi special forces and the Medina Armored Division. The Hammurabi and Tawakalna divisions easily overcame the sole Kuwaiti brigade deployed along the common border, then headed south to Jahrad at the head of the Gulf of Kuwait, before turning east to Kuwait. Kuwaiti armored cars had no chance of stopping the massed Iraqi T-72 tanks.

By 5:00 a.m. fighting had begun for Kuwait. Heliborne elite Iraqi troops were airlifted into the city, preventing any Kuwaiti withdrawal back into it. At the same time, Iraqi seaborne commandoes sealed off the Kuwaiti coast. Meanwhile, the Medina Armored Division screened the Iraqi invasion force against the remote possibility of any intervention by the Gulf Cooperation Council's Peninsula Shield Brigade, situated in northern Saudi Arabia. By evening it was all but over. Four Iraqi infantry divisions moved in behind the mobile forces to occupy the country and conduct mopping-up operations. The three Iraqi heavy divisions then took up defensive positions along the border with Saudi Arabia to the south. Kuwait was completely occupied in fewer than 48 hours. In all, the Iraqis lost in the battle two fighter aircraft, six helicopters, and several armored vehicles. Most Kuwaiti Air Force aircraft took refuge in Saudi Arabia.

Once the battle was won, the Iraqis settled in for a brutal occupation that claimed the lives and property of many Kuwaitis. The Iraqis failed in their effort to seize the emir of Kuwait, Sheikh Jabir al-Ahmad al-Jabir al-Sabah. He managed to escape, but Iraqi commandoes killed his brother, Sheikh Fahd, who was in the palace. The Iraqis then proceeded to loot much of the public and private wealth of Kuwait. Hussein set up a brief puppet government under Ala Hussein Ali before annexing Kuwait outright and installing an Iraqi provincial government.

The U.S. reaction was surprisingly swift. President Bush was deeply concerned over the impact of the invasion on the supply of oil and oil prices, as well as on Saudi Arabia, which possessed the world's largest oil reserves and shared a common border with Kuwait. Bush and others of his generation styled Hussein's aggression as a challenge akin to that of Adolf Hitler and made much of a supposed and quite inaccurate contrast between dictatorship (Iraq) and democracy (Kuwait).

On August 8 Bush ordered the deployment of forward forces to Saudi Arabia in Operation DESERT SHIELD. The troops were to bolster the Saudis and demonstrate resolve in the midst of diplomatic

maneuvering. Hussein proved intransigent, and war loomed between Iraq and a growing coalition headed by the United States, which included Arab states.

SPENCER C. TUCKER

See also

Bush, George Herbert Walker; DESERT SHIELD, Operation; DESERT STORM, Operation; Hussein, Saddam; Iran-Iraq War; Iraq, History of, Pre-1990; Kuwait

References

Crystal, Jill. *Kuwait: The Transformation of an Oil State.* Boulder, CO: Westview, 1992.

Gordon, Michael R., and General Bernard E. Trainor. *The Generals' War: The Inside Story of the Conflict in the Gulf.* New York: Little, Brown, 1995.

Scales, Robert H. *Certain Victory: The U.S. Army in the Gulf War.* Washington, DC: Brassey's, 1994.

Schwarzkopf, H. Norman, with Peter Petre. *It Doesn't Take a Hero: General H. Norman Schwarzkopf, the Autobiography.* New York: Bantam Books, 1993.

Kuwait, Liberation of
Event Date: February 27, 1991

The liberation of Kuwait from Iraqi military occupation occurred on February 27, 1991, and marked the culmination of the Persian Gulf War and Operation DESERT STORM. It occurred during the 100-hour February 24–27, 1991, ground offensive launched by U.S.-led coalition forces, which ended in a crushing defeat for Iraq.

Iraq, with a standing army of 450,000 men in 1990, had invaded Kuwait on August 2, 1990, with 100,000 troops and as many as 700 tanks. The small state of Kuwait was quickly overrun, and Iraqi president Saddam Hussein declared it to be Iraq's "reunited" 19th province. At the same time, Hussein began building up Iraqi forces along the Kuwait-Saudi border.

U.S. president George H. W. Bush led the fight to expel Iraq from Kuwait and received U.S. congressional and United Nations (UN) Security Council approval to reverse Iraq's occupation of Kuwait by all means necessary. U.S. Army general H. Norman Schwarzkopf Jr., commander-in-chief of U.S. Central Command (CENTCOM), oversaw the military operations of the United States and its coalition allies in the Persian Gulf. Meanwhile, the UN Security Council imposed a January 15, 1991, deadline for Iraq's unconditional withdrawal.

Following movement of more than 750,000 military personnel and their matériel to bases in Saudi Arabia and the Persian Gulf, on January 17, 1991 (Kuwaiti time), Operation DESERT STORM began with withering air attacks on Iraqi targets. Coalition forces had complete air superiority and greatly degraded the effectiveness of Iraqi ground force units. However, air power alone failed to coerce Hussein to withdraw from Kuwait unconditionally.

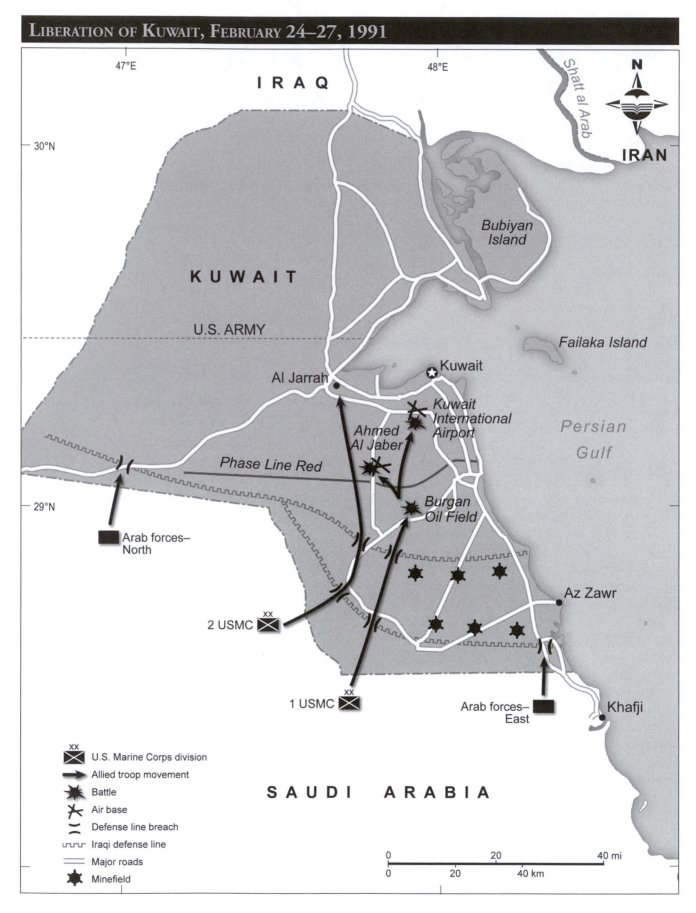

LIBERATION OF KUWAIT, FEBRUARY 24–27, 1991

IRAQ

47°E

48°E

Shatt al Arab

N

IRAN

30°N

KUWAIT

Bubiyan
Island

U.S. ARMY

Failaka Island

Al Jarrah

Kuwait

Kuwait
International
Airport

Ahmed
Al Jaber

Persian
Gulf

Phase Line Red

29°N

Burgan
Oil Field

Arab forces–
North

Az Zawr

2 USMC

1 USMC

Arab forces–
East

Khafji

U.S. Marine Corps division

Allied troop movement

Battle

Air base

Defense line breach

Iraqi defense line

Major roads

Minefield

SAUDI   ARABIA

0   20   40 mi

0   20   40 km

U.S. M-60A1 main battle tanks of the 1st Tank Battalion, 1st Marine Division, advance toward Kuwait City during the third day of the ground offensive phase of Operation DESERT STORM, February 26, 1991. (U.S. Department of Defense)

Given Kuwait's (then) large expatriate Palestinian community, within hours of the start of DESERT STORM on January 17 Iraq sought, ineffectively, to certify its Pan-Arab/pro-Palestinian national unification vanguard credentials by firing Scud medium-range ballistic missiles into Israel and Saudi Arabia. Iraqi forces also began burning what would total 700 Kuwaiti oil wells and dumping hundreds of thousands of barrels of oil into the Persian Gulf, although with no appreciable effect on allied military operations in Kuwait.

The pending assault to liberate Kuwait, as part of Operation DESERT SABRE, the ground component of DESERT STORM, first constituted a distraction to tie down Iraqi forces from the coalition's left-wing outflanking maneuver into southern Iraq by the U.S. Army XVIII Airborne and VII Corps. The U.S. Navy and 5th Marine Expeditionary Brigade, feinting an amphibious landing on the Kuwaiti coast, had tied down as many as 10 Iraqi divisions out of 43. At 4:00 a.m. local time on February 24, after preliminary infiltration operations, the U.S. 1st and 2nd Marine Divisions in Marine Central Command, followed by Joint (Arab) Forces Command-North on their left and Joint (Arab) Forces Command-East, bordering on the Persian Gulf, initiated the ground assault with "pinning" attack operations against Iraqi fortifications in Kuwait. Meanwhile, XVIII and VII Corps, along with French and

British divisions, sought to neutralize reinforcements of the Iraqi Republican Guard, the elite units of the Iraqi armed forces. Of the 14 coalition divisions, 6 (Joint Arab and U.S. Marine) were initially devoted to a northerly attack into Kuwait from Saudi Arabia, directly confronting only 5 Iraqi divisions.

After breaching extensive minefields and taking al-Jaber airfield with 1 dead and 12 wounded from Iraqi rocket fire, both U.S. Marine divisions repulsed repeated Iraqi counterattacks launched from the burning Burgan oil field on February 25, destroying or capturing nearly 200 Iraqi tanks. Joint Arab Forces, both Saudi and Qatari, advanced up the coast on February 24 after heavy shelling by U.S. warships, quickly passing through gaps in the first line of defenses (with 2 Saudis dead and 4 wounded in an air-ground friendly fire incident) to reach the second line, which they overran on February 25. This operation resulted in 6 killed and 21 wounded. Iraqi resistance then collapsed, and the Joint Arab troops reached Kuwait by the evening of February 26. Marine forces approaching on the left from al-Jaber continued to advance and destroyed more than 100 additional Iraqi tanks. Using a combination of U.S. naval gunfire and marine ground units, they eliminated the remnants of the Iraqi armored brigade based at Kuwait International Airport.

Joint Arab Forces-North consisted of Saudi, Kuwaiti, and Egyptian forces, with Syrian forces in reserve. Beginning their northerly advance into western Kuwait on February 24, they encountered very light resistance and took large numbers of Iraqi prisoners, before turning east to reach Kuwait by 5:00 p.m. on February 26.

Iraqi forces now retreated to Kuwait and intermingled with Iraqi occupation troops based there. On February 26 Hussein ordered his surviving forces to evacuate Kuwait, emptying fortifications around the city that may have been more difficult for coalition forces to take. Iraqi units fleeing west and north from Kuwait along the highways linking it with Basra in southern Iraq had already been under continuous air attack from U.S. Navy and Air Force aircraft since the previous night. The planes dropped aerial mines to prevent their advance or retreat on the roads out of Kuwait. The U.S. Army's 1st "Tiger" Brigade, 2nd Armored Division, attacked, cleared, and occupied the 25-foot-high Mutla Ridge outside of the Jahrah suburb of Kuwait next to the juncture of two multilane highways, destroying numerous Iraqi antiaircraft emplacements and adding its firepower to the attacks below on what became known as the "Highway of Death."

The chaotic flight of Iraqi military and commandeered civilian vehicles, as well as Kuwaiti hostages, prisoners, and refugees including Palestinian militiamen, were trapped on the main highway to the north of Jahrah to Basra, as well as on the coastal road spur to Basra, by the continuous and unhindered U.S. and British attacks and the ensuing turmoil. Those who abandoned their vehicles and fled into the desert may also have been killed. Estimates of the casualties among the total of 1,500–2,000 vehicles destroyed along these two conflated stretches of the "Highway of Death" remain in dispute, ranging between a low of 200 to as many as 10,000. Officers of the U.S. Tiger Brigade, the first American unit to arrive at the "Highway of Death," stated that the unit found only about 200 Iraqi corpses among the thousands of destroyed vehicles. The unit captured about 2,000 Iraqi prisoners hiding nearby in the desert. Other reporters and Iraqis who lived through the event reported that hundreds of bodies, including those of women and children, continued to be buried several days later. Commandeered civilian vehicles seized by regular Iraqi army personnel constituted most of the destruction on the northern main highway route. On the coastal spur, predominantly military vehicles belonging to Republican Guards units were destroyed, with the U.S. Army 3rd Armored division joining the assault.

On February 27 Saudi-commanded units passed through Marine Central Command sector to liberate Kuwait, along with Joint Arab Forces Command-North columns. After contacting Egyptian units, U.S. Army Tiger Brigade troops cleared the major military airfield in Kuwait, the Kuwaiti Royal Summer palace, and bunker complexes.

A cease-fire went into effect at 8:00 a.m., February 28. In return for the cease-fire, Iraq accepted unconditionally all 12 UN Security Council resolutions dealing with Iraq's occupation of Kuwait, thereby renouncing for good its annexation of Kuwait.

BENEDICT DeDOMINICIS

See also

DESERT SHIELD, Operation; DESERT STORM, Operation; DESERT STORM, Operation, Coalition Air Forces; DESERT STORM, Operation, Coalition Ground Forces; DESERT STORM, Operation, Coalition Naval Forces; Gulf War Syndrome; Iraq, Army; Iraq, History of, 1990–Present; Kuwait; Kuwait, Iraqi Invasion of; Kuwait, Occupation of by Iraq; Persian Gulf War, Cease-Fire Agreement; Schwarzkopf, H. Norman, Jr.; Topography, Kuwait and Iraq

References

Alberto Bin, Richard Hill, and Archer Jones. *Desert Storm: A Forgotten War*. Westport, CT: Praeger, 1998.

Andersen, Roy R., Robert F. Seibert, and Jon G. Wagner. *Politics and Change in the Middle East: Sources of Conflict and Accommodation*. 8th ed. Upper Saddle River, NJ: Pearson Prentice Hall, 2007.

Cottam, Martha L., and Richard W. Cottam. *Nationalism and Politics: The Political Behavior of Nation States*. Boulder, CO: Lynne Rienner, 2001.

Gregg Robert W. *About Face? The United States and the United Nations*. Boulder, CO: Lynne Rienner, 1993.

Human Rights Watch. *Needless Deaths in the Gulf War: Civilian Casualties during the Air Campaign and Violations of the Laws of War*. New York: Human Rights Watch, 1991.

Schubert, Frank N., and Theresa L. Kraus, eds. *The Whirlwind War: The United States Army in Operations Desert Shield and Desert Storm*. Washington, DC: U.S. Government Printing Office, 1995.

Kuwait, Occupation of by Iraq

Start Date: August 2, 1990
End Date: February 27, 1991

The Iraqi occupation of Kuwait began on August 2, 1990, when Iraqi forces stormed across the Kuwait-Iraq border. The invasion ultimately prompted the deployment to Saudi Arabia of more than 500,000 American troops, along with forces from more than a dozen other countries, including Great Britain, France, Egypt, Syria, Saudi Arabia, and the Arab Gulf states of Kuwait, Bahrain, Qatar, and the United Arab Emirates (UAE). This international coalition ultimately routed Iraq's army during Operation DESERT STORM and expelled Iraqi troops from Kuwait. The first Iraqi troop withdrawals from Kuwait began on February 26, 1991. Two days later, and following the cease-fire agreement on February 27, the Iraqi occupation of Kuwait ended, restoring Kuwaiti independence.

Following the Iraqi incursion into Kuwait, Iraqi president Saddam Hussein moved quickly to consolidate his power over Kuwait, which he held to be a rogue province of Iraq. He thus appointed his first cousin, Ali Hassan Abd al-Majid al-Tikriti, as the governor of Kuwait. He instituted a brutal and repressive occupation, with the support of Hussein. The occupation included the plundering of Kuwaiti resources and infrastructure and the killing of many Kuwaiti citizens. Iraq's military looted, plundered, and pillaged Kuwait's consumer economy almost at will, sending back to Iraq

Iraqi president Saddam Hussein, center, accompanied by aides, tours the front line in Iraqi-occupied Kuwait in January 1991. (AP/Wide World Photos)

large quantities of automobiles and luxury goods. Kuwait became a virtual ghost town of looted and burned shops and stores; in many cases, these establishments were stripped of light fixtures and furniture. Even Kuwait's National Museum was not spared. Its collection of priceless Islamic artifacts was looted, and almost every room in the museum gutted by fire.

Iraqi troops imposed a brutal regime that did not spare the Kuwaiti people. Crimes against the citizenry included murder, rape, and torture. Nor were these limited to Kuwaitis, for expatriates and foreign nationals equally suffered. In the aftermath of the six-month occupation, the Kuwaiti government reported that 5,733 people had been systematically tortured by Iraqi troops. Iraqi documents captured after the liberation of Kuwait revealed orders from Baghdad for the summary execution of home owners whose buildings bore anti-Iraqi or pro-Kuwaiti slogans. Orders also directed troops to kill on sight any civilian caught on the streets after curfew or anyone suspected of being involved in any resistance activity. Iraqi forces were also accused of engaging in extrajudicial killings of government officials and members of the Kuwaiti military. Following the liberation of Kuwait, numerous torture chambers were uncovered. Reports from the few who managed to escape Kuwait following the invasion recounted public executions and bodies left hanging from lampposts or dumped

by the side of the street. According to both the United Nations (UN) and Kuwait, some 600 Kuwaiti nationals were abducted to Iraq and have yet to be accounted for. Iraqi officials also used Westerners captured in Kuwait as hostages, or human shields, until they were released, as an alleged act of goodwill on the part of Iraq, in December 1990.

It is worth pointing out, however, that some allegations by the exiled Kuwaiti government of human rights abuses were later proven false. For example, in the run-up to the war a young Kuwaiti girl testified before the U.S. Congress that she had witnessed Iraqi troops stealing hospital incubators for newborn infants and leaving the babies to die on the cold floor. This account was later proven false. At the time, Congress was unaware that the young woman was the daughter of a member of the Kuwaiti royal family. Despite such false claims, the wanton brutality of Iraq's occupation of Kuwait cannot be denied.

Food and water supplies meant for the Kuwaiti population were routinely diverted to the Iraqi army, yet even this proved insufficient to feed the occupying Iraqi troops. It was reported, for example, that Iraqi troops killed Kuwaiti zoo animals for food as the UN-approved embargo and blockade on Iraq began to strangle its economy. The invasion and occupation of Kuwait also led to the suppression of radio and television broadcasts while electricity was turned off and water supplies from desalinization plants were eliminated. In one final act of defiant revenge, Iraqi troops also set fire to more than 600 Kuwaiti oil wells as they withdrew from Kuwait as a consequence of the ground assault by American and coalition forces. This gratuitous destruction not only crippled Kuwait's oil production for many months but also created an environmental nightmare during which millions of gallons of oil spewed into the ground, and oil-well fires turned the Kuwaiti skies black for weeks.

STEFAN M. BROOKS

See also

DESERT STORM, Operation; Hussein, Saddam; Iraq, History of, 1990–Present; Iraqi Occupation of Kuwait, Atrocities; Kuwait; Kuwait, Liberation of; Majid al Tikriti, Ali Hassan al-

References

Gordon, Michael R., and General Bernard E. Trainor. *The Generals' War: The Inside Story of the Conflict in the Gulf.* New York: Little, Brown, 1995.

Khadduri, Majid, and Edmund Ghareeb. *War in the Gulf, 1990–91: The Iraq-Kuwait Conflict and Its Implications.* Oxford: Oxford University Press, 2001.

Long, Jerry. *Saddam's War of Words: Politics, Religion and the Iraqi Invasion of Kuwait.* Austin: University of Texas Press, 2004.

Sifry, Michah, and Christopher Cerf, eds. *The Gulf Reader: History, Documents, Opinions.* New York: Random House, 1991.

Kuwait, Provisional Free Government of

Short-lived, Iraqi-installed puppet government of Kuwait instituted after the August 1990 Iraqi invasion and occupation of Kuwait. At 1:00 a.m. on August 2, 1990, Iraqi forces invaded Kuwait. In ordering this action, Iraqi president Saddam Hussein hoped to obtain complete economic and political control of his small, oil-rich neighbor. To disguise his objectives, he had the Iraqi media portray the invasion as a response to an indigenous Kuwaiti uprising. Accordingly, the Iraqi media claimed that Kuwaiti revolutionaries had rebelled against the al-Sabah regime of Kuwait and had requested Iraqi intervention. Baghdad radio announced that a Provisional Free Government of Kuwait (PFGK) had been formed but initially provided few details beyond asserting that the PFGK represented the will of the majority of the Kuwaiti people.

In response to the Iraqi invasion, an emergency meeting of the United Nations (UN) Security Council convened at 5:30 a.m. on August 2. The Iraqi delegate reiterated the claim that the events taking place in Kuwait were internal affairs. He asserted that the PFGK had requested Iraqi assistance in order to establish security and protect the Kuwaiti people and that Iraq's intervention ensued. The Iraqi delegate concluded that, according to terms of agreement reached with the PFGK, Iraqi forces would soon withdraw from Kuwait. At an extraordinary session of the Arab League

in Cairo, also held on August 2, the Iraqi delegate repeated this explanation.

Iraq installed a Kuwaiti military officer, 31-year-old Colonel Ala Hussein Ali, as the figurehead ruler of Kuwait with the title of prime minister of the PFGK. Ali also held the positions of commander in chief of the armed forces, minister of defense, and minister of the interior. Four other colonels and four majors joined with him to serve as the nominal leaders of the PFGK.

Following the release of the names of the nine leaders, many Arab diplomats publicly voiced skepticism, saying that the names were either bogus or that they were actually Iraqi names. Their view accorded with opinions expressed by most Arab governments, who were dismayed that Saddam had become the first Arab ruler in modern history to send his army, unprovoked, into another Arab country, overthrow its government, and install a puppet regime.

By midafternoon on August 2, 1990, the PFGK began radio broadcasts from Baghdad announcing that it had deposed Sheikh Jabir al-Ahmad al-Sabah, emir of Kuwait. Indeed, the emir had fled to Saudi Arabia aboard a U.S. helicopter. The PFGK continued to spread its propaganda via Arab language radio broadcasts during the first weeks of August 1990. Thereafter, it was replaced with broadcasts by "The Voices of the Masses."

The charade of a free Kuwaiti government did not last long, however. On August 8, the PFGK called for Iraq to annex Kuwait. The next day, Iraq "complied" with the "request," the PFGK disbanded, and Ali became deputy prime minister of Iraq. This was, in fact, a powerless, figurehead position. After their initial introduction on Iraqi television, the members of the PFGK government seldom appeared in public view. All nine men were held inside a presidential compound in Baghdad, and they exercised no real authority.

During the seven-month Iraqi occupation of Kuwait, very few Kuwaitis rallied to support Iraq. Anti-Iraq graffiti, including derisory comments about the PFGK, appeared within days of the Iraqi invasion. Saddam had apparently overestimated the depth of Kuwaiti political opposition to the emir. Contrary to Saddam's expectations, no important Kuwaiti opposition figures collaborated with the Iraqis.

Soon after the Persian Gulf War ended, eight of the former PFGK leaders returned to Kuwait, where they paid a fine and were allowed to go free. Ali remained in Baghdad until 1997. The restored Kuwaiti government sentenced him to death in absentia in 1993 for heading the puppet government. Ali claimed that Iraqi agents had abducted him at gunpoint and threatened to kill him and arrest his family if he refused to participate in the PFGK. Ali returned to Kuwait in January 2000 and was arrested. At his trial, his former colleagues of the PFGK refuted much of his testimony. In May 2000, the criminal court of Kuwait endorsed Ali's death sentence for treason and collaborating with the enemy in a time of war. The sentence was later commuted to life imprisonment.

JAMES ARNOLD

See also

Hussein, Saddam; Iraq, History of, Pre-1990; Kuwait; Kuwait, Iraqi Invasion of; Kuwait, Occupation of by Iraq; Sabah, Jabir al-Ahmad al-Jabir al-

References

Bulloch, John, and Harvey Morris. *Saddam's War: The Origins of the Kuwait Conflict and the International Response.* London: Faber and Faber, 1991.

Dunnigan, James F., and Austin Bay. *From Shield to Storm: High-Tech Weapons, Military Strategy, and Coalition Warfare in the Persian Gulf.* New York: William Morrow, 1992.

Freedman, Lawrence, and Efraim Karsh. *The Gulf Conflict, 1990–1991: Diplomacy and War in the New World Order.* Princeton, NJ: Princeton University Press, 1993.

Kuwait-Iraq Diplomacy

Start Date: July 1990
End Date: August 1990

High-level discussions between Iraqi and Kuwaiti diplomats in 1990 ultimately failed to avert Iraq's August 2, 1990, invasion and occupation of Kuwait, which precipitated the Persian Gulf War. In 1980, seeking to take advantage of the turmoil following the 1979 Iranian Revolution and hoping to gain better access to the Persian Gulf through the Shatt al-Arab waterway, Iraqi president Saddam Hussein initiated a war with Iran. Initial Iraqi gains were eclipsed by an eight-year, bloody and brutal war that ended in stalemate. Iraq emerged from the war with its economy in ruins, essentially bankrupt and desperate for cash. Because Iraq was a major producer of oil, Hussein depended on the sale of oil to rebuild the Iraqi economy. With the end of the war, Hussein worried that failure to improve economic conditions in Iraq would lead to unrest and threaten his regime.

Casting his war with Iran largely as an effort to protect the Arab Gulf states, especially Kuwait, from the threat of Iranian Shiite Islamic fundamentalism, Hussein came to regard these states as ungrateful for Iraq's wartime sacrifices. To finance the war, Iraq had amassed a debt of some $70 billion, much of it owed to Kuwait. Hussein now pressed for forgiveness of the debt, but Kuwait refused. In February 1990, at the summit meeting of the Arab Cooperation Council in Amman, Jordan, Hussein asked King Hussein of Jordan and President Hosni Mubarak of Egypt to inform the Gulf States that Iraq insisted that its debts be forgiven and that it needed an immediate infusion of some $30 billion. Hussein reportedly said that if he were not given the money, he "would know how to get it." This not-so-veiled threat was accompanied by Iraqi military maneuvers near the Kuwaiti border.

In late May 1990, at the Arab League summit in Baghdad, Hussein claimed that Iraq was being subjected to "economic warfare" and that it would not long tolerate such treatment. This time, he demanded $27 billion from Kuwait. The Kuwaitis replied that they did not have such a large sum to give or lend out. A month later, at an Organization of Petroleum Exporting Countries (OPEC) meeting, Kuwait offered $500 million to Iraq over three years, which Hussein regarded as a paltry and insulting sum when Iraq needed billions.

On July 16, 1990, Iraq publicly accused Kuwait both of violating the OPEC oil-production quota, and thus driving down the price of oil, and of stealing Iraqi oil from the Rumaila oil field, shared by both countries. Hussein claimed that each dollar-per-barrel decrease in the price of oil cost Iraq $1 billion in desperately needed funds. That same day, Iraqi foreign minister Tariq Aziz informed an Arab summit meeting in Tunisia that "we are sure some Arab states are involved in a conspiracy against us" and vowed not to "kneel."

On July 17, in a speech to the Iraqi people, Hussein repeated his claim that Kuwait and the United Arab Emirates (UAE) were violating OPEC oil-production quotas, and he threatened unspecified military action if it continued. In the meantime, Iraq demanded $2.4 billion from Kuwait for oil allegedly "stolen" via slant drilling from the Rumaila oil field. The next day, Kuwait canceled all military leaves and placed its small military on alert. It also called for an emergency session of the Gulf Cooperation Council, a defense group of Gulf States, and also of the Arab League. The Kuwaiti government concluded, however, that Hussein's demands were tantamount to extortion and that acceding to them would only invite more blackmail later. The Kuwaitis also believed that Hussein was bluffing, refusing to believe that he would invade another Arab nation.

On July 21 the U.S. Central Intelligence Agency (CIA) reported that Iraq had moved some 30,000 troops and hundreds of tanks to its border with Kuwait. Kuwait, however, concluded that Iraq's provocative action was a bluff to increase the price of oil and blackmail Kuwait into acceding to Hussein's demands. The next day, Tariq Aziz repeated his criticism of Kuwait and the UAE after Hussein met in Baghdad with Egyptian president Hosni Mubarak, who was acting as a mediator between Iraq and Kuwait. Mubarak claims to have received "assurances" from Hussein that Iraq would not attack Kuwait, but Iraqi officials claimed differently, asserting that Hussein had said that nothing would happen to Kuwait as long as negotiations continued. Meanwhile, Mubarak and other Arab states, such as the UAE, had urged the United States not to get involved in the dispute, fearing that such action would only escalate the crisis, so Washington kept a low profile.

On July 26 Kuwait agreed to lower its oil production quotas, but Hussein had already begun moving another 30,000 troops to the Kuwaiti border. Three days later, the CIA reported that 100,000 Iraqi troops and hundreds of tanks were in position along the border. On August 1, at a crisis meeting at the White House, CIA officials concluded that an invasion of Kuwait was "probable." At the time, the United States had no ground troops in the region and only naval power, which would be unable to prevent a full-scale invasion of Kuwait.

Under Saudi Arabian auspices, Kuwaiti and Iraqi representatives met in Jeddah on July 31 to mediate their differences. Iraq claimed that Kuwait was unwilling to listen or negotiate in good faith. Kuwait, on the other hand, claimed that Iraq did not attend the meeting to negotiate but rather to dictate demands, which included Kuwait ceding disputed territory along the border, increasing Iraq's oil pumping rights, and providing a $10 billion cash payment. Iraqi officials allegedly told Kuwaiti officials to consider Iraq's demands overnight. The next day, the meeting adjourned early because one of the Iraqi diplomats was taken ill, but both sides had agreed to talk again in Baghdad in a few days. The next day, August 2, Iraq invaded Kuwait.

STEFAN M. BROOKS

See also

Aziz, Tariq; Hussein, Saddam; Iraq, History of, Pre-1990; Iraqi Claims on Kuwait; Kuwait; Kuwait, Iraqi Invasion of

References

Freedman, Lawrence, and Efraim Karsh. *The Gulf Conflict, 1990–1991: Diplomacy and War in the New World Order.* Princeton, NJ: Princeton University Press, 1993.

Gordon, Michael R., and General Bernard E. Trainor. *The Generals' War: The Inside Story of the Conflict in the Gulf.* New York: Little, Brown, 1995.

Miller, Judith, and Laurie Mylroie. *Saddam Hussein and the Crisis in the Gulf.* New York: Times Books, 1990.

L

Landing Craft Air Cushion

Hovercraft/air-cushion landing craft employed by the U.S. Navy to aid in amphibious landing operations. Landing Craft Air Cushion (LCAC) craft are designed for ship-to-shore landings and transportation along beaches. With an operational crew of five people, they are capable of carrying cargo, weapons, and personnel.

LCAC craft usually accompany the Marine Air-Ground Task Force. With a 60- to 75-ton payload, each is capable of transporting equipment as large as the M-1 tank, and at relatively high speeds. The air-cushion technology permits the LCAC craft to access as much as 70 percent of the world's coastline, 55 percent of which would be inaccessible to conventional landing craft. Currently, the navy possesses 91 LCAC craft. The only other navy to possess LCAC craft is Japan's Maritime Self-Defense Force.

Design and testing of the first LCAC prototypes began in the early 1970s, and Bell Aerospace's version was ultimately chosen as the preferred design. In 1984 the navy took possession of the first LCAC, and two years later the vehicle was deemed fully operational. In 1987 the Department of Defense authorized the construction of 15 LCAC craft, to be built by Textron Marine and Land Systems and Avondale Gulfport Marine. After the initial delivery of these craft, Textron Marine and Land Systems was granted the contract to build the rest of the LCAC craft. In 2001 the 91st LCAC was delivered to the U.S. Navy.

The LCAC craft, besides its transport capabilities, can also be employed in mine-countermeasure operations. The navy deployed the first operation LCAC craft in 1987, aboard USS *Germantown* (LSD-42, Landing Ship Dock). Each craft features four Allied-Signal TF-40B gas-turbine engines capable of producing up to 4,000 horsepower (hp) each. Two are used for lift, and two are used for forward propulsion. At maximum output of 16,000 hp, the LCAC's engines can propel the craft to a top speed of 40 knots (46 miles per hour [mph]), fully loaded. Each craft measures 87 feet, 11 inches long, and displaces 87.2 tons unloaded and 170–82 tons loaded. The craft's beam is 40 feet. The range of the LCAC is 200 miles at maximum speed, or up to 300 miles at 35 knots (40 mph). Each craft is armed with two 12.7-mm machine guns; gun mounts can also accommodate the M-2HB .50 caliber machine gun, MK-19 40-mm grenade launcher, and the M-60 machine gun. Like other naval vessels, the LCAC has the latest radar and navigational equipment.

LCAC craft were employed with much success during the 1991 Persian Gulf War (Operation DESERT STORM) and the 1993 Operation RESTORE HOPE in Somalia.

PAUL G. PIERPAOLI JR.

See also

DESERT STORM, Operation

References

Department of Defense. *21st Century U.S. Military Documents: World Weapons Guide—Army OPFOR Worldwide Equipment Guide—Infantry Weapons, Vehicles, Recon, Antitank Guns, Rifles, Rocket Launchers, Aircraft.* Washington, DC: Progressive Management, 2003.

Parker, Steve. *The LCAC Military Hovercraft.* Kentwood, LA: Edge Books, 2007.

Landing Craft Air Cushion (LCAC) vehicles are hovercraft employed in amphibious landing operations. (U.S. Department of Defense)

Land Remote-Sensing Satellite

The longest-running U.S. satellite program that provides imagery of earth from space. The Land Remote-Sensing Satellite (LAND-SAT) was used to provide wide-area, multispectral imagery (MSI) of the Persian Gulf theater of operations to coalition forces during Operation DESERT SHIELD and Operation DESERT STORM.

The United States launched the first LANDSAT satellite in 1972; the most recent satellite, LANDSAT 7, was launched on April 15, 1999. Since the first launch, LANDSAT satellites have acquired millions of images, all archived in the United States and at LANDSAT receiving stations around the world. They form a unique resource for global change research and applications in agriculture, cartography, geology, meteorology, forestry, regional planning, surveillance, education, and national security.

Originally called the Earth Resources Observation Satellite Program in 1966, the program's name was changed to LANDSAT in 1975. In 1979 President Jimmy Carter issued Presidential Directive 54, which transferred LANDSAT operations from the National Aeronautics and Space Administration (NASA) to the National Oceanographic and Atmospheric Administration (NOAA), recommended development of a long-term operational system with four additional satellites beyond LANDSAT 3, and transferred the system to the Department of Commerce. In 1985 NOAA selected the Earth Observation Satellite Company (EOSAT) to operate the LANDSAT system under a 10-year contract. EOSAT operated LANDSATs 4 and 5, had exclusive rights to market LANDSAT data, and was scheduled to build LANDSATs 6 and 7.

From 1989 through 1992, NOAA lacked sufficient funding for the LANDSAT program and directed that LANDSATs 4 and 5 be shut down. The U.S. Congress and the users of LANDSAT imagery provided emergency funding for these years. In late 1992 EOSAT ceased processing LANDSAT data because of funding problems, but the program received funding in 1993 to launch LANDSAT 6, which was unfortunately lost during a launch failure in October of that year. Recognizing the limited MSI capabilities of LAND-SAT 5, the Department of Defense worked with NASA to acquire better MSI capabilities for LANDSAT 7. In 1994 EOSAT resumed processing imagery from LANDSATs 4 and 5, and NASA finally launched LANDSAT 7 on April 15, 1999. However, in 2003 LAND-SAT 7 developed a sensor problem that limits its capabilities, and both LANDSATs 5 and 7 will run out of fuel in 2010 or 2011.

Currently, the Future of Operational Land Imaging Working Group, working with representatives from the White House Office of Science and Technology Policy, NASA, U.S. Geological Survey, NOAA, and the departments of State, Energy, Agriculture, Transportation, and Defense, is leading a multiagency effort to develop the LANDSAT Data Continuity Mission, scheduled to launch in 2011.

Before the 1991 Persian Gulf War, LANDSAT was used to image the Persian Gulf region to identify areas of contention between Iraq and Iran during their eight-year war as well as areas of economic contention during the concurrent tanker wars. During Operation DESERT SHIELD, LANDSATs 4 and 5 provided MSI of a 115-mile-wide area with a spatial resolution of 100 feet in the theater of operations on each 16-day pass. The Defense Mapping agency used these images to create maps with a scale of about 1:80,000. The U.S. Air Force also used LANDSAT images to produce engineering drawings for the construction of several very large airfields in Saudi Arabia. Coalition forces used LANDSAT's MSI of the Saudi-Kuwaiti border to determine changes in Iraqi emplacements, fortifications, and significant military movements. During Operation DESERT STORM, battlefield commanders usually preferred the wide-angle LANDSAT imagery to the incredibly large-scale detail of the images from reconnaissance satellites. Although LANDSAT imagery provided good multispectral views of wide areas, it did not always provide timely or accurate data for mission planning, bomb damage assessment, or use of precision-guided weapons.

Because LANDSAT was a commercial satellite system, the Department of Defense paid for its imagery. To prevent Iraq from purchasing LANDSAT images, the Department of Defense convinced EOSAT not to sell LANDSAT images to Iraq between August 1990 and May 1991. Shortly before the ground offensive in late January 1991, the Defense Intelligence Agency intervened to prevent U.S. news media from obtaining LANDSAT data of the Saudi-Kuwaiti border that could have revealed the coalition's preparations for the ground offensive.

During and after the war, LANDSAT images were used to evaluate the environmental damage in Kuwait and the Persian Gulf from oil spills and oil-well fires. The Iraqi army intentionally released some millions of barrels of oil into the Persian Gulf from January to May 1991, polluting more than 800 miles of Kuwaiti and Saudi Arabian coastline. Military pilots had made initial sightings of the oil spills in the early days of the war, and NOAA satellites discovered them on October 3, 1990. LANDSAT first displayed the oil spills in images obtained on February 8, 1991. A detailed examination of successive imagery from LANDSATs and SPOT (Satellite pour l'Observation de la Terre), a French satellite system similar to the LANDSAT satellite, along with computer programs such as the Geographical Information System, allowed analysts to track the progression and extent of the environmental damage from the oil spills. Additionally, Iraqi troops set fire to hundreds of wells throughout Kuwait as they were evacuating the country. The LANDSAT images, taken between January and October 1991, clearly show the oil-smoke plumes, which analysts used to estimate the location and number of burning wells.

In December 1993 the Department of Defense withdrew from the LANDSAT 7 program. Combined with the earlier loss of LANDSAT 6, U.S. military forces became dependent on the aging LANDSAT 5 and foreign remote-sensing satellites, primarily the French SPOT system, to fulfill their MSI needs, particularly wide-area coverage and responsive map-generation capabilities that contributed to successful mission planning and rehearsal, counterdrug operations, terrain analysis, and treaty monitoring. The U.S. Space Command is working with the Office of the Secretary of Defense to determine how national and commercial systems can best meet Department of Defense MSI requirements.

ROBERT B. KANE

See also

Defense Meteorological Satellite Program; Defense Satellite Communications System; Navigation Satellite Timing and Ranging Global Positioning System; Oil Well Fires, Persian Gulf War; Satellites, Use of by Coalition Forces

References

El-Baz, Farouk, and R. M. Makharita, eds. *Gulf War and the Environment.* London: Taylor and Francis, 1994.

Mack, Pamela Etter. *Viewing the Earth: The Social Construction of the Landsat Satellite System.* Cambridge, MA: MIT Press, 1990.

Spires, David N. *Beyond Horizons: A Half Century of Air Force Space Leadership.* 2nd ed. Maxwell Air Force Base, AL: Air Force Space Command and Air University Press, 2007.

Winnefeld, James A., Preston Niblack, and Dana J. Johnson. *A League of Airmen: U.S. Air Power in the Gulf War.* Santa Monica, CA: RAND Corporation, 1994.

Latvia, Role in Afghanistan and Iraq Wars

Baltic nation and former Soviet Republic with a 2008 population of 2.245 million. Independent since August 1991, Latvia borders on Lithuania and Belarus to the south, Russia to the east, Estonia to the northeast, and the Baltic Sea to the west-northwest. The country occupies 24,938 square miles of territory. Latvia has a democratic presidential-parliamentary form of government with a unicameral legislation elected by popular vote every four years. The president is elected by parliament and is head of state, although many of his functions are ceremonial in nature. The president appoints a prime minister, who is head of government. Latvian politics feature numerous parties and coalitions, the largest and most influential being the People's Party (conservative), the Union of Greens and Farmers (centrist-green), the New Era Party (conservative-centrist), and Harmony Centre (socialist-social democratic).

Along with Estonia and Lithuania, Latvia was a staunch supporter of the U.S.-led coalitions in the conflicts in Afghanistan and Iraq. In the aftermath of the Cold War, the Baltic nations endeavored to develop stronger ties with the United States and Western Europe. They particularly sought membership in the European Union (EU) and the North Atlantic Treaty Organization (NATO). Latvia joined both the EU and NATO in 2004. During the 1990s Latvian troops, along with their other Baltic counterparts, were deployed in Bosnia-Herzegovina and later Kosovo, as part of NATO-led peacekeeping missions.

Latvia provided both diplomatic and security support to the United States following the September 11, 2001, terrorist attacks. The Latvians offered the United States and its allies use of the country's airspace, ports, and military facilities for the War on Terror. It also doubled the number of military forces serving as peacekeepers in Bosnia and Kosovo to allow the United States to redeploy troops from those missions to Operation ENDURING FREEDOM. Latvia sent a small contingent of logistics personnel to Kyrgyzstan as part of a Danish-led force that provided transport support to coalition troops during the campaign to overthrow the Taliban and Al Qaeda in Afghanistan during the winter of 2001–2002. In February 2003 Latvia deployed a medical unit in Kabul as part of the NATO-led International Security Assistance Force–Afghanistan (ISAF). Subsequently, Latvian staff officers were stationed as part of ISAF's headquarters force in Kabul, and various units, including infantry troops and ordnance disposal experts, served with the Norwegian-led provincial reconstruction team in Maymana. Latvian forces undertook a variety of humanitarian projects worth more than $1 million, including the construction of water-treatment facilities and security and court buildings. Latvia has maintained about 150 troops in Afghanistan since 2005. It has also dispatched several civilian police trainers and a political adviser. One Latvian soldier had been killed in Afghanistan through 2008.

Latvia also supported the U.S.-led invasion of Iraq in 2003. The first Latvian troops, including ordnance disposal experts and logistical forces, were deployed to Iraq in May 2003. Later, infantry troops were also dispatched to Iraq. The Latvian contingent's peak strength was about 140 soldiers. The Latvians undertook operations in several areas, including Hillah, Kut, Kirkuk, and Diwaniya, and were under the operational command of the Polish-led Multi-National Force. In addition to ordnance demolition and general security operations, the Latvians established a training program for explosive ordnance disposal for Iraqi forces. They also initiated a human rights training program for Iraqi political and security officials. Beginning in June 2007 Latvia began to reduce its contingent; it withdrew its remaining forces from Iraq in November 2008. More than 1,150 Latvians served in Iraq, of whom 3 were killed and 5 were wounded.

TOM LANSFORD

See also

Afghanistan, Coalition Combat Operations in, 2002–Present; International Security Assistance Force; IRAQI FREEDOM, Operation, Coalition Ground Forces; Multi-National Force–Iraq; North Atlantic Treaty Organization in Afghanistan

References

Cockburn, Patrick. *The Occupation: War and Resistance in Iraq.* New York: Verso, 2007.

Feickert, Andrew. *U.S. and Coalition Military Operations in Afghanistan: Issues for Congress.* Washington, DC: Congressional Research Service, 2006.

Keegan, John. *The Iraq War: The Military Offensive, from Victory in 21 Days to the Insurgent Aftermath.* New York: Vintage, 2005.

Lausanne, Treaty of

Peace treaty between the Allied Powers and Turkey signed on July 24, 1923, at Lausanne, Switzerland. Unlike the 1920 Treaty of Sèvres, the terms of which the Allies had dictated to the Ottoman government, the Treaty of Lausanne was a negotiated peace. The Treaty of Sèvres had been a humiliation for Turkey. Under its terms Greece assumed control over Smyrna and the hinterland, as well as all of the Ottoman Europe outside of Constantinople. The treaty also removed the Arabic-speaking lands and Armenia from Ottoman control and established an autonomous Kurdistan under League of Nations guidance. It fixed the size of the Turkish army at 50,000 men, and it also left in place the capitulations treaties that gave foreigners the right of extraterritoriality and established foreign control over many aspects of the Turkish financial system.

The terms of the treaty set off a wave of nationalism in Turkey, personified in Mustafa Kemal, known as Ataturk. On August 19, 1920, the National Assembly, called into session by the sultan to approve the Treaty of Sèvres, instead rejected the treaty and denounced as traitors those who had supported it. The sultan then dissolved Parliament, which led Kemal to establish a rival government in the interior of Anatolia. He soon concluded an agreement with Russia that proved beneficial to both nations. Turkey recognized Russian incorporation of Azerbaijan, Georgia, and half of Armenia. In return, Turkey received surplus Russian arms and Russia's diplomatic support, including its recognition of Turkish control over the other half of Armenia.

Kemal soon took advantage of the Russian arms to go to war against Greece in Smyrna. Although Greek prime minister Eleuthérios Venizélos sent forces into Anatolia, Kemal carried out a brilliant military campaign in the Greco-Turkish War of 1920–1922, during which he retook Smyrna and its hinterland and then turned north against Constantinople. Italy, which had come to see Greece as a more immediate rival than Turkey, agreed to withdraw its own occupation troops after a defeat at Kemal's hands in Central Anatolia. This led the British and French also to depart.

Turkish success on the battlefield produced gains at the bargaining table. In November 1922 a conference to consider revisions to the Treaty of Sèvres opened in the Swiss city of Lausanne. Plenipotentiaries from eight nations negotiated there for seven months. As evidence of their parity at the conference, Turkish diplomats successfully rejected a draft treaty presented in April 1923. The two sides resumed talks until a revision met with the approval of all parties in July.

The Treaty of Lausanne abrogated the terms of the Treaty of Sèvres. It included no provisions for the autonomy of Kurdistan, thus recognizing its reincorporation into Turkey. The capitulations continued in theory, but only a handful of Western legal and medical advisers remained in Turkey after 1923. Eastern Thrace and all of Anatolia returned to Turkish control, settling border disputes with both Greece and Bulgaria. The military terms of the treaty were also favorable to Turkey. Greece agreed not to fortify its Aegean Islands and also promised not to fly military aircraft over Turkish airspace.

The treaty also resolved the delicate issue of the Bosporus and the Dardanelles. The International Straits Committee, established at Sèvres and composed of Great Britain, France, and Italy, remained in place, but Turkey became a member. More importantly, the committee lost the right of intervention granted in the previous treaty. Thereafter, determinations about the security of the straits were the preserve of the League of Nations. In exchange for these concessions, Turkey recognized British control of Cyprus and Italian authority in the Dodecanese Islands.

The Treaty of Lausanne also freed Turkey from reparation payments that the Ottoman government had accepted in the Treaty of Sèvres. In return, Turkey agreed to pay outstanding prewar debts incurred by the Ottomans to the other signatories.

The treaty represented a major triumph for Kemal and the Turkish nationalists. Eleuthérios Venizélos, former prime minister, signed for Greece. He had been one of the most vocal supporters of Greek territorial aims in Turkey, and his signature symbolized the end of Greek designs across the Aegean Sea. The United States had not declared war on Turkey, and therefore did not have a major role when it came to decisions about the dismemberment of the Ottoman Empire. Although not signatories, the United States and Russia lent support.

The treaty also led to one of the largest forced movements of populations in history. It took religion as a basis for defining ethnicity and implicitly argued that religious minorities could not exist within the newly created borders. As a result, more than 1.2 million Eastern Orthodox Christians moved from Turkey to Greece; 150,000 of them were from Constantinople (soon to be renamed Istanbul). Similarly, 380,000 Muslims moved from Greece to Turkey. The flood of refugees caused financial and social problems for both nations.

The Treaty of Lausanne can be understood as a monumental triumph for Turkey. It formally ended any chance of the return of the sultanate, and it established Turkey as a power in the Middle East, Eastern Europe, and Central Asia. The biggest losers under the treaty were the independence-minded Kurds and the Armenians, who now had to live under Turkish and Soviet control. The treaty also significantly reduced tensions in the region among Greece, Italy, and Turkey, thus calming the Balkans considerably.

MICHAEL S. NEIBERG

See also

Mandates; Sèvres, Treaty of; Turkey, Role in Persian Gulf and Afghanistan Wars

References

Busch, Briton Cooper. *Mudros to Lausanne: Britain's Frontier in West Asia, 1918–1923.* Albany: State University of New York Press, 1976.

Kinross, Lord John Patrick Balfour. *The Ottoman Centuries: The Rise and Fall of the Turkish Empire.* New York: Morrow, 1977.

McCarthy, Justin. *The Ottoman Peoples and the End of Empire.* London: Hodde Arnold, 2001.

Lebanon

Middle Eastern nation located on the eastern end of the Mediterranean Sea. Lebanon borders on Israel to the south and Syria to the east and north and covers 4,015 square miles (roughly twice the size of the U.S. state of Delaware). Lebanon's estimated 1948 population was approximately 1.5 million, but that was not based on an official government census. The only government census was conducted in 1932 when France held Lebanon as a League of Nations mandate and counted 861,399 people, which became the basis for the religious composition of the government. This gave a 6-to-5 advantage to Lebanese Christians. The unwritten *mithaq al-watani* (national pact) between Bishara al-Khuri and Prime Minister Riyadh al-Sulh in 1943 formalized this understanding as well as the allocation of leadership positions to specific confessional or religious sects, with, for example, the presidency allocated to the Maronites, the dominant political sect; the office of the prime minister allocated to the Sunni Muslims; the Speaker of parliament allocated to the Shia; and Lebanon's status as nation defined as having an Arab "character." This arrangement continued even though subsequent population figures estimated that demographic trends showed an increase in the Muslim population. A U.S. Central Intelligence Agency (CIA) population estimate in 2003 put the population at 3.72 million, with 70 percent Muslims and 30 percent Christians.

The Lebanese population is further divided among the Sunni, Shia, and Druze sects of Islam and the Maronite, Greek Orthodox, Greek Catholic, Armenian Orthodox, and Syriac denominations of Christianity. The Shia community contained more poor workers and peasants, located in the capital, southern cities, and eastern and southern regions of the country. Because of their depressed economic conditions, Shia were looked down on and discriminated against. A belt of rural poverty also existed in the Sunni north. Certain Christian areas were also impoverished.

Lebanon's population suffered greatly during World War I, leading to high emigration in a pattern repeated during the lengthy civil war of 1975–1991. Remittances from Lebanese abroad were essential to the economy, as were Beirut's services and banking. On the other hand, many areas of the country were dependent on agriculture and were farmed by peasants with small plots or who were landless and worked for large landholders. A neofeudal system remained even after independence whereby the larger landholders, traditional chieftains, counted on the political support of their dependents. Urban counterparts operated like political bosses.

Lebanon declared its independence from France in November 1941 and became a charter member of the United Nations (UN) in 1945, the same year it joined the Arab League. Although independence and international status were welcomed by the Lebanese, sectarian tensions have continually threatened internal peace. The country essentially developed different cultures tied to some degree to educational systems: the private and greatly superior French-language system as opposed to the national system, which in later years increasingly utilized Arabic.

Aerial photograph of the city of Beirut, Lebanon. (Mpalis/Dreamstime.com)

On the basis of the 1932 census and, more importantly, by virtue of their education and political prominence, certain Maronite Christian families maintained a privileged place in Lebanese government. In Lebanon, only a Maronite may become the president, only a Sunni may become the prime minister, and only a Shia may become the Speaker of parliament. As demographic developments led to a Muslim majority by the 1960s, Maronite predominance, at least in legislative representation, came under increasing pressure from various Muslim groups as did other policies, which prevented the consensual nature of politics that was the goal of the Lebanese system. The fact that neither the Christians nor the Muslims were monolithic forces further complicated matters. The Shia outnumbered the Sunnis, but many of the urban Sunni merchant families were far better off than the poverty-stricken Shia peasants or tobacco workers. On top of this, the Arab cold war (or battle between conservative and military progressive states), the overall Cold War, and the ongoing Arab-Israeli conflict all presented Lebanon with very serious challenges.

As a member of the Arab League, Lebanon sent troops to fight Israeli forces when the latter declared its independence in May 1948. Lebanese forces and Lebanese volunteers in the Arab Liberation Army fought alongside those from Syria in the north in the Israeli War of Independence (1948–1949) but were not successful. A series of battles ended with Israel in control of the Jordan River,

the lakes of Galilee and Hulah, and a panhandle of territory jutting north and bordering on both Lebanon and Syria. Lebanon was not a major player in the 1956 Sinai Campaign or the 1967 Six-Day War between Israel and its Arab opponents because the Lebanese Army was so small.

This did not mean that Lebanon remained at peace, however, for sectarian troubles and the evolving Cold War between the United States and the Soviet Union brought their own set of challenges. Both sides sought to support local regimes that they believed would support them in the worldwide conflict. The 1956 Suez War boosted President Gamal Abdel Nasser's popularity, and his declaration that "the Arab nation is one nation" was greeted with considerable enthusiasm by Lebanese Muslims, especially the young. In 1958 the pro-Western monarchy in Iraq fell and was replaced by a government that tilted toward the Soviet bloc. Egypt had already rejected Western support in favor of Soviet aid and was pursuing union with Syria, which still had claims to Lebanon as part of the so-called Greater Syria.

Lebanon's Christian Maronite–dominated government responded to these perceived threats by requesting American aid. President Dwight D. Eisenhower responded by sending U.S. marines to Beirut in the hopes of stabilizing the region. Almost simultaneously, the British sent troops to Jordan to prop up the monarchy there following an alleged coup attempt. The interventions actually

GOVERNORATES OF LEBANON

Mediterranean Sea

Kabir R.

Halba
Qubayyat
Fnaydek
Tripoli
Zgharta
Hermel
Chekka
NORTH
Amioun Sibil
Qaa
Ihdin
Jaoz R.
Douma
Aynata
Al Aqurah
Byblos
Ibrahim R.
L E B A N O N
MOUNT
LEBANON
Afka
Baalbek
Jounieh
BEIRUT
Antelias
BEKAA
Beirut
Hammana
Zahleh
Baabda
Rayak
Litani R.
Damour
Beit ed Dine
SYRIA
Jieh
Joub Jannine
Awali R.
Sidon
El Qaraaoun
Dayr az Zahrani
Jezzine
Hasbani R.
Rachaiya
Nabatieh
NABATIEH
Marjayoun
Tyre
Litani R.
SOUTH
Tibnine Hula
Naqoura
Bint Jbeil
Rmaich

BEKAA   Governorate
★   Governorate capital
✪   National capital

| 0 | 10 | 20 mi |
| 0 | 10 | 20 km |

ISRAEL

heightened tensions and divisions in both nations. The extreme poverty of Lebanon's countryside was in contrast to its attraction for wealthy Arabs who came to vacation in the so-called Switzerland of the Middle East. This mirage of Swiss neutrality belied the politics in Lebanon that simmered just under the surface. The relative degree of freedom of the press meant that political exiles of all types were present, but Lebanon was probably most important in this era as the banking and services capital of the region.

Gradually the Muslim population became the clear majority, and Lebanon could not avoid becoming involved in the Arab-Israeli conflict. Following the Israeli victory in the 1948–1949 war, about 100,000 Palestinian refugees fled to Lebanon, where some of them carried out hit-and-run actions against Israel. Other Lebanese, for example the leaders of the Phalange party, opposed these guerrilla operations, fearing that Israeli reprisals would threaten Lebanese independence. The refugees from 1948 together with those from the Six-Day War in 1967, coupled with the expulsion of the Palestinians from Jordan in 1970 and 1971 (many relocating to Lebanon), increased the overall numbers of Muslims in the country. More important than tipping the sectarian balance, they fueled the conflict between Christian supporters of the political status quo and Christian leftist and progressive and Muslim and Druze challengers to politics as usual. While the Lebanese military tried to maintain order and restrain the Palestinian guerrillas from using Lebanon as a base for attacks against Israel, the effort did not work. This led to clashes between groups of Lebanese Christians and Palestinians and their progressive and Muslim supporters. The progressives linked together in the National Front under the leadership of Kamal Jumblatt also protested Lebanon's failure to democratize and to develop politically or to implement developmental schemes favored by President Shihab that would address deeply rooted economic disparities. Because of their progressive and leftist leanings they saw the problem as one of feudalism and skewed laissez-faire capitalist development. In Lebanon there also was strong dependence on families rather than the state. In addition, many younger Lebanese sought both a role in politics and support for the Palestinian cause.

The result ultimately was a civil war that began in 1975, leading to the deaths of many Lebanese. In sectarian fighting between March 1975 and November 1976 at least 40,000 died and 100,000 more were wounded. The carnage continued. Lebanon was again brought into the larger Arab-Israeli conflict, with disastrous results. Repeated attacks by guerrillas operating in southern Lebanon brought the inevitable Israeli response. In June 1982 Israeli forces invaded Lebanon and even drove north to Beirut, which they occupied by August, leading to an agreement whereby the Palestine Liberation Organization (PLO) departed Beirut for Tunis. The conflict was temporarily ended by international agreements. But with the exodus of the Palestinian fighters and leadership, Lebanese Christian militias massacred scores of Palestinians in the Sabra and Shatila refugee camps in Beirut. Part of the truce agreement involved the United States sending U.S. marines into Beirut, and the French

followed suit in 1983. Israel and Syria maintained significant forces in Lebanon and continued to do so until 2000 and 2005, respectively, long after the United States and France withdrew in response to suicide attacks on their forces in October 1983.

During the civil war the Lebanese government was unable to carry out any of the normal functions of government, whether providing services or security, managing municipalities, or controlling the movement of goods or persons in or out of the country. Israel maintained forces and backed Lebanese allies in the south, ostensibly to prevent raids and rocket attacks against Israeli territory.

The Syrian intervention in Lebanon came about in a piecemeal fashion, first with only 50 troops and then in a much larger force. This was eventually sanctioned by the Arab League as one component of the Arab Deterrent Force, supposedly under the command of the Lebanese president. Syria managed to influence the Lebanese political system as well as became a combatant in the civil war with alliances that shifted over time. In 1993 and in 1996 during the Israeli Operation GRAPES OF WRATH, hundreds of thousands of Lebanese fled their homes in the south to avoid Israeli attacks. Israel decided to withdraw from Lebanon in May 2000 in advance of a previously planned withdrawal under heavy pressure from Hezbollah, which had attained weaponry from Iran. This withdrawal, which many Lebanese regarded as a national victory, brought an end to the 18-year-long Israeli occupation. The withdrawal did not bring stability along Israel's northern border, however, in part because of disputes over the status of a number of Lebanese villages there. After 2000, moreover, Hezbollah's militia further fortified its positions.

Under heavy international pressure as a result of its involvement in a number of assassinations of Lebanese leaders, including former prime minister Rafic al-Hariri, Syria did withdraw its troops from Lebanon in mid-2005, and there was fleeting hope that Lebanon might enter a new era, with foreign forces finally leaving its territory. However, those political and intelligence elements that had relied on Syria in the previous era continued to be active.

Lebanon was plagued by internal conflicts, including the continuing debate over the structure of its government. Hezbollah continued to arm its militia and participated in limited border hostilities with Israel during 2000–2006. As the Lebanese Army could not defend the country, Hezbollah claimed the right to do so. In July 2006 war again erupted between Lebanon and Israel. The Lebanese referred to this 2006 conflict as the Fifth Arab-Israeli War.

On July 12, 2006, Hezbollah miscalculated the Israeli response to a raid in a disputed border village, where it captured two Israeli soldiers, intending to hold them for a prisoner exchange. Israel launched a massive response. Hezbollah leader Hassan Nasrallah later admitted that the raid would not have been launched if he had known the likely Israeli response. The result was a month of war until a tenuous UN cease-fire was negotiated on August 14. Both sides suffered casualties and damage, although they were far more numerous on the Lebanese side. Hezbollah had about 1,000 fighters well dug into positions in southern Lebanon, backed by

An Israeli 155-mm self-propelled gun fires into a Hezbollah camp in Lebanon during the 34-day Israel-Hezbollah conflict in 2006. (iStockPhoto)

other militias and a civilian population who largely supported them, facing up to 30,000 Israel Defense Forces (IDF) troops.

Hezbollah fighters and militias supporting them sustained between 250 and 600 dead during the month-long war, while the Lebanese Army suffered 46 dead and about 100 wounded. Israel reported 119 dead, up to 450 wounded, and 2 captured. UN observer forces in the area also suffered 7 dead and 12 wounded. The worst toll, however, was among Lebanese civilians. Perhaps 1,187 Lebanese civilians died, while 4,080 more were injured. As many as 1 million Lebanese were displaced by the fighting, which brought the destruction of much of the country's infrastructure, especially its bridges and highways. Some Lebanese returned to their homes after Hezbollah issued a call for them to do so, leaving some 255,986 still displaced. Israel suffered 44 civilian deaths and more than 1,300 injured from Hezbollah rockets.

Both sides expended massive amounts of ordnance in the conflict. Israel had complete control of the skies and was able to fly 12,000 sorties over Lebanese territory. In addition to Israeli artillery, the Israeli Navy fired 2,500 shells against Lebanese shore targets. Lebanon suffered damage to its infrastructure that would require billions of dollars and many years to repair.

The effective blockade imposed by Israel until September 2006 exacerbated the problems faced by Lebanon. The power of the Israeli military was not a surprise, but the robust defense put up by Hezbollah was. This militia had used its years of control over southern Lebanon to increase its stocks of weapons and prepare defensive positions. Hezbollah was able to fire 4,000 rockets into Israeli territory. These included not only the short-range Katyushas but also middle-range missiles capable of hitting Haifa and other points believed safe from the usual Hezbollah rockets. In southern Lebanon, Hezbollah was able to resist Israeli armored attacks, destroying 20 main battle tanks in two engagements. Hezbollah's launching of what is presumed to have been a cruise missile against an Israeli warship was also a surprise.

The cease-fire called for a halt in the fighting, an end to the Israeli blockade, and the deployment of UN forces to southern Lebanon to maintain peace, with the Lebanese Army aiding in that effort. Whether these measures would be successful was questionable. Hezbollah soon announced that it had already restocked its missiles (via Iran and Syria).

The political fallout from the summer's war manifested itself in a struggle over the Lebanese cabinet's recommendation that a tribunal be established to hear evidence on the assassination of former prime Hariri and other anti-Syrian individuals. The issues at stake were no longer the future of Syria's government and influence in Lebanon but instead concerned the willingness of Lebanese leaders to compromise and the proper methods to balance disputes among the Aounists, Hezbollah, Saad al-Hariri's Future Party, and other pro- and anti-Syrian Christian elements and the need to diminish sectarianism as spelled out in the Taif Accords but not achieved since the end of the Lebanese Civil War.

In May 2008 following some 18 months of political turmoil and some actual fighting that threatened to become full-scale civil war, an Arab delegation succeeded in brokering an agreement whereby the Lebanese parliament elected General Michel Suleiman, former army chief, as president of Lebanon. The post had been vacant since the previous November, and Suleiman's election, though a foregone conclusion, was seen as a clear victory for Hezbollah. It was, however, also heralded by many quarters in Lebanon as preferable to another round of violence. This election was seen as the first step in an effort to enact a new power-sharing arrangement in the country. Still, the odds against a peaceful arrangement would appear long. Hezbollah has not disarmed, sharp political divisions remain, and the tribunal has gone forward.

DANIEL E. SPECTOR AND SHERIFA ZUHUR

See also

Arab-Israeli Conflict, Overview; Arab League; Hezbollah; Katyusha Rocket; Lebanon, Armed Forces; Lebanon, Israeli Invasion of; Palestine Liberation Organization

References

Hovsepian, Nubar, ed. *The War on Lebanon: A Reader*. Northampton, MA: Olive Branch, 2008.

Hudson, Michael. *The Precarious Republic: Political Modernization in Lebanon*. Boulder, CO: Westview, 1985.

Rabil, Robert G. *Embattled Neighbors: Syria, Israel, and Lebanon*. Boulder, CO: Lynne Rienner, 2003.

Lebanon, Armed Forces

During the French mandate over Lebanon following World War I, the French authorities recruited a special militia force known as the Troupes Spéciales du Levant, which served all Syria (present-day Syria and Lebanon), and functioned as a gendarmerie for internal security. This force was at first largely staffed with French officers, but the number of Arab officers increased over time. Recruitment was higher from rural areas and among the Druze, Circassians, Alawites, Christians, and Kurds. Special squadrons, such as the Druze and Circassian cavalry squadrons, relied entirely on fighters of one sect or ethnicity.

Following the defeat of France by the Germans in June 1940, the Troupes Spéciales of Lebanon came under control of the Vichy French government. After the Allied invasion of Lebanon (Operation EXPORTER) in 1941, some Circassian squadrons led by a Colonel

Collet defected to the Allies, but most Lebanese units fought on the Vichy side. With the Allied victory, by June 1943 the reconstituted Troupes du Levant (the former Troupes Spéciales) operated under British forces in the Middle East. After Lebanon gained its independence in 1945, this 3,000-man force became the cadre of the Lebanese Army.

The Lebanese Army was deliberately a small military force and therefore weak. This was a reflection of the fragmented nature of Lebanese society. Some Christian Lebanese during the 1950s and 1960s feared that a strong army would only embroil Lebanon in the Arab-Israeli wars. Muslim political leaders also feared that a strong military force, commanded primarily by Christians, would be too easily used against Muslim interests, but, conversely, they also wanted the army to be strong enough to play a role in the Arab-Israeli conflict. Finally, all too many Lebanese political leaders, both Christians and Muslims, were also local powers resembling feudal lords or Chicago-style political bosses, with their own strongmen (*abuday*). Certain figures had already put their own militias in place. These individuals saw the possibility of a strong national army's interference in their own interests and disputes as an uncomfortable prospect.

Lebanon committed two battalions to the Israeli War of Independence, which began in earnest on May 15, 1948. The Lebanese also had small detachments of cavalry and a small number of armored cars and tanks. On May 15 Lebanese forces attempted to cross the Palestine border near Rosh Ha-Nikra but were repelled by Israeli troops. When the Arab Liberation Army (ALA) found itself isolated from its Syrian bases, the Lebanese Army performed badly needed logistical services. After the ALA was defeated at the Battle of Sasra in late October 1948, ALA units withdrew to Lebanon for safety. When Israeli forces pursued them into Lebanon proper, Lebanese officials quickly negotiated an armistice, and the Israel Defense Forces (IDF) withdrew.

In 1958 when President Camille Chamoun unconstitutionally extended his presidency and met with political opposition, he requested U.S. military assistance to prevent what he described as a potential takeover by Nasserist elements. The 1958 events exposed the inherent weakness of the Lebanese armed forces, which might have more effectively controlled the situation than did the Americans (who actually did little). However, by that time the army officer corps and leadership, who were predominantly Christian, also had loyalties to their respective political blocs. Lebanese officials made concerted efforts to augment the nation's military strength after 1958, at least to ensure that the Lebanese Army could maintain order and provide some measure of effective defense.

By 1975, the year the Lebanese Civil War broke out, the Lebanese armed forces had expanded considerably. The Lebanese Air Force was equipped with 10 British Hawker Hunter and 9 French Dassault Mirage III aircraft. It also had a helicopter squadron with 16 aircraft, the majority of which were French Aerospatiale Alouette II/IIIs. The Lebanese Navy operated 6 patrol craft. The army had 17,000 combat-ready troops in 20 infantry battalions equipped with either the French Panhard armored personnel carriers or American M-113s. The army also operated 25 French AMX-13 tanks and 18 U.S. M-41 Walker Bulldog tanks. Artillery support consisted of 4 batteries of both 122-mm and 155-mm howitzers and 60 Charioteer self-propelled anti-tank guns. Missile systems included the ENTAC, SS-11, and TOW systems. Antiaircraft support comprised 15 M-42 Duster self-propelled 40-mm twin guns. In addition to the regular forces, the gendarmerie numbered about 5,000 men.

The civil war that began in 1975 effectively led to the dismemberment of the Lebanese Army. In January 1976 Sunni lieutenant Ahmed al-Khatib established the Lebanese Arab Army (LAA). Many of the Muslims who served in the lower ranks followed him, as the LAA joined ranks with the Lebanese National Movement. They mounted an attack on the presidential palace. Some of the recruits to the 140 independent Lebanese militias or small fighting forces that formed during the conflict came from the ranks of the regular army. Others were ordinary citizens. The militias were able to acquire matériel that had been purchased during the civil war by the army from the United States and was worth several billion dollars. Further complicating the situation, Israel, France, Iraq, Syria, other Arab nations, and the Palestine Liberation Organization (PLO) equipped and supported the various competing militias. One of the largest of the predominantly Christian militias was the South Lebanese Army (SLA). The SLA was established after 1982 by Colonel Saad Haddad, who had formed a militia in 1978 while still serving in the Lebanese Army. The SLA was mainly Christian, but later it recruited Shia Muslims who would accept Israeli support in return for control of a sector of southern Lebanon. The Israelis quickly allied themselves with this group, training and equipping many of its fighters. The Phalangist militia also received some funds, assistance, and other support from Israel. In addition, it profited from land speculation and the levying of customs and taxes, through the port of Beirut, under the Sunduq al-Watani.

Druze militias on the opposing side numbered some 4,000 men. They drew closer to Syria until late in the war, when Amal and the Druze came to blows. The Syrian Army also intervened early in the civil war and deployed more than 40,000 troops into the country, inevitably gaining control over many of the militia groups.

The regular Lebanese Army was re-formed in 1982. Toward the end of that year the Lebanese forces were reequipped by the United States with M-16 rifles, M-113 armored personnel carriers, and UH-1H helicopters. Under the reorganization program, Lebanese recruits received limited training from U.S. Marines in the Beirut area prior to their withdrawal. The next phase of the civil war was particularly brutal, with the introduction of snipers paid simply to kill a set number of persons per day, numerous kidnappings and hostage takings, and reprisal actions by militias against not only leading individuals but also their entire families. Various realignments of the Christian political elements, the Syrians, and new groups such as Hezbollah occurred following the expulsion of the Palestinian leadership from Lebanon to Tunis.

By 1988, when the Lebanese Parliament failed to elect a new president, former president Amin Jumayyil (Gemayel) appointed a military government before leaving office. With two competing governments vying for power, the army was split between two different commands according to their location. The result was rapid military deterioration and polarization. In 1989 President Michel Aoun vowed to remove Syrian influence from Lebanon, and the following year the Lebanese Army was again unified. Syrian interference, however, subsequently forced Aoun from office.

In May 1991, after Syrian troops again battled Lebanese forces, most of the militias were dissolved, and the Lebanese Armed Forces began slowly to rebuild as Lebanon's only major nonsectarian institution. The country was not back to normal conditions until after about 1994, and the Israeli/SLA occupation of the South continued. The Lebanese military was not engaged in the 2006 summer war when the IDF bombarded large sections of the country in an effort to neutralize Hezbollah. In the wake of the war, the army was deployed to southern Lebanon in advance and support of the United Nations Interim Force in Lebanon (UNIFIL). However, the mission of UNIFIL was disputed; the LAF believes that its mission is to monitor violence between Israeli forces and Hezbollah, but not to disarm the latter group. The military was also deployed when brief spates of violence emerged between Sunni and Shia youth in the wake of nearly two years of public demonstrations in Beirut against the Fuad Siniura government, and when Hezbollah attacked the Future Party's media outlet.

The LAF engaged in a major operation on the radical Palestinian group Fath al-Islam, allegedly funded and initiated by Syrian-based agents. Because the LAF bombarded the refugee camps, breaking with the Cairo Accords, refugees fled, and the group was contained. This shifted the tenor of debate about the long-lived Palestinian refugee presence in the country.

The present Lebanese Army consists of 11 mechanized brigades, 2 artillery regiments, 5 special-forces regiments, 1 airborne regiment, 1 commando regiment, 1 Republican Guard brigade, and various support brigades. Total army troops number about 55,000. The primary weapons systems include some 100 U.S. M-48 tanks and 200 Soviet T54/55 tanks. With 725 of these, the U.S. M-113 APC is the most common armored fighting vehicle, but the Lebanese also have small numbers of French AMX-13s. Lebanese artillery consists of about 140 towed guns, an assortment of American 105-mm and 155-mm guns, and Russian 122-mm and 130-mm guns. The Lebanese also have approximately 25 BM-21 multiple-rocket launchers. The principal anti-tank weapons include the Milan and TOW.

The Lebanese Navy remains small and is limited to coast patrol activities and a naval commando regiment. During the civil war, the navy remained largely intact and was able to defend the Jounieh naval base from the various militias. Militia forces captured the base in 1991, but the navy's patrol craft were able to escape. The Jounieh base was rebuilt in 1991. The chief vessels are seven British-made Tracker- and Attacker-class patrol boats.

Lebanese Army soldiers patrol the outskirts of the besieged Palestinian Nahr al-Bared camp in northern Lebanon on May 24, 2007. Lebanon's leaders vowed to crush the Islamic fighters holed up in the camp, raising fears of a deadly new showdown after fierce fighting killed 69 people and sent thousands fleeing in the deadliest fighting since the 1975–1990 civil war. (AFP/Getty Images)

The Lebanese Air Force currently has no operational fixed-wing aircraft. The air fleet consists of 4 SA-342 helicopters and a variety of transport helicopters, of which the 30 UH-1Hs are the most common.

Current Lebanese military expenditures amount to $550 million, about 3.5 percent of Lebanon's gross domestic product (GDP).

RALPH MARTIN BAKER, DAVID T. ZABECKI, AND SHERIFA ZUHUR

See also

Chamoun, Camille Nimr; Hezbollah; Lebanon; Lebanon, U.S. Intervention in (1958); Lebanon, U.S. Intervention in (1982–1984); Palestine Liberation Organization; Syria; Syria, Armed Forces

References

Barak, Oren. "Towards a Representative Military? The Transformation of the Lebanese Officer Corps since 1945." *Middle East Journal* 60(1) (Winter 2006): 75–93.

Fisk, Robert. *Pity the Nation: The Abduction of Lebanon*. 4th ed. New York: Nation Books, 2002.

Katz, Samuel, and Lee Russell. *Armies in Lebanon, 1982–84*. Oxford, UK: Osprey, 1985.

Kéchichian, Joseph A. "A Strong Army for a Stable Lebanon." Policy Brief #19. Washington, DC: Middle East Institute, September 2008.

O'Ballance, Edgar. *Civil War in Lebanon, 1975–1992*. London: Palgrave Macmillan, 1998.

Salibi, Kamal. *A House of Many Mansions: The History of Lebanon Reconsidered*. Berkeley: University of California Press, 1990.

Lebanon, Civil War in
Start Date: April 13, 1975
End Date: October 13, 1990

The Lebanese Civil War, which lasted from 1975 to 1990 (and continued unofficially thereafter), was the most devastating event in that country's history. The war had its origin in the conflicts and political compromises of Lebanon's colonial period and was exacerbated by the nation's changing demographics, Christian and Muslim interreligious strife, and Lebanon's proximity to both Syria and Israel. Indeed, the Lebanese Civil War was part and parcel of the wider Arab-Israeli conflict and was emblematic of the inherent volatility and instability of the Middle East after World War II.

Lebanon in its present-day borders dates to 1920, when France exercised a mandate over the region. The French added several districts to the historic *mustashafiyya*, Mount Lebanon, a separate administrative district that had called for Western protection in the 19th century, eventually establishing Greater Lebanon. This meant the inclusion of areas whose populations had always been administered from Syria and did not necessarily support separation from that country. These heavily Sunni and Shia Muslim areas diluted the previous Maronite Christian and Druze majority of Mount Lebanon. When Lebanon won its independence from France in 1943, an unwritten power-sharing agreement was forged among the three major ethnic and religious groups. These included Maronite Christians (then in the majority), Sunni Muslims, and Shiite Muslims.

Lebanon's Muslim groups were discontented with the 1943 National Pact, which established a dominant political role for the Christians, especially the Maronites, in the central government. Druze, Muslims, and leftists joined forces as the National Movement in 1969. The movement called for the taking of a new census, as none had been conducted since 1932, and the subsequent drafting of a new governmental structure that would reflect the census results.

Muslim and Maronite leaders were unable to reconcile their conflicts of interest and instead formed militias, undermining the authority of the central government. The government's ability to maintain order was also handicapped by the nature of the Lebanese Army. It was composed on a fixed ratio of religions, and as members defected to militias of their own ethnicity, the army would eventually prove unable to check the power of the militias, the Palestine Liberation Organization (PLO), or other splinter groups.

Maronite militias armed by West Germany and Belgium drew supporters from the larger and poorer Christian population in the north. The most powerful of these was al-Kataib, also known as the Phalange, led by Bashir Jumayyil. Others included the Lebanese Forces, led by Samir Jaja (Geagea), and the Guardians of the Cedars.

Shiite militias, such as the Amal militia, fought the Maronites and later fought certain Palestinian groups and occasionally even other Shiite organizations. Some Sunni factions received support from Libya and Iraq. The Soviet Union encouraged Arab socialist movements that spawned leftist Palestinian organizations, such as the Popular Front for the Liberation of Palestine (PLFP) and the Democratic Front for the Liberation of Palestine. Prior to the civil war, the rise of Baathism in Syria and Iraq was paralleled by a surge of Lebanese Baathists. Within the civil war these were also reflected in groups such as al-Saiqa, a Syrian-aligned and largely anti-Fatah Palestinian fighting force, and the Arab Liberation Front, an Iraqi-aligned Baathist movement.

In 1970 Jordan's King Hussein expelled the PLO from Jordan after the events of Black September. PLO chairman Yasser Arafat thus regrouped his organization in the Palestinian refugee areas of Beirut and southern Lebanon, where other refugees had survived since 1948. The National Movement attracted support from the PLO Rejection Front faction, prominently including the PFLP, although Arafat and Fatah initially sought to remain neutral in the inter-Lebanese conflict. The National Movement supported the Palestinian resistance movement's struggle for national liberation and activities against Israel, and although Palestinians could not

vote in Lebanon and, being outside of the political system, had no voice in its reformation, they nonetheless lent moral support to the movement's desire for political reformation. By the early 1970s the Palestinian Resistance groups, although disunited, were a large fighting force. Maronites viewed the Resistance and the PLO as disruptive and a destabilizing ally of the Muslim factions.

On the morning of April 13, 1975, unidentified gunmen in a speeding car fired on a church in the Christian East Beirut suburb of Ayn ar Rummanah, killing 4 people including 2 Maronite Phalangists. Later that day Phalangists led by Jumayyil killed 27 Palestinians returning from a political rally on a bus in Ayn ar Rummanah. Four Christians were killed in East Beirut in December 1975, and in growing reprisals Phalangists and Muslim militias subsequently massacred at least 600 Muslims and Christians at checkpoints, igniting the 1975–1976 stage of the civil war.

The fighting eventually spread to most parts of the country, precipitating President Suleiman Franjieh's call for support from Syrian troops in June 1976, to which Syria responded by ending its prior affiliation with the Rejection Front and supporting the Maronites. This technically put Syria in the Israeli camp, as Israel had already begun to supply the Maronite forces with arms, tanks, and military advisers in May 1976. Meanwhile, Arafat's Fatah joined the war on the side of the National Movement.

Syrian troops subsequently entered Lebanon, occupying Tripoli and the Bekáa Valley, and imposed a cease-fire that ultimately failed to stop the conflict. After the arrival of Syrian troops, Christian forces massacred some 2,000 Palestinians in the Tal al-Zaatar camp in East Beirut. Anther massacre by Christian forces saw some 1,000 people killed at Muslim Qarantina.

Some reports charge al-Saiqa, the Syrian-backed Palestinian force or a combination of al-Saiqa, Fatah, and the Palestine Liberation Army along with some Muslim forces with an attack on the Christian city of Damour, a stronghold of Camille Chamoun and his followers. When the city fell on January 20, the remaining inhabitants were subject to rape, mutilation, and brutal assassinations. The civilian dead numbered at least 300, with one estimate being as high as 582. Graves were desecrated, and a church was used as a garage. Also, former camp dwellers from Tal Zatar were resettled in Damour and then evicted again after 1982. As a result of the massacre, other Christians came to see the Palestinian presence as a threat to their survival.

The nation was now informally divided, with southern Lebanon and the western half of Beirut becoming bases for the PLO and other Muslim militias and with the Christians in control of East Beirut and the Christian section of Mount Lebanon. The dividing thoroughfare in Beirut between its primarily western Muslim neighborhoods and eastern Christian neighborhoods was known as the Green Line.

In October 1976 an Arab League summit in Riyadh, Saudi Arabia, gave Syria a mandate to garrison 40,000 troops in Lebanon as the bulk of an Arab deterrent force charged with disentangling the combatants and restoring calm. However, in no part of the

Teenage Christian girls, all members of the right-wing Phalangist Party, fire their weapons in Beirut in November 1975. The Lebanese Civil War of 1975–1990 split the city in half, pitting Maronite Christian Phalangists against an alliance of Muslim militias. (Bettmann/Corbis)

country had the war actually ended, nor was there a political solution offered by the government.

In the south, PLO combatants returned from central Lebanon under the terms of the Riyadh Accords. Then on March 11, 1978, 8 Fatah militants landed on a beach in northern Israel and proceeded to take control of a passenger bus and head toward Tel Aviv. In the ensuing confrontation with Israeli forces, 34 Israelis and 6 of the militants died. In retaliation, Israel invaded Lebanon four days later in Operation LITANI in which the Israel Defense Forces (IDF) occupied most of the area south of the Litani River, resulting in approximately 2,000 deaths and the evacuation of at least 100,000 Lebanese. The United Nations (UN) Security Council passed Resolution 425 calling for an immediate Israeli withdrawal. It also created the UN Interim Force in Lebanon, charged with maintaining peace. Under international pressure to do so, Israeli forces withdrew later in 1978.

However, Israel retained de facto control of the border region by turning over positions inside Lebanon to the group later known as the South Lebanon Army (SLA), led by Major Saad Haddad. Israel meanwhile had been supplying Haddad's forces. The SLA occupied Shia villages in the south, informally setting up a

12-mile-wide security zone that protected Israeli territory from cross-border attacks. Violent exchanges quickly resumed among the PLO, Israel, and the SLA, with the PLO attacking SLA positions and firing rockets into northern Israel. Israel conducted air raids against PLO positions, and the SLA continued its efforts to consolidate its power in the border region.

Syria meanwhile clashed with the Phalange. Phalange leader Jumayyil's increasingly aggressive actions (such as his April 1981 attempt to capture the strategic city of Zahleh in central Lebanon) were designed to thwart the Syrian goal of brushing him aside and installing Franjieh as president. Consequently, the de facto alliance between Israel and Jumayyil strengthened considerably. In fighting in Zahleh in April 1981, for example, Jumayyil called for Israeli assistance, and Prime Minister Menachem Begin responded by sending Israeli fighter jets to the scene. These shot down two Syrian helicopters. This led Syrian president Hafiz al-Assad to order ground-to-air missiles to the hilly perimeter of Zahleh.

In July 1981 Israeli forces attacked Palestinian positions, provoking retaliatory shelling by the PLO. The Israeli response to this shelling culminated in the aerial bombardment of a West Beirut suburb where Fatah's headquarters were located, killing

200 people and wounding another 600, most of them civilians. The PLO rejoinder was a huge rocket attack on towns and villages in northern Israel, leaving 6 civilians dead and 59 wounded. These violent exchanges prompted diplomatic intervention by the United States. On July 24, 1981, U.S. special Middle East envoy Philip Habib brokered a cease-fire agreement with the PLO and Israel. The two sides now agreed to cease hostilities in Lebanon proper and along the Israeli border with Lebanon. The cease-fire was short-lived.

On June 3, 1982, the Abu Nidal organization attempted to assassinate Israeli ambassador Shlomo Argov in London. Although badly wounded, Argov survived. Israel retaliated with an aerial attack on PLO and PFLP targets in West Beirut that led to more than 100 casualties, a clear violation of the cease-fire. The PLO responded by launching a counterattack from Lebanon with rockets and artillery.

On June 6, 1982, Israeli forces began Operation PEACE FOR GALILEE, an invasion of southern Lebanon to destroy PLO bases there. The Israeli plan was subsequently modified to move farther into Lebanon, and by June 15 Israeli units were entrenched outside Beirut. Israel laid siege to Beirut, which contained some 15,000 armed members of the PLO. Over a period of several weeks, the PLO and the IDF exchanged artillery fire. On a number of occasions the Palestinians directed their fire into Christian East Beirut, causing an estimated 6,700 deaths of which 80 percent were civilians. On August 12, 1982, Habib again negotiated a truce that called for the withdrawal of both Israeli and PLO elements. Nearly 15,000 Palestinian militants had been evacuated to other countries by September 1. Within six months, Israel withdrew from most of Lebanon but maintained the security zone along the Israeli-Lebanese border.

Jumayyil was elected Lebanon's president on August 23, 1982, with acknowledged Israeli backing. But on September 14, 1982, he was assassinated. The next day Israeli troops crossed into West Beirut to secure Muslim militia strongholds and stood back as Lebanese Christian militias massacred as many as 2,000 Palestinian civilians in the Sabra and Shatila refugee camps. This event was protested throughout the Arab world, especially because of the Israeli presence in Beirut.

With U.S. backing, the Lebanese parliament chose Amin Jumayyil to succeed his brother as president and focused anew on securing the withdrawal of Israeli and Syrian forces. On May 17, 1983, Lebanon, Israel, and the United States signed an agreement on Israeli withdrawal that was conditioned on the departure of Syrian troops. Syria opposed the agreement and declined to discuss the withdrawal of its troops. In August 1983 Israel withdrew from the Shuf (a district of Mount Lebanon to the southeast of Beirut), thus removing the buffer between the Druze and the Christian militias and triggering another round of brutal fighting. By September the Druze had gained control over most of the Shuf, and Israeli forces had pulled out from all but the southern security zone. The collapse of the Lebanese Army in February 1984

following the defection of many Muslim and Druze units to militias was a major blow to the government. On March 5, 1984, the Lebanese government canceled the May 17 agreement.

This period of chaos had witnessed the beginning of retaliatory attacks launched against U.S. and Western interests, such as the April 18, 1983, suicide attack at the U.S. embassy in West Beirut that left 63 dead. Then on October 23, 1983, a bombing in the Beirut barracks that hit the headquarters of U.S. military personnel left 241 U.S. marines dead. A total of 58 French servicemen also died in the attack. Months later, American University of Beirut president Malcolm Kerr was murdered inside the university on January 18, 1984. After U.S. forces withdrew in February 1984, anti-Western terrorism as well as that directed against Lebanese enemies continued, including a second bombing of the U.S. embassy annex in East Beirut on September 20, 1984, that left 9 Americans dead, including 2 U.S. servicemen.

Between 1985 and 1989 factional conflict worsened as various efforts at national reconciliation failed. The economy collapsed, and the militias that had participated in crime, car theft, hijackings, and kidnappings for ransom expanded their activities. The larger militias were also involved in profiteering, land investment, and sales, and they, rather than the government, also collected tariffs and customs.

Heavy fighting took place in the War of the Camps in 1985 and 1986 as the Shia Muslim Amal militia sought to rout the Palestinians from Lebanese strongholds. Many thousands of Palestinians died in the war. Sabra, Shatila, and Burj al-Barajnah were reduced to ashes. Combat returned to Beirut in 1987 with Palestinians, leftists, and Druze fighters allied against Amal, eventually drawing further Syrian intervention. Violent confrontation flared up again in Beirut in 1988 between Amal and Hezbollah.

Meanwhile, Lebanese prime minister Rashid Karameh, head of a government of national unity set up after the failed peace efforts of 1984, was assassinated on June 1, 1987. President Jumayyil's term of office expired in September 1988. Before stepping down, he appointed another Maronite Christian, Lebanese Armed Forces commanding general Michel Aoun, as acting prime minister, contravening the National Pact. Muslim groups rejected the violation of the National Pact and pledged support to Selim al-Hoss, a Sunni who had succeeded Karameh. Lebanon was thus divided between a Christian government in East Beirut and a Muslim government in West Beirut, each with its own president.

In February 1989 Aoun attacked the rival Lebanese Forces militia. By March he turned his attention to other militias, launching what he termed a War of Liberation against the Syrians and their allied Lebanese militias. In the months that followed Aoun rejected both the Taif Accords that ultimately ended the civil war and the election of another Christian leader as president. A Lebanese-Syrian military operation in October 1990 forced him to take cover in the French embassy in Beirut. He later went into exile in Paris.

The Taif Accords of 1989 marked the beginning of the end of the fighting. In January 1989 a committee appointed by the Arab

U.S. marines search through tons of rubble looking for missing comrades in Beirut, Lebanon, on October 23, 1983. A truck packed with explosives crashed into the building, killing 241 marines. U.S. president Ronald Reagan withdrew all remaining troops. The marines were in Lebanon on a peacekeeping mission during that country's civil war. (U.S. Marine Corps)

League, chaired by a representative from Kuwait and including Saudi Arabia, Algeria, and Morocco, had begun to formulate solutions to the conflict. This led to a meeting of Lebanese parliamentarians in Taif, Saudi Arabia. There in October they agreed to the national reconciliation accord. Returning to Lebanon, they ratified the agreement on November 4 and elected Rene Muawad as president the following day.

Muawad was assassinated 18 days later on November 22 in a car bombing in Beirut as his motorcade returned from Lebanese Independence Day ceremonies. He was succeeded by Elias Hrawi, who remained in office until 1998. In August 1990 parliament and the new president agreed on constitutional amendments. The National Assembly of 128 seats was now divided equally between Christians and Muslims. Because the Muslim sects together now outnumbered the Christians, this decision did not represent a one-vote–one-man solution but was nonetheless an improvement on the previous situation. On October 13 Syria launched a major military operation against Aoun's stronghold around the presidential palace. In the ensuing fighting hundreds of Aoun supporters were killed, and the Syrians took control of the Lebanese capital. Aoun sought refuge in the French embassy. He later announced that the war was over and went into exile in France. Aoun did not return to Lebanon until May 2005.

In March 1991 parliament passed an amnesty law that pardoned all political crimes prior to its enactment. In May 1991 the militias were dissolved, and the Lebanese Armed Forces began to slowly rebuild as Lebanon's only major nonsectarian institution.

MOSHE TERDIMAN

See also

Arab League; Arafat, Yasser; Assad, Hafiz al-; Begin, Menachem; France, Middle East Policy; Habib, Philip; Hezbollah; Hussein ibn Talal, King of Jordan; Israel; Israel, Armed Forces; Lebanon; Lebanon, Armed Forces; Lebanon, Israeli Invasion of; Palestine Liberation Organization; Shia Islam; Suicide Bombings; Sunni Islam; Syria; Syria,

Armed Forces; United Nations; United States, Middle East Policy, 1945–Present

References

Barakat, Halim, ed. *Toward a Viable Lebanon.* London: Croom Helm, 1988.

Collings, Deirdre. *Peace for Lebanon? From War to Reconstruction.* Boulder, CO: Lynne Rienner, 1994.

El-Khazen, Farid. *The Breakdown of the State in Lebanon, 1967–1976.* Cambridge: Harvard University Press, 2000.

Fisk, Robert. *Pity the Nation: The Abduction of Lebanon.* 4th ed. New York: Nation Books, 2002.

Hanf, Theodor. *Coexistence in Wartime Lebanon: Decline of a State and Rise of a Nation.* London: Centre for Lebanese Studies and Tauris, 1993.

Petran, Tabitha. *The Struggle over Lebanon.* New York: Monthly Review Press, 1987.

Picard, Elizabeth. "The Political Economy of Civil War in Lebanon." In *War, Institutions, and Social Change in the Middle East,* edited by Steven Heydemann, 292–322. Berkeley: University of California Press, 2000.

Rabinovich, Itamar. *The War for Lebanon, 1970–1985.* Rev. ed. Ithaca, NY: Cornell University Press, 1986.

Salibi, Kamal S. *Lebanon and the Middle Eastern Question.* Oxford, UK: Center for Lebanese Studies, 1988.

Lebanon, Israeli Invasion of
Event Date: 1982

The Israeli invasion of Lebanon, code-named Operation PEACE FOR GALILEE, began on June 6, 1982, when Defense Minister Ariel Sharon, acting in full agreement with instructions from Prime Minister Menachem Begin, ordered Israel Defense Forces (IDF) troops into southern Lebanon to destroy the Palestine Liberation Organization (PLO) there.

In 1977 Begin had become the first Israeli prime minister from the right-wing Likud Party. He sought to maintain the Israeli hold over the West Bank and Gaza but also had a deep commitment to a Greater (Eretz) Israel, which he defined as the ancestral homeland of the Jews that embraced territory beyond Israel's borders into Lebanon and across the Jordan River.

Israeli defense minister Sharon, also a prominent member of the Likud Party, shared Begin's ideological commitment to Greater Israel. Indeed, Sharon played an important role in expanding Jewish settlements in the West Bank and Gaza. He took a hard-line approach toward the Palestinians, endeavoring to undermine PLO influence in the West Bank and Gaza, and was also influential in the formation of Israeli foreign policy.

In June 1978 under heavy U.S. pressure, Begin withdrew Israeli forces that had been sent into southern Lebanon in the Litani River operation. United Nations Interim Force in Lebanon (UNIFIL) then took over in southern Lebanon. They were charged with confirming the Israeli withdrawal, restoring peace and security, and helping the Lebanese government reestablish its authority in the

area. The Israeli failure to remove Palestinian bases in southern Lebanon was a major embarrassment for the Begin government.

UNIFIL proved incapable of preventing Palestinian forces from operating in southern Lebanon and striking Israel, which led to Israeli reprisals. Attacks back and forth across the Lebanese-Israeli border killed civilians on both sides as well as some UNIFIL troops. Israel meanwhile trained, funded, and provided weapons to the force later known as the South Lebanon Army, a pro-Israeli Christian militia in southern Lebanon led by Major Saad Haddad, and the force used them against the PLO and local villagers.

In July 1981 U.S. president Ronald Reagan sent Lebanese-American diplomat Philip Habib to the area in an effort to broker a truce during the Lebanese Civil War. On July 24 Habib announced agreement on a cease-fire, but it was in name only. The PLO repeatedly violated the agreement, and major cross-border strikes resumed in April 1982 following the death of an Israeli officer from a land mine. While Israel conducted both air strikes and commando raids across the border, it was unable to prevent a growing number of Palestinian fighting forces from locating there. Their numbers increased to perhaps 6,000 men in a number of encampments, as Palestinian rocket and mortar attacks regularly forced thousands of Israeli civilians to flee their homes and fields in northern Galilee and seek protection in bomb shelters.

In London on June 3, 1982, three members of a Palestinian terrorist organization connected to Abu Nidal attempted to assassinate Israeli ambassador to Britain Shlomo Argov. Although Argov survived the attack, he remained paralyzed until his death in 2003. Abu Nidal's organization had been linked to Yasser Arafat's Fatah faction within the PLO in the past, and the Israelis used this as the excuse to bomb Palestinian targets in West Beirut and other targets in southern Lebanon during June 4–5, 1982. The Palestinians responded by attacking Israeli settlements in Galilee with rockets and mortars. It was this Palestinian shelling of the settlements rather than the attempted assassination of Argov that provoked the Israeli decision to invade Lebanon.

Operation PEACE FOR GALILEE began on June 6, 1982. It took its name from the Israeli intention to protect its vulnerable northern region of Israel from the PLO rocket and mortar attacks launched from southern Lebanon. Ultimately, Israel committed to the operation some 76,000 men, 800 tanks, 1,500 armored personnel carriers (APCs), and 364 aircraft. Syria committed perhaps 22,000 men, 352 tanks, 300 APCs, and 96 aircraft, while the PLO had about 15,000 men, 300 tanks, and 150 APCs.

The Israeli mission had three principal objectives. First, Israeli forces sought to destroy the PLO in southern Lebanon. Second, Israel wanted to evict the Syrian Army from Lebanon and bring about the removal of its missiles from the Bekáa Valley. Although Sharon perceived Syrian forces in Lebanon as a major security threat to Israel, he maintained that the IDF would not attack them unless it was first fired upon. Third, Israel hoped to influence Lebanese politics. Israel sought to ally itself with the Maronite Christians, led by Bashir Jumayyil (Gemayel), the leader of the Phalange (al-Kata'ib) and head of the unified command of the Lebanese Forces.

The Phalange was a long-standing militia and political force. Part of the Lebanese Forces, it was an umbrella military organization comprised of several Christian militias. Jumayyil had carried out a series of brutal operations to destroy the autonomy of the other Christian militias and had incorporated them into his Lebanese Forces. He was opposed to relinquishing to the Sunni and Shia Muslims of Lebanon the power held by the Maronites in traditionally Christian-dominated Lebanon. Some in the Phalanges maintained that their heritage was Phoenician, thus predating the Arabs, and they sought to maintain their historic linkages with France and the West. Jumayyil also cooperated closely with Israel because of his desire to preserve a Maronite homeland. Early in the civil war his forces battled the Syrians.

Palestinian militias were not only entrenched in the southern part of the country but were also well established in West Beirut. Understandably, the Israeli cabinet was loath to place its troops into an urban combat situation that was bound to bring heavy civilian casualties and incur opposition from Washington and Western Europe. Begin and Sharon informed the cabinet that the goal was merely to break up PLO bases in southern Lebanon and push back PLO and Syrian forces some 25 miles, beyond rocket range of Galilee.

Once the operation began, however, Sharon quickly changed the original plan by expanding the mission to incorporate Beirut, which was well beyond the 25-mile mark. Many in the cabinet now believed that Begin and Sharon had deliberately misled them. The IDF advanced to the outskirts of Beirut within days. Tyre and Sidon, two cities within the 25-mile limit, were both heavily damaged in the Israeli advance. The entire population was rounded up, and most of the men were taken into custody. Rather than standing their ground and being overwhelmed by the better-equipped Israelis, the Palestinian fighters and PLO leadership withdrew back on West Beirut. Sharon now argued in favor of a broader operation that would force the PLO from Beirut, and for some 10 weeks Israeli guns shelled West Beirut, killing both PLO forces and civilians.

Fighting also occurred with Syrian forces in the Bekáa Valley. Unable to meet Israel on equal footing and bereft of allies, Syria did not engage in an all-out effort. Rather, much of the battle was waged in the air. By June 10 the Israeli Air Force had neutralized Syrian surface-to-air missiles and had shot down dozens of Syrian jets. (Some sources say that the ultimate toll was as many as 80 Syrian jets.) The Israelis employed AH-1 Cobra helicopter gunships to attack and destroy dozens of Syrian armored vehicles, including Soviet-built T-72 tanks. The Israelis also trapped Syrian forces in the Bekáa Valley. Israel was on the verge of severing the Beirut-Damascus highway on June 11 when Moscow and Washington brokered a cease-fire.

In Beirut meanwhile, Sharon hoped to join up with Jumayyil's Lebanese Forces. Sharon hoped that the Lebanese Forces might bear the brunt of the fighting in West Beirut, but Jumayyil was reluctant to do this, fearing that such a move would harm his chances to become the president of Lebanon.

Begin's cabinet was unwilling to approve an Israeli assault on West Beirut because of the probability of high casualties. Meanwhile, the United States had been conveying ambiguous signals regarding its position in the conflict. This only encouraged Arafat to entrench himself and the PLO in West Beirut.

Sharon disregarded cabinet opposition and placed the city under siege from air, land, and sea. He hoped that the Israeli bombardment would cause citizens to turn against the Palestinians, civilians as well as fighters, and drive them eastward, where they could be eliminated. The bombing and shelling resulted in mostly civilian casualties, however, provoking denunciations of Israel in the international press. The PLO believed that it could hold out longer under siege than the Israelis could under international pressure, leading Israel to intensify its attack on Beirut in early August. The PLO then consented to a UN-brokered arrangement whereby American, French, and Italian peacekeeping forces, known as the Multi-National Force in Lebanon, would escort the PLO fighters out of Lebanon by the end of the month, relocating them to Tunis. Habib assured the PLO that the many refugees left behind in camps in Lebanon would not be harmed.

On August 23, 1982, Jumayyil was elected president of Lebanon. He was dead within two weeks, the victim of assassination on September 14, 1982, by a member of the pro-Damascus National Syrian Socialist Party. Jumayyil had indeed paid for his connection to the Israelis. While the National Syrian Socialist Party took responsibility for the murder of Jumayyil, some suspected an Israeli conspiracy to kill him owing to his more recent attempts to disassociate himself from Israel.

Following the assassination of Jumayyil, Israeli forces occupied West Beirut. This was in direct violation of the UN agreement calling for the evacuation of the PLO and protection of the Palestinian refugees who remained behind. With the PLO removed, the refugees had virtually no defense against the Israelis or their Christian allies.

Once Israel had control of the Palestinian refugee camps, in September 1982 Sharon invited members of the Phalange to enter the camps at Sabra and Shatila to "clean out the terrorists." The Phalange militia, led by Elie Hobeika, then slaughtered more than 1,000 refugees in what he claimed to be retaliation for Jumayyil's assassination. Estimates of casualties in the Israeli invasion and subsequent occupation vary widely, although the numbers may have been as high as 17,826 Lebanese and approximately 675 Israelis killed.

Israel had achieved a number of goals. It had accomplished its immediate aim of expelling the PLO from Lebanon and temporarily destroying its infrastructure. It had also weakened the Syrian military, especially as far as air assets were concerned. The Israelis had also strengthened the South Lebanon Army, which would help control a buffer, or security zone, in the south. It had also disheartened the Palestinians in the West Bank and Gaza by the near destruction of their national organization and failure of any international agreement to protect civilians in Lebanon.

Israeli forces invade the city of Beirut, Lebanon, on September 16, 1982, in an attempt to dislodge the forces of the Palestine Liberation Organization (PLO) barricaded in the western part of the city. The city was heavily damaged in the fighting. (UPI-Bettmann/Corbis)

However, the invasion had negative repercussions as well. Much of Beirut lay in ruins, with damage estimated as high as $2 billion, and the tourist industry was a long time in recovering. Operation PEACE FOR GALILEE also became an occupation, which many Israelis protested as immoral or at least the wrong diversion of resources. In May 1983, with assistance from the United States and France, Israel and Lebanon reached an agreement calling for the staged withdrawal of Israeli forces, although the instruments of this agreement were never officially exchanged. In March 1984 under Syrian pressure, the Lebanese government repudiated the agreement. In January 1985 Israel began a unilateral withdrawal to a security zone in southern Lebanon, which was completed in June 1985. Not until June 2000 did Israel finally withdraw all its forces from southern Lebanon.

Rather than producing a stable pro-Israeli government in Beirut, the occupation led to contentious new resistance groups that kept Lebanon in perpetual turmoil. There was also considerable unrest in Israel. A protest demonstration in Tel Aviv that followed the Sabra and Shatila massacre drew a reported 300,000 people. Responding to the furor within Israel over the war, the Israeli government appointed the Kahan Commission to investigate the massacres at Sabra and Shatila. The commission found that Israeli officials were indirectly responsible, and Sharon was forced to resign as minister of defense. Begin's political career also suffered

greatly. Disillusioned by the invasion and the high Israeli casualties, he resigned as prime minister in 1983, withdrawing entirely from public life.

BRIAN PARKINSON AND SPENCER C. TUCKER

See also

Begin, Menachem; Habib, Philip; Lebanon; Palestine Liberation Organization; Sharon, Ariel

References

Friedman, Thomas. *From Beirut to Jerusalem.* New York: Anchor Books, 1995.

Rabil, Robert G. *Embattled Neighbors: Syria, Israel and Lebanon.* Boulder, CO: Lynne Rienner, 2003.

Rabinovich, Itamar. *The War for Lebanon, 1970–1985.* Rev. ed. Ithaca, NY: Cornell University Press, 1986.

Lebanon, U.S. Intervention in (1958)
Event Date: July 1958

In July 1958 the Dwight D. Eisenhower administration in the United States intervened militarily in Lebanon to ensure that the pro-Western regime of Camille Chamoun, president during 1952–1958, would not be overthrown and that the nation would not be plunged into a full-blown civil war. Another reason for sending troops to Lebanon was likely to send a warning to Soviet leaders and their ally, Egypt's President Gamal Abdel Nasser, not to destabilize the Middle East. Finally, Washington hoped to reassure other pro-Western governments in Iran, Pakistan, and Turkey of American resolve in the region. The 1958 intervention, known as Operation BLUE BAT, was officially launched on July 15, 1958, and ended just three months later with the departure of U.S. forces on October 25.

President Eisenhower's decision to dispatch the troops was based in part on his foreign policy stance expressed in a message to Congress on January 5, 1957, which became known as the Eisenhower Doctrine. Asserting that the United States was determined to deny the Soviet Union the opportunity to dominate and control the Middle East, the president pledged to assist both economically and militarily any Middle Eastern nation in the preservation of its independence, to include the deployment of U.S. military forces "against armed aggression from any nation controlled by international Communism."

At the time, the United States regarded with alarm the rise of Arab hostility toward the West and the growing influence of the Soviet Union in the Middle East. Particularly worrisome to Washington were the policies of Egypt and Syria, which had developed great antipathy toward the West. After Nasser had nationalized the Suez Canal in 1956, Britain, France, and Israel invaded Egypt. The resulting 1956 Suez Crisis inflamed Arab hostility toward the West and boomeranged in that it enhanced Nasser's prestige in the region and his Arab nationalist policies, known as Nasserism.

Eisenhower viewed the Suez Crisis as having effectively ended British and French influence in the Middle East, thus creating a power vacuum. To deny the Soviet Union the opportunity to exploit this power vacuum, thwart Nasser's Arab nationalist policies (which later enjoyed Soviet support), and protect the supply of oil, Eisenhower was prepared to intervene militarily in the Middle East should that prove necessary.

The first real test of the Eisenhower Doctrine came in Lebanon in 1958. By the spring of that year, a series of international and domestic events had plunged the country into crisis. Relations with Egypt deteriorated when President Chamoun, a Christian, refused to sever diplomatic relations with Britain and France following their invasion of Egypt during the Suez Crisis, which angered Lebanese Muslims who supported Nasser, including Lebanese prime minister Rashid Karami, a Sunni Muslim. Meanwhile, hostile Egyptian propaganda against Chamoun exacerbated Lebanese Muslim resentment toward his regime. Chamoun's refusal to denounce the 1955 Baghdad Pact and his decision to place Lebanon under the umbrella of the Eisenhower Doctrine further angered Nasser and Lebanon's Muslims. Karami regarded the Baghdad Pact as a threat to Arab unity and an attempt to divide the Arab world.

On February 1, 1958, Egypt and Syria formed a unitary state in the United Arab Republic. Many of Nasser's supporters in Lebanon were enthusiastic about the United Arab Republic and hoped

that Lebanon might join. Chamoun not only refused but was antagonistic toward the Arabists in Lebanon and hoped to keep his country neutral. Lebanese Muslims viewed Chamoun's decision as proof of his desire to remain aligned with the West. The president's position further alienated his Muslim countrymen, however.

In terms of domestic politics, the 1958 Lebanese Crisis grew principally from growing Muslim disenchantment with Christian domination of both the government and the military, especially when Muslims held that Christians were no longer in the majority. Lebanon's only official census, in 1932, had served as the basis for distributing political power among Lebanon's Christians and Muslims (both Sunni and Shiite) as well as other religious faiths such as the Druze. Using dubious statistics, such as counting Christians Lebanese living abroad, the 1932 census showed a slim majority of Christians living in Lebanon. When Lebanon gained its independence in 1943 from France, an informal agreement, known as the National Pact, served as the basis for reconciling religious rivalries by attempting to create a stable, united, and peaceful country among people of different faiths and sought to ensure that no one religion would dominate the government.

Based on the 1932 census, the National Pact stipulated that the president would be a Christian of the dominant Maronite sect (which accounted for approximately 50 percent of the Christians), the prime minister would be a Sunni Muslim, the Speaker of the parliament would be a Shiite Muslim, and the commander of the Lebanese military would be a Maronite. The National Pact also established, per the 1932 census, that the ratio of seats in the parliament, cabinet offices, and positions in the bureaucracy would be awarded on a ratio of six to five, Christians to Muslims. The pact specified that Lebanon was to have an Arab identity but would neither unify with Syria nor invite Western intervention. In sum, the basis of both the government and the idea of a Lebanese national identity was principally a function of religious faith, making national unity tenuous at best and Lebanese democracy an illusion. Although never committed to writing or affirmed by the people, the National Pact was nonetheless accepted by the religious-political elite of the country as the basis for establishing a government and preserving national unity. But as the Muslim population increased, the legitimacy of the political divisions, the relative power of the Christian minority, the powers of the president, and the veto power of the opposition all came into question, and sectarian tensions grew.

Lebanese Muslims generally identified with the Arab world in the sense that they recognized Lebanon as an Arab nation, which was a key point of the National Pact. This agreed with Nasser's Pan-Arabism. One segment of the Lebanese Christian community also identified with Arabism, while another had historically seen itself as a Christian pro-Western enclave. People of the latter segment identified with France, were educated in French and not in Arabic, and were opposed to the leftists and Nasserists. Meanwhile, Middle Eastern politics aggravated the tensions between

A U.S. marine sits in a foxhole and points a machine gun toward Beirut, Lebanon, in the distance, July 1958. (Library of Congress)

the groups, undermining the tenuous unity of this multireligious nation. By the mid-1950s many younger Lebanese, both Christians and Muslims, were opposed to the power of what they called feudalism in Lebanon. They rejected the governing arrangements such as the National Pact and believed that a new census would show that the Muslims were the majority in the country, which should allow them to elect a larger number of deputies in the national assembly. They opposed Chamoun's 1958 decision to amend the constitution that would allow him a second term, and his stance touched off simmering religious tensions.

In May 1958 violent disturbances broke out throughout Lebanon as Chamoun's opponents called for a general strike against the government. Chamoun ordered the commander of the Lebanese Armed Forces, General Fuad Shihab, to intervene. Fearing great bloodshed between Christians and Muslims, Shihab refused. He reasoned that suppressing the rebellion would destroy the military's neutrality, not preserve national unity, and that it would plunge the military into the growing civil war. Indeed, the military was itself composed of both Christians and Muslims, and Shihab knew that any military intervention would dissolve the military into sectarian factions.

Shihab's wise decision to keep the military neutral spared Lebanon a full-scale civil war that summer, and had international events not intruded, Lebanon might have overcome the crisis with

another political solution. The urgency and danger of the crisis, however, increased when on July 14, 1958, Pan-Arab nationalists overthrew and killed King Faisal, the pro-British monarch of Iraq and the key figure behind the Baghdad Pact. Fearing that the coup was part of a concerted effort to take advantage of Lebanon's disorder, overthrow his regime, and turn the country into a solidly Arab-Muslim state with close ties to Nasser and the Soviet Union, Chamoun appealed for American military assistance.

Alarmed at the unexpected coup in Iraq and determined to prevent a friendly regime in Lebanon from suffering the same fate while also seeking to reassure the pro-Western governments of Turkey, Iran, and Pakistan, the American president invoked the Eisenhower Doctrine and dispatched 14,000 U.S. troops to secure Chamoun's regime. Washington made clear to Chamoun, however, that it was not intervening to assist or to endorse his questionable reelection bid.

Of the 14,000 U.S. soldiers who landed in Lebanon, about 8,500 were from the army; the remainder were marines. By mid-July 1958 the United States had 70 warships and support ships in the Mediterranean with an additional 40,000 men at sea, ready to be deployed in short order if necessary.

The presence of U.S. troops as peacekeepers averted other foreign influence in the Lebanon crisis and signaled to all warring factions, including Chamoun, that the United States would not tolerate a civil war in Lebanon. However, many Lebanese regarded the marines as unnecessary and a sign that the president disregarded the balance of powers in the Lebanese political system.

President Chamoun's decision to resign, not amend the constitution, and not seek a second term, along with parliament's selections of General Shihab as Chamoun's successor on July 31, averted a civil war and cooled sectarian tensions. That same day a cease-fire was declared in the city of Tripoli, the scene of some of the worst fighting.

The U.S. troops remained in Lebanon for just 103 days, until October 25, and suffered only 1 combat casualty. Meanwhile, a total of between 2,000 and 4,000 Lebanese had died. This time, at least, Lebanon had been spared a full-scale civil war.

STEFAN M. BROOKS

See also

Arab Nationalism; Chamoun, Camille Nimr; Egypt; Eisenhower, Dwight David; Eisenhower Doctrine; Lebanon; Lebanon, Armed Forces; Lebanon, U.S. Intervention in (1982–1984); Nasser, Gamal Abdel; Syria; United Arab Republic

References

El-Khazen, Farid. *The Breakdown of the State in Lebanon, 1967–1976.* Cambridge: Harvard University Press, 2000.

Fisk, Robert. *Pity the Nation: The Abduction of Lebanon.* 4th ed. New York: Nation Books, 2002.

Harris, William. *The New Face of Lebanon: History's Revenge.* Princeton, NJ: Markus Wiener, 2005.

Mackey, Sandra. *Lebanon: A House Divided.* New York: Norton, 2006.

Lebanon, U.S. Intervention in (1982–1984)

Start Date: 1982
End Date: 1984

The U.S. military intervention in Lebanon began in August 1982 and was prompted by the Israeli invasion of Lebanon on June 6, 1982, during the Lebanese Civil War (1975–1990). In response to continuing raids and attacks on Israeli soil by Palestinian guerrillas—principally those associated with Yasser Arafat's Palestine Liberation Organization (PLO)—from bases in southern Lebanon, the government of Menachem Begin ordered the Israel Defense Forces (IDF) to invade Israel's northern neighbor. Although publicly proclaiming that the goal was only to destroy Palestinian forces in southern Lebanon, Begin and Defense Minister Ariel Sharon expanded the objectives to include eviction of the PLO and as many as Palestinians as possible from all of Lebanon.

As a result, Israeli forces then besieged and blockaded the Lebanese capital of Beirut. Despite heavy Israeli bombardment for 70 days, PLO forces refused to surrender. Israel, however, demurred from invading Beirut proper, fearing heavy casualties from a guerrilla war in the city's rubble-strewn streets and alleys.

Meanwhile, mounting civilian casualties in Lebanon and growing international opposition to the Israeli invasion compelled the United States to intervene in Lebanon in August and September 1982 as part of the international peacekeeping force known as the Multi-National Force (MNF) in Lebanon. With no end in sight to the siege of Beirut, Israel, the PLO, and Lebanon's embattled government all looked to the United States for a settlement. During the intervention, 1,200 U.S. marines from the 1st Battalion of the 8th Marine Regiment and the 2nd Marine Division were to supervise, along with British, French, and Italian troops of the MNF, the evacuation from Lebanon of the PLO. They were also charged with supervising the withdrawal of Israeli and Syrian forces from Beirut and its environs and ensuring the safety of Palestinian civilians. The U.S. marines landed on August 25, 1982, and were based at Beirut International Airport.

The basic terms of the international intervention and PLO evacuation had been negotiated by American envoy Philip Habib. The Habib Agreement stipulated that Israel would end its siege of Beirut and not invade the city or harm Palestinian civilians if PLO fighters withdrew from Beirut and left the country, which they did under the protection of the MNF. By September 1, 1982, U.S. troops had been withdrawn, and the conditions of the Habib Agreement had been fulfilled.

However, the September 14, 1982, assassination of newly selected Lebanese President Bashir Jumayyil, leader of the dominant Christian Maronite faction and an Israeli ally, prompted Israel to invade Muslim-dominated West Beirut that month. During September 16–18 Israeli forces had allowed Jumayyil's Phalange militia to enter two Palestinian refugee camps, Sabra and Shatila, leading to the massacre of as many as 3,500 Palestinians. Many Americans, including President Ronald Reagan, regretted that the U.S. troops had been withdrawn so quickly and called for another multinational force to protect civilians and somehow bring a semblance of peace and stability to Lebanon by separating the warring groups in Lebanon's seven-year-long civil war.

The September massacres at Sabra and Shatila prompted the redeployment of 1,200 U.S. marines to Lebanon later that month, ostensibly to support and stabilize the weak and embattled Lebanese government. The Reagan administration feared that allowing Lebanon's pro-Western government to collapse would turn the

Deaths, by Type, in the U.S. Armed Forces during the Lebanon Peacekeeping Mission (1982–1984)

	U.S. Air Force	*U.S. Army*	*U.S. Marine Corps*	*U.S. Navy*	*Total*
Hostile deaths	0	3	234	19	256
Nonhostile deaths	0	5	2	2	9
Total	0	8	236	21	265

U.S. marines arrive at Beirut International Airport, part of a multinational peacekeeping force deployed to Lebanon during the conflict between Israel and the Palestine Liberation Organization (PLO). (U.S. Department of Defense)

entire country into a hostile Arab state. This, they feared, might allow Syria, aided at the time by the Soviet Union, to control all of Lebanon. Alternatively, Lebanon might have become a client state of Iran's radical Shiite government, which was arming and supporting Lebanese Shiite groups at the time. The marines served in the MNF along with French and Italian troops, arriving in Beirut on September 29 and again setting up headquarters at Beirut International Airport.

U.S. intervention in the civil war and in particular shelling by the battleship *New Jersey,* coming with Israel's invasion of Lebanon and occupation of the southern part of the country, stoked a strong climate of anti-Americanism in Lebanon. Indeed, most Lebanese distrusted the motives behind the American intervention, believing that the Reagan administration had both given its approval of and supported Israel's invasion of Lebanon in June 1982 and its subsequent occupation of Beirut. With such sentiments running high, the United States was dragged into Lebanon's civil war and into conflict with rival neighboring governments, namely Israel and Syria but also Iran. Nevertheless, during the winter of 1982–1983 the MNF was largely successful in limiting the number of attacks by Lebanon's rival groups and the Israeli military.

Not surprisingly, however, with America's military presence in Beirut viewed as not only a tempting target but also an intolerable obstacle to the objectives of the warring groups, the MNF and

U.S. marines came under increasing attack from both Druze and other various Muslim militias. To make matters worse, because the marines were garrisoned at Beirut International Airport they were dangerously exposed to attack, occupying flat terrain with minimal protection behind sandbags and surrounded by heavily armed groups occupying both nearby tall buildings and also the hills and mountains ringing the airport and the city. The U.S. marines also held a strategic target long coveted by the warring factions.

On April 1983 the American embassy in Beirut was bombed, resulting in the deaths of 63 people. The attack was an ominous sign for U.S. forces in Lebanon. In August after the Israelis had withdrawn from Beirut, U.S. forces engaged in fighting with both Druze and Shiite militias.

In September 1983 the United States interceded on behalf of Lebanese president Amin Jumayyil's army, which was battling Druze militias in the village of Suq al Gharb in the mountains above Beirut. This took the form of naval gunfire from ships of the U.S. Sixth Fleet off the Lebanese coast. This was followed up by French aerial bombardments. In so doing, the United States and France had been drawn into the Lebanese Civil War on the side of the Christian-led government. By now, most Lebanese Muslims were outraged by Western intervention in the conflict. In support of President Jumayyil's troops battling Druze fighters, U.S. naval gunfire shelled villages inhabited not only by the Druze but also by

Shiites and some Sunnis, causing significant civilian casualties. To many Lebanese Muslims as well as Muslims throughout the Middle East, America's intervention on behalf of a government they opposed ended any pretense of American neutrality, and in consequence attacks against the U.S. marines, along with the French and Italian forces, increased, as did kidnappings of Westerners.

On October 23, 1983, in apparent retaliation for the American shelling of mountain villages, a massive suicide truck bomb destroyed the U.S. Marine Corps barracks at the Beirut International Airport. The explosion killed 241 marines and wounded more than 100. An attack on the French Army barracks that same day killed 58 French soldiers. Islamic Jihad, a Shiite terrorist group allegedly armed and supported by Iran, claimed responsibility for both bombings. Continued attacks on the U.S. marines, increasing engagements between American and Syrian forces, and resurgent fighting in Beirut led President Reagan to withdraw the U.S. marines on February 26, 1984.

On May 30, 2003, a U.S. federal judge ruled that the suicide truck bombing of the U.S. Marine Corps barracks in Beirut had been carried out by the terrorist group Hezbollah with the approval and funding of Iran's government, giving the survivors and families of those killed in the attack the right to sue Iran for damages. Iran, however, continues to deny any responsibility for the bombing and has dismissed the ruling as nonsense.

STEFAN M. BROOKS

See also

Arafat, Yasser; Habib, Philip; Hezbollah; Islamic Jihad, Palestinian; Lebanon; Lebanon, Civil War in; Lebanon, Israeli Invasion of; Palestine Liberation Organization; Reagan Administration, Middle East Policy

References

El-Khazen, Farid. *The Breakdown of the State in Lebanon, 1967–1976.* Cambridge: Harvard University Press, 2000.

Fisk, Robert. *Pity the Nation: The Abduction of Lebanon.* 4th ed. New York: Nation Books, 2002.

Harris, William. *The New Face of Lebanon: History's Revenge.* Princeton, NJ: Markus Wiener, 2005.

Mackey, Sandra. *Lebanon: A House Divided.* New York: Norton, 2006.

Olson, Steven P. *The Attack on U.S. Marines in Lebanon on October 23, 1983.* New York: Rosen, 2003.

Libby, I. Lewis
Birth Date: August 22, 1950

Attorney, author, leader in the neoconservative movement, and the central figure in the Valerie Plame Wilson incident. I. "Scooter" Lewis Libby was born in New Haven, Connecticut, on August 22, 1950. Lewis has never divulged publicly his actual first name, using only the initial "I." He grew up in an affluent family and graduated from the exclusive Philips Academy (Andover, Massachusetts) in 1968. He enrolled at Yale University, from which he graduated magna cum laude in 1972, and then earned a law degree from Columbia University School of Law in 1975. While an undergraduate at Yale, Libby was greatly impressed and influenced by a young political science professor there, Paul Wolfowitz, who would later become deputy secretary of defense in the George W. Bush administration. Libby began a lifelong friendship and mentorship with Wolfowitz and also began to write a novel during his Yale days, which was ultimately published as *The Apprentice* in 1996. Despite his connection with Wolfowitz, as a young man Libby had Democratic leanings, and he worked in Massachusetts governor Michael Dukakis's gubernatorial campaign.

From 1975 to 1981 Libby practiced law with a prestigious law firm, becoming a junior partner in 1976. With the advent of the Republican Ronald Reagan administration, Wolfowitz invited Libby to join him on the State Department's influential policy planning staff, an opportunity that Libby believed he could not refuse. He remained in the State Department until 1985, at which time he left government service to take up the practice of law. In 1989 he again entered government service, this time with the Department of Defense working for Wolfowitz as deputy undersecretary for strategy and resources. In 1992 Libby became deputy undersecretary for defense policy, a post he held until 1993, at which time he went back to private law practice. During his stints in government, Libby had become allied with both established and up-and-coming neoconservatives, including Secretary of Defense Donald Rumsfeld and future national security adviser and secretary of state Condoleezza Rice. In the late 1990s Libby was active in the Project for the New American Century, a favored group of neoconservatives.

In 2001 Libby joined the George W. Bush administration, serving as an adviser to the president and, more importantly, as chief of staff for Vice President Richard B. Cheney. Libby's role in the West Wing was a large one, and he had considerable access to policy-making decisions. He was a staunch defender of Cheney, and the two men were reportedly very close both professionally and personally. From 2001 to 2003 Libby also played a significant role on the Defense Policy Board Advisory Committee, which was chaired by the vaunted neoconservative Richard Perle. Libby was reportedly much involved in the formulation of U.S.-Israeli policies and had a direct role in the promulgation of the so-called Road Map to Peace in late 2002 and early 2003. Libby, unlike some of his fellow neoconservatives, kept a very low profile while in office; he rarely granted interviews and preferred to work behind the scenes, in which he was especially adept.

Libby's greatest role in the Bush administration came in the Valerie Plame Wilson incident, a multiyear saga that embroiled the White House in a Central Intelligence Agency (CIA) leak case that was allegedly undertaken in retribution for Ambassador Joseph Wilson's unflattering comments made about the Iraq War in July 2003. Valerie Plame, who at the time was a covert CIA operations officer, was Wilson's wife. It was alleged that Libby had a direct role in revealing the identity of Plame during interviews he granted with Judith Miller, a reporter for the *New York*

Times, in July 2003. They took place in the immediate aftermath of an op-ed piece that Wilson wrote for that same newspaper in which he questioned the legitimacy of the Bush administration's claims concerning Iraqi attempts to buy enriched uranium from Niger, claims that had been strongly disputed by Plame and some of her colleagues. Wilson also questioned other justifications for the March 2003 invasion of Iraq. Knowingly revealing the identity of an undercover intelligence officer is a federal offense.

When questioned by Federal Bureau of Investigation (FBI) agents and testifying before a federal grand jury, Libby claimed that he had learned of Plame's identity from a television reporter and had "forgotten" that Vice President Cheney had previously told him about Plame's identity. In September and October 2005 Libby's story began to fall apart. It was soon revealed to the special counsel investigating the case that Libby had had numerous conversations about Plame, including ones with Miller in which he divulged her identity. Other contradicting testimony led investigators to believe that Libby had not, in fact, learned the identity of Plame from a television reporter. As a result, on October 28, 2005, Libby was indicted on five felony counts: obstruction of justice, making false statements to FBI officers (two counts), and perjury in his grand jury testimony (two counts). He immediately resigned from the White House staff. On March 6, 2007, Libby was convicted of four of the five counts against him. Libby's lawyers filed appeals and indicated that they would seek a retrial, although they decided against the latter.

On June 5, 2007, Libby was sentenced to 30 months in prison and a $250,000 fine. He was also disbarred and will not be able to practice law in the future. On July 2 President Bush commuted Libby's sentence, terming it "excessive." While the commutation saved Libby from a prison term, the $250,000 fine remains, as do the felony convictions themselves. Only if Libby were to be issued a full pardon would his record be wiped clean. From January 6, 2006, to March 7, 2007, Libby served as a senior adviser to the Hudson Institute. He is not now actively engaged in work and may be working on his memoirs. Many believed that Libby's conviction was at least in part politically motivated and that he was a scapegoat for higher-ranking members of the Bush White House. Indeed, Cheney never testified at any of the legal proceedings, and it is still unclear who actually initiated the leak.

PAUL G. PIERPAOLI JR.

See also

Bush, George Walker; Cheney, Richard Bruce; Neoconservatism; Niger, Role in Origins of the Iraq War; Perle, Richard; Rice, Condoleezza; Rumsfeld, Donald Henry; Wilson, Joseph Carter, IV; Wilson, Valerie Plame; Wolfowitz, Paul Dundes

References

Plame Wilson, Valerie. *Fair Game: My Life as a Spy, My Betrayal by the White House.* New York: Simon and Schuster, 2007.

Wilson, Joseph. *The Politics of Truth: Inside the Lies That Led to War and Betrayed My Wife's CIA Identity.* New York: Carroll and Graf, 2004.

Woodward, Bob. *State of Denial: Bush at War, Part III.* New York: Simon and Schuster, 2006.

Liberty Incident
Event Date: June 8, 1967

On June 8, 1967, the electronic intelligence-gathering ship USS *Liberty* was attacked by Israeli Air Force and naval units while it was on patrol 13 nautical miles off El Arish on Egypt's Sinai peninsula. The reasons for the attack and charges of a cover-up have been the topics of conspiracy theories, but numerous inquiries in both the United States and Israel have concluded that the attack resulted from mistaken identity, and this remains the official U.S. government position.

The U.S. Navy acquired the 7,725-ton civilian cargo ship *Simmons Victory* and converted it into an auxiliary technical research ship (AGTR). The conversion was completed in 1965, and the ship was renamed the *Liberty* (AGTR-5). Initially it operated off the west coast of Africa. With the Six-Day War in June 1967, the *Liberty* was directed to collect electronic intelligence on Israeli and Arab military activities from the eastern Mediterranean. Commander William L. McGonagle had command.

The attack occurred on the fourth day of the war. On June 4, the day before the start of the war, the Israeli government had asked the United States if it had any ships in the area. Washington responded that it did not because the *Liberty* was only then entering the Mediterranean.

By June 8 the Israelis had routed Egyptian forces in the Sinai Desert and Jordanian forces on the West Bank and were preparing to move aggressively against Syria. The Israelis, aware that their coastlines were vulnerable to naval attack, had warned the United States to keep its ships at a safe distance.

The *Liberty* was off the coast monitoring communications. Responding to the Israeli warning, Washington had sent several warnings to the *Liberty* not to close within 100 miles of the coast, but these messages were rerouted because of an overloaded U.S. Navy communications system and did not reach the ship before the Israeli attack.

A series of explosions in El Arish, which had been recently captured by the Israelis, led the Israelis to conclude that the town was being shelled by an Egyptian ship. It was later determined that the explosions had occurred accidentally in an abandoned ammunition dump. Israeli aircraft patrolling off the coast nonetheless mistakenly identified the *Liberty* as an Egyptian vessel. There was no wind, and a large U.S. flag flying from the *Liberty* was drooping and not identifiable. Identification markings on the side and stern of the ship were apparently not visible to the Israeli pilots, who attacked the ship head-on.

The Israeli attack began at 1:57 p.m. local time on June 8. Two or three Israeli Air Force planes, probably Dassault Mirage IIIs, strafed the ship with 30-millimeter cannon fire. The first Israeli pilot to reach the ship was Yiftav Spector, one of Israel's leading aces. This attack was followed by a comparable number of Dessault Mystères, which dropped napalm. More than 800 bullet holes were later counted in the ship's hull. Some 20 minutes later three Israeli

Gunfire and rocket damage to the U.S. Navy intelligence-gathering ship *Liberty*, inflicted when it came under attack by Israeli forces off the Sinai Peninsula on June 8, 1967. (U.S. Navy)

torpedo boats arrived on the scene, and members of the *Liberty*'s crew opened fire on them with two .50-caliber machine guns in the mistaken belief that the ship was under Egyptian attack.

McGonagle could not signal the Israeli vessels, as all the ship's signal lights had been destroyed. The Israeli torpedo boats fired a number of torpedoes at the *Liberty*, one of which struck the ship on its starboard side and opened a large hole. The torpedo boats then approached to closer range and opened up with machine-gun fire against the American sailors, some of whom were attempting to launch life rafts. The torpedo boats then left the area.

The Israelis claimed that they did not know the *Liberty* was a U.S. ship until a life raft with U.S. Navy markings was found drifting in the water. Three hours after the attack, the Israeli government informed the U.S. embassy in Tel Aviv of events. Although the *Liberty* had been badly damaged, its crew managed to keep the ship afloat. The *Liberty* was able to make its way to Malta under its own power, escorted by ships of the U.S. Sixth Fleet.

Thirty-four American personnel died in the attack, and another 172 were wounded, many seriously. For his heroism and leadership, Commander McGonagle, who was wounded early in the attack, was subsequently awarded the Medal of Honor. His ship received the Presidential Unit Citation. Following stopgap repairs,

the *Liberty* returned to the United States and was decommissioned in 1968. It was scrapped in 1970.

The Israeli government later apologized and paid nearly $13 million in compensation. Those dissatisfied with the official inquiries in the United States and Israel have speculated that the Israelis knew that they were attacking a U.S. ship and did so because they feared that intercepts by the *Liberty* would reveal that Israel was about to attack Syria. But such a theory fails to explain why Israel would risk the anger of its only superpower sympathizer. Knowledge of the imminent Israeli attack on Syria was also widespread and hardly a secret by June 8.

PAUL WILLIAM DOERR AND SPENCER C. TUCKER

See also
Arab-Israeli Conflict, Overview

References
Bamford, James. *Body of Secrets: Anatomy of the Ultra Secret National Security Agency.* New York: Anchor, 2002.

Cristol, A. Jay. *The Liberty Incident: The 1967 Israeli Attack on the US Navy Spy Ship.* Washington, DC: Brassey's, 2002.

Ennis, James M., Jr. *Assault on the Liberty: The True Story of the Israeli Attack on an American Intelligence Ship.* New York: Random House, 1979.

Oren, Michael B. *Six Days of War: June 1967 and the Making of the Modern Middle East.* Novato, CA: Presidio, 2003.

Rabin, Yitzhak. *The Rabin Memoirs.* 1st English-language ed. Boston: Little, Brown, 1979.

Libya

Predominantly Muslim North African nation covering 679,358 square miles whose 2008 population was 6.174 million people. Libya borders Niger, Chad, and Sudan to the south; Tunisia and the Mediterranean Sea to the north; Algeria to the west; and Egypt to the east. The Ottoman Empire ruled Libya for much of the 19th century, but in 1907 Italy began to assert itself in the region. After a brief war with the Turks during 1911–1912, Italy gained control of Libya. A 20-year Libyan insurgency resulted, and Italy did not pacify the colony until 1931.

Libya saw significant fighting in the North African campaigns of World War II until it was ultimately secured by British forces in 1943. At the end of the war Libya's status was immersed in the larger question of the fate of European colonial possessions in the Middle East and Africa. Ultimately, in 1949 the United Nations (UN) passed a resolution in favor of an independent Libya. Negotiations among the varied regions in Libya proved delicate. Those in and around Tripoli supported a large degree of national unity, while the more established government of Cyrenaica preferred a federal system and insisted on choosing the monarch. The process resulted in a constitutional monarchy, an elected bicameral parliament, and a federal system of government. Emir Idris of Cyrenaica was named hereditary king of Libya, and final independence was declared on December 24, 1951.

The new Kingdom of Libya had strong links to the West. Both Britain and the United States maintained military bases on its soil and helped support the state financially. Libya also had a strong Arab identity and joined the Arab League in 1953.

Arab nationalist movements grew in response to the 1948 creation of Israel, and Libya had experienced de-Arabization and a conflict of identity during the oppressive years of Italian colonization. The emergence of Gamal Abdel Nasser's Arab nationalist regime in Egypt by 1954 and its advocacy of Arab unity and socialism encouraged the growth of similar political thought in Libya, and the 1956 Suez Crisis only increased this trend. The discovery of oil in the late 1950s transformed the country, endowing it with wealth and increased geopolitical significance. Oil exports reached $1 billion by 1968.

The June 1967 Six-Day War proved a turning point for Libyan politics. On June 5, 1967, the day hostilities began, anti-Jewish and anti-Western riots broke out in Tripoli. When Nasser claimed that the Arab defeat was because of American and British assistance to Israel, Libyan oil workers refused to load Western tankers. The Libyan prime minister was forced to resign, and the king appointed a new cabinet.

In the months after the war, the Libyan government was under continued pressure from Arab nationalists. Libya pledged financial aid to Egypt and Jordan and demanded the closing of all foreign bases on Libyan soil (although the demand was not pressed). On July 31, 1969, a group of junior army officers seized power while the king was out of the country. The Revolution Command Council, headed by Colonel Muammar Qaddafi, took control with little opposition.

Qaddafi, an adherent of Nasser's version of Arab nationalism, stressed Arab unity, opposition to Western imperialism, and socialist economic policies. Qaddafi maintained that this agenda could be reconciled with a strong emphasis on an Islamic way of life and an Islamic political and economic system. He rejected the Western presence in the Middle East but also rejected communism and socialism. After Nasser's death, Qaddafi actively sought leadership in the Muslim world in the 1970s, promoting his so-called Third International Theory, a claim that Libya and Islam present a middle way between the communism of the Soviet Union and the capitalism of the West. Although he succeeded in convincing more than 30 African countries to reject relations with Israel, he never gained the confidence of certain other Muslim nations, perhaps because of his repression of the Muslim Brotherhood and other Muslim figures in Libya or more likely because of his advancement of radical causes and interference in regional politics.

Always an enemy of Zionism, Qaddafi supported Yasser Arafat's Fatah faction of the Palestine Liberation Organization (PLO) and sponsored terrorist attacks against Israel and related Western targets. As the 1970s progressed Qaddafi voiced his support for anticolonialist movements around the world, including the Irish Republican Army (IRA), and Libya played host to a number of insurgent groups. Qaddafi also sought to build up the Libyan

Residents in the old market in Tripoli, Libya, on August 15, 2000. (AP/Wide World Photos)

military and pursued significant arms purchases from France and the Soviet Union after 1970.

Internally, Qaddafi sought to remake Libyan society, insisting that a mixture of socialism and Islam would ensure social justice. He created a welfare state based on oil revenues and reformed the legal system to include elements of Sharia (Islamic law). His *Green Book* (1976) laid out his political and economic philosophy. In it he rejected representative government in favor of direct democracy. Finally, he transformed Libya's oil industry by insisting on a larger share of profits from international oil companies, setting a pattern that would be imitated by other oil-rich states.

Despite Qaddafi's radical politics, Libya and the United States avoided direct confrontation for much of the 1970s because of their economic relationship. This changed, however, when Libya vehemently opposed the 1978 Camp David Accords. Qaddafi viewed any Arab rapprochement with Israel as a betrayal. In 1977 President Jimmy Carter's administration listed Libya, Cuba, and North Korea as states that supported terrorism. U.S.-Libyan relations continued to sour. On December 2, 1979, rioters targeted the U.S. embassy in Tripoli in imitation of the attack on the U.S. embassy in Tehran earlier that year. As a result, in May 1980 the United States withdrew its diplomatic personnel from Libya.

With the election of President Ronald Reagan in 1980, relations chilled further. On May 6, 1981, the Reagan administration expelled Libyan diplomats from the United States. The administration also pursued a freedom of navigation policy and challenged Libya's 1973 claims of sovereignty over the Gulf of Sidra in the Mediterranean. On July 19, 1981, the *Nimitz* carrier battle group was patrolling near the Gulf when two of the carrier's Grumman F-14 Tomcat fighters were approached and attacked by two Libyan Soviet-made Sukhoi Su-22 fighter jets. The American planes evaded the attack and shot down both Libyan aircraft.

Tensions increased further, and in March 1982 the United States banned the import of Libyan oil. The sanctions had limited effect, however, as European nations did not adopt U.S. policies. Qaddafi continued to support revolutionary and terrorist activity. On April 5, 1986, an explosion in a Berlin nightclub killed 3 and injured 200, including 63 U.S. servicemen. The United States claimed Libyan involvement and retaliated with great ferocity. On April 15, 1986, U.S. Air Force and U.S. Navy planes bombed five targets in Libya. One of the targets was Qaddafi's home. He escaped injury, but an adopted daughter was killed in the raid.

The Reagan administration maintained that the raid resulted in significant disruptions to Libyan-supported terrorism, and such activity did decline for a number of years. However, on December 21, 1988, Pan Am Flight 103 was destroyed over Lockerbie, Scotland, by a terrorist bomb. More than 270 people died, and subsequent investigations pointed to 2 Libyan men as primary suspects. When the Qaddafi regime refused to extradite the men for arrest and trial, the UN imposed sanctions on Libya in 1992. American confrontations with Libya continued, and a second incident over the Gulf of Sidra resulted in the destruction of two Libyan MiG-23 fighter planes in January 1989. At the end of the Cold War, the Qaddafi regime remained steadfast in its support of revolutionary movements and terrorist actions against Israel and the West.

In recent years Qaddafi has reversed himself in many positions in order to reconstitute his relations with the West, including turning over the men responsible for the Pan Am bombing and agreeing to pay restitution to victims' families. However, in August 2009 when Abdelbaset Ali Mohmed Al Megrahi was released from prison in Scotland on compassionate grounds because he was judged not to have long to live, Qaddafi arranged a hero's welcome for the convicted Pan Am bomber on his return to Libya.

After the September 2001 terrorist attacks on the United States, Qaddafi issued a stinging denunciation of the acts and condemned Al Qaeda and other terrorist groups. In February 2004 Libya declared that it would renounce its weapons of mass destruction (WMDs) program and comply with the Nuclear Non-Proliferation Treaty. This began a significant thaw in relations with the United States. The two countries resumed diplomatic relations that June, and the United States and the UN lifted all remaining economic sanctions in September 2004.

The George W. Bush administration has used Libya as an example of how tough policies toward rogue states, such as Iran and North Korea, can have dramatically positive results. Critics of Bush's hard-line foreign policy, however, point out that Libya's behavior was changed not because of an Iraq-style military invasion but rather because of firm diplomatic and economic pressure applied by the international community as a whole.

ROBERT S. KIELY

See also

Arab-Israeli Conflict, Overview; Arab League; Arab Nationalism; Nasser, Gamal Abdel; Palestine Liberation Organization; Qaddafi, Muammar; Suez Crisis; Terrorism

References

Cooley, John. *Libyan Sands: The Complete Account of Qaddafi's Revolution.* New York: Holt, Rinehart and Winston, 1982.
Simons, Geoff. *Libya and the West: From Independence to Lockerbie.* London: I. B. Tauris, 2004.
Wright, John. *Libya: A Modern History.* Baltimore: Johns Hopkins University Press, 1981.

Lifton, Robert Jay
Birth Date: May 16, 1926

Psychiatrist, prolific author, psychohistorian, and critic of modern war. Born in New York City on May 16, 1926, Robert Jay Lifton, the son of a physicist, attended Cornell University and obtained his M.D. degree from New York Medical College in 1948. He interned at Jewish Hospital in Brooklyn (1948–1949) and performed his residency in psychiatry at Downstate Medical Center (1949–1951). Lifton served in the U.S. Air Force from 1951 through 1953, six months of which he served in the Republic of Korea (ROK, South Korea). His study of prisoners of war who had allegedly been subjected to "brainwashing" during the Korean War led to further research on the subject and his first book, *Thought Reform and the Psychology of Totalism: A Study of "Brainwashing" in China* (1961).

On his return to the United States in 1953, Lifton worked on the faculty of the Washington (D.C.) School of Psychiatry (1954–1955). He then received an appointment as associate in psychiatry and in East Asian Studies at Harvard University (1956–1961). In 1961 he was appointed to the Foundation Fund for Psychiatric Research professorship at Yale University, and in 1985 he became distinguished professor of psychiatry and psychology, as well as director of the Center on Violence and Human Survival at John Jay College of Criminal Justice, City University of New York.

Lifton is well known for his work in the 1970s on post-traumatic stress disorder (PTSD). He had previously studied survivors of the World War II Holocaust, the 1945 Hiroshima and Nagasaki atomic bombings, and prisoner-of-war camps in the Democratic People's Republic of Korea (DPRK, North Korea). During the Vietnam War, he participated in a number of antiwar activities, including the 1970 Winter Soldier Investigation, a media event in Detroit at which members of Vietnam Veterans Against the War (VVAW) attested to atrocities they claimed to have committed or witnessed, and the

1971 Operation DEWEY CANYON III, at which veterans discarded their medals on the Capitol steps in Washington, D.C. In December 1970 Lifton began a series of "rap groups," or group therapy sessions, with members of the New York chapter of VVAW. From these sessions grew most of the subsequent definitions and treatment methods for PTSD, including the Vet Centers established in 1979 as part of the Veterans Administration (VA) system.

In 1972, with the National Council of Churches, Lifton sponsored the "First National Conference on the Emotional Needs of Vietnam-Era Veterans," attended by national VA officials. In 1973 he published his landmark book on the subject, *Home from the War,* based on his work with the New York rap groups. The book has since been reissued several times and is frequently cited not only in professional literature but also in the popular media. In 1976 Lifton headed the American Psychiatric Association's task force to develop a description of PTSD for the *Diagnostic and Statistical Manual;* the task force's work, also based on Lifton's own work with the New York rap groups, was published in 1980.

A consistent critic of modern war and the ideology behind it, Lifton next turned his attention to the study of state-sponsored euthanasia and genocide. His 1986 book, *The Nazi Doctors,* was the first in-depth study of how German medical professionals were able to rationalize and justify their roles in medical experimentation and the Holocaust during the 1930s and 1940s. The book was well received and widely read by experts and general readers alike. Lifton also became a vocal opponent of nuclear weapons and nuclear war-fighting strategy, arguing that nuclear war makes mass genocide banal and thus conceivable, raising the likelihood of an actual nuclear exchange.

In his 1999 book, *Destroying the World to Save It,* Lifton posits that the possibility exists for the rise of an apocalyptic terrorist cult, steeped in totalist ideologies, that could hold most or all of the world hostage. After the September 11, 2001, terror attacks on the United States, Lifton rejected the term "War on Terror" as one that has little meaning and destroys "all vulnerability." At the same time, he acknowledged that terrorism in the 21st century is a serious concern, especially with nuclear proliferation. Lifton has spoken out repeatedly against the Iraq War (2003–), arguing that it, like the Vietnam War, is driven by an irrational and aggressive strain in U.S. foreign policy that uses the politics of fear to rationalize wars in which the nation's vital interests are not at stake. His 2003 book, *Superpower Syndrome: America's Apocalyptic Confrontation with the World,* takes up these very themes.

PHOEBE S. SPINRAD

See also

Antiwar Movements, Persian Gulf and Iraq Wars; Global War on Terror; Post-Traumatic Stress Disorder; Terrorism

References

Kimnel, Michael S. "Prophet of Survival." *Psychology Today* (June 1988): 44.

Lifton, Robert J. *Death in Life: Survivors of Hiroshima.* New York: Random House, 1968.

———. *Home from the War: Vietnam Veterans, Neither Victims Nor Executioners.* New York: Simon and Schuster, 1973.

———. *Superpower Syndrome: America's Apocalyptic Confrontation with the World.* New York: Nation Books, 2003.

Lithuania, Role in Afghanistan and Iraq Wars

Baltic nation and Soviet republic until 1991. With a 2008 population of 3.565 million people, Lithuania covers 25,174 square miles. It borders the Baltic Sea, Russia, and Poland to the west; Belarus to the south and east; and Latvia to the north. The Lithuanian government is a presidential-parliamentary republic in which the president is popularly elected; the president in turn appoints the prime minister with the approval of parliament. The Lithuanian presidency is largely ceremonial, as the prime minister holds the preponderance of executive powers. The modern Lithuanian political landscape features numerous political parties, the most influential of them being the Homeland Union/Lithuanian Christian Democrats (conservative-Christian democratic), the Social Democratic Party, the National Resurrection Party (center-right), the Order and Justice (rightist), the Lithuanian Peasant Popular Union (conservative), and the New Union (center-left).

Along with its fellow Baltic states, Lithuania strongly supported the U.S.-led military operations in Afghanistan and Iraq. Following the end of the Cold War and independence, Lithuania pursued a foreign and security policy designed to integrate the former Soviet-occupied state into the broad institutional framework of the West. Successive Lithuanian governments perceived closer ties with the United States as the best means to counter any potential resurgent threat from Russia. Like the other Baltic states, Lithuania joined the North Atlantic Treaty Organization (NATO) Partnership for Peace program in 1994 and subsequently participated in NATO peacekeeping operations in the Balkans as it pursued full membership in the alliance. The nation joined both NATO and the European Union (EU) in 2004.

Lithuania offered the United States the use of its airspace and other logistical support following the September 11, 2001, terrorist attacks. In addition, Lithuania supported the invocation of NATO's collective defense clause, Article 5, in response to the attacks. Lithuania thereafter increased its peacekeeping units in Bosnia and Kosovo to allow U.S. forces to be redeployed to Afghanistan. Lithuania deployed 10 troops as part of a Danish-led contingent of transport handlers, which was stationed in Kyrgyzstan to support Operation ENDURING FREEDOM, and in November 2002 Lithuania sent a 40-member special operations force to Bagram air base in Afghanistan, where they operated under U.S. command. A second 40-member force was rotated into Afghanistan in the spring of 2003, but all combat forces were withdrawn that October. In 2003 Lithuania also dispatched a small medical team and logistics personnel to serve as part of the NATO-led

International Security Assistance Force (ISAF). The country has also provided humanitarian and medical aid to the Afghan national government.

Lithuania endorsed the U.S.-led invasion of Iraq in March 2003. In August 2003 Lithuania deployed elements of the Grand Duchess Birute Motorized Infantry Brigade to Hillah in central Iraq as part of the Polish-led Multi-National Force. The 50 troops were designated the Lithuanian Detachment (LITDET). A second platoon from the Grand Duke Algirdas Mechanized Infantry Battalion was stationed with the British forces in Basra and was deployed as part of a Danish-led unit. These troops were designated as the Lithuanian Contingent (LITCON). Both LITDET and LITCON conducted general security operations, including patrols and checkpoint service. They also supported humanitarian operations and reconstruction efforts. In addition, LITCON undertook ordnance disposal missions and training exercises with Iraqi security forces. Lithuania also dispatched a medical unit to operate on board the Spanish hospital ship *Galicijia* to support coalition operations and stationed staff officers as part of the coalition headquarters unit in Baghdad. There was also an 8-member logistics unit stationed at Tallil air base, south of Nasiriyah. Lithuania's peak troop strength in Iraq was approximately 120 soldiers. Prior to deployment in Iraq, Lithuanian forces underwent training and acclimation in Kuwait. In 2006 LITDET was withdrawn. The bulk of the remaining Lithuanian soldiers were withdrawn in December 2008 after the British announced further reductions to their troop strength in the region. No Lithuanian soldiers were killed during the country's Iraq deployment.

TOM LANSFORD

See also

Afghanistan, Coalition Combat Operations in, 2002–Present; International Security Assistance Force; IRAQI FREEDOM, Operation, Coalition Ground Forces; Multi-National Force–Iraq; North Atlantic Treaty Organization in Afghanistan

References

Cockburn, Patrick. *The Occupation: War and Resistance in Iraq.* New York: Verso, 2007.

Feickert, Andrew. *U.S. and Coalition Military Operations in Afghanistan: Issues for Congress.* Washington, DC: Congressional Research Service, 2006.

Keegan, John. *The Iraq War: The Military Offensive, from Victory in 21 Days to the Insurgent Aftermath.* New York: Vintage, 2005.

Logistics, Persian Gulf War

Logistics involves the procurement, maintenance, and transportation of matériel, personnel, and facilities during a military operation. The Iraqi invasion of Kuwait on August 2, 1990, surprised the United States and its allies. Following the decision to use force if necessary to dislodge the Iraqis, the major logistical challenge facing American military planners, or logisticians, was how to quickly create an infrastructure to support combat troops in Saudi Arabia, where a likely invasion force would be based. Fortunately, numerous preinvasion exercises that envisioned moving combat troops from the United States to Europe to contest a hypothetical Soviet invasion of Western Europe had provided planners with realistic practice. Those exercises had tested the ability to assemble and move large numbers of troops and equipment. Senior commanders such as Lieutenant General John Yeosock and Major General William Pagonis and their subordinates quickly applied their experience to Operation DESERT SHIELD.

The sheer distance from the United States to Saudi Arabia, about 8,000 miles, made the logistical challenge daunting. The head of U.S. Central Command (CENTCOM), General H. Norman Schwarzkopf, made the challenge even harder by insisting that the number of support personnel—the so-called logistical tail—be kept very low. In Schwarzkopf's view, every cook or typist who traveled to Saudi Arabia came at the expense of a combat soldier.

The logistical effort clearly benefited from the reduced threat that the Soviets posed in Europe. Because of the unlikelihood of a Soviet attack in Europe, planners were able to move confidently critical supplies from there to the Middle East. The host country, Saudi Arabia, supplemented the logistical effort by sharing its resources with allied forces. Saudi Arabia provided assets ranging from telecommunications to long-haul trucks and drivers as well as more than 1 million gallons of packaged petroleum products and 20 million meals. Likewise, American industry rallied to help fill critical needs, such as new fuses and warheads for the Patriot PAC-2 antimissile missiles and additional AGM-114A Hellfire antitank missiles.

Still, there were inevitable breakdowns and omissions. The tremendous influx of men and matériel overwhelmed Saudi ports and roads. Traffic clogged the ports and jammed the inland roads that served as the military's main supply routes, and many combat units were based in roadless regions. Movement across rock-strewn or sandy desert terrain destroyed tires and caused engine and transmission troubles. The solution was to exchange older utility cargo vehicles for newer heavy expanded-mobility tactical trucks and rugged, reliable off-road vehicles built by the Oshkosh Company of Wisconsin.

Numerous problems stemmed from the difficulty of communicating tremendous volumes of data from frontline units in Saudi Arabia to sources of supply in far-distant places. Many American logisticians working in Saudi Arabia simply ignored formal procedures and instead worked outside the system to directly contact supply centers back in the United States. In addition, the scale of the demands sometimes exceeded all supplies. For example, desert camouflage material remained in such short supply that most of the soldiers in the U.S. VII Corps entered battle clad in dark green instead of desert camouflage uniforms.

In spite of all the obstacles, during the course of Operation DESERT SHIELD, which lasted from August 1990 to January 1991, the U.S.

military moved and unloaded some 500 ships and 9,000 aircraft in Saudi ports and airfields. These delivered about 1,800 U.S. Army aircraft, 12,400 tracked vehicles, 114,000 wheeled vehicles, 38,000 containers, 1.8 million tons of cargo, 350,000 tons of ammunition, and more than 350,000 service personnel and civilians. From the Saudi ports, the supplies and men moved inland via 3,568 convoys of supply trucks that traveled some 35 million miles. In addition to moving along existing roads, the convoys drove along hundreds of miles of newly constructed roads. It was a stupendous logistical feat, the equivalent of moving the entire city of Atlanta, Georgia, more than 8,000 miles to Saudi Arabia.

During the Persian Gulf War, the military's high-profile combat elements—the Abrams tanks and AH-64 Apache helicopters—rightfully received the majority of attention and praise. However, the logistical effort that supported the combat elements was absolutely critical to victory. According to the official U.S. Army history of the war, the ability of civilians, soldiers, and leaders to demonstrate intelligent initiative made the logistical system work. The experience gleaned from this war led to new concepts and methods to move a large military force to a foreign land and sustain it once it arrived.

Because the Persian Gulf War took place in Iraq and Kuwait, Iraq had a much simpler logistical challenge, and its supply lines were within its own borders. Iraqi logisticians had ample time to prepare before Iraq invaded Kuwait on August 2, 1990. The farthest any unit had to move was about 460 miles. After Iraq conquered Kuwait, truck convoys stocked bunkers inside Kuwait with more than 320,000 tons of ammunition, enough to allow the Iraqi Army to fight for two weeks without supply. About 2 million tons of ammunition remained in Iraq as a reserve supply.

When DESERT STORM began on January 17, 1991, the Iraqi logistical challenges became harder. The allies had absolute control of the air, thus making all Iraqi movements on the ground perilous, and coalition powers had effected a tight naval blockade. However, because the war was so short, lasting only 45 days, the Iraqis seldom suffered from serious supply shortages.

JAMES ARNOLD

See also

DESERT SHIELD, Operation; DESERT STORM, Operation; Pagonis, William Gus; Yeosock, John J.

References

Dunnigan, James F., and Austin Bay. *From Shield to Storm: High-Tech Weapons, Military Strategy, and Coalition Warfare in the Persian Gulf.* New York: William Morrow, 1992.

Matthews, James K., and Cora J. Holt. *So Many, So Much, So Far, So Fast: United States Transportation Command and Strategic Deployment for Operation Desert Shield/Desert Storm.* Washington, DC: Joint History Office, Office of the Chairman of the Joint Chiefs of Staff and Research Center, United States Transportation Command, 1996.

Pagonis, William G., and Jeffrey Cruikshank. *Moving Mountains: Lessons in Leadership and Logistics from the Gulf War.* Cambridge: Harvard Business School Press, 1992.

Lott, Charles Trent
Birth Date: October 9, 1941

Republican U.S. congressman and senator from Mississippi and outspoken critic of Secretary of Defense Donald Rumsfeld's handling of the 2003 Iraq War. Born on October 9, 1941, in Grenada, Mississippi, Charles Trent Lott earned a BA degree and a law degree from the University of Mississippi in 1965 and 1967, respectively. From 1968 to 1972 he was administrative assistant to Congressman William H. Colmer, a leading segregationist in the Democratic Party. When Colmer announced his plans to retire, he supported Lott's campaign to fill his seat, even though Lott ran as a Republican.

Lott, who won the 1972 election by a wide margin, was only the second Republican from Mississippi elected to the U.S. Congress since Reconstruction. He was subsequently reelected to the House of Representatives seven times. From 1981 to 1989 Lott was the House minority whip.

Lott ran successfully for the U.S. Senate in 1989, replacing retiring Senator John C. Stennis. Lott became Senate majority leader in 1996 when Kansas senator Robert Dole resigned to run for president. In 1999 Lott led the unsuccessful impeachment process against President Bill Clinton in the Senate. During January 3–20,

Republican Trent Lott represented the state of Mississippi in the U.S. Senate from 1988 to 2007. He served as both minority and majority leader. He is now a Washington lobbyist. (U.S. Senate)

2001, Lott acted as temporary Senate minority leader because the 50–50 partisan split in the Senate allowed Vice President Al Gore to cast his vote with the Democrats. After George W. Bush became president, Vice President Dick Cheney was able to cast the tie-breaking vote, which once again allowed Lott to resume his position as Senate majority leader.

On December 5, 2002, at a celebration of South Carolina senator Strom Thurmond's 100th birthday, Lott made a speech that was interpreted by many to be an endorsement of Thurmond's earlier support of racial segregation. Following a highly publicized controversy, which included President Bush's criticism of Lott's remarks, Lott resigned as Senate majority leader on December 20, 2002. He subsequently became chairman of the Senate Rules Committee.

In the aftermath of the September 11, 2001, terrorist attacks on the United States, Lott wholeheartedly supported the Bush administration's Global War on Terror. Lott also championed the 2003 U.S.-led invasion of Iraq that removed Saddam Hussein from power. Although most political observers view Lott as neither a moderate nor a maverick Republican, in December 2004 he harshly criticized Secretary of Defense Donald H. Rumsfeld. Lott joined other Senate Republicans who found fault with the Rumsfeld Doctrine, which called for sending only a small force to Iraq to overthrow Hussein. Lott was especially critical of what he called Rumsfeld's failure to properly equip U.S. troops in Iraq and the lack of planning for the occupation of Iraq after the overthrow of Hussein's regime. Most importantly, Lott called for Rumsfeld's resignation within the year. The defense secretary did not resign until late 2006, however, after the Republicans lost control of both houses of Congress in the off-year November elections.

On December 18, 2007, Lott unexpectedly announced his resignation from the U.S. Senate less than one year into his six-year term. He stated that his decision was based on a desire to spend more time with his family and to pursue interests in the private sector. Many believe, however, that Lott's sudden departure had also been motivated by the recent indictment of his attorney brother-in-law Richard Scruggs. Scruggs was accused of having offered a $50,000 bribe to a Mississippi judge. There was no apparent connection between the bribery scheme and Lott, but Scruggs had represented Lott in a suit against an insurance company, which had initially refused to cover the loss of Lott's home in the aftermath of Hurricane Katrina in 2005. Lott is now a lobbyist in Washington, D.C.

MICHAEL R. HALL

See also

Bush, George Walker; Global War on Terror; IRAQI FREEDOM, Operation; Rumsfeld, Donald Henry; September 11 Attacks

References

Krames, Jeffrey A. *The Rumsfeld Way: The Leadership Wisdom of a Battle-Hardened Maverick.* New York: McGraw-Hill, 2002.

Lott, Trent. *Herding Cats: A Life in Politics.* New York: Regan Books, 2005.

Low-Altitude Navigation and Targeting Infrared for Night Targeting Pods

Integrated navigation and targeting pods used by the U.S. Air Force's Boeing F-15E Strike Eagle and General Dynamics/Lockheed F-16C/D Fighting Falcon and the U.S. Navy's Grumman F-14 Tomcat. The Low-Altitude Navigation and Targeting Infrared for Night (LANTIRN) targeting pods permit these aircraft to fly at night, at low attitudes, and in adverse weather to attack ground targets with a variety of precision-guided and unguided weapons.

The LANTIRN system consists of an integrated navigation pod and a targeting pod mounted externally beneath the aircraft. The AN/AAQ-13 navigation pod provides high-speed penetration and precision attack on tactical targets at night and in adverse weather. The navigation pod also has a terrain-following radar and a fixed infrared sensor that provides a visual cue and input to the aircraft's flight control system. As a result, the aircraft can maintain a preselected altitude above the terrain and avoid any obstacles. This sensor displays an infrared image on the pilot's head-up display. With the navigation pod, the pilot can fly following the contours of the terrain at high speed, using geographic features (e.g., mountains, valleys) and darkness to avoid detection. The pod houses the first wide-field, forward-looking infrared navigation system for air force air-superiority fighters.

The AN/AAQ-14 targeting pod has a high-resolution, forward-based infrared sensor that displays an infrared image of the target to the pilot, a laser designator-rangefinder for precise delivery of laser-guided bombs, a missile bore-sight correlator for automatic lock-on of AGM-65D imaging infrared Maverick missiles, and software for automatic target tracking. With Maverick missiles, the pods automatically hand the target off to the missile for launch, with the pilot's consent. For laser-guided munitions, the pilot aims the laser designator and the bomb guides itself to the target. For a conventional bomb, the pilot may employ the laser to determine range; the pod then supplies the range data to the aircraft's fire-control system. These features simplify the functions of target detection and recognition and attack, and permit pilots of single-seat fighters to home in on targets with precision-guided weapons during a single pass.

In September 1980 the air force awarded a research and development contract to Martin Marietta Corporation (now Lockheed Martin, Inc). The contractor completed the initial operational tests and evaluation of the LANTIRN navigation pod in December 1984, and the air force approved low-rate initial production in March 1985 and full-rate production in November 1986. The first production navigation pod was delivered on March 31, 1987.

In April 1986 the initial operational test and evaluation of the LANTIRN targeting pod proved the feasibility of a low-altitude, night, adverse-weather, precision-attack mission. The air force approved low-rate initial production in June 1986. Introduction of the LANTIRN system revolutionized night warfare by denying enemy forces the sanctuary of darkness.

A U.S. Navy F/A-18F Super Hornet conducts a mission over the Persian Gulf in 2005. The Hornet is armed with an AIM-9 Sidewinder missile on the wingtip and an AGM-65 Maverick missile on the pylon. Tucked under the intake is an AAQ-14 LANTIRN (Low-Altitude Navigation and Targeting Infrared for Night) pod. (U.S. Department of Defense)

After the navy decided to phase out the Grumman A-6 Intruder carrier-based ground-attack aircraft by mid-1996, it requested modifications to include a Global Positioning System (GPS) and an inertial navigation subsystem in the AN/AAQ-14 targeting pod so that its F-14 Tomcat could use the LANTIRN pods. Equipped with the LANTIRN system, the VF-103 strike fighter squadron, deployed aboard USS *Enterprise* (CVN-65), became operational with the LANTIRN pods in June 1996 and saw some action in Bosnia (1999) and Iraq (2003). Eventually, the U.S. Navy modified 210 F-14 Tomcat aircraft to utilize the LANTIRN targeting pods to give them ground-attack capability.

In August 1990, when the Iraqi army invaded Kuwait and the United States began Operation DESERT SHIELD and Operation DESERT STORM, the air force had only one precision-guided munitions-capable wing, the 4th Tactical Fighter Wing (TFW), based at Seymour-Johnson Air Force Base, North Carolina. It consisted of two squadrons of F-15E Strike Eagles. One squadron had just received its LANTIRN navigation pods, and the other squadron received its targeting pods in September 1990 and did not deploy to the Persian Gulf theater until December. As a result, the LANTIRN

targeting pod underwent its operational testing in the actual combat of the DESERT STORM air campaign. Additionally, there were only 72 LANTIRN navigation pods available for use by two squadrons of F-16s. As a result, the majority of the F-16s that participated in the air campaign had to rely on General Dynamics F-111 Aardvark and F-15E aircraft to "paint" targets for their laser-guided bombs.

The LANTIRN pods provided aircraft with the ability to conduct low-altitude, high-speed night attacks, a mission for which pre–DESERT STORM air force pilots had not been trained. In December 1990 the U.S. Air Force conducted an in-theater night-training exercise, Operation NIGHT CAMEL, to determine whether infrared-equipped aircraft could carry out night interdiction against supply lines and cluster-bomb attacks against armor. The exercise confirmed the ability of LANTIRN-equipped aircraft to carry out low-altitude interdiction attacks at night. It also led to the discovery of images of armored vehicles on the cockpit video-tapes of F-111s, equipped with the infrared sensor PAVE TACK, (General Dynamics) F-5Es (Tiger IIs), and F-16Cs, equipped with LANTIRN pods. The infrared sensor of the LANTIRN (and the PAVE TACK) targeting pod had picked up the "hotter" signature of the vehicles because desert sand cools faster at night than do metal vehicles.

When the air campaign began in January 1991, the LANTIRN-equipped F-15Es (and the F-111s with the PAVE TACK) used this new information to attack, with GBU-12 500-pound laser-guided bombs, tanks that the Iraqi army had covered with sand, thinking that the sand would camouflage them. This tactic soon became known as "tank plinking," a term that stuck until General H. Norman Schwarzkopf, commander of Central Command (CENT-COM), ordered that the term "tank busting" be used instead. Very quickly the Iraqi tank crews realized that they were no longer safe in their tanks and began sleeping on the ground outside of them. During the air campaign, U.S. Air Force aircraft destroyed up to 500 Iraqi armored vehicles daily. The Iraqis, as well as most other armies and military thinkers, discovered that, with the arrival of the new infrared targeting pods and laser-guided bombs, armies had lost the advantages of digging into the ground and dispersing forces, or massing only at night.

Additionally, LANTIRN-equipped air force aircraft played significant roles in two other DESERT STORM operations. LANTIRN-equipped F-15Es participated in the hunt for Iraqi mobile Scud-missile transporter-erector-launchers (TELs) in the western desert area of Iraq. On January 18, 1991, Iraq initiated a series of Scud missile attacks against Israel, Saudi Arabia, and Bahrain. While these low-accuracy, low-reliability weapons produced few tactical results, the Scud attacks posed a major strategic threat, since the Arab countries would surely desert the fragile anti-Iraq coalition if Israel decided to retaliate militarily.

To counter the Scud threat, the United States sent a number of anti-missile Patriot missile batteries to Israel, deployed U.S. and British special operations teams into the western desert, and allocated some 2,500 sorties (about 8 percent of all combat flights) against the mobile TELs in the western desert of Iraq. Among the aircraft used for the Scud hunt were 12 F-15Es in three flights of two pairs of aircraft each. Usually one of the F-15Es of the pair had a LANTIRN targeting pod to designate prospective targets for attack by a GBU-10 bomb, as required. Unfortunately, the F-15Es could not identify and acquire the TELs, whose infrared and radar signatures were virtually indistinguishable from trucks and other electromagnetic "clutter" in the Iraqi desert and were relatively easy to mask. The difficulty of identifying and destroying the Scud TELs is demonstrated by the fact that on the 42 occasions during the war when orbiting aircraft visually sighted mobile TELs, in only 8 instances could they identify the targets sufficiently to release their weapons. The great Scud hunt was a tactical and operational-level failure, as coalition aircraft destroyed few Scud TELs. However, in the long run, the coalition's overall anti-Scud effort achieved its strategic objective because it sufficiently convinced the Israeli government that it did not have to retaliate against Iraq.

On the night of February 26–27, 1991, a Northrop-Grumman E-8 Sentry Joint Surveillance and Target Attack Radar System aircraft discovered hundreds of Iraqi vehicles on Highway 80 between Kuwait and Basra, Iraq, headed for the Iraqi border to avoid being cut off by the coalition ground offensive. Numerous coalition aircraft, including 12 LANTIRN-equipped F-15Es, attacked the long line of Iraqi military vehicles and stolen Kuwaiti civilian vehicles, destroying in the process more than 2,000 vehicles and killing an unknown and disputed number of Iraqi soldiers and civilians. The scenes of carnage on the so-called Highway of Death remain some of the most recognizable images of the war. LANTIRN pods played a relatively small role during Operation IRAQI FREEDOM in 2003 owing to the short duration of the conflict and the badly degraded condition of Iraqi forces.

ROBERT B. KANE

See also

Aircraft, Attack; Aircraft, Bombers; Aircraft, Fighters; Bombs, Gravity; Bombs, Precision-Guided; DESERT STORM, Operation, Coalition Air Campaign; Scud Missiles, U.S. Search for during the Persian Gulf War

References

Davis, Richard G. On Target: Organizing and Executing the Strategic Air Campaign against Iraq. Washington, DC: U.S. Air Force History and Museums Program, 2002.

Hallion, Richard P. Storm over Iraq: Air Power and the Gulf War. Washington, DC: Smithsonian Institution Press, 1997.

Jamieson, Perry D. Lucrative Targets: The U.S. Air Force in the Kuwaiti Theater of Operations. Washington, DC: U.S. Air Force History and Museums Program, 2001.

Kearney, Thomas A., and Eliot A. Cohen. Gulf Air Power Survey Summary Report. Washington, DC: Department of the Air Force, 1993.

Low-Altitude Safety and Targeting Enhancement System

A computer system developed for the A-10 Thunderbolt II fighter aircraft that allows the pilot to deliver ordnance more accurately. From the advent of aerial warfare, the world's air forces have constantly tried to improve weapons-delivery accuracy. Early attempts began in World War I, with direct pilot inputs to compensate for wind variations. The United States introduced the Norden Bombsight during World War II, which became the first primitive computerized weapons-delivery system. Both world wars witnessed numerous aircraft flying in formation to maximize the destructive power of their bombs. In the last several decades, the U.S. military establishment has made drastic improvements in accuracy and delivery methods, eliminating the need for mass bombardment efforts.

Because the A-10's primary role is to support ground personnel, the safe and accurate delivery of weapons close to friendly forces is crucial. The Low-Altitude Safety and Targeting Enhancement System (LASTE) computer, with its highly accurate delivery system, has allowed one aircraft to do the same job that once required numerous aircraft. While LASTE was not fully operational during Operation DESERT STORM, it proved itself shortly thereafter when a LASTE-equipped A-10 won the U.S. Air Force Gunsmoke competition in 1991. Since then, the LASTE system has been used to support friendly troops in both Operation ENDURING FREEDOM and Operation IRAQI FREEDOM.

Originally designed by General Electric in the late 1980s to improve efficient weapons delivery while keeping pilots safe at low altitudes, the LASTE system consists of several smaller avionics programs that perform crucial functions for the A-10. LASTE's two main components include a Ground Collision Avoidance System (GCAS) and a computerized weapons-delivery system.

The GCAS acts as a warning to the pilot while operating at low altitudes. Information is relayed to the Heads-Up Display (HUD) via a radar altimeter when the aircraft passes through a preset altitude. Radar altitude displays the height above ground and is constantly changing as the aircraft flies. The HUD allows the pilot to focus attention outside the cockpit while flying at extremely low altitudes, attempting to minimize any possibility of colliding with the ground. When the aircraft passes through the designated altitude, a computerized voice tells the pilot to pull up.

The LASTE system also includes a simple autopilot system that can be used in both combat and training environments. The pilot has several different options when employing the Low-Altitude Autopilot (LAAP). If the pilot needs to circle over a specific target area, he or she can select "altitude hold," enabling the aircraft to be placed in a slight turn and allowed to circle overhead. Additionally, the pilot can also select "altitude/heading hold," which maintains a preset altitude and heading determined by the pilot.

The system also greatly improves munitions accuracy through a computerized weapons-delivery system that accounts for wind, aircraft speed, angle of attack, altitude, and bomb trajectory path. These elements are factored into a computer program that gives the pilot an exact aim point in the HUD. Theoretically, the bomb will fall wherever the pilot aims.

Two separate programs offer the pilot different options for ordnance delivery. The Continuously Computed Impact Point (CCIP) program allows the pilot to aim the aircraft at a specific point on the ground using computer symbology in the HUD. This program requires the pilot to dive at the target while almost directly overhead. The Continuously Computed Release Point (CCRP) program allows the pilot to loft or toss free-fall weapons from a greater distance while flying straight and level. This feature minimizes the pilot's exposure to ground-based antiaircraft artillery (AAA) and surface-to-air missiles (SAMs).

Finally, LASTE includes a Precision Attitude Control (PAC) program that compensates for gun vibration, wind variations, and other factors that cause discrepancies beyond the pilot's control. Used specifically when firing the GAU-30-millimeter Avenger Cannon, the PAC program ensures bullet accuracy by keeping the gunsight locked onto the target while the trigger is depressed. When engaged, the PAC program keeps the target on the aim point by moderately locking the flight controls. The aircraft will not stray from the gunsight without significant pilot input. Only when the trigger is released will the aircraft return to normal flight mode.

MATTHEW R. BASLER

See also

Aircraft, Attack; United States Air Force, Afghanistan War; United States Air Force, Iraq War; United States Air Force, Persian Gulf War

References

Department of the Air Force, Technical Order 1A-10–1. *Flight Manual: USAF Series A-10/OA-10A Aircraft.* Washington, DC: U.S. Government Printing Office, 1999.

Reflectone Training Systems. *LASTE V6 Manual: A10PLTIQ Academics, Version 1.1.* Davis-Monthan Air Force Base, AZ: Reflectone, 1999.

Smallwood, William L. *Warthog: Flying the A-10 in the Gulf War.* Washington, DC: Brassey's, 1993.

Loya Jirga, Afghanistan

The Pashto term *loya jirga* ("grand council") has Turco-Mongolian origins and originally meant "great tent." *Loya* (meaning "great" or "grand") and *jirga* (meaning "council, assembly, dispute, or meeting") subsequently became a phrase referring to large meetings held among certain central Asian peoples. In Persian it translated to "grand assembly."

In Afghanistan the councils served as a forum for political consensus-building among tribal elders. In Pashtun tradition, *loya jirgas* were held at critical moments to make or legitimize important decisions. The members of the Jirgas mostly belonged to the royal family, religious leaders, and Afghan tribal chiefs. Pashtun elders dominated the *loya jirgas* throughout most of Afghanistan's history. Eventually, other ethnic groups, including Tajiks and Hazaras, were allowed to attend as observers.

In the twentieth century *loya jirgas* were convened to deliberate about Afghanistan's role in World War I (1915), to approve the rules of business for the national council (1930), to decide Afghanistan's role in World War II (1941), and to resolve the Afghan relationship with Pakhtunistan in 1955 after Pakistan inherited the British role in the region. In 1977 Mohammad Daoud Khan convened a *loya jirga* to legitimize his rule, pass a new constitution, elect a new president, and obtain permission to found a new revolutionary political party. Following the Communist Revolution of 1978, and the subsequent Soviet invasion in December 1979, Afghanistan split into pro-Soviet and anti-Soviet factions.

From time to time during the period of Soviet occupation and subsequent Taliban rule, a variety of factions convened *loya jirgas.* Because the councils were either dominated by or heavily influenced by foreign powers, however, these *loya jirgas* did not enjoy popular credibility. The most influential of the rival *loya jirgas* was in Germany in 2001 and produced the Bonn Agreement,

Women delegates read an official statement during the Loya Jirga's opening session in Kabul, Afghanistan, on June 11, 2002. (AP/Wide World Photos)

which was brokered by the United Nations (UN). The agreement, reached in December, following the U.S. invasion of Afghanistan, established an Afghan Interim Authority and prepared the way for the establishment of a new Afghan constitution.

Following the U.S.-led overthrow of the Taliban on June 13, 2002, an emergency *loya jirga* took place in Kabul to select an interim government. In preparation for this meeting, the UN, in accordance with the Bonn Agreement, had supervised an initial round of elections for delegates to the Loya Jirga in Afghanistan. Local power struggles influenced these elections, leading to inevitable accusations of corruption and coercion. Each of Afghanistan's 362 districts had at least one seat, with a further seat allotted for every 22,000 people. No group was excluded, except for those alleged to have committed acts of terrorism or suspected of crimes. International pressure helped influence the rule that the Loya Jirga would guarantee seats for 160 women.

The Loya Jirga also assigned current government officials 53 seats, reserved 100 seats for Afghan refugees, reserved 6 more seats for internally displaced Afghanis, and provided 25 seats for nomads. The emergency Loya Jirga of 2002 then elected Hamid Karzai as head of state. Karzai won 83 percent of the 1,555 valid votes cast by members of the Loya Jirga. In his acceptance speech, Karzai referred to the historic tradition of the Loya Jirga by saying that "after twenty-five years, all the Afghans are gathering under one tent."

On December 13, 2003, 500 delegates convened at a Loya Jirga to deliberate the drafting of a constitution. The role of women proved particularly contentious. In many districts religious scholars opposed the election of women. Delegates to the Loya Jirga had to seek a balance between Afghanistan's deep-rooted Islamic traditions and its aspirations for democratic rule. Influencing the debate was the struggle for power among rival sects and factions.

International observers have noted that the Loya Jirga is a critical piece in the establishment of Afghanistan's political future. In January 2004 a second Loya Jirga ratified the newly drafted constitution of Afghanistan. The Taliban was not represented, although groups sharing some of their views did participate.

JAMES ARNOLD

See also

Afghanistan; Karzai, Hamid

References

Federal Research Division, Library of Congress. *Afghanistan: A Country Study.* Baton Rouge, LA: Claitor's Publishing Division, 2001.

Hayes, Geoffrey, and Mark Sedra, eds. *Afghanistan: Transition under Threat.* Waterloo, Ontario: Wilfrid Laurier University Press, 2008.

Johnson, Chris. *Afghanistan.* Oxford, UK: Oxfam, 2004.

Sinno, Abdulkader H. *Organizations at War in Afghanistan and Beyond.* Ithaca, NY: Cornell University Press, 2008.

Luck, Gary Edward
Birth Date: Unknown

U.S. Army officer. Gary Edward Luck served in the U.S. Army from 1959 to 1994 and retired as a four-star general in 1994. A Kansas native, Luck attended Kansas State University, where he enrolled in its ROTC program. He graduated in 1959 and was commissioned a 2nd lieutenant in the army shortly thereafter. Luck fought in Vietnam as both a Special Forces officer and a cavalry troop commander.

In the years following the Vietnam War, Luck steadily moved up the military hierarchy. He commanded the 2nd Infantry Division in the mid-1980s, but his most significant assignment in that decade was as commander of Joint Special Operations Command (1989–1990), at which time he held the rank of major general. In that capacity he had a central role in the planning for the 1989 invasion of Panama that overthrew General Manuel Noriega.

Because of Luck's considerable experience in special operations, General Colin L. Powell, then chairman of the Joint Chiefs of Staff (JSC), relied heavily on him in the planning for the Panama invasion, an operation that made much use of special operations units from all three services. Luck was particularly involved in planning for the rescue of American hostages held at Modelo Prison. On October 16, 1989, Luck and Powell briefed President George H. W. Bush on the overall invasion plan. Luck's presentation focused on the special operations capabilities for locating and rescuing American hostages, and his plans eventually formed the basis for the December 1989 invasion.

Luck also played a pivotal role in the Persian Gulf War as commander of the XVIII Airborne Corps. Luck's corps was responsible for the critical left flank and for the wide-sweeping left hook designed to outflank the Iraqi Republican Guard divisions. A longtime friend of General H. Norman Schwarzkopf, Luck was not afraid to speak his mind to the theater commander during the Operation DESERT SHIELD buildup and the planning for Operation DESERT STORM. Luck was particularly critical of the notion of using only one corps for the flanking attack but, after a sharp rebuke from Schwarzkopf, acquiesced. Luck's approach to commanding at the corps level was highly decentralized, leaving the bulk of the operational planning for XVIII Airborne Corps assault into Iraq in the hands of his divisional commanders. With the commencement of the ground war, Luck's divisions advanced rapidly and completed their flanking maneuver despite problems in coordinating their advance with VII corps. Luck saw XVIII Corp's success as a vindication of his decentralized approach to the planning and conduct of operations.

Following DESERT STORM, Luck, now promoted to full (four-star) general, served as commander in chief of United Nations Command/Combined Forces Command in Korea. He retired from the army in 1994. In retirement, he has continued to be engaged in military issues, writing a number of books and articles on the impact of new technologies on command and control. He has also remained an active consultant on current military issues, particularly the war in Iraq that began in March 2003. In the lead-up to the war, he served as a key adviser to Lieutenant General Tommy Franks. Luck has not been afraid of controversy. In late 2004 and early 2005 he led a study group to Iraq to analyze operations and the status of U.S. operations there. The group concluded that the security situation was worse than was being depicted, that the insurgency was gathering momentum, that progress in training Iraqi military and security forces was going slower than expected, and that U.S. intelligence operations were flawed. Needless to say, this did not endear Luck to the George W. Bush administration. Thanks to Luck's activities as both an author and a consultant on military affairs, he has been as influential in retirement as he was on active duty.

WALTER F. BELL

See also

Bush, George Herbert Walker; Bush, George Walker; DESERT SHIELD, Operation; DESERT STORM, Operation; Franks, Tommy Ray; IRAQI FREEDOM, Operation; Iraqi Insurgency; Powell, Colin Luther; Schwarzkopf, H. Norman, Jr.

References

Atkinson, Rick. *Crusade: The Untold Story of the Persian Gulf War.* New York: Mariner Books, 1994.

Ricks, Thomas E. *Fiasco: The American Military Adventure in Iraq.* New York: Penguin, 2006.

Woodward, Bob. *The Commanders.* New York: Simon and Schuster, 1991.

Lugar, Richard Green
Birth Date: April 4, 1932

U.S. Republican senator from Indiana and foreign policy expert who in 2007 broke with the George W. Bush administration over the continuing war in Iraq. Richard (Dick) Green Lugar was born on April 4, 1932, in Indianapolis, Indiana. His family owned a sizable farm near Indianapolis and a company that produced machinery for food processing and preparation that had been founded by his grandfather in 1893. Lugar attended Denison University in Ohio, graduating with distinction in 1954. Awarded a Rhodes Scholarship, he earned a master's degree from Pembroke College–Oxford University in 1956. The following year he entered the U.S. Navy, serving until 1960.

After leaving the navy, Lugar helped run his family's 600-acre farm and was active in the management of the family-owned company. He entered politics in 1964, when he successfully ran for a spot on the Indianapolis School Board of Commissioners. In 1967 he ran for mayor of Indianapolis on the Republican ticket and, at age 35, became one of the youngest men ever elected to head a major American city. As mayor, Lugar earned high marks for his effective management and became known for his unimpeachable integrity and honesty. Lugar ran for the U.S. Senate in 1974 but

Republican Richard Lugar has represented the state of Indiana in the U.S. Senate since 1977. The longest-serving U.S. senator in Indiana history, Lugar broke with the George W. Bush administration over its Iraq policy in 2007. (U.S. Senate)

was unable to unseat incumbent Democratic senator Birch Bayh. Lugar served as Indianapolis mayor until 1975 and the following year launched a successful bid for a U.S. Senate seat. Taking office in January 1977, he immediately set about learning the intricacies of the Senate. Lugar was a moderate Republican who strongly supported the Ronald Reagan administration's efforts to devolve federal power to the state and local levels.

Before long, Lugar had carved for himself a niche as the leading Republican senator with expertise in foreign and military policy. In 1985 he became chairman of the important Senate Foreign Relations Committee but had to give the position up in 1987 after the Democrats regained control of the Senate in the 1986 mid-term elections. This did not dampen his enthusiasm for foreign policy, however, and he was influential in securing ratification of numerous treaties to eliminate or reduce the deployment, stockpiling, and use of weapons of mass destruction (WMDs). In 1991, working in tandem with Democratic senator Sam Nunn, then the chairman of the Senate Armed Services Committee, Lugar helped craft the Nunn-Lugar Cooperative Threat Reduction plan, which helped to finance and plan for the deactivation of Soviet nuclear, biological, and chemical weapons in the wake of the Cold War. Especially important was the management of Soviet weapons then housed in former Soviet satellite states, such as Ukraine and Kazakhstan.

The Nunn-Lugar initiative has more recently increased its scope to include the monitoring of WMDs that might fall into the hands of terrorists and rogue nations. It is believed that almost 6,000 nuclear weapons have been mothballed since the Nunn-Lugar plan went into effect in 1992.

Lugar was also heavily involved in farm legislation as a senator. From 1995 to 2001 he chaired the Senate Committee on Agriculture, during which time he helped end many outdated farm subsidies that dated to the Great Depression of the 1930s. He also led the way toward the development of biofuels, helped to reorganize the Department of Agriculture and the food stamp program, and fought to maintain the school-lunch program when it came under scrutiny in the late 1990s. In 1996 Lugar launched a brief but abortive campaign to win the Republican presidential nomination of that year.

In January 2003 Lugar once again assumed the chairmanship of the Senate Foreign Relations Committee. In that role he was generally supportive of the George W. Bush administration's foreign and military policy concerning the Global War on Terror and the invasion of Iraq in March 2003. Lugar retained this post until January 2007, at which time the Democrats assumed control of Congress.

In June 2007 Lugar publicly broke with the Bush administration over war policy in Iraq. Although Lugar had initially supported the military conflict, he did not believe that the war could be successfully concluded without a major change in strategy. He also did not believe that the surge strategy, first unveiled in January of that year, was working or was likely to bring about a quick or successful end to the fighting. Lugar's comments, made on the floor of the Senate, came as a blow to the White House but buoyed long-term critics of the war. Given Lugar's stature in foreign affairs, his conclusions clearly showed that frustration with the war was growing and that support for it was slipping. Notably, Lugar did not wait until September to make his comments, at which time another progress report on the Iraqi insurgency was to be made to Congress. At the same time, however, Lugar was careful not to endorse an immediate pullout of U.S. troops or even a specific timetable for such a measure. Two days after his speech, he stated that benchmarks and timetables "will not work." Lugar was more circumspect later in 2007 and beyond when some signs of progress in Iraq began to manifest themselves.

PAUL G. PIERPAOLI JR.

See also

Iraqi Insurgency; Surge, U.S. Troop Deployment, Iraq War; United States Congress and the Iraq War

References

Bergner, Jeffrey T. ed. *The Next American Century: Essays in Honor of Richard G. Lugar.* Lanham, MD: Rowman and Littlefield, 2003.

Galbraith, Peter W. *The End of Iraq: How American Incompetence Created a War without End.* New York: Simon and Schuster, 2007.

Lute, Douglas Edward
Birth Date: November 3, 1952

U.S. Army general and assistant to the president and deputy national security adviser for Iraq and Afghanistan (known as the war czar) in the George W. Bush and Barack Obama administrations (2007–present). Born in Michigan City, Indiana, on November 3, 1952, Douglas Edward Lute graduated from the United States Military Academy, West Point, in 1975. As second lieutenant, his first assignment was with the 2nd Armored Cavalry Regiment in the Federal Republic of Germany. Lute earned a master's degree in public administration from the Kennedy School of Government at Harvard University in 1983 and then returned to West Point to teach in the Social Sciences Department. Lute's next assignment was to attend the British Army Staff College before returning to the 2nd Cavalry Regiment, with which he participated in Operation DESERT STORM in 1991.

Following service in the Office of the Chief of Staff of the U.S. Army, Lute commanded a squadron of the 7th Cavalry Regiment at Fort Hood, Texas, during 1992–1994. He returned to Washington assigned to the Joint Staff in the Directorate for Strategic Plans and Policy. After holding a fellowship at the Atlantic Council in Washington, D.C., Colonel Lute commanded the 2nd Cavalry Regiment of the XVIII Airborne Corps at Fort Polk, Louisiana.

Promoted to brigadier general in 2001, Lute was again assigned to Washington as executive assistant to the chairman of the Joint Chiefs of Staff (JCS). In 2002 he became assistant division commander of the 1st Infantry Division in Schweinfurt, Germany. Later that same year he commanded Multinational Brigade East as part of the peacekeeping mission in Kosovo. In early 2003 Lute became deputy director of operations for the U.S. European Command.

Beginning in June 2004 Lute, now promoted to major general, held for more than two years the post of director of operations for the United States Central Command (CENTCOM), during which time he oversaw U.S. operations in Iraq and Afghanistan as well as other parts of the Middle East, Central Asia, and the Horn of Africa. Promoted to lieutenant general in 2006, he became director of operations of the Joint Staff in Washington that September. Lute is married to Jane Holl Lute, who holds a doctorate in political science from Stanford and a JD degree from Georgetown University and is the United Nations (UN) assistant secretary-general for peacekeeping operations.

Although there was some criticism of the George W. Bush administration's decision to create an additional slot in the White House for oversight of the Iraq War and the Afghanistan War (some claimed that this responsibility should rest with the president himself), the Bush administration named Lute as assistant to the president and deputy national security adviser for Iraq and Afghanistan. The assignment called for Lute to work with the commanders in the field to meet their requests and to coordinate

U.S. Army lieutenant general Douglas Lute conducts a Pentagon briefing on February 9, 2007. President George W. Bush selected Lute, formerly the director of operations for the Joint Staff, to serve as the "war czar" for the conflicts in Iraq and Afghanistan. (U.S. Department of Defense)

efforts with the various cabinet members to implement administration strategies for these two theaters of war.

The U.S. Senate confirmed Lute in his new position on June 28, 2007. In the hearings, the senators pressed Lute to demand greater progress by the Iraqis to meet the benchmarks established by the Bush administration. Lute confirmed that the Iraqis had thus far shown little progress toward reconciliation and that violence was likely to continue in that country for the indefinite future. In his new post, while serving as deputy to National Security Advisor Stephen J. Hadley, Lute nonetheless reported directly to President Bush. President Barack Obama kept Lute in his same position.

SPENCER C. TUCKER

See also

Bush, George Walker; Hadley, Stephen John

References

Baker, Peter, and Karen De Young. "Nominee to Coordinate War Offers Grim Forecast on Iraq." *Washington Post,* June 8, 2007.

Roster of Graduates and Former Cadets of the U.S. Military Academy, West Point, New York. West Point, NY: West Point Association of Graduates, 2008.

Woodward, Bob. *State of Denial: Bush at War, Part III.* New York: Simon and Schuster, 2006.

———. *The War Within: A Secret White House History, 2006–2008.* New York: Simon and Schuster, 2008.

Lynch, Jessica
Birth Date: April 26, 1983

U.S. Army soldier who was taken prisoner early in Operation IRAQI FREEDOM and who, upon being rescued, became a national celebrity and a controversial symbol of the Iraq War. Born in Palestine, West Virginia, on April 26, 1983, Jessica Lynch joined the army largely because she was interested in traveling. On the eve of the war she was deployed to Iraq as part of the 507th Maintenance Company. On March 23, 2003, after an element of her supply convoy became separated from other vehicles and became disoriented, she was injured in a Humvee accident during an ambush and taken captive by the Iraqis. The attack took place in the city of Nasiriyah.

After the engagement ended, Private First Class Lynch lost consciousness. She later awoke in an Iraqi military hospital. There, and subsequently at Saddam Hussein General Hospital, Iraqi doctors and nurses treated Lynch for the severe injuries she had sustained. She remained hospitalized until April 1, 2003, when an American Special Forces team raided the hospital and freed her, carrying her out on a stretcher and delivering her to military authorities for medical treatment. Footage of the rescue operation was released to the media, and Lynch quickly became a symbol of American fortitude and resolve in the early days of IRAQI FREEDOM.

Although much of the media portrayed Lynch as a hero, the details of her ordeal remain unclear. Some reports, for example, suggested that during the ambush she had fired her weapon in an effort to fend off the attackers; others maintained that the firing mechanism of her assault rifle was inoperable because it was jammed with sand. The nature of her captivity also became a source of speculation. While there is a great deal of evidence that the Iraqi medical staff treated her professionally and in accordance with the provisions dictated for prisoners of war, questions persist about the possibility that she had been interrogated and abused. Additionally, many critics are skeptical of whether or not the operation to reclaim her was as dangerous as it appeared to be, and there are conflicting reports about whether or not the soldiers encountered any resistance as they entered the hospital. Some have suggested that the George W. Bush administration and the media embellished the story to increase public support for the war and turn her rescue into compelling headlines.

Beyond the disagreement about the details of her captivity, Lynch's story reignited much larger debates about gender, race, and the military. For opponents of the combat exclusion that bars women from frontline duty, Lynch's courage indicated the fitness of women for combat situations. Conversely, for those who support the ban on women in combat, her apparent helplessness proved the rightness of their claims. Other observers wondered why Lynch was the only captive whose cause became famous, particularly because there were two other female casualties of the Nasiriyah ambush, Private First Class Lori Piestewa and Specialist Shoshana Johnson. Piestewa died of injuries sustained during the skirmish, while Johnson was held captive for 22 days. Despite being the first Native American woman to die in combat and the first female African American prisoner of war, respectively, neither woman received as much media attention as did Lynch, and some have claimed that this disparity was a result of race and that mainstream America was more interested in the suffering of a white woman than that of her nonwhite peers.

Whatever the reasons, Lynch became an instant celebrity. Multiple television networks developed her story into full-length programs. In an effort to capitalize on her iconic status, some media outlets may have exaggerated certain aspects of the story, and Lynch later contested the accuracy of an NBC-TV dramatization in particular. Seeking to make her own voice heard, Lynch told her story to Pulitzer Prize–winning journalist Rick Bragg, who developed it into the popular book *I Am a Soldier, Too: The Jessica Lynch Story* (2003). Throughout the text, which covers everything from Lynch's idyllic childhood to her postwar return to her home in Palestine, West Virginia, Lynch resists being labeled a hero and instead tries to provide an accurate account of her life and her time in Iraq. Now a decorated veteran, Lynch has returned to civilian life and is pursuing a college education. She became a mother for the first time in January 2007.

REBECCA A. ADELMAN

See also
IRAQI FREEDOM, Operation; Women, Role of in Afghanistan and Iraq Wars

References
Bragg, Rick. *I Am a Soldier, Too: The Jessica Lynch Story*. New York: Vintage, 2005.

Conroy, Thomas. "The Packaging of Jessica Lynch." In *Constructing America's War Culture: Iraq, Media, and Images,* edited by Thomas Conroy and Jarice Hanson, 61–84. Lanham, MD: Lexington Books, 2008.

Holland, Shannon L. "The Dangers of Playing Dress-Up: Popular Representations of Jessica Lynch and the Controversy Regarding Women in Combat." *Quarterly Journal of Speech* 92 (2006): 27–50.

Takacs, Stacy. "Jessica Lynch and the Regeneration of American Identity and Power Post-9/11." *Feminist Media Studies* 5 (2005): 297–310.

Index

Italy, armed forces of in Iraq and Afghanistan, **644–646**, 645 (image)
  in battles around Nasiriyah, 645–646
  casualties in, 645, 646
  controversy over, 644
  in Operation ENDURING FREEDOM, 644
  in Operation HAVEN DENIED, 644
  in Operation IRAQI FREEDOM, 645–646
  In Operation WARRIOR SWEEP, 644
  against the Taliban, 644–645
  withdrawal of, 646
IVORY JUSTICE, Operation, **646–648**
Iwo Jima (USS), 102

JACANA, Operation, **649–650**
Jad al-Haqq, Sheikh al-Azhar, "Fatwa against
    the Iraqi invasion of Kuwait," 1990,
    1631–1632**Doc.**
Jafari, Ibrahim al-, **650–651**
Jamerson, James L., 999, 1340
JAMES, Operation, 1280
James Forrestal (USS), 70
Janvier, Bernard, 364
Japan, **651–652**, 904, 1252
Japanese Maritime Self-Defense Force
    (JMSDF), 822
Jarhead, film, 459 (image)
Jarrah, Ziyad al-, **652**
Jashinski, Katherine, 313–314
Jawbreaker (Berntsen), 1249
Jean de Vienne (FS), 160
Jeffords, Jim, 1327
Jenkins, Harry W., 364, 1370
Jeremiah, David, 656
Jihad, 324, **653–655**, 654 (image), 772, 1173,
    1177, 1434
  Al Qaeda and, 654
  contemporary Islam and, 653, 655
  declaring of, 653–654
  interpretations of, 653
  martyrdom and, 654
  notable defensive jihads, 653
  participation in, 653
  Qur'anic statements about, 653
  translation of the term, 653
  World Islamic Front, "Jihad against Jews
    and Crusaders Statement," February 23,
    1998 [excerpts], 1698–1699**Doc.**
  See also Islamic Jihad; Islamic Jihad,
    Palestinian
John C. Stennis (USS), 1375
John F. Kennedy (USS), 1377
John Paul II, Pope, **655–656**
Johnson, James, 364
Johnson, Jesse, 1340
Johnson, Louis A., 887
Johnson, Lyndon B., 303, 524, 791, 803
Joint Chiefs of Staff, **656–658**
Joint Direct Attack Munition (JDAM) Small
    Diameter Bomb (SDB), **658–659**, 659
    (image)

See also Satellites, use of by coalition forces
Joint Forces Air Component Commander
    (JFACC), 1339–1340
JOINT GUARDIAN, Operation, 6
Joint Special Operation Task Force Dagger, 416
Joint Special Operation Task Force–North, 291
Joint Special Operations Command (JSOC),
    394, 666
Joint Surveillance and Target Radar System
    Aircraft (JSTARS), **659–660**
Joint U.S.- Soviet statement calling for the
    withdrawal of Iraq forces from Kuwait,
    August 3, 1990, 1639–1640**Doc.**
JointTask Force 2 (Canada), 257
Jonathan Institute, 894
Jones, James L., 889
Jordan, 137, 634, **660–662**
  Black September and, 447, 454, 549, 643
  climate of, 794
  fedayeen and, 454–455
  Israel-Jordan Peace Treaty, **642–643**
  military assistance from Iraq, 437
Jordan, armed forces of, **662–665**
  Air Force, 664, 664 (image)
  Army, 663
  Coast Guard, 664
  relationship with US/UK militaries, 664–665
  Special Forces, 663
JP233 runway-cratering bomb, 1276
Jules Verne (FS), 161
Jumayyil, Amin, 729, 731, 732, 736
Jumblatt, Kamal, 722
Jupiter (HMS), 1226
JUST CAUSE, Operation, 360, 385, **665–667**, 666
    (image), 1124, 1160, 1188

KADESH, Operation, 128, 1170
Kagan, Robert, 424, 695
Kahn, Abdul Qadeer, 1417
Kakar, Mullah, **669–670**
Kalari, Dilshad, 697
Kallop, William, 510
Kamal, Hussein, 1305
Kamiya, Jason K., **670–671**
Kandahar, Battle for, **671–672**
Karameh, Rashid, 729
Karbala, First Battle of, **672**
Karbala, Second Battle of, **672–673**, 673
    (image)
Karbala Gap, **673–674**
Kari Air Defense System, **674–675**
  factors prompting Iraq purchase of, 674
  hierarchical nature of, 674
  implementation of, 674–675
  weaknesses of, 675
Karmal, Babrak, 18–20
Karpinski, Janis, **675–676**, 676 (image)
Karzai, Hamid, 320 (image), **677–678**, 677
    (image)
  Abd al-Rashid Dostum and, 385
  accomplishments of, 677, 678

Afghan Interim Authority (AIA) and, 232
  criticizing NATO and the U.S., 911
  education of, 677
  election of as president of Afghanistan, 20,
    677
  Operation ENDURING FREEDOM and, 677
  Provisional Reconstruction Teams (PRTs)
    and, 1001
  State of the Nation speech, radio
    Afghanistan, April 8, 2003 [excerpts],
    1797–1802**Doc.**
Katyusha rocket, **678**, 679 (image)
  deployment of, 678, 679
  designer of, 678
  as generic term, 678–679
  launch system of, 678
  U.S. counterpart to, 679
Kazakhstan and the Afghanistan and Iraq
    Wars, **679–680**
Kearn, Thomas H., 1100
Keating, Timothy, 610
Keeling, Andrew, 1281
Kelly, David Christopher, 425, **680–681**
Kelo II, Frank B., 656
Kemal, Mustafa, 718, 719
Kennan, George F., 297, 314–315
Kennedy, John Fitzgerald, 301, 302, 523, 524,
    681–683, 682 (image)
  assassination of, 683
  Berlin crisis and, 682
  Cuban Missile Crisis and, 682–683
  deploying troops to Vietnam, 682
  early life of, 681–682
  election of as president, 682
  health problems of, 682
  Operation HARD SURFACE and, 523
  as senator, 682
  support for Israel, 683, 791
Kerr, Malcolm, 730
Kerry, John Forbes, **683–685**, 684 (image)
  early life of, 683–684
  opposition to Vietnam War, 684, 1190
  as presidential candidate, 684
  results of 2004 presidential election, 683
    (table)
  as senator, 684
  service in Vietnam, 1189
  Swift Boat Veterans for Truth campaign
    against, 1189–1190
  See also United States, national elections of
    2004
Keys, William Morgan, 364, **685**, 1370
Khafji, Battle of, **685–686**
Khalid Sheikh Mohammed, 216
Khalifa, Isa bin Salman al-, 189, **686–687**
Khalil, Samir al-, **687–688**
Khalilzad, Zalmay Mamozy, 105, **688–689**
Khamenei, Sayyid Ali, 578
Khan, Bismillah Mohammad, 28
Khan, Yahya, 946, 947
Khoi-al, Abu al-Qasim, 453